FREE AFRICAN AMERICANS
of
MARYLAND and DELAWARE
From the Colonial Period to 1810

SECOND EDITION

By
Paul Heinegg

CLEARFIELD

Published for Clearfield Company by
Genealogical Publishing Company
Baltimore, Maryland
2021

ISBN 9780806359281

CONTENTS

ACKNOWLEDGEMENTS

The Maryland research was made possible by the generous policy of the Maryland State Archives which provides copies of its records for purchase at very reasonable prices and the internet access to all Maryland deeds.

The Family History web site provides pdf copies of original Provincial Court Judgments, Maryland and Delaware wills and Inventories of estates.

ABBREVIATIONS

DB   Deed Book

DW   Deeds, Wills

L.P.   Loose papers at the county courthouse

M804, 805   Microfilm of the Revolutionary War pension files at
            the National Archives

MdHR,   Maryland Hall of Records
MSA   Maryland State Ahives

MHS   Maryland Historical Society

Orders   Order book for the county court of peas and quarter
            sessions

OW   Orders, Wills

MD:, DE:,   Federal census records for the state. Page
NC:, VA: number is for the printed version of thecensus
            in 1790 and the microfilm of the original for all other years.

PPTL   Personal Property Tax Lists at the Library of Virginia (microfilms)

WB   Will Book

W&cO   Wills, etc. Orders

**Note free African Americans are identified by printing their names in bold
except in their own family histories.**

LIST OF FAMILY HISTORIES

Adams	Brown	Cunningham	Fortune
Aldridge	Brumejum	Curtis	Fountain
Alexander	Bryan	Dalton	Fowler
Allen	Bryant	Davis	Francisco
Alsop	Buckwell	Dawson	Frazer
Anderson	Buley	Day	Friend
Annis	Burgess	Dean	Frost
Armstrong	Burke	Delaney	Gale
Anthony	Burton	Devan	Game
Armwood	Butcher	Dias/ Dyer	Gannon
Atkins	Butler	Dobson	Gates
Atlow	Caldwell	Dodson	George
Badger	Callaman	Dogan	Gibbs
Baker	Cambridge	Donaldson	Gibson
Banks	Campbell	Douglas	Giles
Banneker	Cann	Dove	Grace
Barber	Cannady	Downs	Graham
Bantum	Cannon	Drain	Grant
Bardley	Carney	Driggers	Graves
Barrett	Carr	Dublin	Gray
Barton	Carroll	Duffy	Grayson
Bass	Carter	Dulaney	Green
Bates	Carty	Dunlop	Greenwood
Batterton	Case	Durham	Griffin
Bean	Chambers	Dutton	Grimes
Beavin	Chuck	Dyer	Grinnage
Beckett	Churb	Easter	Gurley
Beddo	Clark	Easton	Guy
Bentley	Clayton	Edmunds	Hackney
Berry	Coger	Elbert	Hailey
Bishop	Coker	Ellis	Hall
Black	Cole	England	Hamilton
Blake	Collick	English	Hand
Boarman	Collins	Ennis	Hanser
Bond	Combest	Evans	Hanson
Bone	Conner	Farmer	Harding
Boon	Consello	Faarrell	Harmon
Booth	Cook	Farthing	Harris
Boston	Cooper	Fenton	Harrison
Boswell	Cornish	Fisher	Harwood
Boteler	Cox	Fitzgerald	Hawkins
Bowen	Crass	Flamer	Haws
Bowser	Crawley	Flames	Haycock
Brady	Creek	Fletcher	Heath
Brenning	Cromwell	Ford	Hicks

Hill
Hilton
Hinton
Hitchens
Hodgkin
Hodgskin
Holland
Holly
Holmes
Holt
Hopkins
Horner
Houtson
Howard
Howe
Hubbard
Hughes
Hunter
Hynson
Impey
Jackson
Jacobs
Jeffrey
Jervis
Johnson
Jolley
Jones
Kelly
Kersey
King
Knight
Lacount/
Lacompt
Lamb
Lantern/
Lanthron
Lawder
Lawrence
Leatherby
Lee
Lenkins
Lett
Lewis
Liles
Littlejohn
Lockerman
Longo
McDaniel

McDonald
Madden
Magee
Mahoney
Malavery
Mallory
Marshall
Mason
Massey
Matthews
Mayhew
Mead
Miller
Minor
Mitchell
Molluck
Mongon/
Mongom
Monk
Moody
Moore
Morgan
Morris
Mortis
Morton/
Molton
Mosely
Mungar
Munt(s)
Murray
Myers
Nailor
Natt
Nelson
Newman
Nichols
Norman
Norris
Norwood
Nutts
Okey
Olive
Oneyr
Osborne
Overton
Owens
Palmer
Parker

Parkinson
Parsons
Patteron
Peck
Pennington
Penny
Perkins
Perle
Phillips
Pickett
Plowman
Plummer
Poulson
Pratt
Press
Price
Prichard
Pritchett
Pride
Proctor
Proteus
Prout
Puckham
Quander
Queen
Randall
Ray
Reardon
Redding
Reed
Rhoads
Richards
Ridgeway
Risner
Roach
Roads
Roberts
Robinson
Rogers
Rollins
Ross
Rounds
Russell
Rustin
Sammons
Sampson
Saunders
Savoy

Scarlett
Scott
Sheldon
Shaver
Shaw
Shepherd
Shorter
Simiter
Sisco
Skinner
Smith
Smither
Smothers
Snow
Sockum
Songo
Southwood
Sparksman
Spearman
Spencer
Stanley
Stephens
Stevenson
Stewart
Street
Strickland
Suitor
Summers
Swann
Taylor
Thomas
Thompson
Tills
Tippett
Toney
Toogood
Trout
Trusty
Tunks
Turner
Upton
Valentine
Verdin
Walker
Wallace
Wansey
Ward
Waters

Watson
Webber
Webster
Wedge
Welch
Whittam
Wilkins
Wilkinson
Williams
Willis
Wilson
Wingate
Winslow
Wise
Wiseman
Wood
Woodland
Woodward
Wright
Young
Younger

INTRODUCTION

This is the history of the free African American communities of Maryland and Delaware during the colonial period as told through their family histories.

During the colonial period in Maryland:

- More than 600 free, mixed-race children were born to white women by African American men.

- Relatively few slaves were freed by slave owners.
+
- Less owned land than their counterparts in Delaware, Virginia and North Carolina.

- They had closer relations with the slave population than did their counterparts in Delaware, Virginia and North Carolina.

- Some free African Americans migrated from Maryland to Delaware and West Virginia where there were more opportunities for land ownership.

- During the Jim Crow Period some families, who had developed a culture quite different from the former slaves, were considered Indians.

Descendants of White Women in Maryland
More than 600 mixed-race children were born to white women in Maryland and Delaware during the colonial period. There had been a number of marriages between white women and slaves by 1664 when Maryland passed a law which made them and their mixed-race children slaves for life, noting that,

> *divers freeborne English women forgettfull of their free Condicon and to the disgrace of our Nation doe intermarry with Negro Slaves* [*Archives of Maryland*, 1:533-34].

One such marriage took place in August 1681 between Nell Butler and "Negro Charles," the slave of Major William Boarman of St. Mary's County. The ceremony was conducted by a Catholic priest on the Boarman plantation. Lord Baltimore was said to have been present on the day of the marriage and to have warned Nell of the consequences.[1]

About a month after the wedding however, Maryland passed a law which released white servant women and their mixed-race children from slavery if the marriage was permitted or encouraged by their master [*Archives of Maryland*, 7:203-5; Hodes, *White Women, Black Men*, 19-29].

In 1692 Maryland enacted a law which punished white women who had children by slaves by selling the mothers as servants for seven years and binding their children to serve until the age of twenty-one if they were married to the slave, and till thirty-one if they were not married [*Archives of Maryland*, 13:546-49]. The court records and Prerogative Inventories include at least another nine white women who were married to slaves about 1680 to 1700.

- Mary Davis of Calvert County married a slave named Domingo about 1677 and had two children.

---

[1]This story is based on testimony 84 years later in 1765 [Provincial Judgments 1770-1, 233-44].

• English servant Martha was married to Boatswain in St. Mary's County in 1682 [Prerogative Inventories & Accounts, 8:300].

• an unidentified English woman was listed as the wife of a "Negro" in the 8 August 1691 inventory of the St. Mary's County estate of Cuthbert Scott [Prerogative Inventories & Accounts, 15:38-9]. Perhaps this was Mary, the wife of "Negro" slave Francis Peters, whose petition to the Provincial Court for her freedom was denied on 11 May 1693 as long as her husband lived [Provincial Court Records D.S.#C, p. 241].

• Mr. Robert Mason sold a "Negro man slave," a white woman and a "Mulatto Child" to Mr. Henry Denton, clerk of the Council, before 29 August 1698 when the ministry of King William and Queen Mary Parish in St. Mary's County bound the child to the age of thirty-one and threatened to sue Denton's widow Mary Denton [Proceedings of the Council of Maryland, 1696/7-8, Liber X:128 by *Archives of Maryland Online*, 23:508-9].

• An unidentified English woman was married to a "Negro" in Talbot County in 1692 [Prerogative Inventories & Accounts, 10:256-8].

• Catherine Simiter was married to a "Negro" in Queen Anne's County about 1700-1710.

• Grace MacDonald was married to a "Negro" man in Charles County in 1714.

• "Negro" Grinedge was married to Jane Shoare in Talbot County in 1698.

• Mary Liles was married to Jack, a slave of Hugh Redgley, by Rev. Jacob Henderson about 1712 in Baltimore County and had five children by 1728 [Court Proceedings, 1728-30, Liber HWS#6: 29-30].

• Margaret Madden may have been married to the slave by whom she had six children in Talbot County between 1725 and 1742.

The families in this history descend from 264 white women who had 374 mixed-race children. Another 112 white women had 127 mixed-race children who were not traced to any family in the early census records. Prerogative Inventories indicate that at least another 60 mixed-race children were born to white women in both Calvert and Saint Mary's counties for which there are no surviving colonial court records.(See Endnotes.)

Free mixed-race children of white women were so common that when accountants listed slaves in colonial inventories under the heading "Slaves," some would add "a slave for life" after anyone identified as "Mulatto" [Prerogative Inventories & Accounts 30:60; Inventories 20:9-10].

The inventories indicate that the births of many free, mixed-race children were not recorded by the court–perhaps handled by the churchwardens by order of the vestry. Winifred Jones, servant of Thomas Sheredine of Baltimore County, was prosecuted for having a total of three children by a "Negro," but the inventory of Sheredine's estate indicates that she had five mixed-race children bound to him until the age of thirty-one in 1753 [Prerogative Inventories 50:174]. "Mulatto" Ann Parker's son Robert was bound to Thomas Stockett of Anne Arundel County in 1751, but there is no record of her indenture to Stockett. And the inventory of Stockett's estate in 1763 indicates that she had a sister Susan and six other children bound to Stockett until the age of thirty-one [Prerogative Inventories 15:397; 20:54-9; 48:210].

Some inventories failed to note that a child was free. John Wright of Prince George's County purchased Daniel Lee for thirty-one years in 1717, but Daniel was listed in the

Inventory of Wright's estate in 1729 as "Mullatto Boy named Daniel Lee £18." Priscilla Gray ("Molattoe woman Priss") and her two children were not identified as free in the Prince George's county inventory of Sarah Magruder in 1734. Margaret Cannon's daughter was bound to Isaac Smoot of Charles County for thirty-one years in 1743, but there were two of her children bound to him until thirty-one in the inventory of his estate in 1751. The 3 February 1755 Dorchester County will of Edward Trippe mentions his "mulatto servants," but his inventory merely lists them among the slaves as "1 Mollatto wench, one d° Girl Jealica, one d° Boy Robin, 1 d° girl Sarah, 1 d° girl Rachel, 1 d° Boy Harry and 1 d° boy Charles" [Prerogative Court (Wills), 30:9; (Inventories), 63:465-9; http://freeafricanamericans.com/prerogative.htm].

In November 1728 the Maryland General Assembly made the mixed-race descendants of white women who had children by slaves subject to the same punishments as white women. They were sold as servants for seven years, and their children were bound until the age of thirty-one if they had a child by a slave, either during or after their service. However, if they had a child by a free person, they were charged with fornication and received the same sentence as if both partners had been white: a fine or lashes, and their children were bound until the age of twenty-one (for boys) and sixteen (for girls) [*Archives of Maryland*, 30:289-90; 36:275-76; Kilty, *Laws of Maryland*, 1728, chapter 4].

Elizabeth Grimes, a mixed-race woman, had six children, four by a free person. In June 1721 the Prince George's County court ordered her sold for seven years and sold her child which she had by a slave for 1,000 pounds of tobacco to serve until the age of thirty-one. But the court called her other child her "white" daughter when it bound her until the age of sixteen. Between 1727 and 1750 Priscilla Gray had four children, three bound until the age of thirty-one and one bound until the age of twenty-one.

Many of the prosecutions for bastardy in Delaware are either missing or were not recorded. However, in Kent County there were six recorded cases of white women bearing mixed-race children before 1721: one in 1699, 1703, 1704, two in 1707, and one in 1720. None were recorded in Sussex County, but in 1699 the grand jury presented Adam Johnson's servant woman (Rebecca Saunders) for "lyeing commonly with his Nigroe man as man and wife." Between 1720 and 1751 there were no cases of "Mulatto Bastardy" recorded in Delaware. White women apparently continued to have children by African Americans during this period because in 1726 Delaware passed a law similar to the one in Maryland whereby white women were sold for up to five years and their children by a "Negro or Mulatto" were sold for thirty-one years. In October 1740 the Delaware government found that many such children were being held past their term of service (perhaps because there was no written court record for these cases?) and passed a law allowing them to bring suit in court for their freedom [Laws of Delaware, 1:105-9, 380, cited by Barnes, *Laws of Delaware, Free Blacks & Mulattos*, 7-8, 14-5].

There is a great disparity between the court records of Maryland and those for Delaware. Maryland counties kept judicial records or judicial proceedings which consist of bound volumes of minutes of all that occurred at the county court: cases brought by the county against individuals as well as cases between individuals. They involve bastardy, assault, adultery, slander, public drunkenness, petty theft, failure to pay debts, land disputes, failure to attend church, failure to pay taxes, petitions for relief from taxation, orders to bind children as apprentices, etc., and read almost like a newspaper account of the day-to-day happenings in the county. It is in the Judgment Records of Queen Anne's County that we learn that a white woman named Catherine Simiter was the wife of "Negroe John" and unlawfully dealt with white servants in 1731. Joseph **Guy**, "begot by a Negro man on a white woman," was sold for seven years for marrying a white woman, and Thomas Perlott, a white man, and his wife Sarah, "begot by a Negro man on a white woman," were also sold for seven years in 1735 [Judgment Records 1730-2, 329-30; 1732-5, part 2, 503-4, 535].

In the middle of the eighteenth century some Maryland counties reported the criminal court cases in separate volumes, called criminal records: Baltimore County: 1757-1759, Caroline County: 1774-1784, Cecil County: 1728-1741, Kent County: 1724-1772, Queen Anne's County: 1751-1766, Talbot County: 1747-1775. These contain the cases of white and mixed-race women having children by slaves during those periods as well as cases such as the one in Kent County where the rector of Shrewsbury Parish was fined for marrying Negro Dick, slave of Richard Bennett, Esq., to Amy Nabb [Criminal Record 1728-34, 551-2].

When Mary **Consellah** confessed to bastardy in Kent County, Delaware, in 1728, the clerk wrote in the docket, "Entered in the Criminal Dogget," but there are no surviving colonial court records for Delaware that contain only criminal cases [Delaware Archives RG 3815.031, dockets 1722-32, frames 229, 235].

For Kent County, Delaware, after 1725 and Sussex County after 1709, there are no court minutes. We have only the dockets and whatever case files have survived. The Kent County court dockets record that Hannah Hutt received twenty-one lashes in November 1724 for having an illegitimate child and that the child was bound to Charles Hillyard. However, there is a 1758 Kent County deed in which John **Hutt** petitioned the court that he was bound to Charles Hillyard for thirty-one years and never received his freedom dues, and the Levy Court records indicate that John **Hutt's** "Mulatto" child was supported by the county in 1766 [DSA, RG 3815.031, 1722-1732, frames 65, 153, 206].

In Kent County a white woman named Elizabeth Sheldon had an illegitimate daughter named Rachel by "Negro Phill" in 1743 only received corporal punishment for failure to pay her fine (twenty-nine lashes but no servitude). However, white women Martha Clark (in 1751) and Margery Patterson (in 1753) were convicted under the 1726 law which resulted in their sale into servitude, and on 8 January 1773 "Negro" Jacob was found guilty of begetting a "Male Mulato Bastard" by Hannah Shannon, given thirty-nine lashes and made to stand in the pillory two hours with his ear nailed thereunto and ripped off. But Hannah Shannon's trial was not recorded in the Quarter Sessions dockets [RG 3805.002, 1734-1779, frames 81, 84, 186, 197; RG 3811, Court for the Trial of Negro Slaves, 1764-1773]. The only case recorded in Sussex County was in May 1794 when the court indicted and convicted John **Harmon** "free Mulatto" and white woman Ann Jones for having two illegitimate children [RG 4805, General Court Sessions 1767-94, frames 561-2]. This case received some notoriety because Ann Jones's lawyer objected to the state's witness Rebecca West because she had been convicted of the same offense, but Rebecca's case was not recorded in the Quarter Sessions dockets [Boorstein, *Delaware Cases, 1792-1830*, 1:33-4]. The **Harmon**-Jones case probably influenced the legislature to reconsider the 1726 law which ordered mixed-race children of white women to be bound out until the age of thirty-one. On 23 January 1795 the legislature voided the law of 1726 and ordered the children bound until the same age as white children, it being "unjust and inhuman to punish the child for the offense of the parents" [*Laws of Delaware*, 2:1201].

Descendants of Manumitted Slaves in Maryland
Slaves who were manumitted during the colonial period included a member of the **Guy** family who was free in Talbot County in 1690, a member of the **Grinnage** family who was free on Kent Island before 1698; William **Barton** who was free when he was baptized in Anne Arundel County in 1699; Henry **Quander** who was free and married to his wife Margaret in Charles County by August 1702; Mingo **Savoy** who was free in Anne Arundel County in 1705, Sambo and his wife Betty (**Game**) who were freed by Peter Douty's 1709 Somerset County will, and Robert **Perle** (1720) and James **Callaman** (1730) of Prince George's County who were freed by Richard Marsham's 1713 Prince George's County. Seventeen members of the **Gibbs** family were freed in Queen Anne's County in 1747.

Maryland Landowners
Free African Americans were drawn to Somerset County as early as 1666 when Anthony **Johnson** moved there from the Eastern Shore of Virginia and leased 300 acres in Wicomico Hundred for 200 years. Others from the Eastern Shore followed. The **Driggers** and **George** families were there by 1688. Devorax[1] **Driggers** leased 300 acres in Bogerternorton Hundred in 1707, William **Driggers** owned 100 acres in Baltimore Hundred when he made his will in 1720, and Devorax[2] **Driggers** purchased 75 acres there in 1731. The **Francisco, Harman, Longo,** and **Malavery** followed in the early eighteenth century.

Thomas Davidson noted that Maryland's governor gave Eastern Shore Virginians an opportunity to claim lands in Somerset County in 1661. He traced the development of the free African Americans who owned land in Somerset County, including **Johnson, Driggers, Collick, Cambridge, Dutton, Game, Mungar** and **Puckham,** but observed that it was not a large enough group to form a community [Davidson, *Free Blacks on the Lower Eastern Shore of Maryland* II:27, 30; "Free Blacks in Old Somerset County," *Maryland Historical Magazine* 71:155]. Most moved onto southern Delaware which in 1681 was a frontier region like Somerset County had been twenty years previously.

"Molatto" Robert **Perle** owned land in Prince George's County before 1735, partnered with whites in putting up security for the executors of estates, and was an overseer of the highways in 1748. The **Proctor** family owned land in Charles County before 1762. Jonathan **Curtis** probably owned or leased land in St. Mary's or Charles County in 1746 when he had an account with William Hunter & Company of Spotsylvania County for more than £29. Thomas **Thompson** probably leased or owned land in Charles County in 1774 since he was called a "Mulatto Planter" when he provided security for his daughter's appearance in court. William **Barton** purchased 177 acres in Anne Arundel County in 1711, and Benjamin **Banneker's** father purchased 100 acres in Baltimore County in 1738.

The **Gibbs** families were left 444 acres in Queen Anne's County by the will of their master in 1747. Two members of the family remained in the county and still owned 50 acres each in 1783, but the others sold their land and bought land in Kent County, Delaware. However, in most areas of Maryland free African Americans had little opportunity to own land.

The place of opportunity for free African Americans lay in Kent and Sussex counties in Delaware, North Carolina, and the Virginia Southside which were anxious to attract settlers of any complexion.

Delaware Landowners
Free African American families from Somerset County moved north to Delaware where they formed the mixed-race communities of Sussex and Kent Counties. John **Johnson,** son of Anthony **Johnson** of Accomack County, patented 400 acres in Rehoboth Bay, Sussex County, in 1677.

Aminadab **Hanser** of Accomack County, the son of a white woman and a slave, purchased 200 acres in Rehoboth Bay, Sussex County, in September 1685. Daniel **Francisco (Sisco),** son or grandson of John **Francisco,** a slave freed in Northampton County, Virginia, in 1647, lived in Somerset County between 1707 and 1713 and left an estate in Kent County, Delaware, in 1732.

Other families from the Eastern Shore of Virginia and Somerset County, Maryland, who settled in Delaware included: **Bass, Beckett, Driggers, Game, Hitchens, Hodgskin, Jacobs, Magee, Morris, Perkins, Press, Puckham, Sammons, Scokem/ Sockem, Shaver, Sparksman,** and **Wright.**

The **Butcher** family of Dorchester County was in Kent County, Delaware, by 1693. Settlers from other areas of Maryland included **Fountain, Gibbs, Grinnage, Lacount, Norman, Parsons, Plummer, Poulson, Proctor, Roach, Saunders**, and **Toogood**.

Before coal came into general use, "the **Durhams, Harmons, Clarks, Perkins** and **Sockums**, mostly all related and originally from Delaware," owned nearly all the horses and carts hauling wood in Philadelphia [Minton, *Early History of Negroes in Business in Philadelphia* (1913):18]. Henry **Harmon**, John **Durham** and Francis **Perkins** were heads of "other free" households in Philadelphia in 1810.

Aminadab **Hanser** probably spoke like his mother and dressed and behaved like his white brother. He and his descendants could not have been successful planters in Sussex County unless they had been accepted by the white community. Planters need loans and the cooperation of other planters to succeed.

White communities in Sussex and Kent counties–as well as in some counties in Maryland, Virginia, and North Carolina–developed a culture of acceptance of these free, mixed-race families that had nothing to do with their ideas about slavery. They treated their slaves as property but were good neighbors to free African American landowners. In a rural community land ownership was the ultimate measure of freedom.

Relations with Slave and White Communities
Free African American families in Maryland appear to have had closer relations with the slave population than their counterparts had in other colonies or states, particularly North Carolina and Delaware. Children of white women had difficulty leaving the servant class because they were bound out until the age of thirty-one. If a female child of a white woman indentured until thirty-one had a child by a slave, she was sold for another seven years for each child.

Many early nineteenth-century certificates of freedom describe Maryland descendants as dark-skinned. Nathaniel **Allen**, great-grandson of a white woman, received a Prince George's County certificate of freedom on 11 September 1810 which described him as "a black man." Charles **Allen's** 23 June 1818 Prince George's County certificate described him as, "a Negro boy, tolerably black."

Some free families had relatives who were slaves. Margaret Ruston, a white woman, had a child by her master's slave in Charles County in 1691. Her child was probably Thomas **Rustin** who was free in 1750 when he petitioned the Charles County court to declare his wife Lucy levy-free for the future. But it appears that Margaret Ruston also had slave descendants, possibly Thomas' children by a slave.

Thomas Rustin, Jr., Robert Rustin, and George Rustin, slaves of William Neale of Charles County, were allowed by their master to keep horses as their own property. They were often in trouble with the authorities, perhaps because they "did not know their place."

A slave named Thomas Rustin was indicted by the Charles County court in November 1749 for taking someone's horse. The jury found him guilty, and the court ordered that he be hung. However, he apparently received a pardon because Thomas Rustin, the slave of William Neale, was given thirty-nine lashes seven years later in June 1756 for taking someone's hat. He was called "Thomas Rustain, Junior" in August 1756 when he was indicted for stealing a saddle and called "Molatto Thomas Rustain" in November 1756 when he was acquitted of the charge. In November 1757 he was charged with striking a white man [Court Record 1690-3, 334; 1693-4, 9; 1749-50, 724; 1750, 140; 1756-7, 2, 3, 117-8, 144, 201; 1757-8, 566; 1758-60, 177].

There were also slave and free members of the **Dove** family. John **Dove** was a

"Mulatto" slave charged with felony in Charles County court in November 1727, and free members of the **Dove** family had moved to North Carolina by September 1749 when the Craven County court sent someone to Maryland to confirm that they were free [Charles County Court Record 1727-31, 42; Haun, *Craven County, Court Minutes IV:*11-12, 366]. A member of the **Dove** family owned 75 acres in Craven County in 1775.

Perhaps the principal determinant of relations with slave versus white communities was land ownership. Most free African American families in North Carolina, for example, had at least one member of the family who owned land. Land ownership made for closer relations between free African Americans and whites and fewer social relations with slaves.

Religion-Maryland
During the colonial period St. Paul's Parish in Baltimore County recorded more births and marriages than any other Maryland church [Reamy, *St. Paul's Parish*]. Robert **Banneker** was apparently married to Mary **Lett** in Baltimore County about 1730. And, as noted above, Mary Liles was married to a slave in the county by Reverend Jacob Henderson about 1712. There were seven free African American births or marriages recorded in All Hallows Parish, Anne Arundel County, for the **Barton, Kashier, Lewis, Newman, Oliver, Puckham, Savoy,** and **Williams** families, and ten births or marriages were recorded in Stepney Parish, Somerset County, for the **Dutton, Game** and **Magee** families.

Religion-Delaware
The marriage of Jonas **Hodgskin** and Rhoda **Driggers** and the birth of their two children was recorded in Coventry Parish in Somerset County [Wright, *Anne Arundel County Church Records*, 3, 9, 17, 30-1. 45-7, 51, 86, 105, 155, 200]. However, the births, baptisms and marriages of "Melatos" recorded in Sussex County, Delaware, exceeded all those recorded throughout colonial Maryland, Virginia, North and South Carolina. There were seventy-four marriages, births or baptisms recorded in Sussex County for the **Barton, Beckett, Clark, Cornish, Driggers, Esaw, Friend, Game, Hanser, Harmon, Jackson, Jacobs, Johnson, Morris, Mosely, Norman, Norwood, Okey, Parsons, Parkinson, Ridgeway, Sammons, Street, Verdin** and **Wright** families–the earliest in 1746 [Records of the United Presbyterian Churches of Lewes, Indian River and Cool Spring, Delaware 1756-1855 (transcript at Pennsylvania Historical Society), pp. 274, 279, 282, 284, 286, 288, 294, 298, 302, 304-5, 310-1, 314-6, 318-20, 322-3, 325, 327, 391, 399, 403; Wright, *Vital Records of Kent and Sussex County*, 91-6, 98-104, 106, 109-11, 124, 131]].

This may have been due to the work started by the Reverend William Beckett, a missionary from the Society of the Propagation of the Gospel in Foreign Parts, whose mission at Lewes lasted from 1721 until his death in 1743. Although the society's main mission was to the white residents of the county, it also included the evangelization of slaves [Society for the Propagation of the Gospel in Foreign Parts, Transcripts of Letters Relating to Delaware, University of Delaware Special Collections Department, Manuscript no. 462].

In the early nineteenth century the mixed-race families formed their own churches. Eli **Harmon** made a Sussex County will in 1818 by which he left $10 to the trustees of Harmony Meeting House, and on 13 March 1819 Eli **Norwood** and his wife Ellen gave a half acre of land in Indian River Hundred, Sussex County, for the building of a Methodist Episcopal Church. The church became known as the Harmony Methodist Episcopal Church. Pournelle **Johnson,** Burton **Johnson,** William **Hayes,** John **Cornish** and Mitchell **Johnson** were named trustees for the building of a house of worship for the use of the members of the Methodist Episcopal Church [DB 45:124-6].

In the late 1870s a new preacher, a "Negro," advocated that the church members mingle with the former slaves and include them in their religious services. Part of the congregation was willing to go along with this, but another group was bitterly opposed and withdrew from the church [Zebley, *The Churches of Delaware*, 297-8; Weslager, *Delaware's Forgotten Folk*, 88-9].

Oral History
The origin of mixed-race families has survived in only a very few family oral histories, and those few have been modified. The nineteenth-century biographer of Benjamin **Banneker** reported that Benjamin's grandmother purchased two slaves and married one of them who was an African prince [Bedini, *The Life of Benjamin Banneker*, 19]. John **Harmon**'s family was one of the first African American families free in Northampton County, Virginia (in 1667), but his and other Sussex County, Delaware families came to be known as Moors or Indians during the Jim Crow Period.

In 1855 the **Ridgeway** family of Delaware was said to have descended from a white woman who purchased and later married a "very tall, shapely and muscular young fellow of dark ginger-bread color." The story was modified in the twentieth century to say that he was an African Prince [Fisher, *The So-called Moors of Delaware*].

Some in Virginia and North Carolina tell of a white woman running away with a slave and drinking a drop of blood from a small cut in his finger, so that she could honestly swear to the justice of the peace that she had "Negro" blood in her [Writers' Program, Works Projects Administration, *Slave Narratives*, Project Vol. XI, part 2, pp. 106-8; Taylor, *The Free Negro in North Carolina* (James Sprunt Historical Publications) v. 17, no.1, p.21].

Descendants of families who have believed for generations that they are Indians have an Indian identity no different than if they had Indian ancestors. But the mixed-race families who lived in Indian River Hundred have no connection to the Indians who were described by the Reverend David Humphreys of the Society for the Propagation of the Gospel in 1730: "a small settlement on the utmost Border of the Parish, where it adjoins to Maryland; they were extremely barbarous and obstinately ignorant" [Humphreys, *An Historical Account of the Incorporated Society for the Propagation of the Gospel in Foreign Parts*, 159-168]. By 1748 most of the Nanticokes had moved to Pennsylvania and New York [Porter, *Quest for Identity*, 42].

Anthropologists
After the Civil War, light-skinned African Americans who owned land in the Southeast did not fit into the new society where churches and schools were either white or former slave. Many could vote by the grandfather clause. They had developed a culture very similar to whites because they had gone to school and church with whites since the colonial period and had become part of the local white farming communities.

In 1875 the Democrats in Delaware enacted a law that required all "Colored Persons" to pay a tax of 30 cents on every $100 of property for the erection of separate schools for "Negroes." The families that had been free since the colonial period in Indian River, Sussex County, organized as a "certain class of Colored Persons" and pressured the legislature to allow them to have their own schools so they would not have to attend segregated schools with the former slaves. In 1881 the legislature permitted them to form an "Incorporated Body" under which they would be allowed to construct their own separate schools. They included the **Johnson**, **Norwood**, **Wright**, **Harmon**, **Street**, **Clark** and **Drain** families. They built Warwick School on land donated by the **Harmon** family and Holleyville School on land donated by Samuel **Norwood** [*State Laws of Delaware* XVI, Chapter 364, p. 378 cited by Weslager, *Delaware's Forgotten Folk*, 112-117].

In 1885 Hamilton McMillan of Robeson County, North Carolina's Democratic (Jim

Crow) Party wrote and helped pass a law creating separate school districts for the former free persons of color of the county in an effort to win their votes in a county and state that were about equally divided between Republicans and Democrats. McMillan invented the name "Croatan Indians" and theorized that they had descended from a friendly tribe of Indians on the Roanoke River in eastern North Carolina who had mixed with the whites in Sir Walter Raleigh's lost colony in 1587 and had settled in Robeson County during the colonial period. The law created three castes: white, Negro and Indian and prohibited marriage between them. Later, there would be three sets of water fountains, seating areas, rest rooms, etc. [Blu, *The Lumbee Problem*, 23, 62-3].

This influenced anthropologists like James Moody of the Smithsonian to search for other "lost Indian tribes" among free-people-of-color communities throughout the Southeast. The descendants of white women in Charles and Prince George's counties (the **Proctor, Butler, Newman, Savoy, Swann,** and **Thompson** families) became "Piscataway Indians" or "Wesorts" [Porter, *Quest for Identity*, 99-100; Gilberts, *Surviving Indian Groups of the Eastern United States*].

In 1898 William H. Babcock visited the community in Delaware who became "Nanticoke Indians" and observed that

they have near as many white attributes of mind and body, habit, and temper [Babcock, *American Anthropologist*, 1 (1899): 277-82].

A study of the mixed-race communities of North Carolina in 1886 reached a similar conclusion,

In their habits, manner, and dress, the free negroes still resemble, as they always did, the poorest class of whites much closer than they do the freedman [Dodge, "Free Negroes of North Carolina," *Atlantic Monthly* 57 (January 1886):20-30].

In 1903 the "Incorporated Body" of Sussex County petitioned the legislature to change their name from "a certain class of Colored Persons" to the "Offspring of the Nanticoke Indians," and the legislature complied [*State Laws of Delaware* XXII, Chapter 470, 986 cited by Weslager, *Delaware's Forgotten Folk*, 117].

Anthropologist Frank G. Speck visited the Indian River, Sussex County community in 1911, 1922 and 1942. In 1922 he helped the community to incorporate as the Nanticoke Indian Association. He taught them Plains Indian dances and songs and taught them to prepare costumes, strings of beads and feather headdresses, subjecting them to the ridicule of whites in the area [Porter, *Quest for Identity*, 103, 108-9, 111].

Indian Indentured Servants
The indenture of Indians as servants was not common in Maryland. The governor and his Council were not familiar with the practice on 18 July 1722 when they heard the case of Marcus Andrews who was charged with indenting an Indian boy named James in Somerset County and selling the indenture to someone in Philadelphia. Andrews explained that it was a "Customary thing in Ackamack in Virginia to indent with them for a Time or Term of years" and that he had indented with the boy in Virginia, not in Maryland [*Archives of Maryland* 25:390-1]. Other cases of Indian indentures which appear in the county courts include:

• James Boarman, an Indian servant indentured in Charles County in August 1691 [Court Record 1690-2, 237].

• Joan Kennedy, a two-year-old Indian servant bound until the age of twenty-one in Prince George's County in November 1718 [Judgment Record 1715-20, 719a].

Women convicted of having children by native Indians were prosecuted for the lesser offense of fornication and had to pay a fine or suffer corporal punishment.

• In June 1721 Eliza Lester named an Indian called Sackelah as the father of her child and received a fine or corporal punishment from the Baltimore County court [Court Proceedings 1718-21, 498, 507].

• In March 1732 Mary Ockeley was indicted by the Prince George's County court for "Malatto Bastardy," but she was punished for fornication when it was found that the child was "begot by an Indian" [Court Record 1730-2, 402].

• In August 1736 Catherine Adams of Anne Arundel County was fined for having a child by an Indian [Judgment Record 1736-8, 22].

• In November 1741 Dorothy Smith of Anne Arundel County received corporal punishment for having a child by an Indian [Judgment Record 1740-3, 328].

• In November 1745 Catherine Parsons received ten lashes by the Talbot County court for having an illegitimate child by an Indian named William Asquash [Judgment Record 1745-6, 246-7]. (A William Asquash was one of the Choptank Indians who sold land in Dorchester County in 1727 [Land Records 1720-32, Liber old 8, 153]).

The indenture of East Indian servants was more common:

• an unnamed East India servant boy was valued at 2,500 pounds of tobacco in the 3 July 1676 inventory of the Talbot County estate of Captain Edward Roe [Prerogative Inventories 2:177-8].
• Michael Miller of Kent County, Maryland, purchased an unnamed East Indian from Captain James Mitchel "but for five years" on 28 June 1698 [Court Proceedings 1676-98, 911].
• Francis Mingo of Bengal in the East Indies was set at liberty from Colonel Walter Smith by the Provincial Court on 2 October 1711 [Provincial Court Judgments 1711-2, 193].
• John Forton, born in India and sold as a slave to William Bladen, was freed by the Provincial Court on 12 April 1720 [Provincial Court Judgments 1719-22, 118].
• Thomas Mayhew was free from his indenture in Prince George's County [Judgment Record 1728-9, 413] and was called "An Indian man named Tom" in the inventory of the Prince George's County estate of Thomas Addison in 1727 [Prerogative Inventories 12:295-313].
• Hayfield was free from his indenture in Prince George's County in March 1781 [Judgment Record 1777-82, 671, 712-3].
• John Williams was free from his indenture in Charles County in January 1706/7 [Court Record 1704-10, 272, 288].
• William Creek was free from his indenture to Samuel Chew in Anne Arundel County in March 1736/7 [Court Record 1736-8, 126]. And three members of the Creek family were listed in the inventory of another member of the Chew family in 1737.
• an East Indian named Juba was free from his indenture in Anne Arundel County in 1763 [Judgment Record 1760-2, 166].
• an East Indian named Aron Johnson still had two and a half years to serve when he was listed in the 1 June 1729 inventory of the Anne Arundel County estate of Elizabeth Duhadway [Prerogative Inventories 15:251].
• An unnamed East Indian had about 16 months to serve when he was listed in the 22 January 1732 inventory of the Baltimore County estate of John Stokes [Prerogative Inventories, 18:310].
• an East Indian named George Nulla was 20 years old and valued at £30 in 1759 when he was listed in the Anne Arundel County estate of John Raitt [Prerogative Inventories 69:1-3].

East Indians apparently blended into the free African American population. Peter, an East Indian who was one of the ancestors of the **Fisher** family, had a child by a white woman named Mary Molloyd about 1680 and "became a free Molato after serving some time to Major Beale of St. Mary's County" [Anne Arundel County Judgment Record 1734-6, 83; 1743-4, 11].

Migration Between Maryland and Other colonies
A member of the **Hubbard** family, a descendant of a white woman who had a mixed-race child in Westmoreland County, Virginia, in 1705, married a sister of Benjamin **Banneker** in Baltimore County about 1760. Their children obtained certificates of freedom in Loudoun County, Virginia, in 1795. Families who originated in Maryland but were counted in the 1810 census for Virginia included: **Bates, Chambers, Dawson, Dutton, Easter, Fortune, Grace, Graham, Grimes, Grinnage, Lamb, Lett, Nelson, Nichols, Norman, Osborne, Pickett, Ridgeway, Strickland, Trout, Walker, Webster,** and **Welch.**

Endnotes:
1. Families in these histories who descend from white women include: Adams (4? children), Aldridge, Alexander, Allen (4 children), Anderson (2 families), Annis/ Ennis, Atkins, Banks, Barber, Barton/ Burton, Barrett, Bass, Bates, Beckett, Beddo (2 children), Bentley, Boon, Bond, Bone, Boston, Bowen, Brenning, Brown (3 families, 6 children), Brumejum, Bryan (2 children), Bryant (2 children), Buckwell, Buley, Burgess, Burke (2 families, 3 children), Butcher (2 children), Butler (4 families, 7 children), Caldwell, Cannon (2 children), Cambridge, Campbell, Carney, Carr (2 children), Carty, Case, Chambers (3 children), Chuck (2 children), Churb, Clark (3 families, 4 children), Cole, Collins (2 families), Conner, Cook (2 families, 4 children), Cornish, Cox (2 families), Cromwell, Cunningham, Dalton, Davis (4 families, 6 children), Dawson, Day (2 children), Devan, Dobson (3 children), Dogan, Donaldson (2 children), Downs, Duffy, Dunstan (2 children), Dyer, Easter, Edmunds, Ellis, England, English (3 children), Evans (3 children), Farrell, Farthing, Fisher, Fitzgerald (2 children), Flamer, Fletcher, Ford, Fountain, Frost, Gale, Game, Gannon, Gibson, Grace (3 children), Graham, Grant, Graves (2 children), Gray, Grayson, Green, Grimes (2 children), Grinnage (4 children), Guy, Hall (2 families, 3 children), Hamilton, Hanser, Harding, Harris (2 families, 3 children), Harrison, Harwood, Hawkins, Haws, Heath, Hicks, Hill, Hilton, Hodgkin, Hodgskin, Holland, Holmes, Hopkins (2 children), Howard, Howe (2 children), Hughes (2 families), Impey (2 children), Jackson, Jervice (2 children), Johnson, Jones (5 families, 9 children), Kelly (2 children), Kersey, King, Knight, Lawder, Lee (3 families), Lett, Lewis (3 children), Liles (5 children), Littlejohn (2 children), McDaniel (2 families, 4 children), McDonald (3 children), Madden (6 children), Magee, Mallory (2 children), Miller (2 families), Mitchell (3 children), Moody (3 children), Morgan, Mortis, Munt(s) (6 children), Murray (3 children), Myers, Natt (2 children), Nelson, Newman, Nichols, Nicholson, Norman (3 children), Norris, Nutt, Oliver (2 families), Osborne, Overton, Parker, Parsons (2 children), Patterson (2 children), Peck (2 families, 3 children), Penny, Phillips (2 families, 5 children), Pickett, Plowman, Plummer (2 families), Poulson, Price (2 families), Pritchett, Proctor (2 families, 3 children), Ray (4 children), Reardon, Redding/ Redden, Reed, Rhoads, Richards, Roach, Roberts (2 families, 3 children), Robinson (2 families, 3 children), Rogers, Rollins, Ross, Russell, Rustin, Sammons (4 children), Sampson (2 families, 7 children), Saunders, Scarlet (5 children), Scott (2 families), Shaver, Shaw, Shepherd, Sheldon, Shorter (3 children), Simiter (2 children), Skinner, Smith (2 families, 3 children), Snow, Southwood, Spearman, Spencer, Stanley, Stevenson, Stewart (2 families), Strickland, Suitor, Summers, Taylor (3 children), Thomas (2 families), Thompson (2 children), Tills, Tippett, Tunks, (3 children), Turner (2 families, 4 children), Upton, Walker, Ward, Watson, Webber, Wedge (5 children), Welch, Whittam, Wilkins, Wilkinson (2

families), Williams (3 families), Willis, Wilson (2 children), Winslow, Wise, Wood and Wright.

There were at least another 112 white women who had 127 children by African Americans in colonial Maryland:

- Jane Acron in 1757 [Charles County Court Record 1757-8, 1].
- Adam a "Mulatto" child left at the house of Benjamin Denny in Queen Anne's County in February 1760 [Judgments 1759-62, image 102].
- Jane Addison in 1710 [Charles County Court Record D-2:136, 196, 198].
- Elizabeth Adeline before 1708 [Charles County Court Records B-2:433].
- Mary Alvery in 1706 [Anne Arundel County Judgment Record 1705-6, 378; 1707-8, 568].
- Thomasin Amos (twins) in 1722 [Prince George's County Court Record 1720-2, 648, 653, 659, 661].
- Monica Baggot in 1749 [Charles County Court Record 1748-50, 351, 549, 726; 1750, 59].
- Ursula Banninger in 1768 [Prince George's County Court Record 1766-8, 574; 1768-70, 477].
- Ann Bellows 1734 [Anne Arundel County Judgment Record 1734-6, 3-4].
- Martha Bedworth in 1707 [Charles County Court Record 1704-10, 301].
- Elizabeth Blackbourne in 1705 [Somerset County Liber G-I:251.
- Mary Bowsley in 1742 [Prince George's County Court Proceedings 1742-3, 112; 1743-4, 168].
- Margaret Caine in 1763 [Charles County Court Records 1762-4, 352, 475].
- Elizabeth Cannah in 1753 [Kent County, Maryland Criminal Proceedings 1748-60, 119].
- Chance a "Mulatto" child found at the door of John Faulkner in Queen Anne's County in 1761 [Judgments 1759-62, image 85].
- Ann Christian in 1713 [Somerset County Judicial Record 1713-15, 74, 212].
- Elizabeth Cobham in 1690/1 [Dorchester Judgment Record 1690-2, 176, 157, 156].
- Hannah Coe in 1720 [Kent County, Delaware General Court Record 1718-22, 105].
- Elizabeth Coram in 1750 [Kent County, Maryland Criminal Proceedings 1748-60, 48-9].
- Mary Costos in 1743 [Baltimore County Court Proceedings 1743-6, 71, 88, 155, 163].
- Margaret Crass in 1746 and 1748 [Prince George's County Court Record 1743-6, 532; 1747-8, 331; 1748-9, 44].
- Grace Davison in 1756 [Prince George's County Court Record 1754-8, 218].
- Ann Dazey in 1718 [Queen Anne's County Judgment Record 1718-9, 5].
- Elizabeth Demsey in 1742 [Prince George's County Judicial Record 1742-3, Liber AA:1].
- Rachel Dee in 1755 [Talbot County Criminal record, 1751-5, n.p.; 1755-61, 12-14].
- Ann Dick in 1771 [Charles County Court Records 1770-2, 491; 1772-3, 9, 31].
- Dorothy Dorson in 1736 [Anne Arundel County Judgment Record 1736-8, 18, 36].
- the mother of Fanny Dreaded about 1760 [Frederick County Judgment Records 1780-1, 53-4].
- Ann Dunn in 1773 [Frederick County Judgment Records, 1773-5, 46].
- Jane Disbar in 1714 and 1720 [Prince George's County Court Record 1710-5, 605, 632; 1720-2, 17, 18].
- Sarah Diamond/ Diamant in 1703 [Anne Arundel County Judgment Record 1703-5, 3, 323].
- Jane Duxberry in 1714 and 1720 [Prince George's County Court Record

1710-5, 605, 632; 1720-2, 17, 18].
- Mary Foggett in Cecil County two before November 1734 [Criminal Records 1733-41, 58].
- Eleanor Foggett in 1734 [Charles County Court Records 1735-9, T-2:6].
- Sarah Garner in 1760 [Charles County Court Records 1759-60, 425; 1760-2, 99-100].
- Katherine Gea† in 1715 [Kent County, Maryland Court Proceedings 1714-6, 84].
- Elizabeth Gibbeth in 1770 [Charles County Court Records 1770-2, 128, 254].
- Mary Gorman in 1707 [Talbot County Judgment Record 1706-8, 266-7].
- Sarah Gloster in 1738 [Somerset County Judicial Record 1738-40, 13].
- Isabella Guttery in 1762 and 1767 [Prince George's County Court Record 1761-3, 237; 1766-8, 229].
- Ann Hardie in 1746 [Anne Arundel County Judgment Record 1746-8, 293].
- Ann Haslewood in 1693 [Charles County Court Record 1693-4, 2, 116-7].
- Ann Heather in Somerset County in 1728 [Judicial Record 1727-30, 120].
- Hannah Hockerty in 1770 [Prince George's County Court Record 1768-70, 654].
- mother of Dinah and Dick Hodney in 1774 and 1776 [Montgomery County Court Proceedings 1777-81, 8]
- mother of John Hogson in Queen Anne's County in 1722 [Prerogative Inventories 24:350-1].
- Mary Hoy in 1728 [Queen Anne's County Judgment Record 1728-1730, 37].
- Jane Hudleston in 1682 [Talbot County Court Judgments 1682-5, 22].
- Frances Humphreys in 1744 [Baltimore County Court Proceedings 1743-6, 471, 481-2].
- Martha Hurd in 1739 [Anne Arundel County Judgment Record 1739-40, 11].
- Ann Hyde in 1753 [Prince George's County Court 1751-4, 496, 509].
- the mother of Jane, "Mollatto" servant of Thomas Crow, in 1739 [Kent County, Maryland Criminal Record 1738-9, 226, 230].
- Jenater Jerors in August 1765 [Queen Anne's County Criminal Record 1759-66, n.p.].
- Keturah Jones in 1757 and 1761 [Somerset County Judicial Records 1757-60, 76-7; 1760-3, 76a].
- Joanna Kashier in 1704 [Wright, *Anne Arundel County Church Records*, 155].
- Jane Knock in 1743 and 1747 [Kent County, Maryland Criminal Proceedings 1742-7, 180, 377].
- Sarah Knowlman in 1742 [Talbot County Judgment Record 1742, 171].
- Ann Ladley in 1732 [Talbot County Judgment Record 1731-3, 550].
- Catherine Lands in 1766 [Charles County Court Records 1764-6, 772].
- Margaret Lang in 1731 [Queen Anne's County Judgment Record 1730-2, 162-3; 1735-9, 419].
- Catherine Langsdale in 1761 [Charles County Court Record 1760-2, 229, 275].
- Mary Lavender in 1717 [Kent County, Maryland Court Proceedings 1716-8, 247, 284-5].
- Sarah Leopard in 1716 [Somerset County Judicial Records 1715-17, 145].
- Frances Lewellin in Queen Anne's County in 1771, 1772, and 1774 [Judgments 1771-80, images 46-7, 67, 136-7, 174-5].
- Hannah Litman in 1718 [Kent County Court, Court Proceedings, 1718-20, 153, 210].
- Elizabeth Logan in 1718 [Somerset County Judicial Records EF:17].
- Ann Logan in 1757 [Somerset County Judicial Records 1757-61, 41a].
- Elizabeth Love in 1755 [Charles County Court Record 1755-6, 127].
- Ann McFarthing in 1749 [Charles County Court Record 1748-50, 351, 539, 720].

- Margaret McPherson in 1767 [Charles County Court Records 1766-7, 262].
- Eleanor Mackett in 1723 [Prince George's County Court Record 1723-6, 12].
- Elizabeth Mane in 1716 [Talbot County Judgment Record 1714-7, 147].
- Amis Maney in 1747 [Prince George's County Court Record 1747-8, 258].
- Mary Milner in 1726 [Prince George's County Court Records 1726-7, 4, 10].
- the mother of Lewis Mingo about 1682 [Charles County Court Records 1711-15, 307; Provincial Court 1713-16, 150-2].
- Sarah Moals, alias Grimm, in 1753 [Anne Arundel County Judgment Record 1751-4, 510, 518].
- Ruth Mose in August 1755 [Queen Anne's County Criminal Record 1751-9].
- Susannah Moses on 28 November 1728 [Talbot County Judgment Record 1728, n.p.].
- Elizabeth Mote in 1736 and 1737 [Anne Arundel County Judgment Record 1734-6, 448; 1736-8, 148].
- Elizabeth Moy in 1727 [Prince George's County Court Record 1727-8, 345-6].
- Mary Mutters in November 1757 [Queen Anne's County Criminal Record 1751-9].
- Jane Napier in 1721 [Charles County Court Records 1720-2, 127, 128-9].
- the mother of Newmall in 1717 [Prince George's County Court Record 1738-40, 109, 336-7].
- Sarah Neuth in 1749 [Queen Anne's County Judgments 1750, images 45, 49].
- Jane Nuttle in 1741 [Talbot County Judgment Record 1740-1, 259, 272].
- Sarah Obryan in 1762 [Prince George's County Court Record 1761-3, 181].
- Ann Parrat in 1742 [Charles County Court Records 39:450].
- mother of Sarah who married Thomas Perlott in 1734 [Queen Anne's County Judgments 1732-5, 535].
- Sarah Phillmore in 1705 and 1717 [Prince George's County Court Record 1699-1705, 440; 1715-20, 185].
- Sarah Porter in 1729 [Talbot County Judgment Record 1728-31, 126].
- Sarah Purrey in 1705 [Anne Arundel County Judgment Record 1705-6, 51, 116].
- Jane Repwith/ Rapworth in 1753 and 1763 [Charles County Court Record 1753-4, 149, 221; 1762-4, 351].
- Ann Reyny in 1719 and 1721 [Charles County Court Record 1717-20, 188, 311; 1720-2, 201].
- Christian Robison in 1735 [Charles County Court Record 1734-9, 45-6].
- Mary Rye in 1711 [Baltimore County Liber IS#A, 245].
- Rebecca Sandsbury in November 1754 [Talbot County Criminal Record 1751-5, n.p.].
- Elizabeth Sapcott in 1698 [Prince George's County Court Records, 1696-9, 369].
- Eleanor Shehea in Queen Anne's County in 1775 [Surles, *and they Appeared in Court, 1774-1777*, 57].
- Elizabeth Smith in 1718 [Somerset County Liber EF:170].
- Sarah Smith (mother of John Glover) in 1681 [Charles County Court Records A-2:182, 251].
- Ann Christian Snaw in 1734 and 1735 [Prince George's County Court Record 1736-8, 15].
- Elizabeth Strutt in 1743 [Baltimore County Court Proceedings 1743-6, 20, 82].
- Grace Tacker in 1768 [Prince George's County Court Record 1766-8, 573, 581].
- Martildo Tiror in 1726 [Somerset County Judicial Record 1725-7, 132]
- The mother of Toby in 1742 [Baltimore County Proceedings 1741-2, 29-30]
- Elizabeth Vincent in 1686 [Talbot County Judgment Record 1686-9, 68, 173].

- Ann Wade in 1704 [Kent County, Delaware Court Records 1703-17, 5b].
- Susannah Warburton in 1757 [Baltimore County Criminal Record 1757-9, 32].
- Dinah Wenham in 1714 [Baltimore County Liber IS#A, 505].
- Patience Westall in 1733 [Anne Arundel County Judgment Records 1734-6, 80].
- mother of William Worly about 1688 [Pregogative Court (Inventories & Accounts) 24:71-2].
- Mary Yates about 1767 [Talbot County Criminal Record 1767-74, n.p.].

2. The number of "Mulatto" children born to white women in Maryland by county:
    Anne Arundel County: 61 children in court records. 28 in inventories of estates
    Baltimore County: 24 children in court records. 10 listed in inventories
    Calvert County (no colonial court records): 22 children listed in inventories of estates. Probably about 60 children born in the county.
    Charles County: 84 children in the court records. 31 in inventories.
    Dorchester County: 11 children in court records (Only 15 years of colonial records survived..) 18 in inventories.
    Frederick County: 2 children, 1 child in inventory
    Kent County: 50 children in court records, 16 listed in inventories of estates.
    Prince George's County: 72 children in court records. 26 in inventories.
    Queen Anne's County: 44 children in court records (records before 1709 and from 1720-1729 did not survive. 28 children listed in inventories
    Saint Mary's County (no colonial court records): 43 children listed in inventories of estates. Probably at least 60 children born in the county.
    Somerset County: 36 children in court records.14 listed in inventories
    Talbot County: 64 children in court records. 32 listed in inventories.

3. 5 East Indians were listed in inventories of estates
    18 Indian slaves were listed in inventories of estates
    4 Indian servants were listed in inventories of estates
    23 "Free Negroes" were listed in inventories of estates

4. Thirteen children were born to white women in surviving Kent County, Delaware court records: Alice Bryan in 1696 and 1699, Eleanor Price in 1703, Ann Wade and Mary Plowman in 1704, Ann Burk in 1707 and 1708, Hannah Coe in 1720, Elizabeth Sheldon in 1743, Margery Patterson in 1753 and 1755, Martha Brown in 1766 [Court Records 1699-1703, 4b, 10b; 1703-1717, 5b, 50b, 56b, 72b, 80b; 1718-22, 105; DSA, RG 3805-002, 1734-1739, frames 81, 84, 225; RG 3805, MS case files, Indictments August 1755, Presentments August 1766]. A fourteenth family, the Ridgeways, were identified in 1852 as descended from a white woman.

ADAMS FAMILY

1. Mary[1] Adams, born say 1660, was listed in the inventory of the Honorable William Calvert, Esquire, of St. Mary's County on 13 July 1682:

Mary Adams Marryed to a Negro -	*£13*
William a Negro about 30 years old -	*£30*
Adam a Negro about 21 years old -	*£30*

   .....

Jn° a Mallato boy 2 years old -	*£8*

   [Prerogative Court (Inventories and Accounts) MSA SM 13-11, 1682, 206-16]. The family was living in the household of John Manning when they were listed in the inventory of his St. Mary's County estate in 1716:

1 negro man Called Adam -	*£14*
1 malato man Called Tho[s] Adam -	*£30*
1 malato man Called John Adam	*£30*

   [Prerogative Court Inventories and Accounts, MSA SM 13-56, 1715-16, 36c:219-222].
   And they were listed in the inventory of the St. Mary's County estate of Mr. Cornelius Manning on 14 October 1721:

   Home Plantation

1 Molatto Man called Jack Adams & what is his -	*£35*
1 Ditto called Jackey Boy & what is his -	*£35*
1 Old negro man called Adam at	*£14*

   . There was also a "Mallatto slave named Richard Adams about 40 years old" on 25 February 1722/3 when he was listed in the Charles County estate of Mr. Richard Lewellin [Inventories and Accounts, SM 11-8, 1722-3, 135]. Mary (and Adam?) were apparently the parents of

   i. John[1], born about 1680, two years old when he was listed in the estate of William Calvert, valued at £30 when he was listed in John Manning's estate in 1716, valued at £35 in the estate of Mr. Cornelius Manning on 14 October 1721.

   ii. Thomas, born say 1683, a "malato" valued at £30 in the inventory of John Manning's estate in 1716.

A Maryland law of 1664 made slaves of white women who married slaves. The law was repealed in 1681, but did not affect marriages that took place before 1681. Few St. Mary's County's colonial court records have survived, so it is not possible to determine how the family became free, but Mary Adams (and Adam?) were apparently the ancestors of the following free members of the Adams family:

   i.   Sarah, born say 1733, presented by the Charles County court in November 1753 for having a "Mollatto" child [Court Record 1753-4, 166].

   ii.   Jacob[1], head of a Washington County household of 10 "other free" in 1790.

   iii. Ann[1], "Mulatto" head of a Charles County household of 7 "other free" in 1790.

   iv.   Ann[2], "Mulatto" head of a Charles County household of 6 "other free" in 1790.

2 v.   James[1], born say 1760.

   vi.   Joseph, head of a St. Mary's County household of 8 "other free" in 1790.

3 vii. John[2], born say 1760.

4 viii. Hannah, born say 1760.

5 ix.   John[3], born say 1761.

6 x.   Samuel, born say 1762.

7 xi.   Adam, born about 1763.

   xii. Phoeby, head of a St. Mary's County household of 3 "other free" in 1790 and 5 in 1800 [MD:406].

   xiii. Jenny[1], head of a St. Mary's County household of 3 "other free" in 1790 and 5 in Charles County in 1800 [MD:561].

    xiv. Jane[2], head of a Charles County household of 4 "other free" in 1800 [MD:541] and 6 in 1810 (called Jane, Jr.) [MD:304].

    xv. Jacob[2], head of a Dorchester County household of 4 "other free" and a slave in 1800 [MD:649].

    xvi. James[2], born about 1769, head of a St. Mary's County household of 2 "other free" in 1790 and 6 in 1800 [MD:402], obtained a certificate of freedom in St. Mary's County on 15 July 1812: *aged forty three years or thereabouts...complexion black, hair Short & Curly...born free.*

    xvii. Henry, head of a St. Mary's County household of 4 "other free" in 1810 [MD:177].

    xviii. Joseph, born about 1792, registered in St. Mary's County on 1 June 1812: *aged twenty years or thereabouts...Complexion black - hair short and Curley...born free.*

    xix. William, born about 1783, registered in St. Mary's County on 21 June 1815: *aged thirty two years or thereabouts...Dark Complexion...born free* [Certificates of Freedom 1806-64, 17, 18, 32].

2.   James[1] Adams, born say 1760, was head of a St. Mary's County household of 4 "other free" in 1790, 6 in 1800 [MD:412] and 3 in 1810 [MD:176]. He was the father of

    i. Charles, born about 1782, registered in St. Mary's County on 16 June 1821: *son of James Adams...about twenty nine years, of a yellow complexion...born free* [Certificates of Freedom 1806-64, 57].

3.   John[2] Adams, born say 1760, was a "free Negro" head of a Prince George County household of 8 "other free" in 1800 [MD:268] and 8 in 1810 (called J.B. Adams) [MD:22]. He may have been one of four "Black Persons being Soldiers," Thomas **Thompson**, Leonard **Turner**, Valentine **Murrin**, and John Adams, who were arrested in Orange County, North Carolina, in December 1780 for breaking into someone's house. They were forcibly rescued by their officer Major McIntosh of the Continental Army [Orange County Court Minutes 1777-82, Dec. 19 and 23, 1780].[2] He may have been the father of

    i. Maria B., born about 1788, married Nathan D. **Hale/ Hall**. She registered in Prince George's County on 26 February 1813: *Maria B. Hall, formerly Maria B. Adams, is a bright mulatto woman, about 25 years old, and 4 feet 10 inches tall. She was raised in the town of Piscataway in Prince George's County until she married Nathan D. Hale, her present husband. She was born free.*

    ii. George Clinton, born about 1796, registered in Prince George's County on 15 October 1827: *a dark mulatto man, about 31 years old, and 5 feet 9-1/2 inches tall...born free in Prince George's County* [Provine, *Registrations of Free Negroes*, 14, 71].

4.   Hannah Adams, born say 1760, was head of a Baltimore City household of 3 "other free" in 1800 [MD:125]. She may have been the mother of

    i. James[3], married Agnes **Butler**, "both Negroes," by banns on 21 December 1800 [Piet, *Catholic Church Records in Baltimore*, 126].

5.   John[3] Adams, born say 1761, was a "free Mulatto" head of a Charles County household of 7 "other free" in 1800 [MD:523]. He was a "coloured man" who had a daughter named Elizabeth Ann Adams by Sally Gary, a white woman, according to testimony by Thomas G. Slye for Elizabeth Ann's certificate of freedom in

---

[2]John Adams was not charged but agreed to testify against the others. Their commander Colonel Gunley at Hillsboro agreed to deliver them up to the next session of the Superior Court the following April, but no trial took place.

Washington, D.C., on 23 October 1827. Slye also testified that Polly **Carter**, late Polly Adams, and Eleanor **Davis**, late Eleanor Adams, were born free and were his father's servants in Charles County for many years [Provine, *District of Columbia Free Negro Registers*, 99]. John was the father of
  i.   Elizabeth Ann.
  ii.   ?Polly **Carter**.
  iii. ?Eleanor **Davis**.

6. Samuel Adams, born say 1762, was head of a Talbot County household of 5 "other free" in 1790 and 3 "other free" in 1800 [MD:522]. He may have been the father of
  i.   Deborah, born about 1791, registered in Talbot County on 27 May 1819: *a dark mulatto woman...about 28 years of age, 5 feet high...born free and raised in the County* [Certificates of Freedom 1815-28, 121].

7. Adam Adams, born about 1763, a "free black citizen of Charles County," enlisted May 1777 in Captain Henry Gaither's Company of the 1st Maryland Regiment commanded by General William Smallwood and received his discharge in November 1783. He was head of a Charles County household of 2 "other free" in 1790, 2 in 1800 [MD:551] and 8 "free colored" in 1830. He made a declaration in the First Judicial District Court in Charles County on 28 March 1818 and 5 June 1820 to obtain a pension. He was living at the time with his wife Ann and six children: Pamelia, Eleanor, John, Robert, Richard, and Lydia. He received a pension and 50 acres of bounty land for his service [NARA, S.34623, http://fold3.com/image/10982341]. He was the father of
  i.   Pamelia, born about 1806.
  ii.   Eleanor, born about 1811.
  iii. John[4], born about 1812.
  iv.   Robert, born about 1814.
  v.   Richard, born about 1816.
  vi.   Lydia, born about November 1820.

Other members of the family were
  i.   John, head of a Richmond County, Virginia household of 4 "other free" in 1810 [VA:411]. He was probably identical to "John Adams of Maryland a free Negro, by Trade a Ditcher" who sued Richard **Sherdock**, "a free Mulatto," in Lancaster County, Virginia, on 20 December 1776 for assaulting him [Court Papers 1770-1780, n.p.].

ALDRIDGE FAMILY

1. Jane Eldridge, born say 1733, a white woman, was called "Jane Eldrick" and was the servant of Thomas Marsh of Christ Church Parish in November 1749 when the Queen Anne's County court convicted her of having a "Mulatto" child by a "Negro." The court sold her son Nicholas to Elinor Murphy until the age of thirty-one and called her "Jane Eldridge" when it sold her to Captain Thomas Marsh on 26 March 1754 [Judgments 1749, 260, 263; 1752-4, CD image 556 of 948]. She may have been the ancestor of
  i.   Thomas Aldridge, head of a Talbot County household of 3 "other free" in 1790 and 5 "other free" and a slave in 1800 [MD:509], probably identical to Thomas Auldery, a "free Mulatto" head of a Bay Hundred, Talbot County household of 1 male over 50, 2 males 16-50, 3 under 16 and 1 female under 16 in 1776 [Carothers, *1776 Census of Maryland*, 156].
  ii.   Fredus Aldridge, sued in Queen Anne's County court for assault by James Roberts in March 1770 [Surles, *and they Appeared in Court, 1770-1772*, 8]. He was head of an Elk Neck, Cecil County household of 1 "other free" in 1790.
  iii. John Aldridge, head of a Talbot County household of 5 "other free" in

1790 and 8 in Dorchester County in 1800 [MD:673].

ALEXANDER FAMILY

1. Elizabeth Alexander, born say 1740, the spinster servant of Samuel Hodges, confessed to the Kent County court in June 1761 that she had a "Molatto" child. The court sold her and her child to her master [Criminal Record 1761-72, 8]. She was probably the mother of

    i. Robert, head of a Cecil County household of 8 "other free" in 1810 [MD:248].

    ii. Henry, head of a Cecil County household of 6 "other free" in 1810 [MD:245].

ALLEN FAMILY

1. Hannah[1] Allen, born say 1730, the "Molatto" servant of Joshua Clark, confessed in Prince George's County court to the charge of "Mollatto Bastardy" on four occasions. She was ordered to serve her master an additional seven years for each offense, and her children were bound to her master until the age of thirty-one. Her children were Ignatius (five weeks old on 25 June 1751), Jane (born before 27 November 1753), Frank (six months old on 23 March 1757), and Hannah (three months old on 27 June 1758) [Court Record 1751-4, 71, 512; 1754-8, 411, 412, 636]. Her grandson, Nathaniel Allen, was bound as an apprentice to Richard Higgins in 1772 until the age of thirty-one. In November 1794 when he had passed the age of twenty-one, he petitioned for the Anne Arundel County court for freedom from his indenture, stating that he was the great-grandson of a white woman who had a child named Hannah Allen by a Negro. Hannah, in turn, had a child named Jane Allen who had Nathaniel by a Negro. Nathaniel was bound to Richard Higgins under a law which ruled that the children of free Mulatto women and Negro slaves were to be bound until the age of thirty-one. Nathaniel's lawyer argued that Jane Allen should not have been considered a free Mulatto since she was the daughter of a Mulatto, not a white woman. Nathaniel lost his case in the General Court and had to serve the full thirty-one years [*Cases in the General Court and Court of Appeals of Maryland*, 504]. Hannah was the mother of

    i. Ignatius, born in May 1751, head of a Prince George's County household of 7 "other free" in 1790 and 5 in 1800 [MD:304].

2   ii. Jane, born in 1753.

3   iii. ?Mima[1], born say 1754.

    iv. Frank, born about September 1756, a "free negro" head of a Prince George's County household of 4 "other free" in 1800 [MD:304].

    v. Hannah[2], born March 1757.

2. Jane Allen, born in 1753, was living in Prince George's County in August 1772 when the court ordered her to serve an additional seven years of her indenture for having an illegitimate child "by a negro" and bound her son Nathaniel to serve Richard Higgins for thirty-one years [Court Record 1771-3, 186]. Her son was

    i. Nathaniel[1], born about March 1772, petitioned for his freedom in Anne Arundel County court in September 1794. He registered in Prince George's County court on 11 September 1810: *a black man about 39 years old...raised by Richard Higgins of Anne Arundel County and was born free according to the records of that County Court* [Provine, *Registrations of Free Negroes*, 7].

3. Mima[1] Allen, born say 1754, "a free mulatto woman" of Prince George's County, was the mother of

4   i. Henny, born about 1774.

    ii. Mima[2], born about 1789, registered in Prince George's County on 2 December 1812: *a dark mulatto, nearly black woman, about 23 years old, and 5 feet tall. She has thick lips, a fleshy face, a flat nose, and short wooly hair. She was raised in Prince George's County in the family of Daniel Clarke near Queen Anne and is a free woman, being the daughter of Mima Allen.* Her son Charles Allen registered on 23 June 1818: *a Negro boy, tolerably black, who is about 8 years old...son of Mima Allen.*

4. Henny Allen, born about 1774, registered in Prince George's County on 4 April 1812: *a mulatto woman, about 38 years old, and 4 feet 11 inches tall...rather flat nose, and thick lips. She was raised in Prince George's County in the family of Daniel Clarke near Queen Anne. She is the daughter of Mima Allen, a free mulatto woman.* Henny was the mother of

    i.   Hannah[3], born about 1795, registered in Prince George's County on 4 April 1812: *a dark mulatto woman, about 17 years old, and 5 feet 10 inches tall...flat nose, thick lips and a broad face...born in Prince George's County in the family of Daniel Clarke near Queen Anne...daughter of Henny Allen a free mulatto woman who was born free.*

    ii. Nelly, born about 1797, registered in Prince George's County on 2 October 1812: *about 15 years old, 4 feet 6-1/2 inches tall, and has a yellowish complexion...has woolly hair, a flat nose, full eyes, and good teeth...daughter of Henny Allen, a free woman* [Provine, *Registrations of Free Negroes*, 10, 13, 25].

Other members of the Allen family were

    i.   John, "free negro" head of a Prince George's County household of 9 "other free" in 1800 [MD:299].

    ii. James, "free negro" head of a Prince George's County household of 5 "other free" in 1800 [MD:302].

    iii. Nathan[2], born about 1786, registered in Anne Arundel County on 30 January 1816: *aged about thirty years...brown complexion...free born* [Certificates of Freedom 1810-31, 75].

    iv. Rachel, born about 1788, registered in Anne Arundel County on 6 August 1807: *aged nineteen years...yellowish complexion...raised in Anne Arundel County* [Certificates of Freedom 1806-7, 44].

Another Allen family:

    i.   William, charged by constable Francis Duling in Talbot County court with failing to list his wife Margaret as a taxable person. The court's attorney declined to prosecute [Criminal Record 1755-61, 242-3].

ALSOP FAMILY

Members of the Alsop family of Maryland were

    i.   John, in Captain Bayley's Maryland Regiment commanded by Colonel John Gumby at White Plains on 9 September 1778 [NARA, M246, roll 34, frames 240, 397 of 587]. He enlisted from Frederick County until 10 December 1781 [*Archives of Maryland*, 18:653]. John Allstep was head of an Anne Arundel County household of 4 "other free" in 1810.

    ii. Holsey, head of an Anne Arundel County household of 8 "other free" in 1810, married Juliet **Brown** on 11 December 1807 in Anne Arundel County.

    iii. Tom, born about 1772, head of an Anne Arundel County household of 6 "other free" in 1810. He was counted as a "Mulatto," born in Maryland, married to Elizabeth, born 1788, in the 1850 Dauphin County, Pennsylvania census.

    iv. Alley, married Elisha **Smithers/ Smothers** on 1 May 1802 in Anne Arundel County.

ANDERSON FAMILY

1. Mary Anderson, born say 1716, the "Molatto" servant of Doctor Alexander Adair of Saint Paul's Parish, confessed to the Kent County, Maryland court on 14 November 1738 that she had two illegitimate children. The court bound her daughter Rachel to her master [Criminal Proceedings 1738-9, 36, 84-6]. She was the mother of

    i. Rachel[1], born about 1738, a "Free Molatto" spinster who confessed to the Kent County court that she had a child on 28 January 1759 by a "Negroe" man. In March 1759 the court sold her to Joseph Nicholson for seven years. In March 1766 she confessed that she had another child by a "Negroe," and the court sold her and her child to Josias Ringgold [Criminal Proceedings 1748-60, 219; 1761-72, 70a]. She was head of a Queen Anne's County household of 6 "other free" in 1790.

Other members of an Anderson family were

    i. Joseph, "Negro" head of a Kent County household of 7 "other free" and a slave in 1790 and 6 "other free" in 1800 [MD:157].
    ii. Susannah, head of an Octoraro, Cecil County household of 4 "other free" in 1790.
    iii. James, head of a Cecil County household of 7 "other free" in 1800 [MD:575].
    iv. Hannah, a "free Negroe" living in Kent County on 21 June 1780 when the court ordered her and John Fitzgerald to appear at the next court to testify on behalf of Negro Caesar's petition that he had completed his indenture to Robert Roberts but was still being held as a servant [Court Minutes 1774-1782, n.p.].
2   v. Mary, born say 1750.
    vi. William, born about 1756, about 62 years of age on 15 May 1818 when he appeared in Lebanon, Ohio, to apply for a pension. He stated that he enlisted in the 6th Maryland Regiment under Captain Carberry. His name did not appear on any roster, but Jeremiah Collins, a captain of horse of the French troops, testified that he knew William Anderson, a "black man," who was a servant to Captain West and served part of the time with the French troops and part with the Americans. He received a severe wound to his thigh [NARA, R.203, M804, roll 59, frame 104 of 693].
3   vii. Thomas, born say 1760.
    viii. Stephen, head of a Cecil County household of 4 "other free" in 1800 [MD:247].
4   ix. Ned, born say 1770.
    x. Nathan[1], head of a St. Jones Hundred, Kent County, Delaware household of 6 "other free" in 1800 [DE:48].
    xi. Mary, a "Free Mulatto" indicted by the Kent County, Delaware court in May 1792 [RG 3805.002, 1787-1803, frame 176].
    xii. Nathan[2], head of a St. Jones Hundred, Kent County, Delaware household of 5 "other free" in 1800 [DE:46].
    xiii. John[1], head of a "Coloured" New Castle County household of 9 "free colored" in 1810 [DE:242].
    xiv. John[2], head of a "Coloured" New Castle County household of 4 "other free" in 1810 [DE:242].

2. Mary Anderson, born say 1750, had an illegitimate child named Risdon Anderson in Queen Anne's County by George **Dias** before March 1770 [Surles, *And They Appeared at Court, 1777-2*, 5, 40]. She was a "mulatto" who confessed to the Queen Anne's County court in March 1774 that she had an illegitimate child by a Negro slave [Judgments 1771-80, 144-5]. She was head of a Kent County household of 2 "other free" in 1800 [MD:157]. She was the mother of

    i. Risdon, head of a New Castle County household of 11 "other free" in 1810

[DE:68].
ii. ?George, "Negro" head of a Kent County household of 1 "other free" in 1790.

3. Thomas Anderson, born say 1760, was head of a Talbot County household of 4 "other free" in 1790 and 5 in 1800 [MD:522]. He may have been the father of
    i. Rachel^2, born about 1783, registered in Talbot County on 26 August 1817: *a black woman...about 34 years of age, 5 feet 4 Inches high...born free & raised in the County* [Certificates of Freedom 1814-28, 68].

4. Ned Anderson, born say 1770, and his wife, Lady, were the parents of a "mulatto" girl named "Sale," born in Bohemia, who was baptized by a priest from the Jesuit Mission, Old Bohemia, Warwick, Cecil County, on 14 September 1796. He may have been identical to Edward Anderson who was head of a New Castle County household of 5 "other free" in 1810 [DE:68]. Ned and Lady were the parents of
    i. Sally, born about March 1795, a sixteen-month-old "mulatto" child baptized 14 September 1796 [Wright, *Vital Records of the Jesuit Missions, 1760-1800*, 43].

Another Anderson family:
1. Christian Anderson, born say 1738, was the indentured servant of Robert Horner of Charles County on 6 January 1756 when she delivered a "Molatto" male child which was begotten "by a Negroe." She denied the charge but was convicted in Charles County court in March 1757. The court bound her son Hensey Anderson until the age of thirty-one [Court Record 1760-2, 465-6]. She was the mother of
    i. Hensey, born about 1757, probably identical to Hendley Anderson, "Mulatto" head of a Charles County household of 1 "other free" in 1790.
    ii. ?Caesar, head of an Anne Arundel County household of 5 "other free" in 1790.
    iii. ?Yroek, head of an Anne Arundel County household of 3 "other free" in 1790.

ANNIS FAMILY
(See the Ennis family)

ANTHONY FAMILY

Members of the Anthony family in Maryland were
    i. John, head of a Baltimore City household of 14 "other free" in 1800 [MD:125].
    ii. George, a "free Negro" taxable in the 4th District of Kent County in 1783 [MSA S1161-7-4, p.4].
    iii. Samuel, head of a Baltimore City household of 6 "other free" in 1800 [MD:126].
    iv. James, married Magdalen **Pindare**, "French free Negroes from St. Domingo," 8 February 1796 at St. Peter's Church in Baltimore. Their one month old daughter Mary Joseph was baptized there on 15 December 1799 [Piet, *Catholic Church Records in Baltimore*, 4, 126].

ARMSTRONG FAMILY

Members of the Armstrong family in Maryland were
    i. Bayham, head of a Worcester County household of 5 "other free" in 1790.
    ii. Rachel, head of a Talbot County household of 6 "other free" and a white woman in 1800 [MD:517].
1   iii. Jacob, born say 1760.
    iv. Rachel, head of a Talbot County household of 4 "other free" in 1800 [MD:517].

    v.   Nanny, "Negro" head of a Worcester County household of 7 "other free" in 1800 [MD:735].

    vi. Rhoda, head of a Worcester County household of 10 "other free" in 1800 [MD:832].

    vii. Stephen, head of a Worcester County household of 5 "other free" in 1810 [MD:589].

    viii. George, born before 1776, head of a Worcester County household of 5 "free colored" in 1830.

    ix. Peggy, born before 1776, head of a Worcester County household of 3 "free colored" in 1830.

1.   Jacob Armstrong, born say 1760, made a Worcester County deed of manumission to his daughter Lycia Armstrong who was born of his wife Comfort, a slave to William Selby, on 26 April 1787 [Land Records M:173]. He was head of a Worcester County household of 6 "other free" in 1800 [MD:832] and 6 "other free" and 5 slaves in 1810 [MD:636]. He was the father of

    i.   Lycia.

Delaware

1.   Jacob Armstrong, born say, 1750, was taxable in Kent County from 1773 to 1785: taxable in Murderkill Hundred from 1773 to 1776, called a "F. Neg°" in Duck Creek in 1779, listed as a "Free Negro" in Dover Hundred in 1782, a "N." in Duck Creek Hundred in 1783, a "free Negro" in Dover Hundred in 1785 [RG 3535, Kent County Levy List, 1768-84, frames 187, 224, 281, 370, 373, 439, 527, 540, 544, 568, 571, 580, 604; 1785-97, frame 3]. He may have been the father of

    i.   Joseph, "N." head of a Duck Creek Hundred household of 5 "other free" in 1800 [DE:13].

    ii. James, a "Negro" who paid a £3 fine to the Kent County court in August 1791 for having an illegitimate child by Hannah **Danach** [RG 3805.002, 1787-1803, frame 157, 159, 164, 173]. James was a "N." head of a Duck Creek Hundred household of 4 "other free" in 1800 [DE:11]. Hannah was head of a Duck Creek Hundred household of 5 "free colored" in 1820 [DE:51].

ARMWOOD FAMILY

1.   Jemima Armwood, born say 1726, was a "free negro" (written as Airmwood) who received 25 lashes in Accomack County on 30 August 1743 for bearing an illegitimate child [Orders 1737-44, 497]. She was taxable in John Tull's Pocomoke Hundred, Somerset County household in 1757 [List of Taxables]. She was prosecuted in Somerset County court in 1759 for having an illegitimate child by a "negro slave" [Judicial Records 1757-61, 236]. She (or perhaps a daughter by the same name) was a "Negro" head of a Worcester County household of 3 "other free" in 1800 [MD:733]. She was probably the mother of

    i.   James, head of a Worcester County household of 7 "other free" in 1800 [MD:762], 7 in 1810 [MD:612] and 5 "free colored" in 1830.

2   ii. Daniel, born say 1765.

    iii. Waify, born before 1776, head of a Worcester County household of 8 "free colored" in 1830.

2.   Daniel Armwood, born say 1765, was head of a Worcester County household of 6 "other free" in 1800 [MD:796] and 11 "free colored" in 1830. He was apparently married to a slave since he made a deed of manumission to his children and grandchildren on 4 September 1823. He sold a horse, carriage, harness, cart and six hogs to John Dennis in Worcester County for $100 on 20 April 1832 [Land Records AP:189-190; AY:61]. His children were

    i.   Easter, born about 1797, mother of Zeppa, John, Levi, Ann, Patience and Mill.

    ii.   Nancy, born about 1797.
    iii. Patience, born about 1798,
    iv. Nelly, born about 1802, mother of Henry and Elisa.
    v.   Sally, born about 1802.

ATKINS FAMILY

1.   Eleanor Atkins, born say 1677, was the servant of James Neale on 9 March 1696/7 when she was presented by the Charles County court for having a "Molattoe" child. She did not appear for her presentment because she was pregnant with a second child which she delivered before 8 March 1697/8. The court ordered that she receive twenty-four lashes [Court Records 1696-1701, 162, 280, 306, 334, 376]. She was probably the mother of
    i.   Martha, born say 1697, presented by the Charles County court on 8 November 1726 for having a "Mallatto" child. She confessed to the charge, and the court sold her for seven years and sold her child to Major Robert Hanson until the age of thirty-one [Court Record 1725-7, 409, 494]. Her child was apparently Martha Adkins a "Mullatto" woman who had about nine years to serve when she was listed in the 9 September 1749 inventory of the Charles County estate of Robert Hanson [Prerogative Inventories 1749-50, 217].

They may have been the ancestors of
    i.   Will, head of Cecil County household of 2 "other free" in 1800 [MD:249].

ATLOW FAMILY

1.   Priscilla Atlow, born say 1750, was head of a Frederick County household of 7 "other free" in 1790. She was probably the mother of
    i.   George, born about 1770, obtained a certificate in Frederick County on 6 February 1822: *aged about fifty two years five feet eight and a half inches high...dark Mullatto...free born as appears by the affidavit of Jacob Hoff* [Certificates of Freedom 1806-27, 126].

BADGER FAMILY

Members of the Badger family in Maryland were
    i.   Nan, head of an Anne Arundel County household of 8 "other free" in 1790.
    ii.   Charles, head of an Anne Arundel County household of 7 "other free" in 1790 and 3 in Baltimore City in 1810 [MD:310].
    iii. Nace, head of an Anne Arundel County household of 6 "other free" in 1810 [MD:62].
    iv. Diner, head of an Anne Arundel County household of 6 "other free" in 1810 [MD:66].
    v.   Samuel, born about 1785, registered in Anne Arundel County on 20 May 1807: *free born...about twenty two years, his Complexion a dark Mulatto, was born and bred at the head of South River in Anne Arundel County* [Certificates of Freedom 1806-7, 28].

BAKER FAMILY

1.   Anthony Baker, born say, was a "Mulatto" man living in Kent County, Maryland, on 10 October 1719 when the court found Josiah Crouch innocent of having a child by Anthony's wife Elizabeth Baker [Court Proceedings 1718-20, 510-11]. He may have been the ancestor of
    i.   John, head of a Kent County household of 4 "other free" in 1800 [MD:146] and 4 "free colored" in Dover Hundred, Kent County,

Delaware, in 1820 [DE:40].

BANKS FAMILY

1. Katherine Banks, born say 1705, was the servant of William Ellis on 21 June 1726 when she confessed in Kent County, Maryland court that she had an illegitimate child by Caleb **Hews**, a "free Negroe" [Criminal Record 1724-8, 183, 222-5]. She was probably the ancestor of
    i.   Matthew, head of a Baltimore City household of 6 "other free" in 1800 [MD:144]
    ii. Ann, head of a Dorchester County household of 4 "other free" in 1800 [MD:701].
    iii. Elisha, head of a Dorchester County household of 4 "other free" in 1800 [MD:726].
2   iv. Henry, born say 1770.
    v.   William, born before 1776, head of a Dorchester County household of 4 "free colored" in 1830.
    vi. Sinah, born say 1780, mother of Charlotte Banks who registered in Dorchester County on 17 May 1832: *light chesnut colour...born free...daughter of Sinah also born free, about 31 years of age* [Certificates of Freedom for Negroes 1806-64, 83].

2. Henry Banks, born say 1770, and his wife Rachel, "people of color," baptized their daughter Peggy in St. Paul's Parish, Baltimore. Their daughter was
    i.   Peggy, born about 1793, nine years old when she was baptized on 9 May 1802 [Reamy, *Records of St. Paul's Parish*, II:13].

BANNEKER FAMILY

1. Robert Bannaky/ Banneker, born say 1700, was married to Mary **Lett**, the mixed daughter of a white woman, by 18 May 1731 when she (called Mary Beneca) petitioned the Maryland Provincial Court for her children Sarah, Zachariah and Deborah **Lett** [Provincial Court Judgments, Liber R.B. no.1, fols. 425-426, MSA]. This was probably his second marriage since (his daughter?) "negro" Katherine Bannaker married four years later in May 1735.[3] In March 1736/7 the Baltimore County court exempted Robert Banekey and his unnamed wife from paying taxes during the lifetime of their crippled "Molatto" child Julian, and remitted their taxes for the previous year [Court Proceedings 1736-9, 2]. He and his son Benjamin Bannaky/ Bannaker purchased 100 acres in Upper Patapsco Hundred of Baltimore County called *Stout* from Richard Gist for 7,000 pounds of tobacco on 10 March 1737/8 [Land Records, HWS #IA, 58-9].[4] Robert was taxable on this 100-acre tract and another 25 acres called *Timber Point* in 1737 [MHS, Debt Book, Baltimore County, Calvert Papers No. 904, p.69, cited by Bedini, *Life of Benjamin Banneker*, 29, 347]. Robert was called "Robert Banakey, a Negro free," on 1 November 1743 when the Baltimore County court ordered that his daughters be levy free for the future [Court Proceedings 1743-6, 78]. He owed £1 to the Baltimore County estate of Richard Gist in 1742 and 480 pounds of tobacco to the estate of Charles Christie on 29 June 1762 [Prerogative Inventories 29:20; 78:98-9]. He died on 10 July 1759 according to the entry in his family bible. (His widow) was called Mary Banicker on 27 February 1758 when Mary Welsh, widow of John Welsh, made a Prince George's County deed of release to her for a "Mealato Servant Samuell Morter" (who was the husband of Mary

---

[3]Banaka is the name of a town in Liberia [http://google.com/maps]. The second marriage may have been the origin of the family story that Mary owned two slaves.

[4]Richard Gist bought this land on 19 January 1733/4 for £31.18 [Land Records HWS#M, fol. 26].

Banicker's daughter Molly) [Land Records, PP:104]. On 3 December 1773 John Welsh's widow Mary Welsh also gave Mary Banicker a Prince George's County deed of release to her rights to "Negro Ben (who) had been born free" and was then about 43 years of age [Land Records BB3:325]. Mary apparently used this deed four months later on 19 April 1774 when she was called "Mary the widow of Robert Bannaker" and deposed in Baltimore County that Benjamin was the true and lawful son of Robert Banneker, deceased [Baltimore Chattel Records 4:98].[5] Mary and Robert were the parents of

i. ?Katherine, born say 1728, married James **Boston** (**Barton**?), "negroes," in St. Paul's Parish, Baltimore County, on 22 May 1735 [Reamy, *Records of St. Paul's Parish*, I:32].

ii. ?Esther, born say 1726, married William **Black**, on 22 September 1744 in St. Paul's Parish, Baltimore [Reamy, *Records of St. Paul's Parish*, I:36].

iii. Molly, born say 1730, married a member of the **Morton** family, apparently identical to Samuel Molton, a "molatto" belonging to John Welsh of Prince George's County on 24 February 1748 when Welsh directed that he be free after the death of his wife [Prerogative Court (Wills), Liber 26, folio 40]. Samuel **Moreton** was taxable in Patapsco Upper Hundred of Baltimore County in 1773 [MSA, Tax List] and was listed in the ledger of Ellicott & Company between September 1774 and July 1775.

iv. Benjamin, born 9 November 1731 according to his family Bible [Bedini, *Life of Benjamin Banneker*, 46-7]. He was taxable as a bachelor on an assessment of £300 or more in St. Paul's Parish, Baltimore County, between 1756 and 1762 [Reamy, *Records of St. Paul's Parish*, I:165]. He signed the Baltimore County, Maryland petition of 27 January 1768 to move the county seat from Joppa to Baltimore [*Archives of Maryland Online*, Vol. 61:531]. He was taxable in Patapsco Upper Hundred in 1773 [MSA C428-51, 1773 Tax List]. He sold 20 acres of his land to Greenbury **Morten** on 20 December 1785 and 10 acres to his neighbor John **Barton** on 2 April 1792 [Land Records WG#Y, ff. 653-4; WG#HH. ff. 341-2]. This was land his father had purchased in 1738. He sold 2 acres to Edward **Shugar** (head of a Patapsco Upper Hundred household of 5 "other free" in 1810) on 10 December 1794 and sold the last 72 acres of *Stout* for £180 to Jonathan, Elias, George and John Ellicott on 22 October 1799 [Land Records PP:606-8; WG#60, 408].

v. Julian, born say 1733, the "crippled" child of Robert Banakey, perhaps the daughter who was the mother of John **Hendon** who managed the Ellicott stables. He registered in Baltimore on 16 Oc1811: *light yellow complexion, 5 feet 5 inches high, age 45, born free in Balt° Co°y* (with Alsey Hendon who was 20) [Certificates of Freedom, 1806-16, (not manumitted), no. 70].

vi. a daughter, the wife of William **Hubbard/ Hubert** who was named in a 30 April 1795 entry in the account book of Benjamin **Banneker** [Bedini, *The Life of Benjamin Banneker*, 249]. He was head of a Patapsco Upper

---

[5] George Ely Russell wrote an article in which he refuted Bedini's assertion that Benjamin Banneker's grandmother was Molly Welsh, a servant maid who married a slave and lived on a farm near Benjamin's in Baltimore County. He showed that she was actually the wife of a white man named John Welsh of Prince George's County who signed her own will [*NGSJ* 94 (2006): 305-14]. This additional information raises several questions: why Mary Welsh used the term "my people" when she directed in her 7 January 1752 Prince George's County will that her trustees "see that my people have their right of freedom," why she needed to emancipate her "free born Negro Benjamin" (who had been a co-owner of land in Baltimore County since 1738) and why Mary Banicker, a free woman, sought Mary Welsh's testimony in 1773 that her son Benjamin was free [Wills T#1:30; Land Records BB3:325]. Were Mary Banneker and Mary Welsh related? There is also the coincidence that a woman nmed Mary Welch had a child (named Henry) by a slave in Prince George's County in 1728 (and was sold as a servant for seven years).

Hundred, Baltimore County household of 5 "other free" in 1810 [MD:639] and the father of Henry and Charles **Hubbard** who obtained certificates of freedom in Loudoun County, Virginia, on 24 December 1795: *son of a free woman and grandson of Robert Banneker, whose wife was also a free woman. Robert Banneker lived in Baltimore County about two and a half miles from Ellicott's Mills* [http://lfportal.loudoun.gov/LFPortalInternet/0/edoc/478541/FB1795.02 .pdf]. Perhaps she was Ursula Banninger who was presented by the Prince George's County court in 1768 for having a "Malatto" child on information of the constable of Rock Creek Hundred but not found by the sheriff [Court Records 1766-8, 574; 1768-70, 477].

Other members of the family were
  i.   Mary Ann Benecker, died before 23 June 1803 when the inventory of her Baltimore County estate was recorded. It was valued at $88 and included a writing desk [Inventories, 22, 1801-3, 619-20].
  ii. Nancy, a slave who ran away from her master Abidnigo Hyatt of Frederick County according to an ad he placed in the *Maryland Gazette* on 15 June 1775: *ran away on 15 April last an Irish servant...also went with him a lusty negro woman named Rhoad, now goes by the name Nancy Bannaker* [Windley, *Runaway Slave Advertisements*, II:111-2].

BANTUM FAMILY

Members of the Bantum family of Maryland were
1   i.   James, born say 1730.
      ii.   Gabriel, head of a Caroline County household of 8 "other free" in 1790.
      iii. Delia, said to be over 100 years old when she was head of a Talbot County household of 6 "free colored" in 1830.
      iv.   George, head of a Talbot County household of 3 "other free" in 1790.
      v.   Sally, head of a Talbot County household of 3 "other free" in 1800 [MD:531].
      vi.   Joe, head of a Talbot County household of 3 "other free" in 1800 [MD:527] and 3 "free colored" in 1830.
      vii. Nancy Banthum, "Negro" head of a Kent County household of 1 "other free" in 1790.
      viii. Diana, born before 1776, head of a Kent County household of 6 "free colored" in 1830.

1.   James[1] Bantum, born say 1730, was a "Molatto servant man" listed in the inventory of the Talbot County estate of William Brooke on 7 May 1754 [Prerogative Inventories 60:114-8]. He may have been the father of
2   i.   James[2], born about 1757.

2.   James[2] Bantum, born about 1757, was head of a Talbot County household of 8 "other free" in 1800 [MD:534]. He registered in Talbot County on 24 May 1815: *a Black man...about 58 years of age, 5 feet 10-3/4 inches high, has the top of his head bald...was manumitted & set free by...Wm Thomas*. He may have been the father of
      i.   Levin, born about 1783, registered in Talbot County on 27 May 1807: *a Mullatto Man about twenty four years of age, five feet seven and a half inches high...free born of a white woman and bound to Christopher Bruff until he was twenty one years of age.*
      ii.   Edward, born about 1790, registered in Talbot County on 23 July 1810: *a black man...about 20 years of age, 5 feet 7 ½ inches high...dark complection...free born...raised in this County.*
      iii. Harry, born about 1793, registered in Talbot County on 20 March 1810: *a black man...about 22 years of age, 5 feet 9 inches & an half high,*

complection dark Coffee [Certificates of Freedom 1807-15, 30, 43, 46, 174].

    iv. Moses, born about 1795, registered in Dorchester County on 12 April 1815: *of a light chesnut colour...born free* [Certificates of Freedom for Negroes 1806-64, 24].

BARBER FAMILY

1.   Rebecca Barber, born say 1735, was a spinster white servant of Thomas Ozenent in November 1755 when she admitted to the Talbot County court that she had a "Mulatto" child by a "Negroe." The court sold her four-month-old son Amos until the age of thirty-one for 5 shillings [Criminal Record 1751-5, 14-5]. She was the mother of

    i. Amos, born about July 1755.

Other members of the family were

    i. David, born before 1776, head of a Dover Hundred, Kent County, Delaware household of 3 "free colored" in 1820 [DE:42].
    ii. Simon, born 1776-1794, head of a Dover Hundred, Kent County household of 4 "free colored" in 1820 [DE:42].

BARDLEY FAMILY

Members of the Bardley family in Maryland were

    i. Samuel, born say 1770, head of a Kent County household of 3 "other free" and a slave in 1800 [MD:145].
    ii. Mary, born say 1772, mother of a "mulatto" child who was buried in St. Paul's Parish, Baltimore on 15 September 1792 [Reamy, *Records of St. Paul's Parish*, I:68].

BARRETT FAMILY

1.   Violet Barrott, born say 1720, wife of Darby Barrott, was living in St. Michael's Parish in August 1744 when she was convicted by the Talbot County court of having a child by a "Mulatto slave." The court sold her as a servant for seven years [Judgment Record 1743-4, 352]. She was probably the ancestor of

    i. Ann, born say 1743, a "Mulatto" woman who the constable (tax collector) claimed was married to a white man named John Start who did not list her as a taxable in Talbot County. The jury acquitted him in November 1758 [Criminal Record 1755-61, 254].
    ii. Susannah, a spinster householder who was charged by the constable (tax collector) in Talbot County in November 1758 for failing to pay tax on her person [Criminal Record 1755-61, 243].
    iii. Mary, a "Mulatto" woman who the constable claimed was married to and living with Thomas Condon, a white man, who did not list her as a taxable. The jury found Condon not guilty in June 1759 [Criminal Record 1755-61, 245, 253].
    iv. Jacob, head of a Murderkill Hundred, Kent County, Delaware household of 6 "other free" in 1800 [DE:118].
    v. Isaac, head of a Murderkill Hundred, Kent County, Delaware household of 3 "other free" in 1800 [DE:124], 4 in 1810 [DE:73] and 7 "free colored" in 1820 [DE:17].
    vi. Philip, head of a New Castle County household of 9 "other free" in 1810 [DE:301].
    vii. George, "F.N." head of a Kent County household of 8 "other free" in 1810 [DE:3] and 7 "free colored" in 1820 [DE:39].
    viii. James, "F.N." head of a Kent County household of 6 "other free" in 1800

[DE:6] and 3 "free colored" in 1820 [DE:22].

    ix. Samuel, born before 1776, head of a Talbot County household of 4 "free colored" in 1830.

BARTON FAMILY

1. William[1] Barton, born say 1670, a "free negro," was baptized in All Hallow's Parish, Anne Arundel County, on 9 April 1699. His wife Mary, "belongs to Madam Tayler," was baptized on 30 April 1699. They were probably the parents of Elizabeth Burton, "a negro child," who was baptized on 16 April 1699. Mary was buried in All Hallow's Parish on 7 May 1711 [Wright, *Anne Arundel County Church Records*, 9, 30, 31]. William was called a cooper in 1711 when he purchased two tracts of land in Anne Arundel County: 50 acres called *Essex* and 127 acres called *Kent* for £22. He and his wife Elizabeth made a deed of gift of the 50-acre tract to Anthony **Hill** in 1739 [Land Records 1709-12, PK, 469-74; 1737-40, RD#3, 221, 224]. He was called "Negro William Barton" on 23 July 1729 when he petitioned the Assembly to pass a bill to confirm the right of his heirs to inherit his land [*Archives of Maryland*, 36:329]. In March 1734/5 he petitioned the Anne Arundel County court to be levy-free, stating that he was upwards of seventy years old, that his wife was nearly seventy, and that he had paid taxes for himself for nearly thirty years and nearly that long for his wife. The court granted his petition. She was probably identical to Eliza Barton who petitioned the court in June 1734 that she was aged sixty-six years and unable to labor [Judgment Record 1734-6, 10, 182]. William was the father of

    i. ?Elizabeth, baptized 30 April 1699.

    ii. William[2], "of William and Mary, free negros," buried in All Hallow's Parish on 11 April 1709 [Wright, *Anne Arundel County Church Records*, 30].

2   iii. ?William[3], born say 1710.

3   iv. James[1], born say 1716.

4   v. ?Martha, born say 1728.

2. William[3] Barton, born say 1710, married Sarah **Savoy** in All Hallow's Parish on 25 October 1731 [Wright, *Anne Arundel County Church Records*, 30, 45]. Sarah was presented by the Anne Arundel County court in August 1746 for failing to list herself as a taxable [Judgment Record 1746-8, 214, 285, 468]. They may have been the ancestors of

    i. Henry, born say 1755, living with James Barton in 1810, head of a Baltimore County household of 8 "other free" [MD:493]. He may have been the father of Henry Barton who registered in Baltimore County on 24 April 1832: *about 47 years old, light complexion, born free and raised in Baltimore County* [Negroes Manumitted 1830-32].

    ii. Kizy, head of an Anne Arundel County household of 5 "other free" in 1790.

    iii. Susanah, head of a Baltimore City household of 6 "other free" in 1800 [MD:232] and 9 in 1810 [MD:539].

3. James[1] Barton, born say 1716, married Katherine **Bannaker**, "Negroes," on 22 May 1735 in St. Paul's Parish, Baltimore County (abstracted as James **Boston**) [Reamy, *Records of St. Paul's Parish*, I:32]. He was called James Barton Sr. when he was taxable on his own tithe and Benjamin Barton's tithe in Patapsco Upper Hundred, Baltimore County, in 1773 [MSA C428-51, 1773 Tax List]. He was probably the father of

    i. James[2], a "free Negro" taxable in Elkridge Hundred, Anne Arundel County, in 1783 [MSA S 1161-1-3, p.4] and head of a Patapsco Upper Hundred household of 7 "other free" in 1810 [MD:639].

    ii. John, purchased 10 acres about a mile north of Ellicott City from Benjamin **Banneker** on 2 April 1792 [Land Records, Liber WG #HH:

341-2] and was head of a Patapsco Upper Hundred, Baltimore County household of 5 "other free" in 1810 [MD:639].

4.   Martha Barton, born say 1728, confessed to the Prince George's County court on 24 March 1746/7 that she had a "Mullatto" child. The court sold her to her master, Thomas Charter, for seven years and sold her son William to Charter until the age of thirty-one. On 26 March 1754 the court bound her four-month-old "Mollatto" child named Thomas to George Hardy for thirty-one years and ordered that she serve another seven years. She was living in Piscataway Hundred on 23 August 1757 when the court bound her two-month-old "Mulatto" son John to Henry Hardy and ordered her sold for seven years [Court Record 1746-7, 389; 1751-4, 545; 1754-8, 490, 495]. She was the mother of

   i.   William[4], born in January 1746/7, "free Negro" head of a Prince George's County household of 6 "other free" in 1800 [MD:285] and 5 in 1810 [MD:34].
   ii.   Thomas[1], born 23 November 1753 [Court Record 1751-4, 545], "free negro" head of a Prince George's County household of 3 "other free" and a slave in 1800 [MD:286] and 8 "other free" in 1810 [MD:33].
5 iii.   John, born in June 1757.

5.   John Barton, born in June 1757, was a "free Mulatto" head of a Prince George's County household of 4 "other free" in 1800 [MD:269] and 5 in 1810 (J. Barton) [MD:26]. He may have been the husband of Nancy Barton, a descendant of Rosamond **Bently**, who recovered her freedom by a suit against Anthony Addison in Prince George's County court. Nancy Barton registered in Prince George's County on 22 April 1813: *a bright mulatto woman, about 45 years old, and 5 feet 6 inches tall...descendant of a certain Rosamond Bently who recovered her freedom in the Prince George's County Court in a suit against Anthony Addison.* She was the mother of

   i.   Thomas[2], born about 1791, registered in Prince George's County on 1 September 1818: *a bright mulatto man, about 27 years old, and 5 feet 7 inches tall...descendant of Nancy Barton, a free woman of color.*
   ii.   Elizabeth, born about 1793, registered on 3 November 1813: *a bright mulatto girl, 20 years old, and 5 feet 11 inches tall...daughter of Nancy Barton.*
   iii. William[5], born about 1794, registered on 1 September 1818: *a bright mulatto man, about 24 years old, and 5 feet tall...descendant of Nancy Barton, a free woman of color.*
   iv.   James Richard, born about 1797, registered on 1 September 1818: *a bright mulatto man, about 21 years old, and 5 feet 9 inches tall...descendant of Nancy Barton.*
   v.   Charlotte, born about 1800, registered on 3 November 1819: *a bright mulatto girl, about 19 years old, and 5 feet 4 inches tall...a descendant of Nancy Barton.*
   vi.   Ann Maria, born about 1803, registered on 3 November 1819: *a bright mulatto girl, about 16 years old, and 5 feet 2 inches tall...descendant of Nancy Barton* [Provine, *Registrations of Free Negroes*, 15, 16, 26, 32, 33].

BASS FAMILY

1.   Sarah Bass, born in 1664, was the "Mallatto" daughter of a white woman and a "negro man," the servants of John White of Virginia. Sarah was about eight years old on 13 August 1672 when John White brought her into Somerset County court to have her bound to him as an apprentice. She testified that she was about eight years old and agreed to serve him until the age of twenty-one. White gave her a cow and calf and their increase on the condition that she serve her full term [*Archives of Maryland*, 87:155]. She may have been the ancestor of

    i. Griffin, head of a St. Jones Hundred, Kent County, Delaware household of 15 "other free" in 1800 [MD:44]. He married Nicey/ Unicy **Durham**, widow of Daniel **Durham** before 28 April 1801 when Daniel's Kent County, Delaware will was proved [de Valinger, *Probate Records of Kent County*].

    ii. Phil, head of a Talbot County household of 4 "other free" in 1800 [MD:547].

BATES FAMILY

1. Benjamin Bates, born say 1731, was a "Mullatto Bastard Child" who the Charles County court sold to Peter Harrant on 9 November 1731 [Court Record 1731-4, 41]. He may have been the ancestor of the members of the Bates family who were living in nearby Virginia counties in 1810:

    i. John, head of a Prince William County household of 9 "other free" in 1810 [VA:508]. He may have been the husband of Sophia Bates whose seventeen-year-old daughter registered as a free Negro in Washington, D.C. on 26 July 1827: *a mulatto woman...daughter of Sophia Bates of Dumfries, Virginia, who was born free* [Provine, *District of Columbia Free Negro Registers*, 96-6].

    ii. Cyrus, head of a Prince William County household of 5 "other free" in 1810 [VA:508].

    iii. Fanny, head of a Prince George County, Virginia household of 7 "other free" in 1810 [VA:545].

    iv. Hetty, head of a Prince George County, Virginia household of 7 "other free" in 1810 [VA:545].

    v. Archibald, head of a Prince George County, Virginia household of 1 "other free" in 1810 [VA:545].

BATTERTON FAMILY

1. Elizabeth Batterton, born say 1740, of the Island of Nevis in the Caribbean, placed an ad in the 29 June 1769 issue of the *Virginia Gazette* seeking the whereabouts of her son Joseph Batterton, a free Negro man of the island. She stated that he embarked on the sloop *Sally* which was bound for Maryland, but the ship's captain had made two voyages since Joseph embarked and brought no news or account of him to his parents. She offered a reward of £20 for information about her son [Rind edition, p.4, col. 1]. She was the mother of

    i. Joseph.

    ii. ?Thomas Batterson (Negro), enlisted in the Revolution as a substitute in Anne Arundel County after October 1780 [*Archives of Maryland*, 18:369].

    iii. ?Susa. Batson, "free negro" head of a Prince George County household of 14 "other free" in 1800 [MD:285], probably the mother of Vachel Batson who registered in Anne Arundel County on 27 August 1817: *a negro man...aged about twenty four years...black complexion...free born* [Certificates of Freedom 1810-31, 104].

BEAN FAMILY

1. Jane Bean, born say 1743, was the mother of

    i. Jeremiah, born about 1763, registered in St. Mary's County on 29 September 1828: *son of Jane Bean, aged about sixty five years...bright complexion...born and raised in Saint Mary's County.*

    ii. ?Jacob, a "mulatto" taxable in the Lower District Hundred of Dorchester County in 1783 [MSA S1161-5-4, p.1] and head of a St. Mary's County household of 4 "other free" in 1800 [MD:399].

    iii. ?Lucy, head of a St. Mary's County household of 1 "other free" in 1800 [MD:395].

BEAVIN FAMILY

Members of the Beavin family were
    i. James, a "mulatto" taxable in the 3rd District of Charles County in 1783 [MSA S 1161-4-10, p.2].
    ii. Paul, "Mulatto" head of a Charles County household of 1 "other free" in 1790.
    iii. Susanna, "Mulatto" head of a Charles County household of 1 "other free" in 1790.
    iv. Nancy **Raley**, born about 1779, registered in St. Mary's County on 1 September 1809: *commonly called Nancy Bivans, Complexion very bright - hair long and straight...born free - being born of a free white woman named Jane Cecil and raised in Saint Mary's County* [Certificates of Freedom 1806-64, 8].

BECKETT FAMILY

1. Peter[1] Beckett, born say 1655, was a "Negro" slave who was taxable with Thomas **Driggers** from 1671 to 1677 in the Northampton County, Virginia household of John Eyres [Orders 1664-74, fol.114; 1674-79, 75, 191]. Sarah Dawson, a white servant, was another member of Eyre's household. Her age was adjudged to be sixteen years when Eyre brought her into Northampton County court on 26 November 1677 [OW 1674-79, 203]. Seven years later in 1684 she was given twenty-one lashes and ordered to serve Eyre another six years for having "three bastard Maletto Children by her said Masters Negro slave Peter." On 30 May 1687 and 28 May 1688 she was presented for bastard bearing and the following year on 29 July 1689 was called "Sarah the wife of Peter Beckett slave to Major John Eyre" when the court ordered one of her children released to her, "Shee findinge sufficient security to save the parish harmelesse from the said Childe" [OW 1683-89, 59, 280, 292, 358, 442-3]. On 28 July 1702 she consented to the indenture of their daughter Ann, "daughter of Sarah Beckett," to Mrs. Ann Eyre until the age of eighteen [OW 1698-1710, 96]. Peter was free by 30 November 1703 when "Peter Beckett and Sarah his wife" successfully sued John Morrine for debt in Northampton County court. John Robins brought an action upon the case against him, but neither party appeared when it came for trial on 21 January 1717/8 [OW&c 1698-1710, 176; Orders 1710-6, 55]. Peter and Sarah's descendants were
2   i. ?Peter[2], born say 1683.
    ii. Rebecca[1], born say 1692, taxable in the household of John **Drighouse** in 1726 [Bell, *Northampton County Tithables*, 77].
3   iii. ?William[1], born say 1695.
    iv. Ann, born 10 December 1697, mother of a child by John **Driggers** in Northampton County in 1716.
    v. Jean, born say 1700, common-law wife of Thomas **Driggers** of Northampton County.
    vi. Elizabeth, born say 1705, common-law wife of John **Driggers/ Drighouse**.

2. Peter[2] Beckett, born say 1683, was taxable in Bogerternorton Hundred of Somerset County from 1723 to 1740: listed with Devorix **Driggers** in 1725, with (his son?) William B____ et in 1737, with (his son?) Deverix Becket in 1740 [MdHR C-812, List of Taxables, 1723-1740]. He was fined 2 shillings 6 pence for uttering an oath in Somerset County in 1727. He was special bail for Devorix **Driggers** on 17 November 1730 when Devorix admitted in Somerset County court that he owed Christopher Glass 500 pounds of tobacco and 650 pounds of beef which he had contracted for in writing on 10 November 1729 [Judicial Record 1727-30, 147; 1730-3, 43-4]. The inventory of his Worcester County estate, taken by Arcada **Okey** on 10 May 1751, totaled £129 and listed Bridget

Doves and John Nienburgh as nearest of kin. The second inventory taken on 23 January 1754 by Joseph and his wife Arcada **Okey** included debts from William **Cornish**, Simon **Collock**, and Nathaniel **Morris**. One third of the estate went to Peter's widow Mary Beckett and the remainder to his son Beade Beckett and daughters Arcada **Oakey** and Hannah Beckett. The estate paid Samuel **Handser** 7 shillings [Prerogative Inventories 48:98-100; 60:89; Accounts 37:65-6; Balance Book 1751-5, 1:127 (MSA 533-1)]. William was the father of

    i.   ?William[2], born say 1716.

    ii.   Arcada, married Joseph **Okey**.

    iii.   Hannah.

    iv.   ?Deverix, born say 1723, taxable in Somerset County in 1740, probably named for Deverix **Driggers**.

    v.   ?Solomon, taxable in Mispillion Hundred, Kent County, Delaware, from 1743 to 1762 [Kent County Assessments, 1743-67, frames 10, 109, 125, 154, 174, 201, 204, 216, 247, 270, 349].

    vi.   ?Elizabeth, born say 1737, charged Rike **Miller** in November 1771 with being the father of her illegitimate female child who was born in Little Creek Hundred on 9 February 1769, before she married Jacob **Gibbs** [DSA, RG 3805, MS case files, November 1771 indictments].

4   vii.   Bede[1], born about 1738.

3.   William[1] Beckett, born say 1695, was taxable in Kent County, Delaware, from 1726 to 1756: listed in Little Creek Hundred, charged with the tax of ____ **Drigers** in 1727, called William Beckett Sen. from 1749 to 1756 when he was listed in Dover Hundred near Nehemiah **Hansor** and Samuel Hanson [Kent County Levy List 1743-67]. William was called a yeoman when he purchased two lots of ground within the town of Dover for £12 by Kent County, Delaware deed on 2 April 1754 [DB O:256]. He left a 31-January 1757 Kent County will (signing the letter "B"), proved 7 May 1757, leaving Mary **Concelor** a bed, furniture and a sorrel mare; his daughter Comfort a horse; his son Nathan a gun; his son William a shilling; his daughters Sarah and Mary each a mare; and his wife Comfort all his lands. Nehemiah **Handzor** witnessed the will [WB K-1, 162]. William was probably the father of the illegitimate child Mary **Concelor** had in Kent County in August 1728 [Delaware Archives RG 3815.031, dockets 1722-32, frames 229, 235]. And he was probably related to a "Mulatto" child Abraham Beckitt who was supported by Richard Wells (of Dover Hundred), Esq., from the county levy in November 1757 and Tabitha Beckett, a poor woman, supported by Lydia Wells from Kent County levy in November 1758 [DSA, RG 3200, Levy Court Minutes 1732-, frames 34, 38; RG 3535, Assessments 1743-67, frames 221, 223]. Mary Beckett sold 50 acres in Dover Hundred, Kent County, on the north side of the Dover River on 31 March 1758 [DB P:111]. William was the father of

5   i.   William[3], born say 1720.

    ii.   Comfort, born say 1723.

    iii.   Nathan, born say 1728, taxable in Dover Hundred in 1758 and 1759 [Kent County Levy List, 1743-67, frames 213, 240].

    iv.   Sarah, born say 1734.

    v.   Mary, born say 1737.

4.   Bede[1] Beckett, born about 1738, was a 21-year-old, born in Maryland, who was listed in the 11 May 1759 muster of Captain John Wright's Company in the French and Indian War (abstracted as "Bedy Bullett," in the same list with Samuel and Thomas **Hanzer** of Sussex County, that included mostly men born in Sussex County) [Montgomery, *Pennsylvania Archives, Fifth Series*, 278-9]. He married Ann Butler (no race indicated for either) in Sussex County on 21 April 1763 and their son William was born on 12 July 1768 [Records of the United Presbyterian Churches of Lewes, Indian River and Cool Spring, Delaware 1756-1855, 274]. Bede, a labourer, purchased 118 acres called *Good Luck* on the east side of the

Green Branch in Sussex County on ___ May 1764 from William Reynolds for £37 [DB K-11:60]. He was a delinquent taxable in Sussex County in 1767, taxable in Broadkill Hundred in 1774, a Nanticoke Hundred delinquent in 1787 [Delaware Archives, Levy Assessments RG 2535].[6] He died about 1787 when Peter Beckett was granted administration on his estate [de Valinger, *Calendar of Kent County Probate Records 1680-1800*, 181]. He was the father of

    i.   William, born 12 July 1768, called William Butler Beckett when he was taxable in Sussex County in Nanticoke Hundred near Peter Beckett in 1791 and in Little Creek Hundred in 1796 [Levy Assessment List, RG 2535].

    ii. ?Bede[2], taxable in Nanticoke Hundred adjoining Peter Beckett in 1795.

5.   William[3] Beckett, born say 1720, was taxable in Little Creek Hundred in 1741 and 1742: in the same list as Samuel Hanson; taxable in Dover Hundred from 1748 to 1769: listed in Samuel Hanson's levy in 1748 (called "William Beckitt Ju'"), perhaps deceased in 1769 when he was a Dover Hundred delinquent [Kent County Levy List, 1743-67, frames 437, 494, 508; 1768-1784, 26, 32]. In November 1752 he was fined £5 by the Kent County court for keeping a tippling house without a license [RG 3805.002, Court of General Sessions, frame 214]. He was called William Beckett Jun[r], yeoman, on 13 February 1754 when he purchased 100 acres in the forest of Murderkill Hundred on the north side of Milstons Bridge for £35 [DB O:220]. He may have had a child by one of Samuel Hanson's slaves. On 27 January 1770 Hanson made a deed of manumission by which he freed three slaves named Beckett:

    i.   Charles, born about December 1740, a "Negro" about 30 years and one month old on 27 January 1770 when Samuel Hanson of Kent County set him free by manumission recorded in May 1775 [Historical Society of Pennsylvania, Duck Creek Monthly Meeting, Deed of Manumission of Slaves, 1774-1792, 21]. He was a "Negro" head of a Dover Hundred household of 3 "other free" in 1800 [DE:97].

    ii. Peter[2], born about June 1744, a "Negro" about 25 years and seven months old on 27 January 1770 when Samuel Hanson of Kent County set him free [Historical Society of Pennsylvania, Duck Creek Monthly Meeting, Deed of Manumission of Slaves, 1774-1792, 21]. He served in the First Company of the Delaware Regiment in the Revolutionary War and received pay from 1 August 1780 to 4 November 1783 [DSA, MS Delaware Regiment Pay Records, 1778-1783, certificates 54,483; 54,830; 54,938; 55,184; Public Archives Commission, *Delaware Archives*, 196, 607]. He married Betty **Drigas (Driggers)** on 27 November 1788 in Sussex County [Records of the United Presbyterian Churches of Lewes, Indian River and Cool Spring, Delaware 1756-1855, 302]. He was administrator of the Sussex County estate of Bede Beckett in 1787 [de Valinger, *Calendar of Kent County Probate Records 1680-1800*, 181]. He was taxable in Nanticoke Hundred, Sussex County, in 1791 and 1795 and taxable in Little Creek Hundred, Sussex County, on a horse, cow and calf, and a shoat in 1796. He was a "Negro" head of a Delaware household of 3 "other free" in 1800 [DE:342] and 2 in 1810 [DE:161, 364].

    iii. Isaac, born about November 1747, twenty-three years and 7 months old on 27 January 1770 when Samuel Hanson of Kent County set him free when he reached the age of twenty-five [Historical Society of Pennsylvania, Duck Creek Monthly Meeting, Deed of Manumission of Slaves, 1774-1792, 21]. He was head of a Dover Hundred household of 3 "other free" in 1800 [DE:41].

---

[6]A delinquent taxpayer may have failed to pay his tax or had moved out of the tax collector's district that year.

Another member of the Beckett family was
    i. John, born after 1775, head of a Worcester County household of 10 "free colored" in 1830.

BEDDO FAMILY

1. Martha Badoe, born say 1693, was the servant of Thomas Coleman of Benedict Hundred on 12 June 1711 when she was presented by the Charles County court for having a "Mallato" child. She admitted her guilt in court two months later on 14 August when the court ordered that she serve an additional seven years and bound her child to Coleman until the age of thirty-one. She was presented for the same offense on 9 June 1713, and on 9 August 1713 she bound her four-month-old son James to Coleman. On 9 March 1735/6 the court ordered Coleman to bring her "Mullatto Daughter" Eleanor before the court to have her bound out [Court Record 1710-3, 136, 196-7; 1734-9, 143]. She was the mother of
    i. James[1], born about April 1713, bound as an apprentice to Thomas Coleman of Benedict Hundred, Charles County, on 9 August 1713.
2   ii. Eleanor, born say 1715.

2. Eleanor Bedoe, born say 1715, was the "Mullatto Daughter" of Martha Bedoe. On 12 June 1744 the Charles County court convicted her of having an illegitimate child and ordered that she receive twelve lashes. The court also ordered her son James bound out to Edward Goodrich until the age of twenty-one [Court Record 1744-5, 25]. She was the mother of
    i. James[2], born about 1744, a thirteen-year-old boy bound to serve until the age of twenty-one when he was listed in the inventory of the Charles County estate of Mr. Edward Goodrich on 17 March 1757 [Prerogative Inventories 63:65-6], head of a Charles County household of 9 "other free" in 1800 [MD:522].
    ii. ?William, head of a Charles County household of 10 "other free" in 1810 [MD:303].
    iii. ?Nancy, head of a Charles County household of 4 "other free" in 1810 [MD:321].
    iv. ?M., head of a Prince George's County household of 2 "other free" in 1810 [MD:17].
    v. ?R., head of a Prince George's County household of 3 "other free" and a slave in 1810 [MD:16].
    vi. ?E., head of a Prince George's County household of 3 "other free" in 1810 [MD:16].

BENTLEY FAMILY

1. Mary Davis, born say 1657, the daughter of Richard Davis of London, England, was a white woman who married a "Negroe man" named Domingo, the slave of Joseph Tilley of Calvert County. Mary and Domingo were living with Lord Baltimore when she wrote the details of her marriage and the birth and baptism of her children in a Bible. Her daughter Rose produced a transcription of the Bible in Anne Arundel County court in August 1715 in an unsuccessful petition for her freedom [Court Judgments 1715-7, 93, 178, 244-6]. Mary and Domingo were the parents of
    i. Thomas, born 14 March 1677 on Lord Baltimore's plantation on Lyon's Creek in Calvert County, baptized by Mr. Wessley(?) in the house of Richard Massoms. James and Ann Thompson were the godparents.
2   ii. Rose, born 11 August 1684.

2. Rose **Davis**, born 11 August 1684 at the "Top of the Hill" plantation in St. Mary's County, was baptized at Nottley Hall by a priest named Mr. Richard Hebert with Henry and Rose Wharton as godparents. Rose was thirty-one years old in August

1715 when she brought an unsuccessful suit for her freedom against Henry Darnall in Anne Arundel County court [Court Judgments 1715-7, 93, 178, 244-6]. Rose was listed in the Anne Arundel County inventory of the estate of Henry Darnall (Sr.) in 1713:

Negroes at the Dwelling House	
one Mallata Woman Sue age 33 -	*£28*
At James Watland's 2 Quarter, Negroes	
one Mallata woman Rose age 29 -	*£28*
At the Woodyard, Negroes	
one Mallata David a Carpenter age 45 -	*£40*
one ditto Frank " age 40 -	*£40*
one ditto Jack " age 35 -	*£30*
one ditto Tom a Carpenter age 30 -	*£45*
one ditto Charles do age 15 -	*£25*
one Negro Bently age 20 -	*£30*
one Mallata woman Moll with child a month old age 34 -	*£29*

[Prerogative Court Inventories and Accounts, Vol. 33B, 221-6].
In March 1779 her granddaughter Rosamond Bentley petitioned the Prince George's County court for her freedom, and in August 1781 Rosamond and her brother William and sisters Mary, Eleanor and Margaret Bentley won their cases. In an apparent effort to minimize their African ancestry, Rose's witnesses testified that the family descended from Mary Davis, a white English woman, and an East Indian man - instead of a "Negroe man" as stated in Mary Davis's Bible. And her witnesses described Rose's daughter as "Indian Polly" [Judgment Record 1777-82, 713-5]. Rose was the mother of

3   i.   Polly, born say 1710.

3.   Polly Bentley, born say 1710, called "Indian Polly," was the mother of Rosamond, William, Mary, Eleanor and Margaret Bentley. Polly was the slave of Lettice Thompson when she died of smallpox according to testimony in Prince George's County court [Judgment Record 1777-82, 713-5].[7] Her children were

4   i.   Mary, born say 1731.
5   ii.   Rosamond, born say 1733.
     iii. William[1], born say 1736.
6   iv.   Eleanor[1], born say 1738.
     v.   Margaret, born say 1741.

4.   Mary Bentley, born say 1731, was the slave of William Digges on 27 November 1781 when her and her three children Lucy, Sophia, and William, won their freedom in Prince George's County court. The court also freed her children: Sarah (slave of Mr. Knox of Charles County), Isaac, John and Mary (slaves of Mrs. Eleanor Carroll) and Rose and Eleanor (slaves of John Fitzgerald of Virginia) [Judgment Record 1777-82, 764-5]. She was the mother of

     i.   Isaac[2], born say 1753, a slave of Mrs. Eleanor Carroll.
     ii.   John, born say 1755, a slave of Mrs. Eleanor Carroll.
     iii. Mary, born say 1758, a slave of Mrs. Eleanor Carroll.
     iv.   Rose, born say 1760, a slave of John Fitzgerald of Virginia.
     v.   Eleanor[2], born say 1763, a slave of John Fitzgerald of Virginia.
     vi.   Lucy, born say 1765.
     vii. Sophia, born say 1768.
     viii. William[3], born say 1770.

---

[7]In addition to the slave named Bently in Henry Danall's inventory, there was a "Negro Bently" who sued George Plowden for his freedom in Prince George's County court in January 1697/8 [Court Record 1696-9, Archives of Maryland on-line, 202:72].

5.   Rosamond Bently, born say 1733, recovered her freedom on 28 August 1781 by
     a suit she brought against Anthony Addison in Prince George's County court in
     which she proved she was the granddaughter of Rose **Davis** who was the daughter
     of a white woman [Judgment Record 1777-82, 713-5]. Rosamond was the
     ancestor of
     i.   Nancy **Barton**, born about 1768, registered in Prince George's County on
          22 April 1813: *a bright mulatto woman, about 45 years old, and 5 feet 6
          inches tall...descendant of a certain Rosamond Bently who recovered her
          freedom in the Prince George's County Court in a suit against Anthony
          Addison.*
     ii. Eleanor³/ Nelly **Cooper**, born about 1771, registered in Prince George's
          County on 2 April 1813: *Eleanor Cooper, a bright mulatto woman, about
          42 years old, and 5 feet 5 inches tall. She is free, being the descendant of
          a certain Rosamond Bently who recovered her freedom in the Prince
          George's County Court in a suit against Anthony Addison* [Provine,
          Registrations of Free Negroes, 15, 16].

6.   Eleanor¹ Bentley, born say 1738, and her five children, Polly, William, John,
     Sophia and Bett, were the slaves of John Hawkins on 27 November 1781 when
     they petitioned the Prince George's County court for their freedom [Judgment
     Record 1777-82, 764]. Eleanor's children were
     i.   Polly, born say 1760.
     ii. William², born say 1763.
     iii. John, born say 1765.
     iv. Sophia, born say 1768.
     v.   Bett, born say 1770.

Other members of the family were
     i.   Isaac¹, born say 1735, described as a "mulatto fellow...alias Protus" on 14
          August 1760 when Richard Tilghman Earle of Queen Anne's County
          advertised in the *Maryland Gazette* that he had run away with an English
          convict servant man named Benjamin Williams [Green, *The Maryland
          Gazette, 1727-61*, 251].
     ii. Debora, married Solomon **Haycock**, 14 December 1782 banns by the
          Jesuit Mission in Cordova, Maryland (no race indicated), Peter and
          Protase witnesses [Wright, *Vital Records of the Jesuit Mission*, 19].
     iii. Polly, born say 1773, living in Frederick Town, Frederick County, on 22
          April 1811 when her son William Bentley by Edward **Younger** registered.
          She may have married Edward **Younger**, the Polly who was named as his
          wife when his son obtained a certificate [Certificates of Freedom 1806-27,
          28, 71].

BERRY FAMILY

Members of the Berry family in Maryland were
     i.   William, "Negro" head of a Kent County household of 3 "other free" in
          1790.
     ii. James, head of a Kent County household of 4 "other free" in 1800
          [MD:157].
     iii. Sarah, head of a Kent County household of 6 "other free" in 1800
          [MD:169].
     iv. Henry, head of a Kent County household of 3 "other free" in 1800
          [MD:158].
     v.   Catherine, head of a Kent County household of 2 "other free" in 1800
          [MD:169].
     vi. Polly, born about 1779, registered in Prince George's County court on 24
          August 1819: *Ann Proctor, a white woman, swears that Polly Berry was
          born free, as was Polly's mother. Polly is a bright mulatto woman who is*

about 40 years old. Copy of a registration from the District of Columbia
[Provine, *Registrations of Free Negroes*, 115].

BISHOP FAMILY

1. Thomas Bishop, born say 1700, was an Indian who was credited with one wolf's head by the Talbot County court in November 1723 [Judgment Record 1723-4, 228]. He may have been identical to Thomas Bishop, a Choptank Indian, who sold land in Dorchester County in 1726 and 1727 [Land Records 1720-32, Liber old 8, 141-2, 153]. He, Abram Bishop, Peter Monk, and William Corhonk were Indians who owed the Dorchester County estate of William Pitts about a shilling each on 16 February 1762 [Prerogative Inventories 77:7-8]. He may have been the ancestor of

    i.   Abraham[1], an "Indon" who owed the estate of William Pitts 1 shilling 6 pence on 16 February 1762, head of a Dorchester County household of 3 "other free" in 1800 [MD:740].
    ii. Abraham[2], head of a Dorchester County household of 2 "other free" in 1800 [MD:664].
    iii. Abraham[3] Buship, head of a Dorchester County household of 1 "other free" in 1800 [MD:726].
    iv. Jacob, head of a Little Creek Hundred, Sussex County household of 7 "other free" in 1800 [MD:735].
    v.   London, head of a Kent County, Maryland household of 5 "other free" in 1800 [MD:158] and 3 "free colored" in Little Creek Hundred, Kent County, Delaware in 1820 [DE:25].
    vi. Samuel, "F.N." head of a Kent County, Delaware household of 3 "other free" in 1810 [DE:52].

BLACK FAMILY

Members of the Black family in Maryland were
1
    i.   William, born say 1720.
    ii. Charles, "Negro" head of a Kent County household of 3 "other free" in 1790, 4 in Cecil County in 1800 [MD:215] and 4 "other free" in Gunpowder Hundred, Baltimore County, in 1810 [MD:670].
    iii. James, head of a Cecil County household of 7 "other free" in 1800 [MD:262].
    iv. Lewis, head of a Dorchester County household of 5 "other free" in 1800 [MD:657].
    v.   Joe, "free negro" head of a Prince George's County household of 6 "other free" in 1800 [MD:303] and 4 in 1810 [MD:58].

1. William Black, born say 1720, married Esther **Banneker** on 22 September 1744 in St. Paul's Parish, Baltimore County [Reamy, *Records of St. Paul's Parish*, I:32, 36]. He was taxable in Upper Patapsco Hundred of Baltimore County in 1773 [MSA, 1773 Tax List]. They may have been the ancestors of

    i.   Esther, a "free Negro" taxable in Elkridge Hundred, Anne Arundel County, in 1783 [MSA S 1161-1-3, p.4], head of a Back River Upper Hundred, Baltimore County household of 5 "other free" in 1810 [MD:697].
    ii. Caleb, head of a Back River Upper Hundred, Baltimore County household of 6 "other free" in 1810 [MD:701].
    iii. Charles, head of a Back River Upper Hundred household of 5 "other free" in 1810 [MD:693].
    iv. Fanny, head of an Annapolis household of 5 "other free" in 1810 [MD:117].
    v.   Hannah, head of a Baltimore City household of 4 "other free" in 1810.
    vi. Elizabeth, head of a Pipe Creek and North Hundred, Baltimore County

household of 4 "other free" in 1810 [MD:629].
vii. Reed, head of a Pipe Creek and North Hundred, Baltimore County household of 2 "other free" in 1810 [MD:671].

BLAKE FAMILY

1. George[1] Blake, born say 1685, and (his wife) Hannah were named in the 5 December 1707 Northampton County will of John Robins by which he gave his five sons his part of Chincoteague Island "wth my man and woman, George Blake and Hannah" (who were to continue looking after his cattle, horses and hogs on the island) and gave his son Edward Robins a "Mallatto boy Charles son of Hannah" who was also on his part of the island [DW&c 1708-17, 23-31]. George (£10) and Hannah Blake (£3) were valued in the 14 November 1732 Somerset County inventory of the estate of John Robins's son Thomas Robins with (their children?) Comfort, Samuel, Sarah and Charles Blake [Prerogative Court Inventories 1730-2, 16:717]. Hannah was a spinster charged in Somerset County court with having an illegitimate child in All Hallows Parish on 10 January 1732 but excused because she was a "black woman" and thus not subject to punishment for fornication [Judicial Record 1733-5, 244; 1735-7, 18-19]. A presentment against her by the churchwardens was dismissed in Accomack County on 22 February 1742/3. She was apparently the mother of seven-year-old Harman Blake who was bound out that day to Edward Robins and John Kendall to be a tanner [Orders 1737-44, 467-8]. George and Hannah were probably the ancestors of

    i. Charles, "given" to Edward Robins in December 1707, valued at £3 in 1732, perhaps the Charles Blake who was added to the list of tithables for Accomack County on 27 August 1766 with his wife Jenny "(negro)" and 200 acres of land [Orders 1765-7, 180].

    ii. Comfort[1], valued at £5.10 in 1732.

    iii. Samuel, valued at £10 in 1732, purchased 54 acres in Worcester County called *Partnership* and the house where he was then living from George Blake on 2 March 1763, and on 15 May 1772 he and his wife Mary Blake sold the land to Daniel Miflin [Land Records E:463-4; I:93-4].

    iv. Sarah[1], valued at £1.10 in 1732.

2   v. George[2], born say 1734.

    vi. Harman, born about 1736, "Negro" head of a Worcester County household of 7 "other free" in 1800 [MD:736], probably named for the **Harman** family. He owed £6 to the Worcester County estate of Thomas Robins on 22 December 1770 [Prerogative Inventories 104:56]. He was head of an Accomack County household of 2 "free colored" in 1830.

    vii. Hannah, fined 50 shillings by the Accomack County court on 26 May 1747 for having an illegitimate child [Orders 1744-53].

    viii. Levin[1], bound by the Accomack County court to Jabez Kendall to be a shop joiner on 28 July 1761 [Orders 1753-63, 404]. He sold lot number 60 in the town of Snow Hill by Worcester County deed of 6 September 1782 [Land Records K:468-9] and was head of a Worcester County household of 2 "other free" and a slave in 1800 [MD:790] and 11 "other free" in 1810 [MD:614]. He purchased 20 acres called *Amity* and *Amity's Addition* in Worcester County for £60 on 5 April 1802 [Land Records U:650-1].

    ix. Mary, presented by the churchwardens of Accomack County but dismissed on agreement on 25 September 1765 [Orders 1764-5, 535].

    x. William, a "Mulatto" bound by the Accomack County court to Arthur Rorsley to be a shoemaker on 28 April 1761 [Orders 1753-63, 395], a "Negro" head of a Worcester County household of 8 "other free" in 1800 [MD:732].

    xi. John, born say 1760, purchased his wife Hesther and son Solomon at the sheriff's sale of William Bell's Accomack County estate on 27 September 1790 with Daniel Miflin as witness [DB 1788-93, 408].

2. George[2] Blake, born say 1734, surveyed 1,357 acres in Worcester County between the Pocomoke River and the seaside, near Gibbs Ferry and Littleton Creek, on 29 September 1759 and was called a "Negro," "Malatto," "Negro or Molatter" when he and his wife Esther sold the land called *Partnership* in parcels of about 50 acres each. He sold 54 acres to Samuel Blake and the house where Samuel was then living on 2 March 1763. And he sold the last 100 acres called *Elbon Ridge* and *Blakes Lott* to Bowdoin Robins for £40 on 14 September 1764 [Land Records E:294-5, 302, 463-4, 471; F:236-8, 265]. He may have been the George Blake, Sen[r], "free Molatto," who bound himself as a servant for one year to Mr. John Rock by Worcester County deed of 7 December 1797 for £15 [Land Records S:107]. He was head of a Worcester County household of 4 "other free" in 1790 and 4 in 1800 [MD:732]. He may have been the father of

    i.   George[3], taxable in Mattapony Hundred, Worcester County, in 1783 with Captain John Selby as surety [MSA S1161-11-8, p.2]. He was a "free Mulatto" who bound himself as a servant to Joseph Delastatius in Worcester County for eighteen months for £20 on 3 September 1797 [Land Records S:14-5].

    ii. Charles[2], head of a Worcester County household of 2 "other free" in 1800 [MD:767]. He purchased a "negro man" named Vebo from Affry D. Johnson for $1 by Worcester County deed of 21 April 1832 [Land Records AY:71-2].

    iii. Esther, head of a Worcester County household of 8 "free colored" in 1830.

Other members of the Blake family were

3   i.   Betty, born say 1740.

    ii. Jacob, born about 1756, applied for a pension in Worcester County court on 20 June 1818 and 28 February 1821 for his services in the Revolution. He stated that he enlisted at Snow Hill in 1780 and was discharged at Annapolis. His household consisted of his wife who was 70 years old, a son who was 16, a 19-year-old daughter, another daughter who was blind, and four grandchildren. His property was valued at $40 [NARA, S.34654, M804]. He was head of a Worcester County household of 7 "free colored" in 1820.

    iii. Edward[1], a "molatto" who enlisted and served in the Revolutionary War [*Archives of Maryland* 47:460].

    iv. Oliver, drafted into service in the 3[d] Regiment from Worcester County on 7 May 1781 for 3 years, delinquent on 10 December [*Archives of Maryland* 18:425, 473; NARA, M246, roll 34, frame 450 of 587]. He was taxable in Mattapony Hundred of Worcester County in 1783 with Michael Tarr as his surety [MSA S1161-11-8, 1/4/5/54, http://msa.maryland.gov/msa/stagser/s1400/s1437/html/1437wo.html].

    v.   William, head of a Baltimore Town household of 2 "other free" in 1790.

    vi. Henry, "Negro" head of a Worcester County household of 9 "other free" in 1800 [MD:731].

    vii. James[2], Senior, "Negro" head of a Kent County household of 6 "other free" in 1800 [MD:169].

    viii. James[3], head of a Dorchester County household of 6 "other free" in 1800 [MD:729].

    ix. James[4], born before 1776, head of a Worcester County household of 5 "other free" in 1800 [MD:740], 4 in 1810 [MD:578] and 5 "free colored" in 1830.

    x.   James[5], taxable in Mattapony Hundred, Worcester County, in 1783, John Redding surety [MSA S1161-11-8, p.1]. He was head of a Worcester County household of 5 "other free" in 1800 [MD:731] and 8 in 1810 [MD:629].

    xi. Peter, born before 1776, head of a Worcester County household of 8 "free colored" in 1830.

    xii. Henry, born before 1776, head of a Worcester County household of 3 "free colored" in 1830.

xiii.   Sally[2], born before 1776, head of a Worcester County household of 3 "free colored" in 1830.

xiv.   James[6], Junior, head of a Kent County household of 4 "other free" and a slave in 1800 [MD:169] and 2 "other free" in 1810 [MD:910].

xv.   David, head of a Baltimore City household of 6 "other free" in 1800 [MD:152] and 8 in 1810 [MD:251].

xvi.   Edward[2], born 1776-1794, head of a Worcester County household of 4 "free colored" in 1820.

xvii.   Benjamin, born about 1782, registered in Talbot County on 9 September 1822: *a negro man, about 40 years of age, 5 feet 10 ½ Inch high, born Free and raised in Talbot County* [Certificates of Freedom 1815-28, 168].

xviii.   Standley, born about 1770, head of a Dorchester County household of 4 "other free" in 1800 [MD:728], registered in Dorchester County on 5 August 1806: *Copper colour, born free, raised in Dorchester County, aged about 36 years* [Certificates of Freedom for Negroes 1806-64, 1]. He was probably related to the **Standley** family of Dorchester County.

xix.   Hannah[2], born April 1771, set free by Daniel Miflin in Worcester County on 16 June 1776 [Historical Society of Pennsylvania, Duck Creek Monthly Meeting, Deed of Manumission of Slaves, 1774-1792, 61], head of a Worcester County household of 4 "other free" in 1800 [MD:744].

xx.   Rachel, "Negro" head of a Worcester County household of 3 "other free" in 1800 [MD:731].

4   xxi.   Mary, born in April 1769.

xxii.   Archibald, head of a Kent County household of 1 "other free" in 1800 [MD:169].

xxiii.   James[7], born about 1768, registered in Dorchester County on 6 June 1807: *blackish Colour, long hair, born free, aged about thirty nine* [Certificates of Freedom for Negroes 1806-64, 3].

xxiv.   Lucinda, born before 1776, head of a Talbot County household of 10 "free colored" in 1830.

xxv.   Sarah[3], wife of Salad **Stanley**.

3.   Betty Blake, born say 1740, was set free with her children Suey, John and Comfort Blake by Daniel Mifflin in Worcester County on 16 June 1776 [Land Records I:640 and Historical Society of Pennsylvania, Duck Creek Monthly Meeting, Deed of Manumission of Slaves, 1774-1792, 61]. She was the mother of

i.   Suey.

ii.   John, born about 1759, testified in a Somerset County case against free Negro Jacob, alias Jacob **Purcell**, who was charged with stealing five hogs belonging to Thomas Martin. On 4 March 1806 John testified that he was living at Jacob's house for about a month and saw Jacob and Robert J. H. Handy's slave Moses kill the hogs in Jacob's stables, salt them and bury part of them in a barrel in the garden [Land Records Y:45, 47]. Jacob, a "free Negro," bound himself as a servant to Benjamin Purcell, Jr., by Worcester County deed of 2 July 1779 [Land Records K:187]. Jacob **Purcell** was head of a Worcester County household of 6 "other free" in 1810 [MD:604]. On 28 April 1835 John Blake, called a "Colour man," was about 76 years old when he testified in Philadelphia for the pension application of Daniel **Williams**. He stated that he was born in Accomack County and lived near and was well acquainted with Daniel **Williams**, a "Colour" man who was drafted into the army to drive teams. John had resided in Philadelphia about fifteen years past, where he again met **Williams** and had frequently seen him engaged in driving the team [NARA, R.11569, M804, http://fold3.com/image/28467470].

iii.   Comfort[2], born in December 1776.

4. Mary Blake, born in April 1769, was set free by Daniel Mifflin in Worcester County on 16 June 1776 [Historical Society of Pennsylvania, Duck Creek Monthly Meeting, Deed of Manumission of Slaves, 1774-1792, 61], She was a "Negro" head of a Worcester County household of 2 "other free" in 1800 [MD:724]. She made a Worcester County bond, with John Gunn as surety, to keep the state of Maryland harmless from the illegitimate child named Levin which she bore on 10 January 1783 [Land Records O:326]. She had a child named Peggy by Levin **Cambridge** in November 1790 [Land Records P:301]. She was the mother of
    i.   Levin[2], born 10 January 1783.
    ii. Peggy, born in November 1790.

Members of the Blake family in Delaware were
    i.   James[1] "& Son," head of a New Castle County household of 10 "other free" in 1800 [DE:271].
    ii. Abram, perhaps the unnamed son counted in James Blake's New Castle County household in 1800, head of a New Castle County household of 6 "other free" in 1810 [DE:231] and 6 "free colored" in Mill Creek Hundred, New Castle County, in 1820 [DE:127].
    iii. Edward[2], born 1776-1794, head of a New Castle County household of 7 "other free" in 1810 [DE:301] and 8 "free colored" in Appoquinimink Hundred in 1820 [MD:149].
    iv. John, head of a Little Creek Hundred, Kent County, Delaware household of 4 "other free" in 1800 [DE:35] and 5 "free colored" in Wilmington Borough, New Castle County, in 1820 [DE:185].
    v.   Rosanna, born before 1776, head of a Wilmington, New Castle County household of 4 "free colored" in 1820 [DE:202].

BOARMAN FAMILY

1. James Boarman, born say 1670, was the Indian servant of John Dent of St. Mary's County on 11 August 1691 when the Charles County court ordered that the constable for Port Tobacco Hundred return him to his master [Court Record 1690-2, 237]. He may have been the father of
    i.   Samuel, born say 1695, ran away from his master, Captain Abraham Ewens of Kent County, Delaware, and was brought before the Kent County, Delaware court in November 1718. Samuel was ordered to serve Ewens four years for the expenses in taking him up, and Ewens was ordered to pay £7 to the sheriff of New Castle County for his expenses and £5 to John Cowgil for curing him of divers very bad wounds [General Court Records 1718-22, 12-13].

They may have been the ancestors of
2   i.   Hannah, born say 1775.

2. Hannah Boarman, born say 1775, was the mother of
    i.   Susannah, born about 1800, registered in Prince George's County on 24 April 1816: *a bright mulatto girl...about 16 years old...a free woman being the reputed daughter of Hannah Boarman, a free woman of color.*
    ii. John, born about 1803, registered in Prince George's County on 27 September 1819: *a bright mulatto boy, about 16 years old...is free being the reputed son of Hannah Boarman a free woman of color* [Provine, *Registrations of Free Negroes*, 20, 31].

BOND FAMILY

Baltimore County
1. "Mulatto" Bess, born say 1692, was the servant of the widow Day in August 1711

when she appeared in Baltimore County court and named William Bond as the father of her illegitimate child [Liber IS#A, 247, cited by Barnes, *Baltimore County Families, 1659-1759*, 40]. She may have been the mother of

    i.   Richard, head of an Anne Arundel County household of 6 "other free" in 1790, perhaps the father of Edward Bond who registered in Anne Arundel County on 16 January 1818: *aged about twenty one years...Yellowish Complexion...free born* [Certificates of Freedom 1810-31, 108].

    ii. Harry Bonds, a "free negro" taxable in Spesutia Upper Hundred, Harford County, in 1783 [MSA S1161-6-11, p.54].

Talbot County
1.   Martha Bond, born say 1725, the servant of Francis Pickering of St. Michael's Parish, confessed to the Talbot County court in November 1745 that she had an illegitimate "Mulatto" child [Judgment Record 1745-6, 245]. She may have been the mother of

    i.   John, a "free mulatto" living on Tuckahoe & Kings Creek, Talbot Island, Talbot County, in 1783 [MSA S1161-10-3, p.11].

    ii. Rachel, head of a Caroline County household of 3 "other free" in 1790.

BOON FAMILY

1.   Susanna Middleton, born say 1770, was a white woman who had mixed-race children named Boon in Frederick County. She was the mother of

    i.   Thomas Boon, born about 1794, obtained a certificate in Frederick County on 4 June 1816: *a dark Mulatto Man about Twenty two years, about five feet eight and three quarter Inches high...free born and a Child of Susanna Middleton a white woman as appears by the affidavit of Barbara Ney.*

    ii. Susanna Boon, born about 1795, registered in Frederick County on 4 June 1816: *a bright Mulatto, aged about twenty one years, five feet four Inches and three quarters of an Inch high...child of Susanna Middleton.*

    iii. John Boon, born about 1796, obtained a certificate in Frederick County on 4 June 1816: *a Dark Mulatto aged about twenty years, five feet three inches high...free Born child of Susanna Middleton a white woman as appears by the affidavit of Barbara Ney.*

    iv. Nancy Boon, born about 1801, registered in Frederick County on 4 June 1816: *a Dark Mulatto aged about 15 years, five feet two inches and an half high...free born child of Susanna Middleton* [Certificates of Freedom 1806-27, 59-60].

BOOTH FAMILY

The Booth family won a petition for their freedom from David Weems in the Maryland Court of Appeals about 1793 [*Archives of Maryland on line*, 830:419]. And members of the family won a suit for their freedom from Joseph Mudd in Charles County court in August 1803. Their cases were probably based on descent from a white woman. Members of the family were

    i.   Richard, brother of Edward Booth, obtained his freedom from David Weems, perhaps identical to R. Boothe, head of a Prince George's County household of 2 "other free" in 1810 [MD:24].

1   ii. Hannah, born say 1765.

    iii. Edward, born about 1767, registered in Anne Arundel County on 2 May 1807: *about the age of forty years...his complexion of a nutmeg Colour is the Identical person who petitioned for his freedom in the General Court against David Weems and who as it appears obtained his freedom by the decision of the Court of Appeals in the case on the appeal of Richard Booth who is the Brother of the said Edward Booth, against the said David Weems. The said Edward Booth was born on Herring Bay in Anne*

    Arundel County [Certificates of Freedom 1806-7, 12]. He was head of a Baltimore City household of 4 "other free" in 1810 [MD:28].

    iv. Solomon, head of a Baltimore City household of 10 "other free" in 1810 [MD:309].

    v. James, head of an Anne Arundel County household of 9 "other free" in 1810 [MD:85].

    vi. David, head of a Washington County household of 4 "other free" in 1810 [MD:534].

    vii. Peter, head of an Anne Arundel County household of 1 "other free" in 1810 [MD:90].

1.   Hannah Booth, born say 1765, was freed by Alexander McPherson by deed recorded in Prince George's County on 1 November 1803: *my Negro woman Hannah...descended from the family that calls themselves Booths...and her six children: Margaret, Rachel, Henny, James, Henry and John*. Hannah recorded the manumission in Charles County on 29 March 1804: *Whereas a Family of Negroes claimed by Joseph Mudd of Charles County, calling themselves Boothes, Sued for and obtained their freedom in Charles County Court at August Term 1803 and whereas the Negroes herein after named are of the same family* [Prince George County Land Records JRM #10, 192; IB #6, 83]. Hannah was the mother of

    i. Margaret.

    ii. Rachel, born say 1788, head of a Washington County household of 4 "other free" in 1810 [MD:549].

    iii. Henny.

    iv. James.

    v. Henry.

    vi. John.

BOSTON FAMILY

Members of the Boston family were

1   i. Catherine, born say 1740.

2   ii. Wy, born about 1760.

3   iii. William, born say 1763.

    iv. Violet, born about 1767, registered in Baltimore County on 12 May 1807: *Negro, Dark Colour, 5 feet 1-1/4 inches, age 40, born free in Ann Arundel* [Certificates of Freedom, 1806-16, (not manumitted), no. 18]

4   v. Philip, born about 1772.

    vi. Charles, head of an Anne Arundel County household of 2 "other free" in 1800 [MD:101].

    vii. John, head of a Dorchester County household of 1 "other free" in 1800 [MD:669].

    viii. Clarissa, born about 1784, registered in Anne Arundel County on 5 February 1819: *aged about thirty five years...yellowish complexion...free born* [Certificates of Freedom 1810-31, 127].

1.   Catherine Boston, born say 1740, was described as a yellow woman, being a Portuguese, in a suit brought by her son, Anthony Boston, a slave who was granted his freedom in Anne Arundel County about 1793. The court ruled that the family descended from a Spanish woman named Maria, to her daughter Linah, to Linah's daughter Violet. Linah was described as having a yellow complexion with long black hair [Catterall, *Judicial Cases Concerning Slavery*, IV:51 (Rawlings v. Boston, 3 Har. and McH. 139, May 1793)]. Catherine was the mother of

    i. Anthony, won his freedom about 1793, head of a Prince George's County household of 3 "other free" in 1800 [MD:301].

5   ii. ?Sarah, born say 1785.

2.   Wy Boston, born about 1760, registered in Anne Arundel County on 20 August 1818: *aged about fifty eight years...black Complexion...free born* [Certificates of

Freedom 1810-31, 120]. She may have been the mother of
  i. Peter, born about 1783, registered in Anne Arundel County on 22 August 1818: *aged about thirty five years...black Complexion...free born* [Certificates of Freedom 1810-31, 120].
  ii. Darky, born about 1786, registered in Anne Arundel County on 26 October 1818: *aged about thirty two years...Dark Complexion...free born* [Certificates of Freedom 1810-31, 124].
  iii. Robert, born about 1786, registered in Anne Arundel County on 10 September 1812: *aged about twenty-six years, dark brown complexion, free born* [Certificates of Freedom 1810-31, 25].
  iv. Sarah, born about 1788, registered in Anne Arundel County on 20 August 1818: *aged about thirty years...black Complexion...free born* [Certificates of Freedom 1810-31, 119].

3. William[1] Boston, born say 1763, was head of a Talbot County household of 4 "other free" in 1790 and 5 in 1800 [MD:518]. He may have been the father of
  i. William[2], born about 1788, registered in Talbot County on 27 July 1816: *a dark mulatto man...about 28 years of age, 5 feet 6 ½ inches high...born free & raised in the County* [Certificates of Freedom 1815-28, 39].

4. Philip Boston, born about 1772, was head of an Anne Arundel County household of 8 "other free" in 1800 [MD:109]. He registered in Anne Arundel County on 27 March 1812: *a negro...dark complexion, about forty years of age...obtained his freedom by petition in the late General Court against Richard Sprigg* [Certificates of Freedom 1810-31, 19]. He may have been the father of
  i. Peter, born about 1791, registered in Anne Arundel County on 20 April 1814: *aged about twenty three years dark complexion...free born* [Certificates of Freedom 1810-31, 41].
  ii. David, born about 1793, registered in Anne Arundel County on 3 October 1815: *about twenty two years of age...dark complexion...free born* [Certificates of Freedom 1810-31, 65].
  iii. Caesar, born about 1795, registered in Anne Arundel County on 7 June 1817: *aged about twenty two years...dark complexion...free born* [Certificates of Freedom 1810-31, 100].

5. Sarah Boston, born say 1785, a "free woman of colour," was living in Prince George's County when her children registered as "free Negroes." She was the mother of
  i. Charles Boston **Dulaney**, born about 1804, registered in Prince George's County on 13 August 1825: *bright complexion...about 21 years old...son of Sarah Boston, a free woman of colour.*
  ii. Peter, born about 1806, registered in Prince George's County on 13 September 1826: *a mulatto boy, about 20 years of age...son of Sarah Boston.*
  iii. Betsy, born about 1810, registered in Prince George's County on 13 September 1826: *a mulatto woman, about 16 years old...daughter of Sarah Boston.*
  iv. Mary, born about 1812, registered in Prince George's County on 13 September 1826: *a mulatto girl, about 14 years old, and 5 feet 1 inch tall...daughter of Sarah Boston* [Provine, *Registrations of Free Negroes*, 53, 59, 60].

Notes:
1. A "Negro Man named Boston," a white woman named Nancy who still had 3 years to serve, and a "Mulatto Girl aged 8 years free at the age of 31 years" were listed in the inventory of the Anne Arundel County estate of James Barnes on 16 May 1749 [Prerogative Inventories & Accounts 1749, 176].

BOSWELL FAMILY

Members of the Boswell family were
   i. Terry, head of a Charles County household of 6 "other free" in 1800 [MD:557].
1 ii. Trecy, born say 1775.

1. Trecy Boswell, born say 1775, was a "free woman of colour" and the mother of
   i. Maria, born about 1795, registered in Prince George's County on 12 January 1818: *a black woman about 23 years old, 5 feet 7 or 8 inches tall, and has a brown complexion...a descendant of Trecy Boswell, a free woman.*
   ii. Letty, born about 1799, registered in Prince George's County on 12 January 1818: *a black woman about 19 years old, 5 feet 7 inches tall, and has a brown complexion...the descendant of Trecy Boswell.*
   iii. Henry, born about 1802, registered in Prince George's County on 9 January 1823: *about 21 years old and 6 feet 1-1/2 inches tall...son of Trecy Boswell.*
   iv. Elizabeth, born about 1805, registered in Prince George's County on 9 January 1823: *light complexion, is about 18 years old, and 5 feet 4-1/2 inches tall...daughter of Trecy Boswell, a free woman of colour* [Provine, *Registrations of Free Negroes*, 24, 44].

BOTELER FAMILY

Members of the Boteler family in Maryland were
   i. Black Charles, head of a Prince George's County household of 8 "other free" in 1800 [MD:257].
   ii. Mary, "free Negro" head of a Prince George's County household of 6 "other free" in 1800 [MD:257].
   iii. Letty, "free Negro" head of a Prince George's County household of 4 "other free" in 1800 [MD:279].
   iv. Betty, head of a Washington County household of 6 "other free" in 1800 [MD:555].
   v. Catherine, born about 1801, registered in Prince George's County on 13 August 1822: *a mulatto woman, about 21 years old, and 5 feet 1 inch tall...born free in Prince George's County.*
   vi. John, born about 1807, registered in Prince George's County on 8 July 1828: *a bright mulatto man, about 21 years old, and 5 feet 8 ½ inches tall...son of Negro Betsey, a free woman of color* [Provine, *Registrations of Free Negroes*, 42, 74].

BOWEN FAMILY

1. Alley Bowen, born say 1755, was indicted for "Mollatto Bastardy" by the Kent County, Maryland court in November 1774 [Criminal Dockets, appearances to November 1774, no.17]. She was probably related to
   i. Nathan, head of a Kent County household of 4 "other free" in 1810 [MD:837], perhaps identical to the Nathan Bowen who was head of a Kent County household of 5 "other free" and a slave in 1810 [MD:834].

BOWSER/ BOWZER FAMILY

1. Richard Bowser, born say 1720, was a "free Negroe," who was buried near the ferry to Kent Island on 24 July 1769. His wife may have been Rachel Bowser who was presented by the Queen Anne's County court in March 1770 for failing to list herself as a taxable. She was buried near the ferry to Kent Island on 29 July 1771 [Wright, *Vital Records of the Jesuit Mission, Cordova*, 8, 11; Surles, *And they*

Appeared at Court 1770-1772, 10]]. They may have been related to the Bowser family of Virginia and North Carolina. Their descendants may have been

   i. Elizabeth, born say 1745, presented by the Queen Anne's County court in March 1770 for failing to list herself as a taxable [Surles, *And they Appeared at Court 1770-1772*, 10].

   ii. James, born about 1745, a 105-year-old "Mulatto," born in Maryland, counted in the 1850 census for Frankford, Philadelphia, in 1850, a few households away from a 55-year-old "Mulatto" named James Bowser who was a carpenter, also born in Maryland, with $600 of real estate.

   iii. Thomas, born about 1758, a twelve-year-old orphan boy (no race indicated) bound to David Evans by the Queen Anne's County court in March 1770 until the age of twenty-one, head of a Kent County, Maryland household of 3 "other free" and 4 slaves in 1810 [MD:878]. He was deceased on 10 March 1846 when his only heir William Bowser provided testimony to the Anne Arundel County court that Thomas had served as a private in the Maryland Line during the Revolution [NARA, BlWt. 2385-100, M804-306, frame 0134]. He was listed in the muster of Captain John Hawkins's Company of the 5th Maryland Regiment, engaged to serve 3 years [NARA, M246, roll 34, frame 181 of 587].

   iv. William, married to Sylina, "Neg. (of) Mrs. Mary Jonhns" on 15 September 1805 when their daughter Eliza was baptized at St. George's Parish, Harford County [St. John's and St. George's Parish Registers, p. 192]. Bill Bowser was head of a Harford household of 2 "free colored" males in 1820.

   v. Elias, kept and clothed by John Carcy from 23 December 1770 to November 1771 in Queen Anne's County [Surles, *And they Appeared at Court 1770-1772*, 63].

2   vi. Ruth, born say 1760.

   vii. Percy, head of a Dorchester County household of 6 "other free" in 1800 [MD:691].

   viii. Simon, head of a Kent County, Maryland household of 2 "other free" in 1800 [MD:145].

   ix. Nancy, married Joseph **Wilson**, "free blacks," 8 September 1810 in St. Paul's Parish, Baltimore [Reamy, *Records of St. Paul's Parish*, I:67].

   x. Phil, "Negro" head of a Harford County household of 7 "other free" in 1810 [MD:755].

   xi. Robert, head of a Baltimore City household of 5 "other free" in 1810 [MD:221].

   xii. Lewis, head of a Baltimore City household of 3 "other free" in 1810 [MD:228].

   xiii. Rachel, head of a Kent County household of 2 "other free" in 1810 [MD:853].

2. Ruth Bowser, born say 1760, had an illegitimate child named Ann by Thomas Jackson in Queen Anne's County in 1779 [Judgment Record 1771-80, digital images 176, 221; Surles, *And they Appeared at Court 1779, 1782, 1785, 1786, 1787*, 15-16]. She was head of a Queen Anne's County household of 6 "other free" in 1790. She was the mother of

   i. Ann, born about 1779.

BRADY FAMILY

Members of the Brady family were

   i. Charles, born about 1769, registered in St. Mary's County on 6 March 1809: *aged forty years or thereabouts, complexion very bright, hair long and middling strait...was born free* [Certificates of Freedom 1806-64, 4].

   ii. James, head of a Kent County household of 4 "other free" in 1800 [MD:145].

iii. Nancy, "free negro" head of a Prince George's County household of 1 "other free" in 1800 [MD:275].
iv. Mary, a "Mulatto" who married John, the slave of Mrs. Hoxton, on 20 March 1793 in St. Mary's Mattawoman Parish, Charles County [Colonial Dames of America, *Records of St. Mary's Parish, 1793-1861*, 161].

BRENNING/ BROWNING FAMILY

1. Sarah Brenning, born say 1743, the white spinster servant of William Spencer, was convicted in March 1763 by the Kent County, Maryland court for having a child by a "Negroe man" [Criminal Record 1761-72, 29]. She may have been the mother of
    i. Charles Browning, head of a Kent County household of 4 "other free" in 1810 [MD:907].

BROWN FAMILY

Anne Arundel and Prince George's counties
1. Eleanor Brown, born say 1689, the servant of Thomas Ricketts, confessed to the Anne Arundel County court in November 1709 that she had a child by her master's "Negroe Will." Her son, born October 1709, was bound to Henry Mereday until the age of thirty-one. In March 1718/9 she confessed to having a child by "Negroe Sam belonging to Col. Mahall." The court ordered her to serve her master, Thomas Ricketts, twelve months for the trouble of his house and bound the child to Henry Merryday until the age of thirty-one [Judgment Record 1708-12, 98, 201; 1717-9, 307]. She was the mother of
    i. John[1], born about 1713, a ten-year-old "Mallato" with twenty-one years to serve when he was valued at £15 in the 31 May 1723 inventory of the Anne Arundel County estate of Thomas Ricketts, deceased [Prerogative Court Inventories and Accounts, MSA SM 11, SR 4330-1, 8:196-9].
2   ii. Margaret, born about 1716.
    iii. Philemon, born about 1718, about four or five years of age on 31 May 1723 when he was listed in estate of Thomas Ricketts [Prerogative Court Inventories & Accounts 8:196-9].

2. Margaret Brown, born about 1716, was a seven-year-old "Mallato" with twenty-four years to serve when she was valued at £11 in the 31 May 1723 inventory of Thomas Ricketts [Prerogative Court Inventories and Accounts, 8:196-9]. She was called "Mallatto Margaret at Meredith Davis'" on 27 November 1739 when she confessed to the Prince George's County court that she had an illegitimate child. The court ordered that she receive ten lashes. She was called Margaret Brown (no race indicated), the servant of Meredith Davis, on 28 August 1742 when the court ordered that she receive ten lashes and bound her illegitimate child named John to her master until the age of twenty-one. She had another child named Charity before 16 March 1744/5 (for which she received 10 lashes) and another child before 23 August 1748 [Court Record 1738-40, 435, 515-6; 1742-3, 127; 1744-6, 26; 1747-8, 354]. She was called a "Molatto woman Pegg" and had eighteen months to serve when she was listed in the inventory of the Prince George's County estate of Meredith Davis which was recorded on 23 February 1754 [Prerogative Inventories 58:7-9]. She was the mother of
3   i. ?Ann, born say 1739.
    ii. John[2], born about 1742, perhaps the unnamed "Molatto" boy who still had eleven years to serve when he was listed in the inventory of the Prince George's County estate of Meredith Davis which was recorded on 23 February 1754 [Prerogative Inventories 55:7-9]. He may have been the John Brown, "Free Mulatto," who bound himself to Reverend Mr. Thomas Bacon in Frederick County. Bacon petitioned the court in March 1765 that John had runaway twice since binding himself as an apprentice. The court

ordered that he serve Bacon another year as restitution [Judgments 1763-6, 377]. He was head of a Montgomery County household of 4 "other free" in 1790.

   iii. Charity, born about 1745.

   iv. ? ___ge (George?), head of an Anne Arundel County household of 7 "other free" in 1790.

3.   Ann Brown, born say 1739, confessed to Prince George's County court on 27 November 1753 that she had a five-week-old "Mollatto" child named Eleanor. The court sold the child to Mary Edelen until the age of thirty-one [Court Record 1751-4, 512]. She may have been identical to Nanny Brown who was head of an Anne Arundel County household of 7 "other free" in 1790. She was the mother of

   i. Eleanor[2], born in October 1753.

Other members of the Brown family on the Western Shore were

   i. Henrietta, head of a Charles County household of 8 "other free" in 1800 [MD:523].

   ii. Hannah, head of a Baltimore City household of 6 "other free" in 1800 [MD:148].

   iii. Thomas, head of a Baltimore City household of 5 "other free" and a slave in 1790 and 6 "other free" in 1800 [MD:137].

   iv. Joshua, head of a Baltimore City household of 6 "other free" in 1800 [MD:139].

   v. Benjamin, head of a Baltimore Town household of 7 "other free" in 1790.

   vi. Mary, head of a Baltimore Town household of 3 "other free" in 1790.

   vii. John, "F.M." head of a Back River, Baltimore County household of 4 "other free" in 1790.

   viii. John, head of an Anne Arundel County household of 5 "other free" in 1790.

   ix. Samuel, head of a Frederick County household of 3 "other free" in 1800 [MD:804].

   x. Catherine, head of a Frederick County household of 2 "other free" in 1800 [MD:987].

   xi. Jane, head of a Frederick County household of 2 "other free" in 1800 [MD:979].

   xii. Mary, born about 1789, registered in Anne Arundel County on 21 August 1819: *aged about thirty years...dark Complexion...free born* [Certificates of Freedom 1810-31, 141].

Kent County

1.   Elizabeth Browne, born say 1690, was the servant of John Carville of Kent County, Maryland, on 24 March 1707/8 when she admitted in court that she had a child by William Jenkins, one of her master's slaves. The court ordered that she receive twenty lashes, that her child serve her master according to law, and that her master deliver her to the court at the expiration of her term of service [Court Proceedings 1707-9, fol. 49]. She, her husband and their children were listed in the Kent County estate of John Carvill which was appraised on 30 September 1709:

1 marlatto named Jenkins	£30
1 white woman named Eliza Brown	£12
1 marlatto child abt. 1 year old	£2
1 marlatto boy name Billy	£10

[Prerogative Court Inventories and Accounts, Liber 30:398-406].
They may have been the ancestors of

   i. Margarite, "Negro" head of a Kent County, Maryland household of 6 "other free" in 1790.

   ii. Darky, "Negro" head of a Kent County household of 3 "other free" in

1790.
iii. Harry, head of a Kent County household of 5 "other free" in 1800 [MD:145].
iv. John, head of a Kent County household of 4 "other free" in 1800 [MD:145].
v. Thomas, head of a Kent County household of 3 "other free" in 1800 [MD:145].
vi. Dark, head of a Talbot County household of 7 "other free" in 1790.
vii. Nicholas, a "mulatto" fined 10 shillings by the Queen Anne's County court in March 1774 [Surles, *and they Appeared in Court, 1774-7*, 12], head of a Queen Anne's County household of 7 "other free" in 1800 [MD:325].
viii. Anthony, head of a Queen Anne's County household of 5 "other free" in 1800 [MD:323].
ix. Thomas, head of a Talbot County household of 4 "other free" in 1790 and 5 in 1800 [MD:533].
x. Benjamin, a "free negro" taxable in Gunpowder Hundred, Harford County in 1783 [MSA 1161-6-7, p.58], "Negro" head of a Harford County household of 4 "other free" in 1790.
xi. Major, a "Negro" drafted in the Revolution from Cecil County in May 1781 but listed among those who absconded [NARA, M246, roll 34, frame 447 of 587].
xii. James, head of a North Millford, Cecil County household of 1 "other free" in 1790.
xiii. John, head of a Cecil County household of 5 "other free" in 1800 [MD:236].
xiv. Daniel, head of a Cecil County household of 2 "other free" in 1800 [MD:223].
xv. Perry, born about 1790, registered in Talbot County on 19 August 1815: *a Bright Mulatto man...about 25 years of age, 5 feet 8 inches high...born free & raised in the County* [Certificates of Freedom 1807-15, 12].

Delaware
1. Martha Brown, born say 1746, was living in Duck Creek Hundred, Kent County, Delaware, in August 1766 when the grand jury presented her for having a child by a "Negro or Mulatto" man [DSA, RG 3805, MS case files, Presentments August 1766]. She may have been the ancestor of some of the following members of the Brown family who were "F.N." heads of Kent County households in 1810:
   i. Henry, 4 "other free" [DE:7].
   ii. Abraham, 5 "other free" [DE:156].
   iii. Henry, 5 "other free" [DE:49].
   iv. Anthony, 8 "other free" [DE:49].
   v. Anthony, 6 "other free" [DE:79].
   vi. Philip, 3 "other free" [DE:167].
   vii. Anthony, 9 "other free" [DE:7].
   viii. Isaac, Negro head of a Duck Creek Hundred, Kent County household of 7 "free colored" in 1820 [DE:55].

BRUMEJUM/ BRUMAGEN FAMILY

1. Eliza Brumejum, born say 1692, was presented by the Anne Arundel County court in August 1712 for having a "Mallato" bastard child. She confessed that "a Negroe man called James belonging to Stephen Warman" was the father of the child, and the court ordered that she be sold for seven years and bound her unnamed son to her master for thirty-one years [Judgment Records 1712-15, Liber TB, no. 3, p.5]. She was probably the ancestor of
2.   i. James, born say 1712.
   ii. R. Brumager, head of a Baltimore City household of 1 "other free" in 1810 [MD:75].

2.   James Brumigem, born say 1712, was tried by the Frederick County, Virginia court on 24 January 1746/7 for breaking into the house of Captain John Hite and taking some gunpowder. He was found not guilty of felony but found guilty of petty larceny and given thirty-one lashes, made to stand in the pillory and ordered to post bonds of £40 for his good behavior. He was called a "Mulatto" on 5 March 1746/7 when the court ordered that he receive twenty-five lashes for abusing Lawrence Stevens in a very ill manner. On 6 March 1746/7 the court ordered that the sheriff sell James's goods: a horse, saddle, bridle, coat jacket, leather jacket, rifle, gun powder horn, silver buckles, silver clasps, three axes, a crosscut saw, and a hand saw for a debt of about £8 he owed Jost Hite, John Hite and Lewis Stephens. His estate was attached for debt again on 7 August 1747, 7 June 1748 and 3 August 1748. He died before 6 September 1748 when the court granted administration of his estate to Peter Tostee, his greatest creditor [Orders 1745-8, 201, 213, 224, 301-2, 435, 462, 488]. He may have been the ancestor of

3   i.   Thomas Brumagen, born say 1740.

3.   Thomas Brumagen, born say 1740, was indicted with Jane Clark for fornication by the Frederick County, Virginia court on 7 September 1762. Jane was discharged but Thomas was ordered to pay a fine of 500 pounds of tobacco. Richard Pearis, Gent. , undertook to pay his fine. He was sued by William and Jane Phillips on 5 November 1762, but the case was agreed before coming to trial. He was convicted of stealing a steer belonging to John Shearer on 2 September 1766 and chose to receive 39 lashes corporal punishment rather than be tried at the General Court. Seth Dungen sued him for £3.10 on 8 October 1766 [Orders 1762-3, 156, 393; 1765-7, 172, 224]. He may have been the father of

i.   George Brumagam, taxable in Frederick County, Virginia, in 1787 and 1788 [PPTL 1782-1802].

BRYAN FAMILY

1.   Alice Bryan, born say 1681, confessed in Kent County, Delaware court in September 1699 that she had a "bastard Molattoe Child" by "William Trippits Negro man, Called Jack" and admitted that it was due to "her owne wicked inclinations." She received thirty-nine lashes and was ordered to serve her master, Daniel Rutty, an additional two years. The court bound her "molattoe" son Peter to Rutty for thirty-one years. Later that year in December she came into court and bound her four-year-old illegitimate daughter Elizabeth (no race indicated) to Rutty, for eighteen years [Court Records 1699-1703, 4b, 10b]. Her children were

i.   Elizabeth, born April 1696.

ii.   Peter, born in 1699.

iii.   ?Sarah, born say 1701, "a mulatto woman begotten on a white woman, convicted by the Westmoreland County, Virginia court on 26 January 1708/9 of "haveing a Mulatto bastard Child by a white man" while serving her indenture to a Mr. Westcomb [Orders 1705-21, 108a].

2   iv.   ?Mary, born say 1703.

2.   Mary Bryant, born say 1703, was the "Molattoe" daughter of a free white woman according to testimony by her daughter Daphne in Prince George's County court on 23 November 1756 [Court Record 1754-8, 356]. She was the mother of

3   i.   Daphne, born say 1720.

4   ii.   ?Abigail, born say 1735.

3.   Daphné Bryant, born say 1723, petitioned the Prince George's County court on 23 November 1756 that she and her children: Sarah, Dick, and Hannah, were free but held in slavery by Henry Watson [Court Record 1754-8, 356, 360]. She was the mother of

i.   Sarah, born say 1744.

ii.   Dick, born say 1746.

    iii.   Hannah, born say 1748, head of an Octoraro, Cecil County household of 11 "other free" in 1790.

4.   Abigail Brian, born say 1735, was head of a St. Mary's County, Maryland household of 3 "other free" in 1790. She was the mother of
    i.   Jeremiah, born about 1755, registered in St. Mary's County on 30 April 1822: *son of Abigail...aged sixty seven years, Dark Complexion...born free & raised in Saint Mary's County* [Certificates of Freedom 1806-64, 60].

Other Bryan families:
1.   Ann Bryan, born say 1700, was the servant of the Reverend Mr. Alexander Williamson on 18 June 1718 when the Kent County, Maryland court adjudged her child to be "begot by a negro man," ordered her sold for seven years and bound her child to her master [Court Proceedings 1718-20, 87-8].

1.   Ann Bryan, born say 1730, was called "a spinster white servant" on 20 November 1750 when she confessed to the Kent County, Maryland court that she had a "Mulatto" child by a "Negro." She and her child were sold to her master John Hix, she for seven years and her child until the age of thirty-one [Criminal Proceedings 1748-60, 68]. Perhaps her children were
    i.   John, head of a North Sassafras, Cecil County household of 1 "other free" in 1790.
    ii.   Nathaniel, head of a Kent County household of 4 "other free" in 1800 [MD:157].
    iii.   Charles, head of a Kent County household of 3 "other free" and 2 slaves in 1800 [MD:157].

Other members of a Bryan family were
    i.   David, born about 1757, a six-year-old "Mulatto" boy to be free at twenty-one, listed in the inventory of the Baltimore County estate of Christopher Sutton on 18 September 1763 [Prerogative Inventories 82:191].
    ii.   William, "Mulatto" head of a Charles County household of 1 "other free" in 1790 and 4 in St. Mary's County in 1800 [MD:393].
    iii.   Abraham, head of a Baltimore City household of 8 "other free" in 1800 [MD:138].
    iv.   James, head of an Anne Arundel household of 1 "other free" in 1800 [MD:101].
    v.   Ama, head of a Dorchester County household of 3 "other free" and a slave in 1800 [MD:732].

BUCKWELL/ BUCKELL FAMILY

1.   Susanna Buckwell, born say 1750, a white spinster, confessed to the Kent County court in March 1770 that she had a "Mulatto" child by a "Negroe." The court ordered her sold for seven years and sold her daughter Frances or Fanny to Marmaduke Tilden until the age of thirty-one [Criminal Record 1761-72, 117a; Criminal Dockets 1766-71]. She was the mother of
    i.   Fanny, born about 1768.
    ii.   ?Michael Buckell, head of a Dorchester County household of 7 "other free" in 1800 [MD:717].

BULEY FAMILY

1.   Elizabeth Buly, born say 1710, was a spinster living in Shrewsbury Parish, Kent County, Maryland, on 21 March 1731/2 when she was convicted of having an illegitimate child for which she was fined 30 shillings [Criminal Court Records, 1728-34, 277-8]. She may have been the ancestor of
    i.   Eve, born about 1732, a "negro" taxable in the Nanticoke Hundred,

Somerset County household of Wilson Rider from 1748 to 1759 (called
Eve, Eave, Eavie) [Taxlist, 1729-1759, CR 51864, 23-31]. She was about
thirty-one in 1763 when she sued Wilson Rider for detaining her as a
servant, so she was probably the daughter of a white woman. George
Bennett and William Giles were her witnesses. She was prosecuted in
Somerset County in 1764 for having a child by a "negro slave." On 17
March 1767 she confessed to having another illegitimate child by a free
person, for which she paid a double fine of £3 because she refused to
identify the father [Judicial Records 1760-3, 262; 1763-65, 117; 1766-7,
106-7].

2   ii.   Stephen, born say 1733.

2.   Stephen Buley, born say 1733, was head of a household of a black male 40-50
     years old in the 1776 census for Straights Hundred of Dorchester County with a
     black woman 30-40, a black boy 10-16, 3 black boys under 10, a black girl 10-16
     and a black girl under 10 [MdHR 1419-2-5436]. He was head of a Dorchester
     County household of 5 "other free" in 1800 [MD:682]. He was probably the
     husband of Fortune Beuley whose son Jesse registered in Dorchester County on
     25 September 1816. They were probably the parents of
        i.   Job, born about 1755, enlisted in the 3^d Maryland Regiment on 8 April
             1782: *residence Cambridge, age 27 years, 5'7-1/2" high, stout, black
             complexion, form of hair: wool* [NARA, M881,
             http://fold3.com/image/17229501; M246, roll 34, frame 433 of 587].
        ii. George, born about 1761, a soldier who enlisted in the Revolution in
             Dorchester County and appeared in Dorchester County court at the age of
             72 years on 9 April 1833 and applied for a pension for his services in the
             Revolution. He stated that he was born in Prince George's County about
             1761 and was living in Dorchester County when he entered the service at
             East New Market for 9 months on 10 March 1781. His widow Grace
             Bewley, aged 59, "a free Colored woman," was residing in Baltimore on
             10 July 1855 when she applied for a widow's pension. She stated that they
             were married on 18 June 1824 by a minister of the Methodist Episcopal
             Church in Cambridge, Dorchester County, and her maiden name was
             Grace **Cromwell.** Her husband died on 15 August 1836. Her brother
             Shadrack **Cromwell,** aged 80, stated that she died on 1 March 1872
             [NARA, W.27576, M804, http://fold3.com/image/12028637].
        iii. Jesse, born about 1766, head of a Dorchester County household of 3
             "other free" in 1800 [MD:691]. He registered in Dorchester County on 25
             September 1816: *of a chesnut colour...raised in Dorchester County and
             was born free and is the son of Fortune Beuley who was also born free,
             aged about 50 years* [Certificates of Freedom for Negroes, 1806-64, 34].
        iv. Henry, head of a Dorchester County household of 4 "other free" in 1800
             [MD:663].

Another member of the family was
        i.   Ralph, born about 1794, a 48-year-old farmer from Somerset County who
             emigrated to Liberia aboard the *Lafayette* in 1832 with Nelly (age 40),
             Charlotte (22), Ann (14), Polly Ellen (10), Isaac James (6) and John
             Thomas Buly [http://fold3.com/image/46670387].

BURGESS FAMILY

1.   Margery Burgis, born say 1678, was the servant of John Smith of Prince George's
     County on 26 January 1696/7 when she confessed to the court that she had a
     "Malatta" child by her master's "negroe Cezar." The court ordered that she receive
     twenty-six lashes, serve her master a year for the trouble of his house and ordered
     her master to deliver her up to the vestry of St. Paul's Parish at Charles Town
     when she completed her service to him [Court Records 1696-9, 116-7]. She was

probably the ancestor of

    i. Edward, a "Molatto" who owed £3.7 to the Frederick County estate of Lawrence Owen about 1762 [Prerogative Inventories 77:337-8], probably the husband of Ann **Perle** Burgis who was named in the Frederick County will of her father Daniel **Perle** [Prerogative Court Wills 33:351].

    ii. John, a "Molatto" who owed 8 shillings to the Frederick County estate of Lawrence Owen about 1762 [Prerogative Inventories 77:337-8].

    iii. Mary, born before 1776, head of a Frederick County household of 3 "free colored" in 1830.

BURKE FAMILY

1. Ann Burk, born say 1685, admitted in Kent County, Delaware court in May 1707 that she had a "Mollatoe Bastard Female Child" by a "Certain Negroe Man" on John Walker's plantation. She was given twenty-nine lashes, made to stand two hours in the pillory and ordered to serve her master another six and one-half years. Her daughter was bound to Walker until the age of thirty-one years. A year later in May 1708 her "Mulatto" child, Archibald, born in Walker's house on 1 February 1704, was bound until the age of twenty-one years to Walker's children and executors, John and Daniel Walker [Court Records 1703-17, 56b, 72b]. Her children were

    i. Archibald, born 1 February 1704.

    ii. a daughter, born about 1707.

Another unrelated Burke family in Maryland was

    i. John, born about 1686, a "Mollatto" servant of Mrs. Elizabeth Hawkins, who was twenty-one years old on 10 June 1707 when the Charles County court ordered that he be set free. Mary Elliott, wife of William Elliott, testified that he had been sold to Henry Hawkins by her former husband Henry Brawner [Court Record 1704-10, 326].

Their descendants may have been:

    i. Henry, head of a Queen Anne's County household of 1 "other free" in 1790 [MD:102].

    ii. Charles, head of a Baltimore City household of 4 "other free" in 1800 [MD:148].

BURTON FAMILY

1. Ann Barton/ Burton, born say 1708, was living at the house of James Lindow in Manokin Hundred of Somerset Parish on 11 June 1725 when she had a "molatto" child. The court sold her child to Lindow for 510 pounds of tobacco, and Lindow posted bond of £20 to return her to the parish to be sold for seven years. She had a child by a (white?) man named John Rogers in October 1729. The court sold her child to Edward Rownd [Judicial Record 1725-7, 50-1; 1727-30, 225; 1733-5, 78, 80]. She may have been the ancestor of

2   i. Luke Burton, born say 1745.

    ii. Nace, born about 1786, registered in Baltimore City on 16 May 1832: age 46, *ight complexion, 6 feet high, born free and raised in Dorchester County* (with 48-year-old Deborah Burton) [Certificates of Freedom, 1830-2, no. 116].

2. Luke Burton, born say 1745, and his wife, Patience, registered the 10 May 1769 birth of their "mulatto" son, James, at St. George's Protestant Episcopal Church, Indian River Hundred, Sussex County [Wright, *Vital Records of Kent and Sussex Counties*, 98]. They were the parents of

    i. James, born 10 May 1769.

    ii. ?Joseph, head of a New Castle County, Delaware household of 8 "other free" in 1800 [DE:161].

    iii. ?Peter, head of a Lewis and Rehoboth Hundred, Sussex County household of 6 "other free" in 1800 [DE:414].

    iv. ?William, "Coloured" head of a New Castle County household of 7 "other free" in 1810 [DE:231].

BUTCHER FAMILY

1.   Robert¹ Butcher, born say 1670, was called "Robert Buchery negroe" of Great Choptank Hundred on 2 September 1690 when the Dorchester County court ordered him to pay a fine of 500 pounds of tobacco for begetting an illegitimate child by Elizabeth Cobham, an indentured servant of Andrew Gray. The court also ordered him to pay Gray 800 pounds of tobacco for the nursing of the child. Andrew Gray, Jr., and Philip Pitt were his securities to pay for the tuition and bringing up of the child. Elizabeth Cobham received 25 lashes. In February 1691/2 he was accused of stealing nine deer skins, three new match coats and other items valued at 900 pounds of tobacco from Thomas Wells but was found not guilty. He admitted in February 1692/3 that he owed John Tyley of Talbot County for eight well-dressed deer skins [Judgment Record 1690-2, 176, 157, 156, 93, 87]. He recorded his earmark in adjoining Kent County, Delaware, on 13 February 1692/3 [de Valinger, *Court Records of Kent County, Delaware, 1680-1705*, 89]. He was sued in Kent County by Hugh Durborow on 11 August 1713. In August 1714 he testified that James Dean had counseled him to kill Timothy Hanson and burn his house. In November 1718 he confessed to the charge of battery and was ordered to be flayed and pay a 15-shilling fine. He was sued by Griffin Jones about 1723 and by John Bland in August 1723 [General Court Records 1712-6, n.p.; 1718-22, 20; 1722-3, n.p.; 1722-5, 35]. He was taxable in Duck Creek Hundred, Kent County in 1726, and his name was crossed off the Little Creek Hundred list in 1727 when he was listed with Robert Whud (Wood), Julius **Caesar**, Thomas **Consellor**, William **Beckett**, Winslow **Driggers**, Jacob **Miller**, Richard Poolin, and Daniel **Francisco** [RG 3535, Levy Assessment List, 1726-43, frames 341, 346]. He called himself a "yeoman" in his 26 July 1722 Kent County will which was proved 14 February 1731. He left his son Robert a shilling, left Phillis Asco (no relationship stated) a cow, calf, pewter plates, furniture and one of his three gold rings, and divided the remainder of his estate between his wife Susannah and son-in-law Richard Pulling [DB H-1, fol. 23-24]. His children were

2   i. ?Hannah, born say 1693.
3   ii. Robert², born say 1695.
    iii. the unnamed wife of Richard Pulling.

2.   Hannah Butcher, born say 1693, was convicted of felony by the Kent County, Delaware court on 10 August 1714. She was publicly whipped, made to wear a Roman T, and ordered to pay the owner Timothy Hanson fourfold the 10 shillings value of the goods [Dockets 1680-1725, General Court Records 1712-16, n.p.]. She may have been the mother of

    i. John, born say 1720, taxable in the upper part of Duck Creek Hundred from 1741 to 1743. He died before 29 December 1760 when his wife Sarah was granted administration on his estate. There was a balance of £148 due the estate of which she received half [DSA, RG 3545, frame 182].
4   ii. Susannah, born say 1722.
    iii. Elizabeth, born say 1725, indicted by the Kent County court in May 1743 for having an illegitimate female child which she charged to William **Gonselah** (**Consellor**). In February 1748 she charged George **Hilton** of Duck Creek Hundred, labourer, with being the father of another illegitimate female child. Sarah Butcher was a witness. And Perhaps this or a second case against **Hilton** was the one he submitted to in November 1752 [DSA, RG 3805, MS case papers, May 1743 indictments, November

1748 indictments; Dockets, 1739-79, frames 172, 174, 175, 214, 224]. In August 1775 the Kent County court charged four white men: John Gunard Cox, Charles Robinson, John Ray and James Copper with riotously assaulting her in Little Creek Hundred. Richard Smith, Esq., was her witness [DSA, RG 3505, MS case papers, August 1775 Presentments].

3.   Robert[2] Butcher, born say 1695, was called "Robert Butcher, Junr." in Kent County, Delaware court on 11 August 1713 when he and Thomas **Gonsoaly** (**Consellor**) were fined 15 shillings for being "Deficients on the Highways." He was called "Robert Butcher ye younger" on 15 May 1716 when the Kent County court convicted him of having an illegitimate child by Susanna Stephens [General Court Records 1712-6, n.p.]. His suit against John Harding was dismissed in May 1727 [DSA, RG 3815.031, 1722-1732, frame 154]. He was called "Robert Bucher Junr." when he was taxable in Little Creek Hundred, Kent County in 1729. He was called the administrator of Robert Butcher in May 1732 when Coffey **Hilton** and Richard Pullin brought separate suits against him in Kent County court. Julius **Caesar** sued him in court as the administrator of Robert Butcher claiming that he had paid Robert £10 for two steers which had not been delivered. Julius withdrew the case in May 1733, and Robert sued Julius in August 1733 but the case was agreed in November that year [DSA, RG 3515.031, 1722-32, frame 604; 1733-40, frames 3, 60]. His 14 November 1733 Kent County will, proved 6 December 1733, named his wife Sarah (daughter of Thomas **Conselah**), and left 190 acres of land to his sons, Moses, Benjamin, Robert, Conselah, and Thomas [WB H-1:77]. Sarah was head of a taxable household in Little Creek Hundred, Kent County, from 1740 to 1754. William Rees sued Sarah, Moses, Robert and Consella Butcher for a debt of £65 which they confessed judgment to in March 1747 [RG 3815.031, Common Pleas, Dockets 1744-1750, p.29]. His children were

    i.   Moses[1], born say 1715, taxable in Little Creek Hundred from 1740 to 1748, sued by Hugh Durburow for debt in Kent County in May 1742 and in December 1743 he admitted he owed Cornelius Empson £8 [DSA, RG 3815.031, Dockets 1740-4, frames 255, 319, 507]. He died before 12 September 1749 when his brother Robert was appointed administrator of his Kent County estate [WB K-1:2-3].

    ii.   Benjamin, born say 1718.

    iii.   Robert[3], born say 1720, taxable in Little Creek Hundred from 1745 to 1748, sued Moses Butcher in Kent County court in November 1748 [RG 3815.031, Common Pleas, Dockets 1744-1750, frame 499, 549]. He was appointed administrator of the estate of his brother Moses on 12 September 1749.

5   iv.   Conselah, born say 1722.

    v.   Thomas[1], born say 1723, sued James Maxwell for debt in Kent County court in May 1744 [Docket Volume 1736-85, 43]. He was taxable in Little Creek Hundred from 1754 to 1756.

4.   Susannah Butcher, born say 1722, was a "Molatto free & single woman" who declared in Kent County court on 26 April 1743 that the base born "Molatto" female child which was begotten on her body was by "Negro Jack," who had been the slave of Mrs. Rachel Collins and was then the slave of Mr. James Tybout [DSA, RG 3805, MS case files, April 1743 indictments]. In 1743 Joseph Clayton was allowed 13 shillings for her maintenance [RG 3200, Levy Court minutes]. She may have been the mother of

    i.   Martha, born say 1743, a "free Mulatto," indicted by the Kent County court in August 1771 for having an illegitimate child [DSA, RG 3805, MS case files, August 1771 indictments].

5.   Conselah Butcher, born say 1720, called "Selah" Butcher, was taxable in Little Creek Hundred, Kent County from 1752 to 1780 [RG 3535, Kent County Levy

List, 1743-67, frames 87, 143, 520, 566; 1768-84, frames 26, 103, 334, 366, 368].
Administration on his Kent County estate was granted to Thomas Butcher, his
"next of kin," in 1795 with Jesse **Dean** (signing) surety [WB N-1:117]. He may
have been the father of

 i. Thomas², born say 1750, taxable in Little Creek Hundred from 1773 to
  1776, in Duck Creek Hundred from 1777 to 1782, also in Dover Hundred
  in 1782, a "Negro" taxable in Little Creek Hundred from 1782 to 1785,
  taxable in Dover Hundred in 1785, a "Mulatto" taxable in Little Creek
  Hundred in 1797, taxable on an acre and a log house in 1798 [DSA, RG
  3535, 1768-84, frames 184, 222, 262, 299, 336, 370, 491, 522, 533, 539,
  541, 570, 582, 619; 1785-97, frames 8, 24, 71, 74, 106, 136, 176, 190,
  226, 267, 337; 1797-8, frames 14, 53, 473, 480]. On 14 April 1771 he
  admitted in Kent County court that he owed Archibald Duglass £129
  [DSA, RG 3815.031, 1769-71, frame 423]. He witnessed the 11 May 1776
  Little Creek Hundred, Kent County will of Samuel Whitman [de Valinger,
  Kent County Probate Records, 347]. In November 1792 Mary, Cynthia
  and Elizabeth **Ridgeway** charged him in Kent County court with
  assaulting them. Jesse **Dean** was his surety [DSA, RG 3805.002, Court of
  General Sessions, 1787-1803, frame 226; MS case papers, November
  1792 indictments]. He was head of a Little Creek Hundred household of
  8 "other free" in 1800 [DE:33] and 6 "free colored" in 1820 (called
  Thomas B. Butcher [DE:20].

Other members of the family were

 i. Richard Butcherly, born say 1712, held as a servant by John Stevens of
  Dorchester County contrary to law in August 1733. The court ordered him
  set free [Judgment Record 1733-4, 48].
 ii. Peter Butcherly, born say 1714, servant of Bartholomew Ennalls in
  November 1733 when the Dorchester County court required Ennalls to
  pay security of £10 not to transport him outside the province [Judgment
  Record 1733-4, 178].
 iii. Caesar, born say 1740, taxable in Little Creek Hundred in 1761.
 iv. Robert³, say 1750, taxable in Little Creek Hundred from 1772 to 1781, in
  Duck Creek Hundred in 1785, and a delinquent Murderkill taxable in
  1787, perhaps the Robert Bucher who was a "free" head of a Queen
  Anne's County household of 4 "other free" in 1790 and a Kent County,
  Maryland household of 7 "other free" in 1800 [MD:157].
 v. Jacob, born say 1752, taxable in Little Creek Hundred from 1776 to 1780,
  died before 23 March 1792 when George Frazer was granted
  administration on his Kent County estate. He was apparently the father of
  Susannah Butcher since Frazer wrote a letter saying he was too sick to
  take the inventory on the appointed day and that "her father owes me
  nothing" [RG 3545, Probate Records, reel 28, frames 174-177; WB N-1,
  fol. 15].
 vi. James, a "Negro" taxable in Little Creek Hundred from 1786 to 1789, also
  listed as a "Free Negro" in Dover Hundred from 1789 to 1794 [DSA, RG
  3535, Assessments 1785-97, frames 48, 74, 106, 153, 224, 265, 310]. He
  was called a "Negro" when Robert Hall and Caleb Sipple were granted
  administration of on his estate on 11 August 1808 on a $500 bond [DSA,
  RG 3545, Probate Records, frame 179].
 vii. Rachel, a "free Negro" taxable on a cow in Dover Hundred but struck off
  the list in 1797 [RG 3535, Kent County Levy List, 1785-97, frame 410].
 viii. Moses², born say 1758, taxable in Little Creek Hundred from 1779 to
  1787, listed as a "free Negro" starting in 1781, head of a Montgomery
  County, Pennsylvania household of 5 "other free" in 1790.
 ix. Moses³, born before 1776, a "free Negro" taxable in Dover Hundred, Kent
  County, on 4 acres of land in 1797 [RG 3535, Kent County Levy List,
  1785-97, frame 411], head of a household of 4 "free colored" in 1820

[DE:37]. He died before 26 June 1821 when Whittington Butcher and Henry Butcher of New Castle County were granted administration of his estate. His widow Phebe received $36.84 and his children Whittington and Henry Butcher and Rebecca, wife of Isaac **Maclin**, received $24.56 each [DSA, RG 3545, frames 196-8]. Isaac was head of a Dover Hundred household of 6 "free colored" in 1820 [DE:37].

   x. William, Sr., born say 1760, enlisted in the Revolution on 24 April 1777 and was listed in the muster of the "Independent Company of Foot raised for the safe guard of the...persons...residing near the Town of Lewis and the Coast of Delaware Bay," commanded by Captain William Pary" [NARA, M246, roll 31, frame 322 of 658]. He was a "Mulattoe taxable on 2 horses in Kent County in 1797.

   xi. Peter, head of a Little Creek Hundred, Kent County household of 10 "other free" in 1800 [DE:10].

   xii. James[2], born 1776-1794, head of a Duck Creek Hundred household of 5 "free colored" with one woman over 45 years old in 1820 [DE:48].

   xiii. Henry, head of a New Castle County household of 2 "free colored" in 1820 [DE:199].

   xiv. John, head of a New Castle County household of 6 "free colored" in 1820 [DE:108].

   xv. Whittington, head of a New Castle County household of 2 "free colored" in 1820 [DE:199].

   xvi. Eli, head of a Little Creek Hundred, Kent County household of one "free colored" in 1820 [DE:28].

Another unrelated Butcher family:
1. Susanna Butcher, born say 1734, the servant of Thomas Sellman, was ordered by the Anne Arundel County court in June 1754 to serve seven years for having a "Mulatto" child. The court ordered her child sold to Sellman until thirty-one for 500 pounds of tobacco [Judgment Record 1751-4, 874]. She was identical to Susannah Boucher, the white servant of Thomas Sellman, who had an illegitimate "Mulatto" child named Rachel by a "negro" in Baltimore County before March 1759 [Baltimore County Criminal Record 1757-9, 186-7]. She was the mother of

   i. Rachel, born about 1759.

   ii. Fanny, head of a Baltimore City household of 3 "other free" in 1810 [MD:310].

BUTLER FAMILY

1. Eleanor[1] Butler, born say 1660, was a white woman imported to Maryland by Lord Baltimore. She was the servant of Major William Boarman of St. Mary's County in August 1681 when she married "Negro Charles," one of Boarman's slaves. William Boarman left a St. Mary's County will on 16 May 1708, proved 17 June 1709. He gave his wife slaves Rch[d], Charles & Elliner, his son John Baptiste slave Catherine, his son Francis Ignatius slaves Ann and Margaret, his daughter Mary slaves Sarah and Henry, and his daughter Clare slaves Jane and Susannah [Hodes, *White Women, Black Men*, 33; Charles County Wills No.3: 25]. The inventory of his estate on 11 July 1709 included an "Elderly Negroe man named Charles," an "old Irish woman," a "Mallattoe" slave named Kate, a "Mallattoe" slave Jane, two "Mallattoe girl" slaves, and two "Mullattoe children" slaves. In 1730 members of the family were listed in the inventory of the estate of John Sanders: Charles "very old & lame," Kate, Jenny, Nan and Betty "Negro women," and seven children [Prerogative Court (Inventories) 1729-30, 634].

In August 1749 one of their descendants, Edward Butler, petitioned the Charles County court for his freedom from William Neale. The outcome of the case was not recorded. He may have been identical to Edward Butler who was sentenced to death for robbing Trinity Parish Church but pardoned by the governor on 13

May 1754 [*Archives of Maryland* 31:32]. He apparently had a free "Molatto" wife named Susannah (**Proctor**?) and several children.

On 27 September 1763 two of Charles and Nell's descendants, William and Mary Butler, sued Richard Boarman of St. Mary's County for their freedom in the Provincial Court, and between 1765 and 1767 the court took depositions from sixteen of their elderly white neighbors. Most testified as to what they remembered from their early youth, but a few (Edward Edelen, Benjamin Jamerson, James Jameson, Nathaniel Suit and Thomas Bowling) told what they had heard from their parents. Edward Edelen was probably the son of Richard Edelen, a deponent in Edward Butler's suit for freedom in 1749, and Benjamin Jamerson was probably the son of Mary Jameson, another deponent in the 1749 suit. The deponents told conflicting versions of the Butler family genealogy, but they generally agreed that Nell Butler and Charles were married in a ceremony which was conducted by a Catholic priest on the Boarman plantation. Some reported that Lord Baltimore warned Nell on the morning of the wedding that the marriage would make her and her descendants slaves for life and that Nell replied that she would rather marry Charles than Lord Baltimore himself. The law then in existence enslaved white women who married slaves for the lifetime of their husbands and made slaves of their children. About a month after the wedding Lord Baltimore was apparently influential in passing a law which released such white women and their children from slavery if their marriage was permitted or encouraged by their master. Since the law was passed after Charles and Nell's marriage, the children of Charles and Nell were kept as slaves by Boarman and his descendants [Provincial Court Judgments 1770-1, 233-44].

The Provincial Court decided the case in William and Mary Butler's favor in September 1770, but the decision was reversed by the Court of Appeals in May 1771. In October 1787 their daughter, Mary Butler, sued in the General Court of the Western Shore and won her case [*Cases in the Provincial Court*, 371-7; *Cases in the General Court*, 214-36]. In *The Heritage Within Us, The Butler Family of Pamunkey Neck* a Butler descendant, James Frank Williams, traces a great many Butler descendants through the more than forty court cases which were brought by members of the Butler family following Mary Butler's successful suit as well as estate accounts and wills of the slave owners of the Butler family. Charles and Eleanor's children were

2   i.   Catherine[1]/ Kate, born say 1683.

      ii. Jane[1], born say 1685, a "mallatoe woman slave" listed in the inventory of the Charles County estate of William Boarman in 1709 and a "Negro woman" listed in the inventory of the estate of John Sanders in 1730.

     iii. Ann[1], born say 1687, a "Negro woman" listed in the inventory of the estate of John Sanders in 1730.

3   iv. Elizabeth[1], born say 1693.

2.   Catherine[1]/ Kate Butler, born say 1683, was probably the unnamed "Mallatto Servant" of William Boarman on 10 August 1703 when he accused John Brayfield of dealing and bartering with her [Charles County Court Record 1701-4, 249, 264]. She was bequeathed by William Boarman to his son John Baptiste Boarman in 1709 and was a "mallatoe woman slave" listed in William's Charles County estate in 1709. She was called a "Negro woman named Kate" in the inventory of John Sanders in 1730. Several deponents in the William and Mary Butler vs. Richard Boarman suit testified that she was Charles and Nell's daughter [Provincial Court Judgments 1770-1, 235, 236, 239, 241, 243]. She was the mother of

4   i.   Edward[1], born say 1702.

      ii. ?John[1], born say 1705, a "Negro man Jack" listed in the 1730 inventory of John Sanders. Some deponents in the Butler vs. Boarman suit said that John Butler was Charles and Nell's oldest son, but Mary Crosen, a 74-

year-old woman, said that Jack was one of Catherine's children [Provincial Court Judgments 1770-1, 235, 236, 241, 243].

5   iii.   Margaret[1], born about 1727.

3.   Elizabeth[1] Butler, born say 1693, was not named among the slaves in Major Boarman's 1709 will but was listed as a "Negro woman" in the inventory of the estate of John Sanders in 1730. She was identified as Eleanor's daughter by 76-year-old Ann Whitehorn in her 27 May 1767 deposition in the Provincial Court. Ann also deposed that Elizabeth was somewhat younger than her, that Elizabeth had been dead about 30 years, and that Elizabeth's son William was about 44 years old at the time of the deposition [Provincial Court Judgments 1770-1, 236-7]. Elizabeth was the mother of

6   i.   William[1], born about 1721.

4.   Edward[1] Butler, born say 1702, was identified as the son of Kate Butler by William Simson in his deposition at the Provincial Court on 27 May 1767. The 69-year-old Simson said that he and Ned Butler, one of William Neale's slaves, had played together as children and were about the same age [Provincial Court Judgments 1770-1, 241-2]. Edward was a slave who belonged to Francis Hamersley on 13 June 1738 when he was convicted by the Charles County court of stealing a large quantity of cloth valued at 2,080 pounds of tobacco from the storehouse of Richard Gildart. The court ordered that he sit in the pillory for one hour and receive 39 lashes.[8] In August 1749 he petitioned the Charles County court for his freedom from William Neale. The court ordered that Richard Edelen, Mary Ruthorn, Mary Jameson, and Thomas Osborn be deposed for the next session of the court in November 1749, but the outcome of the case was not recorded [Court Record 1734-9, 474; 1748-50, 414]. (Perhaps the case was heard in adjoining St. Mary's County whose colonial court records have not survived.) Edward was sentenced to death for robbing Trinity Parish Church but was pardoned by the governor on 13 May 1754 [*Archives of Maryland* 31:32]. He may have been the husband of Susannah (**Proctor**?) Butler, a free woman, who was sued by William Neale (Edward Butler's master) for a debt of 1,631 pounds of tobacco in November 1753. She was also sued for a debt of 1,662 pounds of tobacco by William Parker in Charles County court on 9 March 1756. Most of the debt was for 1,500 pounds of tobacco which Parker paid for her to Thomas Clark, Esquire. She was identified as a "Molatto" in Parker's accounts, called a spinster in the court document, and called a widow on 14 March 1758 when she had a counter suit against Parker. He sold her security which consisted of 3 cows and 2 calves, 2 steers, 7 shoats, a bed, dishes, and other household items for 3,113 pounds of tobacco [Court Record 1753-4, 186; 1755-6, 423-4; 1756-7, 161, 404; 1757-8, 149]. Edward and Susannah may have been the parents of

7   i.   John, born say 1720.
        ii.   Joseph, born say 1722, sued William Parker for his freedom (no race indicated) [Court Record 1753-4, 369].
       iii.   Edward[2], born say 1732, called "Edward Butler, Junior, Planter" and "Labourer" in August 1753 when William Parker was security for his appearance in Charles County court to answer a presentment for stealing an ax from Benjamin Fendall and Robert Gates. He was found guilty, made to stand in the pillory for one hour and given thirty-nine lashes [Court Record 1753-4, 75, 82, 84-5]. He may have been identical to Edward Butler who was counted with Henry **Gray** in the 1800 census [MD:568].
       iv.   Matthew, born say 1740, a "Mulatto," owed 396 pounds of tobacco to the St. Mary's County estate of Philip Key on 2 March 1765 [Prerogative Inventories 102:101].

---

[8]Since this was a capital offense, he could have received the death penalty.

5. Margaret[1] Butler, born about 1727, was a "Negro Girle about 3 years old" who was listed in the estate of John Sanders in 1730. William McPherson (aged 60 years) and Joseph Jameson (aged 52) deposed on 27 May 1767 that Margaret was the daughter of Kate Butler and the mother of Mary Butler, the petitioner in the Butler vs. Richard Boarman suit [Provincial Court Judgments 1770-1, 239, 243]. Margaret's daughter was

    i. Mary, married William Butler. They sued for their freedom from Richard Boarman of St. Mary's County in 1763.

6. William[1] Butler, born about 1721, was a 9-year-old boy listed in the inventory of John Sanders' estate in 1730. He married his second cousin Mary Butler, the granddaughter of Catherine Butler. They brought suit for their freedom from Richard Boarman of St. Mary's County in 1763. They were the parents of

    i. Mary, brought a successful suit for her freedom from Adam Craig in the General Court for the Western Shore in October 1787 [*Cases in the General Court*, 214-36].

8   ii. ?Prudence[1], born say 1748.

7. John[2] Butler, born say 1720, (no race indicated) won a suit for his freedom against William Parker in Charles County court on 13 August 1754. He may have been identical to John Butler, "Molato," who was presented by the Charles County court on 13 August 1768 for concealing a tithable (probably his wife) on information of constable Daniel McPherson. In November 1770 he accused William **Gray**, a "Mulatto," of killing one of his unmarked hogs [Court Record 1753-4, 368-9, 1767-70, 246; 1770-2, 130]. He may have been the father or grandfather of

9   i. John[3], born say 1770.

        ii. Elizabeth, born say 1772, married Isaac **Proctor** at St. Mary's Roman Catholic Church 29 September 1794. The couple required a dispensation because they were related within the second degree of consanguinity which was equivalent to being first cousins [Colonial Dames of America, *Records of St. Mary's Parish, 1793-1861*, 162].

        iii. Henry[1], head of a Charles County household of 8 "other free" and 4 slaves in 1800 [MD:530] and 9 "other free" and a slave in 1810 [MD:342]. He was one of the drafts and substitutes from Charles County who were discharged from service in the Revolutionary War on 3 December 1781 [*Archives of Maryland* 48:10].

8. Prudence[1] Butler, born say 1748, was freed by the estate of Wilfree Neale of St. Mary's County. She was in Washington, D.C., on 24 December 1817 when she testified that Lydia Butler, aged about 58, was free. She was the mother of Monica Butler according to the Washington, D.C., certificate of freedom granted to her granddaughter Letitia [Provine, *District of Columbia Free Negro Registers*, 66, 67]. Prudence was the mother of

10   i. Monica, born about 1767.

9. John[3] Butler, born say 1770, married Elizabeth **Proctor** at St. Mary's Roman Catholic Church in Charles County on 10 February 1793. The couple required a dispensation because they were related within the third degree of consanguinity which was equivalent to being second cousins. Their children were baptized in St. Mary's Parish:

    i. Joseph, born 2 January, baptized 7 June 1793, "Mulatto" son of John and Elizabeth, sponsors: Charles Boarman and Elizabeth Butler.

    ii. Mary, born 2 February 1795, daughter of John and Elizabeth Butler.

    iii. John, born 18 September, baptized 7 December 1806 [Colonial Dames of America, *Records of St. Mary's Parish, 1793-1861*, 6, 9, 15, 161].

10. Monica Butler, born about 1767, was head of a St. Mary's County household of 3 "other free" in 1810 [MD:189]. She was a "Negro woman" about 60 years old on 23 October 1827 when she registered in Washington, D.C., with her children: Letty, Joe, Thomas, Ellen, Catherine, and Robert. Henry C. Neale swore that Monica had once been the property of his father and that she obtained her freedom "by law in Maryland" [Provine, *District of Columbia Free Negro Registers*, 66, 100]. She was the mother of

11   i. Letitia, born say 1785.
      ii. Joseph, born about 1785, registered in St. Mary's County on 30 December 1807: *about twenty two years of age, dark complexion, was born free & raised in the County* [Certificates of Freedom 1806-64, 2].
     iii. Thomas.
     iv. Ellen.
      v. Catherine.
     vi. Robert.

11. Letitia Butler, born say 1785, registered in Washington, D.C., with her daughters, Mary and Prudence, on 11 September 1826 [Provine, *District of Columbia Free Negro Registers*, 67]. She was the mother of
     i. Henry, called "son of Letty Butler" when he registered on 28 April 1826 [Provine, *District of Columbia Free Negro Registers*, 62].
     ii. Mary, born about 1805, about twenty-one when she registered in Washington, D.C., on 11 September 1826.
     iii. Prudence[2], born about 1808, about eighteen years old when she registered in Washington, D.C., on 11 September 1826.

Other members of the Butler family were:
     i. Charles[2], born say 1730, called "Mulatto Charles, late of Prince George's County Labourer, the Slave of a certain James Campbell, otherwise called Charles Butler" when he was sentenced to death by the Court for the Western Shore for stealing a mare from William Elson. On 28 April 1756 the Council of Maryland recommended him to the governor for a pardon. He was called "Charles Butler Junr....the Slave of James Campbell" on 13 June 1758 in Charles County court when he was convicted of breaking into the storehouse of Andrew Buchanan & Company and stealing a large quantity of cloth worth over £9. He was found guilty and sentenced to be hung. On 7 August 1758 the Council again recommended him for a pardon, but he had escaped from Charles County jail before 10 August 1758 when the sheriff advertised his escape in the *Maryland Gazette* [*Archives of Maryland* 31:119, 291-2; Charles County Court Record 1757-8, 407-8; Green, *The Maryland Gazette, 1727-61*, 213].
     ii. Stephen[2], born about 1734, a 50-year-old "mulatto slave" who ran away from Leonard Boarman of Charles County according to the 8 December 1784 issue of the *Virginia Journal and Alexandria Advertiser* [Headley, *18th Century Newspapers*, 51].
     iii. Will **Ferrall**, aka Will Butler and Will **Curtis**, a "yellow slave," a house carpenter who ran away from Edward Mattingly of St. Mary's County and was seen in Virginia according to the 22 September 1768 issue of the *Virginia Gazette* [Rind edition, p. 3, col. 2].
     iv. Josias, "Mulatto" head of a Charles County household of 5 "other free" in 1790 and 5 in Baltimore City in 1800 [MD:137].
     v. Charles[3], "F.N." head of a Charles County household of 1 "other free" in 1790 and 7 in 1800 [MD:560].
     vi. Rhody, "Mulatto" head of a Charles County household of 1 "other free" in 1790.
     vii. Mary, head of a Charles County household of 10 "other free" in 1800 [MD:505].
     viii. Sarah, head of Charles County household of 7 "other free" in 1800

[MD:561].

ix. Phillis, head of a Charles County household of 6 "other free" in 1800 [MD:518] and 4 "other free" and a slave in 1810 [MD:321].

x. Lewis, freed by John Landler in 1792, perhaps the Lewis Butler who was head of a Charles County household of 5 "other free" in 1800 [MD:563].

xi. Betsy, head of a Charles County household of 5 "other free" in 1800 [MD:563].

xii. Eleanor, head of a Charles County household of 7 "other free" in 1800 [MD:505].

xiii. Henry[2], head of a Charles County household of 7 "other free" in 1800 [MD:559].

xiv. Milly, head of a Charles County household of 5 "other free" in 1800 [MD:528]. Her son Perry Butler, born about 1788, registered in St. Mary's County on 10 November 1829: *son of Milly Butler, aged about 41 years of age...bright complexion...born and raised in St. Mary's County* [Certificates of Freedom 1806-64, 82].

xv. Catherine, head of a Charles County household of 3 "other free" in 1800 [MD:551].

xvi. Charles[3], born say 1745, freed by William Bond of St. Mary's County, head of a St. Mary's County household of 7 "other free" in 1800 [MD:421].

xvii. Anthony, freed by Clement Gardiner. He was head of a St. Mary's County household of 7 "other free" in 1800 [MD:402]. He and his wife Charity were the parents of Nelly **Jackson** who registered in St. Mary's County on 28 October 1823: *daughter of Charity & Anthony Butler, aged about twenty four years...bright complexion...her hair long & bushy...genteel appearance, was born free* [Certificates of Freedom 1806-64, 64].

xviii. Ignatius[1]/ Nace, born say 1760, died on 6 August 1809 according to testimony on 30 July 1840 by his widow Mary Butler, aged seventy-six, who was residing in the 1st Election District of Anne Arundel County when she appeared in court to apply for a pension for his services as a musician in the Revolution. She stated that they were married when he was on furlough on 30(?) November 1782 by Parson Hickenbottom and that her husband died on 6 August 1809. He was listed at the Land Office in Annapolis in an "Alphabetical list of the 2nd Regiment in 1782: Butler, Nace Fifer, entered 1776 for the War, disch[d] in 1783." William **Calder**, a "coloured man," testified in Anne Arundel County on 11 August 1840 that he was acquainted with Nace Butler, a Mulatto, and that his widow Mary Butler was an Irish woman who was known in their neighborhood to be the wife of Nace Butler. R. Welsh, a white man, testified that he had often heard officers say that Nace had been a good soldier, had been long time absent from Maryland, and upon his return brought with him an Irish woman who he represented as his wife. Isaac **Stevens**, a "free Colored Man" aged between 70 and 80 years, also testified on Mary's behalf that she was an Irish woman and always reputed to be the wife of Nace Butler. Her application was denied because they were not legally married. On 31 January 1853 their nephew Charles Butler of Annapolis applied for any pension due his aunt Mary Butler [NARA, M804, roll 438, R.1549, http://fold3.com/image/12741094].

xix. Ignatius[2], born about 1763, ran away from Nat Ewing of St. Mary's County on 1 February 1785 according to an ad Ewing placed in the *Maryland Gazette*: *Ran away on the first instant, from the subscriber, living near the Queen-tree, in St. Mary's County, a dark mulatto man named Nace, who calls himself Nace Butler, about 22, combs his hair back, which is pretty long for one of his complexion, 5'8"...an artful designing rogue; he lately petitioned the general court for his freedom, which petition still remains undetermined. His father lives with Mrs. Bradford, at Bladensburg, where he has been since he ran away. He went last October to Annapolis, where he passed as a freeman* [Windley, *Runaway Slave Advertisements*, II:150-1]. He was head of a St. Mary's County household of 5 "other free" in 1800 [MD:421]. He was a "Black man" taken up as a runaway slave in Culpeper County, Virginia, on 20 October 1800 but released on 16 December after examining his papers and hearing the testimony of William Howe [Minutes 1798-1802, 279]. He was called a "free man of colour" on 8 March 1804 when he made a Charles County deed of manumission by which he freed his wife "a Mulatto woman called Nanny (late the property of Edward Sanders of Charles County of whom I purchased her)" and their four children: Ignatius (age 17), James (7), Alexius (4) and Martena (2) [Land Records IB #6, 53].

xx. Leonard, freed by Jerome Jordon. He was head of a St. Mary's County household of 3 "other free" in 1800 [MD:421] and 7 in 1810 [MD:168].

xxi. Abigail, freed with her seven children by Henrietta Plowman of St. Mary's County in 1792. Abigail was head of a St. Mary's County household of 3 "other free" in 1800 [MD:407]. She was the mother of Hopey Butler, perhaps the Hopewell[2] Butler who was head of a St. Mary's County household of 1 "other free" in 1800 [MD:417].

xxii. Clement, freed by Henry Pyke in 1792, perhaps the Clem Butler who was head of a St. Mary's County household of 8 "other free" in 1800 [MD:419].

xxiii. Hopewell[1], head of a St. Mary's County household of 8 "other free" in 1800 [MD:427] and 5 in 1810 [MD:189].

xxiv. Jacob, freed by Elizabeth Taney. He was a "Mulatto" head of a Charles County household of 1 "other free" in 1790, perhaps the Jacob Butler who was head of a St. Mary's County household of 5 "other free" in 1800 [MD:433].

xxv. Giles, freed by John Somerville. He was head of a St. Mary's County household of 7 "other free" in 1800 [MD:420].

xxvi. Edward[3], head of a St. Mary's County household of 9 "other free" in 1800 [MD:417] and 6 "free colored" in Charles County in 1830.

xxvii. Henry[5], head of a St. Mary's County household of 5 "other free" in 1800 [MD:411].

xxviii. John, head of a St. Mary's County household of 5 "other free" in 1800 [MD:402].

xxix. George, ran away from Edmund Plowden before 31 July 1789 when Plowden advertised for his return in the *Maryland Gazette*: *Ran away from the subscriber on Saturday last, a negro man calls himself George Butler, and is one of those who has petitioned the general court for freedom, whence he has but lately returned, and said the court set him free, and that Mr. J.T. Chase, his attorney, told him he might go work where he pleased. As soon as I was informed the Butler cause did not come on at the last term, I ordered him into my service, and on a complaint being made against him by my overseer, I had him corrected for his ill behavior. He has an order of the court with him signed by Mr. Gwinn, which I have no doubt he will produce* [Windley, *Runaway Slave Advertisements*, II:183-4]. He was head of a St. Mary's County household of 3 "other free" in 1800 [MD:406].

xxx. Nat, head of a Baltimore City household of 9 "other free" in 1800 [MD:136].

xxxi. Abraham, head of a Baltimore City household of 6 "other free" in 1800 [MD:137].

xxxii. Nancy[1], head of a Baltimore City household of 6 "other free" in 1800 [MD:156].

xxxiii. Luke, head of a Baltimore City household of 3 "other free" in 1800 [MD:137].

xxxiv. Peggy, head of a Baltimore City household of 6 "other free" in 1800 [MD:143].

12 xxxv. Benjamin, born say 1755.
13 xxxvi. Sarah, born say 1758.
  xxxvii. Prudence[2], born about 1764, registered in Anne Arundel County on 16
      June 1807: *aged above forty years...Complexion yellow...raised in Saint
      Mary's County* [Certificates of Freedom 1806-7, 39].
  xxxviii. Thomas, head of an Anne Arundel County household of 3 "other free" in
      1800 [MD:101].
  xxxix. Tobias, head of a Frederick County household of 6 "other free" in 1800
      [MD:843].
    xl. Mary, head of a Frederick County household of 3 "other free" in 1800
      [MD:917].
    xli. Henry[4], "free negro" head of a Prince George's County household of 7
      "other free" in 1800 [MD:286].
   xlii. Menehy, head of a Washington, D.C., household of 6 "other free" in 1800.
   xliii. Nelly, head of a Washington, D.C. household of 5 "other free" and 2
      slaves in 1800.
   xliv. Sarah, head of a Washington, D.C. household of 5 "other free" in 1800.
14 xlv. Henny, born say 1770.
15 xlvi. Nell, born say 1770.
16 xlvii. Jane, born say 1770.
  xlviii. Rebecca, born about 1770, registered in St. Mary's County on 14 June
      1819: *forty nine years of age, of a dark complexion...obtained her freedom
      in the late General Court of Maryland for the Western Shore* [Certificates
      of Freedom 1806-64, 51].
   xlix. Phillis, born about 1771, registered in St. Mary's County on 15 March
      1810: *aged thirty nine years or thereabouts...Complexion dark, hair short
      and nappy...and was on the 14 day of March 1810 manumitted by a
      certain John Lothoron by a deed of manumission* [Certificates of Freedom
      1806-64, 9].
    l. Lucy, head of a Washington, D.C. household of 3 "other free" in 1800,
      grandmother of Maria **Shorter** (born about 1814) who registered in
      Washington, D.C., on 29 October 1827 [Provine, *District of Columbia
      Free Negro Registers*, 164].
    li. Nathan, head of a Washington, D.C. household of 2 "other free" in 1800.
17   lii. Anna, born about 1774.
18   liii. Joanna, born say 1775.
19   liv. Susannah, born about 1776.
20   lv. Nancy[2], born say 1778.
21   lvi. Charles[4], born about 1778.
   lvii. Elizabeth, born about February 1779, a sixteen year old "Negro" who was
      jailed as a runaway in Dumfries, Virginia, according to the 12 June 1795
      issue of the *Republican Journal and Dumfries Advertiser*. She said she
      was raised on the Eastern Branch in Maryland near the Federal City
      [Headley, *18th Century Newspapers*, 51].
22 lviii. Fanny, born say 1780.
   lix. Anthony, a "free Negro," married Ruth **Middleton**, a "free Mulatto," on
      16 April 1797 at St. Peter's Church in Baltimore [Piet, *Catholic Church
      Records in Baltimore*, 128].
    lx. John, a "free mulatto," died 21 November 1800 and buried the same day
      at St. Peter's Church, Baltimore [Piet, *Catholic Church Records in
      Baltimore*, 164].
   lxi. Francis, born about 1780, a twenty-year-old "free negro" who died on 26
      July 1800 and was buried the next day at St. Peter's Church in Baltimore
      [Piet, *Catholic Church Records in Baltimore*, 164].
   lxii. Thomas, born about 1781, registered in St. Mary's County on 13
      September 1821: *son of Eleanor Butler...aged about forty years, of a dark
      complexion...born free* [Certificates of Freedom 1806-64, 57].
   lxiii. Peter, born about 1788, registered in St. Mary's County on 13 March 1810:

aged twenty two or thereabouts...Complexion dark, hair short...aquiline nose, thick lips...obtained his freedom in Saint Mary's County Court at March Term 1809 against John Lothoron & others [Certificates of Freedom 1806-64, 9].

12. Benjamin Butler, born say 1755, was head of a Baltimore City household of 3 "other free" in 1800 [MD:157]. He and his wife Ann were the parents of
    i. Henry, born about 1780, a 20-year-old "free Negro" who died on 29 October 1800 and was buried the next day at St. Peter's Church, Baltimore [Piet, *Catholic Church Records in Baltimore*, 164].

13. Sarah Butler, born say 1758, of St. Mary's County was the mother of
    i. John, born about 1774, registered in St. Mary's County on 19 October 1824: *aged about fifty years...of a dark complexion, short hair...got his freedom by a suit instituted in the General Court by his mother Sarah Butler of Henry Gardiner* [Certificates of Freedom 1806-64, 68].
    ii. Clement, born abut 1798, registered in St. Mary's County on 14 June 1819: *son of Sally Butler...about twenty one years of age, of a dark complexion...born free* [Certificates of Freedom 1806-64, 51].
    iii. George, born about 1803, registered in St. Mary's County on 22 March 1819: *son of Sally Butler...aged about sixteen years, Dark complexion...born free* [Certificates of Freedom 1806-64, 45].

14. Henny Butler, born say 1770, recovered her freedom at the General Court of Maryland in a suit against Thomas Clagett in May 1792. She was the mother of
    i. Mariah, born about 1791, registered in Prince George's County on 18 September 1821: *a colored woman, about 30 years old, and 5 feet 5 inches tall...dark complexion...daughter of Henny Butler who recovered her freedom from the General Court of Maryland in a suit against Thomas Clagett at May Term 1792.*
    ii. Elizabeth, born about 1794, registered in Prince George's County on 18 September 1821: *a black woman, about 27 years old, and 5 feet 7 inches tall...daughter of Henny Butler.*
    iii. Mary, born about 1796, registered in Prince George's County on 18 September 1821: *a black woman, about 25 years old, and 5 feet 2-1/2 inches tall...daughter of Henny Butler.*
    iv. Augustus[2], born about 1796, registered in Prince George's County between November and December 1819: *a black man about 23 years old, and about 5 feet 6 inches tall...son of Henny Butler.*
    v. Nancy[3], born about 1798, registered in Prince George's County on 18 September 1821: *a black woman, about 23 years old, and 5 feet 3 inches tall...daughter of Henny Butler.*
    vi. Francis, born about 1801, registered in Prince George's County on 11 December 1819: *about 18 years old and 5 feet 3 inches tall...son of Henny Butler.*
    vii. Lucy, born about 1804, registered in Prince George's County on 18 September 1821: *a black woman about 17 years old and 5 feet 4 inches tall...daughter of Henny Butler* [Provine, *Registrations of Free Negroes*, 33, 40].

15. Nell Butler, born say 1770, was head of a Baltimore City household of 8 "other free" in 1800 [MD:157]. She was the "free Negro" mother of
    i. Eleanor, born 28 July 1798, baptized 5 August 1798 at St. Peter's Church in Baltimore.
    ii. Henry, a five-week-old baptized on 9 June 1799 and buried on 3 August 1799 at St. Peter's Church in Baltimore [Piet, *Catholic Church Records in Baltimore*, 19, 164].

16. Jane Butler, born say 1770, obtained her freedom from Robert Lawson of Charles County. She was the mother of
    i.   Eleanor, born about 1791, a dark-complexioned woman who registered in Washington, D.C., on 1 November 1831.
    ii. George, born about 1810, "yellow complexioned" son of Jane who registered in Washington, D.C., on 1 November 1831 [Provine, *District of Columbia Free Negro Registers*, 210, 211].

17. Anna Butler, born about 1774, registered in St. Mary's County on 29 March 1819: *about forty five years of age, Dark Complexion...obtained her freedom in the late General Court at May Term 1792 of Jno. DeButts* [Certificates of Freedom 1806-64, 46]. She was the mother of
    i.   Susanna, born about 1801, registered in St. Mary's County on 29 March 1819: *daughter of Ann Butler...about Eighteen of age, Dark Complexion...born free* [Certificates of Freedom 1806-64, 46].
    ii. Nancy[4], born about 1804, registered in St. Mary's County on 29 March 1819: *daughter of Anna Butler...about sixteen years of age, Dark Complexion...born free* [Certificates of Freedom 1806-64, 46].

18. Joanna Butler, born say 1775, was a "free Mulatto" who had children by Henry, a slave of Robert Walsh. She was the mother of
    i.   George, born about February 1795, a 19-month-old child who died 5 September 1796 and was buried the next day at St. Peter's Church in Baltimore.
    ii. William, born 6 August 1797, baptized 15 August 1797 at St. Peter's Church [Piet, *Catholic Church Records in Baltimore*, 19, 164].

19. Susannah Butler, born about 1776, registered in St. Mary's County on 14 March 1809: *aged thirty years or thereabouts, complexion rather bright, hair short & woolly...obtained her freedom in Saint Mary's County Court at March Term 1809.* She was the mother of
    i.   Elizabeth, born about 1798, registered in St. Mary's County on 8 August 1820: *daughter of Susanna...about twenty two years of age, of a bright complexion.*
    ii. Sarah, born about 1804, registered in St. Mary's County on 8 August 1820: *Daughter of Susanna...about sixteen years of age, bright complexion* [Certificates of Freedom 1806-64, 4, 55].

20. Nancy[2] Butler, born say 1778, was head of a Baltimore City household of 4 "other free" in 1800 [MD:142]. She was the "free Mulatto" mother of
    i.   David, born in March 1797, one month old when he was baptized on 13 April 1797 at St. Peter's Church in Baltimore [Piet, *Catholic Church Records in Baltimore*, 19].

21. Charles[4] Butler, born about 1778, registered in St. Mary's County on 7 May 1807: *about twenty nine years of age, black complexion, was freed in Saint Mary's County Court August Term 1793 & raised in the County aforesaid.* He was apparently married to a slave since he freed his children. He was a "blk." head of a St. Mary's County household of 8 "other free" in 1810 [MD:164]. He was the father of
    i.   Harriot, born about 1796, registered in St. Mary's County on 29 March 1819: *daughter of Charles, aged about twenty three years...light Complexion...was on the 26 January 1807 manumitted by a certain Charles Butler.*
    ii. Catherine, born about 1798, registered in St. Mary's County on 9 August 1820: *daughter of Charles, aged about twenty two years...very bright complexion...was on the 17 April 1819 manumitted by a certain Charles Butler by deed of manumission* [Certificates of Freedom 1806-64, 1, 46,

55].

22. Fanny Butler, born say 1780, was a "free woman of colour," and mother of
    i. Elizabeth, born about 1798, registered in Prince George's County on 25 May 1821: *a colored woman, about 23 years old, and about 5 feet 2 inches tall...dark complexion...daughter of Fanny Butler, a free woman of colour* [Provine, *Registrations of Free Negroes*, 37].

Anne Arundel County:
1. Lydia Butler, born say 1735, the servant of John Mercer, confessed to the Anne Arundel County court in November 1755 that she had a "Mulatto" child. The court ordered that she serve seven years and that her master deliver her "to the Court for which she was transported into the Province of Maryland in order to be sold" [Judgment Record 1754-6, 260]. She may have been the mother of
    i. Thomas, head of an Anne Arundel County household of 3 "other free" in 1800 [MD:101] and 2 in 1810 [MD:79].
    ii. Patrick, head of an Anne Arundel County household of 1 "other free" and 4 slaves in 1800 [MD:101].

Eastern Shore of Maryland
1. Ann Butler, born say 1670, was the white servant of Samuel Hersey on 15 January 1690 when she admitted in Somerset County court that she had a "Molatta" child by "Emanuel Negro" a slave of William Coulborne. She promised to pay Hersey 1,200 pounds of tobacco for his expenses in raising the child. Emanuel was given 39 lashes on 10 June 1690 when he was convicted of stealing a hog [Judicial Records 1689-90, 36, 57, 60a, 106, 200].

1. Anne Butler, born say 1728, was the servant of Jeremiah Buchner of Shrewsbury Parish on 10 March 1747 when she confessed to the Kent County court that she had a "Mulatto" child by a "Negroe." The court ordered her sold for seven years [Criminal Records 1748-60]. She was probably the ancestor of
    i. James, taxable in the 4th District of Kent County in 1783 [MSA S1161-7-4, p.3], head of a Kent County household of 5 "other free" in 1800 [MD:153].

CALVELL/ CALWELL/ CALDWELL FAMILY

1. Isabella Colvill, born say 1706, the servant of Mr. Daniel Sherwood of St. Michael's Parish, Talbot County, admitted in court in November 1726 that she had a "Mallatto" child by Sherwood's "Negroe" slave Jack on 1 September 1726. The court ordered that she serve her master another six months for his trouble and then be sold for seven years [Judgment Record 1726, 346-7; 1726 (reverse), 87]. She was the mother of
2   i. Martha, born about 1726.
3   ii. Martin Collwell, born say 1745.

2. Martha Calvell, born about 1726, said to have been the "Mullatto" daughter of Elizabeth Calvel but corrected to Esabel Calvel, was sold to Daniel Sherwood until the age of thirty-one in November 1726 [Judgment Record 1726, 326]. She was called "Martha Colvin, a Mallatto woman" in November 1751 when the Talbot County court convicted her of having an illegitimate child by a "Negroe." The court sold her for seven years and her child for 31 years for a total of 650 pounds of tobacco to Joseph Dawson. She was called Martha Calvell in November 1753 when she admitted to the same offense and was ordered to be sold for another seven years after the completion of her service to Joshep Dawson [Criminal Record, 1751-5, n.p.]. Martha Caldwell was head of a Talbot County household of 2 "other free" in 1790. She may have been the mother of
    i. Lucy Caldwell, born say 1743, a spinster living in Talbot County in

August 1763 when she was convicted of having a child by a "Negro." The court sold her and her child to Cornelius Dailey for 4,400 pounds of tobacco [Criminal Record 1761-7, 212-3].

3.   Martin Collwell, born say 1745, was head of a taxable "free Mullotes" household of two "blacks" in Bay Hundred, Talbot County, in August 1776 [Carothers, *1776 Census of Maryland*]. He may have been the father of

    i.   Ary, born about 1768, registered in Talbot County on 11 September 1809: *a black woman...about 41 years of age, 5 feet & three quarters of an inch high...free born...raised in the County.*

    ii.   Joseph, born about 1780, registered in Talbot County on 12 September 1812: *a Mullatto man...about thirty two years of age, five feet Seven and one quarter inches high...born free and raised in the County.*

    iii.   Jeremiah, born about 1787, registered in Talbot County on 29 January 1811: *about 23 years of age, five feet nine inches high...dark yellow complexion was born free...raised in the county.*

    iv.   Sally, born about 1795, registered in Talbot County on 21 August 1815: *a Black Girl...Sally Caldwell...about 20 years of age 5 feet ½ inches high...born free, & raised in the County* [Certificates of Freedom 1807-15, 17, 18, 40, 124].

Members of the family in Delaware were

    i.   Palin, head of a Murderkill Hundred, Kent County household of 10 "other free" in 1800 [DE:126] and 5 in 1810 [DE:12].

    ii.   Solomon, head of a Kent County household of 5 "other free" in 1800 [DE:65] and 7 in 1810 [DE:75].

    iii.   Tobias, head of a Kent County household of 6 "other free" in 1800 [DE:65] and 5 in 1810 [DE:75].

    iv.   Peter[1], head of a New Castle County household of 5 "other free" in 1800 [DE:279].

    v.   Peter[2], head of a Kent County household of 3 "other free" in 1800 [DE:147].

    vi.   Philip, head of a Mispillion Hundred, Kent County household of 5 "other free" in 1800 [DE:110] and 3 in 1810 [DE:49].

    vii.   Oliver, head of a Kent County household of 7 "other free" in 1810 [DE:12].

    viii.   Richard, head of a Kent County household of 8 "other free" in 1800 [DE:46].

    ix.   Prince, head of a Murderkill Hundred, Kent County household of 7 "other free" in 1800 [DE:126].

    x.   Timothy, head of a Murderkill Hundred, Kent County household of 5 "other free" in 1800 [DE:126].

    xi.   Stephen, head of a St. Jones Hundred, Kent County household of 5 "other free" in 1800 [DE:50].

    xii.   Joseph, head of a St. Jones Hundred, Kent County household of 4 "other free" in 1800 [DE:50].

    xiii.   Anthony, head of a Murderkill Hundred, Kent County household of 4 "other free" in 1800 [DE:50].

CALLAMAN FAMILY

1.   James Callaman, born say June 1695, was probably identical to "James a malatto" who was about seventeen years old on 14 April 1713 when Richard Marsham of Prince George's County devised him his freedom at age thirty-five. He was listed in the 15 June 1713 Prince George's County inventory of Marsham's estate:
Negroes:
one Malato Man Robin 7 years to serve, age 27   *£16*
(Robert Pearl)

one Malato boy Jemmy 17 years to serve, age 18 £20

[Prerogative Wills 13:514-20; Prerogative Inventories and Accounts, 35A:299-308].

Robert **Pearl's** sons Thomas and James **Pearl** were called the kinsmen of James Colemore when they approved the inventory of his Prince George's County estate which was filed by their brother Daniel **Pearl** on 23 June 17__ [Prerogative Court Inventories 96:336]. And on 17 August 1768 Daniel **Pearl** sold a thirteen-year-old slave named Rob who had formerly been the property of James Caulmore, late of Prince George's County deceased, by Frederick County bill of sale of 17 August 1768 [Land Records B:6]. He may have been the ancestor of

    i.   Moses Callaman, head of a Frederick County household of a free white male and two free white females [MD:242], father of Mary Calliman who married Benjamin **Lett**, 4 January 1809 Frederick County, Virginia bond.

    ii.   John, head of a Frederick County household of 9 "other free" in 1790 [MD:218].

    iii. Zilpha Calliman, married Thomas **Perrill (Pearl)**, 5 March 1791 Frederick County, Maryland bond.

    iv. Benjamin Callaman, married Elizabeth **Perrill**, 2 September 1813 Frederick County, Maryland bond.

CAMBRIDGE FAMILY

1.   Anne Hunt, born say 1694, was the servant of Mr. Robert Nearn/ Nairn, merchant of Coventry Parish, on 2 June 1713 when she admitted in Somerset County court that she had a child by a "Negroe." The court ordered that she receive thirty lashes and that her master give security to return her to court to be sold for seven years at the completion of her indenture. Her master Robert Nearn purchased her unnamed son for thirty-one years [Judicial Record 1711-13, 283-4]. Ann was apparently the mother of

    i.   William Cambridge, born about 1713.

2.   William[1] Cambridge Hunt, born about 1713, was called William Cambridge when he was taxable in the Pocomoke Hundred, Somerset County household of Robert Nairn in 1727 and 1728: called Will and taxable in James Nairn's Pocomoke household from 1730 to 1743: called William Cambridge in 1730 and 1743, called either "Will" or "Cambridge" in the intervening years [List of Taxables]. He was called William Hunt Cambridge in 1752 when he was granted a patent for 50 acres in Worcester County called *William's Choice* which he expanded to 128 acres in 1754 (called William Cambridge Stuart). He was called "William Cambridge a Molatto" in 1783 when he was taxable in Acquango Hundred, Worcester County, on 128 acres called *William's Choice enlarged* [MSA S1437, p.2]. He called himself William Cambridge Hunt in his 11 March 1784 Worcester County will, proved 5 January 1787, by which he left his plantation to his wife Esther during her widowhood and then to son Levin, or to son George if Levin died before attaining the age of twenty-one. He also left his daughter Leah a feather bed, furniture and a place and materials to build a house and divided some of his possessions among "all my children" [WB JW 13:109-11]. His widow Esther sold and released *William's Choice* for £30 on 9 March 1798 [Land Records S:286-7]. Their children were

    i.   Leah, born say 1763.

    ii.   Levin, born say 1765, called himself a "free Mollater" on 25 March 1794 when he and George Cambridge gave bond of £30 to support the illegitimate child Peggy he had by Mary **Blake** in Worcester County in November 1790 [Land Records P:301]. He called himself "Levin Cambridge (alias Hunt)" on 24 April 1795 when he sold (signing) the 128 acres of land he received by his father's will to Charles Godfrey for about £11 and then repurchased the land from Godfrey for the same price on 25 December the same year. He mortgaged the property to James Bowdoin

Robins on 4 November 1796 for £50 and then completed the sale to Samuel Handy, Sr., on 6 April 1798 [Land Records Q:172-3; R:56, 374; S:284].

iii. George, born say 1767, head of a Bracken County, Kentucky household of 3 "free colored" in 1830, in the same county as William Cambridge, born before 1776, who was head of a household of 4 "free colored."

iv. ?Charles, "Negro" taxable in Little Creek Hundred, Kent County in 1789, in Mispillion Hundred in 1797, and head of a Mispillion Hundred household of 4 "other free" in 1800 [DE:76]. He died before 6 May 1806 when his widow Mary gave up her right to administer his estate which was valued at $201 [DSA, RG 3545, Reel 31, frames 521-4].

v. ?Isaac, head of a New Castle County, Delaware household of 5 "other free" in 1810 [DE:301].

vi. ?William^2, died about 1806-12 when the inventory of his estate was recorded in Kent County, Delaware.

CAMPBELL FAMILY

1.   Sarah Campbell, born say 1712, was the servant of Thomas Davis on 1 August 1731 when she bore a "mullatto" by a "negro" in Queen Anne's County. The court ordered her sold for seven years to William Price and sold her son James to Price until age thirty-one for 732 pounds of tobacco [Judgment Record 1730-2, 323-4]. She was the ancestor of

i. James, born 1 August 1731, perhaps the James Campbell who was head of a West Sassafras, Cecil County household of 1 "other free" in 1790.

ii. ?William, head of a West Sassafras, Cecil County household of 1 "other free" in 1790.

iii. ?Henry, head of a New Castle County household of 8 "other free" in 1800 [DE:207] and 3 "other free" in Kent County, Delaware, in 1810 [DE:178].

CANN FAMILY

1.   James Cann, born say 1715, was called a "free Mallatto Man" on 28 November 1738 when "Mallatto Nan," the servant of Thomas Gantt, Jr., testified in Prince George's County court that he was the father of her eight-month-old child named Nasey [Court Record 1738-40, 269]. He was probably the ancestor of

i. Cross, head of an Anne Arundel County household of 3 "other free" in 1790.

ii. William, head of an Anne Arundel County household of 2 "other free" in 1800 [MD:97].

CANNADY FAMILY

Members of the Cannady family of Maryland were

1   i. Thomas, born say 1760.

ii. Cuffy, "Negro" head of a Kent County household of 2 "other free" in 1790.

1.   Thomas^1 Cannady, born say 1760, was head of a Queen Anne's County household of 3 "other free" in 1790 and 6 in Kent County in 1810 [MD:845]. On 22 March 1790 Jacob Walter set him free by Queen Anne's County deed "for the love of freedom." On 10 June 1791 he made a deed of manumission in Queen Anne's County to "a Negro Woman (now my wife) known by the name of Liby." He was called "Thomas Kennedy free Negro" when he made a second deed of manumission about a year later on 21 May 1792 to "one Negro Boy named Joshua about Eight Years Old," no relationship stated [Liber [STW-1:394; 2:106, 224]. He was probably the father of

i. Joshua, born about 1784.

CANNON FAMILY

1. Margaret Cannon, born say 1725, was the indentured servant of Isaac Smoot on 10 August 1743 when she was convicted by the Charles County court of having a child by a "Negro." The court bound her five-month-old daughter Nelly as an apprentice and ordered that she serve her master an additional seven years [Court Record, 1741-3, 627-8]. She was the ancestor of
    i.   Eleanor, born about March 1743, an eight-year-old "Mulatto" girl bound until the age of thirty-one when she was listed in the inventory of the Charles County estate of Isaac Smoot on 14 October 1751 [Prerogative Inventories 48:210].
    ii. Robert, born about 1748, a three-year-old "Mulatto" boy bound until the age of thirty-one when he was listed in the inventory of the Charles County estate of Isaac Smoot on 14 October 1751 [Prerogative Inventories 48:210].
    iii. ?Patrick, head of an Elk Neck, Cecil County household of 1 "other free" in 1790.

CARNEY FAMILY

1. William[1] Karney, born say 1689, was taxable in Daniel Robbeson's Murderkill Hundred, Kent County, Delaware household in 1734, taxable in his own household in 1736 and 1738, and a taxable free "Malato" in 1748 and 1751. He was not taxable in 1752 ("struck out" by the court) [RG 3535, Kent County Levy List, 1726-42, frames 380, 398; 1743-67, frames 10, 380]. He was probably the ancestor of
    i.   Thomas[1], born say 1731, taxable in Murderkill Hundred, Kent County, from 1752 to 1767, taxable in Little Creek Hundred from 1768 to 1770, in Duck Creek Hundred from 1778 to 1785: called a "N."(egro) starting in 1781, taxable on personal tax only in 1798 [RG 3535, Kent County Levy List, 1743-67, frames 317, 327, 386, 523, 575; 1768-84, frames 10, 65, 336, 370, 552, 568; 1785-97, frames 6; 1798-9, frame 350], head of a Duck Creek Hundred, Kent County household of 2 "other free" in 1800 [DE:15]. He admitted in Kent County court in February 1771 that he owed John Smith £90 [DSA, RG 3815.031, 1769-1771, frames 372, 390].
    ii. John, head of a Duck Creek Hundred, Kent County household of 6 "other free" in 1800 [DE:24] and 7 "other free" in Sussex County in 1810 [DE:442].
2   iii. Thomas[2], Jr., born about 1758.
    iv. William[2], born say 1760, a "Negro" taxable in Duck Creek Hundred from 1781 to 1783 and in 1797 [RG 3535, Kent County Levy List, 1767-84, frames 522, 568, 475], head of a Duck Creek Hundred, Kent County household of 2 "other free" in 1800 [DE:26].
    v.   James, born say 1768, a Mulator" taxable in Mispillion Hundred in 1789, a "melato" in the list of "Free Negroes" in 1793 [RG 3535, Kent County Levy List, 1785-97, frames 141, 298].
3   vi. Robert, born say 1776.
    vii. Nathan, head of a Duck Creek Hundred, Kent County household of 2 "other free" in 1800 [DE:24].
    viii. Jacob, head of an Appoquinimink, New Castle County household of 7 "other free" in 1810 [DE:442].

2. Thomas[2] Carney, Jr., born about 1758, a man of color, was about 60 years old on 24 February 1818 when he appeared in Caroline County court to apply for a pension for his services in the Revolution. He enlisted in the 5th Maryland Regiment in June 1781 and served for 3 years. He appeared in court again on 7 March 1822 at the age of 63 and listed his property which included a pair of cart

wheels and shafts, five pigs, a sheep and lamb, 3 barrels of corn, some household items and a debt of $92.50 to the estate of Risdon Fountain. He was a farmer with a 57 or 58-year-old wife named Grace, a 17-year-old daughter Alice, and a 14-year-old daughter Rebecca living with him [NARA, S.35203, M804, roll 473, frame 552]. He was head of a Duck Creek Hundred, Kent County household of 4 "other free" in 1800 [DE:24] and a "negro" head of a Caroline County household of 7 "other free" in 1810 [MD:190]. He was the father of

    i. ?Elizabeth, born about 1790, a "molatto woman," registered in Caroline County on 16 September 1815.

    ii. ?Levi, born about 1793, "molatto complexion," registered in Caroline County on 16 September 1815.

    iii. ?Montgomery, born about 1791, registered in Caroline County on 16 September 1815.

    iv. ?Lydia, born about 1801, a "negro woman" who registered in Caroline County on 23 September 1826.

    v. Alice, born about 1804.

    vi. Rebecca, born about 1808 [Certificates of Freedom 1806-27, 77, 186, 215]..

3.   Robert[1] Carney, born say 1776, was a "Mulatto" taxable in Duck Creek Hundred in 1797 and a "Negro" taxable in 1798 [RG 3535, Kent County Levy List, 1785-97, frame 561; 1797-8, frame 350], head of a Duck Creek Hundred, Kent County household of 3 "other free" in 1800 [DE:24] and 10 "free colored" in 1820 [DE:49]. He died before 6 January 1824 when his widow Elizabeth deposed that her husband died on 25 of the previous month and left a movable estate which was valued at $847. Simon Spearman was administrator. She received her third of about $230 and the remainder amounted to about $50 to each of the eight heirs: James Carney, Thomas Carney, Rachel **Sisco** (wife of Isaiah **Sisco**), Debrix **Miller**, Ann Carney, Robert Carney, Miller Carney and John Carney on 13 February 1826 [RG 3545, roll 33, frames 134-147]. He was the father of

    i. James.

    ii. Thomas.

    iii. Rachel **Sisco**, died before 13 February 1826 when John Carney, Jr., of New Castle County was granted administration on her Kent County estate [WB Q-1:78].

    iv. a daughter who married Debrix **Miller**.

    v. Ann.

    vi. Miller.

    vii. John, born 1795-1806, head of a Little Creek Hundred household of 5 "free colored" in 1830.

    viii. Robert[2], born about 1814, head of a Dover Hundred household of 5 "free colored" in 1840 and a 36-year-old "Mulatto" laborer living in Dover Hundred with wife Phebe in the 1850 census [DE:348].

CARR FAMILY

1.   Elizabeth Carr, born say 1705, the white servant of Thomas Strong of Shrewsbury Parish, confessed to the Kent County, Maryland court in March 1725/6 that she had a "Mollatoe" child by Jacob **Miner**, a "free Negroe," on 1 October 1725. She was the servant of Joseph Young on 17 March 1729/30 when she confessed to the same offense [Criminal Records 1724-8, 155-7; 1728-34, 108]. Elizabeth and Jacob were probably the ancestors of

    i. John, born about 1791, obtained a certificate in Talbot County on 16 August 1814: *about 23 years of age...of a dark Complexion...born free and raised in the County* [Certificates of Freedom 1807-15, 88].

Members of the Carr family on the Western Shore may have been descendants of John Carr who had a child by Eliza **Norman** before 24 March 1712/3 when the Prince

George's County court ordered that she receive 20 lashes [Court Record 1710-15, 285].
Members of the family were

    i.   Isaac, born about 1758, enlisted in the 2nd Maryland Regiment on 6 April
1782: *residence: Montgomery County, age 24, 5'7" height, complexion:
yellow Molato* [NARA, M246, roll 34, frame 430 of 587].

1   ii. Ann, born say 1759.

1.   Ann[1] Carr, born say 1759, "the property of Mrs. Mary Berry," was indicted by the
Prince George's County court on 26 October 1777 for having a "Molatto" child
on information of William Berry. The court ordered that she serve nine months
for the trouble of her present mistress, be sold for seven years, and that her three-
month-old child Ann be sold. Mary Berry was the highest bidder [Court Records
1777-82, 9, 23-4]. She was the mother of

    i.   Ann[2], born about July 1777, registered in Prince George's County on 17
June 1808: *a mulatto woman, 31 years old...bright yellow complexion. She
is a free woman...sold by Prince George's County Court at its August term
1777 to a certain Mary Berry until the age 31, under the conviction of her
mother of mulatto bastardy, being at that time a child of three months*].
She was probably the Nancy Carr whose daughter Milley registered in
Prince George's County on 25 September 1816: *a bright mulatto girl,
about 20 years old...daughter of Nancy Carr, a free woman of color.*
Provine, *Registrations of Free Negroes*, 1, 22].

CARROLL FAMILY

Members of the Carroll family in Maryland were
1   i.   James, born say 1720.
2   ii. William[1], born about 1733.

1.   James Carroll, born say 1720, was a "black man" who rented land from Mrs.
Gallaway's in Baltimore County in 1750 [Wright, *Inhabitants of Baltimore
County*, 45]. He was probably the ancestor of

    i.   Peter[1], head of a Baltimore City household of 8 "other free" in 1800
[MD:160].
    ii. Peter[2], head of a Baltimore City household of 6 "other free" in 1800
[MD:170].
    iii. Maryan, head of a Baltimore City household of 1 "other free" in 1800
[MD:164].
    iv. H., head of a Baltimore City household of 7 "other free" in 1810
[MD:310].

2.   William[1] Carroll, born about 1733, ran away from Notley Young before 21
January 1762 when Young placed an ad in the *Maryland Gazette*: *living near the
mouth of the Eastern Branch of Patowmack, a Mulatto Man, about 28 or 29 years
of Age, nigh 6 feet high, calls himself Billy Carroll, and is a Carpenter by Trade*
[Windley, *Runaway Slave Advertisements* II:43]. He may have been the father of

3   i.   William[2], born say 1775.
    ii. Margaret, "free Negro" head of a Prince George's County household of 2
"other free" in 1800 [MD:261].
    iii. Ann, head of a Montgomery County household of 4 "other free" in 1810
[MD:977].

3.   William[2] Carroll, born say 1775, was a "free Negro" head of a Prince George's
County household of 2 "other free" in 1800 [MD:294] and 5 in 1810 [MD:53]. He
was the father of

    i.   Christiana **Scott**, born about 1798, registered in Prince George's County
on 14 September 1827: *a bright mulatto woman, about 29 years old, and
5 feet 3 inches tall...freed by William Carroll by manumission this day*

acknowledged and recorded.

ii. William[3], born about 1803, registered on 14 September 1827: *a bright mulatto man, about 24 years old, and 5 feet 7-1/2 inches tall...freed by his father, William Carroll Sr. of this county, by manumission this day.*

iii. Charles, born about 1808, registered on 14 September 1827: *a bright mulatto boy, about 19 years old, and 5 feet 9 inches tall...set free by William Carroll Sr. of this county my manumission this day.*

iv. John, born about 1812, registered on 14 September 1827: *a dark copper-colored boy, about 15(?) years old, and 5 feet 5 inches tall...set free by William Carroll* [Provine, *Registrations of Free Negroes*, 68].

CARTER FAMILY

Members of the Carter family were

i. Hannah, "Mulatto" head of a Charles County household of 4 "other free" in 1790.

ii. Anthony, head of a St. Mary's County household of 3 "other free" in 1790 and 10 in 1800 [MD:405].

iii. William[1], "Mulatto" head of a Charles County household of 1 "other free" in 1790.

iv. Charles, "Mulatto" head of a Charles County household of 1 "other free" in 1790.

v. Rachel, head of a Baltimore City household of 4 "other free" in 1800 [MD:171].

vi. Pall, "free negro" head of a Prince George's County household of 8 "other free" in 1800 [MD:258].

vii. Peter, head of a Baltimore City household of 6 "other free" in 1800 [MD:161].

viii. Nelly, head of a Montgomery County household of 5 "other free" in 1800 [MD:235].

ix. Jane, head of a St. Mary's County household of 5 "other free" in 1800 [MD:437].

x. Anne, head of a St. Mary's County household of 5 "other free" in 1800 [MD:436].

xi. Stacie, head of a St. Mary's County household of 4 "other free" in 1800 [MD:402].

xii. Polly, "free Mulatto" head of a Prince George's County household of 2 "other free" in 1800 [MD:264].

xiii. Philip, born about 1779, registered in St. Mary's County on 26 July 1814: *aged thirty years or thereabouts...complexion yellow - hair woolly...born free.*

xiv. William[2], born about 1784, registered in St. Mary's County on 54 November 1807: *about twenty three years of age, very bright complexion, was born free.*

xv. Enoch, born about 1788, registered in St. Mary's County on 5 April 1838: *aged about fifty years...bright complexion...born free* [Certificates of Freedom 1806-64, 2, 27, 115].

CARTY FAMILY

1. John Cartey, born say 1715, was called John Cartey of St. Peter's Parish, Labourer, "being a Mulatto man begotten by a Negroe man upon the body of a white woman" in Talbot County court in November 1741 when he was convicted of marrying a white woman named Margaret Deepup on 10 September 1739. Margaret was sold to John Jones, tanner, for seven years. The court fined Margaret, wife of John Cartey, 1 shilling for assaulting John Jones in February 1742, and in November 1742 Jones sued John Cartey for being absent from his service a total of fifty-seven days in 1741 and 1742 [Judgment Record 1740-2,

327-9; 1742, n.p.]. They were probably the ancestors of

   i. Samuel, head of a Harford County household of 1 "other free" in 1790.

  ii. Solomon, a "free Negro" sued in Kent County, Delaware court by Henry Farsons on 7 October 1796 [DSA, RG 3830.004, Supreme Court 1791-1821, frame 108], head of a Kent County household of 8 "other free" in 1800 [DE:20], called Solomon Carter in 1820, head of a Duck Creek Hundred, Kent County household of 4 "free colored" [DE:49].

 iii. Peter, head of a New Castle County, Delaware household of 6 "other free" in 1800 [DE:275] and 4 in 1810 [DE:302].

 iv. Nathan, head of a Kent County, Delaware household of 2 "other free" in 1800 [DE:26].

  v. Isaac, head of an Appoquinimink Hundred, New Castle County household of 4 "free colored" in 1820 [DE:148].

CASE FAMILY

1. Mary[1] Case, born say 1683, was the servant of John West on 3 December 1701 when the churchwardens of Accomack County Parish presented her for having a "Mullatto Bastard Child." She was presented for having another child on 6 April 1703 [Orders 1697-1703, 122a, 126a, 144]. She was probably the mother of

2   i. Mary[2], born say 1724.

2. Mary[2] Case, born say 1724, was added to the list of tithables in Accomack County on 26 November 1740. She admitted in Accomack County court on 26 November 1754 that she stole a gammon of bacon and received 20 lashes [Orders 1737-44, 415: 1753-63, 44, 70]. She may have been the mother of

   i. George[1], called George Case alias Bristol when he was bound as an apprentice caulker to William Tilney on 28 October 1754 [Orders 1753-63, 65].

  ii. Charles[1], born Christmas 1752, called Charles Case alias Bristol when he was bound as an apprentice tailor to Edward Jones on 39 July 1754, called Charles Bristol a free Negro Boy when he was bound to Thomas Wise to be a shoemaker on 30 January 1760, called Charles Case alias Bristol when he was bound to Charles Snead in St. George's Parish to be a mariner on 29 August 1769 [Orders 1753-63, 58, 327; 1768-70, 220]. He was seen in the Philadelphia Work House by David Bowman, a member of the Accomack County court, and claimed by Daniel Henderson of New Jersey (as a slave or servant) when Walter Hatton, Gent., appeared in Accomack County court on 28 February 1775 and certified that Charles Case, a "Mulatto," was a free person born of free parentage in the county and was of full age [Orders 1774-7, 320].

 iii. William, born say 1756, bound as an apprentice in St. George's Parish to Reuben Giddon to be a cooper on 29 December 1767 [Orders 1767-8, 371], a "Mulatto," who died while serving in the Revolution [NARA, Bounty Land Warrant 1826-100, http://fold3.com/image/12751811].

 iv. John, born say 1758, bound as an apprentice cooper in St. George's Parish to William Shipham on 26 May 1767 [Orders 1767-8, 89], a "Mulatto" and brother of William Case who died while serving in the Revolution according to the 11 June 1807 deposition of John Cropper, Jr., of Accomack County, former lieutenant colonel of the 9th Virginia Regiment. He stated that William and John had no wives or children, and Betty Case "of this county," who was an infant during the war, was their only legal representative [LVA, Digital Collections, Case, John, Revolutionary War Bounty Warrants].

3   v. Elizabeth, born say 1765.

3. Elizabeth Case, born say 1765, was head of a St. George Parish, Accomack County household of 3 "other free" and a slave in 1800 [*Virginia Genealogist*

2:130]. She was probably the mother of
  i.   Major, head of an Accomack Parish, Accomack County household of 3 "other free" in 1800 [*Virginia Genealogist* 1:105].
 ii.   Bridget, head of an Accomack County household of 5 "other free" in 1810 [VA:17].
iii.   George², bound as an apprentice farmer to Peter Hack in Accomack County in January 1790 [Indentures, 1786-96, http://familysearch.org/search/catalog/332865, film 8620585, images 529-30], a "fn" taxable in Accomack County in 1809, listed with his wife Bridget in 1813 [PPTL 1783-1814, frames 682, 789, 857], head of a household of 2 "other free" in 1810 [VA:16].
 iv.   Charles, in a list of free Negroes and Mulattos for Accomack County in 1813 with his wife Polly [PPTL 1783-1814, frame 857].
  v.   Sabra A., born say 1795, made a power of attorney (signing) in Accomack County on 11 August 1831 as the only heir-at-law of Betty Case who was the only heir-at-law of William and John Case who enlisted in the Revolution. She stated that she had never received bounty land for their services [NARA, Bounty Land Warrants, 1826-100, http://fold3.com/image/12751843].

Other members of the family were
  i.   Betty, head of a Dorchester County household of 5 "other free" in 1800 [MD:692].
 ii.   James, head of a Dorchester County household of 6 "other free" in 1800 [MD:692].

CHAMBERS FAMILY

1.   Mary Chambers, born say 1698, was the servant of William Frisby of Worton Hundred, Kent County, Maryland, on 22 November 1716 when she appeared in court and confessed that she had two "Mollatoe Children" by a "Negro." The court ordered her to serve an additional seven years and bound her children, a boy and a girl, to her master until the age of thirty-one. She was the servant of William Frisby on 22 April 1718 when the court ordered her to serve him another seven years [Court Proceedings 1716-8, 85-6; 1718-20, 142]. She was apparently the ancestor of
  i.   William, head of a Kent County household of 7 "other free" in 1800 [MD:147].
 ii.   Deb, head of a Baltimore City household of 8 "other free" in 1800 [MD:161].
iii.   Edward, born say 1760, "a man of color," who received arrears of pay for his service in the Revolution from 1 August 1780 to 15 November 1783. He appeared in Anne Arundel County court on 20 June 1818 and 21 April 1820 to make a declaration to obtain a pension for his service. He stated that he enlisted in the 3rd Regiment about July 1777 in New Town, Chester [NARA, S.534684, http://fold3.com/image/19897567]. He was head of an Anne Arundel County household of 1 "other free" in 1790.
 iv.   Isaac, head of a Queen Anne's County household of 6 "other free" in 1800 [MD:331].
  v.   Robert, head of a Queen Anne's County household of 5 "other free" in 1800 [MD:331].
 vi.   Elizabeth¹/ Betsy, head of a Kent County household of 4 "other free" in 1800 [MD:147].
vii.   Elizabeth², head of a Kent County household of 3 "other free" in 1800 [MD:147].
viii. James, head of a Kent County household of 2 "other free" in 1800 [MD:159].
 ix.   Tom "& Co.," head of a New Castle County, Delaware household of 16 "other free" in 1800 [DE:253].

    x. Joseph, head of a New Castle County household of 8 "other free" in 1800 [DE:277].

    xi. Peter, head of a New Castle County household of 9 "other free" in 1810 [DE:282].

CHUCK FAMILY

1. Margaret Chuck, born about December 1743, was a "Mullatto" child sold by the Prince George's County court to Lingan Wilson, Gent., for thirty-one years in March 1743/4. She was the servant of Margaret Gibson on 22 August 1775 when the Prince George's County court indicted her on two cases of "Mulatto bastardy" for having children by a "Negro slave named Tom." The court found her not guilty (of having the children by Tom) but ordered her to serve her mistress additional time for having illegitimate children. Benjamin Brookes was her security [Court Record 1743-4, 270; 1775-7, 169-73]. She was apparently the mother of

    i. Richard, born about March 1772, bound by the Prince George's County court to Elizabeth Brookes until the age of twenty-one [Court Record 1775-7, 165].

    ii. George, born about April 1773, bound by the Prince George's County court to Elizabeth Brookes until the age of twenty-one [Court Record 1775-7, 165].

CHURB/CHUBB FAMILY

1. Mary Chirb, born about 1736, was a "Mulatto" (called Mary Churl) with about six years and four months to serve when she was listed in the inventory of the Prince George's County estate of Mr. Turner Wooten on 25 February 1761 [Prerogative Inventories 73:52-4]. On 25 August 1761 the Prince George's County court presented her for having a "Molatto" bastard child. On 22 November 1763 she had another illegitimate child whose father was probably a free man since the court ordered that she serve her master and mistress, William Turnor Wootton and Elizabeth Wootton, only nine months for the trouble of their house. On 25 March 1766 she confessed to the court that she had another "Mulatto" child, and the court sold her son Natt to Wootton to serve until the age of thirty-one [Court Record 1761-3, 69; 1763-4, 9; 1765-6, 386, 390]. She was the mother of

2   i. Margaret, born say 1756.

    ii. John Chubb, born about 1758, enlisted in the Revolution in Loudoun County, Virginia, on 19 March 1781 and was sized on 28 May: *age 23, 5'5-1/2" high, black complexion, planter, born in and residing in Montgomery County, Maryland* [The Chesterfield Supplement or Size Roll of Troops at Chesterfield Court House, LVA accession no. 23816, by http://revwarapps.org/b81.pdf (p.67)]. He may have been identical to Jonathan Chubb who enlisted in the 3rd Maryland Regiment on 1 January 1782 [NARA, M246, Roll 34, frame 398 of 587]. He served in 6th Virginia Regiment under Lieutenant Colonel Thomas Posey from 1 April to 1 September 1782, served in Captain Clough Shelton's Company of the 1st Virginia Battalion from 1 December 1782 to 1 May 1783 and received 100 acres bounty land [NARA, M246, roll 113, frame 712; M881, Roll 1089, frames 323-6 of 1808].

    iii. ?Dick, born about February 1760, a one-year-old "Mulatto" child bound until the age of thirty-one when he was listed in the Prince George's County estate of Turner Wooten on 25 February 1761.

    iv. Natt, born say 1766.

2. Margaret Churb, born say 1756, a free woman, was the ancestor of

3   i. Esther, born about 1772.

    ii. ?Robert[1], born say 1775, "free Negro" head of a Prince George's County household of 2 "other free" in 1800 [MD:282].

iii. ?George, born say 1777, "free Negro" head of a Prince George's County household of 1 "other free" in 1800 [MD:282].

3. Esther Churb, born about 1772, registered in Prince George's County on 26 May 1817: *about 45 years old...has a dark complexion. She was raised in Prince George's County and is free, being a descendant of a free woman named Margaret Churb.* She was the mother of

    i. Louisa, born about 1793, registered in Prince George's County on 28 February 1813: *a Negro woman, about 20 years old...has a dark complexion. She was raised in Prince George's County and is free being the reputed daughter of Esther Churb, a free woman of color.*

    ii. Robert[2], born about 1801, registered in Prince George's County on 7 January 1822: *a colored man, about 21 years old...light complexion...son of Easter Chu(r)b* [Provine, *Registrations of Free Negroes*, 14, 41].

CLARK FAMILY

Delaware:

1. Martha Clark, born say 1727, was sold by the Kent County court for seven years on 28 August 1746 for payment of fees and charges for murdering her illegitimate child [RG 3815.031, Common Pleas, Dockets 1744-1750, frame 234]. She was the servant of Robert Buchanan of Kent County, Delaware, in May 1761 when she was convicted of having an illegitimate "Molatto" male child and ordered to serve her master one year for the trouble of his house. The court sold her son, born 4 July 1759, to her master for £7 [RG 3805.002, Quarter Sessions, 1734-79, frame 197]. She may have been the mother of

2   i. Thomas, born 4 July 1759.

2. Thomas Clark, born 4 July 1759, married Elizabeth **Morris** ("Mustees, free"), on 1 July 1773 in Sussex County [Records of the United Presbyterian Churches of Lewes, Indian River and Cool Spring, Delaware 1756-1855, 286]. He was a soldier in the Revolution from Sussex County who died about 1819. On 13 August 1833 his children and legal heirs Whittington Clark, Nathaniel Clark, John Clark, Comfort **Miller**, Elizabeth **Rigware** and Levina **Harmon** applied for bounty land for his service. Comfort **Miller** testified on 22 June 1834 that Thomas died about 1819, leaving a widow who was deceased when his children made their application. Comfort named his surviving children listed above and grandchildren: Nelly **Morris** (daughter of Mary **Morris**, deceased), Nancy **Curley**(?) and Robert Clark (children of Morris Clark, deceased), Major and Whittington **Johnson** (children of Nancy **Johnson**, deceased) and Rebecca and Miens **Miller** (children of Zepporah **Miller**, deceased) [NARA, B.L.Wt. 2047-100, M804, roll 566, frames 463, 474 of 782]. (His widow) Comfort Clark was head of "free colored" household of a woman over 55 in 1830. Thomas was the father of

    i. Whitington, born before 1776, head of an Indian River Hundred, Sussex County household of 9 free colored" in 1820 [DE:222].

    ii. Mary **Morris**, mother of Nelly **Morris**.

    iii. Morris, born 1776-1794, head of an Indian River Hundred, Sussex County household of 6 "free colored" in 1820 [DE:222], father of Mary **Morris**, Nancy **Curley**(?) and Robert Clark.

    iv. Nancy **Johnson**, mother of Major and Whittington **Johnson**.

    v. Zepporah **Miller**, mother of Rebecca and Miens **Miller**.

    vi. Nathaniel, born about 1794, head of an Indian River Hundred, Sussex County household of 3 "free colored" in 1820 [DE:206], a "Mulatto" listed in the 1850 Lewis and Rehoboth Hundred, Sussex County census with Unicey (age 56), children, 73-year-old John **Ridgeway** and Edward **Morris**.

    vii. John.

viii. Comfort **Miller**.
ix. Elizabeth **Rigware**, perhaps the wife of John **Ridgeway/ Rigware**.
x. Levina **Harmon**, perhaps the Levina **Harmon**, a 45-year-old "Mulatto"counted in the 1850 Sussex County census with Jonathan **Harmon** (45) and children.

Other members of the family were
i. Miens, born 1776-1794, married Nancy **Hanzor**, "(Colour'd)" on 26 January 1815 in Sussex County [Records of the United Presbyterian Churches of Lewes, Indian River and Cool Spring, Delaware 1756-1855, 325]. He was head of a Sussex County household of 4 "free colored" in 1820.

Kent County, Maryland:
1. Mary Clark, born say 1745, a white spinster, confessed to the Kent County court in June 1765 that she had a child by a "Negroe." The court sold her and her "Molatto" daughter Hannah to Joseph Nicholson, Jr. [Criminal Record, 1761-72, 59b]. She was the servant of Joseph Nicholson, Jr., in June 1769 when she confessed to the same offense. The court sold her two-month-old son Moses until the age of thirty-one to her master for 5 shillings [Criminal Dockets, 1766-71, August 1769 appearance no. 27]. She was the mother of
i. Hannah, born about 1765.
ii. Moses, born about June 1769.

Other members of the Clark family on the Eastern Shore of Maryland were
i. Elizabeth, head of a Talbot County household of 7 "other free" in 1800 [MD:526].
ii. Lucretia, head of a Talbot County household of 5 "other free" in 1800 [MD:527].
iii. William, head of a Talbot County household of 1 "other free" in 1790 and 4 in 1800 [MD:533].
iv. Jere, head of a Talbot County household of 5 "other free" in 1790 and 4 in Baltimore City in 1810 [MD:74].
v. John, head of an Octoraro, Cecil County household of 3 "other free" in 1790 and 6 "other free" in Talbot County in 1800 [MD:527].

Charles County:
1. Mary Clarke, born say 1732, was presented by the Charles County court on 9 June 1752 for bearing a "Molatto" child, but the case was struck off the calendar in November 1752 [Court Record 1752-3, 65, 228]. She may have been the mother of
i. Elizabeth, "Mulatto" head of a Charles County household of 5 "other free" in 1790.
ii. Richard, "Mulatto" head of a Charles County household of 1 "other free" in 1790.
iii. Shadrack, "free Negro" head of a Prince George County household of 6 "other free" in 1800 [MD:311].
iv. Benjamin, had of a Charles County household of 7 "other free" in 1810 [MD:337].

Other members of the Clark family on the Western Shore were
i. Julia, head of a Baltimore City household of 4 "other free" in 1800 [MD:170].
ii. William, head of a Baltimore Town household of 6 "other free" in 1790.
iii. Isaac, head of an Anne Arundel County household of 6 "other free" in 1790 and 6 in 1810 [MD:63].
iv. Jenny, a "Negro" taxable in Elkridge Hundred, Anne Arundel County in 1783 [MSA S1161-1-3, p.3].

CLAYTON FAMILY

1. Jeffrey Clayton, born say 1753, was head of a Kent County, Maryland household of 6 "other free" in 1800 [MD:158]. He may have been the father of
   i. Solomon, born say 1774, husband of Clarissa "free blacks"who registered the birth and baptism of their daughter Priscilla at St. Paul's Parish, Baltimore on 28 March and 8 April 1787 [Reamy, *Records of St. Paul's Parish*, I:115].

COGER FAMILY

1. Margaret Coger, born say 1740, was presented by the Queen Anne's County court in November 1771 for failing to list herself as a tithable [Surles, *and they Appeared at Court 1770-1772*, 45]. She may have been related to Coger, a "Negro" taxable in Island District of Queen Anne's County in 1783 [MSA S1161-1-8-10, p.74, 1/4/5/51]. And she may have been the mother of
   i. Samuel, a "black" head of a Queen Anne's County household of 9 "Blacks" in 1776 [Carothers, *1776 Census of Maryland*, 148], charged with assault and battery by William **Haycock** in Queen Anne's County court in July 1786 [Surles, *and they Appeared at Court, 1779, 1782, 1785, 1786, 1787*, 71, 121]. He was head of a Queen Anne's County household of 7 "other free" in 1790.
   ii. Isaac, head of a Queen Anne's County household of 3 "other free" in 1790.
   iii. James, head of a Queen Anne's County household of 5 "other free" in 1800 [MD:329]. He was called a blacksmith when he charged Solomon and William **Haycock** with assault and battery in Queen Anne's County in 1787. He posted a bond of £10 in 1787 for his appearance to answer the suit of Solomon **Haycock**'s wife Dorcas [Surles, *and they Appeared at Court, 1779, 1782, 1785, 1786, 1787*, 128-9].
   iv. William, head of a Queen Anne's County household of 7 "other free" in 1810 [VA:155].
   v. Sarah, a 101-year-old "Mulatto woman born in Maryland and counted in the 1850 census for Washington, D.C. [Ward 7, family 783].

COKER FAMILY

Members of the Coker family may have been related to the Coger family of Queen Anne's County. Members of the Coker family in Maryland and Delaware were
   i. Daniel[1], born about 1766, head of a Caroline County household of 11 "free colored" in 1820, an 84-year-old "Mulatto," born in Maryland, living in Little Creek Hundred, Kent County, Delaware, in 1850 with (wife?) Sarah in the household of James Coker who was also born in Maryland [family no. 348].
   ii. Moses, born about 1774, a "Negro," purchased three tracts of land in Kent County, Delaware, totaling 150 acres partially in Caroline County, called *Old Fields Enclosure, Long Range* and *Hickory Hill* for $140 on 21 January 1817 [Land Records R-2:155]. He was head of a Caroline County household of 11 "other free" in 1820 and a 76-year-old "Mulatto" farmer with $3,400 worth of real estate in Caroline County in 1850 [MD:82].
   iii. Philip, born before 1776, head of a Caroline County household of 4 "other free" in 1820.
   iv. David, born about 1775, a 75-year-old "Mulatto" counted in the 1850 census for Greenwich, Cumberland County, New Jersey, with "Black" (wife?) Harriet, both born in Maryland [family no. 121].
   v. Daniel[2], born 1776-1794, head of a Talbot County household of 4 "free colored" in 1820.
   vi. Thomas Cooker, born 1776-1794, head of a Little Creek Hundred, Kent County, Delaware household of 8 "free colored" in 1830.

Endnote:
1. Another Daniel Coker, born about 1780, was the son of a white woman named Susan Coker and a slave of Frederick County, Maryland. He was elected but declined to be the first bishop of the African Methodist Church. He went to Liberia as a missionary and died there in 1846 [Berlin, *Slaves Who Were Free*].

COLE FAMILY

Members of the Cole family who registered in Alexandria, Virginia, claimed their freedom through descent from a white woman [Brown, *Free Negroes in the District of Columbia*, 30]. They may have been related to a "Mullatto Boy," aged fifteen years, bound to serve until the age of thirty-one, who was listed in the inventory of the St. Mary's County estate of John Cole on 21 May 1718 [Prerogative Court (Inventories), 1718-1777, SR4328, Liber 1, pp.315-6]. And the inventory of the estate of Mrs. Elizabeth Cole of St. Mary's County had a "Mallato Boy" named Will who had four years to serve on 1 March 1734 [Prerogative Court Inventories, 1734, Vol. 18, pp. 335-7].

Also, William Cole in his 7 February 1732 St. Mary's County will, proved 31 March 1733, left his slaves to his wife Elizabeth during her lifetime, but after her death gave them and their increase their freedom and all his lands. They were: Sam, Moll, Tom, Sarah, and Job [Prerogative Court WB 20:632-3].

Members of the Cole family in Maryland were

	i.	Thomas[1], born say 1730, a "free Negro" who owed the estate of John Clark of St. Mary's County 2 shillings on 28 April 1755 [Prerogative Inventories 59:213].
1	ii.	Araminta, born about 1764.
	iii.	Ann, born say 1766, head of a St. Mary's County household of 2 "other free" in 1790.
2	iv.	Milly, born say 1772.
	v.	Frances, head of a St. Mary's County household of 2 "other free" in 1800 [MD:417].
	vi.	Cava, head of a St. Mary's County household of 7 "other free" in 1810 [MD:217].
	vii.	Monica, head of a St. Mary's County household of 4 "other free" in 1810 [MD:232].
	viii.	Joe, "blk." head of a St. Mary's County household of 3 "other free" in 1810 [MD:191].
	ix.	Jesse, "blk" head of a St. Mary's County household of 3 "other free" in 1810 [MD:208].

1. Araminta Cole, born about 1764, registered in St. Mary's County on 10 April 1809: *aged 45 years or thereabouts...complexion yellowish, hair short & curley...raised in Saint Mary's County and obtained her freedom in the late General Court for the Western Shore.* She was a "blk." head of a St. Mary's County household of 2 "other free" in 1810 [MD:215]. She was the mother of
    i. Cornelius, born about 1795, registered in St. Mary's County on 17 November 1823: *son of Minty Cole, aged about twenty eight years...dark complexion...born free.*
    ii. Sandy, born about 1802, registered in St. Mary's County on 29 December 1826: *aged about 24 years, born free, and born and raised in Saint Mary's County, being the son of a free woman of colour named Minta Cole...dark complexion* [Certificates of Freedom 1806-64, 4, 64, 72].

2. Milly Cole, born say 1772, was head of a St. Mary's County household of 3 "other free" in 1800 [MD:413]. She was the mother of

   i. Thomas[2], born about 1793, registered in St. Mary's County on 28 March 1820: *son of Milly Cole...twenty seven years of age, of a Dark Complexion...born free.*

Other members of the Cole family were

   i. Frances[2], born about 1785, registered in St. Mary's County on 25 May 1807: *about twenty years of age, dark complexion, was born free and raised in the County aforesaid, she has Woolly hair, large features, cheerful countenance.*

  ii. Mary, born about 1787, registered in St. Mary's County on 29 April 1817: *aged thirty years or thereabouts...Dark Complexion, short hair...born free.* She was head of a St. Mary's County household of 4 "other free" in 1810 [MD:216].

 iii. Lewis, born about 1799, registered in St. Mary's County on 10 June 1823: *Son of Nelly Cole, about twenty four years of age and is of a dark complexion...born free* [Certificates of Freedom 1806-64, 1, 38, 54, 61].

COLLICK/ KOLLOCK FAMILY

Members of the Collick family were

1   i. Samuel, born say 1718.

  ii. Simon, born say 1720, taxable in the Mattapony Hundred, Somerset County household of Emanuel **Harman** in 1736 and 1737, called "Simon" in 1736, "Simon Colleck" in 1737 [List of Tithables, 1736, 1737]. He owed the Worcester County estate of Peter **Beckett** £1 on 23 January 1754 and the Worcester County estate of Alexander Buncle 6 shillings on 3 February 1761 [Prerogative Inventories 60:89; 72:137-42]. He was a "Negro" taxable on 100 acres called *Spences Venture* and another 12 acres called *Conveniency's Addition* in Bogerternorton Hundred of Worcester County in 1783 [MdHR MSA S1161-11-6, p.2]. He was head of a Worcester County household of 6 "other free" in 1790 (Simon Kollok). He was charged with assault and battery in Sussex County court in May 1773 and November 1778 [RG 4805, General Sessions Court, 1767-94, frames 133, 204].

 iii. Mary Kollock, head of a Worcester County household of 5 "other free" in 1790.

 iv. William, head of a Worcester County household of 6 "other free" and a slave in 1810 [MD:622]. He mortgaged a sailboat and a yoke of oxen to Levin Conner on 14 February 1823 and sold a yoke of steers and the service of his son Benjamin until the age of twenty-one for $19.25 by Worcester County deed of 24 February 1823 [Land Records AO:391-2, 419-20].

1.   Samuel Collick, born say 1718, purchased 49 acres in Worcester County called *Red Oak Ridge* on the north side of the Pocomoke River in Indian Town on 6 June 1744 [Land Records A:193]. He was a "Mollato" taxable on 49 acres in Acquango Hundred in 1783 [MSA S1161-11-5, p.2]. He died before 16 October 1801 when his wife Esther and children: Charles Collick, Leah **Roberts**, Comfort Collick, Betsy Collick, and Hetty Collick sold *Red Oak Ridge* and an adjoining 8-1/2 acres called *Equantico Savannah* which Esther had purchased [Land Records, U:405]. Esther was head of a Worcester County household of 4 "other free" in 1800 [MD:828]. (There was also an Esther Collick counted as head of a Worcester County household of 3 "other free" in 1800 [MD:814]). Samuel and Esther's children were

   i. Charles, head of a Worcester County household of 4 "other free" in 1800 [MD:830].

  ii. Leah **Roberts**.

 iii. Comfort.

    iv. Betsy.
    v. Hetty.

COLLINS FAMILY

1.   Christian Collins, born say 1697, had three years remaining on her indenture to William Smith on 24 March 1718/9 when she confessed in Prince George's County court that she had an illegitimate child. The court adjudged that the child was "begott by a Negroe man" and ordered her master William Smith to deliver her up to the court to be sold when her indenture was completed and ordered that the child serve Smith until the age of thirty-one [Court Record 1715-20, 809]. She may have been the ancestor of

2   i. Henry², born say 1765.
    ii. Sarah, head of an Anne Arundel County household of 3 "other free" in 1790.
    iii. Israel, head of a Baltimore City household of 3 "other free" in 1800 [MD:174].

2.   Henry² Collins, born say 1765, was a "free Mulatto" head of a Prince George's County household of 4 "other free" in 1800 [MD:263] and 9 in 1810 [MD:18]. He may have been the husband of Susannah Collins who registered in Washington, D.C., on 21 June 1821: *a woman of colour...swarthy complexion, aged about fifty-five or sixty years*. On 10 June 1817 she testified that Thomas **Wiseman** was free. She was the mother of

    i. Mary **Douglass**, born 1782-1787, registered in Washington, D.C., on 13 October 1827: *a mulatto woman...about forty or forty-five years old, daughter of Susannah Collings...born free and raised in Prince George's County* [Provine, *District of Columbia Free Negro Registers*, 82].

1.   Mary Collins, born about 1699, was a "Mollatto woman" who had six more years to serve when she was listed in the inventory of the St. Mary's County estate of Mr. John Blackiston on 18 January 1724/5 [Prerogative Inventories & Accounts 1724-1725, 292-5]. She may have been the ancestor of

    i. Henry¹, head of a St. Mary's County household of 4 "other free" in 1800 [MD:411].
    ii. Eleanor, born about 1772, registered in St. Mary's County on 4 June 1817: *aged forty five years or thereabouts...dark complexion, hair short & gray...born free*.
    iii. Elizabeth, born about 1787, registered in St. Mary's County on 24 October 1817: *aged about thirty years...Dark Complexion...born free* [Certificates of Freedom 1806-64, 39, 41].

Members of the Collins family in Charles County were

    i. Samuel, head of a Charles County household of 9 "other free" in 1800 [MD:561], perhaps the Sam Collins who was a "Molatto" servant listed in the inventory of the St. Mary's County estate of Mr. Edward Diggs with three more years to serve on 10 March 1770, valued at £18 [Prerogative Inventories 103:230].
    ii. Samuel, Sr., head of a Charles County household of 2 "other free" in 1800 [MD:562].
    iii. Samuel, Jr., head of a Charles County household of 10 "other free" in 1800 [MD:562] and 13 in 1810 [MD:298].
    iv. George, "Mulatto" head of a Charles County household of 1 "other free" in 1790 and 4 in 1800 [MD:522]. On 9 February 1804 he made a Charles County mortgage of seven hogs, a cow, a cow yearling and his household goods for £22 to Gabriel Moran who agreed to pay George's rent of 1,740 pounds of tobacco due to his landlord Richard Edelen, deceased. George was called a "mulatto" the same day when he indentured himself to serve

Moran for eleven months to compensate him for the £22. Moran also agreed to bring down from the fishing landing on the Potomac River as much fresh fish as George wanted for his wife and children at George's cost [Land Records IB #6, 37-40].

Members of the Collins family on the Eastern Shore of Maryland were
  i.   George, "Negro" head of a Kent County household of 1 "other free" in 1790.
  ii. Peter, head of a Dorchester County household of 5 "other free" in 1800 [MD:673].
  iii. Spindells, head of a Talbot County household of 3 "other free" and 3 slaves in 1800 [MD:530].
  iv. Grace, head of a Dorchester County household of 2 "other free" in 1800 [MD:673].

COMBESS/ CUMBEST FAMILY

1. John[1] Combess/ Combest, born say 1670, was taxable in Spesutia Hundred, Baltimore County, in 1695 [Court Proceedings1693-6, 521]. He was the father of
    i.   Sarah, born 17 January 1693, "d/o John Combest," in St. George's Parish, Baltimore County. She married William Robinson on 8 December 1713 at St. George's Parish.
    ii. Ketturah, born 10 October 1695, the daughter of John Combest of St. George's Parish, Baltimore County. She was head of a household and taxable on herself and John Combess on 2 tithes in Spesutia Lower Hundred, Baltimore County, in 1737.
    iii. Mary, born 20 April 1698, "d/o of John Combest," at Swan Creek, St. George's Parish.
2   iv. Martha, born 9 September 1700.
    v.   John[2], born about December 1704, a "Mulatto," aged eleven years and six months in June 1716 when he was bound to George Wells by the Baltimore County court [Court Proceedings 1715-8, 12].

2. Martha Combest, born 9 September 1700, was the daughter of John Combest who lived at the head of Collats Creek in St. George's Parish [Reamy, *St. George's Parish Register, 1689-1773*, 1, 3, 7, 16, 21]. She was head of a household, taxable on herself and her son Jacob Combess on 2 tithes in Spesutia Lower Hundred, Baltimore County, in 1737 [Wright, *Inhabitants of Baltimore County*, 16]. She was the mother of
    i.   Jacob, born 10 November 1718, "son of Martha Combest" in St. George's Parish. He was taxable on 46-3/4 acres in Spesutia Hundred, Harford County, in 1783 [MSA S1161-6-10, p.124].

Some of their descendants were in South Carolina in 1770:
    i.   Josiah[1] and Penelope, witnesses in a murder case against William Fust and Christopher Davis in the South Carolina Court of General Sessions on 19 January 1770 [Journal of the S.C. Court, p.41].
3   ii. Winna, born say 1752.

3. Winna Combest, born say 1752, was a "Mulatto" head of a Cheraw District, South Carolina household of 3 "other free" in 1790. She may have been the mother of
    i.   Josiah[2], born about 1770, a twelve-year-old "poor Boy" bound to Joseph Booth until the age of twenty-one on 3 August 1782 in St. David's Parish, South Carolina.
    ii. Mary, born about 1776, a six-year-old girl bound to Thomas Lankford in St. David's Parish on 3 August 1782.
    iii. Joans, born about 1777, a five-year-old girl bound to Francis Robertson in St. David's Parish, South Carolina on 3 August 1782 [Holcolm, *Saint*

David's Parish Vestry, 24, 25].

iv. John[3], head of an Edgefield District, South Carolina household of 4 "other free" in 1810 [SC:766].

CONNER FAMILY

1. Margaret Conner, born say 1699, was the servant of Captain Edward Hammond of All Hallows Parish on 3 March 1712/3 when she admitted to the Somerset County court that she had an illegitimate child for which she received twenty-five lashes. On 5 August 1712 she admitted in court that she had a child by her master's slave Jeffrey. Jeffrey received twenty-five lashes, and the court sold Margaret to her master for seven years in March 1714/5. She received twenty lashes in June 1716 for having a child by a white man Jeremiah Venie [Judicial Records 1713-15, 177, 204, 259; 1715-17, 74, 235]. She may have been the ancestor of
    i. Abner, head of a Worcester County household of 2 "other free" in 1790 and 7 in 1800 [MD:741].
    ii. ?David, head of a Talbot County household of 5 "other free" in 1800 [MD:517].
    iii. ?Thomas, head of a Kent County household of 3 "other free" in 1800 [MD:159].

CONSELLOR FAMILY

The Consellor family of Delaware may have descended from John Gonsolvos, an Accomack County, Virginia tithable in 1676 [Orders 1676-8, 33]. The Accomack County court dismissed a suit against Grace Gonsolvo (his widow?) on 11 February 1689 [Orders 1678-82, 59]. A William Comsloe admitted in Dorchester County court in August 1691 that he owed Alexander Fisher 3,200 pounds of tobacco [Court Proceedings in Land Records Liber 4-1/2, p.120].

1. Thomas[1] Consellor/ Gonseala, born say 1670, purchased 120 acres on the north side of Little Creek Hundred, Kent County, Delaware, from Griffin Jones by deed acknowledged in court in December 1699. He recorded his earmark on 30 April 1700 and sued Dennis Dyer on 8 September 1702 [de Valinger, *Court Records*, 90, 150, 233; Land Records C-1:243]. He was sued in Kent County court on 11 August 1708 and was fined 15 shillings on 11 August 1713 (called Thomas Gonsoaly). In February 1720 John Mar and Simon Irons posted £228 bail for him when he was sued for debt by William Rodeney. The suit was discontinued in May 1721 [Court Dockets 1680-1725, 75; General Court Records 1712-6, n.p.; 1718-22, 110, 121]. He died before 6 August 1726 when administration on his Kent County estate was granted to his widow Joanna [WB F-1, fol. 14]. He was probably the father of

2   i. Thomas[2], born say 1690.

2. Thomas[2] Consellor, born say 1690, was called Thomas Gonsela of Kent County in November 1721 when he posted £14 bail in Kent County court for Robert **Butcher** [General Court Records 1718-22, fol. 169]. He was taxable in Little Creek Hundred, Kent County, in 1727 and 1734 [RG 3535, Kent County Levy List, 1726-42, frames 301, 346, 378]. His 26 September 1739 Kent County will, proved 20 October the same year, left a mare to his grandson William Conseelah and named daughters Elizabeth **Francisco**, Sarah **Butcher**, and Mary Conselah who was his sole executor [WB I-1, p.10 - fol. 10]. His children were

3   i. Mary, born say 1708.
      ii. Elizabeth **Francisco**, probably the wife of Daniel[1] **Francisco**.
      iii. Sarah, wife of Robert **Butcher**, Jr.

3.   Mary Conselah, born say 1708, was the executor and heir of her father's 26 September 1739 will. She was called Mary Gonsola when she sued Abraham Amley in Kent County court in February 1726/7 and called Mary Gonzalo or Gonzales in August 1728 when she confessed to having an illegitimate child in Kent County. John Craig sued her in August 1737 [Delaware Archives RG 3815.031, dockets 1722-32, frames 148, 266, 229, 235; 1733-40, frame 346]. She was head of a taxable household in Little Creek Hundred in 1743 and 1745 [RG 3535, Kent County Levy List, 1726-42, frame 301; 1743-67, 16, 43]. She received a bed, furniture and a mare by the 31 January 1757 Kent County will of William **Beckett** [WB K-1, 162]. **Beckett** was probably the father of her illegitimate child William Conseelah who was named in her father's will. Mary was apparently the mother of

4   i.   William[1], born about 1728.

4.   William[1] Consellor, born about 1728, was found not guilty by the Kent County court in May 1743 of having an illegitimate child sworn to him by Eliza **Butcher**. Mary Gonselah came into court and promised to pay his court fees [DSA, RG 3805.002, Quarter Sessions, 1734-79, frame 80; MS case files]. He was not taxable in the Little Creek Hundred, Kent County list for 1745, but was taxable in the next surviving list for 1748 (called William Gonsella) until 1755, taxable from 1759 to 1764 in Little Creek Hundred, from 1765 to 1774 in Duck Creek Hundred, and taxable again in Little Creek Hundred from 1776 to 1778 when he was called William Conselo S[r]. According to the Little Creek Hundred tax lists for 1772 and 1773, he owned 130 acres in Little Creek Hundred, 70 acres of which were in the possession of Thomas Consellor [Levy List 1743-67, frames 51, 87, 107, 136, 143, 240, 490, 517, 549, 566; 1768-84, frames 22, 73, 125, 180, 186, 220, 310, 342]. He died before 1 May 1780 when John **Durham** was granted administration on his Kent County estate [WB L-1, fol. 217]. His children were probably Whittington and William Conselor whose support was listed in the account of the estate. His widow Mary was a witness to John **Durham**'s will. His children were most likely

        i.   Thomas[3], born say 1748, taxable in Little Creek Hundred from 1768 to 1778. According to the levy assessments for 1772 and 1773 he was living on about 70 acres of land which belonged to William Consellor. He married Elizabeth, daughter of John **Durham**. The Kent County court indicted John Spruance for assaulting him on 15 August 1783 in Duck Creek Hundred, and Joseph Wyatt sued him for a debt of £10 in April 1793 [DSA, RG 3805, MS November 1783 Indictments; RG 3815, MS April 1793 case papers].

5   ii.   Elijah[1], born say 1750.

        iii.   Charles, born say 1758, a taxable in Little Creek Hundred from 1779 to 1783: listed as a "Negro" in 1780 [RG 3535, Kent County Levy List, 1768-84, frames 366, 368, 442, 445, 502, 541, 570, 582].

        iv.   Jonathan, born say 1758, a "Mulatto" taxable in Duck Creek Hundred in 1779 and 1781, called John in Murderkill Hundred from 1782 to 1788, crossed off the list in 1789 [RG 3535, Kent County Levy List, 1767-84, frames 370, 522, 546, 573, 595, 628; 1768-84, frames 10, 28, 52, 123, 147]. John Conselor's estate was administered on 8 August 1791 when Thomas Nixon certified that John had settled a debt he owed Ann Adams's "Negro George" [RG 3545, reel 44, frames 846-62].

        v.   William[2], born say 1758, taxable in Little Creek Hundred from 1778 (called William Concealor, Jun[r]) to 1780 and in Duck Creek Hundred in 1781 [RG 3535, Kent County Levy List, 1767-84, frames 342, 366, 445, 522].

        vi.   Whittington.

5.   Elijah[1] Consellor, born say 1750, was taxable in Murderkill Hundred from 1775 to 1785, listed as a "N." taxable in 1785, a "Mulattoe" listed with 83 acres under

the care and management of James **Dean** and 2 mares, 4 horses, a yoke of oxen, a steer, 7 cows, 4 yearlings, 3 cattle, 5 calves, 18 sheep, 2 sows, 2 hogs, and 5 shoats in 1797, in a list of "Negroes and Mulattoes" with 150 acres in 1798 [RG 3535, Kent County Levy List, 1768-84, frames 254, 267, 299, 370, 522, 568, 607; 1785-97, 127, 470; 1797-8, frame 25]. He married Hannah **Durham**, daughter of John **Durham**, before 9 April 1788 when she was named in her father's Kent County will [RG 3545, roll 68, frames 612-23; WB M-1, fol. 170-1]. He purchased 38 acres on the road from Fast Landing to Dover from John **Durham** on 14 February 1788 for £116 and another 46 acres from Francis Denney, administrator of John **Durham**'s estate, on 14 May 1789 for £60; and he purchased 120 acres adjoining John **Durham**'s land for $1,066 on 7 February 1798 [DB Z:199; A-2:155; F-2:82]. His widow Hannah was granted administration on his estate on 29 December 1801. About £500 was divided amongst his widow Hannah and five children: Jeremiah, Elijah, Sarah **Miller**, Elizabeth and Benjamin [DSA, RG 3545, roll 45, frames 10-20]. Hannah was head of a Little Creek Hundred household of 1 "free colored" woman over the age of 45 in 1820 [DE:24]. Their children were

6   i.   Jeremiah[1], born say 1777.

       ii. Elijah[2], Jr. named in the final settlement of the estate of his father. His estate was administered by Elisha **Durham** (signing) and by his widow, Elizabeth Conselor. He was a "Mulatto" taxable in Little Creek Hundred in 1798 [RG 3535, Kent County Levy List, 1797-8, frame 483] and head of a Little Creek Hundred household of 7 "free colored in 1820 [DE:24].

     iii. Sarah, widow of Debrix **Miller**.

     iv. Elizabeth, married John **Durham**.

      v. Benjamin, born say 1780, still a minor when his father died. He was a "N." head of a Duck Creek Hundred household 9 "free colored" in 1820 [DE:49].

6.   Jeremiah[1] Concellor, born say 1777, was a "Mulatto" taxable on a minor's property of £37 in Little Creek Hundred in 1798 [RG 3535, Kent County Levy List, 1797-8, frames 473, 483]. He died before 29 April 1811 when Elizabeth Conceler was granted administration on his estate on $1,000 bond by Jeremiah's brother Elijah Conceler (signing) who married Jeremiah's widow Elizabeth. The estate paid various bills to Jesse **Dean**, Deberix **Mller**, Peter **Beckett**, Benjamin **Sisco**, William **Sisco**, and John **Durham** and distributed about $500 between the widow and children: Esther, Elijah, Hannah, Harrietta (Henrietta), and Jeremiah [RG 3545, reel 44, frames 856-62]. His children were

       i. Esther, married Jesse **Dean** (signing) bond of 29 August 1814 with Benjamin Concealor bondsman [DSA, Marriage Bonds 20:157].

      ii. Elijah.

     iii. Hannah.

     iv. Harrietta.

      v. Jeremiah[2].

Another member of the family was

       i. William[3], born about 1769, a 91-year-old "Mulatto" farm laborer counted with (wife?) Esther in Concordville, Delaware County, Pennsylvania, in the 1860 census, both born in Delaware [PA:296].

COOK FAMILY

1.   Margaret Cook, born say 1715, was a white woman living with William Robinson of Westminster Parish on 11 March 1734/5 when the Anne Arundel County court presented her for having two "Mollatto" children. She confessed her guilt to the court on 10 June 1735, and the court sold her and her son, born 19 December 1734, to William Ghisolin. On 8 March 1736/7 she confessed to having another

child which was adjudged by the court to be "begot by some Negro." Margaret was ordered to serve another seven-year term, and her child, a two-month-old girl, was bound to Ghiselin until the age of thirty-one [Judgment Record 1734-6, 238; 1736-8, 138]. Margaret may have been the ancestor of
  i. Jack, a "mulatto boy" who Patriarch Creagh of Annapolis gave to his wife Frances until the age of twenty-one by his 5 June 1747 will, proved 12 January 1761 [Prerogative Court (Wills), 31:336].
  ii. Thomas, head of a Baltimore City household of 9 "other free" in 1810 [MD:433].
  iii. Dian, head of a Baltimore City household of 7 "other free" in 1810 [MD:310].
  iv. Benjamin, "of Caller," head of a Baltimore County household of 4 "other free" in 1810 [MD:680].

Dorchester County:
1. Mary Cook, born say 1714, was the servant of James Woolford of Choptank Parish, Dorchester County, in March 1733/4 when the jury convicted her of having a "Mulatto" child for which the court ordered her to serve seven years [Judgment Record 1733-4, 240-4]. She may have been the ancestor of
  i. Jacob, head of a Queen Anne's County household of 10 "other free" in 1790.
  ii. Aaron, head of a Dorchester County household of 7 "other free" in 1800 [MD:692].
  iii. Nathan, "Negro" head of a Caroline County household of 3 "other free" in 1810 [MD:680].

COOPER FAMILY

Members of the Cooper family in Maryland were
  i. Ben, head of a Talbot County household of 9 "other free" in 1790.
  ii. Dick, head of a Talbot County household of 4 "other free" and a slave in 1790, perhaps the Richard Cooper who was head of a Little Creek Hundred, Kent County, Delaware household of 5 "other free" in 1800 [DE:34].
  iii. John/ Jack, head of a Talbot County household of 5 "other free" in 1790 and 7 in 1800 [MD:534].
  iv. James^1, head of a Kent County household of 11 "other free" in 1800 [MD:146].
  v. James^2, head of a Kent County household of 4 "other free" in 1800 [MD:146].
  vi. Harry, head of a Kent County household of 4 "other free" in 1800 [MD:147].
  vii. Peter, head of a Baltimore City household of 3 "other free" in 1800 [MD:174].
  viii. Caesar, head of a Kent County household of 1 "other free" in 1800 [MD:158].
  ix. Nace, born about 1762, living in Prince George's County on 18 July 1782 when a twenty-year-old "mulatto" slave ran away from Henry Neale of St. Mary's County and passed as a freeman using his name [*Maryland Gazette* (Green); http://2.vcdh.virginia.edu/gos/explore.html].
1 x. Eleanor, born about 1771.

1. Eleanor/ Nelly Cooper, born about 1771, registered in Prince George's County on 2 April 1813: *Eleanor Cooper, a bright mulatto woman, about 42 years old, and 5 feet 5 inches tall. She is free, being the descendant of a certain Rosamond Bently who recovered her freedom in the Prince George's County Court in a suit against Anthony Addison.* She was the mother of
  i. Patience, born about 1793, registered in Prince George's County on 27

August 1823: *light complexion, is about 30 years old, and about 5 feet 5-1/2 inches tall...child of Nelly Cooper, a free woman of colour*.

   ii. Mary, born about 1795, registered in Prince George's County on 27 August 1823: *light complexion, is about 28 years old, and about 5 feet 5-3/4 inches tall...child of Nelly Cooper*.

  iii. William, born about 1799, registered in Prince George's County on 27 August 1823: *light complexion, is about 24 years old, and about 5 feet 7 inches tall...son of Nelly Cooper*.

  iv. Matilda, born about 1802, registered in Prince George's County on 27 August 1823: *dark complexion, is about 21 years old, and about 5 feet 6 inches tall...daughter of Nelly Cooper*.

   v. Rosetta, born about 1807, registered in Prince George's County on 27 August 1823: *a bright mulatto girl, about 16 years old, and 5 feet 4 inches tall...daughter of Nelly Cooper* [Provine, *Registrations of Free Negroes*, 15, 46].

CORK FAMILY

1. "Negroe Cork" was listed in the account of the Kent County, Maryland estate of John Connor on 29 January 1753, owing a debt of 3 shillings [Prerogative Inventories 52 (1752-3), 124-7]. He may have been the ancestor of

   i. Isaac, a "free negro" taxable in the 4th district of Kent County, Maryland, in 1783 [1783 Assessment MSA S1437, p.4], head of a Kent County household of 6 "other free" in 1800 [MD:158]

  ii. Moses, "negro" taxable in the 3rd district of Kent County, Maryland, in 1783 (called Moses Caulk) [1783 Assessment MSA S1437, p.2]. He was "Negro" head of a Kent County household of 3 "other free" and a slave in 1790 and 7 "other free" in 1800 [MD:171].

  iii. William, a "Negro" taxable in Duck Creek Hundred, Kent County, Delaware, in 1797 [Assessments 1785-97, frame 470]. He and Joseph **Oliver**, "people of Colour," bought 7 acres called *Killmanins Plains* in Queen Anne's County for $45 from Jacob **Jeffreys**, a "Man of Colour," on 15 September 1810. They sold the same land back to him for $50 on 25 May 1811 [Land Records STW-9:369].

  iv. Jacob[1], a "Negro" head of a Kent County, Maryland household of 3 "other free" in 1790 and 8 in 1800 [MD:158].

   v. Jacob[2], head of a Kent County, Maryland household of 4 "other free" in 1800 [MD:170].

  vi. Samuel[1], a "N." head of a St. Jones Hundred, Kent County, Delaware household of 9 "other free" in 1800 [DE:48]

  vii. John, head of an Indian River, Sussex County household of 4 "other free" in 1800 [DE:437].

 viii. Samuel[2], head of a Little Creek Hundred, Kent County, Delaware household of 2 "other free" in 1800 [DE:40].

CORNISH FAMILY

1. Jack Cornish, born about 1682, was a "Negro" man slave, 77 years old, listed in the inventory of the Dorchester County estate of Colonel John Eccleston in 1759 [Prerogative Inventories, 68:59-68]. He may have been the ancestor of

   i. William[1], born say 1715, a brick maker sued in Dorchester County by John Carville in March 1755 for a debt of £2.8 which William had owed since 1753 [Judgment Records, 1754-5, 241-3], probably identical to the William Cornish who was imprisoned for debt in Sussex County, and petitioned the court in February 1750 to serve Jacob Kollock, Esq., to pay the debt. The court charged him with assault in August 1757 [RG 4815.017, General Sessions Court, 1741-53, frame 516; 1753-60, 381, 384, 403, 421, 446]. He owed the estate of Peter **Beckett** of Worcester

County £2.5 on 23 January 1754 [Prerogative Inventories 60:89]. He died before 19 March 1760 when his debt of £4.4 to the Dorchester County estate of Colonel Joseph Ennalls was determined to be unrecoverable because of his death. Perhaps his widow was Elizabeth Cornish who owed the estate 9 shillings [Prerogative Inventories 76:169-183].

2   ii.   Esau, born say 1718.
3   iii. Samuel[1], born say 1720.
       iv.   John[1]/ Jack, born about 1728, living in Dorchester County on 20 October 1745 when Charles Hudson and Thomas Stewart posted bond for his good behavior and appearance in November court [Judgment Record 1744-5, 468]. He ran away from his master John Turner in September 1762 according to an ad placed by Turner in the 28 April 1763 issue of the *Pennsylvania Gazette*: *run away from the subscriber, living in Dorchester County, Maryland, in September last, a Mulatto Fellow, called Jack Cornish, about 35 Years of Age, and by Trade a Weaver, about 5 feet high, his Visage is round, his Complexion light for a Mulatto, and his Carriage very stately, pretending to be very genteel, talkative and complaisant* [*Pennsylvania Gazette*, http://accessible.com]. He was head of a Transquakin Hundred, Dorchester County household of 2 "Negroes" in 1776 [Carothers, *1776 Census of Maryland*, 53]. He may have been the John Cornish who was charged with felony by the Kent County, Delaware court in August 1790. He pled guilty and was ordered to wear a Roman T [RG 3805.002, 1787-1803, frame 156].
4   v.   Sidney, born say 1724.
5   vi.   Rebecca, born say 1742.

2.   Esau Cornish, born say 1718, was bondsman for the appearance of (his brother?) Samuel Cornish in Dorchester County court in November 1742 [Judgment Record 1742-3, 43-4]. He owed 5 pounds of tobacco to the Dorchester County estate of Howels Goldsbrough in 1761 [Prerogative Inventories 75:303-5]. He was taxable in Indian River Hundred, Sussex County, in 1770. He left a 7 December 1770 Sussex County will in which he named his wife Mary, son Samuel, son Amos, and daughters Sarah and Elener. His wife Mary and son Samuel were executors [WB B:408-9]. He was the father of

6   i.   Samuel[2], born say 1742, taxable in Indian River and Angola Hundred, Sussex County, from 1773 to 1790 [RG 2535, Levy List 1767-83; 1780-96] and head of an Indian River, Sussex County household of 11 "other free" in 1800 [DE:437].
       ii.   Amos, charged with felony in Sussex County court in February 1773. Mary Curley was a witness against him [RG 4805, General Sessions 1767-94, frames 126, 154, 167, 181]. He called himself a "Mollatto" in the 14 July 1786 Worcester County deed by which he sold half the corn and crop on Thomas Benston's land that he owned by agreement with Benston for £8.13 [Land Records L:400].
       iii. Sarah, head of a Sussex County household of 4 "other free" in 1810 [DE:458].
       iv.   Eleanor.

3.   Samuel[1] Cornish, born say 1720, was sued in Dorchester County court in November 1742 for a £32 debt [Judgment Record 1742-3, 43-4]. He may have been identical to _____ Cornish who married _____ in Lewes and Coolspring Presbyterian Church, Sussex County, in 1768 [Wright, *Vital Records of Kent and Sussex Counties*, 124]. He was taxable in Indian River Hundred, Sussex County, from 1773 to 1790 and head of an Indian River Hundred, Sussex County household of 11 "other free" in 1800 [DE:437]. He may have been the father of
       i.   Sally, born say 1750, married Moses **Parkinson** ("Molattoes") on 7 January 1771 in Sussex County [Records of the United Presbyterian Churches of Lewes, Indian River and Coolspring, 1756-1855, 282].

4. Sidney Cornish, born say 1724, a "Spinster," was living in Dorchester County in March 1744/5 when she was found not guilty of having an illegitimate child by a "Negroe." She was assessed court costs which Lewis Griffith agreed to pay [Judgment Record 1744-5, 347]. She may have been the mother of

7   i.   Ann[1], born say 1744.
8   ii.   Christianna, born say 1747.
       iii. Daniel, born about 1749, a "Mullatto Boy" aged fifteen years and bound until the age of thirty-one on 4 December 1765 when he was listed in the Queen Anne's County estate of Henry Costin, J[r] [Prerogative Inventories 94: 211-2].
       iv.   Ebby, head of a Dorchester County household of 1 "other free" and a slave in 1800 [MD:684].
       v.   Samuel[3], head of a Dorchester County household of 4 "other free" in 1790.
       vi.   Sol, head of a Dorchester County household of 4 "other free" in 1800 [MD:684].

5. Rebecca Cornish, born say 1742, was the spinster servant of John Ross of Talbot County in November 1763 when the court convicted her of having a child by a "Negro." The court ordered that she be sold for seven years after the completion of her indenture to her master and sold her son Levin Cornish to her master for £3. She admitted in August 1766 that she had another child by a "Negro" and paid twice the normal fine of £1.10 because she would not identify the father. In June 1767 she was convicted of fornication and found guilty of stealing gloves, brass buttons, a handkerchief and several other items from Cornelius Dailey. The court ordered that she receive 15 lashes, stand in the pillory and pay four times the value of the goods or 1,500 pounds of tobacco. She was convicted of assaulting Elizabeth Heels in November 1770 and ordered to pay a shilling fine [Criminal Record 1761-7, 235-6, 465; 1767-74, n.p.]. She was a "free Mulatto" head of a Bay Hundred, Talbot County household of 1 male under 16, 1 female under 16 and a "Black" in 1776 [Carothers, *1776 Census of Maryland*, 156]. She was the mother of

       i.   Levin, born about 1763, indicted for an unspecified offense in Sussex County in May 1780 [RG 4805, General Sessions 1767-94, frame 243], a delinquent taxable in Lewes and Rehoboth Hundred, Sussex County, in 1781, head of a Mispillion Hundred, Kent County, Delaware household of 8 "other free" in 1800 [DE:83].
9   ii.   ?Charles, born say 1764.

6. Samuel[2] Cornish, born say 1742, was taxable in Indian River and Angola Hundred, Sussex County, from 1773 to 1790 [Levy List 1767-83; 1780-96] and head of an Indian River, Sussex County household of 11 "other free" in 1800 [DE:437]. He died before 12 April 1811 when his Sussex County estate was administered by Rachel and William Cornish. His heirs were Rachel, William, John, Elon, Mary, Samuel, Rachel, Hetty and James Cornish, Sarah **Morris** and Nancy **Gurley**. Rachel was head of a Sussex County household of 4 "other free" in 1810 [DE:468] and an Indian River, Sussex County household of 2 "free colored" in 1820 [DE:222], perhaps the Rachel Cornish who was head of a Talbot County household of 4 "free colored" in 1830 or the one who was head of a Dorchester County household of 7 "free colored" in 1830. Their children may have been

       i.   Nancy **Gurley**, probably the wife of Bryan **Gurley**, head of a Sussex County household of 5 "other free" in 1810 [DE:425] and 8 "free colored" in 1820 [DE:218].
       ii.   William, taxable in Indian River Hundred in Sussex County in 1797 [RG 4200.027, Levy Court, reel 2, frame 176].
       iii. John[2], born 1776-1794, head of a Sussex County household of 4 "other free" in 1810 [DE:427] and head of an Indian River, Sussex County household of 7 "free colored" in 1820 [DE:220].

    iv. Rachel.
    v. Samuel.
    vi. Hetty.
    vii. Sarah, married Nathaniel **Morris**, "free Mulattoes," on 5 December 1802 [Records of the United Presbyterian Churches of Lewes, Indian River and Cool Spring, Delaware 1756-1855, 315, 318].
    viii. James.

7.   Christianna Cornish, born say 1747, was the mother of
10   i. David, born about 1768.
11   ii. ?Henny, born say 1770.

8.   Ann[1] Cornish, born say 1744, paid a £1.10 fine in Talbot County court in November 1761 for having an illegitimate child [Criminal Record 1755-61, n.p.]. She was head of a Dorchester County household of 7 "other free" in 1790 and 6 in 1800 [MD:685]. She was the mother of
    i. ?Elisha, head of a Dorchester County household of 1 "other free" and a slave in 1800 [MD:684]. On 15 August 1806 he manumitted his forty-year-old slave Thomas **Jolly** by Dorchester County deed [Land Records HD 23:446].
    ii. Lisbon, born about 1790, registered in Dorchester County on 13 September 1815: *of a blackish colour...born free...son of Ann Cornish who was also born free, aged about 25 years* [Certificates of Freedom for Negroes 1806-64, 29].

9.   Charles Cornish, born say 1764, was listed as one of the recruits from Caroline County in the Revolution "to the 10th December" on 14 August 1781 [*Archives of Maryland*, 18:385]. He was head of a Talbot County household of 3 "other free" in 1790 and 6 in Baltimore City in 1800 [MD:169]. He may have been the father of
    i. Rachel, a "free black" who married Isaac **Elzey**, the slave of George Hall in St. Paul's Parish, Baltimore on 28 June 1795 [Reamy, *Records of St. Paul's Parish*, I:88].

10. David Cornish, born about 1768, registered in Dorchester County on 24 September 1821: *of a light chesnut colour...free born and is the son of Christianna Cornish who was free born, was raised in Somerset County...aged about 53 years.* He was head of a Dorchester County household of 4 "free colored" in 1830. He and his wife Nancy were the parents of
    i. Ann[2], born about 1806, registered in Dorchester County on 10 September 1822: *yellow complection...raised in Dorchester County and born free and is the Daughter of David Cornish and Nancy his wife, aged about 16 years* [Certificates of Freedom for Negroes 1806-64, 45, 47].

11. Henny Cornish, born say 1770, was the mother of
    i. Amelia, born about 1791, registered in Dorchester County on 24 October 1816: *of a chesnut colour...born free and is the Daughter of Henny Cornish who was also born free, aged about 25 years.*
    ii. Milley, born about 1794, registered in Dorchester County on 10 August 1821: *of a dark chesnut colour...born free and is the daughter of Henny who was also born free, aged about 27 years* [Certificates of Freedom for Negroes 1806-64, 34, 44].

Other members of the family in Maryland were
    i. Curtis, head of a Dorchester County household of 7 "free colored" in 1830.
    ii. Ann, head of a Montgomery County household of 4 "other free" in 1790.
    iii. Beck, head of a Talbot County household of 2 "other free" in 1790.

 iv. Ned, born about 1785, registered in Dorchester County on 25 July 1806: *blackish colour...born free, raised on Taylor's Island.*

 v. Jack, born about 1788, registered in Dorchester County on 15 August 1806: *blackish Colour...born free, raised in Dorchester County, aged 18 years.*

 vi. Delia **Evans**, born abut 1803, registered in Dorchester County on 11 September 1822: *of a dark chesnut colour...raised in Dorchester County and born free and is the daughter of Lucy Cornish, a free negro woman, aged about 19 years* [Certificates of Freedom for Negroes 1806-64, 1, 47].

COTT FAMILY

1. John[1] Cott, born say 1750, may have been identical to "Negro Jack" who successfully petitioned the Kent County, Delaware court for his freedom from Thomas Collins, Esquire, (of Duck Creek Hundred) on 23 May 1770. The court ruled that he be discharged and "Enjoy all the benefits a free Negro or Molato may or can within this government" [DSA, RG 3815.031, 1769-1771, frames 222, 235, 247]. John Cott was taxable in Little Creek Hundred from 1771 to 1780 except for 1775 when he was taxable in Duck Creek Hundred. He was a delinquent taxable in Dover Hundred in 1781 [RG 3535, Kent County Levy List, 1768-84, frames 103, 128, 184, 220, 262, 310, 334, 366, 445, 482]. He may have been the husband of Deborah **Cott**, daughter of William **Durham** who died before 27 July 1797 when administration on his Kent County estate was granted to (his wife) Mary **Durham** [WB N-1:179]. He may have been the father of

 i. John[2], a "Mulatto" taxable in Little Creek Hundred in 1797 [RG 3535, Kent County Levy List, 1785-97, frame 13], head of a Little Creek Hundred household of 3 "other free" in 1800 [DE:33] and 4 "free colored" in 1820 [DE:29], married to Sally Ann **Dean**, daughter of Jesse **Dean**, a "colored man," when Jesse made his Kent County will which was proved in December 1839 [WB R-1:160]. He was a 76-year-old "Mulatto" counted in the 1850 census for Little Creek Hundred living with 78-year-old Mary Cott [family no. 202].

COX FAMILY

1. Elizabeth Cox, born say 1688, was the white servant of Thomas Coleman on 12 November 1706 when the Charles County court ordered her to serve him an additional 250 days for running away. Later that day in the same court she confessed to having an illegitimate "Mollatto" child for which she was sold to Jacob Miller for 2,000 pounds of tobacco [Court Record 1704-10, 271, 274]. She may have been the ancestor of

 i. Abner, head of a Baltimore City household of 3 "other free" in 1800 [MD:174].

Members of the Cox family on the Eastern Shore of Maryland were

1 i. Jemima, born about 1741.
2 ii. Ann, born say 1748.

1. Jemima Cox, born about 1741, was a "Mulatto Wench" with twelve years and nine months to serve when she was listed in the Dorchester County estate of Margery Gibb on 30 December 1760 [Prerogative Inventories 76:333]. She may have been the mother of

 i. Stephen, head of a Dorchester County household of 5 "other free" in 1800 [MD:684].

2. Ann Cox, born say 1748, was bound as a "Mulatto" servant bound to Mary Hatcheson for thirty-one years in March 1769 when she confessed to the Kent County court that she had two illegitimate children during her service. The court

ordered that she be brought to court to be sold when she arrived to the age of thirty-one [Criminal Dockets 1766-71, nos. 8,9]. She was probably related to

    i. Levin, head of a Talbot County household of 7 "other free" in 1790.

    ii. Jacob, head of a Talbot County household of 6 "other free" in 1790.

    iii. Tom, head of a Talbot County household of 3 "other free" and 2 slaves in 1800 [MD:531].

CRASS FAMILY

1. Margaret Crass, born say 1728, was the servant of John Rawlings on 24 June 1746 when she confessed to the Prince George's County that she had a "Molatto" child. The court sold her child named Fryday to her master until the age of thirty-one for £5. The court convicted her of having another "Mulato" child on 23 August 1748, and on 22 August 1749 sold her for seven years to Kenedy Farrill [Court Proceedings, 1744-6, 517-8, 532; 1747-8, 331]. John Rawlings made a 10 March 1754 Frederick County will, proved 10 September 1756, by which he left "mulatto Friday" and "mulatto Robinson Crusoe" to his children [Liber A#1, folio 95]. Margaret was the mother of

    i. Friday, born 1 March 1746.

    ii. ?Robinson Crusoe, head of a Frederick County household of 8 "other free" in 1800 [MD:808].

CRAWLEY FAMILY

Members of the Crawley family of St. Mary's County were

    i. William, born say 1755, head of a St. Mary's County household of 7 "other free" in 1790 and 2 in 1800 [MD:422].

    ii. Benjamin, born say 1760, head of a St. Mary's County household of 5 "other free" in 1790.

    iii. Winnifred, born say 1770.

1. Winnifred Crawley, born say 1770, was the mother of

    i. ?Ann, born about 1792, registered in St. Mary's County on 13 March 1826: *aged about 34 years...a bright Mulatto...born free.*

    ii. Nealey, born about 1800, registered in St. Mary's County on 8 January 1824: *son of Wenefred Crawley, aged twenty four years...dark complexion...born free.*

    iii. John **Barton**, born about 1803, *registered in St. Mary's County on 8 January 1824: son of Winefred Crawley, aged about 21 years, bright complexion...his hair long & bushy* [Certificates of Freedom 1806-64, 65, 69].

CREEK FAMILY

1. William Creek, born say 1710, and members of his family were listed in the inventory of the Anne Arundel County estate of Samuel Chew on 6 January 1718:

2 East India Indians -	£30

and the inventory of the Anne Arundel and Calvert County estate of another Samuel Chew on 15 October 1737:

Negroes Age:	
Peg Creek 40 -	*£54*
. *Wm Creek 8 -*	*£41*
Ned Creek 6 -	*£30*

[Prerogative Inventories 1718, 464-9; 1737-1739, 218-223]. He successfully petitioned the Anne Arundel County court for his freedom from his master Samuel Chew on 8 March 1736/7. He testified that he was born in the East Indies and was carried as a young boy to England where he was apprenticed to an apothecary. Chew's nephew testified that William played a prank by giving someone a love potion. This so offended the apothecary's wife and daughter that the apothecary consigned William to the captain of a ship headed to Maryland [Judgment Record 1736-8, 126]. William was probably the ancestor of

- i. Jane[1]/ Jenny, head of a Washington County household of 5 "other free" in 1800 [MD:572] and 4 in 1810 [MD:535].
- ii. Richard, head of a Baltimore City household of 9 "other free" in 1810 [MD:271].
- iii. Jane[2], head of an Anne Arundel County household of 8 "other free" in 1810 [MD:86].
- iv. Hagar, head of an Anne Arundel County household of 6 "other free" in 1810 [MD:85].
- v. James, head of a Baltimore City household of 5 "other free" in 1810 [MD:529].
- vi. William[2], born before 1776, head of a Washington County household of 2 "free colored" in 1830.
- vii. Catherine, born before 1776, head of a Washington County household of 5 "free colored" in 1830.

CROMWELL FAMILY

1. Isaac Cromwell, born about 1709, was the forty-year-old "Mulatto servant" of Thomas Cresap of the old town of Potomac, Frederick County, when Cresap advertised in the 1 June 1749 issue of the *Pennsylvania Gazette* that he and Ann Greene, a forty-five-year-old English servant, had run away. Nine years later on 23 February 1758 Cresap advertised in the *Maryland Gazette* that Isaac spoke a little Dutch and English, that Anne Green was his wife, that they took their five or six-year-old daughter Susanna with them, and that they spent some time in Baltimore County but had since moved on [Scott, *Abstracts of the Pennsylvania Gazette, 1748-55*, 49; Green, *The Maryland Gazette 1727-61*, 206]. They were the parents of

2
- i. ?Mary, born say 1740.
- ii. Susanna, born about 1752.

2. Mary Cornwell/ Cromwell, born say 1740, the servant of Dr. Charles Neel, Sr., was presented by the Frederick County court for having a "base born mulatto child" in August 1760 for which the court ordered her sold for seven years in November 1760 [Court Minutes 1750-7, 151; 1758-62, 292-3]. Her children were most likely

- i. David, head of a Talbot County household of 8 "other free" in 1800 [MD:534].
- ii. George, head of a Talbot County household of 6 "other free" in 1800 [MD:531].
3
- iii. Milly, born say 1780.
- iv. William, head of a Baltimore County household of 6 "other free" in 1810 [MD:463].
- v. Charles, head of an Anne Arundel County household of 5 "other free" in 1810 [MD:97].

3. Milly Cromwell, born say 1780, was the mother of

- i. Mary, born about 1803, registered in Frederick County on 26 November 1819: *a bright Mulatto Girl, aged about Sixteen years...the daughter of a certain Milly Cromwell who was a free born woman as appears by the affidavit of Jacob Hoff* [Certificates of Freedom 1806-27, 102].

CUNNINGHAM FAMILY

1. Mary Cunningham, born say 1730, was living at John Kinsman's on 13 November 1750 when the Charles County court presented her for bearing a "Mullatto Child"

by information of constable Alexander MacPherson [Court Record 1750, 140]. She may have been the ancestor of

    i.   Waters, a "Mulatto" child bound as an apprentice to John Williams in Frederick County on 9 March 1753 [Orders 1751-3, 449].

    ii. John, head of a Washington County, Maryland household of 3 "other free" in 1800 [MD:570].

    iii. Benjamin[1], head of a Hampshire County, Virginia household of 10 "other free" in 1810 [VA:818].

    iv. Philip[1], head of a King George County, Virginia household of 8 "other free" in 1810 [VA:193].

    v. Benjamin[2], head of a King George County, Virginia household of 5 "other free" in 1810 [VA:193].

    vi. Cyrus, born about 1777, registered in King George County, Virginia, on 28 May 1799: *of a dark yellow Colour aged about twenty two years and about five feet ten inches high is now a free man, has served William Hooe, Gent., of this County twenty one years* [Register of Free Persons, no.10].

    vii. Philip[2], Jr., head of a King George County household of 2 "other free" in 1810 [VA:195].

    viii. Jas.(?), head of a King George County household of 1 "other free" in 1810 [VA:195].

CURTIS FAMILY

Members of the Curtis family in Maryland were

    i. Jonathan, born say 1720, called a "Free Negro" on 6 November 1744 when the Spotsylvania County, Virginia court ordered him to post bond of £20 for his good behavior because John Doncastle complained that he had broken open some of his locks [Orders 1738-49, 286]. He was called "Jonathan Curtis late of Charles County, Planter," in March 1749/50 in Charles County court when William Hunter and Company of Spotsylvania County sued him for a debt of £10.12. He was called a "free Negroe" in Hunter's accounts which were copied into the court record. The accounts were from October 1746 to 18 November 1747 and included a pocket book, shoes, rum, cloth, sheeting, buttons, thread, handkerchiefs, and a padlock. Samuel Luckett was Jonathan's security [Charles County Court Records 1748-50, 630-2].

    ii. Cloe, born say 1740, a "free Negro," married Isaac, "negro of Jane Taney," in St. Mary's County in 1761 [Parsons, *Marriage Register of Rev. Joseph Mosley*, 24].

    iii. Will **Ferrall**, aka Will **Butler** and Will Curtis, a "yellow slave," a house carpenter who ran away from Edward Mattingly of St. Mary's County and was seen in Virginia according to the 22 September 1768 issue of the *Virginia Gazette* [Rind edition, p.3, col. 2].

1   iv. Lucy, born say 1753.

    v. Joseph, head of a St. Mary's County household of 7 "other free" in 1790 and 4 in Charles County in 1800 [MD:514].

    vi. Esther, head of a St. Mary's County household of 7 "other free" in 1790 and 5 in 1800 [MD:424].

    vii. Mary[1], born say 1730, a "negro" who owed £5 to the St. Mary's County estate of Thomas Phillips on 23 November 1757 [Prerogative Inventories 65:152-3], head of a St. Mary's County household of 5 "other free" in 1790 and a "blk." head of a St. Mary's County household of 5 "other free" in 1810 [MD:189].

2   viii. Sarah, born about 1759.

3   ix. Milly, born about 1759.

    x. Samuel, "F.N." head of a Charles County household of 2 "other free" and a slave in 1790.

xi. Margaret[1], born about 1764, head of a St. Mary's County household of 10 "other free" in 1800 [MD:417] and 3 in 1810 [MD:217], registered in St. Mary's County on 10 August 1808: *forty four years of age, black complexion, was born free & raised in the County* [Certificates of Freedom 1806-64, 2].

xii. Mary[2], head of a St. Mary's County household of 2 "other free" in 1790 and 2 in Charles County in 1800 [MD:537], perhaps the mother of Gerard Curtis who registered in St. Mary's County on 20 February 1822: *son of Mary Curtis...about twenty two years of age, of a dark complexion...born free* [Certificates of Freedom 1806-64, 58].

4 xiii. Rebecca[1], born say 1760.

xiv. James, head of a St. Mary's County household of 3 "other free" in 1800 [MD:402].

xv. Mary[3], born say 1774, married Francis **Savoy** on 16 February 1795 in St. Mary's Mattawoman Parish, Charles County [Colonial Dames of America, *Records of St. Mary's Parish, 1793-1861*, 162].

5 xvi. Elizabeth, born about 1779.

6 xvii. Ann, born about 1782.

xviii. Nance, born about 1783, registered in St. Mary's County on 8 August 1806: *about twenty three years of age, dark complexion, was free born.*

xix. Sophia, born about 1784, registered in St. Mary's County on 9 November 1808: *by birth a free woman, about twenty four years of age...light complexion.*

xx. Minta, born about 1785, "blk." head of a St. Mary's County household of 5 "other free" in 1810 [MD:176], registered in St. Mary's County on 20 February 1817: *aged thirty two years or thereabouts...Dark Mulatto, long hair.*

xxi. Mary, born about 1786, registered in St. Mary's County on 2 August 1814: *aged about twenty eight years or thereabouts...Complexion Black - hair short & Curley...born free.*

xxii. Matilda, born about 1788, registered in St. Mary's County on 8 August 1806: *about eighteen years of age, dark complexion, was free born.*

xxiii. Cornelius, born about 1788, registered in St. Mary's County on 20 September 1808: *about twenty years of age, black complexion, was born free & raised in the county...big mouth & thick lips, large boney hands, low forehead, short Woolly hair.*

xxiv. Rebecca[2], born about 1789, registered in St. Mary's County on 8 August 1806: *about seventeen years of age, of a dark complexion, was free born.*

xxv. Henry, born about 1796, registered in St. Mary's County on 29 April 1818: *son of Nancy Curtis, aged about thirty two years...dark complexion* [Certificates of Freedom 1806-64, 1, 2, 3, 28, 38, 76].

1. Lucy Curtis, born say 1753, was head of a St. Mary's County household of 6 "other free" in 1800 [MD:416]. She was the mother of

    i. Gustavus[1], born about 1773, registered in St. Mary's County on 16 May 1820: *son of Lucy Curtis...about 47 years - of a dark complexion...born free.* Gusty Curtis was a "blk." head of a St. Mary's County household of 5 "other free" in 1810 [MD:198].

    ii. Nancy, born about 1784, registered in St. Mary's County on 29 March 1819: *daughter of Lucy Curtis...about thirty five years of age, Black complexion...born free* [Certificates of Freedom 1806-64, 47, 55].

2. Sarah Curtis, born about 1759, was head of a St. Mary's County household of 5 "other free" in 1790, 10 in 1800 [MD:411] and 9 in 1810 [MD:189]. She registered in St. Mary's County on 20 August 1814: *aged fifty five years or thereabouts...Complexion rather Black - hair short & gray...born free.* She was the mother of

    i. Margaret[2], born about 1792, registered in St. Mary's County on 22 June

             1814: *Daughter of Sarah Curtis, aged about twenty two years, complexion dark.* She was called Margaret Curtis alias **Shorter** when she registered on 14 August 1833.

    ii. Susanna, born about 1802, registered in St. Mary's County on 10 April 1823: *daughter of Sarah Curtis, aged about twenty one years...light complexion...born free* [Certificates of Freedom 1806-64, 26, 61, 99].

3.   Milly Curtis, born about 1759, was a "blk." head of a St. Mary's County household of 6 "other free" in 1810 [MD:192]. She registered in St. Mary's County on 14 August 1812: *aged fifty three years or thereabouts...complexion black - hair short and curley...born free.* She was the mother of

    i.   Sarah, born about 1776, registered in St. Mary's County on 14 August 1812: *aged thirty two years or thereabouts...complexion dark - hair short & curley...born free being the Daughter of Milly Curtis.*

    ii. Mary, born about 1789, registered in St. Mary's County on 14 August 1812: *aged twenty three years...complexion black - hair short & woolly...born free being the Daughter of Milly Curtis.*

    iii. Gustavus[2], born about 1794, registered in St. Mary's County on 14 August 1812: *aged eighteen years...Complexion black...born free being the son of Milly Curtis* [Certificates of Freedom 1806-64, 20, 21].

4.   Rebecca[1] Curtis born say 1760, was head of a St. Mary's County household of 7 "other free" in 1800 [MD:410] and 9 in 1810 [MD:197]. She was the mother of

    i.   Henry, born about 1782, registered in St. Mary's County on 6 September 1820: *son of Rebecca...about thirty eight years of age, of a dark complexion...born free.*

    ii. Nancy, born about 1793, registered in St. Mary's County on 8 April 1819: *Daughter of Rebecca Curtis...about twenty six years of age, of a Dark Complexion...born free.*

    iii. Harriot, born about 1797, registered in St. Mary's County on 20 February 1822: *daughter of Rebecca Curtis...about twenty four years of age, of light complexion...born free.*

    iv. Sarah Ann, born about 1800, registered in St. Mary's County on 8 April 1819: *daughter of Rebecca Curtis...about nineteen years of age, of a Dark Complexion...born free.*

    v.   Elizabeth, born about 1803, registered in St. Mary's County on 4 May 1819: *daughter of Rebecca Curtis, about sixteen years, of a bright complexion...born free.*

    vi. Joseph, born about 1805, registered in St. Mary's County on 29 July 1828: *son of Rebecca, aged about twenty three years...dark complexion...born free* [Certificates of Freedom 1806-64, 49, 50, 56, 58, 78].

5.   Elizabeth Curtis, born about 1779, registered in St. Mary's County on 7 June 1814: *aged thirty five years or thereabouts...complexion dark, hair short and wooly...born free.* She may have been identical to Betty Curtis who was head of a Charles County household of 2 "other free" in 1810 [MD:334]. She was the mother of

    i.   John, born about 1798, registered in St. Mary's County on 8 April 1819: *son of Elizabeth Curtis...about twenty one years of age, dark complexion...born free.*

    ii. Eleanor, born about 1801, registered in St. Mary's County on 13 September 1821: *daughter of Elizabeth Curtis...aged about twenty years, of a bright complexion...born free.*

    iii. Rebecca, born about 1803, registered in St. Mary's County on 8 April 1819: *Daughter of Elizabeth Curtis...about sixteen years of age, of a dark complexion...born free.*

    iv. Nancy, born about 1805, registered in St. Mary's County on 13 September 1821: *daughter of Elizabeth Curtis...about sixteen years of a age, of a dark complexion...born free* [Certificates of Freedom 1806-64, 26, 49, 58].

6.   Ann Curtis, born about 1782, was head of a St. Mary's County household of 6 "other free" in 1800 [MD:409]. She registered in St. Mary's County on 10 August 1812: *aged thirty years...complexion not very black - hair short...born free*. She was the mother of
   i.   Bednego, born about 1799, registered in St. Mary's County on 4 May 1819: *son of Ann Curtis...about twenty years of age, of a dark complexion...born free.*
   ii. Joseph, born about 1800, registered in St. Mary's County on 4 September 1820: *son of Ann Curtis...aged about twenty, dark complexion* [Certificates of Freedom 1806-64, 19, 50, 55].

DALTON FAMILY

1.   Henry[1] Dalton, born 8 September 1750, a "mulatto" and apparently the son of a white woman, was bound to Samuel Pruitt until the age of thirty-one years in Frederick County court in August 1750 [Rice, *Frederick County, Maryland Judgment Records 1748-65*, 49]. He was probably the son of Ann Dorton who was presented by the Prince George's County court on 27 March 1750 for having a base born child (no race indicated) on information of Jane Martin [Court Record 1749-50, 128]. He was a "Mulatto" who petitioned the Frederick County court on 23 November 1775 that he had been bound to Samuel Pruitt in 1750 but that Pruitt had since died and that his present master John Randle had no other claim to him than his marrying the widow of the deceased. The court ordered that he be at his liberty [Minutes 1773-5, 420]. He married Eleanor **Russell** on 4 June 1781 [Barnes, *Maryland Marriages, 1778-1800*]. Eleanor was probably a descendant of James **Russell**, a "Mallatto" who won his freedom in Charles County court on 13 March 1721 because he was the son of a white woman and had reached the age of thirty-one [Court Records K-2:236]. He was living in Prince George's County by 26 August 1729 [Court Record 1729-30, 136]. Henry was taxable in Monongalia County, Virginia, from 1791 to 1821: called "Henry Dorton Senr. a man of color" starting in 1810, listed with 2 tithables starting in 1802, his profession a farmer in 1820 [PPTL 1783-1821, frames 91, 101, 177, 216, 264, 319, 373, 455, 536, 611, 679, 898, 787, 856]. He was head of a Eastern District, Monongalia County household of 12 whites for 1810 [VA:495], 8 "free colored" in 1820 [VA:169] and 8 "free colored" in 1830 [VA:344]. He was granted a pension for his service in the Revolution, stating in his application on 31 November 1832 that he was born in Bladensburg, Maryland, in 1748, enlisted in 1777 at Redstone settlement near Brownsville, Pennsylvania, resided in Prince George's County for nine years after the Revolution and then moved to Monongalia County. He died on 11 June 1836 [NARA, S.5362; http://fold3.com/image/16979121]. He was probably the father of
   i.   Daniel Dorton, born before 1776, head of a Harford County household of 3 "free colored" in 1830.
   ii.   Levi, born about 1785, a "man of color" taxable in Monongalia County from 1805 to 1821: his profession a mason in 1820 [PPTL 1783-1821, frames 406, 583, 629, 787, 856, 916, 976]. He married Hannah Billey, 12 January 1806 Monongalia County bond and was head of an Eastern District, Monongalia County household of 3 whites in 1810 [VA:495], 9 "free colored" in 1820 [VA:169] and 12 "free colored" in 1830 [VA:344], a "Mulatto," born in Maryland, listed in the 1850 census for Monongalia County with (wife?) Ann and with $500 real estate [VA:481].
   iii. Elizabeth, born 1776-1796, head of a Monongalia County household of 2 "free colored" in 1820 [VA:169].
   iv.   John, a "man of color" taxable in Monongalia County from 1810 to 1821: his profession a mason in 1820 [PPTL 1783-1821, frames 536, 787, 856, 916, 976]. He was head of an Eastern District, Monongalia County

household of 3 "free colored" in 1820 [VA:169] and 7 in 1830 [VA:344].
v.   Henry[2], Jr., born about 1794, a "man of color" taxable in Monongalia
County from 1812 to 1821, his profession a stone mason in 1820 [PPTL
1783-1821, frames 611, 787, 856, 916, 976]. He was head of an Eastern
District, Monongalia County household of 4 "free colored" in 1830
[VA:344] and a "Mulatto" head of a Decatur, Washington County, Ohio
household with white wife Elizabeth in 1850 [family no. 76], a "Mulatto"
farmer, born in Virginia, counted in the 1870 census for Troy Township,
Athens County, Ohio, in 1870 with "Mulatto" (wife?) Hannah (born in
Ohio) and $400 real estate [OH:20].
vi.   Bethuel, born about 1797, a 53-year-old "Mulatto" counted in the Eastern
District, Monongalia County census of 1850 with $600 real estate with
white (erased?) wife Nancy [VA:469, family no. 185], a "Mulatto"
widower living in Clinton District, Monongalia County in 1880 [VA:17].
vii.   Nimrod, born 1794-1806, head of a Monongalia County household of 1
"free colored" in 1820 [VA:169].
viii.   ?Malachi, born about 1796, head of a Wilkes Township, Gallia County,
Ohio household of 7 "free colored" in 1840 [VA:53], a "Mulatto" farmer,
born in Virginia, counted in the 1850 Wilkeson, Vinton County, Ohio
census with (wife?) Mahala Dorton [OH:589, family no. 1026].

DAVIS FAMILY

1.   Mary Davis, born say 1657, the daughter of Richard Davis of London, England,
was a white woman who married a "Negroe man" named Domingo, the slave of
Joseph Tilley of Calvert County. Mary and Domingo were living with Lord
Baltimore when she wrote the details of her marriage and the birth and baptism
of her children in a Bible. Her daughter Rose produced a transcription of the Bible
in Anne Arundel County court in August 1715 in an unsuccessful petition for her
freedom [Court Judgments 1715-7, 93, 178, 244-6]. Mary and Domingo were the
parents of
i.   Thomas, born 14 March 1677 on Lord Baltimore's plantation on Lyon's
Creek in Calvert County, baptized by Mr. Wessley(?) in the house of
Richard Massoms with James and Ann Thompson as godparents.
2   ii.   Rose, born 11 August 1684.

2.   Rose Davis, born 11 August 1684 at the "Top of the Hill" plantation in St. Mary's
County, was baptized at Nottley Hall by a priest named Mr. Richard Hebert with
Henry and Rose Wharton as godparents. Rose was thirty-one years old in August
1715 when she brought an unsuccessful suit for her freedom against Henry
Darnall in Anne Arundel County court [Court Judgments 1715-7, 93, 178, 244-6].
Rose was listed in the Anne Arundel County inventory of the estate of Henry
Darnall (Sr.) in 1713:

At the home house	
one Mallata woman Sue 33 yrs. old -	£28
At James Watland's Quarter	
one Mallata woman Rose 29 yrs. old -	£28
At the Woodyard	
one Mallata David a Carpenter 45 yrs. -	£40
one do Frank do 40 yrs. old	£40
one do Jack do 35 yrs. old -	£30
one do Tom a Carpenter 30 yrs. old -	£45
one do Charles do 15 yrs. old -	£25
one Negro Bently 20 yrs. old -	£30
one Mallata woman Moll with child a month old 34 yrs. old -	£29

[Prerogative Court Inventories and Accounts, Vol. 33B, 221-6].
In March 1779 her granddaughter Rosamond **Bentley** petitioned the Prince
George's County court for her freedom, and in August 1781 Rosamond and her

brother William and sisters Mary, Eleanor and Margaret **Bentley** won their cases. In an apparent effort to minimize their African ancestry, Rose's witnesses testified that the family descended from Mary Davis, a white English woman, and an East Indian man–instead of a "Negroe man" as stated in Mary Davis's Bible. And her witnesses described Rose's daughter as "Indian Polly" [Judgment Record 1777-82, 713-5]. Rose was the mother of

    i. Polly, born say 1710.

Anne Arundel County:
1. Elizabeth Davis, born say 1736, confessed to the Anne Arundel County court in August 1758 that she was the mother of two "Molatto" children named Sam and David. The court sold her children to James Barnes until the age of thirty-one and ordered that she serve a total of fourteen years [Judgment Record 1757-60, 320, 324]. She was the mother of

    i. Sam, born June 1754, head of an Anne Arundel County household of 2 "other free" in 1810 [MD:81].
    ii. David, born in February 1757.
    iii. ?John, head of an Anne Arundel County household of 6 "other free" in 1790 and 5 "other free" and 5(?) slaves in 1810 [MD:78].

Queen Anne's County:
1. Belvidera Davis, born say 1731, was a white spinster woman who was convicted by the Queen Anne's County court for having "Mulatto" child by a "Negroe." The court sold her "Mollatta" child Anne to Nathaniel Wright for 2,520 pounds of tobacco in June 1751 [Judgments 1750-1, 269; Criminal Record 1751-9, 27-8]. She may have been the ancestor of

    i. Abraham, head of a Caroline County household of 5 "other free" in 1790 and 5 in Talbot County in 1800 [MD:517].

1. Eleanor Davis, born say 1755, was fined 30 shillings by the Queen Anne's County court in March 1774 for having a child by a "Negroe" slave in May 1772 [Judgment Records 1771-80, 137-9]. She ran away from her master James Buller of Queen Town, Queen Anne's County, before 27 September 1775 when he put an ad in the *Pennsylvania Gazette* offering a reward for her return: *an English servant woman, has been in the country about 8 or 9 years, she was sold for a mulatto bastard; she is a well set woman, about 5 feet 3 or 4 inches high, had dark coloured hair* [*Pennsylvania Gazette*, http://accessible.com].

Other members of a Davis family were

    i. Charles, born about 1763, enlisted in the 2nd Maryland Regiment on 23 April 1782: *residence: Baltimore, age 19, 5'4-1/2" height, complexion Negro* [NARA, M246, roll 34, frame 434 of 587].
    ii. Moses, head of a Baltimore City household of 16 "other free" in 1800 [MD:190].
    iii. Abraham, "Mulatto" head of a Charles County household of 7 "other free" in 1790, perhaps the Abraham Davis who was head of a St. Mary's County household of 8 "other free" in 1800 [MD:431].
    iv. Daniel, head of a Baltimore City household of 4 "other free" in 1800 [MD:186].
    v. William, "free negro" head of a Prince George's County household of 2 "other free" in 1800 [MD:301], perhaps the William Davis who was head of an Annapolis household of 3 "other free" in 1810 [MD:116].
    vi. James, head of a Frederick County household of 2 "other free" in 1800 [MD:835].

DAWSON FAMILY

1. Jane Dawson, born say 1695, was presented by the Charles County court on 9 November 1714 for having an illegitimate "Mallatto" child by information of constable John Dodson and on evidence of (her master and mistress?) William and Elizabeth Midellton [Court Record 1711-5, 469]. She was probably the mother of

    i. Ann, mother of a "Mallatto" child Jenny, born 9 August 1748, sold by the Prince George's County court to William Hardy for 750 pounds of tobacco on 22 November 1748 [Court Record 1748-9, 30]. Jenny was a "Mallato" girl bound until the age of thirty-one when she was listed in the Prince George's County estate of William Hardy on 26 June 1758 [Prerogative Inventories 64:439-41].

Talbot County

Members of a Dawson family in Talbot County were

    i. Tom, head of a Talbot County household of 2 "other free" in 1800 [MD:540], perhaps the husband of Patty Dawson who registered in Talbot County on 13 June 1818: *a negro woman...about 45 years of age, 5 feet 2 ½ Inches high...born free and raised in the County.*

    ii. Isaac, born about 1780, registered in Talbot County on 19 July 1806: *five feet, one inch high, twenty six years of age, of a yellowish complextion...raised in Talbot county...free born* [Certificates of Freedom 1807-15, 84, 150].

    iii. Stepney, head of a Kent County household of 1 "other free" in 1800 [MD:172].

DAY FAMILY

1. Elizabeth Day, born say 1695, was the indentured servant of John Sanders on 13 March 1710/1 when she admitted in Charles County court that she had an illegitimate "Malatto" child by a "Negro man named Quasey belonging to her master." And on 11 August 1713 she admitted to the court that she had a second mixed-race child [Court Record 1710-3, 62, 70; E-2:301, 304]. Her descendants may have been

    i. Mary, born say 1744, confessed to the Prince George's County court on 27 March 1764 that she had a "Mulatto" child. The court ordered that she be sold for seven years and that her five-week-old daughter Lydia be sold to her master, Henry Purdie, until the age of thirty-one [Court Record 1763-4, 60].

    ii. Benjamin[1], "Mulatto" head of a Charles County household of 6 "other free" in 1790. Samuel Hanson sued him and Thomas **Thompson** in Charles County court for a debt of 4,020 pounds of tobacco on 13 November 1770. (He was called Benjamin Davis in his first appearance, but called Benjamin Day in the index and in his second appearance) [Court Record 1770-2, 216; 1772-3, 577].

    iii. Henrietta, "Mulatto" head of a Charles County household of 3 "other free" in 1790.

    iv. Vinney, "Mulatto" head of a Charles County household of 4 "other free" in 1790.

    v. William[1], "Mulatto" head of a Charles County household of 1 "other free" in 1790.

    vi. Henry, born before 1776, head of a Charles County household of 4 "free colored" in 1830.

Other members of a Day family were

    i. Jacob[1], head of a Kent County household of 4 "other free" in 1800 [MD:148].

ii. Jacob[2], head of a Talbot County household of 3 "other free" and 2 slaves in 1800 [MD:521].

DEAN FAMILY

Delaware
1. James[1] Dean, born say 1737, was taxable in Kent County, Delaware, in 1755. He was called a carpenter on 25 May 1762 when he purchased 5 acres in Little Creek Hundred for £30 with Jonas Miller and Edward **Norman** (signing) as witnesses [DB Q:57, 89]. His 2 June 1787 Little Creek Hundred, Kent County will, proved 26 June 1787, left his land, house, and personal estate to his wife Sarah (**Hughes**), daughters Rebecca and Keziah, and son Jesse [WB M, fol. 144-5]. His children were

    iii. Rebecca.

    iv. Keziah, born 4 May 1757, sued Thomas Murphy in Kent County court on 12 May 1773 for unjustly detaining her seven days past the time she was bound to him as an apprentice "for relief of the poor." She stated that she was born on 4th May and should have been released on her birthday. Mary Freeman was her witness. She had an illegitimate child by Peter **$ern/ Lantron** about December 1773 [DSA, RG 3505, MS case files, Petitions-Apprentices May 1773; Indictments May 1774].

2   v. Jesse[1], born say 1762.

2. Jesse[1] Dean, born say 1762, was taxable in Little Creek Hundred, Kent County, in 1783 and a "Mulattoe" taxable on 15 acres and a wooden house in 1797 and 1798. He was head of a Little Creek Hundred, Kent County household of 5 "other free" in 1800 [DE:34]. He was married to Elizabeth **Durham** by 2 January 1806 when he was paid her share of the estate of her father William **Durham**. In his Kent County will, proved in December 1839, he called himself a "colored man." He left his land and other estate to his wife Rebecca, sons William and Jesse, Elisha **Durham** "colored man," daughter Sally Ann **Cott** (wife of John **Cott**) granddaughter Mary, and Elijah **Concealor**, son of his previous wife. He also adopted his sons William and Jesse who were born to his wife Rebecca before their marriage. Perhaps Elisha **Durham** was his illegitimate son since he left him furniture, carpets, his best cow, and other stock and listed him in the will before his daughter [WB R-1, 160]. His children were

    i. William.

    ii. Jesse[2].

    iii. Sally Ann, wife of John **Cott** who was head of a Little Creek Hundred household of 3 "other free" in 1800 [DE:33] and 4 "free colored" in 1820 [DE:29].

Other members of the Dean family were

    i. James[2], born say 1770, a "Mulattoe" taxable in 1797 on 3 acres and a small house in Kent County, Delaware, and farming another 83 acres which belonged to Elijah **Concellor**. He was head of a Duck Creek Hundred, Kent County household of 7 "free colored" in 1820 [DE:54].

    ii. James[3], born 1776-1794, head of a Duck Creek Hundred, Kent County, Delaware household of 9 "free colored" in 1820 [DE:54].

    iii. Michael, head of a Caroline County household of 4 "other free" in 1790 and a "negro" head of a Caroline County household of 6 "other free" in 1810 [MD:188].

    iv. David, born before 1776, head of a Murderkill Hundred, Kent County household of 5 "free colored" in 1820 [DE:14].

    v. Jessa, born before 1776, head of a Little Creek Hundred, Kent County household of 9 "free colored" in 1820 [DE:28]. She may have been the mother of "Free man of color" Jesse Dean who died intestate in Kent County, leaving 50 acres of land before 1843 when his half brothers John

Dean and Thomas **Butcher** petitioned the legislature for title to the property, stating that they were the children of the same white man by different women of color [Schweninger, *Race, Slavery, and Free Blacks, Series 1*, 33].

Maryland
1.   Richard Dean, born say 1720, sold a black cow to Richard Smith by Frederick County bill of sale on 6 March 1758, making his mark "RD" [Land Record F:458]. He purchased lot no. 66 in Sharpsburg from Joseph Chapline by Frederick County deed of 21 January 1764. The word "Negro" followed his name in the two places it appeared on the original deed and in the three places it appeared in Joseph Chapline's original acknowledgment of the deed. But it was crossed out, and the clerk did not transcribe anything about race when he recorded the deed. The word "Black" was inserted in place of "Negro" in the three places on Joseph Chapline's acknowledgment, perhaps at some later time [Land Record J:232-3; MSA Special Collections 2477-5-47, location 00/66/09/28]. The deed may have identified Richard by race in order to distinguish him from a white Richard Dean who lived in the same area. Richard and his wife Catherine Dean sold this land to Griffith James for 55 shillings on 16 June 1764, making his mark "RD" [Land Record J:652-3]. Catherine was apparently the daughter of Robert **Perle/ Pearl** who named her in his 3 September 1765 Frederick County will [Prerogative Court Wills 33:351]. They were probably married and living at Monocacy Hundred on 24 November 1747 when the Prince George's County court quashed a grand jury presentment against Katherine **Perle** for bastardy [Court Record 1747-8, 90, 297]. On 2 August 1777 Richard purchased 50 acres in Washington County from Moses Chapline for £20 Pennsylvania currency, and the deed was recorded with "Del'vrd to Massom Dean" in the margin. On 23 January 1779 Massam Dean, his wife Ann Dean and (his mother) Catherine Dean sold 50 acres called *Resurvey on Roots Hill* in Washington County to Christian Road for £425.10 Maryland currency [Land Record A:13-5; B:448-9]. Richard and Catherine's children were identified in the Washington County chancery court suit of Toby heirs vs. Chapline from 1810 to 1812 [MSA accession no. 17,898-638-1/2; location 1/35/5]. They were
   i.   Massam, born say 1747, apparently named for Robert **Pearl's** former master Richard Marsham. He enrolled in the first militia company organized for the Revolutionary War in the Elizabeth Town District of Frederick County on 6 January 1776 [Peden, *Revolutionary Patriots of Washington County, Maryland*]. He purchased 26 acres in Washington County on the Old Town Creek for £32.10 on 24 March 1781 from Francis Deakins [Liber B:498-9]. He was taxable on 52 acres called *Town Creek* in the assessment for Skipton and Fifteen Miles Creek District of Allegany County in 1793 [Assessment Record, Maryland Archives digital file, image 46]. He was head of an Allegany County household of 9 "other free" in 1800 (called Marsham Dean) [MD:3] and was counted as a white male over the age of forty-five in Perry County, Ohio, in 1820 [OH:5]. He left a 16 June 1825 Perry County, Ohio will which named his children Massom, Jr., Catherine (later married George Higgins), Mary Ann (never married) and James Dean as well as his granddaughter Elizabeth Jemiah, daughter of Massom, Jr., and Mary Brooks [WB AB:52].
   ii. Catherine, born say 1753, married Charles Dowd, a Revolutionary War veteran who died 14 June 1821 in Monongalia, Virginia [Pierce, *Selected Final Pension Payment Vouchers--Maryland*, 51]. About 1800 she and her brother James Dean testified about the location of a fence on the tract of land called *Resurvey on Hills, Dales and the Vineyard* in Washington County which was the property line of Michael Toby and Massam Dean [MSA accession no. 17,898-638-1/2; location 1/35/5, depositions of Jonas Hogmire and Frederick Rohrer]. She and Nancy **Dowd** were called "free persons of color" on 13 November 1818 when a group of white men were indicted by the Monongalia, Virginia court for committing a riot on them

by the information of Charles Dowd [Zinn, *Monongalia County Records of the District, Superior and County Courts*, 8:136].

iii. James, born say 1755, enrolled in the first militia company organized for the Revolutionary War in the Elizabeth Town District of Frederick County on 6 January 1776 [Peden, *Revolutionary Patriots of Washington County, Maryland*]. He was head of a Washington County household of 5 "other free" in 1790 and 5 in 1800 [MD:641]. About 1810 he made a deposition in the Washington County chancery case of Toby heirs vs. Chapline about events which had taken place before 13 July 1779 when Joseph Chapline sold part of a tract of land called *Resurvey on Hills, Dales and the Vineyard* near Little Antietam Creek to Michael Toby. James stated that his brother Massam Dean purchased part of the tract from Joseph Chapline, and not obtaining a deed from Chapline, sold the land to Michael Toby. He deposed that his father had fenced a road that ran along the property line into "Richard Dean's Meadow" [MSA accession no. 17,898-638-1/2; location 1/35/5].

Endnotes:
1. Many thanks to Beverly Dean Peoples of Raleigh, North Carolina, for her research of the Richard Dean family
   hhtp://freepages.genealogy.rootsweb.com/~ladeanxx/richarddeane.htm.

DELANEY/ DULANEY FAMILY

Members of the Delaney/ Dulaney family of Maryland were
    i. Isaac, head of a Baltimore City household of 8 "other free" in 1800 [MD:184].
1   ii. Mary, born say 1770.

1. Mary Dulaney, born say 1770, a "free woman of colour," was living in Prince George's County from 1813 to 1820 when her children obtained certificates of freedom. She was the mother of
   i. Elizabeth, born about 1790, registered in Prince George's County on 25 November 1813: *a bright mulatto woman, about 23 years old...raised in the family of John T. Wood of Prince George's County...daughter of Mary Dulany, a free woman of color.*
   ii. William, born about 1792, registered in Prince George's County on 25 November 1813: *a bright mulatto man, about 21 years old...son of Mary Dulany.*
   iii. Moses, born about 1798, registered in Prince George's County on 30 March 1815: *a dark mulatto youth, about 17 years old...son of Mary Dulany.*
   iv. Nancy, born about 1801, registered in Prince George's County on 15 May 1820: *a Negro woman of dark complexion who is about 19 years old...daughter of Mary Dulany* [Provine, *Registrations of Free Negroes*, 16, 34].

DEVAN FAMILY

1. William Devan, born about 1767, registered in Frederick County in 1817: *a Mulatto Man aged about fifty years, about five feet five Inches high...born of a white woman in the family of Richard Simpson to Whom said William Devan was bound by the Orphans Court of the County aforesaid as appears by the affidavit of Charles Simpson.* He may have been the father of
   i. Lydia, born about 1786, registered in Frederick County in 1817: *a Mulatto woman about five feet Eight Inches high...about thirty one years of age is a free born woman, she being the issue of a free born woman as appears by the affidavit of John Rene* [Certificates of Freedom 1806-27, 78]

DOBSON FAMILY

1.   Margaret Dobson, born say 1722, the white servant of Nicholas Goldsborough of St. Peter's Parish, confessed to the Talbot County court in November 1742 that she had a child by a "Negroe." The court ordered her sold for seven years and bound her daughter Diana to her master until the age of thirty-one. In March 1744/5 she was sold for a second term of seven years, and the court bound her "Mulatto" son James to her master until the age of thirty-one. She was living in St. Michaels Parish on 20 October 1747 when she was convicted of having her son Jethro by a "Negro" [Judgment Record 1742, 293-4; 1744-5, 238-9; Criminal Record 1747-50, n.p.]. She was the mother of

2   i.   Diana, born 6 May 1742.
     ii. James, born in 1745, head of a Talbot County household of 4 "other free" in 1800 [MD:507].
     iii. Jethro, born about January 1747, nine months old on 20 October 1747 when he was sold to Nicholas Benson for the £4 which was due to him for keeping Jethro for the first nine months of his life [Judgment Record 1747-50, n.p].

2.   Diana Dobson, born 6 May 1742, was called Dido Dobson, the servant of Nicholas Goldsborough, Sr., in November 1761 when she admitted to the Talbot County court that she had a child by a "Negro." The court sold her son John for thirty-one years to her master for £5. She was called Diana Dobson in November 1764 when she was convicted by the Talbot County court of having two illegitimate children [Criminal Record 1761-7, 311-3]. She was the mother of

     i.   John, born about 1761.
     ii. ?Abram, head of a Talbot County household of 5 "other free" in 1800 [MD:537].
     iii. ?Benjamin, born before 1776, head of a Sussex County household of 5 "other free" in 1810 [DE:444] and 5 "free colored" in 1820 [DE:324].

They was also a Dobson family that were slaves in adjoining Queen Anne's County:
     i.   Jemmy, born about 1704, a "Negroe" tanner listed in the inventory of the estate John Sayer Blake on 18 May 1750.
     ii. Jenny, born about 1717, listed in the inventory of John Sayer Blake.
     iii. Phil, born about 1739, listed in the inventory of John Sayer Blake [Prerogative Inventories 1750, 176-185].
     iv. Isaac, born about 1766, manumitted by Archelus Price of Talbot County on 16 August 1808, registered on 29 September 1812: *a Mullatto Man...named Isaac Dobson who is now about 46 years of age, 5 feet 5-3/4 in. high...set free by him the said Archelus Price on the 16 August 1808* [Certificates of Freedom 1807-28, 40].

DODSON FAMILY

Members of the Dodson family in Maryland were
1   i.   John[1], born say 1765.
     ii. Anthony, head of a Kent County household of 2 "other free" in 1810 [MD:854].

1.   John[1] Dodson, born say 1765, was head of a Prince George's County household of 5 "other free" in 1810 [MD:43]. He was the father of
     i.   John[2], born about 1787, registered in Prince George's County on 14 July 1810: *black man...about 23 years old...raised in the family of John Henry Hall and was born free, being the son of John Dodson, Sr., and his wife Nancy who were free persons of color.*
     ii. Nancy, born about 1791, registered in Prince George's County on 9 May 1821: *a colored woman, about 30 years old...is free being the reputed*

      daughter of Ann(?) Dodson a free woman of color.

iii. William, born about 1795, registered in Prince George's County on 25 May 1821: *a colored man about 26 years old...light complexion. He is free being the reputed daughter (sic) of Margary Dodson, a free woman of color.*

iv. Henry, born about 1797, registered in Prince George's County on 13 July 1812: *a black boy, about 15 years old, with thick lips and flat nose...raised in Prince George's County...son of Margary Dodson who was a free born woman of color.*

v. Jane, born about 1798, registered in Prince George's County on 7 June 1819: *a Negro girl, about 21 years old...dark complexion. She is free, being the reputed daughter of John Dodson and Margary, his wife.*

vi. Margaret, born about 1800, registered in Prince George's County on 22 July 1815: *a mulatto girl, about 15 years old...large flat nose and thick lips. She is free and the reputed daughter of John Dodson and Margary, his wife, free people of color.*

vii. Mary Ann, born about 1806, registered in Prince George's County on 22 Jun 1821: *a colored woman, about 14 years old...has rather a light complexion. She is free, being the reputed daughter of Margary Dodson, a free woman of color* [Provine, *Registrations of Free Negroes*, 6, 10, 18, 28-9, 36-7].

DOGAN FAMILY

1. Alice[1] Dogan, born about 1685, was called the "Mallato" servant of Captain Thomas Dickson of Coventry Parish in March 1711/2 when the Somerset County court convicted her of having a child in 1703 by "Harry her Master's Negroe" at Annemessex. On 9 November 1711 the court presented her for having a child about September 1711, and on 4 March 1713/4 she confessed to the court that she had a child by "Abram, Mrs. Coulbourne's Negro," in Stepney Parish. The court sold her child to Samuel Handy, Gent., until the age of thirty-one for 1,000 pounds of tobacco and ordered her to serve another four years. On 4 August 1713 she complained to the court that she was about twenty-eight years old and ought to be free, and in June 1714 the court sold her children Shelly, over five years old, and George, to be two, to her master for 1,500 pounds of tobacco [Judicial Records 1711-13, 91-2, 132; 1713-5, 27, 69, 299]. She was the ancestor of

    i. Shelly, born about 1709.

    ii. George, born about 1712.

2   iii. ?Catherine[1], born say 1714.

    iv. ?Leah, a spinster (no race indicated), confessed to the Somerset County court on 15 November 1768 that she had an illegitimate child. She refused to name the father and paid a fine of £3 [Judicial Record 1767-9, 70, 237].

2. Catherine[1] Dogan, born say 1714, had an illegitimate child named Toby who was born on 2 October 1732 and bound out until the age of twenty-one by the Somerset County in March 1732/3. She was apparently identical to "Kate free mollatto" of Coventry Parish, the servant of William Coulbourn, who confessed to the Somerset County court on 15 March 1736/7 that she had a child named Alice, born six months previous, by a "negro." The court sold Alice to William Colebourn, Jr., until the age of thirty-one for 50 shillings. The court indicted her again for fornication in August 1737 [Judicial Record 1737-8, 2-3, 126]. She was the mother of

    i. Alice[2], born about September 1736, head of a Talbot County household of 3 "other free" in 1800 [MD:529].

    ii. ?Catherine[2], head of a Talbot County household of 5 "other free" in 1790.

DONALDSON FAMILY

1. Sarah Donalson, born say 1734, the spinster servant of Abigail Wilson, admitted
    to the Somerset County court in March 1757 that she was guilty of "Inordinate
    Copulation" by having a child by a slave the prior month. The court ordered that
    she be sold for seven years and bound her daughter Sarah to James Wilson until
    the age of thirty-one. In June 1763 she confessed that she had a "Negro Bastard"
    child by "Negro Bristo," a slave of Elizabeth Waters, and the court bound their
    daughter Rhoda to James Wilson for thirty-one years and ordered Sarah to be sold
    for seven years after the completion of her service [Judicial Record 1757-60, 2-3].
    She was the mother of

    2   i.   ?Bridget, born say 1752.
          ii. Sarah, born February 1757.
          iii. Rhoda, born 20 December 1762.

2. Bridget Donaldson, born say 1752, the "free Mulatto" servant of James Wilson,
    admitted to the Somerset County court that she had a child by a "Negro slave."
    The court ordered her sold for seven years and sold her son Levin to her master
    until the age of thirty-one [Judicial Record 1769-72, 139]. She was the mother of

        i.   Levin, born in 1770.

DOUGLASS FAMILY

Members of the Douglass family in Virginia and Maryland were
1   i.   Gabriel, born say 1760.
      ii. Daniel, head of a Harford County household of 5 "other free" in 1790.

1. Gabriel Douglass, born say 1760, was head of a Washington County household
    of 7 "other free" in 1800 [MD:636] and was the father of Thomas Douglass who
    registered as a free Negro in Washington, D.C., on 3 October 1821: *son of Gabriel
    Douglass, a free man, and his wife, who is also free. Douglass has passed as free
    in Harper's Ferry for some years past* [Provine, *District of Columbia Free Negro
    Registers*, 10]. He was the father of

        i.   Thomas, head of an Anne Arundel County household of 9 "other free" in
           1810 [MD:63].
        ii. ?James, head of a Prince George's County household of 9 "other free" in
           1810 [MD:44].

DOVE FAMILY

Members of the Dove family in Maryland were
    i.   John, born say 1702, the "Mallatto slave" of Doctor Gustavus Brown on
      14 November 1727 when he was brought before the Charles County court
      on suspicion of burglary [Court Records 1727-31, 42]. Vincent Askin, by
      his 1 October 1745 Charles County will, proved 22 October 1745, directed
      that at his death his "mulatto man John Dove" was to have his freedom
      [Prerogative Court (Wills), Liber 24, fol. 229]. And "John Dove Mullatto"
      was valued at £60 in the inventory of Askin's estate in 1745 [Prerogative
      Court (Inventories), Liber 32, pp. 36-7].
1   ii. Mary, born say 1710.
    iii. Hannah, born say 1720, petitioned the Prince George's County court on
      27 August 1754 that she was born free but was held in slavery by Ignatius
      Wheeler. Her case was struck off the docket on 25 March 1755 [Court
      Records, 1751-4, 626; 1754-8, 57].
    iv. Dolly, "Negro" head of a Kent County household of 3 "other free" in 1790.
    v.   Jim, head of a Talbot County household of 5 "other free" and a slave in
      1800 [MD:531].

1. Mary Dove, born say 1710, was a "Negro woman" slave listed in the Anne Arundel County inventory of the estate of Eleazar Birkhead on 28 April 1744 [Prerogative Court (inventories) 1744-5, 43]. Birkhead's widow married Leonard Thomas, and Mary Dove sued him in Anne Arundel County court for her freedom in June 1746 [Judgment Record 1746-8, 118]. The outcome of the suit is not recorded, apparently because Thomas took her with him when he moved to Craven County, North Carolina.

    In September 1749 the Dove family was living in Craven County when William Smith complained to the court on their behalf that Leonard Thomas was detaining them as slaves:

    > *Moll, Nell, Sue, Sall, & Will, Negroes Detained as Slaves by Leonard Thomas That they are free born Persons in the Province of Maryland and brought to this Province by the said Leonard Thomas*

    William Smith traveled to Maryland to prove their claim, and they were free by November 1756 when James Dove, "~~a free negro~~ a "Negro Servant," complained to the Craven County court that Smith was mistreating him, Nelly, Sue, Sarah, Moll, and William Dove [Haun, *Craven County Court Minutes*, IV:11-12, 366]. The Dove family owned land in Craven County by 1775.

    William **Dowry**, a grandson of Mary Dove, was still held in slavery in Anne Arundel County in 1791 when he sued for his freedom in the General Court. In October 1791 a white woman named Ann Ridgely testified in Anne Arundel County that the family descended from Mary Dove, of brown complexion, who was the granddaughter of:

    > *a Yellow Woman and had long black hair, but this deponent does not know whether she was reputed to be an East Indian or a Madagascarian, but she has understood that she was called in the family Malaga Moll* [Craven County Miscellaneous Records, C.R. 28.928.10].[9]

    Mary died before 6 April 1763 when the Craven County court appointed her son James Dove administrator of her estate on security of £100 [Minutes 1762-66, 13d].

DOWNS FAMILY

1. Eliza Downes, born say 1708, was the servant of Sarah Dashiell of Stepney Parish on 15 March 1725/6 when the Somerset County court ordered that she be sold for seven years for having an illegitimate child [Judicial Record 1725-7, 97]. She may have been the ancestor of
    i.   Paddy, "N." head of a Muddy Branch, Little Creek Hundred, Kent County household of 4 "other free" in 1800 [DE:31].
    ii. James, "N." head of a St. Jones Hundred, Kent County household of 8 "other free" in 1800 [DE;46].
    iii. James, head of a Little Creek, Kent County household of 7 "other free" in 1800 [DE:40].
    iv. Isaac, head of a Dover Hundred, Kent County household of 3 "free colored" in 1820 [DE:35].
    v.   Charles, (Negro) head of a Caroline County household of 7 "other free" in 1810 [MD:194].
    vi. Ben, "Negro" head of a Caroline County household of 7 "other free" in

---

[9]Claiming descent from an East Indian in order to minimize the African Ancestry of a petitioner was not without precedent in Maryland. See the Bentley and Davis families.

         1810 [MD:195].
    vii. Daniel, "Negro" head of a Caroline County household of 5 "other free" in
          1810 [MD:195].

Prince George's County
1.   William Downs, born say 1765, was a "free negro" head of a Prince George's
     County household of 8 "other free" in 1800 [MD:303]. He was probably the father
     of
         i. Robert, born about 1792, registered in Anne Arundel County on 3
             September 1816: *aged about twenty four years...brown complexion...free
             born and...raised in the County* [Certificates of Freedom 1810-31, 89].

DRAIN FAMILY

Members of the Drain family in Delaware were
         i. Solomon, born before 1776, "N." head of a Lewis and Rehoboth Hundred,
             Sussex County household of 9 "free colored" in 1820 [DE:310]. He was
             a "Coloured" man who left a 12 May 1851 Sussex County will, proved 27
             November 1851, by which he left 10 acres of land to his wife Sinah and
             sons Robert, Jacob and James; left $2 each to sons Abram and David and
             left daughters Eliza, Hannah and Mary 25 cents each [DSA, RG 4545.009,
             reel 72, frames 128-131].
        ii. Martain, born before 1776, "N." head of a Broadkill Hundred, Sussex
             County household of 5 "free colored" in 1820 [DE:322].

DRIGGERS FAMILY

The Driggers family originated in Northampton County, Virginia, and spread to
Maryland, Delaware, North Carolina and South Carolina during the colonial period.
See the Virginia section for the entire Driggers history. Listed below are the branches
of the family which lived in Maryland and Delaware.

1.   Emmanuel Driggers, "Negroe," born say 1620, was the slave of Francis Pott on
     his plantation in Magotha Bay, Northampton County, Virginia. He was free by 27
     May 1645 when he purchased a cow and calf from Pott and recorded the sale in
     Northampton County court [DW 1645-51, 82]. His children were
2   i. Thomas, born about 1644.
3   ii. Devorick/ Devorix[1], born say 1656.
       iii. ?Mary, born say 1658, mother of an illegitimate child in 1674, probably
             the Mary Driggers whose tax was paid by the parish that year [Orders
             1664-74, 254, 273-4]. She may have married Peter **George**.

2.   Thomas Driggers, born about 1644, remained a slave in Northampton County. He
     married a free woman named Sarah **King**, daughter of "King Toney Negro." She
     was in Somerset County before 23 April 1688 when she, called "negroe Woman
     & wife to Thomas Griggers Negro," complained to the Somerset County court that
     Margaret Holder had stolen some of her goods. Peter **George**, "Negroe" of
     Wicomico Hundred, posted £5 security for Sarah's appearance. The court heard
     testimony from Peter **George**, Mary **George**, Mary **Johnson**, and Sarah Driggers,
     Jr., and found in favor of Margaret Holder. By 14 August 1688 Sarah, Peter
     George, three unnamed women, and an unstated number of men petitioned the
     Somerset County court to stop taxing them as slaves since they were free born.
     The court ruled that for that year the women should be exempt, but the men
     should pay taxes. The court also ordered that they obtain certificates from where
     they formerly lived to prove that they were free born [*Archives of Maryland*
     91:47; Judicial Record, 1687-89, 58]. In 1689 she was back in Northampton
     County [Orders 1679-89, 463]. Their children were free because their mother was
     free. Two of their children who moved to Delaware and Maryland were

i. Sarah[1], born say 1667, raised by John and Christian **Francisco** until she was twenty-one years old. She testified in Somerset County court on 13 June 1688. In 1691 she was in Northampton County when she was bound to William Kenny "to go to the Southward with him" [OW 1689-98, 121, 125]. He may have been the William Kenning, Jr., who sued Sarah Drigers for defamation in Sussex County, Delaware court on 3 June 1691 [Court Records 1680-99, 497]. She brought a successful suit against Edward Fetlock(?) in Kent County, Delaware court on 14 November 1717 [Court Dockets 1680- February 1725, fol. 119].

4   ii. William[2], born say 1682.

3.   Devorick/ Devorix[1] Driggers, born say 1656, was the son of Emmanuel Driggers, a slave who was freed in Northampton County, Virginia. Deverax received a bay mare from his father by a 1673 Northampton County deed [D&c 1668-80, fol.59-60]. He moved to Somerset County about 1677 when he was one of the headrights claimed by Stephen Cosden in his patent [Maryland Provincial Patents, Liber 15:433]. In 1689 he signed a Somerset County address of loyalty to King William and Queen Mary [Torrence, *Old Somerset on the Eastern Shore*, 349]. On 12 January 1701/2 he provided security in Somerset County court for Deborah Wildgoose who had an illegitimate child by Samuel Webb. He and several whites were presented for being drunk on the Sabbath in All Hollows Parish, but he was acquitted after paying court costs [Judicial Records 1702-5, Liber G-I, 21; 1707-17, 16].[10] He was renting a 300-acre plantation in Bogerternorton Hundred of Somerset County in 1707 [Somerset County Rent Roll, 1707, Calvert Papers, ms. 174, MHS]. He received a cow from his sister in Somerset County on 27 July 1708 [Wright, *Maryland Eastern Shore Vital Records, Book 1* (Somerset County Livestock Marks), 160]. He died before 2 March 1708/9 when court suits against him by David Hudson and John Swann & Co. were suspended by his death [Judicial Record 1707-11, 176, 215]. His estate was valued at about £37 [Inventories and Accounts, Liber 30:88]. His administrator John Jermain was sued by a number of Deverix's creditors to whom he had written promissory notes at Snow Hill, one of them his lawyer for six cases between March 1698 and March 1706. Jermain recovered 1,600 pounds of tobacco that William Godard of Wicomico had owed Deverix [Judicial Record 1706-11, 223-4, 228, 256-60, 434; 1711-13, 57]. He may have been the father of

5   i. Devorax[2], born about 1680.

4.   William[2] Driggus, born say 1682, was probably the son of Thomas Driggers, a Northampton County slave, and his wife Sarah **King**. William was called the "Maletto Servant" of Daniel Neech when he recorded his cattle mark in Northampton County court in 1698 [DW 1651-54, 30 at the end of volume]. He was living in Somerset County in April 1708 when he was presented for carrying Mary Winslow out of the county to avoid prosecution for having an illegitimate child by Daniel **Francisco**. The court ordered that he, a "Mollatto," receive twenty-five lashes when he told the justices that

they had no more to do with sd Woman than his Arse

Edward Winslow and David Hudson were security for him [Judicial Records 1707-11, 94, 96, 102; 1713-5, 5, 26]. William signed his 7 January 1720 Somerset County will which was proved 7 May 1722. He left his 100-acre plantation called

---

[10]Davidson determined that this was a far more serious case than is apparent from the county court records. The May 1707 Provincial Court records indicate that Driggers was assisting prominent vestryman Captain Edward Hammond to break into the home of Enoch Griffin and carry off his wife (who had been accused of committing adultery with Hammond) and one of her children [Provincial Court Judgments Liber P.L. nol.1, 198-206; Davidson, *Free Blacks on the lower Eastern Shore*, IV:71].

Drigus Adventure to his son William and mentioned unnamed children under eighteen years old and his wife, Jane. He specified that his children were to be cared for by their uncle John Driggus of Accomack County if his wife remarried. The inventory of his estate included a parcel of old books [Prerogative Wills, 17:285; Inventories 8:65]. Jane was called a "maleto widow" in 1724 when Winslow Driggus (William's son by Mary Winslow?) was taxable in her Baltimore Hundred, Somerset County household [List of Taxables]. William's children were

   i.   William[3], born about 1702.
6 ii. ?Winslow[1], born say 1705.
   iii. Sabra, born say 1722, presented by the Somerset County court on 17 November 1741 for having an illegitimate child [Judicial Record 1740-2, 175].

5. Devorax[2] Driggers, born about 1680, was a "Molatto" Accomack County tithable in Jonathan Owen's household in 1696. He was sued by Robert Houston in Accomack County court on 7 August 1704 [Orders 1690-7, 222a, 224, 235; 1703-9, 30a]. He and (his wife?) Arendia Driggas were witnesses with Thomas Purcell to the 24 December 1720 Somerset County will of Henry Hudson, Sr., a wealthy planter [Prerogative Wills 16:279-3]. He was taxable in Thomas Purcell's household in Bogerternorton Hundred, Somerset County, in 1723 and 1724 and in Peter **Beckett**'s household in 1725, listed in Baltimore Hundred from 1730 to 1733 [List of Taxables]. He was called a carpenter on 17 November 1730 when he admitted in Somerset County court that he owed Christopher Glass 500 pounds of tobacco and 650 pounds of beef which he had contracted for in writing on 10 November 1729. Peter **Beckett** provided special bail for him [Judicial Record 1730-3, 43-4]. On 16 June 1731 he purchased 75 acres in Somerset County on St. Martins River in present-day Worcester County [Land Records, Liber SH:324]. He and his wife Ann sold this land in 1734 and were renting it in 1748 [Worcester County Debt Book, 1748, 190]. They may have been the parents of an apprentice named Davarix Drigus who was valued at £6 in the inventory of the estate of Thomas Parnall in June 1723 [Prerogative Inventories & Accounts 1724-1725, 263]. He may have been the father of

   i.   John, taxable in Bogerternorton Hundred, Somerset County, from 1734 to 1740.
   ii. Deverix[3], perhaps identical to Drake Driggers who was taxable in Indian River and Angola Hundred, Sussex County, from 1770 to 1787 [DSA, RG 2535]. His 2 September 1788 Sussex County estate named his sister Rhoda **Hodgskin** [de Valinger, *Calendar of Sussex County Probate Records*, 195].
   iii. Rhoda, sister of Drake Driggers, married Jonas **Hodgskin**.
   iv. Sarah, indicted for bastardy in Sussex County court in February 1758 but not found by the sheriff [RG 4815.017, General Sessions Court, 1753-60, frames 403, 422, 447].

6. Winslow[1] Driggers, born say 1705, was taxable in the Baltimore Hundred, Somerset County household of Jane Drigus in 1724 and in the household of Isaac **Perkins** in 1725. He was called Winsley Drigers when his Little Creek Hundred, Kent County, Delaware taxes were charged to William **Beckett** in 1727 (listed with ~~Robert Butcher~~, Robert Whud (Wood), Julius **Caesar**, Thomas **Consellor**, Jacob **Miller**, and Daniel **Francisco**) and in Murderkill Hundred, Kent County, when his taxes were charged to Isaac **Perkins** in 1729 and 1730 [Kent County Assessments, Film RG 3535, reel 1, frames 354, 360, 364]. He was sued in Kent County by Hugh Durburow in August 1729, by John McDowell in May 1733 but was not found by the sheriff, and he sued the executors of Robert Wood in November 1733. The sheriff's warrant for McDowell's case read "William Grigers" [RG 3815.031, Common Pleas, Dockets 1722-32, frame 363; 1733-1740, frames 12, 37, 73, 131; May Term 1733 case papers, executions #41-86]. He may

have been the ancestor of

i. Jacob, born say 1733, a "Negro" indicted in the November 1754 session of the Kent County court for stealing a dark bay gelding worth £10 from John **Durham** on 1 October 1754 [DSA, RG 3805.0, MS case files, November 1754 indictments].

ii. Richard, taxable in Dover Hundred, Kent County, in 1773 [Kent County Assessments, frame 0183] and taxable in Duck Creek Hundred in 1779 when an "X" was placed next to his name [DSA, MS Kent County Papers, 1680-1800, Official Tax lists, etc., Duck Creek Hundred 1779-1781].

iii. Luke, taxable in Lewes and Rehoboth Hundred, Sussex County, in 1774. He was indicted by the Sussex County court in February 1775 for an unstated offense. Lydia **Coursey** gave £40 recognizance to appear to give evidence against him [RG 4805, General Sessions, 1767-1794, frame 164].

iv. Benjamin, taxable in Indian River and Angola Hundred, Sussex County in 1777.

v. James, born say 1758, listed in the pay roll of Captain Matthew Manlove's Company in the Revolutionary War on 1 October 1776, having served a month and seventeen days and paid £3.16 [Public Archives Commission, *Delaware Archives*, 70-1].

vi. William[5], born say 1765, a delinquent taxpayer in Little Creek Hundred, Sussex County, in 1787, taxable in Dover, Kent County in 1788, and head of a Sussex County household of 6 "other free" in 1800 [DE:425]. He purchased 13 acres leading to Thomas's Chapel in Murderkill Hundred for £8 on 5 December 1799 [DB F-2:234-5].

vii. Betty, married Peter **Becket** on 27 November 1788 in Sussex County [Records of the United Presbyterian Churches of Lewes, Indian River and Cool Spring, Delaware 1756-1855, 302].

viii. Noval, head of a Sussex County household of 3 "other free" in 1800 [DE:425].

ix. Mary/ Molly, purchased 15 acres called *Second Chance* on Gabriels Branch in Worcester County, the crop of corn, a cow, nine hogs, ten pigs, two beds and furniture, an ewe and lamb, all his household furniture and 40 shillings of paid accounts from William Jarman (of W[m]) for £6 on 11 September 1794 [Land Records P:493].

x. Elizabeth, "Negro," mother of an illegitimate child by "Negro" Moses **Wall** in Dover Hundred in June 1785 [DSA, RG 3805, MS November 1785 Indictments]. Moses was a "Negro" taxable in Little Creek Hundred from 1782 to 1784 [RG 3535, Levy Assessment List 1768-84, frames 542, 620].

DUBLIN FAMILY

Members of the Dublin family were

i. Benjamin, born say 1725, the husband of Hannah **Gibbs** who named him and her children Rebecca, Alice, Martha and Sarah in her 16 February 1785 Queen Anne's County deed by which she left her portion of *Kilmannin's Plains* and *Knowles's Range* to them at her death [Liber CD-2:317]. He was taxable on 50 acres of *Killman's Plains* in 1783 [Assessment of 1783, MSA S1437, p.2].

ii. Catherine, head of a Kent County, Maryland household of 11 "other free" in 1800 [MD:171].

iii. Jo., head of a Kent County household of 3 "other free" in 1810 [MD:844].

iv. George, born before 1776, head of a Baltimore County household of 6 "free colored" in 1830.

DUFFY FAMILY

Members of the Duffy family were
  i. Sarah, born about 1782, registered in Somerset County on 25 October 1822: *descendant of Susan Dove who was a white woman...bright yellow Complexion...about forty years of age* [Certificates of Freedom 1821-32, 11].
  ii. Ziposah, head of a Worcester County household of 6 "other free" in 1800 [MD:828] and 4 in 1810 [MD:602].
  iii. Leah, head of a Worcester County household of 5 "other free" in 1800 [MD:828] and 5 "other free" and a slave in 1810 [MD:602].
  iv. Isaac, head of an Accomack County household of 9 "other free" and 3 slaves in 1810 [VA:91].

DUNLOP FAMILY

1. Mary Dunlop, born say 1717, was living in St. Paul's Parish, King George County, Virginia, in 1735 when the birth and baptism of her son James was recorded (no race indicated). She was the mother of
   i. James, born 6 August 1735, baptized September 29, 1735 [St. Paul's Parish Register, 60].

Members of the family who moved to Prince George's County were
2   i. Joseph, born about 1768.
    ii. Naney, head of a Richmond City household of 4 "other free" in 1810 [VA:333], perhaps the mother of Nancy Dunlap who registered in Prince George's County on 7 July 1819: *about 5 feet 3-1/4 inches tall, about 22 years old, and of a yellow complexion...daughter of Nancy Dunlap, a free woman of color...born in King George County, Virginia and has been residing in Prince George's County for about a year* [Provine, *Registrations of Free Negroes*, 29]

2. Joseph[1] Dunlop, born about 1768, registered in King George County on 25 September 1798: *a mulatto man about thirty years old and five feet three inches high was born free* [Register of Free Persons 1785-1799, no.9]. He had moved to Prince George's County before 7 August 1817 when his son George registered there. He was the father of
    i. Winny, born say 1788, registered in Prince George County on 7 July 1819: *a black woman about 5 feet 2-1/2 inches tall, and about 51 (31?) years old...free and the daughter of Joseph Dunlap and Lydia his wife free people of color, born in Virginia King George County, who have been residing in Prince George's County for the last twelve months.*
    ii. ?Ann, born about 1794, registered in Prince George's County on 16 December 1825: *a dark mulatto woman, about 31 years old, and 5 feet 3-1/2 inches tall.*
    iii. George, born about 1796, registered in Prince George's County on 7 August 1817: *a dark mulatto man, 5 feet 8 inches tall, and 21 years old...the son of Joseph Dunlop Sr. of Prince George's County, a respectable colored freeman.*
    iv. Joseph[2], born about 1797, registered in Prince George's County on 14 September 1818: *a colored man of dark complexion, about 21 years old, and 5 feet 8 inches tall. He is a free man, being the legitimate son of Joseph Dunlop Sr., a free man of color.*
    v. Treasy, born about 1803, registered in Prince George's County on 19 February 1825: *a mulatto woman, about 22 years old, and 5 feet 1 inch tall...daughter of Joseph Dunlop Sr.* [Provine, *Registrations of Free Negroes*, 23, 27, 29, 50, 54].

DUNSTAN FAMILY

1. Ann Dunstan, born say 1727, was the servant of Edward Pearson of Piscataway Hundred in Prince George's County on 24 June 1746 when she was presented by the court for having a "Malato" child. She confessed, was presented for the same offense on 23 August 1748, and on 22 November 1748 the court sold her to her master William Hardy for the nine-months trouble of his house and ordered that she be delivered to the court after the completion of her indenture to be sold for seven years [Prince George's County Court Record 1746-7, 20; 1747-8, 331; 1748-9, 47-8]. She was the mother of
    i. Sarah Donstan, a "Molatto" girl valued at £12 in the Prince George's County estate of Mr. Edward Pearson on 9 September 1749 (not identified as free) [Prerogative Inventories 1749-50, 166].

DURHAM FAMILY

1. Daniel[1] Durham, born say 1690, was taxable in Mispillion Hundred, Kent County, Delaware, between 1729 and 1740 and taxable in Little Creek Hundred from 1745 to 1748. He may have died sometime between 1753 and 1754 when (his son?) Daniel Durham was no longer called "Jr." in the levy assessment lists [Kent County Levy List, 1743-67, frames 24, 43, 51, 87, 143, 168]. He may have been identical to Daniel Doron/ Durrum/ Derham who was taxable in Somerset County from 1723 to 1725 [List of Taxables, 1723-1725]. He was probably the father of
2.   i. John[1], born say 1710.
3.   ii. Daniel[2], born say 1718.
      iii. Sarah, married William **Hanser** about 1757 and died before 8 February 1771 when her "next of kin" (brother?) John Durham was granted administration on her Kent County, Delaware estate [WB L-1, fol. 91].

2. John[1] Durham, born say 1710, was taxable in Mispillion Hundred from 1741 to 1742 (called a shoemaker in 1741), was taxable in Dover Hundred in 1743 and 1744, and taxable in Little Creek Hundred from 1745 to 1789: in 1768 listed with John Durham Jun[r] who was called his son in the list for 1772 which included a third John Durham. Only his estate listed in 1789 [RG 3535, Kent County Levy List, 1743-67, frames 499, 503; 1743-67, frames 12, 44, 51, 87, 107, 143, 168; 187, 196, 209, 226, 240, 263, 269, 290, 316, 347, 377, 383, 397, 437, 520, 552; 1768-84, frames 26, 65, 103, 128, 184, 222, 262, 310, 334, 342, 366, 368, 442, 445, 502, 541, 570, 582, 619; 1784-97, frames 8, 24, 48, 71, 74]. He purchased 54 acres in Little Creek Hundred on the westside of Ellingsworth Branch adjoining Andrew Tybout's and Israel Alston's land for £40 on 8 February 1750 [DB P-3:4]. He was named in the 19 January 1763 will of his mother-in-law, Isabell **Hughes** [WB K-1, fol. 301-3]. In February 1773 the Kent County court indicted six white men: James Cockrell, Andrew Jenkins, William Hawkins, William Maddin, John Brown and Edward McConnaway for riot and assault and battery when they attacked him at his home and damaged his rush-bottomed chair and other property on 19 November 1772 at Little Creek Hundred. William Durham, Whittington Durham, John **Cott**, Elijah **Consiglio** (**Consellor**) and Margaret **Sisco** were his witnesses [DSA, RG 3505, MS case papers, Indictments February 1773]. On 14 February 1788 he sold 38 acres adjoining the road from Fast Landing to Dover to Elijah **Consellor** of Duck Creek Hundred for £116, and on 24 February 1788 he sold a lot of 3 acres adjoining this to James **Dean** for £45 [DB Z:198-9]. By his 9 April 1788 Little Creek Hundred, Kent County will, proved 14 May 1788, he gave his sons William, Isaiah, and Whittington Durham his estate except for £5 each to his daughters Sarah **Sisco**, Letitia **Lacount**, Elizabeth **Concilar**, and Hannah **Concilar** as well as £5 for four years to Rebecca Durham for raising his son John Durham's children. He also gave £10 to Clayton Durham until he came of age but did not state their relationship. Mary **Concilar**, Eleanor **Puckham**, and John Durham witnessed the will. The account of the estate

included payments to John **Cott**, Ephraim **Francisco**, William and Daniel **Songo**, Jesse **Dean**, Mary **Consellor**, Stephen **Sparksman**, and Jacob **Gibbs** [RG 3545, roll 68, frames 612-23; WB M-1, fol. 170-1]. His children were

4   i.   William[1], born about 1730.

5   ii.   Isaiah, born say 1740.

       iii. Whittington[1], born say 1741, taxable in Little Creek Hundred from 1759 to 1772, in Duck Creek Hundred from 1773 to 1783, and in Little Creek Hundred from 1784 to 1791, a "N." in 1790 and in 1791 when he was listed as delinquent [RG 3535, Kent County Levy List, 1743-67, frames 240, 263, 269, 290, 316, 347, 377, 383, 437, 520, 552; 1768-1784, frames 65, 103, 128, 180, 220, 299, 336, 370, 522, 568, 619; 1785-97, frames 6, 24, 48, 71, 74, 106, 136, 197, 226]. He was charged with contempt by the Kent County court in February 1789 for failing to comply with a judgment of the court in August 1779 regarding his conviction for fornication with Elizabeth **Hughes**, and he sued Philip Denny in court in November 1769 [DSA, RG 3805.002, 1787-1803, frame 52, 54; RG 3815.031, frame 135]. He was administrator of Charles Clark's 20 October 1785 Kent County estate [WB M-1, fol. 68].

       iv. Sarah, married John **Sisco** according to the distributive account of her father's estate.

       v.   John[2], born say 1747, called "John Derham Jun. deceased" on 19 June 1776 when administration on his Kent County estate was granted to his father [WB L-1:180].

       vi. Letitia, married Thomas **Lacount** according to the distributive account of her father's estate.

       vii. Elizabeth, married Thomas **Conselar** according to the account of her father's estate.

    viii. Hannah, married Elijah **Conselar**.

       ix. ?Clayton, born say 1773, a "Negro" taxable in Duck Creek Hundred in 1797 and 1798 [RG 3535, Kent County Levy List, 1785-97, frames 483, 572; 1797-8, frame 351].

3.   Daniel[2] Durham, born say 1718, applied for a warrant for 150 acres in Mispillion Hundred on 27 October 1739 [Warrant Book A:64]. He was called Daniel Doram, Jnr., when he was taxable in Mispillion Hundred in 1740 and 1741 and on 17 May 1744 when he purchased 100 acres in Little Creek Hundred [DB N:1:46]. He was taxable in Little Creek Hundred from 1742 to 1776. He sued Spencer Cole in Kent County court in August 1741, the executor of John Hammett (of Mispillion Hundred) sued him in November 1741 and he admitted he owed a debt to Isaac Pounds in May 1743 [RG 3815.031, Common Pleas, Dockets 1740-1744, frame 208, 213, 296, 414, 480, 510]. He sold an acre of land adjoining John **Hansor** on the west side of Landing Road to Thomas **Butcher** on 12 February 1783 [DB Y:206]. By his 4 December 1779 Kent County will, proved 17 August 1786, he divided his land, a boy named George until he reached twenty-one years of age, and goods among his wife Eleanor, sons Benjamin, Daniel and Thomas, and daughters Joanah, Hester, Rachel, Mary, Eleanor, and Sarah. His estate paid debts due to Charles **Cambridge** and Sabella **Hanser** [WB M-1, fol. 118; RG 3545, roll 68, frames 494-8]. His children were

6   i.   Benjamin[1], born say 1747.

       ii.   Joanah, born say 1749.

       iii. Hester, born say 1751.

       iv. Rachel, born say 1753.

7   v.   Daniel[3], born say 1755.

       vi. Mary, born say 1757.

       vii. Eleanor, born say 1759, perhaps the Eleanor **Puckham** who witnessed John Durham's 9 April 1788 Kent County will.

8   viii. Thomas[1], born say 1761.

       ix. Sarah.

4. William[1] Durham/ Derham, born about 1730, was a "Mulatto" mason about twenty-three years of age on 15 November 1753 when his master, Griffith Griffith, a mason of Bristol Township, Pennsylvania, advertised in the *Pennsylvania Gazette* that he had run away [Scott, *Abstracts of the Pennsylvania Gazette 1748-55*, 261]. He was called a "malatto" when he married Mary **Waldrek**, "malatto both free," on 17 January 1756 in St. Michael's and Zion Lutheran Church, Philadelphia, Pennsylvania [St. Michael's and Zion Church Marriage Register 1745-1784, microfilm of original at Historical Society of Pennsylvania]. He was taxable in Little Creek Hundred, Kent County, Delaware, from 1765 to 1768 and taxable in Duck Creek Hundred from 1770 to 1777 and in 1785 and 1788, a "N." taxable in Little Creek Hundred in 1790 and 1792, in the list of "Mulatto's and Negroes" in 1797 [RG 3535, Kent County Levy List, 1743-67, frames 508, 552; 1768-84, frames 10, 74, 107, 119, 180, 220, 254, 299; 1785-97, frame 6, 127, 267; 1797-8, frame 75]. He died before 27 July 1797 when administration on his Kent County estate was granted to (his wife) Mary Durham on £500 bonds posted by Joseph Farrow [RG 3545, reel 68, frame 733; WB N-1:179]. Mary was called "Mulatto (widow of William Durham, Senr.)" in the levy list for 1798 [RG 3535, Kent County Levy List, 1797-8, frame 479]. The account of his estate names heirs: Ibba (Isabella), Benjamin, and Mary Durham, Elizabeth **Dean**, Mary **Hughes**, Deborough **Cott** and Susannah **Hansor** [RG 3545, reel 68, frames 733-44; de Valinger, *Kent County Probate Records*, 528]. His children named in the distribution of the estate, dated 24 September 1805, were
   i. William[2], born say 1762, called William Durham, Jr., in the list of taxables for Duck Creek Hundred in 1783, a "Mulatto" taxable in the lists for 1797 and 1798 [RG 3535, Kent County Levy List, 1768-84, frame 568; 1797-8, frames 12, 75].
   ii. Elizabeth, born say 1767, wife of Jesse **Dean** who was paid her share of her father's estate on 2 January 1806.
   iii. Sarah, born say 1769, wife of John **Derram**.
   iv. Mary **Hughes**, born say 1771.
   v. Deborah **Cott**, born say 1773.
   vi. Susannah **Hansor**, born say 1775.
   vii. Benjamin[2], born say 1778.
   viii. Isabella, born say 1780.

5. Isaiah[1] Durham, born say 1740, was taxable in Duck Creek Hundred from 1775 to 1783, in Little Creek Hundred from 1785 to 1800: listed as a "N." starting in 1790, a "mulattoe" in 1797 [RG 3535, Kent County Levy List, 1768-84, frames 254, 267, 299, 336, 370, 522, 568; 1784-97, frames 8, 24, 48, 71, 74, 106, 136, 226, 267; 1797-8, frames 7, 473]. He died before 19 May 1800 when administration on his Kent County estate was granted to Mary Durham and William Vanstavoren. The inventory of his estate was taken by Joseph Farrow and totaled £195. Mary "of Isaih" was head of a Muddy Branch, Little Creek Hundred household of 10 "other free" in 1800 [DE:31]. She was married to John **Francisco** by 2 February 1803 when the estate was distributed among Isaiah's children. On 24 February 1806 Vanstavoren petitioned the court that Isaac Derham "Mulatto" died seized of land, a widow and nine children; his widow had married John **Francisco** a "Mulatto," but no guardian had been appointed for the children [RG 3545, roll 68, frame 600; Brewer, *Kent County, Delaware, Guardian Accounts, Caton to Edinfield*, 153, 203]. His children who received their share of the estate were
   i. Pheby.
   ii. William[3].
   iii. Elijah.
   iv. Margaret.
   v. Isaiah[2].
   vi. Rebecca, perhaps the Rebecca Durham who married Asa **Street**, 23 January 1811 Delaware bond, Asa **Street** and Daniel **Songo** bondsmen

[DSA, Marriage Records 18:292].

vii. Jeremiah.

viii. John³, born 1794-1776, head of a Duck Creek Hundred, Kent County household of 3 "other free" in 1800 [DE:11] and 4 "free colored in Little Creek Hundred in 1820 [DE:28].

ix. George², born 1794-1776, head of a Duck Creek Hundred, Kent County household of 8 "free colored" in 1820 [DE:46]. On 21 February 1821 he and his wife, late Susan **Handsor**, widow of William **Handsor** late of Jones Hundred, deceased, petitioned the court saying her deceased husband William **Handsor** had died intestate after conveying a 75-acre tract of land in the forest of Jones Hundred to Jacob Stout on 16 January 1804 while she was still an infant under twenty-one. She had not signed over her rights to the land which was then in the possession of free David **Hopper**, alias **Henby** [Brewer, *Kent County, Delaware, Guardian Accounts, Edmonson to Hopkins*, 21]. David **Hopper** was head of a Dover Hundred household of 7 "free colored" in 1820 [DE:35].

6. Benjamin¹ Durham, born say 1756, was taxable in Little Creek Hundred in 1777 and 1778, in Dover Hundred from 1779 to 1781, in Little Creek Hundred from 1782 to 1789, in Dover Hundred from 1789 to 1798: called a "N." in 1789 and 1790, a "Mulattoe" in 1797 when he was taxable on 87-1/2 acres of land with a log dwelling house, a cow, a yearling, a calf, a sow and a shoat [RG 3535, Kent County Levy List, 1768-84, frames 310, 334, 363, 413, 449, 452, 499, 539, 541, 571, 582; 1784-1797, frames 2, 71, 74, 106, 133, 136, 193, 224, 264, 309, 438; 1797-8, frames 62, 118, 530]. As executor of the estate of his father Daniel Durham he called himself a yeoman of Little Creek Hundred on 1 December 1786 when he made a deed for 1 acre of land, on the west side of Landing Road which led from Carbines Bridge and adjoined John **Hanzor**, to Thomas **Butcher**, stating that Thomas had paid his father £11 for it [DB Z:37-8]. He married Elizabeth **Hansor**, daughter of William and Bridget **Hansor**, after 1791. He was taxable on 87-1/2 acres in Jones Hundred, Kent County, in 1798 and head of a Kent County household of 8 "other free" in 1800 [DE:45]. Benjamin and his first wife had Daniel and Elizabeth. He died intestate owning 15-3/4 acres in Jones Hundred and a widow and seven children: Daniel, Elizabeth, Handsor, William, Susan, Hannah and Eleanor Durham before 14 August 1815 when James **Williams**, "mulatto" labourer of Little Creek Hundred, petitioned the court that he had purchased the right of Handsor Durham, Daniel Durham, and William Durham (who had since died intestate without issue) and asked the court to lay out the dower land. The court ruled that the land did not bear division and sold the entire plot to him for $45. Elizabeth and Daniel Durham were named administrators of the estate on 8 February 1810, providing $2,000 security with the assistance of Jeremiah **Consellor** and John **Hughs**. The estate paid S. **Sparksman** $4.50, Esther **Sisco** $27.30, Mary **Cambridge** $2.12, and Hugh Durham $4.65 [Brewer, *Kent County, Delaware, Guardian Accounts, Caton to Edinfield*, 202-3; RG 3545, roll 68, frames 466-9]. Benjamin was the father of

i. Daniel⁴, died about 19 February 1815 after making a nuncupative will to John McCoy. He divided his estate equally between his sister Elizabeth Durham and two half-sisters Hannah and Eleanor Durham and appointed Hugh Durham his executor. On 9 March 1815 Hugh Durham was granted administration on the will on $700 bond. The estate owed money to Mary **Cambridge** [WB P-1:68-9; RG 3545, roll 68, frames 519-523].

ii. Elizabeth.

iii. Handsor, born say 1794, married Margaret **Consilor**, 1 June 1815 Kent County bond. He and his wife Margaret sold part of a tract called *Jolly's Neck* in Saint Jones Hundred to Hugh Durham on 13 May 1817 [DB R-2: 97, 321].

iv. Hannah.

v. Eleanor.

7. Daniel[3] Durham, born say 1755, was taxable as Daniel Durham, Jun[r], in Little Creek Hundred, Kent County, in 1772, in Duck Creek Hundred in 1773, in Little Creek in 1774, delinquent in 1775, listed in Little Creek in 1778, in Dover Hundred from 1780 to 1792 [RG 3535, Kent County Levy List, 1768-84, frames 128, 180, 220, 222, 238, 342, 452, 499, 539, 571, 580; 1784-1797, frames 2, 9, 108, 110, 133, 224, 264]. He made a 1 October 1795 Kent County will (signing) which was proved 8 April 1801 by Lewis Gano and Benjamin Durham. He gave his son Hugh a mare and divided the rest of his personal estate between Parker, Hannah, Hugh, Joseph and Sarah Durham, the child his wife was pregnant with and his wife Nicy Durham. His wife Nicey/ Unicy was head of a St. Jones Hundred household of 6 "other free" in 1800 [DE:44]. She married Griffin **Bass** before 28 April 1801 when the will was proved. His heirs Parker Durham, Hannah **Williams**, Hugh, Joseph, Sarah, and Mary Durham each received over £11 [RG 3545, roll 68, frames 505-515; WB O-1:25]. His children were

    i. Parker.

    ii. Hannah **Williams**, perhaps the wife of James **Williams** who purchased Benjamin Durham's land in Little Creek Hundred.

    iii. Hugh, born say 1765, head of a Kent County, Delaware household of 7 "other free" in 1810 [DE:41]. He purchased land in Saint Jones Hundred called Jolly's Neck from Hanzor Durham on 13 May 1817 [Land Records R-2:97, 321].

    iv. Joseph.

    v. Sarah.

    vi. Mary, born say 1796.

8. Thomas[1] Durham, born say 1761, was underage when his father made his 4 December 1779 Kent County will. He was a delinquent taxable in Duck Creek Hundred in 1786 and taxable in Little Creek Hundred from 1790 to 1794 [RG 3535, Kent County Levy List, 1768-84, frame 607; 1785-97, 226, 267, 337]. He died before 10 August 1795 when administration on his estate was granted to Thomas **Hughes** who married his widow Mary [RG 3545, roll 68, frame 709; WB N-1:126; de Valinger, *Probate Records of Kent County*, 494]. Mary was head of a Little Creek Neck, Kent County household of 6 "other free" in 1800 [DE:38]. His children were

    i. Jemima, born say 1786.

    ii. Joseph, born say 1788.

    iii. Sarah, born say 1790.

    iv. Whittington[2], born say 1792, married Hester **Sisco**, 27 August 1817 Delaware bond, John **Durham** surety [DSA, Marriage Records 19:62].

    v. Thomas[2], born say 1794.

Other members of the family were

    i. Ann, born say 1737, confessed in Kent County court in August 1753 that she had an illegitimate child named Jonathan. John and Daniel Durham were her securities to support the child [RG 3805.002, Common Pleas, Dockets 1734-1779, frame 226].

    ii. Isaac, born say 1750, a laborer indicted in Kent County court in August 1768 for having an illegitimate female child by Ann **Songo** of Little Creek Hundred [DSA, RG 3805, case papers, August 1768 indictments]. He sued Aaron Hart in court in February 1779 [DSA, RG 3815.031, 1769-71, frames 20, 39]. He was taxable in Dover Hundred from 1770 to 1779 when he was delinquent, listed as a "Free Negro" from 1780 to 1800: a delinquent taxable in 1780, taxable in Dover Hundred in 1781, in Little Creek Hundred in 1782, in Dover Hundred from 1783 to 1800, taxable in 1797 on two cows, two yearlings, and a calf said by Isaac to be in his care for his children, taxable in what was then St. Jones Hundred in 1800 [RG 3535, Kent County Levy List, 1768-84, frames 69, 183, 216, 240, 298,

339, 413, 428, 500, 540, 571, 580; 1784-1797, frame 10, 45, 411; 1798-1800, frame 328], head of a Kent County, Delaware household of 9 "other free" in 1800 [DE:50] and a "negro" head of a Caroline County household of 6 "other free" in 1810 [MD:212], perhaps the Isaac Durham, born before 1776, who was head of a Baltimore County household of 5 "free colored" in 1830.

9   iii. Richard, born say 1745.

     iv. Ezekiel, taxable in Duck Creek Hundred, Kent County, in 1774.

     v. Charles, a "N." taxable in Duck Creek Hundred in 1788, in Little Creek Hundred from 1790 to 1794, in Duck Creek Hundred in 1797 and 1798 [RG 3535, Kent County Levy List, 1784-97, frames 127, 226, 267, 337, 347, 484, 572; 1798-9, frames 351, 382], head of a Duck Creek Hundred household of 6 "other free" in 1800 [DE:18]. Administration on his Kent County estate was granted to Thomas **Consellor** and Thomas Hawkins on 6 May 1812 [RG 3545, roll 68, frame 492].

9.   Richard Durham, born say 1745, was taxable in Jones Hundred, Kent County, in 1770 and also taxable that year in the south side of Broadkill Hundred, Sussex County. He was taxable in Little Creek Hundred, Kent County, from 1773 to 1781, and a "Free Negro" taxable in Dover Hundred in 1782. He witnessed the 2 May 1787 Sussex County will of Elias Johnson and the 30 May 1787 Sussex County will of James Wilkins. He was granted administration on the 6 March 1793 Sussex County estate of George[1] Durham [de Valinger, *Sussex County Probate Records*, 207, 208, 280]. He may have been the father of

     i. George[1], born say 1763, taxable in Duck Creek Hundred, Kent County, in 1783. Administration on his Sussex County estate was granted to Richard Durham on 6 March 1793 [de Valinger, *Sussex County Probate Records*, 280].

     ii. Miller, born say 1765, taxable in Little Creek Hundred in 1785 and a delinquent taxable in 1786.

     iii. Betty, born 1 October 1768 [Wright, *Vital Records of Kent and Sussex Counties*, 98].

DUTTON FAMILY

Members of the Dutton family in Maryland, Delaware and Virginia were

1   i. Mary, born say 1740.

2   ii. Isaac, born say 1742.

     iii. Stephen[1], born say 1744, father of an illegitimate child by Early **Wright**, a spinster of Coventry Parish, Somerset County, before June 1767 [Judicial Record 1766-7, 152].

3   iv. David[1], born say 1745.

     v. Stephen[3], born about 1769, an eight-year-old "negro" bound as an apprentice in Harford County to Benjamin Richardson in October 1777 [*Maryland Historical Society Bulletin*, vol. 35, no.3].

     vi. Guy, born before 1776, head of a Harford County household of 6 "free colored" in 1830.

     vii. Eleanor, "free negro" head of a Fairfax County, Virginia household of 2 "other free" and a slave in 1810 [VA:251].

     viii. Levin, born about 1793, registered in Somerset County on 4 June 1821: *born free...dark brown complexion...in the twenty eighth year of his age* [Certificates of Freedom 1821-32, 1-2].

1.   Mary Dutton, born say 1740, was a "Mulatto" who registered the 13 June 1759 birth of her daughter Leah and the 18 August 1762 birth of her son Stephen in Stepney Parish, Somerset County [Wright, *Maryland Eastern Shore Vital Records*, III:43, 46]. She was a spinster of Coventry Parish on 16 June 1767 when she confessed to the Somerset County court that she had an illegitimate child (by

an unnamed free person) and was fined £3 [Judicial Record 1766-7, 152]. She was the mother of

    i.   Leah, born 13 June 1759.

    ii. Stephen[2], born 18 August 1762, taxable on 100 acres in Wicomico Hundred, Somerset County, in 1783 [MSA S1161-9-10, p.68], head of a Sussex County household of 5 "other free" in 1800 [DE:391], 7 in 1810 [DE:325], and 6 "free colored" in 1820 [DE:396].

    iii. ?David[3], born before 1776, head of a Sussex County household of 3 "other free" in 1810 [DE:307] and 4 "free colored" in 1820 [DE:414].

    iv. ?Hanabel, born before 1776, head of a Nanticoke, Sussex County household of 6 "free colored" in 1820 [DE:224].

2.   Isaac Dutton, born say 1742, was bound as an apprentice blacksmith in Somerset County in 1759 [Judicial Record 1757-61, 225]. He married Elizabeth **Hill**, "(both free Mulattoes)," on 13 October 1763 in Stepney Parish, Somerset County [Wright, *Maryland Eastern Shore Vital Records*, 47]. They may have been the parents of

    i.   David[2], head of a Sussex County household of 6 "other free" in 1810 [DE:321].

3.   David[1] Dutton, born say 1745, married Bethia **Bibbons** on 17 September 1766 at Stepney Parish, Somerset County [Wright, *Maryland Eastern Shore Vital Records*, 49].[11] He sued Benjamin Gilliss (blacksmith) for £7.4 in Somerset County court on 19 November 1771 [Judicial Record 1769-72, 268]. He was a "free Mulatto" who purchased a total of 91 acres in 1772 and 1775 in the part of Somerset County which later became Wicomico County. He was taxable on 50 acres called *Crooked Chance* and 40 acres called *Poor Chance* in Rewastico, Somerset County, in 1783 [MSA S1161-9-10, p.40]. David died in 1798 not long after purchasing a larger tract of land in Nanticoke Hundred, Somerset County [Land Records Liber F-2, 395; Liber O-32, 206]. David and Bethia were the parents of

    i.   Nancy, born 7 August 1768, "daughter of David and Bethier," registered in Stepney Parish.

    ii. Suckey, born 14 March 1771, "daughter of David and Bethyer," registered in Stepney Parish.

    iii. Betheyer, born 20 January 1774, "daughter of David and Betheyer," registered in Stepney Parish [Wright, *Maryland Eastern Shore Vital Records*, 49, 50, 52, 53].

DYER/ DIAS FAMILY

1.   Priscilla Dyer, born say 1699, was a "Molatto" woman having 10 more years to serve and valued at £14 when she was listed in the Queen Anne's County inventory of Doctor Thomas Godman in 1730 [Prerogative Court Inventories 1729-30, 15:723]. She was called Priscilla Dias, the servant of Thomas Godman of Christ Church Parish, Queen Anne's County, in March 1730 when she confessed that she had an illegitimate child named Rachel. She received twenty lashes and was ordered to serve her master an additional eighteen months. She had six more illegitimate children between 1731 and 1740 (called Priscilla Dyer in 1732, Priscilla Doyas in March 1741). No race was mentioned in the court records [Judgment Record 1728-30, 221-2; 1730-1, 154-5; 1732-5, 13, 485-6; 1735-9, 146-7, 452; 1740-2, 92-3]. On 2 August 1787 the court allowed her £6 for her annual support [Surles, *And They Appeared at Court, 1774-7*, 89, 117]. She was the ancestor of

---

[11]The **Bibbens** family descended from a white woman who had a child by a slave in Accomack County in 1718 [Orders 1717-19, 23, 28].

  i. Rachel, born before March court 1730 when the court bound her to serve James Ringold until the age of twenty-one with the consent of her mother [Judgment Record 1728-30, 222].

  ii. George[1] Dias, born say 1740, convicted in Queen Anne's County court in March 1770 of having an illegitimate child named Risdon **Anderson** by Mary **Anderson** [Surles, *And They Appeared at Court, 1777-2*, 5, 40]. Risdon was head of a New Castle County, Delaware household of 11 "other free" in 1810 [DE:68].

  iii. George[2] Dias, born about 1761, petitioned with Thomas **Hopkins** for their freedom from Vinson Benton in Queen Anne's County court in 1774 [Surles, *And They Appeared at Court, 1774-7*, 18, 50, 73]. He was a "man of Colour" who was residing in Lancaster County, Pennsylvania, on 5 May 1818 when he appeared in court to apply for a pension for his services in the Revolution (called George Dias). He stated that he enlisted in Queen Anne's County and served until 1783. He received a land warrant and pension. On 14 July 1820 he was residing in Philadelphia when he made a further application (called George Dice, signing), stating that he was a shoemaker and had only one son who was 18 years old and still learning a trade [NARA, M804, S42,161, Bounty Land Warrant no. 618-100, http://fold3.com/image/15490549]. He was head of a Queen Anne's County household of 8 "other free" in 1790 (called George Dice) [MD:509] and 2 "free colored" males in the Middle Ward of Philadelphia in 1820 (called George Dies).

  iv. ?Ann Dyer, head of a Worcester County household of 10 "other free" in 1810 [MD:608].

  v. ?John Dyer, a "free Negro" taxable in Dover Hundred, Kent County, Delaware, in 1783 and 1785 [Levy Assessments 1768-84, frame 571; 1785-1850, frame 46].

EASTER FAMILY

1. Frances Easter, born say 1730, was presented by the Charles County court on 13 March 1749/50 for bearing an illegitimate "Melato" child by information of John Franklin, constable for the lower part of Durham Parish. On 12 June 1750 she was convicted of the charge, and the court bound her four-month-old son John to Bayne Smallwood [Court Record 1748-50, 604, 720]. She was the mother of

  i. John, born February 1749/50.

EASTON FAMILY

Members of the Easton family were

  i. Clem, "Mulatto" head of a Charles County household of 1 "other free" in 1790.

  ii. Samuel, "Mulatto" head of a Charles County household of 1 "other free" in 1790 and a "free Negro" head of a Prince George's County household of 2 in 1800 [MD:271].

  iii. John, born about 1784, registered in Anne Arundel County on 12 June 1816: *aged about thirty two years...yellowish complexion...free born* [Certificates of Freedom 1810-31, 85], perhaps the John Easton who was head of a Hampshire County, Virginia household of 1 "other free" in 1810 [MD:805].

EDMUNDS FAMILY

1. Elizabeth Edmunds, born say 1700, was the mother of "Mallatoe" Francis Edmunds who was sold by the Prince George's County court to Samuel Perrie until the age of 30 years on 25 November 1718 when Francis was five months old. The court ordered that William Mattingly be paid for keeping Elizabeth and her

child for five months, and on 25 August 1719 the court ordered that Richard Bevans or John Gardiner be paid 600 pounds of tobacco for keeping Elizabeth [Court Record 1715-20, 722, 934]. Elizabeth was the mother of

i. Francis, born about July 1718, a "Molatto man" with about 6-1/3 years to serve and valued at £20 when he was listed in the 25 July 1737 inventory of the Prince George's County estate of Richard Beaven [Prerogative Court Inventories 1739-41, 24:189-90]. Richard Bevan gave Frank Edmund, "alias Mollatto Frank," his freedom by his 27 February 1738/9 Prince George County will which was proved 21 May 1739 [Prerogative Court Wills, 22:58].

ELBERT FAMILY

Members of the Elbert family were

i. Isaac, "free negro," taxable in the 4th District of Kent County, Maryland, in 1783 [MSA 1161-7-4, p.6].

ii. William Elbut, aka **Hughes**, born about 1745, a forty-year-old "mulatto" who claimed to be a Revolutionary War soldier when he was jailed in Williamsburg, Virginia, according to the 9 July 1785 issue of the *Virginia Gazette and General Advertiser* [Headley, *18th Century Newspapers*, 113]. He was a taxable "negro" in the Upper District Hundred of Dorchester County in 1783 [MSA S1161-5-6, p.7] and head of a Dorchester County household of 3 "other free" in 1800 [MD:693]. He was probably related to the **Hughes** family of Dorchester County.

iii. Phil, head of a Caroline County household of 3 "other free" in 1810 [MD:210].

iv. Lydia, born about 1794, obtained a certificate in Talbot County on 28 April 1819: *25 years of age...four feet 11 ½ Inches high....born free and raised in the County.*

v. Nicholas, born about 1798, registered in Talbot County on 12 April 1819: *a negro man...about Twenty one years of age, 3 feet and a half Inches high, dark complexion...born free and raised in the County* [Certificates of Freedom 1815-28, 105, 109].

ELLIS FAMILY

1. Margaret Ellis, born say 1739, was a white woman who confessed to the Kent County, Maryland court in March 1759 that she had a child by a "Negroe" man on 10 February 1759. The court sold their child named Jonas to Charles Tilden until the age of thirty-one [Criminal Proceedings 1748-60, 219]. Margaret was the mother of

i. Jonas, born 10 February 1759.

ii. ?Richard, head of a Kent County household of 8 "other free" in 1800 [MD:148].

iii. ?Joseph, "Negro" head of a Murderkill Hundred, Kent County, Delaware household of 3 "other free" in 1800 [DE:117] and 3 in 1810 [DE:15].

iv. ?Cuffy, "Negro" head of a Murderkill Hundred Kent County, Delaware household of 6 "other free" in 1800 [DE:115] and 3 in 1810 [DE:54].

ENGLAND FAMILY

1. Elizabeth England, born say 1725, was living in Kent County, Maryland, in August 1746 when she submitted in court that she had a "Mulatto" child by a "Negro." The court ordered her to serve Peter Cole Jun[r] for seven years [Criminal Records 1742-4, 318-9]. She was probably the ancestor of

i. Rebecca, born 11 April 1770, a "Mola." bound to Phebe Gale by indenture in Kent County court on 24 April 1774 [Court Minutes 1774-82, n.p.].

ii. Thomas, a "Negro" taxable on 50 acres in Duck Creek Hundred, Kent

County, Delaware, in 1798 [Assessments 1798-9, 352].

ENGLISH FAMILY

1. Margaret[1] English, born say 1705, a spinster servant woman of Edward Worrell of St. Paul's Parish, confessed to the Kent County, Maryland court on 15 June 1725 that she had a "Mullatto" child by a "Negroe." The court ordered that she serve her master four months after the expiration of her service and that she and her child be sold by the county to Jervis Spencer, she to serve seven years and her child until the age of thirty-one. The court also referred to a prior conviction for the same offense in March 1721. In June 1727 she confessed to having a child by "Negroe Robin" [Criminal Records 1724-8, 82-4, 303-4]. She may have been the mother of

2   i.   Margaret[2], born say 1721.

2. Margaret[2] English, born say 1721, was called "Pegg English a Mollatto Woman of St. Paul's Parish," the servant of Edward Worrell, on 21 August 1739 and 18 March 1739/40 when the Kent County court ordered that she receive corporal punishment for having illegitimate children (by a free person). On 17 June 1740 she (or her mother?) was called "Margt. English spinster" when she confessed to having an illegitimate child (by a slave), and the court ordered her sold for seven years and her child bound to her master, Edward Worrell, until the age of thirty-one. On 17 November 1741 she confessed to having a child by a free person and received fifteen lashes [Criminal Proceedings 1738-9, 152; 1739-42, 66, 72, 225-6]. She may have been the ancestor of

     i.   Peter, (no race indicated) petitioned the Kent County court that he was unjustly detained as a servant by Bastus Wilkins [Court Minutes 1774-1782, n.p.].

     ii.   Susanna, born say 1750, indicted by the Kent County court in November 1774 and August 1775 for not giving in her tax [Criminal Dockets, 1774-6, August 1775 appearance no. 89].

ENNIS FAMILY

1. Eliza Hannis, born say 1692, had a child by "Negro Cesar," the servant of John Menekin, before August 1712 when Menekin was ordered to bring Caesar before the Anne Arundel County court [Judgment Record 1712-15, 6]. Eliza and Caesar may have been the ancestors of

2   i.   "Mulatto Sue," born say 1730.

2. "Mulatto Sue, born say 1730, was the mother of a five-year-old boy named Jonathan Annis who was bound by the Anne Arundel County court to Charles Frissel on 13 August 1751 until the age of twenty-one [Judgment Record 1751-4, 85]. She was the mother of

     i.   Jonathan, born March 1746/7, perhaps identical to John Annis who was married to Sarah when their daughter Mary was born on 9 May 1774 and baptized "a few days after" in St. Anne's Parish, Anne Arundel County [Wright, *Anne Arundel County Church Records*, 105].

     ii.   ?Peggy, head of a Baltimore County household of 7 "other free" in 1810 [MD:452].

The Annis family was probably identical to the Ennis family:

     i.   Anthony, head of an Anne Arundel County household of 8 "other free" in 1810 [MD:85].

     ii.   Judy, head of an Annapolis household of 3 "other free" and a white male in 1800.

     iii.   Samuel, head of an Anne Arundel County household of 5 "other free" in 1810 [MD:85].

iv. Jane, born about 1759, a ninety-one-year-old "Mulatto" counted in the 1850 census for Annapolis in the household of William **Bishop**.

v. Hector Enos, head of an Anne Arundel County household of 5 "other free" in 1810 [MD:98].

vi. Joshua, head of a Baltimore City household of 4 "other free" in 1810 [MD:61].

vii. Benjamin, head of a Baltimore City household of 4 "other free" in 1810 [MD:183].

viii. Charles, head of a Baltimore City household of 3 "other free" in 1810 [MD:109].

ix. R. Enness, head of a Baltimore City household of 2 "other free" in 1810 [MD:507].

x. Winney, "F. Negroe" head of a Fauquier County, Virginia household of 1 "other free" in 1810 [VA:420].

xi. William, born about 1788, obtained a certificate of freedom in Charles County on 15 September 1814 and registered it in the Court of the District of Columbia in Alexandria: *a bright mulatto man, about twenty six years of age...a free born person and was born and raised in New Port Parish, twenty-three years of age, a bright mulatto* [Arlington County Register of Free Negroes, 1797-1861, p. 23].

xii. James, born 1776-1794, heads of an Indian River, Sussex County household of 3 "free colored" in 1820 [DE:214].

EVANS FAMILY

1. Elizabeth Dennis, alias Evans, born say 1687, was convicted of having a "Mullattoe" child by the Anne Arundel County court in November 1707. She charged the child to a white man named Jeremiah Connelly, but he was acquitted and she was ordered to serve her mistress, Madam Biggs, twelve months for the trouble of her house. She confessed to having another child in August 1709 which she admitted was fathered by Mrs. Biggs's "Negroe Dick." She had another "Malato" child who was about five weeks old in November 1711 when he was sold to James Carroll to serve until the age of thirty-one [Judgment Records 1707-8, 649-50; 1708-12, 75, 374, 411]. She may have been the ancestor of

    i. David, born about 1710, a "Mulatto" with 5 years left to serve when he was listed in the Cecil County estate of Dominck Carroll on 23 August 1736 [Prerogative Inventories 22:359-60].

2   ii. Hannah, born say 1760.

    iii. Mary Evens, head of a Montgomery County household of 6 "other free" in 1810 [MD:914].

2. Hannah Evans, born say 1760, was born free in Dorchester County. She was head of a Dorchester County household of 5 "other free" in 1800 [MD:669]. She was the mother of

    i. Lucy **Cornish**, born about 1781, registered in Dorchester County on 13 November 1826: *of a dark chesnut colour...born free and is the daughter of Hannah Evans who was also born free, aged about 45 years.*

    ii. James, born about 1798, registered in Dorchester County on 24 August 1826: *of a chesnut colour...born free and is the son of Hannah Evans who was also born free, aged about 28 years.*

    iii. Hooper, born about 1802, registered in Dorchester County on 19 June 1824: *chesnut colour...son of Hannah Evans, who was born free, about 22 years of age* [Certificates of Freedom for Negroes 1806-64, 50, 55].

FARMER FAMILY

1. William[1] Farmer, born say 1711, was a "Mallato" taxable in the Pocomoke Hundred, Somerset County household of widow Elizabeth Davis from 1727 to

1733, taxable in the Bogerternorton household of Daniel Wells in 1734 and in the Pocomoke Hundred household of Isaac Morris in 1738 [List of Taxables]. He may have been the William Farmer who was sued by Archibald Smith in Kent County, Delaware court but not found by the sheriff in August 1727 [DSA, RG 3815.031, 1722-1732, frames 170, 171] and he may have been the William Farmer who was taxable in Little Creek Hundred, Kent County, Delaware, in 1768 and in Dover Hundred in 1772 [RG 3535, Kent County Levy List, 1768-84, frames 10, 151, 159] and he may have been the father of

 2   i. John^1, born say 1740.
 3   ii. William^2, born say 1745.

2. John^1 Farmer, born say 1740, was taxable in Little Creek Hundred, Kent County, Delaware, in 1768 and in Dover Hundred from 1772 to 1779 when he was listed without assessed tax [RG 3535, Kent County Levy List, 1768-84, frames 10, 151, 159, 222, 303, 345, 374]. He died before 29 February 1785 when administration on his estate was granted to Thomas Nixon, Esq., and James McClement [RG 3545, roll 74]. He may have been the father of

   i. John^2, born say 1761, a "free Negro" taxable in Murderkill Hundred, Kent County, in 1782 and taxable there in 1783 and 1784, taxable in Little Creek Hundred in 1787 and 1788, taxable in Murderkill Hundred in 1789 and 1791, taxable in Little Creek Hundred in 1792 and 1794, a "Molattoe" taxable in Little Creek Hundred in 1797 and 1798 [RG 3535, Kent County Levy List, 1768-84, frames 550, 595, 628; 1785-96, frames 71, 74, 106, 147; 230, 267, 337; 1797-8, frames 473, 483], head of a Mispillion Hundred household of 7 "other free" in 1800 [DE:105].
   ii. Nancy, head of a Caroline County household of 9 "other free" in 1810 [MD:188].
   iii. Adam, born say 1777, a "Mulatto" or "Negro" single man, taxable in Little Creek Hundred in 1798 and 1800 [RG 3535, Kent County Levy List, 1797-98, frames 473, 482; 1800-2, frame 326]. He married Betty **Buck**, 16 October 1805 Sussex County bond, John Callosa bondsman [DSA, Marriage Records 16:36].

3. William^2 Farmer, born say 1745, was taxable in Little Creek Hundred, Kent County, Delaware in 1768, called William Farmer, Jr., and taxable in Murderkill Hundred from 1770 to 1786: listed as a "free Negro" in 1782 [RG 3535, Kent County Levy List, 1768-84, frames 10, 80, 188, 281, 300, 345, 374, 457, 508, 544, 550, 595, 628; 1785-1796, frames 11, 52]. He was a "Negro" living on 100 acres of land belonging to Vincent Lockerman, Jr., deceased, on 13 December 1793 when the annual rent of the land was valued at £22 [Brewer, *Kent County Guardian Accounts, Houston to McBride (v.4)*, 147]. He was head of a Mispillion Hundred household of 7 "other free" in 1800 [DE:111]. He may have been the father of

   i. William^3, born say 1767, called Wm Farmer Junr when he was taxable in Murderkill Hundred in 1786, in Little Creek Hundred in 1787 and 1788, and in Murderkill Hundred in 1789, perhaps the William Farmer who was taxable in Murderkill Hundred in 1791, a "Mulatto" taxable in Little Creek Hundred in 1798, taxable in Mispillion Hundred in 1798 [RG 3535, Kent County Levy List, 1785-97, frames 52, 74, 106, 147, 230; 1797-8, frames 473, 478].

Their descendants in Delaware were

   i. Abel, born 1776-1794, head of a Dagsboro Hundred, Sussex County household of 4 "free colored" in 1820 [DE:372].
   ii. Gilbert, born 1794-1806, head of a Little Creek Hundred, Kent County household of 3 "free colored" in 1820 [DE:24].

FARRELL FAMILY

1. Margaret Ferrell, born say 1753, was a spinster servant of Mr. Edward White of Caroline County in November 1774 when she had a "Mulatto" child by a "Negro." The court ordered her master to deliver her up to the court at the expiration of her service to be sold for seven years and sold her child to Daniel Godwin until the age of thirty-one for 102 pounds of tobacco [Criminal Record 1774-8, 61]. She may have been the mother of
    i. Adam, head of a Caroline County household of 3 "other free" in 1810 [MD:216].

FARTHING FAMILY

1. Ann Farthing, born say 1718, was living in Saint Paul's Parish, Kent County, Maryland, on 19 June 1739 when the court convicted her of having a "Mollatto" child by a "Negro" [Criminal Record 1738-9, 178-180]. She was probably the ancestor of
    i. Ann, head of a Kent County, Maryland household of 4 "other free" in 1810 [MD:844].
    ii. Henrietta, a "mulatto" child living in Fairfax County, Virginia, on 17 February 1761 when the court ordered the churchwardens of Truro Parish to bind her as an apprentice to James McKensy [Orders 1756-63, 553].

FENTON FAMILY

1. Margaret Fenton, born say 1728, was the servant of David Evans on 9 August 1748 when he brought her into Anne Arundel County court where she confessed to having two "Molatto" children. The court bound her children Eleanor and Charles to her master for thirty-one years. She had another "Molatto" child, also called Charles, when she was the servant of Henry Howard who brought her into court on 13 August 1751 [Court Record, 1748-1751, 65; 1751-54, 85]. She was the mother of

  2
    i. Eleanor, born 28 July 1746.
    ii. Charles[1], born in May 1748.
    iii. Charles[2], born 21 June 1749, enlisted in the Revolution on 20 July 1776 [*Archives of Maryland*, 18:41]. He was head of a Patapsco Hundred, Baltimore County household of 5 whites in 1790 and head of a Soldiers Delight Hundred, Baltimore County household of 4 "other free," a white woman 16-26 and 2 slaves in 1810.

2. Eleanor Fenton, born 28 July 1746, was probably the mother of
    i. Margaret, born about 1767, a sixteen-year-old "mulatto wench" living in Prince George's County near Baldwin's tavern on 19 July 1783 when she ran away from William Merriken according to an ad he placed in the *Maryland Gazette* [Windley, *Runaway Slave Advertisements*, II:138].

FISHER FAMILY

1. Mary[1] Molloyd, born say 1660, was an Irish woman who came to Maryland as the indentured servant of Madam Vansweringen and was later the servant of Thomas Beale. According to the petition for freedom brought by her grandchildren in Anne Arundel County court in June 1743, she had an illegitimate child named Mary by Peter, an East Indian servant who lived with Lord Baltimore in St. Mary's County. Peter "became a free Molato after serving some time to Major (Thomas) Beale of Saint Mary's County" [Judgment Record 1734-6, 83; 1743-4, 11]. They were the parents of

  2
    i. Mary[2], born say 1680.

2. Mary[2] Molloyd, born say 1680, was kept as a slave by Thomas Beale's son, John Beale, Gentleman, of Anne Arundel County. She married Francis Fisher, a "Negro slave" of Beale's, in a ceremony performed by a Roman Catholic priest named Robert Brooke [Judgment Record 1734-6, 83; 1743-4, 11]. Richard and Mary Fisher had

3   i. Ann, born about 1702.

      ii. Robert, born say 1704, held as the slave of Thomas Jennings of Anne Arundel County in June 1743.

     iii. James, born say 1706, held as the slave of John Dorsey, son of Caleb Dorsey, Gentleman, of Anne Arundel County in June 1743.

     iv. Richard, born say 1708, held as the slave of Richard Dorsey, Gentleman, of Anne Arundel County in June 1743.

      v. Mary, born say 1710, held as the slave of Richard Warfield, Jr., Gentleman, of Anne Arundel County in June 1743.

     vi. Frances, born say 1712, held as the slave of Colonel Henry Ridgely of Anne Arundel County in June 1743.

    vii. Edward[1], born say 1714, held as the slave of Philip Hammond, Esq., of Anne Arundel County in June 1743.

    viii. Charles, born say 1716, held as the slave of Elizabeth Beale, widow, of Anne Arundel County in June 1743 [Judgment Record 1743-4, 11-12].

3. Ann Fisher, born about 1702, was about thirty-two years old when she petitioned for her freedom from John Beale of Anne Arundel County in August 1734. She was held as the slave of Thomas Gassaway of Baltimore County in June 1743 when she and her brothers and sisters brought an unsuccessful suit in Anne Arundel County court for their freedom [Judgment Record 1734-6, 83; 1743-4, 11-12]. On 26 May 1783 her daughter Eleanor **Toogood** sued for her freedom by reason of her descent from a free white woman and won her case. The Court of Appeals affirmed the judgment in Eleanor's favor and also ruled that Eleanor's grandmother, Mary Fisher, should have been free. Ann was the mother of

      i. Eleanor **Toogood**, born say 1750, won her freedom in a suit in the General Court against Doctor Upton Scott in October 1782 by reason of her descent from a free white woman [*Cases in the General Court and Court of Appeals of Maryland*, 26-31; Catterall, *Judicial Cases Concerning Slavery*, IV:49-50].

     ii. ?Edward[2] Fisher, head of a Queen Anne's County household of 16 "other free" in 1800 [MD:341].

     iii. ?Henry Fisher, head of a Kent County, Maryland household of 5 "other free" in 1800 [MD:160].

     iv. ?Joseph Fisher, a "Free Negro" taxable in Little Creek Hundred, Kent County, Delaware in 1787 and 1789, head of a Little Creek, Kent County household of 5 "other free" in 1800 [DE:35] and 7 "free colored" in 1820 [DE:27].

Another member of the Fisher family was

      i. Catherine, a free "Negro" who sued Richard Starbuck, cutter, in Anne Arundel County court in August 1765 for £2 for cash and other articles she had lent him [Judgment Record 1765, 296-7].

FITZGERALD FAMILY

Members of the Fitzgerald family in Charles County were

      i. Elizabeth, born say 1697, a "Free Mollatto girl" maintained by the Charles County court in 1711 because she was troubled with convulsions. She was placed with Daniel Murphey in 1711, with Thomas Austin in 1712 and with Henry Franklin in March 1712/3 [Court Record 1710-14, 126, 137, 209].

     ii. Peter, born about 1708, a "Mallatto...born of a white woman," eighteen years old and the former servant of Cleborn Lomax on 14 June 1726 when he was sold by the Charles County court to Thomas Harris until the age of thirty-one for 500 pounds of tobacco. He was about twenty five on 14 August 1733 when the court rejected his complaint that he was still detained as a servant by the widow of Thomas Harris [Court Record 1725-1727, 236; 1731-4, 378].

Dorchester County
1.   Alex Fitzgerald, born say 1763, was the mother of
      i.   Polly **Young**, born about 1784, registered in Dorchester County on 25 November 1829: *of a chesnut colour...born free, raised in Dorchester County and is the Daughter of Alex Fitzgerald who was also born free, aged about 46 years* [Certificates of Freedom for Negroes 1806-64, 65].

FLAMER/ FLAMES FAMILY

Members of the Flamer family were
      i.   John[1], born say 1717, a "Molatto" servant man having "eleven months and 15" to serve and valued at £4 in the inventory of the Queen Anne's County estate of William Hernsley on 28 October 1737 [Prerogative Inventories 1737-1739, 45-6]. He had an illegitimate child by Elizabeth **Grinnage** in September 1736 [Judgment Record 1735-9, 344, 382]. He may have been identical to Jonathan Flamar who owed 994 pounds of tobacco to the Queen Anne's County estate of Solomon Clayton (who died in 1739) [Prerogative Inventories 98:18-22].
      ii. William, born say 1717, a "Molatto" servant man having "eleven months and 15" to serve and valued at £4 in the inventory of the Queen Anne's County estate of William Hernsley on 28 October 1737 [Prerogative Inventories 1737-1739, 45-6].
      iii. Rachel, born say 1720, a "poor old Woman," supported from public funds by the Queen Anne's County from 12 December 1775 to 1787. She was called a "poor molatto woman" by the court when it approved her allowance for 1777 [Surles, *and they Appeared at Court, 1774-1777*, 65, 80; *1779, 1782, 1785, 1786, 1787*, 35, 53, 89, 96, 117].
1   iv. Judith, born say 1722.

1.   Judith Flamer, born say 1722, was the servant (no race indicated) of Mark Hargadine of Saint Paul's Parish in March 1745 when the Queen Anne's County court convicted her of having an illegitimate child named John in 1742 and another child in 1743. In August 1750 she confessed to having other children in 1748 and 1749 [Judgment Record 1744-6, 161-2; 1750, 40-2]. She was a spinster living in St. Paul's Parish when she received 30 lashes and was ordered to pay fourfold the value for stealing a hog worth 40 pounds of tobacco [Criminal Record 1751-9, n.p.]. She owed the estate of Thomas Kendall £4.19 on 10 August 1756 [Prerogative Inventories 73:243]. She was the mother of
      i.   John[2], born on 10 October 1742, a "black" taxable in the Upper Hundred of Kent Island, Queen Anne's County, in 1776 [Carothers, *1776 Census of Maryland*, 148], married to Sherry **Grinnage**'s daughter Sarah on 1 November 1790 when Sherry gave her £5 by his Caroline County will [WB JR B:168-70].
      ii. ?Ann, mother of William and John Flamer (no race indicated) who were with George Sweat on 26 January 1774 when the Queen Anne's County court ordered him to bring them to court [Surles, *and they Appeared at Court, 1774-1777*, 41], perhaps identical to the "Molatto girl named Nan" who was valued at £16 in the inventory of the Queen Anne's County estate of William Hernsley on 28 October 1737 [Prerogative Inventories 1737-1739, 45-6].
      iii. ?Solomon, head of a Queen Anne's County household of 9 "other free" in 1790 [MD:99] and 9 in 1800 [MD:341]. He was married to Sherry **Grinnage**'s daughter on 1 November 1790 when Sherry gave her £5 by his

Caroline County will [WB JR B:168-170].
iv.   ?William, head of a Talbot County household of 1 "other free" and 3 slaves in 1800 [MD:506].

FLETCHER FAMILY

1. Polly Fletcher, born say 1745, was an Irish servant who was indentured to Matthew Whiting, Esq., of Prince William County, Virginia. Whiting's executor, E. Brooke, Sr., certified in the Court of the District of Columbia in Alexandria that Polly was the mother of Betsy, Mary, and Alice Fletcher, "Mulatto" women [Arlington County Register of Free Negroes, 1797-1861, nos. 57, 59, 61, 62, pp.51-3]. Her children were

2   i.   ?Ann, born say 1764.
      ii.   Betsy, born about 1775, registered in Alexandria on 2 May 1820: *a forty-five-year-old "bright Mulatto" woman born on the Prince William County estate of Matthew Whiting.*
     iii.   Mary, born about 1780, registered in Alexandria on 8 December 1820: *a forty-year-old "bright Mulatto" woman born on the Prince William County estate of Matthew Whiting.*
      iv.   Alice, born about 1795, registered in Alexandria on 2 May 1820: *a twenty-five-year-old "bright Mulatto" woman born on the Prince William County estate of Matthew Whiting.*
       v.   ?Peter, head of an Accomack County household of 7 "other free" in 1810 [VA:94].
      vi.   ?John, "F. Negroe" head of a Fauquier County household of 7 "other free" in 1810 [VA:398].
     vii.   ?Cloe, head of a Petersburg household of 2 "other free" in 1810 [VA:334].

2. Ann Fletcher, born say 1764, was head of a St. Mary's County household of 3 "other free" in 1790. She may have been the mother of
       i.   Jane, born about 1784, a thirty-seven-year-old "stout negro woman" who registered in Alexandria, Virginia, on 6 August 1821 and registered in Washington, D.C., on 3 November 1834. Sarah Harper swore that Jane was born free in St. Mary's County and was bound to Sarah's mother, Catherine Cheveller, to serve until she came of age. Harper testified that she and Jane "grew up and were girls together" and that Jane's parents were free as were her several brothers and sisters [Provine, *District of Columbia Free Negro Registers*, 254].

1. Ann Fletcher, born say 1711, was a spinster living in St. Stephen's Parish, Cecil County, in March 1732/3 when she was convicted of having a child by a "Negro." The court ordered her sold for seven years [Criminal Record 1733-41, 3].

FORD FAMILY

1. Amy[1] Ford, born say 1698, was the servant of John Southern on 12 November 1706 when the Charles County court presented her for having an illegitimate "Molatto" child [Court Record 1704-10, 273]. She may have been the mother of

2   i.   Aptha, born say 1742.

2. Aptha Foard, born say 1742, confessed to the Prince George's County court on 22 November 1763 that she had an illegitimate "Mulatto" child. The court ordered her sold for seven years and bound her ten-month-old daughter Amey to her master, John Billingsley, until the age of thirty-one. On 25 March 1766 she confessed to having another "Mulatto" child. The court ordered her sold for a second seven-year term and bound her one-month-old daughter Ally to her master until the age of thirty-one. She was called Appey Ford on 23 August 1768 when the court ordered her to serve another seven-year term and sold her daughter Sarah, born 10 May 1768, to John Mitchell [Court Record 1763-4, 8; 1765-6, 385-6; 1768-70, 34-5]. She was the mother of

      i.   Amy[2], born January 1763.

3   ii.   Ally, born February 1766.

4   iii.   Sarah, born in 1768.

     iv.   ?Rachel, head of a Montgomery County household of 3 "other free" in 1790.

      v.   ?Mary[1], head of a Baltimore Town household of 3 "other free" in 1790.

     vi.   ?Ninian, "Mulatto" head of a Charles County household of 2 "other free" in 1790, perhaps identical to N. Ford, head of a Prince George's County household of 2 "other free" and 3 slaves in 1810 [MD:6].

    vii.   ?Philis, "F.N." head of a Charles County household of 1 "other free" in 1790.

   viii.   ?Jacob, head of a Kent County household of 6 "other free" in 1800 [MD:160].

     ix.   ?William, head of a King George County, Virginia household of 5 "other free" in 1810 [VA:199].

      x.   ?George, head of a Westmoreland County, Virginia household of 4 "other free" in 1810.

3.   Ally[1] Ford, born February 1766, was bound to John Billingsley on 25 March 1766 until the age of thirty-one. She was a "free woman of colour" living in Prince George's County between 1819 and 1826 when her children obtained certificates of freedom. She was the mother of

5   i.   Chloe, born about 1777.

     ii.   Daphney, born about 1783, registered in Prince George's County on 28 September 1826: *a mulatto woman, about 43 years old...born free in Prince George's County, being the daughter of Ally Ford, a free woman of colour.* Her son Henry registered on 28 September 1826: *a mulatto man, about 24 years old...son of Daphney Ford, a free woman of color.*

    iii.   Mary[2], born about 1785, registered on 28 September 1826: *a very dark mulatto woman, about 41 years old...born free in Prince George's County...daughter of Ally Ford.*

    iv.   Thomas[1], born about 1792, registered on 19 January 1819: *a yellow man, about 27 years old...descendant of Ally Ford.*

     v.   John, born about 1794, registered on 19 January 1819: *a black man, about 25 years old...has thick lips...descendant of a free woman named Ally Foard.*

     vi.   Benjamin, born about 1801, registered on 28 September 1826: *a copper-colored man, about 25 years old...son of Ally Ford.*

    vii.   Jane[2], born about 1806, registered on 28 September 1826: *a black woman, about 21(?) years old...daughter of Ally Ford.*

   viii.   Nancy, born about 1808, registered on 28 September 1826: *about 18 years old...daughter of Ally Ford.*

     ix.   Rebecca, born about 1809, registered on 28 September 1826: *a copper-colored girl, about 17 years old...daughter of Ally Ford* [Provine, *Registrations of Free Negroes*, 27, 28, 61, 62].

4.   Sarah Ford, born in 1768, was a free woman living in Prince George's County in 1817 when her son Charles registered. She was the mother of

     i.   Charles, born about 1794, registered in Prince George's County on 2 April 1817: *a black man, about 23 years old...descendant of a free woman named Sarah Ford who lived in the family of Benjamin Wood* [Provine, *Registrations of Free Negroes*, 23].

5.   Chloe Ford, born about 1777, registered in Prince George's County on 18 September 1819: *a black woman, about 42 years old...raised in the family of John Billingsly of Prince George's County...daughter of Ally Foard.* She was the mother of

     i.   Thomas[2], born about 1798, registered in Prince George's County on 18 September 1819: *a black man, about 21 years old...son of Chloe Foard.*

     ii.   Alley[2], born about 1796, registered on 18 September 1819: *a mulatto*

> *woman, about 25 years old...daughter of Chloe Foard.*
>
> iii. Jane[1], born about 1800, registered on 18 September 1819: *a mulatto woman, about 19 years old...daughter of Chloe Foard.*
> iv. Mary[3], born about 1808, registered on 17 February 1825: *about 17 years of old...daughter of Chloe Foard* [Provine, *Registrations of Free Negroes*, 31, 50].

Other members of a Ford family in Maryland were

> i. Rachel, born say 1760, a witness for the state against Patrick **Hopkins** who was charged with fornication by the Queen Anne's County court in 1782. On 3 August 1787 the court allowed £5 per annum from public funds to support Henry Ford, "mulatto orphan of Rachel Ford" [Surles, *and they Appeared at Court, 1779, 1782, 1785, 1786, 1787*, 95].
> ii. Thomas, head of a Cecil County household of 7 "other free" in 1800 [MD:252].

FORTUNE FAMILY

1. Fortune **Game**, born say 1687, was called Fortune **Magee**, the servant of Mrs. Mary Day, on 15 June 1705 when the Somerset County court ordered that she serve Mrs. Day until the age of thirty-one, explaining that she was the "mulatto" daughter of Maudlin Magee, a white woman living in Somerset County who was married to George Magee at the time [Judicial Records 1702-5, in Land Records GI:251]. In 1712 she bound her children, Ross, Sue, and Perlina to Mrs. Day [Judicial Records 1702-5, 251; 1711-3, 220]. She was called Fortune **Game**, a taxable head of a Nanticoke Hundred, Somerset County household from 1728 to 1735, with Betty **Game** in 1728 and 1731, and with Betty and Rose **Game** in 1733. She was the mother of

> i. Rose, born March 1703.
> ii. Sue **Magee**, born in April 1705.
> iii. Perlina, born in April 1707, five years old "next April" in March 1712 when she was bound as an apprentice. She was probably identical to "Ner Game," a taxable in Nanticoke Hundred in 1734 and to Polina Gam who was a taxable head of a Nanticoke Hundred, Somerset County household with Sarah Gam in 1759.

2 iv. ?Betty, born say 1712.
3 v. ?Sarah Fortune, born say 1715.
> vi. ?Anville, born say 1722, taxable in Fortune Game's Nanticoke Hundred household in 1738 and 1740 and taxable in Isaac Bebbings' Nanticoke Hundred household in 1744.

2. Betty **Game**, born say 1712, was taxable in Nanticoke Hundred, Somerset County, in the household of Fortune **Game** from 1728 to 1731. Betty **Game** purchased 50 acres on the south side of the Nanticoke River in Somerset County in 1753. By his 14 June 1753 Somerset County will, proved 17 August 1757, George Day Scott left Betty Fortune the 50-acre tract where she was then living if she paid the balance due [WB 1756-61, 58]. She was probably identical to Betty Fortune who was a taxable head of household in Nanticoke Hundred with (her daughter?) Fortune Fortune in 1757. Betty was probably one of "Two Women of a Dark Complection Live at the Head of Tippin(?)" listed by the constable as having refused to pay the discriminatory tax on free African American women in 1743. The constable reported further that "they are full as Dark as most Mallatos. They are of the Breed of old fortune and Robt. Game" [List of Taxables, 1743]. Betty was head of a taxable household in Little Creek Hundred, Sussex County, in 1777 and 1790. She may have been the mother of

> i. George[1] **Game**, born say 1733, taxable in Betty **Game**'s household in Nanticoke Hundred in 1749.
> ii. "Negro Patience **Thomson**," a taxable in Betty **Game**'s Nanticoke Hundred household in 1756, called Patience **Game** in 1783, taxable in

Nanticoke Hundred [MSA S1161-9-10, p.45].

 iii. ?Fortune Fortune, born say 1740, taxable in Betty Fortune's household in Nanticoke Hundred in 1757.

 iv. Levin[2] **Game**, taxable in Little Creek Hundred in 1777 and from 1788 to 1791, perhaps identical to Levin **McGee/ Magee** and Levin Fortune.

 v. John **Game**, taxable in Indian River, Sussex County, in 1789, called a "Mulato" in the list of delinquents: "not Settled anywhere," and taxable there in 1790 and 1791.

3. Sarah Fortune, born say 1715, was a "Mullatto" living "at Widow Ann Fooks" on 11 March 1734/5 when the Charles County court presented her for having an illegitimate child [Court Record 1734-9, 1].[12] Sarah may have been identical to Sarah **Gam**, a taxable in the Nanticoke Hundred, Somerset County household of (her sister?) Polina **Gam** in 1759. Sarah was the mother of James Fortune, "a Mulatto of Sarah Fortune," who bound himself as an apprentice to James Laws until the age of twenty-one in Somerset County in March 1761 to learn the trade of light cooper [Judicial Records 1760-3, 63b]. She was the mother of

 i. James, born say 1745.

4. James Fortune, born say 1745, bound himself as an apprentice until the age of twenty-one in Somerset County in March 1761. He may have been the ancestor of

 i. Major, born say 1783, a "BM" taxable in Accomack County in 1807 [PPTL 1783-1814, frame 677], head of a household of 5 "other free" in 1810 [VA:95].

 ii. William, a "BM" taxable on a horse in Accomack County in 1809 [PPTL 1783-1814, frame 710].

1. John Fortin, born say 1715, was an Indian taxable in Pocomoke Hundred of Somerset County in 1735 [List of Tithables]. He may have been the ancestor of

2 i. Levina, born say 1740.

 ii. Mary, presented by the Accomack County court on 24 June 1760 fo rnot listing herself as a tithable. Jacob Broadwater undertook to pay her court costs [Orders 1753-63, 352].

2. Levina Fortune, born say 1740, was presented by the Accomack County court on 24 June 1760 fornot listing herself as a tithable. The court ordered that she remain in the custody of the sheriff until she paid her court costs which Jacob Broadwater undertook to pay. She may have been the mother of

 i. Leah, an Indian formerly bound to Jacob Broadwater who was bound by the court to Anne Pitt on 2 June 1763 [Orders 1753-63, 352, 558, 597].

 ii. Scarburgh, bound by the Accomack County court to Robert Polk on 27 July 1768.[Orders 1767-8, 124].

FOUNTAIN FAMILY

1. Mary Fountain, born say 1675, the servant of Emanuel Ratclife, was presented by the Charles County court on 13 March 1693/4 for having an illegitimate child. She was living at Penelope Land's on 14 June 1698 when she was presented for the same offense. And she was the servant of Penelope Land on 14 January 1700/1 when she was presented for having a "Mollatto" child. She confessed to the fact on 11 March 1700/1 [Court and Land Record 1692(3)-94, 242; Court Record 1696-1701/2, 373, 397; 1698(9)-1699/1700, 176]. She was probably the mother of

---

[12]The Fooks family was from Somerset County [1783 Worcester County Tax List, MSA 1161-11-5, p.4].

2   i.   Thomas[1], born in May 1698.

2.   Thomas[1] Fountain, born in May 1698, a "Mallattoe," was almost six years old on
     14 March 1703/4 when the Charles County court bound him to Joseph Douglass
     until the age of thirty-one. He had been purchased from the William and Mary
     Vestry by Mrs. Land and given to her daughter, Penelope Douglass, wife of
     Joseph Douglass. Thomas was the "Mallatto Servant" of Captain Joseph Douglass
     on 11 March 1728/9 when the Charles County court ordered that he serve his
     master an additional ten days for each of the thirty days he had absented himself
     from his master's service [Court Record 1701-4, 327; 1727-31, 231]. He was
     probably the ancestor of
          i.   Thomas[2], head of a Talbot County household of 3 "other free" in 1800
               [MD:512].
          ii. William, head of a Caroline County household of 4 "other free" in 1810
               [MD:188].
          iii. Sam, head of a Caroline County household of 6 "other free" in 1810
               [MD:188].
          iv. James, born 1794-1776, head of a Murderkill Hundred, Kent County,
               Delaware household of 6 "free colored" in 1820 [DE:13].

FOWLER FAMILY

Members of the Fowler family were
          i.   Freeman, head of an Octoraro, Cecil County household of 1 "other free"
               in 1790.
          ii. Sarah, born say 1767, mother of Elizabeth Fowler who registered in St.
               Mary's County on 20 September 1823: *daughter of Sarah, aged about
               thirty five years...of a bright complexion...born free*. Elizabeth was the
               mother of Louisa Fowler who registered in St. Mary's County on 30 April
               1822: *Daughter of Eliz. Fowler...aged about fifteen years, bright
               complexion....born free & was born & raised in Saint Mary's County*
               [Certificates of Freedom 1806-64, 60, 63].

FRANCISCO/ SISCO FAMILY

1.   John[1] Francisco, born perhaps 1630, was the slave of Stephen Charlton for whom
     Charlton claimed a headright in Northampton County, Virginia, in August 1647
     [DW 1645-51, 97 by Deal, *Race and Class*]. In July 1648 Charlton made a deed
     of manumission to free him ten years later in November 1658: *and then the said
     Negro is to bee a free man*. He was called "Black Jack" in Charlton's October
     1654 will by which he received his freedom. Charlton also agreed to free John's
     wife, Christian, a "Negro woman," three years after his death or within six months
     if she paid 2,500 pounds of tobacco [DW 1645-51, 150-2; 1654-55, fol.57]. John
     and Christian were tithable in their own household in Northampton County from
     1665 to 1671. Grace Susanna (Sebastian **Cane**'s wife?) was in their household in
     1667. In 1668 the court agreed to have the "Negro" child of Thomas **Driggers**,
     then living with him, bound to him until the age of twenty-one [Orders 1657-64,
     198; 1664-74, fol.14, p.42, 53, fol.54, fol.115]. He was called "John Francisco
     Negroe" on 7 July 1685 when the Accomack County court ordered him to pay his
     debt of 5,090 pounds of tobacco to Colonel William Kendall [W&c 1682-97,
     66a]. He was taxable in Accomack County from 1674 to 1695: called a "negro"
     in 1676 and 1686. In 1684 one of his three tithables was identified as his unnamed
     wife [Orders 1676-78, 33, 57; 1678-82, 18, 99; W&c 1682-97, 191, 258;
     Nottingham, *Accomack Tithables*, 12, 16, 18, 19, 22, 23, 25, 27, 28, 31, 33, 35,
     37, 40, 42, 44, 47, 50, 52, 54, 60]. John was probably the ancestor of
2   i.   Daniel[1], born say 1680.
3   ii. Elizabeth, born say 1695.
          iii. Thomas[1] Frisco, born say 1700, a Northampton County taxable with Ann

Frisco in 1724 and tithable without Ann in Nathaniel Anders' household in 1725 [L.P. 1724, 1725]. He may have been identical to Thomas[2] Sisco of Kent County, Delaware.

2. Daniel[1] Francisco, born say 1680, was sued for debt in Northampton County, Virginia, on 28 November 1706, but the case was dismissed because neither part appeared [Orders, Wills, Etc., 1698-1710, 308]. Daniel was probably in company with William **Driggers** because Daniel had a child by Mary Winslow in Somerset County sometime in 1708, and William **Driggers** helped him by carrying her out of county to avoid prosecution. Daniel was called a Somerset County planter when he admitted to being the father of Mary's child when he appeared in court seven years later in March 1713/4. He was probably living with Elizabeth Francisco, "of Somerset County," who was sued for a debt of 500 pounds of tobacco on 5 June 1712 by Samuel Daughty with whom she had contracted to pay by 7 May 1712 at Pocomoke. On 7 August 1712 her bail was forfeited to pay the debt [Judicial Records 1707-11, 94-6, 103; 1711-13, 167, 225; 1713-5, 5, 26]. Daniel was in Accomack County on 6 July 1715 when the court ordered that he, John Smith, John Martiall, and Richard Rowle/ Rowlin be summoned to the next court for disobeying constable Hill Drummond while he was trying to break up a fight. The other parties were fined when they appeared at the next court on 4 October, but there was no further mention of Daniel [Orders 1714-17, 10a, 11]. He was sued for debt by Evan Jones in Kent County, Delaware court in November 1724, by Nicholas Greenway in May 1725, by Jonathan Griffin in May 1731 and by Nicholas Nixon for £16 in August 1731 [RG 3815.031, Dockets 1722-1732, frames 83, 84, 492, 498, 519, 593 ; MS case papers]. He was listed in the Little Creek Hundred, Kent County, Delaware tax assessments from 1727 to 1733: listed near Winslow **Drigers**, Thomas **Comsoloe**, Julius **Caesar**, William **Beckett**, and Jacob **Miller** in 1727 [RG 3535, Assessments 1726-42, frames 346, 352, 358, 363, 369], apparently identical to David Francisco who died before 22 September 1732 when the inventory of his Kent County, Delaware estate was taken. (This inventory is not the original, but a copy made in 1752. Perhaps the clerk wrote David for Daniel). Daniel may have married the daughter of Thomas **Consellor** who named his daughter Elizabeth Francisco in his 26 September 1739 Kent County will. "Elisabeth Siscom" was head of a household in Little Creek Hundred, Kent County, in 1738, taxable on her son Thomas. Doctor Ridgely was allowed £7 for her maintenance by the Kent County levy court on 18 December 1766 [Kent Count Levy List, 1727-67, frame 531]. Daniel and Elizabeth may have been the parents of

4   i. Daniel[2], born say 1700.
     ii. Tabitha, born say 1705, sued by Jacob **Miller** in Kent County court but withdrawn in August 1731 [RG 3815.031, Common Pleas, Dockets 1722-1732, frame 509].
5   iii. Thomas[2], born say 1715.
6   iv. John[2], born say 1723.
     v. Rebecca, sued in Kent County court in August 1748 by John Clayton in a case decided out of court [RG 3815.031, Common Pleas, Dockets 1744-1750, frame 423].

3. Elizabeth Francisco, born say 1695, a "negro," bound out her daughter Rachel to Robert Nottingham in Northampton County on 17 March 1717/18 [Orders 1716-18, 84] and bound out her daughter Sabra, "a Negro Child," to Abraham Bowker on 18 August 1719 [Orders 1719-22, 31]. On 13 September 1722 she was accused of murdering her child but was acquitted of the charge [Orders 1719-22, 183]. In November 1722 Bowker sued her to recover his costs for looking after her during her childbirth. She may have left the county since Ralph Pigot forfeited the bail he posted for her appearance in court to answer Bowker [Mihalyka, *Loose Papers 1628-1731*, 37, 42]. Her children were

7   i. Rachel[1], born perhaps 1715.

ii.   Sabra, born perhaps 1717.

4.   Daniel² Francisco, born say 1700, was taxable in Little Creek Hundred in 1748, listed next to John Francisco [Assessments 1743-48 (RG 3535-2), frame 51], but not listed in later assessments, so he may have been the brother of John Francisco who petitioned the Kent County Orphans Court on 26 February 1756 that his brother had died "some years ago," as had his brother's wife Catherine, leaving an infant. Perhaps Daniel's widow was Ruth Fransisscoe who was being maintained by James Starling on 18 November 1766 when the Kent County levy court allowed him £10 for her maintenance [Levy List 1727-67, frame 530], and perhaps he was the father of

8   i.   Ephraim Sisco, born say 1745.

5.   Thomas² Francisco, born say 1715, was taxable in the Little Creek Hundred, Kent County household of his mother Elisabeth Siscom in 1738 and taxable in his own household from 1740 to 1745. He died before 16 July 1748 when his widow Patience Sisco was granted administration on his Kent County estate. The 29 November 1750 account of his estate included the payment of a bond to Daniel **Durham** for £18 [WB I-1:231; RG 3845.000, roll 80, frames 332-3]. Thomas and Patience may have been the parents of

9   i.   Benjamin, born say 1735.

6.   John² Francisco, born say 1723, was taxable in Little Creek Hundred from 1743 to 1758 [1743 to 1767 Levy Assessments, frames 16, 24, 43, 51, 107, 136, 143, 187, 226]. On 26 February 1756 he petitioned the Kent County Orphans Court that his unnamed brother (Daniel?) had died "some years ago" as had his brother's wife Catherine, leaving an infant in the care of John Swaney who was unable to care for it. The court placed the child in John's care. He married Sarah **Durham**, the Sarah Sisco who was named in the 9 April 1788 Kent County will of her father John **Durham** [WB M-1, fol.170-1]. John Francisco died before 24 October 1798 when administration of his Kent County estate was granted to (his son?) Charles Francisco. The inventory of his estate totaled over £942 and included 80 acres of wheat worth £90 and another 35 acres of crops worth £20. On 10 November 1800 the estate was divided among his widow Elizabeth Francisco and Charles, Lydia, and Esther Francisco [RG 3845.000, roll 80, frames 196-208]. His children were most likely

         i.   John³, Jr., born say 1740, taxable in Little Creek Hundred from 1758.
         ii. James, born say 1742, sued Isaac Carty in Kent County in a case discontinued by the plaintiff before trial in February 1762 [RG 3815.031, Common Pleas, Dockets 1760-1762, frame 406]. He was taxable in Little Creek Hundred in 1770.
10   iii. Lydia, born say 1743.
11   iv. Charles, born say 1745.
         v.   Esther, born say 1752, made an 11 February 1813 Kent County will, proved 21 March 1815, by which she left all her personal estate and 4-1/4 acres to Giloca **Lockerman**, requiring her to pay Susan **Derham**, George **Derham**'s wife, within four years [WB P-1:69].

7.   Rachel¹ Sisco, born say 1715, was bound as an apprentice by her mother Elizabeth Francisco in Northampton County, Virginia, on 17 March 1717/18. She was tithable in Ann Batson's Northampton County household in 1738. Her children were

         i.   Phillis¹, born about 1737, five-year-old "Negro" daughter of Rachel Sisco who was bound as an apprentice in Northampton County in March 1741/2 [Orders 1732-42, 484].
         ii. Bridget, born about 1739, three-year-old "Negro" daughter of Rachel Sisco, bound as an apprentice in September 1742 [Orders 1732-42, 484].
         iii. ?Rachel², born about 1760, nine years old when she was bound as an

apprentice in August 1769 [Minutes 1765-71, 306].

Other likely descendants of Rachel Sisco were
   i. Phillis[2], born about 1758, a five-year-old "Negro" bound as an apprentice in Northampton County on December 1763 [Minutes 1761-65, 111]. She was the mother of Isaiah Sisco who was nine years old when he was bound as an apprentice by the Northampton County court on 1 May 1785 [Orders 1783-87, 284].
  ii. James, born about 1768, four years old in July 1772 when he was bound as an apprentice in Northampton County [Minutes 1771-77, 44].
 iii. Daniel[3] Cischo, born about 1771, five years old on 19 August 1776 when he was bound as an apprentice in Northampton County [Minutes 1771-77, 372]. He was head of an Accomack Parish, Accomack County household of 3 "other free" in 1800 [*Virginia Genealogist* 2:14].

8. Ephraim Sisco, born say 1745, was taxable in Little Creek Hundred, Kent County, from 1765 to 1783 when he was crossed off the list [RG 3535, Kent County Levy List, 1743-67, frames 509, 521, 553, 566; 1768-84, frames 27, 129, 185, 223, 263, 310, 335, 341, 367, 368, 443, 503, 542, 583]. He was indicted by the Kent County court in November 1765 for having an illegitimate male child by Rachel Sisco, Jr., about May 1764. The court ordered Ephraim to support the boy for five years. Daniel **Durham** was his security [DSA, RG 3805.002, 1734-79, frame 446; MS case files November 1765]. He was a "Molattoe" taxable on a mare, two horses, eight cows, two calves and eight sheep in Little Creek Hundred in 1800 [RG 3535, Kent County Levy List, 1800-1, frame 413] and head of a Little Creek Hundred household of 11 "other free" in 1800 [DE:36]. He was the father of
   i. John[5], born say 1764, called "son of Ephr." from 1788 to 1790 when he was taxable in Little Creek Hundred [RG 3535, Kent County Levy List, 1785-97, frames 75, 107, 191]. He was head of a Little Creek Hundred, Kent County household of 7 "other free" in 1800 [DE:33].
  ii. ?Amelia[2] Cisco, born say 1770, married Jeremiah **Shad** in July 1790. Jeremiah was head of a New Castle County household of 8 "other free" in 1800 [DE:161].

9. Benjamin Sisco, born say 1735, was taxable in Little Creek Hundred, Kent County, from 1754 to 1756, taxable in Duck Creek Hundred from 1761 to 1767 and taxable in Little Creek Hundred in 1768 [DSA, RG 3535, 1743-67, frames 136, 143, 168, 187, 315, 345, 354, 381, 396, 427, 436, 491, 518, 534, 551, 566; 1767-84, frames 10, 26]. Benjamin Wynn sued him in Kent County court in November 1769 [DSA, RG 3815.031, 1769-71, frame 43]. He may have been the father of
   i. William, born say 1750, taxable in Little Creek Hundred in 1770 and 1771, in Duck Creek Hundred in 1773, in Little Creek Hundred in 1776 and 1778 and in Dover Hundred in 1778 [DSA, RG 3535, Assessments 1768-84, frames 66, 129, 180, 263, 335, 341].
  ii. Amelia[1], born say 1755, married **Hanser**, perhaps the Nehemiah[2] **Hanser** who was taxable in Dover Hundred from 1785 to 1788. Amelia died before 9 December 1814 when administration on her Kent County estate was granted to John Francisco [WB P-1:61].
 iii. Mary, born say 1758, mother of an illegitimate male child in Little Creek Hundred in December 1775 [RG 3805.0, MS case papers, May Term 1776]. She died before 29 May 1808 when administration papers were filed on her estate which amounted to $41.61 [DSA, RG 3845.000, roll 80, frames 325-8].
  iv. George, born say 1763, father of an illegitimate daughter by Ann **Munt** in Duck Creek Hundred in 1782 [DSA, RG 3805.0, MS Kent County Court case papers, August 1782 Indictments]. He was taxable in Little Creek Hundred from 1785 to 1789, a "Mulattoe" taxable in 1797 and 1798. By

his 10 November 1814 Kent County will, proved two weeks later on 26 November, he divided his estate between his sister Emela (Amelia) **Hanser** and his brother William Sisco. Jacob **Trusty** paid cash to the estate [RG 3845.000, roll 201, frames 819-24; WB P-1:59].

10. Lydia Francisco, born say 1743, was charged in Kent court in February 1770 with having an illegitimate child [DSA, RG 3805.002, 1734-79, frames 547, 551]. She was named in her brother Charles's 20 January 1798 Kent County will. By her 7 November 1798 Little Creek Neck, Kent County will, proved 18 December 1798, she left her daughter Elizabeth all her interest in her father's estate [WB N-1, fol. 221-2]. She was the mother of
    i.   Elizabeth, born say 1770.

11. Charles Sisco, born say 1745, was taxable in Little Creek Hundred from 1765 to 1785. He was granted administration on the estate of (his father?) John Francisco on 24 October 1791 [WB N-1, fol. 5]. By his 20 January 1798 Little Creek Neck, Kent County will, proved 9 February 1798, he gave his sister Lydia his part of his father's estate and all his own estate to his sister Lydia's daughter Elizabeth Francisco [WB N-1, fol. 195-6]. Charles was the father of
    i.   John[4], born say 1764, taxable in Little Creek Hundred in 1785 and called "son of Chrls." in the list for 1787.

Other Delaware descendants were
    i.   Comfort, head of a Little Creek, Kent County, Delaware household of 2 "other free" in 1800 [DE:37].
    ii. Isaiah, husband of Rachel Sisco who died before 13 February 1826 when John **Carney**, Jr., of New Castle County was granted administration on her Kent County estate [WB Q-1:78].

FRAZER FAMILY

Members of the Frazer family in Delaware were
    i.   Frazer, a "Mulato" woman freed by Rebecca Steel of Philadelphia by Kent County peititon on 22 April 1782. Her mistress stated that she had known her about the year 1733 and that she was found to be free at a court in Dover about 44 or 45 years previous [Delaware Archives RG 3815.35].
    ii. William Frazer, head of a Mispillion Hundred, Kent County household of 5 "other free" in 1800 [DE:81].

FRIEND FAMILY

Members of the Friend family were
1   i.   Job, born say 1750.
2   ii. John, born say 1765.
    iii. Isaac, head of a Caroline County household of 7 "other free" in 1810 [MD:197]. He was called a "negro" in the 7 February 1814 Caroline County deed by which he purchased 130 perches of land near Brown's Saw Mill on 7 February 1814, 8-1/2 acres called *Alcock's Fancy* on the northeast side of Robins Saw Mill Branch and 6-1/2 acres called *Holb's Folly* on 1 August 1817 [Land Records L:166-7; M-6, 7].
    iv. Pattey, born say 1780, mother of Charles Friend who registered in Dorchester County on 16 November 1827: *of a chesnut colour, was born free, raised in Dorchester County and is the son of Pattey Friend who was also born free, aged about 24 years* [Certificates of Freedom for Negroes 1806-64, 57].

1.   Job Friend, born say 1750, married Patience **Jackson**, "Melattoes" on 8 June 1772 in Sussex County [Records of the United Presbyterian Churches of Lewes, Indian

River and Cool Spring, Delaware 1756-1855, 284]. They were the parents of

    i.   Jackson, born 19 September 177_, "mulatto" son of Job and Patience Friend, baptized at St. George's Protestant Episcopal Church, Indian River [Wright, *Vital Records of Kent and Sussex Counties*, 101]. He was head of a Mispillion, Kent County household of 5 "other free" in 1800 [DE:92], 3 in 1810 [DE:46], and a Dover household of 2 "free colored" in 1820 [DE:32].

2.   John Friend, born say 1765, was head of a Caroline County household of 4 "other free" in 1790. He may have been the father of

    i.   Henry, born 4 April 1781, a free born "coloured man" who registered in Caroline County on 29 April 1826 [Certificates of Freedom 1806-27, 192]. He purchased 33 acres in Caroline County called *Harris's Hazard* and *Edmondson's Desire* on the road from Hunting Creek Mill to Fowling Creek Mill for $218 on 27 February 1821. On 3 January 1833 John Friend "(negro)" sold this land which descended to him by the death of Henry Friend, for $50 [Land Records N:216-7; R:333-4].

FROST FAMILY

1.   Sarah Frost, born say 1746, was the servant of James Wilson on 23 August 1766 when she confessed to the Somerset County court that she had a child by "Bristo a Negro man belonging to Betty Waters." The court ordered her sold for seven years and sold her son Planner to her master until the age of thirty-one [Judicial Record 1766-7, 9-10]. Sarah and Bristo were the parents of

    i.   Planner, born about 1766, head of a Somerset County household of 7 "other free" in 1800 [MD:467].

GALE FAMILY

1.   Ann Gale, born say 1740, was the servant of Susannah Cox of Cecil County in March 1760 when the court convicted her of having a "Molata" child [Judgment Record 1759-61, 92]. She may have been the ancestor of

    i.   Capn, head of an Octoraro, Cecil County household of 8 "other free" in 1790.

    ii.   Ben, head of an Anne Arundel County household of 2 "other free" in 1790.

    iii.   Robert, head of an Anne Arundel County household of 6 "other free" in 1810 [DE:75].

    iv.   T., head of a Frederick County household of 7 "other free" in 1810 [DE:610].

GAME FAMILY

1.   Sambo Game, born say 1670, was the slave of Peter Douty of Somerset County. While still a slave, Sambo may have had a child by a white woman named Mauldlin Magee. Her daughter Fortune Game/ **Magee** was the servant of Mrs. Mary Day on 15 June 1705 when the Somerset County court ordered her to serve Mrs. Day until the age of thirty-one, explaining that she was the "mulatto" daughter of Maudlin Magee who was married to George Magee at the time [Judicial Records 1702-5, 251]. Sambo and his wife Betty were "Negro" slaves freed by Peter Douty's 1709 Somerset County will. Douty also allowed them the use of his 150 acre plantation called *Paris* in the Nanticoke Hundred of Somerset County during their lives [Wills Liber 5:142; Land Records Liber CD:416]. They were free by 1713 when they petitioned the Somerset County court to allow Betty to be tax free [Liber AC:17]. He was called "Sambo Gam a Negro" when he was paid £5.19 by the executor of Peter Douty's estate [Prerogative Court Inventories and Accounts, Vol. 36B, 245]. He was taxable in Nanticoke Hundred, Somerset

County, from 1724 to 1733, listed in a household adjoining Fortune Game in 1728. "Negro" Grace, a taxable in his household in 1724 and 1727, may have been his slave; and Robert Game, a taxable in his household in 1728, was probably his son. Patrick Makeala and Samuel Clark, who were probably white, were taxables in his household in 1727 [List of Taxables, 1724-33]. He probably died before 1735 when Betty paid quit rents on their land [Somerset County Debt Book 1734, 79; 1735, 47 cited by Davidson, *Free Blacks on the lower Eastern Shore*]. Sambo may have been the father of

2   i.   Fortune **Magee**, born say 1687.
3   ii. Robert, born say 1710.
4   iii. Harry, born say 1720.

2.   Fortune Game, born say 1687, was called Fortune **Magee**, the servant of Mrs. Mary Day, on 15 June 1705 when the Somerset County court ordered that she serve Mrs. Day until the age of thirty-one, explaining that she was the "mulatto" daughter of Maudlin Magee, a white woman living in Somerset County who was married to George Magee at the time [Judicial Records 1702-5, 251]. In 1712 she bound her children, Ross, Sue, and Perlina to Mrs. Day [Judicial Records 1702-5, 251; 1711-3, 220]. She was called Fortune Game, a taxable head of a Nanticoke Hundred, Somerset County household from 1728 to 1735: with Betty Game in 1728 and 1731, and with Betty and Rose Game in 1733. She was the mother of

5   i.   Rose, born March 1703.
6   ii. Sue **Magee**, born in April 1705.
7   iii. Perlina, born in April 1707.
8   iv. ?Betty, born say 1712.
        v. ?Anville, born say 1722, taxable in Fortune Game's Nanticoke Hundred household in 1738 and 1740 and taxable in Isaac Bebbings' Nanticoke Hundred household in 1744.
      vi. ?Sarah , born say 1723. See the **Fortune** family history.

3.   Robert Game, born say 1710, was taxable in the Somerset County household of Sambo Game in 1728. He was head of his own Nanticoke Hundred, Somerset County household in 1733 with (his wife?) Ellender Game until 1749 and taxable by himself in 1750. He was in Murderkill Hundred, Delaware, when he made his September 1782 will, proved 17 October 1782. He left his wife Elizabeth his largest bed which was to go to her daughter Mary **Lanthorn** after her death and left his wife a cow which was to go to her daughter and Sarah **Lanthorn** (**Lantern**) after her death. His inventory included two mares, a colt and corn in the field [RG 3545, roll 82, frame 425; DB L-1, fol. 267-8]. Robert may have been the father of

        i.   Levin[1], born say 1740, convicted of murder in May 1767. Betty and Sarah Game/ **Tompson**/ **Fortune** testified against him. The governor issued a death warrant for him on 13 June 1767 [Provincial Court Judgments, May Term 1767, 648-52; *Archives of Maryland* 32:200].
       ii. Ephraim[1], taxable in George Scott's Nanticoke Hundred household in 1759. He was a recruit from Dorchester County in the Revolutionary War on 25 July 1780 [*Archives of Maryland* 18:339].
     iii. Henry[2], listed in Colonel Thomas Couch's 2nd Battalion of Delaware Militia in 1776 [NARA, M246, roll 29, frame 199 of 694]. He was head of a St. Mary's County household of 3 "other free' in 1800 [MD:340].

4.   Harry[1] Game, born say 1720, was probably identical to "Harry Negro," a taxable slave in the Nanticoke Hundred household of Priscilla Dashiell in 1738. He may have been related to Sambo Game since Priscilla Dashiell was one of Peter Douty's heirs [Land Records, Liber A-2, 150]. He was probably the "negro physician...Doctor Harrey" whose services were advertised in the 7 November 1750 issue of the *Maryland Gazette*. He, called Henry (Doctor) Game, and his wife Rose were free before 10 August 1751 when they registered the birth of their

son Daniel at Stepney Parish, Somerset County. They were taxable in Somerset County in 1752. In 1757 Harry purchased for £70 a 150 acre plantation called *Covington's Choice* in Wicomico Hundred and petitioned the Somerset County court to have his slave, Tite, tax exempt [Land Records, Liber B:173; Judicial Records 1757-61, 18]. Harry left a will in 1781 naming his sons, Daniel and Jeremiah [Wills, Liber EB 1:144]. His children were

    i.   Daniel, born 10 August 1751 in Stepney Parish [Wright, *Maryland Eastern Shore Vital Records*, Book 3:42]. He sued Stephen Adams in 1785 in Somerset County for £12 for "attending, curing and healing a negro woman slave of said Stephen of divers diseases and infirmities" [Judicial Record 1786-88, 87].

    ii. Bridget, born 20 February 1754 in Stepney Parish, daughter of Doctor Henry and Rose Game [Wright, *Maryland Eastern Shore Vital Records*, Book 3:42].

    iii. Jeremiah, born say 1758, taxable on 60 acres of *Covington's Choice* in Rewastico, Wicomico Hundred, Somerset County, in 1783.

    iv. ?Samuel, taxable on 55 acres of *Covington's Choice* in Rewastico, Wicomico Hundred, in 1783 [MSA S1161-9-10, p.42].

5.   Ross Game, born in March 1703, child of Fortune Game, was apparently identical to Rose Game, a taxable in Fortune Game's Nanticoke Hundred household in 1733. She owed £9.11 to the estate of Day Scott of Somerset County on 8 September 1757 [Prerogative Inventories 77:42-44]. Her children, whose births were registered in Stepney Parish, Somerset County, were

    i.   Stephen **Magee**, born 25 June 1737, alias Game of Mulatto Rose or Rose **Magee** [Wright, *Maryland Eastern Shore Vital Records*, Book 2:128]. Stephen Game was charged with assault in Queen Anne's County court in November 1771 [Surles, *And they Appeared at Court 1770-1772*, 55, 88]. He was head of a Queen Anne's County household of 3 "Blacks" in 1776 [Carothers, *1776 Census of Maryland*, 143] and a "Free Mulatto" head of a Queen Anne's County household of 2 "other free" in 1790.

    ii. Isaac[1] **Magee** Game, born 25 June 1741, son of Mullato Rose or Rose Game alias **Magee** [Wright, *Maryland Eastern Shore Vital Records*, Book 2:128]. He owed a shilling to the estate of Day Scott of Somerset County on 8 September 1757 [Prerogative Inventories 77:42-44]. He may have been identical to Sax Game, a taxable in Nanticoke Hundred in 1759. He was taxable in Little Creek Hundred, Sussex County, in 1777.

    iii. Joe **Magee**, a "molatto" bound by Rose **Magee** to Edward Rownds on 19 March 1722/3 [Judicial Record 1723-5, 3].

6.   Sue **Magee** alias Game, born in April 1705, was a "mulatto" woman living in Somerset County from 1741 to 1754 when the births of her "mulatto" children Belindor, Davey, James, Jenney, and Nelly **Magee** were registered at Stepney Parish [Wright, *Maryland Eastern Shore Vital Records*, Book 2:126; 3:42]. Her children were

    i.   ?Ned, born say 1737, a "Mullatto" (no last name) with eleven months to serve when he was listed in the inventory of the Somerset County estate of Day Scott on 8 September 1757 [Prerogative Inventories 63:562-74].

    ii. Belindor **Magee**, born September 1741, "otherwise Belinder Game dau of Mollatto Sue otherwise Sue **Magee** or Game." She was probably the "Mullatto" Belinda listed in the inventory of the Somerset County estate of Day Scott on 8 September 1757 with fourteen years to serve [Prerogative Inventories 63:562-74]. She may have been identical to "Blinda" (no last name) who was a taxable with Ephraim Game and James Right in George Scott's Nanticoke Hundred household in 1759.

    iii. Davey **Magee**, born 14 March 1745, "otherwise Davey Game son of mollato Sue otherwise Sue **Magee** or Game." He was probably the "Mullatto" David listed in the inventory of the Somerset County estate of

Day Scott on 8 September 1757 with sixteen and one half years to serve [Prerogative Inventories 63:562-74].

iv.   Janney **Magee**, born 13 October 1746, "otherwise Janney Game son of mollato Sue other wise Sue **Magee** or Game" [Wright, *Maryland Eastern Shore Vital Records*, Book 2:126; 3:42].

v.   James **Magee**, born 28 July 1750, "otherwise James Game son of mullato Sue other wise Sue **Magee** or Game" [Wright, *Maryland Eastern Shore Vital Records*, Book 2:126; 3:42]. He enlisted in the 2nd Delaware Regiment on 9 March 1781 and was in the same list as Edward **Harmon** [NARA, M246, roll 31, frames 498, 504].

vi.   Nelly **Magee**, born 9 _ , 1754, alias Game (dau of Mullato Sue) [Wright, *Maryland Eastern Shore Vital Records*, Book 2:126; 3:42].

7.   Perlina Game, born in April 1707, was five years old "next April" in March 1712 when she was bound as an apprentice in Somerset County court. She was probably identical to "Ner Game," a taxable in Nanticoke Hundred in 1734, and Polina Gam, a taxable head of a Nanticoke Hundred household with Sarah Gam in 1759. She may have been the mother of

9   i.   Sarah, born say 1730.

8.   Betty Game, born say 1712, was taxable in Nanticoke Hundred, Somerset County, in the household of Fortune Game from 1728 to 1731. She had an illegitimate child in Stepney Parish on 1 September 1732 for which she received ten lashes. Stephen Winwright was her security for payment of the court costs. She was indicted for another illegitimate child in March 1735, but the court decided that she was a "black woman and doth not come within the act of assembly for punishment of adultery and fornication" [Judicial Record 1730-3, 262-3; 1735-7, 135]. She was identical to Betty **Fortune** who was a taxable head of household in Nanticoke Hundred with (her daughter?) Fortune **Fortune** in 1757. On 22 October 1754 Betty Game purchased 50 acres called *Georges Pleasure* on the southside of the Nanticoke River in Somerset County from Day Scott for £5, and on 5 December 1772 Betty sold this land for £33 [Land Records B:42-3; O:26-7]. By his 14 June 1753 Somerset County will, proved 17 August 1757, George Day Scott left Betty **Fortune** the 50 acre tract where she was then living if she paid the balance due [WB 1756-61, 58]. Bess **Fortune** owed 9 shillings to the Somerset County estate of Day Scott on 8 September 1757 [Prerogative Inventories 77:42-44]. Betty was probably one of "Two Women of a Dark Complection Live a the Head of Tippin(?)" listed by the constable as having refused to pay the discriminatory tax on free African American women in 1743. The constable reported further that "they are full as Dark as most Mallatos. They are of the Breed of old fortune and Robt. Game" [List of Taxables, 1743]. She was head of a taxable household in Little Creek Hundred, Sussex County, in 1777 and 1790. She may have been the mother of

i.   George[1] Game, born say 1733, taxable in Betty Game's household in Nanticoke Hundred in 1749.

ii.   "Negro Patience **Thomson**," a taxable in Betty Game's Nanticoke Hundred household in 1756, called Patience Game in 1783, a taxable in Nanticoke Hundred [MSA S1161-9-10, p.45].

iii. ?Fortune **Fortune**, born say 1740, taxable in Betty **Fortune**'s household in Nanticoke Hundred in 1757.

iv.   Levin[2], taxable in Little Creek Hundred, Sussex County, in 1777 and from 1788 to 1791. Levin McGee enlisted in the 1st Company of the 2nd Battalion of Colonel Williams's Delaware Regiment and was listed in the muster for July and August 1780, transferred in September, delivered a coat at Lewis Town in March 1780, delivered clothing in Dover on 13 June 1780 [NARA, M246, reel 29, frames 312, 393, 402, 495]. He may have been identical to Levin **Thompson**.

v. John Game, taxable in Indian River, Sussex County, in 1789, called a "Mulato" in the list of delinquents: "not Settled anywhere," and taxable there in 1790 and 1791.

9. Sarah Game, born say 1730, was taxable in Perlina Game's Nanticoke Hundred, Somerset County household in 1759. She was living in Stepney Parish in March 1762 when she confessed to having a child by an unnamed "Negro slave." The court sold her son Ephraim to her master George Scott for thirty-one years and ordered her master to return her to court at the completion of her indenture so she could be sold for seven years. In June 1762 Scott was the highest bidder for her servitude at 3,150 pounds of tobacco [Judicial Records 1760-3, 130b, 151]. She was the mother of a "Melatto" son Lovewell who was baptized at St. George's Protestant Episcopal Church in Indian River Hundred, Sussex County, in May 1770 [Wright, *Vital Records of Kent and Sussex County*, 100]. She had another illegitimate child in Stepney Parish before 15 March 1768 and paid a double fine to avoid naming the father [Judicial Records 1767-9, 70, 146]. She was head of a Little Creek Hundred, Sussex County household of 3 "other free" in 1810 [DE:309] and 1 "free colored" in 1820 [DE:408]. She was the mother of
   i. Ephraim^2, born in January 1762.
   ii. Lovewell, baptized in May 1770.

Other Game descendants were
   i. Isaac^2, an orphan bound by the Somerset County court until the age of twenty-one with his own consent as an apprentice to Mathias Hobbs to be a cordwainer in March 1763 [Judicial Records 1760-3, 198b].
   ii. George^2, an orphan bound by the Somerset County court until the age of twenty-one with his own consent as an apprentice to Mathias Hobbs to be a cordwainer in March 1763 [Judicial Records 1760-3, 198b]. He married Leah **Noble**, 6 December 1799 Worcester County bond, and was head of a Little Creek Hundred, Sussex County household of 4 "free colored" in 1820 [DE:410]. Leah may have been related to Mark **Noble**, head of a Kent County, Delaware household of 4 "other free" in 1800 [DE:17]. George Game "of Geo." (age 25) and Spenser Game "of Geo." (age 25) emigrated to Liberia from Somerset County aboard the ship *Lafayette* in 1832 [http://fold3.com/image/46670390].
   iii. Levin^3, born about 1786, sold (signing) 50 acres called *Pembertons Goodwill* in Somerset County on 14 February 1818 for $50 [Land Records JD-3:336-7]. He was head of a Little Creek Hundred, Sussex County household of 3 "free colored" in 1820 [DE:412] and registered in Somerset County on 27 May 1825: *born free in Somerset County...bright Mollatto Complexion...about thirty nine years of age* [Certificates of Freedom 1821-32, 48].

GANNON FAMILY

1. Charles Gamon, born about 1694, petitioned the Charles County court for his freedom on 9 March 1724/5, stating that he was born of a free white woman and a "Mallatto" and had served Mr. Lynes and his executor, John Marten, thirty-one years. The court ruled that he was free [Court Record 1723-4, 443-4]. He may have been the "Mullatto boy ab^t 16 years old" who was listed in the inventory of the Charles County estate of Madame Ann Lynes on 1 January 1711/12 [Prerogative Inventories 1711-12, 71]. And he may have been the ancestor of
   i. Absalem Gannon, head of a Talbot County household of 5 "other free" in 1790, perhaps identical to Abraham Gannon, head of a Talbot County household of 9 "other free" in 1800 [MD:532].
   ii. Abner Gannon, head of a Talbot County household of 6 "other free" in 1790.

iii.   Rachel Gannon, head of a Baltimore City household of 4 "other free" in 1800 [MD:215].

iv.   Noble Gannon, born about 1788, registered in Talbot County on 1 November 1809: *a Mulatto Man...between twenty & twenty one years of age, about five feet nine inches & an eighth...is a free born Mulatto Man* [Certificates of Freedom 1807-28, 38].

GATES FAMILY

1.   Margaret[1] Gates, born say 1692, was a "free Mulatto Woman" living in Charles County on 9 November 1742 when the court exempted her from paying levy because she was infirm and "Distempered." She may have been identical to "a Certain Margrett a Mallatto Liveing with Wm Boarman" who was presented by the Charles County court on 13 August 1728 for having an illegitimate Child by information of constable William Chapman. She was called Margaret Yates, the "Mullatto" servant of William Boarman, on 12 November 1728 when she confessed in Charles County court that she had an illegitimate child, and the court ordered that she receive fifteen lashes [Court Record 1727-31, 147, 196; 1741-3, 563]. She may have been the mother of

2   i.   James, born say 1735.

2.   James Gates, born say 1735, was a taxable "Malata" head of a Trinity Parish, Upper Hundred, Charles County household in 1758 and a "mulatto" taxable in the 3rd District of Charles County in 1783 [MSA 1161-4-10, p.6]. He may have married Elizabeth **Thompson**. On 8 March 1768 the Charles County court excused her from her presentment for having an illegitimate child because she had married James Gates. No race for either was indicated in the records [Court Records 1767-70, 60]. He may have been the father of

   i.   Sam, "free negro" head of a Prince George's County household of 4 "other free" in 1800 [MD:303].

   ii.   Eliza, "free negro" head of a Prince George's County household of 4 "other free" in 1800 [MD:305].

   iii.   Edward, "free negro" head of a Prince George's County household of 2 "other free" in 1800 [MD:304].

   iv.   Benjamin, head of a Washington County household of 12 "other free" in 1810 [MD:457].

   v.   Margaret[2], born say 1765, mother of Elizabeth (born 29 December 1782) who was born before Margaret's marriage to Caleb[1] **Overton** (born 14 July 1750). Caleb obtained certificates of freedom for their children in Washington, D.C., in October 1814 [Provine, *District of Columbia Free Negro Registers*, 378-9].

GEORGE FAMILY

1.   Peter George, born say 1620, was the "Negro" slave of Nathaniel Littleton of Northampton County in 1640. About 1676 Peter received his freedom from Captain Francis Pigot on the promise to pay 10,000 pounds of tobacco. He completed the last payment in 1682 [DW&c 1680-92, 53]. He must have been a free man when he was a witness to the will of King **Tony**, "Negro," proved 28 February 1677/8 [Orders 1674-79, 247]. In 1679 he rented land near Emmanuel **Driggers** [OW 1683-9, 150-1]. In March 1687/8 he was duped into thinking that "free Negroes should be slaves againe" by one of his white neighbors, Robert Candlin. He left all his household goods and livestock with Candlin and fled to Somerset County with his neighbor, Sarah **Driggers**, and several other unidentified free African Americans. He was called "Peter George of Wiccocomoco Hundred Negro" on 23 April 1688 when he posted £5 surety and he and (his wife?) Mary George were witnesses in a Somerset County court case for "Sarah Driggers Negro woman wife of Thomas Driggers Negro" [*Archives of*

Maryland 91:47]. Perhaps (his wife?) Mary was Mary **Rodriggus** whose Northampton County tax was paid by the parish in 1674 [DW 1664-74, 273]. He and Sarah **Driggers** returned to Northampton County about three years later and successfully sued Candlin's widow for the recovery of his livestock [OW 1689-98, 106, 115-116]. His descendants in Maryland may have been

    i.   America, head of a Worcester County household of 6 "other free" in 1790 and 15 "other free" in 1800 (called George America Negro) [MD:735]. He made a deed of manumission in Worcester County on 13 January 1800 by which he set free a "certain Negro woman called Jib" [Land Records T:43].

    ii. Martha, head of a Kent County household of 6 "other free" in 1800 [MD:161].

    iii. America, head of a Worcester County household of 6 "other free" in 1800 (called George America) [DE:718].

    iv. Patience, Negro head of a Worcester County household of 6 "other free" in 1800 [MD:725].

    v.   Betty, Negro head of a Worcester County household of 4 "other free" in 1800 [DE:718].

    vi. Mary, head of a Worcester County household of 4 "other free" in 1800 [MD:738].

GIBBS FAMILY

John Gibbs, a white resident of Queen Anne's County, purchased 200 acres which was part of a tract called *Killmannin's Plain* on Unicorn Branch of the Chester River on 6 February 1712. And he purchased another 244 acres in the same area, called *Knowles's Range*, adjoining Rothbottom's Park on 19 February 1740 [Land Records IK, no. A, fol. 15; RT, no.B, fol. 323]. By his 26 August 1747 Queen Anne's County will, proved 22 October the same year, he set his slaves free and divided the land between them in lots of one fourth to four groups, perhaps different family units. They were

1   i.   Richard[1], Absalom[1], Thomas, and Elizabeth Jr.
2   ii. Hannah, Alice, Martha, and Sarah.
3   iii. Ann, Peter, Abraham[1], Isaac[1], and Jane.
4   iv. Wealthy, William, Jacob, and Rachel [WHN #1:420-423, MdHR 8878-784].

Absolem, Thomas, Bethia, Nan, Alce, Peter, Abraham, William, Isaac, Jacob, Rachel, Jane, and Martha Gibbs sold the 244 acres called *Knowles's Range* twelve years later on 20 March 1759 for £195 [Land Records RT, no.F:24]. William Gibbs, one of the heirs, sold 12-1/2 acres of *Killmannin's Plains* on 18 June 1768 (leaving about 187 acres), and Absolem and Isaac Gibbs were each taxable on 50 acres of *Kilmannin's Plain* in 1783.

1.   Richard[1] Gibbs, born say 1705, was freed by the 26 February 1740 Queen Anne's County will of John Gibbs. He may have been deceased by 20 March 1759 when the Gibbs family sold the land devised to them by John Gibbs, and he may have been the father of

5   i.   Absolem[1], born say 1735.

       ii. Thomas, a "Negro," confessed judgment in Queen Anne's County court to Joseph Bennett for £6.9 in June 1756. Henry Lowe accused him of killing his mare with a knife, but the court found Thomas not guilty in March 1757. In June 1757 he (called Free Negro) admitted that he owed Giles Cooke £8.10 [Judgment Record 1755-6, 204; 1756-7, 221, 316]. He was living in Kent County, Delaware, on 2 August 1766 when he sold 15 acres, his rights to *Kilmannin's Plain*, to Absolem Gibbs for £18 [Liber RT-G:281]. He was a taxable "Negro" in Duck Creek Hundred, Kent County, Delaware, in 1770 and head of a Queen Anne's County household of 5 "other free" in 1800 [MD:345].

       iii. Bethia (Elizabeth, Jr.).

2.   Hannah Gibbs, a "free Negro," was sued by Thomas Ringgold for £9.9 due by account in Queen Anne's County court in November 1754 [Judgment Records 1755-6, digital images 14-16]. On 16 February 1785 she made a Queen Anne's County deed to James Tilghman of Chester, Kent County, by which her one-fourth part of *Kilmannin's Plain* and *Knowles's Range* would pass at her death to her common-law husband Benjamin **Dublin** and her children Rebecca, Alice, Martha and Sarah [Liber CD-2:317]. Benjamin **Dublin** was taxable on 50 acres of *Killman's Plains* in 1783 [Assessment of 1783, MSA S1437, p.2]. Hannah was the mother of
       i. Rebecca.
       ii. Alice.
       iii. Martha.
       iv. Sarah[1].

3.   Ann Gibbs made a Queen Anne's County deed of gift for her rights to *Kilmannin's Plain* and *Knowles Range* to her son Isaac Gibbs on 2 November 1796 [Liber STW-4: 97-8]. She was the mother of
       i. ?Peter, a tithable "free Negro" in Murderkill Hundred, Kent County, Delaware, from 1771 to 1783, a "Negro" charged with assaulting Sarah Clarke in Kent County in November 1785 [DSA, RG 3805.002, 1787-1803, frames 4, 147, 152].
       ii. ?Abraham[1], a "Negro," admitted in Queen Anne's County court in August 1765 that he owed Benjamin Jacobs £8.16 due by note [Judgment Record 1765, 61-2]. He sold his rights to *Kilmannin's Plain* to Isaac Spencer by Queen Anne's County deeds of 16 February 1785 [Liber RT-K:34; CD-1:189-90] and was head of a Queen Anne's County household of 3 "other free" in 1790 [MD:100].
6   iii. Isaac[1], born say 1740.
       iv. Jane.

4.   Wealthy Gibbs, born say 1710, was freed by the 26 February 1740 Queen Anne's County will of John Gibbs. She was probably deceased by 20 March 1759 when the heirs sold part of their land, and she may have been the mother of
       i. William, "one of the Free Negroes and Heirs or Legatees of John Gibbs" who sold 12-1/2 acres, called *Killmanning's Plains* by Forge Road to William Clark on 18 June 1768 [Land Records RT-H:266]. On 9 February 1767 he called himself "William **Trusty**, otherwise called William Gibbs of Kent County in Delaware" when he sold to Richard **Jeffereys**, "free Negroe formerly servant to John Willson of Kent County in Maryland," for £10 whatever remaining interest he had in 12-1/2 acres called *Kilmannin's Plain* sold by him to William Clark [Land Records RT-H:56-7], perhaps the William Gibbs who was taxable in Duck Creek Hundred, Kent County, Maryland, from 1779 to 1780, called a "Negro" in 1780 [DSA, MS Kent County Papers, 1680-1800, Official Tax lists, etc., Duck Creek Hundred 1779-1781].
       ii. Rachel.

5.   Absolem[1] Gibbs, born say 1735, was among thirteen members of the Gibbs family who sold land on 20 March 1759 which had been devised to them by John Gibbs's will. He was called "Negro Absalom" in June 1761 when he petitioned the Queen Anne's County court that he had property called *Killmanam's Plains* whose boundaries had decayed and required depositions to certify where the boundaries had been. One person testified that it was on the east side of Unicorn Branch [Land Commissions 1756-68, digital images 61, 75 of 269]. He purchased land called *Discord* on a branch of the Chester River adjoining *Killmanins Plains* from John Seale for 5 shillings on 3 February 1767. On 9 February 1767 he made a

deed of emancipation to his wife Judith, sons Nathan and Richard and daughter Elizabeth whom he had purchased from Thomas Burroughs late of Kent County, Delaware. He mortgaged his 58-1/2 acre portion of *Kilmannin's Plain* to Eleazar Massey for 3-1/2 years, and Massey foreclosed on the land on 7 February 1786 [Liber RT H:34, 54, 56; CD-1:440]. He was taxable on 50 acres of *Kilmanin's Plains*, in the Upper District of Queen Anne's County in 1783 [MSA S1161-9-1, p.3] and head of a Queen Anne's County household of 6 "other free" in 1790 [MD:100]. He was also a tithable "N." (Negro) in adjoining Murderkill Hundred, Kent County, Delaware from 1783 to 1787, head of Kent County household of 6 "other free" in 1800 [DE:106] and 4 in 1810 [DE:17]. He was granted administration of the estate of Absalom Gibbs, Jr., "free Negro," in Kent County, Delaware, on 15 May 1809 [Brewer, *Probate Records of Kent County, 1801-1812*, 172]. He was the father of

    i.   Nathan.

    ii. Elizabeth.

   iii. Absolem², born before 1776, head of a Kent County, Delaware household of 6 "other free" in 1810 [DE:19] and 2 "free colored" in Dover Hundred in 1820 [DE:40]. He was called a bricklayer on 26 February 1790 when he purchased 75 acres adjoining Charles Emory in Kent County, Delaware, for £200 [DB B-2:83], perhaps the Absalom Gibbs (free Negro) who purchased 5 acres called *Harris's Ramble* in Queen Anne's County for £25 on 5 February 1814 [Land Records JB-2:250].

   iv. Jacob, taxable in Duck Creek Hundred, Kent County, Delaware, from 1779 to 1788, called a "Negro" starting in 1780 [DSA, MS Kent County Papers, 1680-1800, Official Tax lists, etc., Duck Creek Hundred 1779-1781]. Esther and John Rees sued him and Andrew Gibbs in Kent County, Delaware court for a debt of £29 which they confessed judgment to in August 1770, and Thomas Murphy sued him and Andrew Gibbs for a debt of £30 which they confessed judgment to in November 1770 [DSA, RG 3815.031, 1769-1771, frames 275, 291, 323, 332]. He married Elizabeth **Beckett** sometime between 9 February 1769 when she had an illegitimate female child by Rike **Miller** in Little Creek Hundred, Kent County, and November 1771 when **Miller** was charged in court [DSA, RG 3805, MS case files, November 1771 indictments]. He was head of a Queen Anne's County household of 5 "other free" in 1800 [MD:345].

    v. Stephen, taxable in Duck Creek Hundred, Kent County, Delaware from 1783 to 1798, head of a Kent County household of 6 "other free" in 1800 [DE:21] and 4 in 1810 [DE:45]. He died before 17 February 1809 when letters of administration were granted on his estate to Cornelius Comegys and Lucy Gibbs [Brewer, *Probate Records of Kent County, 1801-1812*, 169].

   vi. Richard², a tithable "Negro" in Duck Creek Hundred, Kent County, Delaware, in 1783, taxable on 75 acres in Duck Creek Hundred in 1798, living that year on 3/8 of an acre and a log dwelling house in good repair [1797 Levy Assessments, frames 354, 394]. He was head of a Kent County, Delaware household of 7 "other free" in 1800 [DE:21]. He and Absalom Gibbs petitioned the Kent County court on 23 February 1809 that their brother Stephen died intestate seized of 60 acres in Duck Creek Hundred leaving a widow, two brothers, children of another brother Jacob and three sisters then deceased. He asked that the court assign the lands to him because his brother Absalom, to whom the right of acceptance belonged, had refused to accept the lands. He died before 17 August 1815 when his widow Mary Gibbs renounced her right to administer the estate. He owned about 140 acres in Duck Creek Hundred when he died and his estate was valued at $1,238, but his land was sold for $1,080 to pay his debts [DSA, RG 3545, reel 83, frames 791-8; Brewer, *Kent County, Delaware, Guardian Accounts, Edmonson to Hopkins*, 66-7].

6.   Isaac[1] Gibbs, born say 1740, was born before 26 August 1747 when he was named
     in John Gibbs' will. He admitted in Queen Anne's County court in August 1766
     that he owed John Vansant £17.19. In March 1774 the court fined him 6 shillings
     for assaulting Isaac Scrivener and fined his wife Catherine 1 shilling for assaulting
     Christopher Simmons [Judgment Record 1766-7, digital images 77, 137-40]. He
     was taxable on 50 acres of *Kilman Plains* in the Upper District of Queen Anne's
     County in 1783 [MSA S1161-9-1, p.3], head of a Queen Anne's County
     household of 5 "other free" in 1790 [MD:100], and 3 in 1800 [MD:345]. He
     received a deed of gift from his mother Ann Gibbs for her right to *Kilmannin's
     Plain* and *Knowles Range* in 1796 and made a deed of gift returning the land to
     her on 2 September 1796. He sold property by deed recorded in Queen Anne's
     County in 1805 [Liber STW-4:54, 56, 97-8; STW-8:339]. He may have been the
     father of

    i.   Isaac[2], born before 1776, head of a Kent County, Delaware household of
     6 "other free" in 1810 [DE:45] and 5 "free colored" in 1820 [DE:11].

   ii.   Joseph[1], head of a Kent County, Delaware household of 6 "other free" in
     1800 [DE:106]. He died before 9 May 1804 when administration was
     granted on his Kent County estate to (his wife?) Priscilla Gibbs with
     Absalom Gibbs as security [Brewer, *Probate Records of Kent County,
     1801-1812*, 169].

Their descendants in Maryland and Delaware were

    i.   Abraham[2], born say 1752, discharged from the service of William
     Newnam by the Queen Anne's County court in March 1774 [Surles, *and
     they Appeared in Court, 1770-1777*, 17].

   ii.   Ned, a taxable "Negro" in Duck Creek Hundred, Kent County, Delaware,
     from 1779 to 1781 [DSA, MS Kent County Papers, 1680-1800, Official
     Tax lists, etc., Duck Creek Hundred 1779-1781].

   iii. Andrew, a taxable in Duck Creek Hundred from 1779 to 1781, called a
     "Negro" in 1780 [DSA, MS Kent County Papers, 1680-1800, Official Tax
     lists, etc., Duck Creek Hundred 1779-1781]. Thomas Murphy sued him
     and Jacob Gibbs for £30 debt in Kent County which they confessed
     judgment to in November 1770 [DSA, RG 3815.031, 1769-1771, frames
     323, 332].

   iv. Coffer/ Coffee, head of a Kent County, Maryland household of 6 "other
     free" in 1790 [MD:83] and 6 in 1800 [MD:149].

    v.   John, a "Negro" taxable in Kent County, Delaware, in 1780 and 1781
     [DSA, MS Kent County Papers, 1680-1800, Official Tax lists, etc. , Duck
     Creek Hundred 1779-1781], head of a Cecil County household of 1 "other
     free" in 1790, 4 "other free" in Murderkill Hundred, Kent County,
     Delaware, in 1800 [DE:113] and a "Coloured" head of a New Castle
     County household of 5 "other free" in 1810 [DE:253].

   vi. James, a "Negro" charged with felony in Kent County, Delaware court in
     August 1785 [DSA, RG 3850.002, 1787-1803, frames 4, 152], head of a
     Murderkill Hundred, Kent County household of 5 "other free" in 1800
     [DE:131], perhaps identical to the James Gibbs who was a laborer counted
     in the 1800 census for Alexandria, Virginia, with his wife Ustley and six
     children, "free Negroes" [*Virginia Genealogist* 4:58]. A James Gibbs, a
     "man of color," was taken up as a runaway in Petersburg, Virginia, when
     Edward Stokes and Emos H(?)arland testified on 13 November 1817 that
     Gibbs served his time with John Thomas Ricketts of Maryland and was
     always reputed to be a free person [Gibbs, James, (M): Free Negro
     Affidavit, Chesterfield County, 1817, African American Narrative Digital
     Collection, LVA].

   vii. Solomon, head of a Lewis and Rehoboth Hundred, Sussex County
     household of 4 "other free" in 1800 [DE:412].

   viii. Absolem[3], head of a Kent County, Delaware household of 6 "other free"
     in 1810 [DE:17] and 6 "free colored" in Murderkill Hundred in 1820

[DE:15].
ix. Jo[2], a "Coloured" head of a New Castle County household of 4 "other free" in 1810 [DE:257].

GIBSON FAMILY

1. Mary Gibson, born say 1699, was the servant of Carpender Lillington on 10 May 1719 when the Queen Anne's County court convicted her of having an illegitimate "molatto" child. The court ordered that she serve her master additional time after her servitude for sixty-six days runaway time [Judgments 1718-19, images 219-20 of 252]. She may have been the ancestor of
    i. Ben, head of a Talbot County household of 4 "other free" in 1790 and 4 "other free" in Kent County in 1800 [MD:173].
    ii. Richard, head of a Cecil County household of 5 "other free" in 1790 and 2 "other free" in New Castle County, Delaware, in 1810 [DE:266].
    iii. Joe, head of a Talbot County household of 3 "other free" in 1800 [MD:531].
    iv. Jacob, head of a Talbot County household of 2 "other free" in 1800 [MD:522] and 2 "free colored" in Newark, Delaware, in 1820 [DE:102].
    v. Robert, "N" head of a Mispillion Hundred, Kent County, Delaware household of 3 "free colored" in 1820 [DE:79].

GILES FAMILY

Members of the Giles family in Maryland were
    i. Hannah, married Henry **Williams** near Poplar Spring, Anne Arundel County, on 14 August 1785 according to her application for bounty land for his services in the Revolution [NARA, M804, roll 2588, W3638].
    ii. Richard, head of a Baltimore City household of 3 "other free" in 1800 [MD:212] and 8 in the 1st Ward in 1810 [MD:309].
    iii. James, head of a 7th Ward, Baltimore City household 5 "other free" in 1810 [MD:86], perhaps identical to the James Giles who was head of an Anne Arundel County household of 3 "other free" in 1810 [MD:96].
    iv. Jacob, head of a Baltimore City household of 2 "other free" in 1810 [MD:155].

GRACE FAMILY

1. Joan Grace, born say 1714, an indentured servant to William Penn, admitted in Charles County court on 8 June 1731 that she had a "Mullatto" child "by a Negroe." And she admitted to a second mixed-race child on 13 March 1732/3. Her son William Grace, born 6 November 1732, was bound to serve Penn until the age of thirty-one. On 10 June 1735 her "Mullatto" son Thomas was bound to serve Penn for thirty-one years and on 10 August 1736 the court ordered that she be sold for twenty-one years as punishment for having three "Mullatto" children [Court Record 1727-31, 521; 1731-4, 297-8; 1734-9, 2, 37-38, 220]. She and her "2 Molatto children" were valued at £28 in the inventory of the Charles County estate of William Penn on 12 May 1737 [Prerogative Inventories & Accounts 1736-1739, 271]. She was the mother of
    i. William[1], born 6 November 1732, perhaps the William Grace who was head of a Caroline County household of 6 "other free" in 1810 [MD:219].
    ii. Thomas[1], born about March 1735, head of a Dorchester County household of 4 "other free" and 4 slaves in 1800 [MD:736].
    iii. ?Ann[1], head of a Kent County, Maryland household of 2 "other free" in 1800 [MD:161].
    iv. ?Betsey, head of a Baltimore City household of 8 "other free" in 1800 [MD:215].

Descendants counted in adjoining Stafford County, Virginia were
  i.   Annie[2], head of a household of 6 "other free" in 1810.
  ii. Thomas[2], head of household of 4 "other free" in 1810.
  iii. Rachel, head of a household of 4 "other free" in 1810.
  iv. William[2], head of a household of 3 "other free" in 1810.
  v.   Polly, born about 1767, registered in Stafford County on 13 August 1804:
       a black woman aged about thirty seven years...appearing to the
       satisfaction of the Court to have been born free and registered a copy in
       King George County [King George County Register of Free Persons,
       no.39].

GRAHAM FAMILY

1. Elizabeth Graham, born say 1696, appeared in Prince George's County court on
    26 June 1716 with her child who was adjudged to be a "Mallato." She was ordered
    to serve Thomas Wells, Sr., until November court. Later that year on 27
    November the court sold her and her child to Thomas Clagett for 3,000 pounds
    of tobacco. She was called the "Servant woman of Thomas Wells" (no last name)
    on 25 November 1718 when the court bound her seventeen-month-old daughter
    Margaret to Edward Marlow. On 24 March 1718/9 she confessed to having
    another illegitimate child [Court Record 1715-20, 87, 143; 1715-20, 721, 814].
    She was probably the mother of
2   i.   Catherine, born about 1715.
      ii. Margaret, born about June 1717.

2. Catherine Graham, born about 1715, appeared in Prince George's County court on
    28 June 1732 and admitted that she had a child by "negro or Mallatto Nasy"
    belonging to Henry Darnall, Jr. The court sold their six-week-old daughter
    Hannah to Sarah Clagett until the age of thirty-one. Nasy was convicted of the
    offense on 22 August the same year [Court Record 1732-4, 13, 544]. She was
    listed in the inventory of the Prince George's County estate of Thomas Clagett on
    26 June 1733: "1 Mulatto Woman named Kate 12 years to serve" [Prerogative
    Inventories & Accounts 1732-1734, 277-8]. Catherine appeared in court again on
    25 March 1735 and admitted that she had an illegitimate child by "Negro Taff
    Belonging to Daniel Carroll of Upper Marlborough Town." She was ordered to
    serve an additional seven years after completing her indenture, and her child was
    bound to Mary Clagett until the age of thirty-one. The court ordered that Taff be
    whipped. She was called "Yellow Cate" on 22 November 1737 when the court
    ruled that her son Moses was "Begotten by a Negro" and ordered that the child be
    sold to Mary Clagett. And on 28 November 1738 she confessed that she had a
    child by Yarrow, a "Negro" slave of Thomas Gantt. The court sold her and her
    four-year-old son Dick to Doctor John Haswell. In March 1738/9 she confessed
    to having two illegitimate children: Ann, born on 28 February 1736/7, and
    Charles, born in October 1738. On 25 August 1747 the court sold Catherine to
    sheriff Osborn Sprigg for twenty-eight years [Court Record 1734-5, 357; 1735-6,
    11; 1736-8, 597-8; 1738-40, 198, 286-7, 662; 1747-8, 108]. She was called a
    "Mulatto Woman Cate about 31 years old supposed to have 21 years to serve"
    when she was listed in the inventory of the Prince George's County estate of
    Doctor John Haswell on 31 May 1750 [Prerogative Inventories 48:226-230]. She
    was the mother of
      i.   Hannah, born in May 1732.
      ii.   Dick, born in 1734, sixteen years old on 31 May 1750 when he was listed
            in the Prince George's County estate of Doctor John Haswell.
      iii. Ann, born 28 February 1736/7, fourteen years old on 31 May 1750 when
            she was listed in inventory of the Prince George's County estate of Doctor
            John Haswell.
      iv.   Moses[1], born about November 1737.
      v.   Charles, born in October 1738, a twelve-year-old "Mulattoe" boy bound

until the age of thirty-one who was listed in the inventory of the Prince George's County estate of Osborn Sprigg in 1750 [Prerogative Inventories 48:190-6].

3   vi. Sarah[1], born in April 1740.
4   vii. ?Eleanor, born say 1742.

3.   Sarah[1] Graham, born in April 1740, was the two-month-old "Mallatto" child of Catherine Graham who was bound to John Clagett of Rock Creek on 24 June 1740. She was apparently the ten-year-old "Mulattoe" girl bound until the age of thirty-one who was listed in the inventory of the Prince George's County estate of Osborn Sprigg in 1750 [Prerogative Inventories 48:190-6]. She was called a "Malato Wench Liveing in Mount Calvert Hundred" on 23 August 1757 when the court ordered her sold for seven years and bound her five-month-old son James to Thomas Clagett until the age of thirty-one [Court Record 1738-40, 662; 1754-8, 490, 495]. She was the servant of John Clagett of Frederick County in August 1762 when he presented a bill to the county court "for expenses for support of Sarah Graham's bastard Mulatto Child" from 29 November 1761 to 18 August 1762. Sarah admitted in court that the child was "begot by a Negro," and the court bound the child to Clegatt for thirty-one years. She appeared in court again on 21 August 1764 and confessed to having a female "Mullatto Bastard Child" who was also bound to Clagett [Judgment Record 1763-6, 277, 279; Court Minutes 1763-8, August 1764 (n.p.)]. She was the mother of

    i.   James, born March 1757, a 22-year-old Negro in the household of Thomas Clagett in the 1776 census for St. John's and Prince George's Parishes of Prince George's County [Brumbaugh, *Maryland Records*, I:1], head of a Frederick County, Virginia household of 8 "free colored" in 1830.
    ii.   ?Amos, head of a Kent County, Maryland household of 5 "other free" in 1800 [MD:149].
    iii. ?Roger, head of a Dover, Kent County, Delaware household of 6 "free colored" in 1820 [DE:42].
    iv. ?Lethy, head of a Wilkes County, North Carolina household of 3 "free colored" in 1820 [NC:524].

4.   Eleanor Graham, born say 1742, confessed in Prince George's County court on 24 November 1761 that she had a "Mulatto" child. The court ordered that she be sold for seven years and sold her one-month-old son Aaron to her master, Zachariah Lyles, until the age of thirty-one. On 22 November 1763 the court ordered that she be sold for a second seven-year term and ordered her two-month-old "Mulatto" son Moses bound to Zachariah Lyles until the age of thirty-one. On 25 March 1766 the court ordered that she be sold for a third seven-year term and bound her five-month-old "Mulatto" child Sandy to Lyles until the age of thirty-one. On 25 August 1767 the court ordered that she be sold for a fourth seven-year term and sold her six-week-old daughter Sarah to her master until the age of thirty-one. On 27 June 1769 the court ordered her sold for a fifth seven-year term and ordered her five-week-old daughter Kitty sold to Margery Lyles until the age of thirty-one [Court Record 1761-3, 140; 1763-4, 8-9; 1765-6, 385; 1766-8, 322; 1768-70, 286]. Nell, Aaron, Moses, Sandy and Sarah were listed in the 20 April 1768 Prince George's County estate of Zachariah Lyles [Prerogative Inventories, 96:339-40]. She was the mother of

    i.   Aaron, born in October 1761.
    ii.   Moses[2], born in September 1763, ordered by the Frederick County, Virginia court in April 1792 to serve his master Ignatius Perry an additional two years and four months for time lost and expenses in taking him up [Orders 1791-2, 430].
    iii. Sandy, born in November 1765, head of a Frederick County, Virginia household of 4 "other free" in 1810 [VA:511].
    iv. Sarah[2], born in July 1767.
    v.   Kitty, born in July 1769.

vi.   Thomas, born about 1773, registered in Prince George's County on 6 May 1811: *has a yellow complexion, is about 38 years old...has pale eyes, thick lips...was raised in Prince George's County in the family of Ignatius Perry and is free, being descended from a free woman named Elenor Graham* [Provine, *Registrations of Free Negroes*, 7].

GRANT FAMILY

1.   Margaret Helen Grant, born say 1740, was the servant of James Elgin on 11 March 1760 when the Charles County court presented her for bearing a "Mollatto Child." She may have been identical to Eleanor Grant who was presented by the grand jury of Charles County on 12 March 1765 for bearing a "Molatto" child by information of constable John Moran [Court Record 1759-60, 425; 1764-6, 181]. Her children may have been
      i.   John, head of a Talbot County household of 1 "other free" in 1790.
      ii. Hugh, head of a Bohemian Manor, Cecil County household of 1 "other free" in 1790.

GRAVES FAMILY

1.   Mary Graves, born say 1724, the "free Mollatto" servant of Arthur Miller, confessed to the Kent County, Maryland court that she bore two illegitimate "Mullatto" children, one about six weeks old and the other about two years old. The court ordered her sold for seven years and sold her children to her master until the age of thirty-one [Criminal Proceedings 1728-34, 465, 478-9, 481]. She was probably the ancestor of
      i.   Abigail, born about March 1741, a "Mullatto Woman" with about 13 years and 7 months to serve when she was listed in the inventory of the Kent County estate of Samuel Miller on 7 August 1758 and 11 years to serve on 28 April 1761 [Prerogative Inventories 66:42-8; 76:211-4].
      ii.   Moses, born about 1745, a twenty-six-year-old "Mulatto" who escaped from jail in Newtown on the Chester River in Maryland according to the 17 October 1771 issue of the *Virginia Gazette*. He was jailed in Lancaster County, Virginia, according to the 12 March 1772 issue [Rind edition, p. 4, col.1].
      iii. Harry, "Negro" head of a Kent County household of 2 "other free" in 1790 and 4 in 1800 [MD:173].
      iv.   Elizabeth, "Negro" head of a Kent County household of 2 "other free" in 1790 and 2 in Cecil County in 1800 [MD:584].
      v.   Henny, head of a Kent County household of 9 "other free" in 1800 [MD:173].
      vi.   Stepney, head of a Kent County household of 8 "other free" in 1800 [MD:173].
      vii. Judy, head of a Baltimore City household of 6 "other free" in 1800 [MD:212].
      viii. Stephen, head of a Talbot County household of 2 "other free" and 2 slaves in 1800 [MD:539].
      ix.   George, born about 1764, a ten-year-old "Molatto" boy who was bound by the Kent County, Maryland court by indenture to Elizabeth Williamson on 25 November 1774 [Court Minutes 1774-1782, n.p.]. He was head of a Kent County household of 1 "other free" in 1800 [MD:160].
      x.   Nancy, "F. Negroe" head of a Fauquier County, Virginia household of 9 "other free" in 1810 [VA:343].

GRAY FAMILY

1.   Priscilla Gray, born say 1708, was a "malatto" servant of Mrs. Sarah Magruder, Sr., of Prince George's County in November 1727 when she confessed to the court

that she had an illegitimate child by a "negroe." On 23 March 1730/1 the court presented her for having another child by information of the constable for Mount Calvert Hundred. She admitted her guilt, and the court ordered that she receive five lashes and serve her mistress an additional nine months. The court called her "Priscilla Gray alias Malatto Priscilla" when it bound her son Dick, aged about three months, to Lingaw Wilson until the age of twenty-one years. In November 1732 she was called a "Mollatto Woman born of a white Woman" when she confessed to having a child by "Malatto George belonging to Mr. William Digges." The court ordered her to serve an additional seven years and bound her son William for thirty-one years [Court Record 1726-7, 626; 1730-2, 2, 5; 1732-4, 118]. She and her two sons were listed in the inventory of the Prince George's County estate of Sarah Magruder on 3 September 1734 (not identified as free):

1 Molattoe woman Priss - £15
1 D° Boy 6 years old - £10
1 D° D° Boy 2 years old - £2

[Prerogative Inventories & Accounts 1734-1735, 54-9]. She was presented for the same offense in March 1735, and on 28 November 1738 the court bound her "Mallatto" son Joseph, born 9 August 1738, to her master William Magruder until the age of thirty-one. She may have had a common-law marriage with a member of the **Grimes** family since she was called "Priscilla Grimes Als Gray" on 26 November 1745 when she confessed to having an illegitimate child named Kate who was bound to William Magruder until the age of thirty-one. On 27 November 1750 she confessed to "Mollatto Bastardy," and the court ordered that she serve seven years and bound her daughter Ann to William Magruder until the age of thirty-one [Court Records 1734-5, 357; 1738-40, 199; 1744-6, 298-9; 1749-50, 244]. She was the mother of

    i.   Richard, born about December 1730, "free Negro" head of a Prince George's County household of 3 "other free" in 1800 [MD:281] and 5 in 1810 [MD:8].

    ii.   William, born 3 August 1732, bound as an apprentice for thirty-one years. He was probably the William Gray, a "Mulatto," who was presented by the Charles County court in November 1770 for killing one of John **Butler's** unmarked hogs [Court Records 1770-2, 130]. He was a "Mulatto" who owed 11 shillings to the Prince George's County estate of Henry King on 29 November 1770 [Prerogative Inventories 104:253-4], perhaps identical to William Gray "a Mulatto" who was one of James Lewis's tithables in Loudoun County, Virginia, in 1782 [Tithables 1758-1799, 1110].

2   iii.   ?Hannah, born say 1735.

    iv.   Joseph, born 9 August 1738, bound to William Magruder until the age of thirty-one. He was head of a Montgomery County household of 1 "other free" in 1800 [MD:202].

3   v.   Catherine[1], born about August 1745.

    vi.   Ann, born in 1750.

2.   Hannah Gray, born say 1735, was the "Mollatto" servant of merchant Enoch Magruder on 23 March 1756 when she confessed to the Prince George's County court that she had an illegitimate child named Benjamin who was bound by the court to her master until the age of thirty-one [Court Record 1754-8, 218]. She was the mother of

    i.   Benjamin, born 20 November 1755, "free negro" head of a Prince George's County household of 6 "other free" in 1800 [MD:271], 4 in 1810 [MD:40] and 3 "free colored" in Frederick County, Virginia, in 1830.

4   ii.   ?Elizabeth, born say 1760.

3.   Catherine[1] Gray, born about August 1745, was the three-month-old child of Priscilla **Grimes**, alias Gray, who was bound to William Magruder by the Prince George's County court on 26 November 1745. She was called "Catherine Gray a Mullatto Woman" on 22 August 1769 when she was presented by the court for

having an illegitimate child on information of George Magruder [Court Record 1768-70, 385, 528-9]. She was a "free negro" head of a Prince George's County household of 7 "other free" in 1800 [MD:303]. She was the mother of

5   i.   Catherine³, born about 1778.
6   ii. ?Mary, born about 1781.
       iii. Rezin, born about 1787, registered in Prince George's County on 7 April 1807: *a dark mulatto lad, about 20 years old...a free man and the son of Cate Gray of Prince George County, a free woman of color.*

4.   Elizabeth Gray, born say 1760, was head of a Baltimore City household of 6 "other free" in 1800 [MD:221]. She may have been the mother of
       i.   Phillis, mother of a child named Ruth Gray (born in October 1803) by Ezekiel **Williams** ("free mulattoes"). Her parents had Ruth baptized on 12 March 1804 in St. Paul's Parish, Baltimore [Reamy, *Records of St. Paul's Parish*, II:27].

5.   Catherine³ Gray, born about 1778, registered in Prince George's County on 21 September 1809: *a dark mulatto woman, about 31 years old...a free woman, being the daughter of Cate Gray, a free woman of color.* She was the mother of
       i.   Eliza, born about 1793, registered on 28 April 1818: *a dark mulatto girl, about 25 years old...daughter of Catherine Gray, who was the daughter of Cate Gray.*
       ii. Erasmus, born about 1797, registered on 22 March 1819: *a black man...about 22 years old...son of Catharine Gray Jun.*

6.   Mary Gray, born about 1781, was a "free negro" head of a Prince George's County household of 5 "other free" in 1800 [MD:302]. She registered in Prince George's County on 19 June 1821: *a colored woman, about 40 years old...the descendant of a white woman.* She was the mother of
       i.   John, born about 1800, registered on 19 June 1821: *a black man about 21 years old...son of Mary Gray, a free woman of color* [Provine, *Registrations of Free Negroes*, 1, 5, 24, 28, 38].

Other members of the Gray family were
       i.   Isaac, head of a Talbot County household of 8 "other free" in 1800 [MD:526].
       ii.   Henry, head of a Charles County household of 10 "other free" in 1800 with Edward **Butler** in his household [MD:568].
       iii. Cate², head of a Montgomery County household of 4 "other free" in 1800 [MD:194].
       iv.   Milly, head of a Prince George's County household of 3 "other free" in 1800 [MD:281], perhaps identical to Milby Gray, head of a Prince George's County household of 3 "other free" in 1810 [MD:4].
       v.   Thomas, head of a Prince George's County household of 1 "other free" in 1800 [MD:281].
       vi.   Peter, head of a Prince George's County household of 1 "other free" in 1800 [MD:271].
       vii. Simon, head of a Prince George's County household of 3 "other free" and 3 slaves in 1810 [MD:4].

GRAYSON FAMILY

1.   Ann Grayson, born say 1700, the servant of William Harris, confessed to the Prince George's County court on 23 August 1720 that she had a "Mallatoe" child by Clement Brooke's "Negro man" John. John confessed to the charge when he appeared in court on 28 March 1720/1, and the court ordered that he receive twenty-five lashes [Court Record 1715-20, 1032, 1040-1; 1720-2, 91-2]. She was probably the ancestor of

    i. William, head of a Stafford County, Virginia household of 7 "other free" in 1810.

    ii. Matilda, head of a Stafford County household of 3 "other free" in 1810.

    iii. Winney, "F. Negroe" head of a Fauquier County, Virginia household of 4 "other free" in 1810 [VA:355].

    iv. Nice, head of a Spotsylvania County, Virginia household of 2 "other free" in 1810.

    v. David, head of a Prince William County, Virginia household of 1 "other free" in 1810 [VA:498].

GREEN FAMILY

1.   Elizabeth Green, born say 1712, was convicted in Queen Anne's County court in March 1731 for delivering a "mullatto" child on 1 November 1730 begotten by a "negroe." The court sold her daughter Sarah to Mr. Thomas Hynson Wright for 600 pounds of tobacco in March 1731 and sold her to Wright for £50 in November 1731 [Judgment Record 1730-2, 161-2, 264]. She was probably the ancestor of

    i. Sarah, born 1 November 1730, petitioned the Queen Anne's County in August 1772 to be levy free for the future [Judgments 1771-80, 64].

    ii. Edward, head of a Queen Anne's County household of 7 "other free" in 1800 [MD:345].

    iii. Solomon, married Mary **Protase**, "free Negroes," by 4 November 1783 banns [Parsons, *Marriage Register of Rev. Joseph Mosley*, 133]. He was head of a Kent County, Maryland household of 8 "other free" in 1800 [MD:161].

    iv. Elisha, head of a Queen Anne's County household of 4 "other free" in 1800 [MD:345].

    v. Henry, head of a Queen Anne's County household of 4 "other free" in 1800 [MD:343].

    vi. Valentine, head of a Queen Anne's County household of 2 "other free" in 1800 [MD:345].

    vii. Isaac, head of a Queen Anne's County household of 2 "other free" in 1800 [MD:345].

    viii. James, head of a Harford County household of 1 "other free" in 1790.

GREENWOOD FAMILY

Members of the Greenwood family in Maryland were

    i. Jacob, "Negro" head of a Kent County household of 3 "other free" and 2 slaves in 1790 and 7 "other free" in 1800 [MD:160].

1   ii. Perry, born say 1768.

1. Peregrine[1] Greenwood, born say 1768, and his wife Henrietta, "both free mulattoes," buried their two-year-old son Jonathan in the Catholic Church Yard at the head of Little Bohemia, Cecil County, on 6 March 1792. They were probably identical to Peregrine and Henny Wood, "free mulattos," whose son Peregrine was born in Bohemia on 1 January 1793 [Wright, *Vital Records of the Jesuit Mission, Warwick*, 39, 50]. Their children were

    i. Jonathan, born about 1790, died in 1792.

    ii. Peregrine[2], born 1 January, baptized 31 March 1793.

GRIFFIN FAMILY

Members of the Griffin family in Maryland and Delaware were

    i. Peter, "Negro" head of a Kent County household of 5 "other free" in 1790 and 4 in 1800 [MD:161].

    ii. Ann, born say 1755, mother of an illegitimate male child by Nehemiah

> **Hanser** in Dover Hundred, Kent County, Delaware, about January 1774
> [DSA, RG 3505, MS case files, February 1775 indictments].

1   iii.   Robert, born say 1775.
      iv.   Joseph, head of a Charles County household of 2 "other free" in 1800
         [MD:161].
      v.   Catherine, head of a Kent County household of 2 "other free" in 1800
         [MD:172].

1.   Robert Griffin, born say 1775, was free and married to Priscilla Griffin on 10
    March 1821 when his son Matthew registered in Dorchester County. Robert and
    Priscilla were the parents of
      i.   Matthew, born about 1799, registered in Dorchester County on 10 March
         1821: *of a yellow complection...free born, was raised in Dorchester*
         County and is the son of Robert and Priscilla Griffin who were both free,
         aged about 22 years [Certificates of Freedom for Negroes 1806-64, 43].

GRIMES FAMILY

1.   Susanna[1] Grimes, born say 1670, ran away from Prince George's County to Anne
    Arundel County with her "Malatta" child Elizabeth in 1704 after the death of her
    master, Colonel Hollyday. She was arrested and returned to Prince George's
    County court on 23 August 1704 when the court sold her and her four-year-old
    daughter to Edward Willett [Court Record 1699-1705, 321a]. She was the mother
    of
2   i.   Isabella, born say 1690.
3   ii.   Elizabeth, born 15 October 1700.

2.   Isabella Grimes, born say 1690, completed her indented time by 27 November
    1711 when her mistress Sarah Magruder delivered her to the Prince George's
    County court. The court sold her to Major Thomas Spriggs for seven years as
    punishment for a prior conviction of "Mulatto Bastardy." She had another child
    before 25 August 1713 when the court punished her for having an illegitimate
    child and running away from her master for eleven days. On 23 March 1713/4 the
    court sold her "Mallatto" child to John Henry until the age of thirty-one [Court
    Record 1710-5, 124, 386, 388, 540, 542]. She may have been the mother of
      i.   a son, born about 1713, may have married Priscilla **Gray** who was called
         "Priscilla Grimes Als. Gray" when she confessed to the Prince George's
         County court that she had an illegitimate child [Court Record 1744-6, 298-
         9].
4   ii.   Susanna[2], born say 1719.

3.   Elizabeth Grimes, born 15 October 1700, was sold to Edward Willett, her
    mother's master, by the Prince George's County court on 23 August 1704. She was
    called a "Mallatoe woman belonging to Edward Willett" on 27 June 1721 when
    she confessed to having two illegitimate children. The court ruled that the oldest
    child was "begotten by a Negroe," ordered the child sold to her master until the
    age of thirty-one and sold the youngest, called her "white" daughter, to Willett
    until the age of sixteen. She was called "Malatto Bess" on 24 June 1729 when she
    confessed to having a child by "a Certain Negro or Malatto Frank at William
    Digges'." Their child, born on 25 March 1728/9, was bound to Willett until the
    age of thirty-one. She had another child by a free person before 28 March 1731/2
    when the court ordered that she serve twelve months and bound her illegitimate
    child, Rachel, to her master until the age of sixteen. And she had a child by a free
    person before 22 November 1737 when the court ordered that she receive ten
    lashes. On 23 March 1737/8 John Smith Prather, innholder, was security for her
    presentment for selling liquor without a license. The case was postponed several
    times until 26 June 1739 when Edward Willett became her security. On 26 August
    1740 she was called "Elizabeth Grimes alias Malatto Bess" when James Russell

had a case against her which was agreed between the parties before it came to trial. On 24 March 1740/1 she confessed to having an illegitimate child (by a free person), and the court ordered that she receive ten lashes [Court Record 1699-1705, 321a; 1720-2, 264-6; 1729-30, 9, 401; 1730-2, 301; 1736-8, 415, 595-6, 659, 660; 1738-40, 444, 518; 1740-2, 76, 93, 203]. She was the mother of

- 5   i. Catherine, born say 1717.
- 6   ii. ?Lettice, born say 1728.
-     iii. ?Moses, born say 1730, a "mulatto" who served in the Virginia Regiment commanded by Colonel Gibson and waited on Colonel Brent during the Revolution. He was listed as a wagoner in the July 1779 muster of Captain Thomas Ewell's Company in the 1st Virginia Regiment commanded by Colonel George Gibson [NARA, M246, roll 93, frame 565]. He was married to a 45-year-old "mulatto" woman named Jane **Wilson** on 2 October 1779 when Cuthbert Bullitt of Dumfries, Virginia, placed an ad in the *Maryland Journal and Baltimore Advertiser* which stated that she had run away, perhaps to her husband or to the plantation of her former master, Colonel George Mason, or to Mrs. Page, among whose slaves she had a number of relations [Windley, *Runaway Slave Advertisements* II:232-3].
-     iv. Rachel, born about 1732.
-     v. ?John, born 25 March 1736/7, seven years old on 25 March 1743/4 when the Prince George's County court bound him as an apprentice to William Willett until the age of twenty-one. The court ordered that his master teach him to read the Bible and give him a suit of clothes at the completion of his indenture [Court Record 1743-4, 275].
-     vi. ?Philip, born about 1740, a three-year-old orphan bound to William Willett on 22 November 1743. The court ordered that he serve until the age of twenty-one and receive one year of schooling [Court Record 1742-3, 156].

4.   Susanah^2 Grimes, born say 1719, admitted in Prince George's County court on 28 August 1739 that she had a "Mallatto" child. The court ordered that she be sold for seven years and bound her daughter Nelly, born 25 June 1739, to Edward Willett until the age of thirty-one. In March 1742 she confessed that she had an illegitimate "Molatto" child named John who was bound as an apprentice until the age of thirty-one [Court Record 1738-40, 442; 1742-3, 375]. Her children were

- i. Nelly, born 25 June 1739.
- ii. John, born about January 1742, two months old in March 1742 when he was bound as an apprentice by the Prince George's County court. He was said to have been eighteen years old (born 20 December 1744) on 22 June 1762 when the court bound him to Charles Pearl until the age of twenty-one [Court Record 1761-3, 188]. He was head of a Washington County household of 7 "other free" in 1790.

5.   Catherine Grimes, born say 1717, was the "Molato" servant of William Bowie of Mount Calvert Hundred on 26 November 1745 when she was convicted by the Prince George's County court of having an illegitimate child by a free person. The court bound her six-week-old child Ann to William Bowie until the age of sixteen. She may have had a common-law marriage with a member of the **Graham** family. She was called "Mulatto Kate belonging to William Bowie" on 28 June 1748 when she confessed to having another illegitimate child. The court ordered that she serve seven years and ordered her two-month-old "Mulatto" son Philip **Graham** bound to her master until the age of thirty-one. She was called "Mollatto Cate" on 26 November 1751 when she confessed to having an illegitimate child and was fined thirty shillings, the penalty for having a child by a free person. On 27 November 1753 she was called "Molatto" Catherine **Graham**, "servant to William Bowie," when the court ordered that she serve seven years and bound her one-year-old son Charles until the age of thirty-one

[Court Record 1744-6, 248, 278, 298-9; 1746-7, 434; 1747-8, 168; 1751-4, 72, 174]. She was the mother of

7   i. Ann, born in October 1745.

      ii. Philip **Graham**, born in April 1748.

     iii. Charles **Graham**, born 29 October 1752, "free negro" head of a Prince George's County household of 3 "other free" in 1800 [MD:281].

6. Lettice Grimes, born say 1728, was called "Negroe Lettice" in Prince George's County court on 23 June 1747 when the court ordered her daughter Dido sold to Thomas Willett until the age of thirty-one [Court Record 1746-7, 620]. She was a "Free-Born Mulatto" listed in the inventory of the Frederick County estate of Thomas Willett on 18 September 1751 [Prerogative Inventories 48:325]. She was a "free-born Mullatto woman" who claimed to be close to forty years old in August 1764 when she petitioned the Frederick County court for her freedom from her indenture to Isabella Willet. She stated that she was born of a white woman and should have been entitled to her freedom at the age of thirty-one. Three months later on 20 November 1764 the court ordered her released from Willet's service but also convicted her of "Mullatto Bastardy" and ordered her sold to Samuel Beall for two years and four months. The same court ordered her daughter Lucy and (her daughter?) Lydia Grimes sold to Samuel Beall until the age of thirty-one. On 18 March 1766 she confessed to having another illegitimate child. Samuel Beall paid her fine and court costs [Judgment Record 1763-6, 285, 320, 323, 324, 503, 639]. She was the mother of

8   i. ?Benjamin[1], born say 1744.

      ii. Dido, born about August 1747, a "Free-Born Mulatto" girl listed in the inventory of the Frederick County estate of Thomas Willett on 18 September 1751 [Prerogative Inventories 48:325].

     iii. Lydia, born about 1754, a ten-year-old "Mullatto" girl (no parent named) sold by the Frederick County court to Colonel Samuel Beall in November 1764 for thirty-one years [Judgment Record 1763-6, 324].

     iv. ?William, head of a Frederick County household of 6 "other free" in 1800 [MD:538].

      v. Lucy, born about 1760, a five-year-old child "begott on the body of Lettice Grimes a Free born Mullato Woman by a Negro" who was sold to Samuel Beall on 20 August 1765 to serve until the age of thirty-one [Judgment Record 1763-6, 324, 503].

     vi. ?Nace, head of a Loudoun County, Virginia household of 11 "other free" in 1810 [VA:258].

7. Ann Grimes, born in October 1745, confessed to "Mulatto Bastardy" in Prince George's County court in June 1761 and in March 1763. The court ordered that she serve seven years for each offence and bound her two-month-old daughter Catherine to her master, William Bowie, until the age of thirty-one [Court Record 1761-3, 47-8, 414]. She was the servant of John Fletcher in March 1773 when the Frederick County court convicted her of having a child by a "Negro," sold her for seven years and sold her eleven-month-old daughter Alice to Colonel Samuel Beall until the age of thirty-one for £4 [Court Minutes 1773-5, 22, 41]. She was the mother of

    i. Catherine, born January 1763.

    ii. Alice, born about April 1772.

8. Benjamin[1] Grimes, born say 1744, and his wife Elizabeth Grymes, "free Mulattas," registered the birth of their daughter, Frances, in Bruton Parish, James City County, Virginia, on 11 February 1765 [Bruton Parish Register, 26]. Benjamin's children were

    i. Frances, born 11 February 1765.

    ii. ?Daniel, born about 1777, head of a Norfolk County, Virginia household of 8 "other free" in 1810 [VA:538], registered in York County on 21

September 1812: *a person of light complexion about 35 years of age...short hair, large nostrils & very fierce Eyes...Born of free parents on Queens Creek in the parish of Bruton* [Free Negro Register 1798-1831, no.67].

   iii. ?Benjamin[2], born 1776-94, head of an Ash County, North Carolina household of 1 "other free" in 1800 [NC:79] and 3 "free colored" in Salisbury, Rowan County, in 1820 [NC:283].

   iv. ?Thomas, head of a Cumberland County, North Carolina household of 2 "other free" in 1810 [NC:625] and 3 "free colored" in 1820 [NC:224].

GRINNAGE FAMILY

1.   Grinedge, born say 1670, was called the "Former Negroe" of Thomas Marsh (constable of the Lower Hundred of Kent Island) on 15 March 1697/8 when he and a white woman named Jane Shoare, daughter of William Shoare, were presented by the Talbot County court for "haveing Carnell Copulation" the previous October and for living together. Grinage was called a "planter" in March 1698/9 when he posted 2,000 pounds of tobacco and Richard Kempton posted 1,000 pounds of tobacco as security for his appearance in court. Perhaps he and Jane were married since he was acquitted of the charge on 20 June 1699 on the condition that he pay the court fees [Judgment Record 1696-8, 524; 1699, 37, 49, 54-5]. Jane and Grinage's children or grandchildren may have been those listed in the inventory of the Kent Island estate of Thomas Marsh, Gentleman, on 5 September 1716: *One Mallatoe Garl named beck 4-1/2 years old, one Mallatoe D° named Kate 1-1/2 years old, one D° named Rachel 1 years old* [Prerogative Inventories 1717-1718, 41-2]. Their descendants who used the last name Grinnage were:

2   i. Mary Grenidge, born say 1700.
3   ii. Rebecca[1], born about 1712.
      iii. Catherine[1], born about 1714.
      iv. Rachel, born about 1715, a "black" head of an Upper Hundred, Kent Island, Queen Anne's County household of 3 Blacks in 1776 [Carothers, *1776 Census of Maryland*, 149] and head of a Queen Anne's County household of 1 white woman and 1 "other free" in 1790 [MD:103].
4   v. Elizabeth, born say 1717.
      vi. Walter[1], called Walter Greenwich, "very aged and decripit," in November 1735 when the Queen Anne's County court exempted him and his wife Mary from paying taxes in the future [Judgment Records 1735-9, part 1, digital images 13-14], called Walter Grinedge, Sr., on 3 April 1745 when he owed 11 shillings to the Kent Island, Queen Anne's County estate of Benjamin Elliott, called Walter Greenage when he owed 5 shillings to the Queen Anne's County estate of Mr. Jacob Winchester per John Elliott's book, called Walter Greenwich on 13 December 1746 when he owed 6 pence to the Queen Anne's County estate of Robert Wilson [Prerogative Inventories, 1745, 31:51-60, 243-4; 1746, 33:308-12].
      vii. Walter[2], called Walter Grinedge, Jr., when he owed 1 shilling to the Kent Island, Queen Anne's County estate of Benjamin Elliott, on 3 April 1745, called Walter Greenwith on 9 July 1751 when he owed 2 shillings to the Queen Anne's County estate of Joseph Evens and called Walter Greenwich when he owed 800 pounds of tobacco to the Queen Anne's County estate of Thomas Hampton on 3 April 1752 [Prerogative Inventories, 31:51-60; 48:414-8; 49:9-10]. He was taxable in Island District of Queen Anne's County in 1783 [MSA S1161-8-10, p.65].
     viii. Sarah, sued by Nathan Williams in Kent County, Delaware court in August 1754 in a case which was discontinued before coming to court [DSA, RG 3815.031 1754-7, frame 46].
      ix. Thomas, head of a Queen Anne's County household of 5 "other free" in 1790 [MD:100].

      x. Cusby, head of a Queen Anne's County household of 5 "other free" in 1790 [MD:100].

     xi. Jacob, taxable in Corsica District of Queen Anne's County in 1783 [MSA S1161-8-9, p.51], a "free Mulatto" head of a Queen Anne's County household of 4 "other free" in 1790 [MD:100], a "N" taxable in Murderkill Hundred, Kent County, Delaware, in 1798 [RG 3535, reel 6, frame 208], 6 "other free" in Murderkill Hundred in 1800 [DE:132], and 4 in 1810, perhaps counted twice [DE:18 & DE:64]. He purchased 2 acres in Kent County for $12 by deed proved on 2 December 1808 [DB L-2:40]. He was probably related to Abraham Grinnage, "free Negro," who was ordered to be hanged for burglary in Kent County on 2 August 1803 [DSA, RG 3825.002, 1751-1939, frame 91].

     xii. Catherine²/ Kitty, born say 1758, mother of an illegitimate child in Queen Anne's County on 10 March 1778 [Judgment Record 1771-80, images 106-7].

5   xiii. John¹, born say 1750.

    xiv. John³, born say 1770, perhaps the John Grinage who was head of a Kent County, Delaware household of 6 "other free" in 1810 [DE:8]. His uncle Sherry Grinnage, by his 1 November 1790 Caroline County will, gave him 40 acres in Caroline County called *Stock Range* and a log house with feather-edged shingles when he reached the age of twenty-one [WB JR B:168-70]. He was living in Queen Anne's County on 19 August 1812 when he sold the land to Sherry's son John (senior) [Land Records K:610-1]. He was a 90-year-old "Mulatto" living in the Caroline County household of Solomon Grinnage in 1860.

     xv. Sampson, head of a Stafford County, Virginia household of 3 "other free" in 1810.

2.   Mary Grenidge, born say 1700, was a poor old woman who was allowed 800 pounds of tobacco by the Queen Anne's County for her support from 9 December 1772 to November court 1773 [Surles, *And they Appeared at Court* 120]. She testified in Queen Anne's County court on 11 April 1776 that she delivered the birth of twin sons to Ann Derochbrane, wife of Joseph Derochbrane, on Kent Island forty-eight years previous [Land Records RT L:353]. She may have been the mother of

6   i. Sherry, born say 1722.
7   ii. James¹, born say 1725.

3.   Rebecca¹ Grinnage, born about 1712, a "spinster," was convicted by the Queen Anne's County court in March 1734 for having an illegitimate child on 10 March 1733. She may have been living on the land of Arthur Emory, Gentleman, who gave bond of 10,000 pounds of tobacco that her child Benjamin would not become a charge to the county [Judgment Record 1732-5, 392-3]. She owed 530 pounds of tobacco to the estate of Benjamin Elliott of Kent Island, Queen Anne's County, on 3 April 1745. [Prerogative Inventories 1745, 31:57-40]. She was a "black" head of an Upper Hundred, Kent County household of 3 "Blacks" in 1776 [Carothers, *1776 Census of Maryland*, 148]. She was the mother of

8   i. Benjamin¹, born 10 March 1733.

4.   Elizabeth Grinnage, born say 1717, was a spinster living in Christ Church Parish, Queen Anne's County, in June 1737 when she was convicted of having an illegitimate child on 10 September 1736. She was not found by the sheriff when he went to arrest her in November that year, so she may have been living on the land of Robert Lloyd of Talbot County, Gentleman, who posted bond of £30 that her child Rebecca would not become a charge to the county. John **Flamer** was the father of her child [Judgment Record 1735-9, 343-4, 382]. She may have been the mother of

     i. Rebecca², born say 10 September 1736, a spinster "free Negroe" woman living in Talbot County in November 1756 when she admitted to the court that she had a child by a white man. The court sold her for seven years to her master and mistress Philip and Rebecca Palmer for £11 to commence after she completed her indenture to them [Criminal Record 1755-61, 69].

5. John[1] Grinnage, born say 1750, rented 2 acres of land in Queen Anne's County from Richard Hall on 18 November 1785 [Liber CD no.2, fol.52], made a deed of gift in Queen Anne's County for a horse, mare, bed and furniture, gun and pots to his children Nicholas and Mary Grinage on 22 March 1788 and a bill of sale to William Hall for a mare for $60 in 1813 [Liber STW-1, 25; IB-2, 198]. His children were

    i. Nicholas.
    ii. Mary.

6. Sherry Grinnage, born say 1722, was owed £2 due by note by the Queen Anne's County estate of Mr. Jacob Winchester on 28 August 1747, owed the estate of Joseph Evens a little over a shilling on 9 July 1751 and owed 230 pounds of tobacco to the Queen Anne's County estate of Thomas Hampton on 3 April 1752 [Prerogative Inventories 31:243-4; 48:414-8; 49:9-10]. He was allowed 600 pounds of tobacco by the Queen Anne's County court for the annual support of his poor old mother in December 1775 [Surles, *and they Appeared in Court, 1774-1777*, 66], head of an Upper Hundred, Kent Island, Queen Anne's County household of 16 Blacks in 1776 [Carothers, *1776 Census of Maryland*, 148], taxable in Island District of Queen Anne's County in 1783, taxable on 103 acres called *Copartnership* and 52 acres called *Streets Circumvention* in River District of Caroline County in 1783 [MSA S1161-8-10, p.74; MSA S1161-3-5, p.28] and head of a Caroline County household of 6 "other free" and 4 slaves in 1790 [MD:37]. On 15 February 1785 he purchased 94 acres which was part of a tract called *Copartnership* and another tract of 48 acres called *Street Circumvention* for £620 (called Sherry Greenwich). The following day he paid £7 for 9 acres called *Sherwood Friendship* adjoining *Copartnership* [Land Records A:848-9, 856-7]. He made a 1 November 1790 Caroline County will, proved 23 December 1790, by which he gave his daughter Susannah Greenage a "negro" girl Daffney, 2 beds and furniture, bedstead, horse, cow, heifer, calf, five sheep, a sow and pig, one-third his pewter, pots and pans, earthen ware, chairs and tables; gave son John Greenage all his lands except for 40 acres called *Stock Range* near Ann White's which his son John should make over to Sherry's nephew John Greenage when he should arrive at the age of twenty-one as well as build a log house for him about the size of the widow Ward's house and cover it with feather-edge shingles. He gave £5 each to his daughter Sarah **Flamour** (wife of John **Flamour**), daughter Mary **Flamour** (wife of Solomon **Flamour**), Rachel **Willson** (wife of Solomon **Willson**), grandson Thomas **Willson** (son of daughter Ann **Willson**, dec[d]), but if nephew John Greenage dies, Sherry **Flamour** son of ___ **Flamour** to receive the part of John Greenage. He also gave his nephew Sherry **Wansey Willson** one negro boy Dick, and his son John Greenage all his plantations, utensils, Negroes, stock and household furniture [WB JR B:169-70]. He was the father of

    i. Sarah **Flamour**.
    ii. Mary **Flamour**.
    iii. Rachel **Wilson**.
    iv. John[2], taxable in River District Hundred of Caroline County in 1783 [MSA 1161-3-5, p.28], called a farmer of Caroline County when he purchased all the lands, improvements and personal estate of William Miller, including two horses, a yoke of oxen and other farm stock, and household furniture by two Caroline County deeds of 18 January 1798 for $400. He purchased 212 acres in Caroline County called *Stock Range* for £198 on 14 October 1802 [Land Records F:198-200; H:223]. He was a "negro" head of a Caroline County household of 4 "other free" and a white woman over 45 years of age in 1810 [MD:168]. On 19 August 1812 he

purchased for £35 the 40 acres called *Stock Range* which his father had given his cousin John Grinage, Jr., of Queen Anne's County [Land Records K:610-1], and on 18 January 1823 he (signing) and William Hughlett sold parts of *Streets Circumstance, Shearwood Friendship, Copartnership* and *Stock Range* for $800, explaining in the deed that Hughlett had bought the property of John Grinage at a sheriff's sale. On 6 January 1823 John Grinage and William Hughlett sold *Stock Range* adjoining *Honeysuckle* and *Neighbor Kindness* for $160 [Land Records O:28-9; 62-3].

  v.   Ann **Wilson**.

7.   James[1] Grinage, born say 1725, owed 500 pounds of tobacco to the Queen Anne's County estate of Thomas Hampton on 3 April 1752 [Prerogative Inventories, 49:9-10]. He was a "black" head of an Upper Hundred, Kent Island, Queen Anne's County household of 4 Blacks in 1776 [Carothers, *1776 Census of Maryland*, 149]. He, Sarah Grinage, Cassia Grinage and William Baxter were witnesses for the State against James Ringold who was fined for assault and battery and breaking and entering a house in Queen Anne's County in 1782 [Surles, *And they Appeared at Court 1779, 1782, 1785, 1786, 1787*, 37], perhaps the James Grinnage who was convicted by the Kent County, Delaware court of stealing a horse from Simon Hawkins. In November 1792 the court ordered that he pay double the £15 assessed value of the horse, receive 39 lashes, stand in the pillory for an hour and have the soft part of his ear cut off [DSA, RG 3825.002, Oyer & Terminer, 1751-1939, frame 205]. He may have been the father of

9   i.   James[2], born say 1745.
   ii.   Zachariah, "free Mulatto" head of a Queen Anne's County household of 8 "other free" in 1790 [MD:100] and 10 in 1800 [MD:345].

8.   Benjamin[1] Grinnage, born 10 March 1733, owed 300 pounds of tobacco to the Queen Anne's County estate of Thomas Hampton on 3 April 1752 and £1.18 to the estate of Nathaniel Moore in 1763 [Prerogative Inventories, 49:9-10; 81:88]. He was called Benjamin Greenage, S[r], in March 1765 when the administrators of the Queen Anne's county estate of Edward Brown sued him for £36 [Judgments 1764-5, 345-7]. He made a bill of sale in Queen Anne's County to Thomas Meloyd on 16 August 1773 for a black mare, cow and heifer to serve as security for his payment of his rent for a plantation belonging to William Ringgold, and he mortgaged a mare, horse, two cows, a steer and four rooms of tobacco hanging in a tobacco house to John Rosette for £30 on 12 January 1785 [Liber RT-K, 172; CD-1, 163]. He was a "free Mulatto" head of a Queen Anne's County household of 6 "other free" in 1790. He may have been the father of

  i.   Benjamin[2], served in the Revolution as a substitute from Queen Anne's County, described as "a poor man with children but never applied for his discharge" [*Archives of Maryland* 48:11; NARA, M246, roll 34, frame 446 of 587]. He, a "molatto," and a white woman named Isabella Forbes alias Forbush were presented by the Queen Anne's County court in 1779 for marrying [Surles, *And they Appeared at Court 1779, 1782, 1785, 1786, 1787*, 9]. He was taxable in Island District of Queen Anne's County in 1783 [MSA S1161-8-10, p.65], a "free Negro" head of a Queen Anne's County household of 6 "other free" a white woman in 1790 and 5 "other free" and 2 white women in 1800 [MD:345]. He purchased two milk cows, hogs and household furniture from Greenberry Pritchett by Queen Anne's County deed recorded on 5 September 1822 [Liber STW-3, 40].
  ii.   William, paid £100 bounty on 7 March 1779 for enlisting in the 5th Maryland Regiment [NARA, M246, roll 34, frame 557 of 587].
  iii.   James, enlisted for 3 years and was in the roll of Captain Josias Johnson's Company in the 5th Maryland Regiment on 8 September 1778 [NARA, M246, roll 34, frame 183 of 587].

9.   James[2] Grinnage, born say 1745, died before 29 September 1767 when the inventory of his Queen Anne's County estate was taken. James and Zachariah Grinage were nearest of kin. His inventory, signed by the administrator Sherry Grinage, totaled £13 and included a bed, bedstead and other household furniture, two mares, two cows, a sow, ewe and lamb, and some shoemaker's tools. The account of his estate filed by Sherry Grinnage on 24 November 1768 called him James Grenage, Jr., and stated that he was survived by his widow Elizabeth, by then wife of Peter **Bentley**, and one child Ann Grenage [Prerogative Inventories 94:133-4; Queen Anne's County Administration Accounts 1756-69, 347-8 (MSA C1335-2)]. James and Elizabeth were the parents of

     i.   Ann, born say 1765.

A member of the family may have had a child by a slave. A "Negro Lad Named Grinage" was valued at £45 in the inventory of the Queen Anne's County estate of Thomas Wilson on 31 May 1745 [Prerogative Inventories 1745, 31:245-6].

GURLEY FAMILY

Members of the Gurley family were
1   i.   Francis, born say 1760.
     ii.   Bryan, head of a Sussex County household of 5 "other free" in 1810 [DE:425] and 8 "free colored" in 1820 [DE:218], probably the husband of Nancy **Cornish**.

1.   Francis Gurley, born say 1760, was taxable in Wicomico Hundred of Worcester County in 1783 [Assessment of 1783, MSA S1437, p.4]. He purchased 25 acres in Worcester County called *Castle Fine* for £12 on 11 June 1793, 7 acres on 3 May 1794, and 50 acres on the north side of Aydolet's branch for £28 on 12 September 1800. He sold 25 acres leading to Captain Winder's Mill at Salisbury for $250 on 14 April 1810 and he and his wife Nelly sold 156 acres called *Hard Fortune, Gurley's Choice* and *Hazel Ridge* for $300 on 1 April 1812 [Land Records P:31-2, P:372-3, AB:78, AC:282]. He was head of a Worcester County household of 9 "other free" in 1790, 9 in 1800 [MD:914] and 3 in 1810 [MD:486]. He left a 22 March 1830 Sussex County will in which he named his wife Ellender and sons William and Robert [DSA, RG 4545.9]. He was the father of

     i.   William.
     ii.   Robert.

GUY FAMILY

1.   Guy, born say 1660, was a "Negroe" who was living in Island Hundred, Talbot County, on 15 November 1687 when the court ordered that he serve James Downs for two years as punishment for begetting an illegitimate child by Downs's servant Elizabeth Vincent sometime before 15 March 1685/6. Their daughter Barbara Vincent was bound to Downs until the age of twenty-one. Downs gave Guy his freedom on 2 May 1690 [Judgment Record 1686-9, 68, 173; Chattel Records 1689-92, 320]. They may have been the ancestors of

2   i.   Joseph[1], born say 1702.
     ii.   Richard[1], born say 1704, living in Queen Anne's County on 26 August 1735 when the court found in his favor in a suit brought against him by James Earle. He was called Richard Guy alias Williams in March 1738 when the court ordered him to serve James Earle another 5 years for running away for a total of 104 days in 1736 and 1737 [Judgment Record 1732-5, 541; 1735-7, 47].

2.   Joseph[1] Guy, born say 1702, was a "free mulatto man begot by a Negro man on a white woman" living in Saint Paul's Parish on 10 August 1733 when the Queen Anne's County court convicted him of marrying a white woman named Bridget

Jones and ordered them sold for seven years. Thomas Hynson Wright was highest bidder at £18.10. He may have been identical to Joseph Williams alias Guy who John Emory won a suit against for 9,586 pounds of tobacco in June 1735. In November 1737 he confessed to running away for a total of 141 days in 1736 and 1737 and was ordered to serve an additional 1,410 days [Judgment Record 1732-5, 503-4, 513, 526]. They may have been the parents of

    i.   Joseph[2], head of a Kent County, Maryland household of 6 "other free" in 1800 [MD:173].

    ii.   Richard[2], head of a St. Jones Hundred, Kent County, Delaware household of 8 "other free" in 1800 [DE:47].

    iii.   John, head of a Murderkill Hundred, Kent County household of 2 "other free" in 1800 [DE:118] and a "F.N." head of a Kent County household of 3 in 1810 [DE:64].

    iv.   Samuel, head of a Little Creek Hundred, Kent County household of 4 "other free" in 1800 [DE:35].

    v.   George, "F. N." head of a Kent County household of 6 "other free" in 1810 [DE:19].

HACKNEY FAMILY

Members of the Hackney family in Maryland and Virginia were

    i.   Samuel, born say 1767, a "free Negro" taxable in Frederick County, Virginia from 1793 to 1813: listed with his unnamed wife and daughter in 1813, perhaps the father of Samuel Hackney, Jr., who was listed in 1813 [PPTL 1782-1802, frames 451, 629, 728, 766, 805, 856].

    ii.   Margaret, born about 1769, registered in Anne Arundel County on 13 March 1819: *aged about fifty years...dark complexion...free born...raised in the County* [Certificates of Freedom 1810-31, 128].

HAILEY FAMILY

1.   Honour Haley, born say 1714, confessed in Somerset County court in November 1730 that she had a "negro Bastard Child" at the house of Captain William Turpin in Somerset Parish on 1 August 1730. The court ordered her to serve for seven years and sold her child to William Turpin for thirty-one years. On 25 August 1733 she confessed that she had an illegitimate child by "Jupiter a Negro man belonging to Jonathan Stanton," and the court sold her "Mollatto" daughter named Sarah to William Gray of Monacan until the age of thirty-one for 500 pounds of tobacco [Judicial Record 1730-3, 28; 1733-5, 61]. She was the ancestor of

    i.   Sarah, born 24 July 1733.

    ii.   ?Stephen Hailey, head of a Worcester County household of 5 "other free" and a slave in 1810 [MD:645].

HALE/ HALL FAMILY

Anne Arundel and Baltimore Counties

1.   Elizabeth Hall, born say 1690, servant of John Hammond, confessed to the Anne Arundel County court in June 1710 that she had an illegitimate child by her master's "Negroe" slave James. The court bound her child, born the Sunday before Shrove Tuesday in 1709, to her master until the age of thirty-one [Judgment Record 1708-12, 156]. She was probably the ancestor of

2   i.   William[1], born say 1740.

2.   William[1] Hall, born say 1740, was head of a Patapsco Upper Hundred, Baltimore County household of 13 "other free" in 1810 [MD:639]. In 1836 his son Jacob told Martha Tyson, the biographer of Benjamin **Banneker**, that his father had been granted his freedom and 13 acres in Baltimore County by Walter Hall of Anne Arundel County. He also told her that he was Benjamin **Banneker's**

classmate (which is unlikely since Benjamin lived from 1731 to 1806, and Jacob died in 1843) [Bedini, *The Life of Benjamin Banneker*, 40, 261].[13] William was the father of

    i. ?James, head of a Patapsco Upper Hundred, Baltimore County household of 10 "other free" in 1810 [MD:641].

    ii. Jacob[1], head of a Patapsco Upper Hundred household of 8 "other free" in 1810 [MD:641]. He was employed for more than forty years as the keeper of the graveyard of the Society of Friends of Elkridge Landing, Baltimore County. He died in 1843 [Bedini, *The Life of Benjamin Banneker*, 40, 261]

    iii. ?Levin, head of a Baltimore County household of 5 "other free" in 1810 [MD:565].

    iv. ?Thomas[2], head of a Baltimore City household of 7 "other free" in 1810 [MD:276].

Members of the Hall family in Baltimore City and Anne Arundel County were

    i. William[2], head of an Anne Arundel County household of 2 "other free" in 1790 and 10 in 1810 [MD:84].

    ii. Jane, head of a Baltimore City household of 7 "other free" in 1800 [MD:244].

    iii. Betsey, head of a Baltimore City household of 5 "other free" in 1800 [MD:232].

    iv. Thomas[1], head of an Anne Arundel County household of 8 "other free" in 1810 [MD:80].

    v. Penby, head of a Baltimore City household of 5 "other free" in 1810 [MD:31].

    vi. Hy., head of a Baltimore City household of 3 "other free" in 1810 [MD:187].

    vii. Jacob[2], head of an Anne Arundel County household of 2 "other free" in 1810 [MD:80].

    viii. Sampee, head of an Anne Arundel County household of 1 "other free" in 1810 [MD:60].

Prince George's County

The Hall/ Hale family of Prince George's County moved there from King George County, Virginia, about 1800 according to the "free Negro" registration of Nathan D. Hale [Provine, *Registrations of Free Negroes*, 14]. They were probably related to Nathan Hall, head of a Prince George's County household of 8 "other free" and a slave in 1810 [MD:75], and William, Elijah, and James Hall (born about 1769-1781), alias **Deen**, who registered as "free Negroes" in King George County in 1800 [Register of Free Persons, nos. 11, 15, 19]. They may have been related to Abraham Hall, a "free Molatto," who appeared in adjoining Westmoreland County, Virginia court between 1744 and 1750.

1. Abraham Hall, born say 1720, was sued in Westmoreland County, Virginia court on 28 February 1743/4. He appeared in Westmoreland County court a number of times as plaintiff and defendant between 1744 and 1750. He was identified as a "free Molatto" on 24 February 1747/8 in his suit against John Crabb for which he was awarded £15 damages by a jury and on 30 November 1749 when he sued William Cox [Orders 1743-7, 14a, 23a, 66a, 67; 1747-50, 57, 95a, 113a, 133, 174a, 198; 1750-2, 8a]. He may have been the father of

2   i. John, born say 1755.

2. John Hall, born say 1755, moved from King George County, Virginia, to Prince George's County about 1799. He was head of a Prince George's County household of 14 "other free" in 1800 [MD:282]. He was the father of

---

[13]No will for Walter Hall has been located in Anne Arundel County after 1777.

3   i.   ?Trecy Hale, born say 1775.
   ii. ?Nathan D. Hale, born about 1781 in King George's County, Virginia,
       married Maria B. **Adams**. He registered as a free Negro in Prince George's
       County on 26 February 1813: *a bright mulatto man, about 31 or 32 years*
       old...born in King George's County in Virginia and resided there until he
       reached the age of 18 when he moved to Maryland where he lived for
       many years as a free man. He was born free. His wife Mary B. Hall, born
       about 1788, registered the same day: *formerly Maria B. Adams, is a bright*
       mulatto woman, about 25 years old...raised in the town of Piscataway in
       Prince George's County until she married Nathan D. Hale, her present
       husband. She was born free.
   iii. James D. Hale, born about 1793, registered in Prince George's County on
       22 October 1813: *a dark mulatto man, about 20 years old...son of John H.*
       Hale, a free person of color.

3.   Trecy Hale, born say 1775, was a "free woman of colour" of Prince George's
     County. She was the mother of
     i.   Mary Ann Hale, born about 1796, registered in Prince George's County on
        9 May 1821: *Polly who calls herself Mary Ann Hale, is about 25 years*
        old. She has a bright complexion...daughter of Trecy Hale, a free woman
        of color [Provine, *Registrations of Free Negroes*, 14, 16, 36].

<u>Eastern Shore of Maryland</u>
Members of a Hall family in the Eastern Shore of Maryland were
     i.   Jane, one of "2 "mulato girls" bound to Edward Harris of Queen Anne's
        County when the inventory of his estate was taken on 28 January 1741/2,
        each with nine years to serve and valued at £20.
     ii. Ann, one of "2 mulato girls" bound to Edward Harris on 28 January
        1741/2 when the inventory of his Queen Anne's County estate was taken
        on 28 January 1741/2 [Prerogative Court Inventories 1741-2, 26:490].
     iii. Sarah, head of a Talbot County household of 8 "other free" in 1800
        [MD:521].
     iv. Isaac, head of a Kent County household of 6 "other free" in 1810
        [MD:892].
     v.   Augustin, head of a Kent County household of 3 "other free" in 1800
        [MD:149] and 5 in 1810 [MD:905].
     vi. Fulbury, head of a Worcester County household of 10 "other free" in 1810
        [MD:608].

Other members of the Hall family in Maryland were
     i.   Frederick, born 6 March 1736 according to his pension file, head of a
        Montgomery County household of 1 "Free Negro or Mulatto" over 16, 3
        under 16 and 2 female "Free Negroes or Mulattos" in 1790 [MD:235] and
        4 "free colored," including a man and woman over 45, and a female slave
        over the age of 45 years in Fairfax Township, Fairfax County, Virginia, in
        1820. He applied for a pension for his service in the Revolution while
        living in Washington, D.C., on 24 September 1833, stating that he enlisted
        in the 3[d] Maryland Regiment on 8 May 1777 and served a total of six
        years. He was born in Port Tobacco, Charles County, and had a record of
        his age in the book of the Episcopalian Church there. He lived principally
        in Fairfax County, Virginia, since the Revolution before moving to
        Washington. Adam **Adams** made a deposition in Charles County in his
        favor on 12 March 1833. His name appeared on the muster rolls on 11
        May 1777 but was listed as a deserter on 10 January 1778; enlisted again
        on 25 March 1779 and was on the rolls to April 1780, so his application
        was denied [NARA, R.7569, M804, roll 1160, frame 686 of 1020].
     ii. Richard, "Mulatto" head of a Charles County household of 6 "other free"
        in 1790.

iii. John, head of a Charles County household of 6 "other free" in 1800 [MD:564].
iv. Jane, head of a Charles County household of 7 "other free" in 1800 [MD:505].
v. Bridget, head of a Charles County household of 5 "other free" in 1800 [MD:533].
vi. Tamer, head of a St. Mary's County household of 5 "other free" in 1800 [MD:418].
vii. Sarah **Moore**, born about 1795, registered in St. Mary's County on 30 March 1819: *Daughter of Ann Hall...about twenty five years of age, complexion dark...born free* [Certificates of Freedom 1806-64, 47]. Sarah was probably married to the son of Leonard **Moor**, head of a St. Mary's County household of 8 "other free" in 1800 [MD:419].

HAMILTON FAMILY

1. Isabell Hambleton, born say 1718, was living at Colonel George Dent's when the Charles County court presented her for bearing a "Molatto" child by information of George Thomas, the constable for William and Mary Parish [Court Record 1734-9, 263]. She may have been the ancestor of
   i. Charles, head of a Hampshire County, Virginia household of 4 "other free" in 1810 [VA:805].
   ii. Dido, head of a Hampshire County, Virginia household of 5 "other free" in 1810 [VA:793].

HAND FAMILY

1. Jane Hand, born say 1745, was a "Mulatto" head of a Charles County household of 6 "other free" in 1790. She paid a 30 shillings fine for bastardy in Charles County on 10 November 1772 [Court Record 1772-1773, Liber U, no.3, 169-70]. She may have been the mother of
   i. George, "Mulatto" head of a Charles County household of 1 "other free" in 1790.
   ii. John, "Mulatto" head of a Charles County household of 1 "other free" in 1790 and 4 in 1800 [MD:560].
   iii. James, head of a Charles County household of 5 "other free" in 1800 [MD:173].
   iv. Jonathan, head of a Sussex County household of 10 "other free" in 1810 [DE:406].

HANSER/HANZER FAMILY

1. Mary Vincent, born say 1648, was a neighbor of the **Johnson** family in Accomack County [DB 1651-54, 133]. In 1665 Richard **Johnson** and Thomas Tunnell agreed to support Mary's child by Aminadab, a slave of Southy Littleton, a planter on Nandua Creek in Accomack County [DW 1663-66, fol. 91]. The elder Aminadab died before 14 April 1665 when Southy Littleton of Accomack County gave the younger Aminadab "ye sonne of my servant Aminadab negro deceased and Mary Vincent Three cows and there female increase wch were formerly given to my said servant" [DW 1664-71, fol. 20]. On October 1666 Mary married John Okey, and they moved to Somerset County and then to Sussex County with the **Johnson** family [Torrence, *Old Somerset*, 399-400, 453, 474]. Mary's child by Aminadab was

2   i. Aminadab^1, born about 1664.

2. Aminadab^1 Hanser, born about 1664, apparently adopted the name Hanser sometime before April 1683 when he recorded his cattle mark in Sussex County [Horle, *Records of the Sussex County Court*, 222]. He was about twenty-four

years old in September 1688 when he, John Okey and Mary Okey testified in Sussex County court that they had helped John Barker move his cattle from Accomack County to Sussex County. His wife Rose Hanser also testified [Court Records 1680-99, 262]. In March 1689/90 he was called "Aminidab Hanger Negro," a twenty-six-year old, and his wife was called Rose Hanjaw, an eighteen-year old, when they testified in Accomack County court about this same court case in which John Barker was convicted of appropriating seven cattle belonging to William Burton and Thomas Bagwell. Rose testified that in 1684 she lived in John Barker's house on the land of William Burton and Thomas Bagwell [W&c 1682-97, 181, 181a]. Rose may have been Rose Matthews who testified with Aminadab in another case concerning John Barker which was held in Sussex County court on 8 September 1685 [Court Records 1680-99, 93]. In February 1690 Aminadab acted as attorney for William Burton and Thomas Bagwell in their Sussex County court case, and on 2 September 1696 he and Edward Carey each purchased 200 acres of a 400 acre tract in Sussex County [Horle, *Records of the Sussex County Court*, 682, 1025-6; DB A-198]. He was found not guilty in Sussex County court of stealing a fishing boat valued at £20 on 4 November 1706 [RG 4815.017, dockets 1707-41, frame 3]. John Burton mentioned him in his 10 February 1708/9 Sussex County will [de Valinger, *Sussex County Probate Records*, 21]. He sued Aminadab **Oaky** (perhaps his half-brother?) in Sussex County court on 3 May 1704 over some damage which their neighbors were ordered to inspect and report back to the court [Horle, *Records of Sussex County*, 1191]. On 9 April 1713 Aminadab **Oaky** posted £100 security in Sussex County court to guarantee Aminadab Handsor that he would abide by the arbitrators' decision regarding the removal of a fence. He sold his 200 acre tract to Thomas Marriner on 28 May 1715. Aminadab and Rose were still living on 16 October 1717 when their son Aminadab, Jr., mentioned them in his Sussex County will. Aminadab, Sr., died before 8 December 1725 when Rose Hanzer was called the "widow, relict, and administrator of the estate of Aminadab Hanzer...Deceased" in the deed by which she sold for £33 to Job Barker 150 acres being part of 200 acres (part of a larger tract of 400 acres which Aminadab Hanzer and Edward Carey purchased from Sarah Painter on 3 September 1695). Rose died before 5 May 1752 when their descendants, Bridget **Norman**, William Handsor "who lives in Kent County" (signing), Samuel Hansor (signing), Elias Hansor, and Mary **Brown** sold to Benjamin Burton 50 acres which was part of 400 acres in Little Creek Hundred called *Ebonezer* "being the Dwelling place of Rosanna Hanzor Deceased." On 2 February 1773 Thomas and William Handzer, "Mallatos," made a quit claim deed for 350 acres on Ivey Branch which had been granted to "Aminadab Handzer Malatto Deceasd" [DB D-4:225-7; F-6:220-2; H-1, 329-30; L-11, 314-5]. Aminadab and Rose's children are

- i. Aminadab[2], born 23 January 1688/9 [Turner, *Records of Sussex County*, 146], made a Sussex County will on 15 March 1717 by which he left a saddle and bridle to his brother Samuel, a yearling steer to his sisters Ann and Mary, and the remainder to his father and mother, Aminidab and Rose Handzer [WB A-1:122].

3   ii. William[1], born say 1692.

4   iii. Thomas[1], born say 1693.

5   iv. Samuel[1], born say 1695.

- v. Ann, born say 1710. She may have married Edward **Norman**, a "mulatto," who baptized his son, Edward, on 16 May 1747 at St. George's Protestant Episcopal Church, Indian River [Wright, *Vital Records of Kent and Sussex Counties*, 92], and they may have been the parents of Bridget **Norman** who sold land in Sussex County in 1752 "where Rosanna Hanzor formerly lived."

- vi. Mary, perhaps the Mary **Brown** who sold land in 1752 where (her mother?) Rosanna Hanzer had lived.

6   vii. Elias, born say 1712.

3. William[1] Handsor, born say 1692, purchased 100 acres called *Bottle and Cake* at the head of Long Neck in Indian River Hundred by deed proved in Sussex County court on 1 November 1715 and recorded a survey for *Bottle & Cake* in 1716 [DB A-1:301; Shankland's Surveys & Warrants, p.55]. He patented land in Dover Hundred, Kent County, and was taxable there from 1733 to 1765. His son Nehemiah was taxable near him from 1758 to 1765. By his 28 August 1756 Kent County will, proved 16 December 1767, he left his land called *Jolly's Neck* to his youngest son Cornelius (son of Mary), left his gun to his son William, an iron pot to son Jonathan, and his shoemaker's tools to his son Nehemiah. He also named his daughter Naomy (daughter of Mary) [WB L-1:39-40]. The account of the estate named heirs: Cornelius, Naomi, Rhoda, Rachel, and Sarah Handsor [de Valinger, *Kent County Probate Records*, 238]. His wife Mary apparently died before the will was proved on 16 December 1767 since his wife was called Sarah Hansor when she and (her brother?) John **Durham** were granted administration on the estate until Cornelius Hansor arrived to the age of seventeen. Sarah, John **Durham**, William **Conselor**, and Daniel **Durham** posted bond for its administration. Sarah was probably "the widow Handser" who was head of a taxable household in Dover Hundred in 1768. She sued her son Cornelius in Kent County court in February 1771 but the case was abated by her death [DSA, RG 3815.031, frame 395]. She died before 8 February 1771 when administration on her estate was granted to her "next of Kin" John **Durham** [WB L-1, fol. 91]. William was the father of

7   i.   William[2], born say 1713.
8   ii. Jonathan[1], born say 1715.
9   iii. Nehemiah[1], born say 1720.
   iv. ?Jacob[1], born say 1721, taxable in Dover Hundred from 1742 to 1751. In 1748 he was a "Malatto" taxable in adjoining Murderkill Hundred. He and Nehemiah Hanser testified in the Kent County trial against "Negro" Phil who was found not guilty of robbing Thomas Parker on 25 August 1749 [Delaware Archives RG 3811.1, 1749-1750, Court for the Trial of Negro Slaves]. He may have died before 1756 when his father made his will.
   v.   Naomi, died before 24 December 1793 according to the account of her father's estate.
   vi. Cornelius, born say 1752, not yet seventeen years old on 15 February 1768 when Sarah Hansor and John **Durham** were granted letters of administration of the Kent County estate his father William[1] Hansor [WB L-1, fol. 41]. He was indicted by the Kent County court in 1778 to keep the peace [DSA, RG 3505.003, 1735-1779, frame 685]. He was taxable in Dover Hundred, Kent County, in 1776, taxable on a cow and calf in Duck Creek Hundred in 1798, and head of a Little Creek Hundred, Kent County household of 5 "other free" in 1800 [DE:32]. He died before 6 January 1814 when administration of his Kent County estate was granted to William Collins.
   vii. Rhoda, born say 1764, born after her father made his will on 28 August 1756. She assigned her right to her father's Kent County estate to Gabriel **Harmon** before 24 December 1793 when this part of the account of her father's estate was included in the account of the estate of John **Durham** [RG 3545, reel 68, frame 621].
   viii. Rachel, born say 1768, born after her father's death, called a minor above the age of fourteen years in Orphans Court on 28 August 1783 [Orphans Court Book C:255]. She was living in Dover Hundred on 11 October 1788 when she sold 200 acres which had been granted to her father William Hansor on 9 November 1734 and laid out for him on 21 November 1737 in the forest of Dover Hundred called *Jolly's Neck* adjoining the main branch of the head of Dover River and Chances Branch [A-2:95]. She was taxable on 87-1/2 acres in St. Jones Hundred, Kent County in 1798 and head of a St. Jones Hundred household of 5 "other free" in 1800 [DE:45].

4.   Thomas[1] Hanzer, born say 1693, brought a successful case against Samuel Cary in Sussex County court for assault in November 1727. Richard Poultney withdrew a case against him for debt in Sussex County court in February 1727/8 and he was sued for debt in May 1735 and by Christopher Topham in May 1737. In November 1742 the Sussex County court allowed him £2 for the support of Ann **Oakey**. He called himself a house carpenter on 22 March 1743 when he petitioned the Sussex County court to be adjudged a servant to his creditors for three years in order to pay a total of £50 debt (a not uncommon request). The court agreed and allowed him to retain enough of his earnings to support his family [RG 4815.017, 1707-41, frames 63, 164, 168, 170, 175, 355, 469, 485; 1741-53, frame 153]. He received a warrant for 150 acres in Sussex County on 20 October 1735 and another 205 acres, called *The Addition* in 1754. He sold (signing) to Benjamin Burton land in Indian River Hundred in Long Neck called *Ebonezer*, "part of a tract formerly belonging to Rosanna Handzer the mother of the sd Thomas," by deed proved in 1749 [Warrants, C 1776, p.329; DB H-8, 253]. He and his wife Hester registered the birth and baptism of their son Job at St. George's Chapel, Indian River Hundred, in 1753. He made an Indian River Hundred, Sussex County quit claim deed (signing) with William Handzer (who made his mark) for 350 acres on Ivey Branch in Indian River Hundred, Sussex County, on 2 February 1773. They called themselves called "Mulattos and yeoman" in the deed for land for which "one Aminadab Handzer Molatto Deceasd" had been granted a patent [DB L-11, 314-5]. Thomas and Hester were the parents of

   i.   Job, born 17 June 1753, baptized 9 December 1753 at St. George's Protestant Episcopal Church, Indian River [Wright, *Vital Records of Kent and Sussex Counties*, 96].

5.   Samuel[1] Hanzer, born say 1695, was named in the 16 October 1717 Sussex County will of his brother, Aminidab. He was involved in a fight with Elias Fisher at the widow **Johnson**'s harvest. Fisher claimed in Sussex County court in May 1723 that Samuel struck and kicked him. However, the sheriff testified that Samuel had tried to avoid a confrontation with Fisher, and Albert Jacobs and James Bailey swore that Fisher called Hanser a "Black son of a Bitch" and struck Hanser first. The jury found Samuel not guilty. Perry Fordham sued him for debt in Sussex County court in May 1729, Thomas Stockley, Joseph Pemberton and Richard Poultney sued him in August 1733, Thomas Petty in November 1730, and Serjeant Smythies sued him for debt in August 1736 [RG 4815.017, dockets 1707-41, frames 56, 69, 244, 281, 285, 289, 404, 414, 460]. On 20 May 1733 he and his wife Ann (both signing) sold 124 acres of land in Sussex County which his father had owned and which he had purchased from the administrator of his father's estate. It was described as being on Fishing Creek or Goldsmith Creek, proceeding out of Rehoboth Bay, bordering land of Robert **Okey** on the south side of Herring Branch, called *Ebenezer*. This was land which had been part of Aminadab **Okey**'s Sussex County estate. Samuel received a warrant for 200 acres in Sussex County on 20 October 1735 and sold this land called *Hanzors Lookout* on 13 April 1744 [DB G-7:18-19, 34, 35; Warrants C 1776, p.329; DB H-8:76]. He sued (his brother) Thomas Hanzer in Sussex County court in November 1742. The court, with the consent of the parties, appointed a committee of Benjamin Stockley, Daniel Nunez and Woodman Stockley to rule on the matter [RG 4815.017, General Sessions Court, 1741-53, frames 74, 100, 116]. He may have been the father of

10   i.   Samuel[2], born about 1735.

6.   Elias Hanzer, born say 1712, was married to Nancy before 1 April 1747 when their "mulatta" son John was born [Wright, *Vital Records of Kent and Sussex Counties*, 106]. Thomas and Peter Robinson sued him in Sussex County court in November 1765 [RG 4815.017, General Sessions Court, 1761-71, frame 292]. Their children were

   i.   John[1], born 1 April 1747, married Eliza **Norman** at Lewes and Cool

Springs Presbyterian Church on 21 September 1768 [Records of the United Presbyterian Churches of Lewes, Indian River and Cool Spring, Delaware 1756-1855, 279]. He was taxable in Indian River, Sussex County, from 1770 to 1791 and head of an Indian River Hundred household of 6 "other free" in 1800 [DE:437]. He made a 7 October 1806 Sussex County will, proved 6 January 1807, by which he left his land to his wife Leviney during her widowhood and then to nephew Robert Handser, son of William Handser, and if Robert died, then to John Handser, son of Isaac Handser [RG 4545.009, reel 100, frame 193; WB F-6:249].

11   ii.   William⁴, born say 1752.

7.   William² Hanser, born say 1713, purchased 212 acres in Indian River Hundred on the east side of *Hanzer's Lookout* for £30 on 7 November 1752 [DB H-8:339-40]. He was called "William Handzer of ye County of Sussex...Yeoman" when he purchased 200 acres in Sussex County on 4 March 1767. This was land that (his uncle) Samuel¹ Handsor had owned from 1735 to 1744. He sold 100 acres of *Handsor's Lookout* on the west side of Delaware Bay in Indian River Hundred for £30 on 4 March 1767. He was probably the William Handzer who made an Indian River Hundred, Sussex County quit claim deed with Thomas Handzer, "Mallatos," on 2 February 1773 [DB K-10, 242-3; L-11, 314-5]. He was taxable in Dover Hundred, Kent County in 1773 and 1774 and taxable in Indian River Hundred, Sussex County, in 1777 and 1784. By his 26 October 1784 Sussex County will, proved in 1801, he left a gun to his son David, his land to son Thomas, a bed to son Peter, a bed to wife Jane, and a shilling to grandchildren Aaron, Isabel, Thomas, Elise, and Cary Hanzer and divided the remainder between Elizabeth **Roads**, Agnes Hanzer, Easter Hanzer, Jane **Rigwah** and Ann **Salmons** who was apparently the wife of Henry **Sammons**. The estate paid Elisabeth Rawles, Nany Rawles, Elizabeth **Morris**, John Rawles, and David **Hodgskin** [WB E:312; RG 4545.009, reel 100, frames 107-112]. His children were

12   i.   David¹, born say 1734.
13   ii.   Thomas², born about 1740.
     iii.   Peter, born say 1750.

8.   Jonathan¹ Hanser, born say 1715, was sued by James Prettyman in Sussex County court in November 1742. The sheriff sold some of his property which included a horse, a sow and pigs and a saddle. Cornelius Stockley sued him, Nehemiah Handzer and Jonathan Handzer, Jr., in court in August 1769 [RG 4815.017, General Sessions Court, 1741-53, frame 72; 1761-71, 510, 582]. He was listed in the account of the Sussex County estate of Cord Hazard, Jr., on 12 March 1750 [Orphans Court 1744-51, 80]. He was taxable in Indian River Hundred, Sussex County, from 1770 to 1789: called "Jona. Hanzer a poore Melato" when he was a delinquent taxable in 1789. He may have been the father of

     i.   Sarah, born say 1748, married Levi **Morris** in Sussex County in September 1768 [Records of the United Presbyterian Churches of Lewes, Indian River and Cool Spring, Delaware 1756-1855, 279].
14   ii.   Jonathan², born say 1749.
     iii.   Caleb, born say 1760, a delinquent taxable in Lewes and Rehoboth Hundred, Sussex County, in 1781 and 1782.
     iv.   Aminadab³, born say 1763, married Hannah Pettyjohn on 13 November 1784 in Sussex County [Records of the United Presbyterian Churches of Lewes, Indian River and Cool Spring, Delaware 1756-1855, 298]. He was taxable in Indian River Hundred, Sussex County, in 1784 and 1789. Perhaps his widow was Hannah Hansor, head of an Indian River Hundred household of 4 "other free" in 1800 [DE:438].

9.   Nehemiah¹ Hansor, born say 1720, was taxable in Dover Hundred from 1738 to 1785 [Kent County Levy Assessments]. On 16 May 1752 he purchased 80 acres,

formerly owned by John Chance, on the northwest side of the main branch of the Dover River in Little Creek Hundred from Nicholas Lockerman (written as Nehemiah Handson) [DB O:213]. He witnessed the 31 January 1757 Kent County will of William **Beckett** [WB K-1:62]. By his 15 December 1785 Kent County will, proved 20 November 1787, he left his land on the north side of a branch of the Dover River to his son Nehemiah, Jr. (where Nehemiah, Jr., was then living) and left the remainder of his land and estate to his wife Johannah and his two grandchildren Elizabeth and Jemima Handzer. His wife Johannah and friend Peter Miller, Sr., were executors [WB M-1, p. 89 - fol. 90]. Johannah was probably the "Widow Handsor" who was charged for John **Hagins'** tax in Dover Hundred in 1785 [Levy Assessments, frame 45]. She married Sanders **Oakey** before 12 November 1787 when she and Saunders **Oakey** were ordered to return an account of her husband's estate [Orphans Court Book D:144]. Nehemiah's children were

15   i. William^3, born say 1740.
       ii. Nehemiah^2, born say 1750, taxable in Dover Hundred from 1772 to 1788: called Nehemiah, Jr., from 1772 to 1785. He had an illegitimate male child by Ann **Griffin** in Dover Hundred about January 1774 [DSA, RG 3505, MS case files, February 1775 indictments; RG 3805.003, 1735-79, frame 597]. He may have married Amelia **Sisco**.

10. Samuel^2 Hansor, born say 1735, was 24 years old when he was listed in the muster of Captain John Wright's Company of Delaware recruits in the French and Indian War on 11 May 1759 [Public Archives *Commission, Delaware*, 25]. He was married to Comfort Hanzer before 15 April 1770 when their "Melatto" daughter Ann was baptized at St. George's Chapel, Indian River Hundred. He had married Mary before 14 August 1784 when they registered the birth of their son Samuel at St. George's Chapel [Wright, *Vital Records of Kent and Sussex Counties*, 99, 106]. He was taxable in Indian River Hundred, Sussex County, from 1770 to 1791 and head of an Indian River Hundred household of 4 "other free" in 1800 [DE:438]. He was apparently married to Bridget Hanzer by 7 March 1805 when she and William **Rigwaw** (signing) administered his estate which was valued at £7 [RG 4545.009, reel 100, frame 156]. His children were
        i. Ann, born 16 M(arch?), baptized 15 April 1770.
       ii. Nisa, born 18 February 1772, "melatto" daughter of Samuel and Comfort Hanzor [Wright, *Vital Records of Kent and Sussex Counties*, 101].
      iii. Samuel^3, born 14 August 1784, baptized 31 July 1785.

11. William^4 Hanzer, born say 1752, was taxable in Indian River Hundred, Sussex County, from 1773 to 1787: called "Wm Hanzor of Elas" in 1787 when he was a delinquent taxable, perhaps the Wm. H. Hanzer who was taxable in Indian River Hundred from 1789 to 1791. He and his wife Easter/ Hester registered the 15 March 1773 birth of their son Joshua at St. George's Protestant Episcopal Church, Indian River [Wright, *Vital Records of Kent and Sussex Counties*, 101]. William was head of an Indian River Hundred household of 3 "other free" in 1800 [DE:437] and 3 in 1810 [DE:455]. He may have been the William Handzor who died before 24 December 1816 when Jane Handzor was granted administration on his estate [RG 4545.009, reel 100, frame 122]. William was the father of
        i. Joshua, born 15 March 1773.
       ii. Alce, born 3 September 1777, married Nathaniel **Morris**, "Two free Mulatoes," in Sussex County, on 24 December 1799 [Records of the United Presbyterian Churches of Lewes, Indian River and Cool Spring, Delaware 1756-1855, 315].
      iii. Agnes, born 1 February 1784, baptized 31 July 1785 [Wright, *Vital Records of Kent and Sussex Counties*, 103, 104], perhaps the mother of Jane and Isaac Handzor who received her share of William Handsor's estate in 1803 [RG 4545.009, reel 100, frames 107-112].
       iv. Robert, son of William and nephew of John Handzer who named him in his 7 October 1806 Sussex County will.

12. David[1] Handzer, born say 1734, was listed in the account of the Sussex County estate of Thomas Waples on 2 September 1766 [Orphans Court 1761-72, 138]. He served in the First Company of the Delaware Regiment and died before the February 1780 muster. His administrator received his pay from 1 August 1780 to 1 November 1782 [DSA, MS Delaware Regiment Pay Records, 1778-1783, certificates 54,358, 54,816, 54,479, 55,180; Public Archives Commission, *Delaware Archives*, 196; also NARA, M246, roll 31, frame 496]. On 8 December 1784 (his son?) David Handzer, Jr., was granted administration on his Sussex County estate. He was the father of
    i. ?David[2], born say 1765, a delinquent taxable in Indian River Hundred in 1787.
    ii. ?Aaron, born say 1767, a delinquent taxpayer in Indian River in 1787 and a "poore Melato" taxable in Indian River Hundred in 1789, head of an Indian River Hundred household of 8 "other free" in 1800 [DE:437].
    iii. William[5], born say 1769, taxable in Indian River Hundred from 1787 to 1790, called "Wm Hanzer of David" in 1789 when he was a delinquent taxable, probably the William who died intestate about 1804 according to the petition of his widow Susan **Durham** on 21 February 1821 which stated that he had conveyed a 75 acre tract of land in the forest of Jones Hundred to Jacob Stout on 16 January 1804 while she was still an infant under twenty-one [Brewer, *Kent County, Delaware, Guardian Accounts, Edmonson to Hopkins*, 21].
    iv. ?Mary, born say 1774, married William **Harmon**, "free Mulattoes," on 11 May 1795 in Sussex County [Records of the United Presbyterian Churches of Lewes, Indian River and Cool Spring, Delaware 1756-1855, 311].

13. Thomas[2] Hanzer, born about 1740, was 19 years old when he was listed in the muster of Captain John Wright's Company of Delaware recruits in the French and Indian War on 11 May 1759 [Public Archives *Commission, Delaware*, 25]. He was married to Priscilla before 22 April 1784 when they registered the birth of their son Thomas at St. George's Chapel, Indian River Hundred [Wright, *Vital Records of Kent and Sussex Counties*, 106]. He was head of an Indian River Hundred, Sussex County household of 3 "other free" in 1800 [DE:437]. His Sussex County will, proved 18 May 1821, named his sons, Peary, John, Alexander, Nehemiah, and William. They were the parents of
    i. Jane, born before 1776, wife of Woolsey **Foster** who was head of a Dagsboro, Sussex County household of 7 "free colored" in 1820 [DE:370].
    ii. Thomas[3], born 22 April 1784, baptized 31 July 1785, married Katherine **Jackson**, 4 February 1808 at Lewes and Cool Spring Presbyterian Church [Records of the United Presbyterian Churches of Lewes, Indian River and Cool Spring, Delaware 1756-1855, 320].
    iii. Ann, born 1775-1794, probably the Nancy Hanzor who married Myers **Clark** on 26 January 1815 at Lewes and Cool Spring Presbyterian Church [Records of the United Presbyterian Churches of Lewes, Indian River and Cool Spring, Delaware 1756-1855, 325].
    iv. Peery, born 5 February, baptized 12 August 1792 at St. George's Protestant Episcopal Church, Sussex County, son of Thomas and Priscilla Hanson [Wright, *Vital Records of Kent and Sussex Counties*, 109], married Mary **Butcher** in Kent County in 1812.
    v. John[2], born say 1794.
    vi. Alexander, born say 1796.
    vii. Nehemiah[3].
    viii. William[6].
    ix. Sarah Lack.

14. Jonathan[2] Hanser, born say 1749, was taxable in Indian River Hundred, Sussex County, from 1770 to 1791 (called Jonathan, Jr.) and a "Negro" head of an Indian River Hundred household of 4 "other free" in 1800 [DE:437]. He and his wife

Agnes registered the 5 September 1772 birth of their son Jacob and the 23 November 1777 birth of their daughter Jane at St. George's Protestant Episcopal Church, Indian River [Wright, *Vital Records of Kent and Sussex Counties*, 101, 103]. Jonathan and Agnes were the parents of

    i.   Jacob[2], born 5 September 1772, head of an Indian River, Sussex County household of 1 "other free" in 1810 [DE:455] and 6 "free colored" in 1820 [DE:214].

    ii. Jane, born 23 November 1777.

    iii. ?Polly, married Israel **Jackson**, "free Mulattoes," on 18 April 1802 at Lewes and Cool Spring Presbyterian Church [Records of the United Presbyterian Churches of Lewes, Indian River and Cool Spring, Delaware 1756-1855, 318].

15. William[3] Hanzer, born say 1740, was called William Hanzer, Jr., when he was taxable in Indian River Hundred, Sussex County, from 1773 to 1777. He died before 6 March 1784 when his widow Bridget Handzer and William **Rigwaw** administered his Sussex County estate which was valued at £11 [RG 4545.009, reel 100, frame 160]. On 15 December 1785 his father Nehemiah[1] Hanser made his will naming grandchildren Elizabeth and Jemima. Elizabeth was called the "daughter of William Handsor deceased" in 1788 when she chose her guardian in orphan's court [Orphans Court Book D:152]. His wife Bridget was head of an Indian River Hundred, Sussex County household of 2 "other free" in 1800 [DE:437]. William and Bridget were the parents of

    i.   Elizabeth, born say 1773, a minor above the age of fourteen years in 1788 when she chose William Pierce as her guardian in Kent County Orphans Court [Book D:152]. She and her sister Jemima were named in the will of her grandfather William[1] Hansor. She married Benjamin **Durham**.

    ii. Jemima, born say 1775.

Another member of the family was

    i.   Sibilla/ Isabell, sued Thomas Hanzer, Junr., in a Sussex County court case that was agreed to before coming to court [RG 4815.017, General Sessions Court, 1771-93, frame 529].

HANSON FAMILY

Members of the Hanson family in Maryland were

    i.   Harry, born say 1755, head of a Kent County, Maryland household of 7 "other free" in 1800 [MD:149].

1   ii. Milley, born say 1775.

    iii. Mary, born before 1776, head of a Charles County household of 2 "free colored" in 1830.

1. Milley Hanson, born say 1775, was living in Prince George's County from 1815 to 1825 when her children registered as "free Negroes." She was the mother of

    i.   William, born about 1796, registered in Prince George's County on 14 July 1815: *a dark mulatto youth, about 19 years old, and 5 feet 4-1/2 inches tall...son of Milley Hanson, a free born woman of color.*

    ii. Eleanor, born about 1807, registered on 18 April 1825: *a dark mulatto woman, about 18 years old, and 5 feet 1 inch tall...daughter of Milly Hanson.*

    iii. Caroline, born about 1810, registered on 18 April 1825: *a dark mulatto girl, about 15 years old, and 5 feet tall...daughter of Milly Hanson* [Provine, *Registrations of Free Negroes*, 19, 50].

HARDING FAMILY

1. Alice Hardin, born say 1682, was the servant of William Coursey on 4 November 1701 when she was convicted by the Talbot County court of having an illegitimate "Mullato" child. The court ordered that she serve her master an additional year for the trouble of his house, that she be sold for seven years and that her child be sold for the benefit of the county [Judgment Record 1701-2, 85b]. She was probably the mother of

2   i.   William, born say 1701.

2. William Harding, born say 1701, a "free mullatto" laborer, was living in Saint Paul's Parish on 26 August 1735 when the Queen Anne's County court sold him for seven years as punishment for marrying a white woman named Mary Harding on 10 March 1734 [Judgments 1732-5, 535]. They may have been the ancestors of

     i.   Susanna, "Negro" head of a Kent County, Maryland household of 1 "other free" in 1790 and 9 in 1800 [MD:161].
     ii.   Mrs. Harden, head of a Baltimore City household of 8 "other free" in 1800 [MD:228] and 8 in 1810 [MD:358].
     iii. Ann Harden, head of a Baltimore City household of 4 "other free" in 1800 [MD:228].
3   iv. Abraham, born say 1768.

3. Abraham Harding, born say 1768, was head of a Baltimore Town household of 2 "other free" in 1790. He was married to Mary Harding, "free blacks," on 6 April 1795 when their son, William, was baptized in St. Paul's Parish, Baltimore. Abraham was buried at St. Paul's Parish on 7 August 1801 [Reamy, *Records of St. Paul's Parish*, I:88, II:6]. Their children were

     i.   William, born 6 April, baptized 24 May 1795.
     ii.   Mary, born 21 September 1797, baptized 7 February 1798, daughter of Abraham and Mary Harding, "free blacks" [Reamy, *Records of St. Paul's Parish*, I:115].

HARMAN FAMILY

1. William[1] Harman, born about 1632, was called "William Harman Negro" in the court and tax records before and after he became free. He arrived in Virginia as a slave sometime before 1648 when he was claimed as one of the headrights of planters Lewis Burwell and Thomas Vause [Nugent, *Cavaliers & Pioneers*, I:171-2]. In 1654 he was called the slave of William Andrews when he recorded his purchase of a calf in Northampton County court. William Andrews died about this time and his widow, Mary, married William Smart [DW 1654-55, 38, 85, fol.85]. In 1660 Smart sold William Harman to William Kendall who, on the same day he purchased Harman, agreed to sell him his freedom if he could provide sufficient security for the payment of 5,000 pounds of tobacco within two years [DW 1657-66, 70, 74, cited by Deal, *Race and Class*, 398-412]. This was 1,000 pounds more than his purchase price. He was still listed in Kendall's household in 1664 and 1665 [Orders 1657-64, 198; 1664-74, 15].

In March 1666 he sold a colt to Jane **Gossall**, the twenty-two-year-old daughter of Emmanuel **Driggers** and widow of free "Negro" John **Gossall**, and stated in the deed that he intended to make her his wife, promising that the colt would be her sole property as long as she lived [DW 1655-68, pt.2, fol.12]. He had married Jane by June 1666 when he submitted the letters of administration on her first husband's estate to the court. He was head of his own household with his wife Jane in the Northampton County list of tithables from 1667 to 1677 [Orders 1664-74, fol. 24, pp.24, 42; 1674-79, 190].

He appeared to have been equally friendly with slaves, free African Americans, and whites. According to the court deposition of a neighbor, he spent New Years Eve of 1672 drinking rum and sugar with the slaves on John Michael's plantation. He was about forty years old when he made a deposition in court about an argument he had witnessed while at the home of John **Francisco** [Orders 1664-74, ff. 125, 138, 143, 146, 156a-f, 157]. And in the summer of 1683 there was a court hearing about an argument among six of his white neighbors who were gathered at his house to help him harvest his crop [OW 1683-9, 15-16].

On 29 July 1675 he was involved in a dispute with William Gray over the possession of a gun that once belonged to Francis **Payne**. **Payne**'s widow, Amey, had delivered the gun to Harman, perhaps as a gift, and her second husband, William Gray, white like her, protested and took it back. The court ordered the gun returned to Harman [OW 1674-79, 58-59].

In September 1673 Jane Harman was the wet nurse for the illegitimate child of Nicholas Silvedo, a Portuguese servant, and English maidservant Mary Gale [Deal, *Race and Class*, 405]. William Harmon "Negro" and Jane were tithables in their own Northampton County household in 1677 [OW 1674-9, 190]. William was still living in April 1699 when he recorded the livestock mark of his son, Manuel Harman [DW 1651-4, 31 at end of volume]. Jane may have been identical to Jane Harman who bought a "parcel of cloathes" in the 15 June 1700 sale of the estate of Philip **Mongon**, deceased [Orders 1692-1707, 262]. William and Jane's children were

>   i.   Frances, born say 1667. She had an illegitimate child by a white man, Samuel Johnson, in 1685 [OW 1683-9, 112], another in 1686 by Jarvis Cutler, and two more before 1692 [OW 1683-9, 358, 386; OW 1689-98, 160-1]. In May 1690 Thomas **Carter** was security for her fine for fornication [OW 1689-98, 35, 58]. She married a slave, Anthony **George**, by 1693 when she recorded her livestock mark in Northampton County court [DW 1651-4, 26 at end of volume]. See further the **George** history.

2   ii.   Manuel^1, born say 1670.
3   iii. Edward^1, born say 1672.
       iv. John^1, born say 1674.
4   v.   William^2, born say 1676.

2.   Manuel^1 Harman, born say 1670, recorded his livestock mark in Northampton County court with his father in April 1699 [DW 1651-4, 31 at end of volume]. He was a tenant on land in Accomack County on 7 December 1714 [Orders 1714-17, 2]. He was taxable in Mattapony Hundred of Somerset County from 1723 to 1738: with John Harmon in his household in 1729, taxable on Simon **Collick** in 1736 and 1737 [List of Tithables, 1723-38]. He was about "seventy odd years of age and "almost past Labour" on 19 June 1739 when the Somerset County court granted his petition to be discharged from paying taxes [Judicial Record 1738-40, 121]. He may have been the father of

>   i.   John^2, born say 1712, taxable in Bogerternorton Hundred, Somerset County, in the household of Emanuel Harman in 1729, in Edward Franklin's household in 1737, taxable in his own household in 1739 and with his unnamed "melotto" wife in 1740 [List of Tithables].

3.   Edward^1 Harman, born say 1672, was living in Northampton County in 1702 when he and (his brother?) John Harman, Johnson **Driggus**, John **Driggus**, and Samuel **George**, "Free Negroes," were convicted of stealing a hog and then abusing and threatening several whites "in an insolent manner" [Orders 1698-1710, 102, 106]. He moved to Accomack County where he purchased 100 acres of land a few miles from Chincoteague in the northeastern part of the county in 1711. He and his wife, Patience, sold this land 25 years later [DW 1729-37, fol. 235-p.236; Whitelaw, *Virginia's Eastern Shore*, 1333]. He may have been

identical to Edward Harman who was taxable in Bogerternorton Hundred, Somerset County, from 1738 to 1740. Edward and Patience may have been the ancestors of some of the family members who were in Maryland and Delaware:

    i. Zachariah, taxable in Bogerternorton Hundred, Somerset County, in William Smith's household in 1733, in Ursley Greer's household (with William Harman) in 1734, in Presgrave William's household in 1735, in Edward Franklin's household in 1737, in Edward Harman's household in 1738, and in Edward Franklin's household in 1739.

5   ii. William³, born say 1715.

    iii. John², born say 1718, taxable in Bogerternorton Hundred, Somerset County, in Edward Franklin's household in 1737 and taxable in his own household with his unnamed "melotto" wife in 1740 [List of Tithables].

    iv. Edward³, born say 1720, taxable in Bogerternorton Hundred, Somerset County, in the household of (his brother?) William Harman in 1739 and the household of (his father?) Edward Harman in 1740. Gershom Mott sued him for debt in Sussex County court in November 1748 when the garnishee William Bryan reported that he had only £2.17 belonging to Edward. He was indicted by the court in February 1748/9 for an unspecified offense for which Gershom Mott provided £40 security. He died before May 1750 court when his death was reported in the court record [RG 4815.017, General Sessions Court, 1741-53, frames 374, 376, 404, 411, 415, 424, 452, 453, 469, 486, 500].

    v. Jane, born say 1722, living in All Hollow's Parish, Somerset County, in June 1738 when she was indicted for having an illegitimate child but found not guilty. Edward Harmon, planter, was her security for the payment of court fees [Judicial Record 1738-40, 43]. She was a taxable "mulato" in the Bogerternorton Hundred household of Robert Warren in 1740 [List of Tithables, 1740]. On 18 November 1740 she was again indicted for having an illegitimate child, but this time confessed that John **Jackson** was the father. Robert Warren was her security [Judicial Record 1740-2, 59-60, 310].

6   vi. Daniel¹, born say 1725.
7   vii. Job, born say 1726.

4. William² Harman, born say 1676, was a tithable head of his own household in the Northampton County list of Hillary Stringer in 1720 and a "Negro" tithable head of a household in Stringer's list for 1721 [L.P. 1720, 1721]. He was called William Harmon "Negro" in December 1721 when he paid Hannah **Carter**'s fine of 500 pounds of tobacco for having an illegitimate child [Orders 1719-22, 144]. He died before 26 January 1725/6 when his Northampton County estate was valued at £32 by Philip **Mongong** [DW 1725-33, 32]. Two of his children, Edward and Jane, chose Philip **Mongon** as their guardian [Orders 1722-9, 226]. His children were

    i. ?Dinah **Mongon**, wife of Philip **Mongon**.

8   ii. Jane, born about 1706.

    iii. Edward², born say 1707, a "Negro" tithable in his father's household in the list of Jacob Stringer in 1723 and 1724 [L.P. 1723]. He was tithable in Philip **Mongon**'s household in 1726, a "negro" tithable in Matthew Welch's Northampton County household from 1727 to 1731, and taxable in the household of Henry Speakman from 1737 to 1744 [L.P. 1726 - 1744].

    iv. ?Nan, born say 1710, a "negro" taxable in Thomas Moor's household in the list of Matthew Harmonson from 1726 to 1728.

    v. ?Jeffry, born say 1712, taxable in Abraham Bowker's Northampton County household in 1727 and 1728.

    vi. ?George, born about 1717, a ten-year-old "orphan Mulatto" bound as an apprentice in Accomack County on 5 March 1727 to Jeptha Perry and then bound instead to Benjamin Salmon on 3 August 1736 when Salmon complained to the court that Perry neither taught him a trade nor "put him to School" [Orders 1724-31, 95a; 1731-36, 190]. He was taxable in Robert Scott's household in Annamessex Hundred, Somerset County, in 1743. On 30 September 1766 the Accomack County court ordered that he be added to the list of tithables [Orders 1765-67, 235].

5. William[3] Harman, born say 1715, was taxable in Bogertemorton Hundred, Somerset County, in Ursley Greer's household in 1734, in Robert Warren's household in 1737, in his own household from 1738 to 1739 (with his brother? Edward Harman), and taxable with his wife Betty in 1740 "by order of Court" [List of Taxables]. Worcester County was formed from this part of Somerset County in 1742, so his descendants may have been those members of the family counted as "other free" in Worcester County. He and William Butcher owned land adjoining Nathan Brittingham in Broadkill Hundred, 15 miles southwest of Lewes, on 30 April 1759 when Brittingham sold the land to Solomon Parrimore [DB I-9:239]. Jonathan Vaughan sued him and Joshua Bucher in Sussex County court in February 1764 with Daniel Nunez as security for his costs, and Joshua Rocher sued him in August 1764. His death was suggested when Vaughan's case against him came before the court in May 1768. Perhaps his widow was Tabitha Harmon who was sued by Robert Lacey in May 1770 [RG 4815.017, General Sessions Court, 1761-71, frame 130, 146, 165, 205, 275, 407, 428, 446, 480, 512, 549, 562, 567, 575]. His descendants may have been

    i.   Jeremiah, head of a Worcester County household of 6 "other free" in 1790 [MD:124].
    ii. Abel, purchased 50 acres in Worcester County called *Scarborough's Castle* from Samuel and Kendall Scarborough for £50 on 11 February 1791 [Land Records O:67-8]. On 26 February 1799 he and Edward Scarborough posted bond of £30 to indemnify Worcester County against any charges from an illegitimate child Abel had by Jenny **Handby**, free single woman [Land Records T:140-1]. He was head of a Worcester County household of 10 "other free" in 1800 [DE:744].
    iii. Sophia, head of a Worcester County household of 7 "other free" in 1800 [MD:830].
    iv. Sally, head of a Worcester County household of 5 "other free" in 1800 [MD:745].
    v.   Lazarous, born about 1758, served in the 6th Company of the 1st Maryland Regiment from 1 August 1780 to 15 November 1783 [*Archives of Maryland* 18:356, 539]. He was head of a Worcester County household of 6 "other free" in 1790 [MD:124], 9 in 1800 [MD:745] and 7 "other free" and a slave in 1810 [MD:623]. He mortgaged two cows, two heifers, two calves, seven sheep and a sow to James B. Robins for $130 by Worcester County deed on 24 October 1803 [Land Records W:1-2]. He made a declaration in Worcester County court on 10 April 1818 to obtain a pension for his service in the Revolution. On 28 July 1821 he stated that he was about 60 years old and was living with his wife Betty and their sons John, aged 18 years, and Joseph, aged 12 years [NARA, S.34911, M805-399].
    vi. Elizabeth, a 60-year-old woman from Somerset County who emigrated to Liberia in 1832 aboard the *Lafayette* with (her son?) Nathan G. Harman, a farmer, and his family [http://fold3.com/image/46670390].
    vii. Levin, born after 1775, head of a Worcester County household of 4 "other free" in 1810 [MD:612] and 4 "free colored" in 1830.
    viii. Daniel[3], head of a Worcester County household 3 "other free" in 1810 [MD:612].

6. Daniel[1] Harman, born say 1725, was a Little Creek Hundred, Kent County, Delaware taxable from 1766 to 1773. He pled guilty to assault and battery in Kent County court in February 1764 and was ordered to pay a fine of £10 or be sold by

the sheriff [RG 3805.002, Common Pleas, Dockets 1734-1779, frame 397]. He died before 10 May 1774 when his widow Elizabeth was granted administration of his Kent County, Delaware estate. She married Joseph **Lantern** [de Valinger, *Kent County, Delaware Probate Records*, 289]. Daniel may have been the father of

    i.   Daniel[2], a "Mulatto" taxable in the Kent County levy assessments about 1820.

    ii. Gabriel, born say 1760, married Rhoda **Hanser** who assigned her right to the estate of her father William **Handsor** to Gabriel before 24 December 1793 when this part of the account of her father's estate was included in the account of the estate of John **Durham** [DSA, RG 3545, reel 68, frame 621]. Gabriel was a "free Negro" taxable in Murderkill Hundred in 1787 and in Little Creek Hundred in 1798 [RG 3535, Kent County Levy List, 1785-97, frames 80, 98, 475, 515], head of a St. Jones Hundred, Kent County household of 3 "other free" in 1800 [DE:45] and 3 "free colored" in Dover in 1820 [DE:36].

7.   Job Harman, born about 1725, was a 21-year-old, born in Sussex County, who was listed in the muster of Captain John Shannon's Company of foot solders in King George's War in September 1746 [Montgomery, *Pennsylvania Archives, Fifth Series*, 142-3]. He had an account with merchant John Shannon for about £12.18 for items such as a checked shirt and for cash paid to Mr. Curry in Shannon's account book which is found in the Kent County, Delaware court dockets [DSA, RG 3505.003, 1735-1779, frame 642]. He was the father of Jemima who was baptized at St. George's Protestant Episcopal Church, Indian River, on 16 April 1750. He was indicted by the Sussex County court for an unspecified offense in February 1759 that was continued through August 1762. John Lockwood sued him in November 1765 [RG 4815.017, General Sessions Court, 1753-60, frames 496, 516, 534, 555, 594, 622; 1761-1771, 17, 41, 72, 85, 109, 287, 376, 404]. He was probably married to Comfort and they were probably the parents of Shepherd Harmon: "Mulattoes: Shepherd son of Job and Comfort _____ b. 15 Apr 177(2)" at St. George's Protestant Episcopal Church, Indian River [Wright, *Vital Records of Kent and Sussex Counties*, 95, 101]. They were the parents of

    i.   Jemima, baptized 16 April 1750, daughter of Job Harmon, at St. George's Protestant Episcopal Church, Indian River.

    ii. ?Eunice, born say 1752, married Suthy **Pride**, "Melattoes," on 13 May 1772 in Sussex County [Records of the United Presbyterian Churches of Lewes, Indian River and Cool Spring, Delaware 1756-1855, 284].

9   iii. ?Edward[4], born about 1758.

    iv. Shepherd, born 15 April 177_ (probably 1772), "mulatto" son of Job and Comfort ___. He married Lina **Oakey**, "free Mulattoes," on 10 October 1802 in Sussex County [Records of the United Presbyterian Churches of Lewes, Indian River and Cool Spring, Delaware 1756-1855, 318] and was head of a Sussex County household of 7 "other free" in 1810 [DE:458].

    v. ?Adonijah, married Sarah **Jacobs**, "free Mulattoes," on 19 January 1795 in Sussex County [Records of the United Presbyterian Churches of Lewes, Indian River and Cool Spring, Delaware 1756-1855, 310]. He died before 5 March 1811 when Edward Harmon administered his estate which was valued at $40 [RG 4545.9, reel 100, frame 479].

    vi. ?Kesiah, married Aron **Esaw**, "Malattoes," on 25 February 1790 in Sussex County [Records of the United Presbyterian Churches of Lewes, Indian River and Cool Spring, Delaware 1756-1855, 305]. Aaron **Nezor** was head of an Indian River, Sussex County household of 5 "other free" in 1800 [DE:438].

8.   Jane Harmon, born about 1706, was twenty-one years old in February 1727/8 when she petitioned the Northampton County court to allow her to take control

of the remaining part of her father's estate which was then in the hands of her guardian, Dinah **Mongong** (Philip **Mongong's** widow) [L.P Pk#12, February 1727/8]. She was a "Negro" tithable in Philip **Mongon's** household in the 1727 list and in the household of Richard **Malavery** (Dinah's second husband) in the 1728-31 lists of John Robins. She may have been the Jane Harmon who was living in Accomack County on 25 April 1749 when her children Elijah, Harman, Solomon, and Nimrod, were bound as apprentice shoemakers [Orders 1744-53, 327]. Her children were

10   i.   ?John^2, born say 1727.
       ii.   Elijah^1, born about 1735, a fourteen-year-old bound to Hezekiel Purnoll on 25 April 1749.
      iii.   Harman, born about 1738, an eleven-year-old bound to Hezekiel Purnoll on 25 April 1749.
       iv.   Solomon, born about 1743, a six-year-old bound out on 25 April 1749.
        v.   Nimrod, born about 1747, a two-year-old bound out in Accomack County on 25 April 1749, head of a Worcester County household of 6 "other free" in 1790 [MD:124].

9.   Edward^4 Harman, born about 1758, received pay from 1 August 1780 to 4 November 1783 for service in the Delaware Regiment in the Revolution [DSA, MS Delaware Regiment Pay Records, 1778-1783, certificates 54,359; 54,480; 54,860; 54,935; 55,181; Public Archives Commission, *Delaware Archives*, 196, 607]. He married Agnes **Jackson** on 27 November 1788 in Sussex County [Records of the United Presbyterian Churches of Lewes, Indian River and Cool Spring, Delaware 1756-1855, 302]. He and his wife Agnes registered the 11 January 1792 birth of their son Benjamin at St. George's Protestant Episcopal Church in Sussex County. He was head of an Indian River, Sussex County household of 6 "other free" in 1800 [DE:438], 8 in 1810 [DE:437] and 5 "free colored" in Lewis and Rehoboth Hundred in 1820 [DE:308]. He was about 60 years old on 20 April 1818 when he appeared in Sussex County court to apply for a pension for his service in the Revolution. He stated that he enlisted under Captain Kirkwood in the 1st Company of the Delaware Regiment in 1777. Lieutenant Colonel Mitchell Kirkwood of the 9th Delaware Regiment, testified in his favor. Hezekiah Lacey testified that Edward worked for his father when he enlisted. He was about 70 and a resident of Lewes and Rehoboth Hundred on 16 November 1820 when he stated that had a wife named Agnes who was about 50, a 25-year-old son Benjamin and a 23-year-old son Dirickson who did not live with him, a 21-year-old son Paynter, 12-year-old son Woolsey and a 10-year-old daughter Eliza [NARA, S.36000, M805-399]. Edward and Agnes were the parents of

        i.   Benjamin, born 11 January 1792, "son of Edward and Agness" [Wright, *Vital Records of Kent and Sussex Counties*, 110].
       ii.   Dirickson, born about 1797.
      iii.   Paynter, born about 1800.
       iv.   Woolsey, born about 1808.
        v.   Eliza, born about 1810.

10. John^2 Harmon, born say 1727, was taxable in Northampton County, Virginia, in 1743 and 1744 [L.P. 1743, 1744] and head of a Halifax County, North Carolina household of 4 "other free" and a white man over 16 years of age in 1790 [NC:63] and 9 "other free" in 1800 [NC:316]. On 30 October 1795 he sold 100 acres, tools, furniture, cattle, and hogs in Halifax County to Joseph **Lantern**, Moses Matthews, and John Kelly [DB 17:920] and sold 100 acres near the road from Halifax Town to Enfield old courthouse to Joseph **Lantern** on 3 December 1795 [DB 18:130].^{14} John may have been the father of

---

^{14}Joseph **Lantern** was taxable in Dover Hundred, Kent County, Delaware from 1776 to 1785.

i. James, born say 1755, a "Mullatto" bound as an apprentice house
    carpenter to George Chappel until the age of twenty-one in Princess Anne
    County, Virginia, on 17 July 1759, no age or parent named [Minutes
    1753-62, 357]. He and his son James were named in the 30 December
    1792 Princess Anne County will of his father-in-law, William **Shoecraft**
    [WB 1:210].
ii. Eleanor, bound to George Chappel to read, sew, and knit in Princess Anne
    County, Virginia, on 17 July 1759, no age or parent named [Minutes
    1753-62, 357].
iii. Thomas, a "Negro" taxable on 130 acres and 5 "Negroes" in Prince
    Frederick Parish, South Carolina, in 1786 [S.C. Tax Returns 1783-1800,
    frame 119], head of a Georgetown District, Prince Frederick's Parish,
    South Carolina household of 5 "other free" in 1790 [SC:51].
iv. Abraham, head of a South Orangeburg District, South Carolina household
    of 3 "other free" in 1790 [SC:101].

Other descendants in Delaware were
i. Benjamin[1], born say 1725, indicted by the Sussex County court in
    February 1749/50, apparently for selling liquor without a license since the
    clerk made a notation in the case about awarding a license to another
    person. Robert Fraim sued him for debt in February 1750/1 and Benjamin
    petitioned the court to serve Frame to pay his debt. He was indicted for an
    unspecified offense in August 1752, and there were continuances for this
    and possibly other offenses until August 1758 when he pled guilty and
    was fined 2 shillings [RG 4815.017, General Sessions Court, 1741-53,
    frames 437, 470, 515, 537, 555, 579, 608; 1753-60, frames 158, 182, 236,
    259, 284, 303, 317, 336, 359, 382, 401, 418, 444]. He was head of a Kent
    County household of 4 "other free" in 1800 [DE:23].
ii. Thomas, head of a New Castle County household of 8 "other free" in 1810
    [DE:303].
iii. Abraham, head of a Broadkill Hundred, Sussex County household of 5
    "other free" in 1800 [DE:328].
iv. John, born say 1745, required to provide £20 security in February 1773 for
    his appearance in Sussex County court [RG 4805, General Sessions, 1767-
    94, frame 124]. He made a 6 April 1776 Sussex County will, proved 24
    April 1776, in which he left all his estate to his wife Saborah during her
    widowhood, left a mare and the increase of one young cow to his daughter
    Saborah and advised that his wife should leave his daughter Saborah as
    much as any of her other children. Elizabeth, daughter of Argal Harmon
    was a witness [RG 4545.9, reel 100, frame 570-1]. The state indicted
    Thomas Marvel of Dagsboro Hundred for assaulting Sabra Harmon on 8
    October 1789 [DSA, RG 4805.021, 1755-1791, MS case files, 1790
    Indictments]. She died before 23 December 1794 when William Rigley
    and Isaac Morris administered her estate [RG 4545.9, reel 100, frame
    463].
v. Argel, sued for debt by James Stephenson, Jr., in Sussex County court in
    November 1762 [RG 4815.017, General Sessions Court, 1771-93, frame
    117], a delinquent taxable in Sussex County in 1767, taxable on the south
    side of Broadkill Hundred in 1770, head of a Broadkill Hundred, Sussex
    County household of 3 "other free" in 1800 [DE:327], 6 in 1810 [DE:427]
    and 1 "free colored" in Dagsboro in 1820 [DE:382]. His daughter
    Elizabeth was a witness to the 6 April 1776 Sussex County will of John
    Harmon [RG 4545.9, reel 100, frame 570-1].
vi. Eli[2], head of a Sussex County household of 3 "other free" in 1810
    [DE:404]. He made a 17 November 1818 Sussex County will, witnessed
    by John **Rigwah**, by which he left his house to his brother William, left a
    dollar to his brother Argel, a dollar to each of his sister Milly **Mosely**'s
    four children, a dollar to his sister Ann's daughter Jane **Street**, a dollar to

his sister Ann's son Ephraim Harmon and $30 to his apprentice Cary **Hanshaw (Hanser)**. He also left $10 to the trustees of Harmony Meeting (the Harmony Methodist Episcopal Church) [RG 4545.9, reel 100, frames 519-527].

vii.   Ann, named in the will of her brother Eli Harmon, mother of Jane **Street** and Ephraim Harmon, born 1776-1794, head of a Dagsboro Hundred, Sussex County household of 4 "free colored" in 1820 [DE:392]. Ephraim was a "Mulatto" who died before 4 August 1840 when administration on his estate was granted to John West [RG 4545.009, reel 100, frame 449].

viii.   Henry, charged by the Sussex County court with fornication in November 1777 with Esther **Hanzer** as witness against him and charged with stealing a mare from Hugh Vestry in August 1791 [RG 4805, General Sessions Court, 1767-94, frames 168, 480; MS Case Files 1791].

ix.   William, born say 1770, married Mary **Hanser**, "free Mulattoes," on 11 May 1795 in Sussex County [Records of the United Presbyterian Churches of Lewes, Indian River and Cool Spring, Delaware 1756-1855, 311]. He was a "Negro" taxable in St. Jones Hundred, Kent County, in 1798 and head of an Indian River, Sussex County household of 3 "other free" in 1800 [DE:437], 5 "other free" in Cedar Creek Hundred in 1810 [DE:303], and 9 "free colored" in Indian River Hundred, Sussex County, in 1820 [DE:220].

x.   Betsey, head of a Broadkill Hundred, Sussex County household of 8 "other free" in 1800 [DE:327].

xi.   John, a "free Mulatto" convicted in November 1794 of having two illegitimate female children by a white woman Ann Jones of Broadkill Hundred, one in 1792 and the other in 1794. He was whipped and ordered to wear a four inch high red Roman T for six months as a mark of dishonor [RG 4805, General Sessions, 1767-94, frames 561-2]. He was head of a Nanticoke Hundred, Sussex County household of 4 "other free" in 1800 [DE:342], perhaps the Jonathan Harman who was head of a Sussex County household of 7 "other free" in 1810 [DE:458] and 4 "free colored" in Dagsboro in 1820 [DE:376]. He manumitted slaves "old Arter" and Candis (signing) by Sussex County deed on 30 July 1808 [DB AD-27:359].

xii.   Nathan[1], head of a Dagsboro Hundred, Sussex County household of 4 "other free" in 1800 [DE:424], 9 in 1810 [DE:410] and 12 "free colored" in 1820 [DE:372].

xiii.   Nathan[2], born before 1776, purchased 5 acres in Worcester County from "Negro" Jacob **Purnall** for £30 on 15 January 1810 [Land Records X:542-3]. He was head of a Dagsboro Hundred household of 4 "free colored" in 1820 [DE:374].

xiv.   Jacob, born before 1776, head of a Worcester County household of 7 "free colored" in 1830.

xv.   Benjamin[2], head of a Duck Creek Hundred, Kent County, Delaware household of 3 "other free" in 1800 [DE:7].

xvi.   James, head of a St. Jones Hundred, Kent County, Delaware household of 3 "other free" in 1800 [DE:45] and 3 "free colored" in Dover in 1820 [DE:34].

xvii.   William, head of a St. Jones Hundred, Kent County, Delaware household of 2 "other free" in 1800 [DE:43], 5 in New Castle County in 1810 [DE:303] and 6 "free colored" in Appoquinimink Hundred in 1820 [DE:147].

xviii.   Manuel[3], head of a Sussex County household of 12 "other free" in 1810 [DE:437].

xix.   Manuel[4], head of a Sussex County household of 10 "other free" in 1810 [DE:426] and a Dagsboro Hundred household of 5 "free colored" in 1820 [DE:374].

xx.   Peter, head of a Sussex County household of 5 "other free" in 1810

[DE:452].
xxi. Jethro, head of a Sussex County household of 7 "other free" in 1810 [DE:363].

HARRIS FAMILY

1. Jane Harris, born say 1679, was the servant of William Barton in November 1697 when she confessed to the Prince George's County court that she had a "basterd Mallatta Child." The court ordered that she receive sixteen lashes [Court Record 1696-99, 262].

1. Ann Harris, born say 1730, confessed to the Charles County court in November 1750 that she had an illegitimate "Mullatto" child. The court ordered her sold to Jacob Andrew Minitree for seven years and ordered her six-month-old daughter Alice to serve Minitree until the age of thirty-one. On 9 June 1752 the court ordered that she serve an additional fifteen months for running away for twenty-four days. In November 1753 she confessed to having another "Mollatto" child. The court ordered her to serve seven years for the offense and bound her six-month-old son Joseph to her master until the age of thirty-one [Court Record 1750, 151; 1752-3, 60; 1753-4, 75, 220-1]. She was the mother of
    i. Alice, born about May 1750, a ten-year-old "Mulatto" serving to the age of thirty-one when she was listed in the Charles County estate of Jacob Andrew Minitree which was recorded on 13 August 1761 [Prerogative Inventories 76:280-2].
    ii. Joseph, born about June 1753, head of a Baltimore City household of 3 "other free" in 1800 [MD:244].
    iii. ?Joan, born about 1753, an 8-year-old "Mulatto" listed in the inventory of the Charles County estate of Jacob Andrew Minitree on 13 August 1761 [Prerogative Inventories 76:280-2].

Members of the Harris family in adjoining St. Mary's County were
    i. Zachariah, head of a household of 8 "other free" in 1800 [MD:431].
    ii. Robert, head of a household of 5 "other free" in 1800 [MD:412].
    iii. Elizabeth, head of a household of 3 "other free" in 1800 [MD:412].

Eastern Shore of Maryland
1. James Harris, born say 1710, was a "Mollatto planter" living in Kent Count on 20 November 1739 when he confessed that he had assaulted Bulman Medford and was fined 30 shillings [Criminal Records, 172, 1739-60]. He may have been the ancestor of
    i. Joseph, head of a Queen Anne's County household of 1 "other free" in 1790.
    ii. Isaac, head of a Kent County household of 7 "other free" in 1800 [MD:149] and 5 in 1810 [MD:905].
    iii. Stephen, head of a Kent County household of 3 "other free" in 1800 [MD:162].
    iv. Edith, head of a Kent County household of 4 "other free" in 1810 [MD:905].

HARRISON FAMILY

1. Dorothy Harrison, born say 1750, was presented by the Charles County court on 14 June 1769 for bearing a "Mulatto" child [Court Record 1767-70, 434]. She was probably the ancestor of
    i. Sarah, born say 1775, head of a Kent County household of 4 "other free" in 1800 [MD:162].
    ii. Nicholas, born about 1788, registered in Talbot County on 23 July 1816: *about 28 years of age...born free and raised in the County* [Certificates of

        Freedom 1815-28, 37].
iii.   Thomas, born about 1788, registered in Anne Arundel County on 30 May
       1816: *aged about twenty eight years...brown complexion...free born.*
iv.   Edward, born about 1797, registered in Anne Arundel County on 30 May
       1816: *aged about nineteen years...brown complexion...free born*
       [Certificates of Freedom 1810-31, 82, 83].

HARWOOD FAMILY

1.   Anne Harwood, born say 1686, was living in Anne Arundel County in November
     1706 when she was convicted of having a "Molato" child "gott by a Negroe." The
     court ordered that she serve seven years as well as a year and a half for court fees
     and the trouble of her master's house [Judgment Records 1705-6, 440-1]. She may
     have been the ancestor of
       i.   David, "F.M." head of a Queen Anne's County household of 7 "other free"
            in 1790.

HAWKINS FAMILY

1.   Catherine Hawkins, born say 1690, alias "Catherine Binmeter," was the servant
     of John Hawkins of St. Paul's Parish, Queen Anne's County, on 24 November
     1709 when she admitted that she had a "Mullatto" child who was born on 10 July
     1708. The child was bound to her master until the age of thirty-one, and Catherine
     was ordered to serve an additional seven years [Judgment Record 1709-16, 7].
     She was probably the ancestor of
       i.   Francis, head of a Caroline County household of 6 "other free" in 1790.
       ii. Joseph, head of a Queen Anne's County household of 5 "other free" in
            1800 [MD:349].
2   iii. Daniel[1], born say 1756.
       iv. Daniel[2], head of a Queen Anne's County household of 4 "other free" in
            1800 [MD:337].
       v.   Sarah, head of a Murderkill Hundred, Kent County, Delaware household
            of 5 "other free" in 1800 [MD:114].

2.   Daniel[1] Hawkins, born say 1756, was head of a Talbot County household of 5
     "other free" in 1800 [MD:520]. He may have been the father of
       i.   Daniel[3], born about 1781, registered in Talbot County on 29 July 1812: *a
            Mullatto Man...about 31 years of age...born free & raised in the County.*
       ii. Levin, born about 1789, registered in Talbot County on 11 July 1815: *a
            Slender made black man...raised in the County and is about twenty Six
            years of age* [Certificates of Freedom 1807-15, 16, 22].

Anne Arundel County
Members of a Hawkins family in Anne Arundel County were
1   i.   Lucy, bon say 1758.
       ii. John, head of a household of 5 "other free" in 1800 [MD:101].
       iii. Hannah, head of a household of 5 "other free" in 1800 [MD:99].
       iv. Richard, born before 1776, head of a household of 6 "free colored" in
            1830.
       v.   Emanuel, born before 1776, head of a household of 2 "free colored" in
            1830.

1.   Lucy Hawkins, born say 1758, obtained her freedom from James Williams in the
     General Court of the Western Shore in May 1780. She died in Annapolis before
     1803 when her children obtained certificates of freedom from the clerk of the
     Court of Appeals for the Western Shore: *Lucy Organs otherwise Lucy Hawkins
     being descended from a free Woman, obtained her freedom in the late General
     Court for the said Shore on her petition...against James Williams of the City of*

Annapolis at May Term in the year 1780...Lucy Organs otherwise called Lucy Hawkins Commonly called Hominey Lucy died in the City of Annapolis and had at the time of her death several Children and among others the following: Abigail now twenty years of age of a yellowish Complexion, Lucy about Eighteen years of age and nearly the same complexion. Harry about seventeen years of age of a dark Complexion, Hagar about sixteen years of age also of a dark Complexion and Joe about twelve years of age also of a dark complexion. Her daughters Hagar and Sal registered the certificate in Anne Arundel County court about four years later in May 1807 when Hagar was twenty years old: *Hagar, daughter of Lucy Hawkins, about twenty years of a Yellowish Complexion and was born and raised in the City of Annapolis...Sal about 12 years of a dark complexion* [Certificates of Freedom 1806-7, 21-4]. She was the mother of

    i.   ?Susanna, born about 1782, registered in Anne Arundel County on 30 April 1807: *about the age of twenty five years...Complexion Yellow...born free...born and bred in the City of Annapolis* [Certificates of Freedom 1806-7, 12].

    ii. Abigail, born about 1783, twenty years old in 1803.

    iii. Lucy, born about 1785, eighteen years old in 1803.

    iv. Harry, born about 1786, seventeen years old in 1803.

    v. Hagar, born about 1787, sixteen years old in 1803 and twenty years old in May 1807.

    vi. Joe, born about 1791, twelve years old in 1803.

    vii. Sal, born about 1795, twelve years old in May 1807.

HAWS FAMILY

1.   Winefred Haws, born say 1700, the servant of John Welsh, confessed to the Anne Arundel County court in March 1720/1 that she had a child by her master's "Negroe" Jack. She was ordered to serve her master seven years, Jack was given twenty-five lashes, and their child was bound to their master until the age of thirty-one [Judgment Record 1720-1, 88-9]. He was listed in the inventory of the Anne Arundel County estate of John Welsh on 19 July 1734:

    1 Molato Boy Jack ab¹ 13 years old to serve till 31 years -   £21

    [Prerogative Inventories & Accounts 1734-1736, 38-42]. Winefred and Jack may have been the ancestors of

2   i.   Peter, born say 1750.

    ii. William, born say 1752, a seaman aboard the *Dragon* according to an affidavit by a fellow seaman aboard the ship, John **Davis**, who testified for the bounty land claim of James Jennings on 7 February 1834 and named five of the officers and fifty-two members of the crew who served faithfully for three years and were discharged at the Chickahominy Ship Yard [Revolutionary War Bounty Warrants, Jennings, James (p.9), Digital Collection, LVA]. He was listed aboard the ship *Gloucester* on 5 July 1779 and aboard the *Dragon* on 2 September 1779. He served three years and was entitled to bounty land [Brumbaugh, *Revolutionary War Records*, 8, 14, 68].

    iii. Amy Haw, head of a St. Mary's County household of 3 "other free" in 1790.

2.   Peter Haw(s)/How, born say 1750, and William Hawes were serving aboard the galley *Gloucester* on 4 November 1777 when the keeper of the public store was ordered to deliver them articles of clothing, "on their paying for the same" [U.S. Government Printing Office, *Naval Documents of the American Revolution*, 11:160; http://ibiblio.org/anrs//docs/E/E3/ndar_vl1p05.pdf]. He was head of a Lancaster County, Virginia household of 9 "Blacks" in 1783 [VA:56] and 6 "other free" in 1810 [VA:349]. He was taxable on a horse in Lancaster County from 1783 to 1814: not charged on his own tithe after 1785, in the list of "free Negroes & Mulattoes" in 1813 and 1814 [PPTL, 1782-1839, frames 15, 30, 44, 72, 119,

187, 385, 399]. On 1 November 1834 Peter's heirs applied for bounty land for his and his brother William's services in the Revolution. They stated that William Haw entered the State Navy in 1776, was on board the *Dragon* in 1777 under the command of Captain James Markham, and died in the service. William was from Lancaster County and had only one brother Peter Haw. Their petition included an affidavit that Peter Haws' name was on the army register as receiving £60.10 as the balance of his pay as a seaman on 9 March 1787. Peter died many years previous to the petition and left four children: Rachel, Peter, Alice and Betsy. The petition was signed by Rachel **Jones**, Milly **Jones**, Peter Haw, Alice Haw, and William Haw [Revolutionary War Rejected Claims, Haw, William, Digital Collection, LVA]. He was listed on 25 November 1834 as a seaman who served three years and was due bounty land [Brumbaugh, *Revolutionary War Records, Virginia*, 216].. He was the father of

    i.   Rachel Howe, "daughter of Peter Howe," married Daniel **Jones**, 13 June 1794 Lancaster County bond.

   ii.   ?Nancy Howe, spinster over 21, married Robert **Nickens**, 5 March 1793 Lancaster County bond.

  iii.   ?Jane Haws, married Holland **Wood**, 15 October 1821 Lancaster County bond.

   iv.   Sally, a 19-year-old "free light mulatto woman" who ran away with a "Negro man named Syphax" from Lancaster County according to the 30 September 1795 issue of the *Virginia Gazette* [Headley, *18th Century Newspapers*, 156].

   v.   Peter^2.

   vi.   Alice.

  vii.   Betsy, mother of William^2 and Milley Haw (wife of William **Jones**). William^2 Haw married Fanny **Toulson**, 8 January 1827 Northumberland County bond, William **Toulson** security.

HAYCOCK FAMILY

Members of the Haycock family were

1   i.   John, died before 27 March 1765 when the inventory of his Queen Anne's County estate was taken. The estate totaled £20.9 and was witnessed by his brother James Haycock and sister Ruth Lance [Prerogative Inventories 88:90].

      ii.   James^1, born say 1738, owed the Queen Anne's County estate of Mr. John Sayor Blake 82 pounds of tobacco on 8 September 1761 [Prerogative Inventories 76:230], perhaps the James Haycock who was head of a Queen Anne's County household of 2 "other free" in 1790.

2   iii.   Ann, born say 1740.

1.   Ann Haycock, born say 1740, was presented by the Queen Anne's County court in March 1770 for having an illegitimate child. The child had died before she appeared in court in March 1771 and refused to identify the father. Nicholas Griffin and James Haycock were her securities. In November 1770 she was presented for failing to list herself as a tithable but was discharged by the court the following November. On 9 December 1771 she was called a poor woman when the court appointed Rachel Imbert to clothe and maintain her until the following November for 600 pounds of tobacco [Judgments 1771-80, 15-16; Surles, *And they Appeared at Court 1770-1772*, 2, 10, 42, 78]. Other members of the Haycock family of Maryland were

2   i.   Solomon, born say 1760.

      ii.   James^2, Jr., head of a Queen Anne's County household of 7 "other free" in 1790 and 6 in 1800 [MD:351].

     iii.   William, head of a Queen Anne's County household of 2 "other free" in 1790. He may have been identical to William Haycock who married Sally **Mason**, 29 October 1791 Fairfax County, Virginia bond. He was called a "free Mulatto" on 19 November 1792 when he purchased 5 acres of land where he was then dwelling in Queen Anne's County called *Darbara's Inlett* for £10. On 13 March 1798 he leased a parcel of land called *Balled Eagle* which was part of a tract of land called *Fandenboy Enlarged* for 5 shillings per year from Christopher McCarradine for the term of "his and his present wife's natural lives" [STW2:312-3; STW-5:280].

2. Solomon Haycock, born say 1760, served in the Revolution from Queen Anne's County and was discharged on 3 December 1781 [*Archives of Maryland* 48:11]. He married Debora **Bently**, 14 December 1782 banns by the Jesuit Mission in Cordova, Maryland (no race indicated), Peter and Protase (slaves) witnesses [Wright, *Vital Records of the Jesuit Mission,* 19]. He and William Haycock posted £5 bond each when they were charged with assault and battery by James **Coger** in Queen Anne's County court in 1787. And Solomon paid £5 for the appearance of his wife Dorcas Haycock to give evidence in her suit against James **Coger** [Surles, *and they Appeared at Court, 1779, 1782, 1785, 1786, 1787*, 128-9]. He was head of a Queen Anne's County household of 6 "other free" in 1790, 6 in 1800 [MD:349] and 6 "free colored" in Harford County in 1830. He, or perhaps a son by the same name, was married to Eleanor by 23 December 1807 when their daughter Eliza was born. They registered the births and baptisms of their daughters in St. Paul's Parish, Baltimore. They were the parents of

    i.   Eliza, born 23 December 1807, baptized 22 May 1808, "d/o Sol. & Elenor Haycock."
    ii. Sarah, born 16 December 1814, baptized 6 August 1816, "dau. of Solomon and Nelly Haycock (mulatto)" [Reamy, *Records of St. Paul's Parish*, II:39, 53].

HEATH FAMILY

1. Mary Heath, born say 1695, was the servant of Thomas Price of St. Michael's Parish in November 1716 when she confessed to the Talbot County court that she had a child by "Negro Jack," one of her master's slaves. The court bound her "Mallattoe" son William to Thomas Price until the age of thirty-one [Judgment Record 1714-7, 147, 154]. She was the mother of

    i.   William, born about January 1715/6.

They may have been the ancestors of

    i.   Aggy, head of a Petersburg Town, Virginia household of 3 "other free" and a slave in 1810 [VA:336a].
    ii. Lewis, head of a Petersburg Town, Virginia household of 2 "other free" in 1810 [VA:330b].

HICKS FAMILY

1. Mary Hicks, born about 1726, confessed to the Anne Arundel County court in August 1741 that she had a child by "Negro Cupid," a slave of her mistress Margaret Moore. The court ordered that she serve her mistress one year when she arrived to the age of sixteen, then serve another seven years, and bound her daughter Prudence Hicks to her mistress until the age of thirty-one. In August 1743 Richard Moore purchased her seven years of service on behalf of his mother Margaret Moore [Judgment Record 1740-3, 249-50; 1743-4, 161]. She was the mother of

    i.   Prudence, born before 11 August 1741.

Their descendants my have been

    i.   James, head of a Baltimore City household of 8 "other free" in 1800 [MD:234], perhaps the J. Hicks who was head of a Baltimore City household of 9 "other free" in 1810 [MD:359].

    ii.   Jesse, head of a Baltimore City household of 4 "other free" in 1800 [MD:240].

   iii.   John, "Mulatto" head of a Charles County household of 1 "other free" in 1790, perhaps the John Hicks who was head of an Annapolis household of 4 "other free" and a slave in 1810 [MD:117].

   iv.   Robert, head of a Prince George's County household of 7 "other free" in 1810 [MD:44].

HILL FAMILY

1.   Anthony¹ Hill, born say 1700, a cooper, was a "mulatto man" servant of Captain Richard Smith on 22 March 1725/6 when he was convicted by the Prince George's County court of stealing cider. The court ordered that he receive 30 lashes and stand in the pillory for a half hour. On 25 August 1730 his mistress Elizabeth Smith, wife of Richard, a Quaker, petitioned the court that Anthony was a "Mallatto born of a white woman" and had unlawfully absented himself from their service for six months. The court was undecided how to rule on the issue [Court Record 1723-6, 557; 1729-30, 456]. He married Sarah **Williams** in all Hallow's Parish, Anne Arundel County, on 18 December 1732 [Wright, *Anne Arundel County Church Records*, 46]. He was called Anthony Hill, carpenter, in Anne Arundel County in 1732 when he mortgaged livestock and household goods to Samuel Roberts. He received a deed of gift from William **Barton** for a 50 acre tract of land called *Essex* in Anne Arundel County in 1739. The sheriff sold this land in 1743 to settle Anthony's debts and imprisonment fines [Land Records 1H & T1, 427; RD #3, 224; RB #1, 310-11]. John Darnall sued him for 3,220 pounds of tobacco in June 1746, but he failed to prosecute and had to pay Anthony's costs. In August 1746 he was presented by the court for failing to list his wife and daughter as taxables. In March 1752 he was acquitted of stealing goods from Ann Salyer [Judgment Record 1746-8, 149-50, 213, 285, 353; 1751-4, 243]. He may have been the ancestor of

    i.   the husband of Elizabeth **Williams**, called "Daughter in Law" of Anthony Hill in Anne Arundel County court in August 1741 when she was presented for bastardy. The court ruled that the law did not apply to her since she was a "free Negro." Anthony Hill was security for her appearance in court in June 1745 on a presentment for assaulting Elizabeth Jacobs [Judgment Record 1740-3, 248-9; 1744-5, 322].

    ii.   Anthony², head of a Frederick County household of 8 "other free" in 1790.

   iii.   William, "Mulatto" head of a Port Tobacco, Charles County household of 8 "other free" and 2 slaves in 1790.

   iv.   Humphrey, head of a Montgomery County household of 8 "other free" in 1790 and 4 "other free" and 4 slaves in Charles County in 1810 [MD:301].

    v.   William, "Mulatto" head of a Newport, Charles County household of 6 "other free" in 1790 and 6 in 1800 [MD:534].

   vi.   Ignatius, head of a Charles County household of 4 "other free" in 1800 [MD:562] and 3 in 1810 [MD:319].

   vii.   Sarah, head of a Charles County household of 5 "other free" in 1800 [MD:524].

  viii.   Charity, head of a Charles County household of 3 "other free" and 2 slaves in 1800 [MD:537], perhaps identical to Charity Hill who was head of a Charles County household of 3 "other free" in 1800 [MD:541] and 6 "other free" and 2 slaves in 1810 [MD:349].

   ix.   James, head of a Charles County household of 4 "other free" and a white woman 16-26 years old in 1810 [MD:312].

    x.   Charles, head of a Prince George's County household of 8 "other free" in 1810 [MD:32].

Members of the Hill family in Dorchester County were

2   i.   Levin, born say 1768.

    ii. Daniel, head of a household of 1 "other free" and 6 slaves in 1800 [MD:641].

    iii. Henry[1], head of a household of 2 "other free" in 1800 [MD:685].

    iv. Henry[2], head of a household of 1 "other free" in 1800 [MD:683].

    v. Robinson, born about 1796, registered in Dorchester County on 18 July 1818: *of a bright yellow complection...born free and raised in Dorchester County and is the son of Margaret Robinson, now deceased...about 22 years old* [Certificates of Freedom for Negroes 1806-64, 38].

2.   Levin Hill, born say 1768, was head of a Dorchester County household of 6 "other free" in 1800 [MD:684]. He and his wife Milley were the parents of

    i. Litha, born about 1800, registered in Dorchester County on 15 July 1820: *yellow complection...raised in Dorchester County and is the Daughter of Levin Hill and Milley Hill who was free born, aged about 20 years* [Certificates of Freedom for Negroes 1806-64, 42].

Other members of the Hill family in Maryland were

    i. John, "free negro" taxable in the 5th District of Kent County in 1783 [MSA 1161-7-5, p.5], perhaps the John Hill who was head of a Cecil County household of 4 "other free" in 1800 [MD:259].

    ii. William, "free negro" taxable in the 5th District of Kent County in 1783 [MSA 1161-7-5, p.5].

    iii. Stephen[1], head of a Baltimore City household of 14 "other free" in 1800 [MD:238].

    iv. Stephen[2], head of a Baltimore City household of 6 "other free" in 1800 [MD:228].

    v. James[1], head of a Baltimore Town household of 4 "other free" in 1790.

    vi. Margaret, head of an East Nottingham, Cecil County household of 1 "other free" in 1790.

    vii. James[2], head of an Elk Neck, Cecil County household of 1 "other free" in 1790.

HILTON FAMILY

1.   Coffey[1] Hilton, born about 1699, was apparently identical to Coffey who was manumitted with his wife Sue by Evan Jones of Kent County, Delaware, in 1720. Jones gave them his farm, an additional 50 acres, a cow, ewe, horse and gun [WB D:50, cited by Williams, *Slavery & Freedom in Delaware*, 80]. Coffee Hilton purchased 50 acres in Duck Creek Hundred from John Reynolds on 2 December 1725 [DB 9:117]. He sued Robert **Butcher**, administrator of Robert **Butcher**, in Kent County court in May 1732, and he was indicted by the court in February 1735 for assault, but the person he was supposed to have assaulted was not identified [DSA, RG 3815, dockets 1722-32, frame 604; 3805.003, 1735-79, frame 12]. He was taxable in Duck Creek Hundred from 1729 to 1763, probably considered elderly by 1764 when his name was crossed off the list [RG 3535, Kent County Levy List, 1727-42, frames 351, 357, 362, 368, 379, 395, 405, 419, 468, 483, 513; 1743-67, 22, 56, 85, 140, 169, 184, 198, 228, 244, 261, 291, 314, 344, 353, 381, 395, 426]. On 24 December 1754 he confessed in Kent County court that he owed Thomas Green £60 [RG 3815.031, 1754-7, frame 132]. On 26 August 1755 he sold 50 acres called *Coffes Purchase* on the northside of Frenchmans Branch of Duck Creek and another 50 acres called *Cristiana* to Nicholas Lockerman for £70 [DB O:310], and on 19 March 1771 he confessed judgment in Kent County court of £90 to Caesar Rodney, trustee of the Land Office of Kent County [RG 3815.031, 1769-71, frame 423]. The sheriff sold approximately 153 acres of his land on Frenchmans Branch to merchant Vincent Lockerman, Sr., of Dover to satisfy the £90 judgment on the property [DB T:97]. He was seventy-two years old on 11 September 1771 when he petitioned (signing) the Kent County court that he had raised his grandson John, son of his deceased

son John, since the age of five, and now that he was sixteen and able to help his grandfather, he had been bound out as an apprentice to Charles Cahoon. The court dismissed the case [DSA, RG 3805, MS court papers, September 1771 Petition]. He was the father of

2   i.   ?Coffee[2], born say 1722.

    ii.   ?Phillis, indicted by the Kent County court in May 1750 for felony but not found by the sheriff in August 1750, reported to be deceased in November 1750 court [DSA, RG 3805.002, frames 189, 191, 193].

    iii.   ?Elizabeth, indicted by the Kent County court in May 1750 for felony, case dismissed in November 1752 when she was said to have runaway [DSA, RG 3805.002, frames 189, 193, 196, 198, 204, 208, 212].

    iv.   ?George[1], born say 1727, a "labourer" of Duck Creek Hundred who confessed in Kent County court in February 1748 to being the father of an illegitimate female child by Elizabeth **Butcher**. Cuffee Hilton was his security to support the child. He had an illegitimate male child by Elizabeth in 1752 for which Thomas Green was his security to support the child [DSA, RG 3805, MS case papers, November 1748 indictments; RG 3805.002, frames 213, 214, 219, 224]. He was taxable in Duck Creek Hundred from 1748 to 1777 [RG 3535, Kent County Levy List, 1743-67, frames 56, 85; 1768-84, frames 23, 26, 66, 220, 256, 269, 299], head of a Kent County household of 8 "other free" in 1800 [DE:17] and 9 in New Castle County in 1810 [DE:301].

    v.   ?Emanuel, taxable in Duck Creek Hundred from 1748 to 1774, a "Free Negroe" in Dover Hundred from 1781 to 1783 [RG 3535, Kent County Levy List, 1743-67, frames 56, 85, 140, 354, 381, 395, 427, 490, 518, 532, 534, 566; 1768-84, frames 23, 26, 66, 74, 107, 119, 180, 220, 500, 540, 580].

    vi.   John, born say 1733, died about 1760 when his son John was five years old.

2.   Coffee[2] Hilton, born say 1722, was taxable in Duck Creek Hundred from 1762 to 1781: called "Coffee Hilton, Jr." until 1771, a "N." taxable in 1781 [RG 3535, Kent County Levy List, 1743-67, frame 345, 354, 381, 395, 426, 436, 490, 518, 550, 565; 1768-84, frames 23, 26, 66, 74, 107, 119, 180, 220, 299, 371, 523] and head of a Little Creek Hundred, Kent County household of 3 "other free" in 1800 [DE:40]. He may have been the father of

3   i.   George[2], Jr., born say 1755.

    ii.   John, born say 1757, in the list of taxables in Duck Creek Hundred in 1778 with his tax crossed off [RG 3535, Kent County Levy List, 1767-84, frame 337], probably identical to John Hilton who was head of a New Castle County household of 4 "other free" in 1800 [DE:282].

    iii.   Charles, a "Free Negro" taxable in Dover Hundred in 1785 [RG 3535, Levy List 1727-1850, reel 4, frame no. 108], a "man of Colour" taxable in Harrison County, Virginia, from 1813 to 1818 [PPTL 1809-18, frames 193, 219, 292, 384, 407].

    iv.   James, head of a New Castle County household of 4 "other free" in 1800 [DE:207] and 7 in 1810 [DE:178].

    v.   William[1], taxable in Harrison County, Virginia, from 1805 to 1818: taxable on 3 tithes in 1805 and 1806, 2 tithes and a horse in 1807, a tithe and 2 horses in 1809, called a "man of Colour" starting in 1813 [PPTL 1785-1808, frames 425, 494, 517; 1809-18, frames 28, 69, 84, 407].

3.   George[2] Hilton, born say 1755, was taxable in Duck Creek Hundred from 1774 to 1777 and a "N." taxable in Duck Creek Hundred in 1781, a "Free Negro" in Dover Hundred from 1786 to 1788 [RG 3535, Kent County Levy List, 1768-84, frames 220, 256, 269, 299, 523; 1785-97, frames 46, 108 111]. He was taxable in Harrison County, Virginia , from 1803 to 1818: taxable on 1 tithe and 3 horses in 1803, 2 tithes in 1805, 3 tithes and 2 horses in 1806, called a "man of Colour"

starting in 1813 [PPTL 1785-1808, frames 366, 425, 494, 517; 1809-1818, frames 28, 69, 84, 123, 193, 219, 292, 317, 384, 407]. He may have been the father of

    i.   Mark, taxable in Harrison County, Virginia, from 1811 to 1818: taxable on a horse in 1812, called a "man of Colour" starting in 1813 [PPTL 1809-18, frames 84, 123, 193, 219, 292, 384, 407].

    ii. William², Jr., a "man of Colour" taxable on a horse in Harrison County, Virginia, from 1813 to 1818 [PPTL 1809-18, frames 193, 219, 292, 407].

Maryland

1.   Ann Hilton, born say 1738, was the servant of Henry Gaither on 2 August 1758 when the Frederick County court bound her "Molatto" son John to him until the age of thirty-one. She was the mother of

    i.   John, born 2 August 1758 [Court Minutes 1758-62, 77], ran away before 7 July 1778 when his master Henry Gaither placed an ad in the *Pennsylvania Gazette*: *a mulatto boy named John Hilton, about eighteen years old, had on a leather hat, coarse shirt and long breeches* [*Pennsylvania Gazette*, http://accessible.com].

    ii. ?Dave, born before 1776, head of a Harford County household of 5 "free colored" in 1830.

HINTON FAMILY

1.   Charles Henton, born about 1750, was a 19-20 year-old "Mulatto" who ran away from Henry Howard of Elkridge, Maryland, according to the 7 December 1769 issue of the *Virginia Gazette* [Rind edition, p.3, col.1]. He may have been the ancestor of

    i.   Jube, head of a Baltimore City household of 9 "other free" in 1800 [MD:244].

    ii. Rose, head of a Baltimore City household of 7 "other free" in 1800 [MD:242].

HITCHENS FAMILY

1.   Jarret¹ Hitchens, born say 1675, received an Accomack County deed of gift from his parents Edward and Elizabeth Hitchens on 19 September 1692 for 170 acres which Edward had patented on 9 October 1672 [DW&c, 1682-97, 250]. Jarret made a 13 November 1708 Accomack County deed, proved 1 February 1708/9, by which he left his son Major the 170 acres where he was then living, gave daughter Abigail Hitchens a cow, gave daughter Rosanna Hitchens a cow when she reached the age of 16, and gave his son Edward a bed that he had with Edward's mother Mary when Edward reached the age of 21, and 2 iron pots after his mother Mary's death [Wills &c 1692-1715, 466a]. He was the father of

2   i.   Major¹, born say 1686.

    ii. Abigail, born say 1688

3   iii. Edward, born say 1692.

    iv. Rosanna, born say 1698, perhaps identical to Anne Hutchins who was taxable in the Northampton County household of Major Hitchens in 1733. The Northampton County court presented her on 8 November 1737 for bastard bearing, for which Major Hitchens paid her fine [Orders 1732-42, 284, 291].

2.   Major¹ Hitchens, born say 1700, was living in Accomack County on 1 April 1718 when he sold 170 acres for 10,800 pounds of tobacco, noting in the deed that he received the land from his father Jarett Hitchens who received it by deed of gift from Major's grandfather Edward Hitchens [DW 1715-29, 41]. He was head of a Northampton County, Virginia household of 4 tithables in 1733 and 1744 and head of a household of 4 free tithables and 2 slaves, Nan and Sue, from 1737 to 1744 [Bell, *Northampton County Tithables*, 232, 237, 262, 274, 280, 312, 325,

330, 362]:

Master of family	tithable names nubr.
Major Hitchens :	*Tamar, Edward and Anne Hutchins*
nann & Sue negros	*6*

On 12 May 1747 the Northampton County court presented him for intermarrying or cohabiting with a "Molattoe" woman and presented Siner Bennett alias Hitchens for cohabiting with Major Hitchens, a "Molattoe man." The King's attorney discontinued the suit against Major on 10 June 1747 and discontinued the suit against Siner on 9 September 1747 [Orders 1742-8, 402-3, 422, 429, 445, 457]. He died before 20 December 1766 when Tamer Hitchens presented his inventory in Worcester County court. Edward Hitchens and Peter Dolbee were nearest of kin [Prerogative Inventories 91:135-6]. By his 10 November 1765 Worcester County will, proved 18 June 1766, he left his wife Tamer the use of his 100-acre plantation which was then to descend to his son Edmon, and gave a shilling each to his sons Edward, Major, Edmond and Jard [Wills, JW-3, 121]. He was the father of

i. James[1], born say 1722, tithable in Major's household in 1738 and 1743.

ii. Major[2], Jr., born say 1724, tithable in Major's household in 1740 and 1741 and in Edward Hitchens's household in 1743. He was listed in the Muster Roll of Recruits to the Delaware Regiment at the Port of Christiana Bridge on 20 June 1781 with Caleb Hitchens, Peter **Beckett**, Levin **Magee** Presley/ Preston **Hutt**, George **Lehea** (a slave) and David **Hanser** in an undated list of the 1st Delaware Company. Major and Caleb were paid for their services [NARA, M246, roll 30, frame 283 of 532, roll 31, frame 495 of 658; *Delaware Archives*, I:135].

iii. Jared[2], born say 1726, tithable in Major's household in 1743 and 1744. He was called Garret Hitchens, a "mulato," on 12 May 1747 when the Northampton County court presented Mary Filby for intermarrying and cohabiting with him. The case was dismissed by the King's attorney on 12 August 1747 [Orders 1742-8, 402-3, 429, 444]. He was taxable in Broad Creek Hundred, Sussex County, in 1777.

3.   Edward[1] Hitchens, born say 1692, was tithable in the Northampton County household of Major Hitchens in 1737. He married a white woman named Tamer Smith before 10 October 1738 when the sheriff was ordered to take her into custody, keep her in the county jail for six months without bail, and to discharge her after she paid a fine of £10 as punishment for marrying Edward Hitchens, a "Mulatto man" [Orders 1732-42, 334; Deal, *Race and Class*, 216]. On 1 January 1773 he sold for £90 (signing) 200 acres of a 215 acre tract called *Hitchens Choice* in Worcester County near Indian River which was land he received by patent of 22 August 1762 and on the same day sold another 50 acres of *Hitchens Choice* for £15 [Land Records I:209-11]. He was taxable in Broad Creek Hundred, Sussex County, in 1777 and also listed that year in Baltimore Hundred. He was probably the father of

i. Edward[2], Jr., taxable in Baltimore Hundred, Sussex County, in 1777, listed in Captain William Peery's muster raised to guard the Town of Lewes and the coast of the Delaware Bay, enlisted on 6 May 1777 [NARA, M246, roll 31, frame 322 of 653].

ii. Isaac, taxable in Baltimore Hundred, Sussex County, in 1777.

And they were likely the ancestors of

i. Milly, born 1776-1794, head of a Dagsboro Hundred, Sussex County household of 6 "free colored" in 1820 [DE:388].

ii. Eli, born 1776-1794, head of a Dagsboro Hundred, Sussex County household of 9 "free colored" in 1820 [DE:378]. He married Hester **Jackson** on 9 September 1802 in Sussex County.

iii. James[2], born about 1778, registered in Baltimore County on 14 May 1832: *age about 54 years, light complexion, 5 feet 9 inches high, born free in Somerset County*. (Registered with 20-year-old John Hitchens and Mary **Ward** (24) who were born free in Dorchester County) [Certificates of Freedom, 1830-2, no. 116].

HODGKIN FAMILY

1. Elizabeth Hodgkin, born say 1737, was presented by the Prince George's County court for "Mulatto Bastardy" on 22 November 1757 by information of Ruth Vermillion [Judgment Record 1754-8, 528]. She was probably the mother of
    i. Robert, (no last name) a "Molatto" child maintained by Giles Vermillion from November 1757 until the next court [Judgment Record 1754-8, 539].
    ii. Nanny Hogskins, head of an Anne Arundel County household of 1 "other free" in 1790.

HODGSKIN FAMILY

1. Jonas Hodgskin, born say 1720, a "Mallatto," confessed on 19 August 1739 in Somerset County court that he was the father of an illegitimate child by Dorcas **Malavery** and was fined 30 shillings [Judicial Record 1738-40, 171]. He was taxable in Pocomoke Hundred of Somerset County in the household of Sue Hogskin (his white mother? who was not a taxable) in 1736, in Henry Schofield's household in 1737, in Seward Tomlinson's in 1738, in Solomon Tomlinson's in 1739, with slaves Robin and Sarah in Annamessex Hundred in 1740, and taxable in his own Pocomoke household from 1746 to 1759 [List of Tithables 1736-1759]. He married Rodey **Driges (Driggers)** on 23 December 1747 at Coventry P.E. Church, Somerset County [Wright, *Maryland Eastern Shore Vital Records*, 2:104]. Rhoda was taxable in his Pocomoke Hundred household from 1756 to 1759. He was granted 50 acres in Worcester County on 12 March 1764 called *Flemings Pleasure* on the east side of Dividing Creek, and he and his wife Rhoda sold this land on 15 June 1770. He owed £5.9.1 to the Worcester County estate of James Smythe in 1766 [Prerogative Inventories, 1766, 325]. On 5 August 1769 he mortgaged to William Lane a crop of corn on the plantation whereon Lane's wife was then living and ten hogs on 5 August 1769 [Land Records H:79-80, 339-40]. He was taxable in Little Creek Hundred, Sussex County, in 1777 and a delinquent taxpayer in 1787 [Sussex County Levy Lists, n.p.]. His wife Rhoda Hodgskin was called the sister of Drake **Driggers** in the administration of Drake's 2 September 1788 Sussex County estate. They were the parents of
    i.   John, born 10 February 1747/8, "son of Jonas and Rodey Hodgskin [Wright, *Maryland Eastern Shore Vital Records*, 2:104].
    ii. Devericks/ Debrix, born 4 February 1748/9, "son of Jonas and Rodey Hodgskin" [Wright, *Maryland Eastern Shore Vital Records*, 2:104], a taxable in Little Creek in 1788, 1790, 1791, and 1795 [Sussex County Levy Lists] and head of a Sussex County household of 8 "other free" in 1800 [DE:375].
    iii. ?Stephen, born say 1770, a delinquent taxable in Little Creek, Sussex County, in 1787 and a taxable in Little Creek in 1788 and 1790 [Sussex County Levy Lists]. The Sussex County court charged him with assault in February 1786 [RG 4805, General Sessions, 1767-1794, frame 383, 388, 403].
    iv. ?David, born say 1772, a delinquent taxable in Little Creek in 1787.
    v.   ?Winder, head of a Sussex County household of 3 "other free" in 1800 [DE:391].

Endnote:
1. Dorcas **Malavery** called him Jonas Miller, but he was called Jonas Hogskin when he confessed. A James Hogskin alias Miller married Mary Hobbs in Somerset

County on 25 July 1815.

HOLLAND FAMILY

Members of the Holland family were

    i.   ?Elizabeth Hallin, born say 1730, presented by the Prince George's County
         court on 24 March 1747 for having a "Malato Bastard" by information of
         Sarah Johnson [Court Record 1747-8, 259].
1   ii. Barbara, born say 1736.

1. Barbara Holland, born say 1736, the "Mollatto" servant of Thomas Standish,
    confessed to the Prince George's County court on 25 March 1755 that she had an
    illegitimate "Mollatto" child named James who was born 20 August 1754. The
    court ordered that she serve seven years and sold her son to her master until the
    age of thirty-one [Court Record 1754-8, 57]. She was the mother of

    i.   James, born 20 August 1754, head of a Baltimore Hundred, Sussex
          County household of 2 "other free" in 1800 [DE:402], 7 in 1810 [DE:452]
          and 7 "free colored" in 1820 [DE:280].
    ii.   ?Rachel, head of a Montgomery County household of 6 "other free" in
          1790.
    iii. ?Jacob, head of an Anne Arundel County household of 2 "other free" in
          1790.
    iv.   ?Robert, head of a Murderkill Hundred, Kent County, Delaware
          household of 4 "other free" in 1800 [DE:127] and 3 in 1810 [DE:22].
    v.   ?Margaret, born about 1777, registered as a free Negro in Washington,
          D.C., on 24 October 1827: *aged about fifty, was born of a white woman*
          [Provine, *District of Columbia Free Negro Registers*, 96].

HOLLY FAMILY

Members of the Holly family in St. Mary's County were
1   i.   Joseph[1], born say 1745.
2   ii.   Phebe, born say 1750.
3   iii. Elizabeth, born say 1758.
    iv.   Enoch, head of a St. Mary's County household of 8 "other free" in 1810
          [MD:231].
    v.   Matilda, head of a St. Mary's County household of 3 "other free" in 1810
          [MD:174].

1. Joseph[1] Holly, born say 1748, was head of a St. Mary's County household of 8
    "other free" in 1790. His widow may have been Mary Holly, head of a St. Mary's
    County household of 3 "other free" in 1800 [MD:441]. She was the mother of

    i.   Ignatius, born about 1766, head of a St. Mary's County household of 3
          "other free" in 1800 [MD:407] and 6 in 1810 [MD:222], registered in St.
          Mary's County on 19 April 1826: *son of Mary Holly, aged about 60
          years...light Complection...born free.*

2. Phebe Holly, born say 1750, was the mother of
4   i.   Sarah, born about 1769.
    ii.   Lewis, born about 1794, registered in St. Mary's County on 17 February
          1829: *son of Phebe Holly, aged about thirty five years...bright
          complexion.*

3. Elizabeth Holly, born say 1758, was the mother of

    i.   Susan **Butler**, born about 1779, registered in St. Mary's County on 19
          October 1824: *aged about forty five years...bright complexion, long
          hair...born and raised in Saint Mary's County being the daughter of Betsy
          Holly.*

4. Sarah Holly, born about 1769, registered in St. Mary's County on 7 April 1819: *daughter of Phebe Holly...about fifty years of age, bright complexion...born free* [Certificates of Freedom 1806-64, 48]. She was the mother of

   i. Anna, born about 1794, registered in St. Mary's County on 7 April 1819: *daughter of Sarah Holly...dark complexion...about twenty five years of age, was born free.*

   ii. Miley, born about 1794, registered in St. Mary's County on 7 April 1819: *son of Sarah Holly...about twenty five years of age, bright complexion...born free.*

   iii. Phebe[2], born about 1802, registered in St. Mary's County on 7 April 1819: *daughter of Sarah Holly...aged about seventeen years...born free.*

Other members of the Holly family were

   i. Tot, born about 1779, registered in St. Mary's County on 7 September 1809: *aged thirty seven years or thereabouts, Complexion bright - hair short...born free and raised in Saint Mary's County.*

   ii. Sarah **Mason**, late Holly, born about 1786, registered in St. Mary's County on 2 August 1814: *aged twenty eight years or thereabouts Complexion bright yellow - hair short & Curley...born free.*

   iii. Joseph[2], born about 1795, registered in St. Mary's County on 25 March 1822: *about 27 years of age...dark complexion...born free being the son of a free black woman by the name of Becky Holly.*

   iv. George, born about 1798, registered in St. Mary's County on 12 March 1819: *son of Ann Holly, aged about twenty one years, bright complexion, born free.*

   v. Leanna, born about 1804, registered in St. Mary's County on 16 March 1825: *aged twenty one years or thereabouts...bright complexion, long hair...born free, daughter of Priscilla Holly* [Certificates of Freedom 1806-64, 8, 27, 45, 48, 59, 67, 68, 74, 79].

HOLMES FAMILY

1. Mary Holmes, born say 1723, was the servant of James Presbury on 6 March 1743/4 when she confessed to the Baltimore County court that she had an illegitimate "Molatto" child. She was probably a mixed-race woman who had a child by a free person since her punishment was a fine of thirty shillings [Court Proceedings 1743-6, 72, 170]. She was probably the ancestor of

   i. Easther, born about 1769, an eight-year-old "Mulatto" bound as an apprentice to Thomas Presbury of Harford County in March 1777 [*Maryland Historical Society Bulletin*, vol. 35, no.3].

   ii. Allen, born say 1773, head of a Talbot County household of 4 "other free" in 1800 [MD:531].

   iii. Thomas, born about 1792, registered in Talbot County on 29 August 1815: *a dark mulatto man...about 23 years of age, 5 feet 9 3/4 inches high...born free & raised in the County* [Certificates of Freedom 1807-15, 207].

HOLT FAMILY

Members of the Holt family were

   i. Henny, head of a St. Mary's County household of 11 "other free" in 1800 [MD:408] and 7 in 1810 [MD:181].

   ii. Betty, head of a St. Mary's County household of 5 "other free" in 1800 [MD:408].

   iii. William, born say 1775, head of an Accomack County household of 4 "other free" in 1800 [*Virginia Genealogist* 2:154], and 9 in 1810 [VA:29].

   iv. John, born about 1778, registered in St. Mary's County on 26 May 1809: *aged about thirty one years, complexion rather dark...hair in some*

degrees resembles that of a Mulatto's...raised in Saint Mary's County, was born free.
  v. Henry Leonard, born about 1787, registered in St. Mary's County on 27 September 1810: *aged twenty three years or thereabouts - complexion yellowish, hair short & Curley...born free.*
 vi. John, born about 1802, registered in St. Mary's County on 24 September 1834: *aged about 32 years...dark complexion* [Certificates of Freedom 1806-64, 5, 11, 107].

HOPKINS FAMILY

1. Ann Hopkins, born say 1711, was the servant of John Granger in June 1730 when the Queen Anne's County court sold her "mollato" child Chloe to Colonel Ernaut Hawkins until the age of thirty-one for 209 pounds of tobacco [Judgment Record 1730-32, 1]. She was the servant of George Cooley in June 1731 when she was convicted by the Talbot County court of having a child by a "Negro." The court bound her son Thomas to her master until the age of thirty-one [Judgment Record 1728-31, 428-9]. She was the mother of
  i. Chloe, born about March 1730, three months old when she was bound to Colonel Hawkins in June 1730.
 ii. Thomas, born about 1731, called a "Malatto child 20 years to serve" when he was listed in the inventory of the Talbot County estate of George Cooley on 23 April 1732 [Prerogative Inventories & Accounts 1732-1734, 72-4], a "Negro" head of a Harford County household of 10 "other free" in 1810 [MD:738].

They were probably the ancestors of
  i. Abram, "F.M." head of a Queen Anne's County household of 1 "other free" and a slave in 1790 [MD:100] and 5 "other free" in 1800 [MD:347].
 ii. Esther, head of a Kent County household of 6 "other free" in 1800 [MD:162].
iii. Edward, head of an Octoraro, Cecil County household of 1 "other free" in 1790.
 iv. James, head of a Queen Anne's County household of 1 "other free" in 1800 [MD:349].
  v. George, "Negro" head of a Harford County household of 4 "other free" in 1810 [MD:764].
 vi. Margaret, head of a Montgomery County household of 1 "other free" and 4 slaves in 1810 [MD:934].
vii. Gerard, head of a Montgomery County household of 1 "other free" in 1810 [MD:931].

HORNER FAMILY

1. George[1] Horner, born say 1690, was the common-law husband of Matilda, a "free mulatto woman," in Somerset County. She was the servant of Captain Arnold Elzey of Monacan Hundred on 10 March 1707/8, 8 November 1710, and 7 March 1710/11 when she was presented by the Somerset County court for having an illegitimate child. She identified George Horner as the father in each case. The court ordered her to serve her master additional time for the trouble of his house and fined George 600 pounds of tobacco for each offense. She was called "Martilldo...a certain Mollato Woman servant to Capt. Arnold Elzey" when she petitioned the Somerset County court on 26 November 1713 that she was about twenty-two to twenty-three years old and should have been free at age sixteen. The court ruled that she serve six years for fines, court costs, and the trouble of her master's house (for having children). They had another child before 12 November 1714 for which Martildo was ordered to receive ten lashes and serve another six months [Judicial Record 1707-11, 69, 100-1, 431, 451, 453; 1711-13,

299-300; 1713-15, 12, 127-8, 176; 1715-17, 57]. George was living on land belonging to John Bozman on 26 April 1716 when Bozman made his Somerset County will. He was taxable in Manokin Hundred from 1723 to 1740: taxable on William Horner in 1725, on Martilder and William in 1727, on Martilder, William and George Horner in 1728. He was called George Horner, Sr., in 1739 when he was head of a household with Mertildo and John and Arnold in Manokin Hundred. He died before 14 April 1744 when the inventory of his Somerset County estate was valued at over £112. By her 8 June 1745 account of the estate, Martildar divided the proceeds among herself (£31.6) and £10.8 each to his adult children: Arnold, Elizabeth, and Charles and named his underage children: Samuel, Robert, and Mary [Land Records Liber AC-25:12; Prerogative Court (Inventories), 29:207-9; Prerogative Accounts, Liber 21:413-4; Davidson, *Free Blacks on the Lower Eastern Shore of Maryland*, 52]. Matilda was head of an Annamessex Hundred household with Samuel and Robert Horner in 1749. George and Matilda's children were

    i. ?George[2], Jr., born say 1710, taxable head of his own household in Somerset County in 1733, not mentioned in the distribution of his father's estate in 1744. The Somerset County court indicted him for stealing 30 pounds of tobacco from William McClemmey on 1 August 1740, and in November 1749 the court convicted him of stealing a calf which belonged to George Irven and ordered him to pay four times the value [Judicial Record 1740-2, 36; 1749-51, 15].

    ii. Arnold[1], born say 1712, taxable in Manokin Hundred in 1739. He was living on *Manlowe's Lot* in 1748 when he was sued in Somerset County court for four years back rent. In March 1749/50 David Wilson sued him for £4 due by promissory note [Judicial Records 1747-49, 161, 232; 1749-51, 59, 156].

    iii. Elizabeth[1], born say 1716.

    iv. Charles, born say 1722, taxable in John Rigsby's Somerset County household in 1748.

    v. Samuel, born say 1728, underage in 1744, taxable in his mother's household in 1749.

    vi. Robert, born say 1730, underage in 1744, taxable in Somerset County in 1749.

    vii. Mary, born say 1732, underage in 1744.

Their descendants were

    i. Arnold[2], Jr., charged in Somerset County court on 16 June 1767 with assaulting William Luke, called Arnold Horner, Jr., planter, on 20 August 1771 when he admitted that he owed John Bell £10.15 [Judicial Record 1766-7, 160; 1769-72, 208].

    ii. Elizabeth[2], confessed to the Somerset County court on 5 August 1766 that she had a child by James Shingwich and confessed to a child by James Ring on 17 March 1767. She was acquitted of stealing petticoats from Mary Caldwell in March 1769 but convicted of stealing articles worth 992 pounds of tobacco in June 1769. The court ordered that she stand in the pillory for thirty minutes, receive thirty-nine lashes and be sold for fourfold the value of the articles [Judicial Record 1766-7, 14a, 106; 1767-9, 257; 1769-72, 50]. She was sentenced to death by hanging but pardoned by the governor on condition she leave Maryland [*Archives of Maryland* 32:315].

HOUSTON FAMILY

1.   Fortune Magee, born say 1687, was a servant of Mrs. Mary Day on 15 June 1705 when the Somerset County court ordered that she serve Mrs. Day until the age of thirty-one, explaining that she was the "mulatto" daughter of Maudlin Magee, a white woman living in Somerset County who was married to George Magee at the

time. On 7 March 1710/11 the court presented her for having four illegitimate children: one about seven years old, one five, one three and one three months old. On 8 August 1711 she confessed that Penny, "negroe" servant to Mr. Benjamin Wailer, was the father of her child. On 6 August 1712 she bound her children Ross, Sue, and Perlina to Mrs. Day [Judicial Records 1698-1701, 134; 1702-5, 251; 1707-11, 454; 1711-13, 40, 220]. Fortune was taxable in Baltimore Hundred, Somerset County, in 1735 [List of Tithables]. Her children were

    i. Rose, born in March 1703, mother of Joe Magee, born 12 March 1722/3, who she bound as an apprentice to Edward Rownd in Somerset County in March 1722/3 until the age of twenty one [Judicial Records 1723-5, 3b].

2   ii. Sue Magee alias **Game**, born in April 1705.

    iii. Perlina, born in April 1707, five years old "next April" in August 1712 when she was bound as an apprentice.

2.   Sue **Magee** alias **Game**, born in April 1705, was a "mulatto" woman living in Stepney Parish, Somerset County, from 1741 to 1754 when her "mulatto" children Belinder, Davey, Jenney, James, and Nelly **Magee** were born. She was the mother of

3   i. Belinder, born say 1747.

    ii. David.

    iii. James.

    iv. Nelly.

3.   Belinder **Magee**/ Houston, born say 1737, was called a "Mollatto woman" Bellinder **McGhee** on 19 May 1768 when she was listed in the inventory of the Worcester County estate of John Houston with five weeks remaining to serve [Prerogative Inventories 95:312]. She may have taken the name of her master John Houston and been identical to Bellinder Houston, a "Negro" head of a Broad Creek Hundred, Sussex County household of 4 "other free" in 1800, living near Susannah **Magee** [DE:391]. She was probably the mother of

    i. Lydia Houston, born say 1755, married Nathan **Norwood** on 22 March 1775 in Sussex County [Records of the United Presbyterian Churches of Lewes, Indian River and Cool Spring, Delaware 1756-1855, 288].

    ii. Susannah **Magee**, born say 1764, called "Sue a Molatto" girl with twenty-seven years to serve when she was listed in the Worcester County inventory of the estate of John Houston on 19 May 1768 [Prerogative Inventories 95:312], called Susannah **Magee**, a "Negro" head of a Broad Creek Hundred, Sussex County household of 3 "other free" in 1800 [DE:391].

    iii. David Houston, born before 1776, head of a Sussex County household of 6 "other free" in 1810 [DE:324] and 2 "free colored" in Dagsboro Hundred in 1820 [DE:374].

    iv. Jacob Houston, head of a Sussex County household of 3 "other free" in 1810 [DE:367].

HOWARD FAMILY

1.   Barbara Howard, born say 1718, was the mother of Sarah Howard, a five-year-old "Mulatto" who was bound by the Anne Arundel County court in June 1737 to Robert Perry until the age of thirty-one [Judgment Record 1736-8, 171]. She was the mother of

    i. Sarah, born 25 December 1731.

They may have been the ancestors of

    i. Poll, head of an Anne Arundel County household of 2 "other free" in 1800 [MD:93].

    ii. Harry, head of a Baltimore City household of 6 "other free" in 1810 [MD:403].

iii. William, head of a Baltimore City household of 4 "other free" in 1810 [MD:507].
iv. Charles, head of an Anne Arundel County household of 3 "other free" in 1810 [MD:66].
v. Rachel, head of a Baltimore City household of 2 "other free" in 1810 [MD:432].

HOWE FAMILY

1. Elizabeth How/ Hough, born say 1700, the servant of Daniel Richardson, confessed to the Anne Arundel County court in June 1718 that she had a child by "Negroe Sam belonging to her Master." The court bound their son to John Maccubbins until the age of thirty-one. She was called Elizabeth Hough in November 1721 when she confessed to having another child by Sam. She was sold for seven years and Sam received twenty lashes [Judgment Record 1717-9, 202, 210-11; 1720-1, 22-3, 214-5]. They may have been the ancestors of
   i. Robert, head of a Baltimore City household of 2 "other free" in 1810 [MD:504].
   ii. Anthony, head of a Baltimore City household of 2 "other free" in 1810 [MD:504].
   iii. H., head of a Baltimore City household of 2 "other free" in 1810 [MD:506].
   iv. Sarah, head of a Baltimore City household of 2 "other free" in 1810 [MD:218].

HUBBARD FAMILY

1. Jane Hubbard, born say 1685, was the mother of a "Mulatto" daughter named Elizabeth who was bound out by the churchwardens of Washington Parish, Westmoreland County, Virginia, before 30 October 1705 [Orders 1705-21, 3]. They were probably the ancestors of
   i. Ruth, born about 1722, a 54-year-old "mulato" head of Broad Creek Hundred, Harford County household with (her children?) Belt (13 years old), Joe (10), and Hanna (6) in 1776 [Carothers, *1776 Census of Maryland*, 88].
2 ii. William, born say 1750.
   iii. Abram, counted with his wife Dorcas and four children in a "List of Free Mullatoes and Negroes" living in Westmoreland County in 1801 [*Virginia Genealogist* 31:41]. He was head of a Westmoreland County household of 11 "other free" 1810 (called Abram Herbert) and 12 "free colored" in 1830, perhaps the father of Talbert Hubbard, head of a Westmoreland household of 3 "free colored" in 1830.

2. William Hubbard/ Hubert, born say 1750, was listed in a 30 April 1795 entry in the account book of Benjamin **Banneker** [Bedini, *The Life of Benjamin Banneker*, 249]. He was head of a Patapsco Upper Hundred, Baltimore County household of 5 "other free" in 1810 [MD:639]. He married a daughter of Robert and Mary **Banneker**. He and his wife were the parents of
   i. Henry, born say 1770, registered in Loudoun County, Virginia, on 24 December 1795 on testimony of Henry Jarvis that: *he was the son of a free woman and grandson of Robert Banneker, whose wife was also a free woman. Robert Banneker lived in Baltimore County about two and a half miles from Ellicott's Mills.*
   ii. Charles, born say 1772, called brother of Henry Hubbard on 24 December 1795 when he registered in Loudoun County [Certificates of Freedom in Loudoun County courthouse, cited by *Journal of the AAHGS* 11:123]. He (called Charles Hubbert) was head of a Loudoun County household of 8 "other free" in 1810 [VA:288].

Other possible descendants were
  i.   Isaac Hubbert, "negro" head of a Caroline County household of 5 "other free" in 1810 [MD:165].
  ii. Isaac, head of a Halifax County, North Carolina household of 5 "other free" in 1810 [NC:26].
  iii. ?Anthony Herbert, head of a Kent County, Virginia household of 6 "other free" in 1810 [VA:755].
  iv. Nancy Herbert, head of a Norfolk County, Virginia household of 3 "other free" and 2 slaves in 1810 [VA:832].

HUGHES FAMILY

Members of the Hughes family of Maryland and Delaware were
1   i.   Isabell, born say 1700.
     ii.   Caleb, born say 1704, a "free Negroe" father of an illegitimate child by a white woman named Katherine Banks before 21 June 1726 when she confessed to the Kent County, Maryland court [Criminal Record 1724-8, 183, 222-5]. He or perhaps a son by that name was taxable in Little Creek Hundred of Kent County, Delaware, in 1767 [Kent County Levy List, 1743-67, frames 552, 566].
2   iii. Mary, born say 1727.
     iv.   James[1], born 1726-1736, a 40-50 year old "Black Man" counted in the 1776 census for Nanticoke Hundred, Dorchester County [Carothers, *1776 Census of Maryland*, 40], a taxable "negro" in the Upper District of Dorchester County in 1783 [MSA S 1161-5-6, p.10], and head of a Dorchester County household of 2 "other free" and 4 slaves in 1790. He purchased 36 acres called *Greenland* in Dorchester County on 28 March 1782 [Land Records NH 2:35].
     v.   William **Elbut**, aka Hughes, born about 1745, a forty-year-old "mulatto" who claimed to be a Revolutionary War soldier when he was jailed in Williamsburg, Virginia, according to the 9 July 1785 issue of the *Virginia Gazette and General Advertiser* [Headley, *18th Century Newspapers*, 113]. He was a taxable "negro" in the Upper District Hundred of Dorchester County in 1783 [MSA S1161-5-6, p.7] and head of a Dorchester County household of 3 "other free" in 1800 [MD:693].
     vi.   Christina, born say 1754, mother of David Hughes who registered in Dorchester County on 11 December 1816: *of a blackish colour...raised in Dorchester County, born free and is the son of Christina Hughes who was also born free, aged about 42 years* [Certificates of Freedom for Negroes 1806-64, 34].
     vii. Joseph, born about 1750, enlisted in the Revolution in Culpeper County, Virginia, before December 1781 when he was sized: *age 31, 5'9-1/4" high, black complexion, a planter, born in Newcastle, Pennsylvania* [The Chesterfield Supplement or Size Roll of Troops at Chesterfield Court House, LVA accession no. 23816, by http://revwarapps.org/b81.pdf (p.79)].
     viii. James[2], a "Negro" set free by William Vinson in Dorchester County on 4 September 1804 [Land Records HD-21:295].
     ix.   James[3], born about 1774, a "Negro" set free for $30 by Robert Traverse in Dorchester County on 17 May 1816 [Land Records ER-4:285].

1.   Isabell Hughes, born say 1700, and (her daughter?) Sarah Hughs were summoned to testify in Kent County, Delaware, for "Mulatto Moll alias Molly Gibbs." Moll was a slave who claimed she and her children were entitled to their freedom from Waitman Sipple and Andrew Caldwell because she was the daughter of a white woman named Fleetwood Gibbs. Isabel deposed in Dover on 1 July 1760 that she knew Moll but not as Moll Gibbs, she did not know that Moll was the issue of a

free woman, she had seen Moll suckle (her children) Joseph and Flora about twenty-five years past, she had heard that Moll won her freedom in a court of law but did no know of her own knowledge anything that would benefit Moll's case [Delaware Archives RG 1225, chancery case G#1].[15] She was a widow on 3 June 1757 when she made her Little Creek Hundred, Kent County will, proved 19 January 1763. She named her son John, son-in-law John **Durham**, and daughter Sarah Hewes who was her executrix. Edward **Norman** witnessed the will [WB K-1, fol. 301-3]. Her children were

    i. a daughter, wife of John **Durham**.

    ii. Sarah, confessed to the Kent County court in February 1743/4 that she was delivered of an illegitimate female child two months previous but refused to identify the father. John Hughes paid her fine [RG 3805.002, Quarter Sessions, 1734-79, frame 92]. She was subpoenaed to appear to testify in favor of "Mulatto Moll" in 1760 but not deposed. She married James **Dean** [de Valinger, *Kent County Probate Records*, 205] and was granted administration of his Kent County estate on 4 August 1787.

3   iii. John[1], born say 1736.

2. Mary Hughes, born say 1727, a "Spinster," was living in Dorchester County on 13 August 1745 when she admitted to having an illegitimate child by a "Negroe Slave." The court sold her two "Molatta Children" to Henry Hooper, Jr., to serve until the age of thirty-one [Judgment Records 1742-5, 409]. Her descendants were most likely:

    i. Harry[1], head of a Dorchester County household of 3 "other free" and 2 slaves in 1790. He set free "a certain child he bought of Henry Anderson" named Territa **Buley** by Dorchester County deed of manumission on 15 June 1801 and mortgaged two horses, six sheep, a sow and four pigs and six Windsor chairs for $22.72 on 15 February 1808. He freed his "Negro" wife Ruth on 14 December 1816 and sold a bull, sow, and household furniture to Levin Keys for $50 on 14 July 1817 [Land Records HD-17:230; 24:604; ER-4:297, 478].

    ii. Harry[2], head of a Dorchester County household of 1 "other free" in 1790.

    iii. Shadrick, head of a Dorchester County household of 6 "other free" in 1800 [MD:684].

    iv. Mary, head of a Dorchester County household of 3 "other free" in 1800 [MD:687].

    v. Mary, head of a Cecil County household of 1 "other free" in 1790.

    vi. Hannah, purchased a "Negro" slave named Joseph from the administrator of the Dorchester County estate of Charles Muir on 11 November 1790 for £30 [HD 2:732].

    vii. Enoch, born about 1788, registered in Dorchester County on 6 May 1809: *of a Chesnut colour...born free...aged about 21 years* [Certificates of Freedom for Negroes 1806-64, 7].

    viii. Nancy, born about 1796, registered in Dorchester County on 7 May 1816: *of a blackish colour...born free in Dorchester County and is the daughter of Milcah Hughes who was also born free, aged about 20 years* [Certificates of Freedom for Negroes 1806-64, 32].

---

[15]Moll "Gibbs" lost her case. Depositions were taken in Queen Anne's County from the family that had owned Moll before she was sold to Waitman Sipple. Their testimony as well as Moll's indicate that she was first owned by Evan Jones, then Charles Hilliard, then John Whittington, then John Dempster of Queen Anne's County who sold Moll and her husband Weymouth to Waitman Sipple of Kent County, Delaware. Waitman Sipple answered that Moll was the daughter of an Indian slave. In August 1713 the New Castle County court convicted Fleetwood Gibbs, servant of Peter Mackfareland, of bearing a bastard child [RG 2805.015, reel 1, frame 13]. No race was indicated for the child, but the race of the child or father would not have been relevant in 1713.

3.   John[1] Hughes, born say 1736, was taxable in Dover Hundred, Kent County, Delaware, in 1752 and taxable in Little Creek Hundred from 1754 to 1767 [Kent County Levy List, 1743-67, frames 82, 136, 187, 226, 344, 437, 566], head of a Little Creek Hundred, Kent County, Delaware household of 7 "other free" in 1800 [DE:34] and 3 "free colored" in 1820 [DE:29]. He may have been the father of

    i.   Thomas, born say 1764, a "Mulattoe" taxable in Kent County in 1797 and 1798 [Tax Assessments, frames 15, 479], head of a Little Creek, Kent County household of 7 "other free" in 1800 [DE:33], administrator of the estate of Thomas **Durham**. He married Mary **Durham** [de Valinger, *Kent County Probate Records*, 494].

    ii.   John[2], head of a Murderkill Hundred, Kent County household of 4 "other free" in 1800 [DE:126] and a Duck Creek Hundred household of 9 "free colored" in 1820 [DE:54]. On 27 April 1802 he purchased 5 acres on the northside of the northwest branch of the Dover River in the forest of Little Creek Hundred for £29 [DB G-2:232].

    iii.   William, born before 1776, head of a Duck Creek Hundred, Kent County household of 4 "free colored" in 1820 [DE:53].

Members of a Hughes family on the Western Shore of Maryland were

    i.   John, a "Mollatto Child" living with James Heap of Charles County in August 1749 when the court allowed Heap 300 pounds of tobacco for the child's support until the next court session in November 1749 [Court Record 1748-50, 413].

    ii.   George, head of a St. Mary's County household of 2 "other free" in 1790 and 2 in 1800 [MD:427].

HUNTER FAMILY

Members of the Hunter family in Maryland were

    i.   William, head of a Talbot County household of 5 "other free" in 1790.

    ii.   James, head of a Talbot County household of 5 "other free" in 1790.

    iii.   Thomas, head of an Octoraro, Cecil County household of 1 "other free" in 1790.

    iv.   Henry, head of a Talbot County household of 3 "other free" in 1800 [MD:518].

HUTT FAMILY

1.   Hannah Hutt, born say 1705, received twenty one lashes by the Kent County court in November 1724 for having an illegitimate child. Charles Hillyard agreed to pay her fine and court fees in exchange for three years service after the completion of the time she was then engaged to serve. In May 1728 her unnamed child was bound to Hillyard until the age of eighteen, he having maintained the child for six years [DSA, RG 3815.031, 1722-1732, frames 65, 153, 206]. She was the mother of

2   i.   John, born say 1722.

2.   John Hutt, born say 1722, was taxable in Duck Creek Hundred, Kent County (the same district as Charles Hillyard), from 1755 to 1759 and in Little Creek Hundred from 1760 to 1763 [RG 3535, Levy Assessments 1743-67, frames 140, 169, 184, 198, 212, 228, 244, 264, 269, 305, 315, 383]. He sued John Lawrence for debt in Kent County court in February 1754, and Samuel Hand and Silvester Luck sued him for debt in November 1762 [RG 3815.031, dockets 1750-54, frame 588; 1760-2, frame 515]. On 25 May 1758 he petitioned the Kent County court that he had been bound out by the justices until the age of thirty-one to Charles Hilyard, Sr., who died and left him to his widow who married Presly Raymond. John claimed that Raymond died before paying him his freedom dues [Brewer, *Kent County Guardian Accounts, Houston to McBride*, 30]. He was the father of a

"Mollatto" child who was being kept by Jacob Gay (Guy) on 18 November 1766 when the Kent County levy court allowed him £1.16 for taking care of the child the previous three months and another 12 shillings per month for the ensuing year, perhaps identical to the "Negro Child nam'd Hutt" who John Ham agreed to have bound to him by the Kent County levy court on 15 November 1768 [DSA, RG 3535, Kent County Levy List, 1743-67, frame 529; 1768-84, frame 6]. Perhaps his wife was Sarah Hutt, head of a Kent County, Delaware household of 5 "other free" in 1800 [DE:26]. He may have been the father of

    i.   Presley, born say 1760, received pay for service in the Delaware Regiment in the Revolutionary War from 1 August 1780 to 4 November 1783 [DSA, MS Delaware Regiment Pay Records, 1778-1783, certificates 54,361; 54,861; 55,018; 55,273], a delinquent "Negroe" taxable in Duck Creek Hundred in 1780, 1781, 1788, delinquent in 1789, a "Negro" taxable on a cow and a calf in 1797 [Levy List 1768-84, frame 425, 491; 1785-98, frames 104, 128, 174, 516], head of a Duck Creek Hundred, Kent County household of 4 "other free" in 1800 [DE:13].

    ii. John, born say 1762, enlisted in the Revolution in Delaware on 17 March 1781 and died in June 1781 [NARA, M246, roll 31, frame 502].

    iii. David[1], sued by John Farson in Kent County court on 20 May 1796 [RG 3815, MS case files, 1-20]. He was head of a Kent County household of 6 "other free" in 1800 [DE:24] and 8 "free colored" in 1820 [DE:28].

    iv. James, a "free Negro" taxable in Murderkill Hundred in 1787 [Kent County Tax List, 1785-89, frame 98], head of a Kent County, Delaware household of 2 "other free" in 1800 [DE:16].

    v. Charles, taxable in Little Creek Hundred in 1784, a "Negro" taxable in Duck Creek Hundred in 1788 and from 1797 to 1798 [Kent County Levy Lists, 1768-1784, frame 620; 1785-1797, frames 104, 128, 174, 492, 574; 1798-9, 401]. The Kent County court charged him with assault and battery on Sarah Loller and charged him and (his wife?) Sarah Hutt with riot in November 1792. Sarah Hutt accused Phillis Hutt of assaulting her in Duck Creek Hundred on 1 May 1787 [RG 3805.002, 1787-1803, frames 228-9; MS Indictments May 1787]. James Morris sued him for a debt of £26 in April 1793 [RG 3815, MS case papers].

    vi. David[2], head of a Kent County household of 2 "other free" in 1800 [DE:43].

IMPEY FAMILY

1.   Sarah Empy/ Impee, born say 1685, confessed to the Anne Arundel County court on 11 June 1717 that she had two illegitimate "Mollatto" children by Mark **Williams**. The court ordered that she receive twenty-five lashes [Judgment Record 1717-19, 10-1]. She was buried in All Hallows Parish, Anne Arundel County, two years later on 28 June 1719 [Wright, *Anne Arundel County Church Records*, 200]. She was probably the mother of

2   i. Peter, born say 1705.

2.   Peter Impey, born say 1705, a "free mallatto," married Phillis **Emerson**, "negro servant to Thomas Gassaway," in All Hollow's Parish on 11 July 1725. He married, second, ___ in All Hollow's Parish on 21 January 1731. In August 1741 he and his wife and Anthony **Hill** were summoned to testify against Arthur **Savoy** in a case in which **Savoy** was convicted of stealing a mare from Robert Killeson. In August 1743 Peter was imprisoned for a debt he owed Stephen Higgins [Judgment Record 1740-3, 237, 248, 251; 1743-4, 169]. Peter may have been the ancestor of

    i. Jacob, head of a Baltimore City household of 7 "other free" in 1810 [MD:67].

    ii. David, head of an Anne Arundel County household of 4 "other free" in 1810 [MD:98].

    iii. Jane, born before 1776, head of a Frederick County household of 3 "free colored" in 1830.

JACKSON FAMILY

Charles County:
1.   Elizabeth Jackson, born say 1688, was living at Samuel Cookleys on 11 June 1706 when she was presented by the Charles County court for having a "Mollatto Child" [Judicial Records Liber B-2:211, 244-5]. She may have been the ancestor of

      i. Mary, a "free Mullatto" whose petition to be exempt from paying taxes was rejected by the Charles County court on 9 November 1742 but accepted on 10 November 1747 [Court Record 1741-3, 461; 1746-7, 179].

      ii. William[1], "Mulatto" head of a Charles County household of 13 "other free" in 1790 and 6 in 1800 [MD:487].

      iii. Benjamin, a "free Mulato of Montgomery County" who took the oath of allegiance on 30 March 1778 [*Archives of Maryland*, 16, 559].

      iv. Samuel, "Mulatto" head of a Charles County household of 4 "other free" in 1790 and 6 in 1800 [MD:521].

      v. Susanna, "Mulatto" head of a Charles County household of 4 "other free" in 1790.

      vi. John, "Mulatto" head of a Charles County household of 4 "other free" in 1790 and 4 in 1800 [MD:520].

      vii. John B., "Mulatto" head of a Charles County household of 2 "other free" in 1790.

      viii. Barton, "Mulatto" head of a Charles County household of 2 "other free" in 1790.

      ix. James, "Mulatto" head of a Charles County household of 1 "other free" in 1790 and 11 in 1800 [MD:568].

      x. William[2], head of a Charles County household of 6 "other free" in 1800 [MD:529].

      xi. Abednego, born in 1758 in St. Mary's County and residing there when he enlisted for nine months in the 2nd Maryland Regiment on 25 May 1778. He was discharged on 3 April 1779. After the war he moved to Georgetown where he was employed by and lived at the Catholic College. He was 76 on 29 August 1833 when he appeared in the District of Columbia court to apply for a pension [NARA, S.10909, M804, roll 1397, frame 662 of 1069]. He was a "Mulatto" head of a Charles County household of 4 "other free" in 1790 and apparently the A. Jackson who was head of a Washington, D.C. household of 2 "free colored" and 6 slaves in 1830.

      xii. Edward, "free Negro" head of a Prince George's County household of 9 "other free" in 1800 [MD:286].

      xiii. Wall, "free Negro" head of a Prince George's County household of 5 "other free" in 1800 [MD:296].

      xiv. Charles, born about 1765, registered as a free Negro in Prince George's County on 20 December 1825: *a very dark mulatto, about 60 years old, and 5 feet 4-1/4 inches tall...obtained his freedom by petition to the Prince George's County Court at its September Term 1785* [Provine, *Registrations of Free Negroes*, 54].

Baltimore:
1.   Dorcas Jackson, born say 1755, was the mother of

      i. Hezekiah, born about 1775, a seventeen-year-old "free mulatto" who was baptized in St. Paul's Parish, Baltimore on 23 December 1792 [Reamy, *Records of St. Paul's Parish*, I:64]

Queen Anne's, Dorchester and Kent counties:
1. Anne[1] Jackson, born say 1723, was a "free molatto" spinster living in Saint Paul's Parish when the Queen Anne's County court ordered that she receive 10 lashes for having an illegitimate child on 10 January 1743. She (no race indicated) had another child on 5 July 1746 [Judgment Record 1744-6, 166; 1747-8, 49]. They may have been the ancestors of
    i.   Joseph, head of a Kent County, Maryland household of 7 "other free" in 1800 [MD:150] and 4 in 1810 [MD:848].
2   ii. Anna, born say 1777.
    iii. Adam, "Negro" head of a Caroline County household of 5 "other free" in 1810 [MD:216].

2. Anna Jackson, born say 1777, was the mother of
    i.   Nancy, born about 1797, registered in Dorchester County on 12 September 1816: *of a yellowish colour...raised in Dorchester County and was born free and is the daughter of Anna Jackson who was also born free, aged about 19 years.*
    ii. Sally, born about 1799, registered in Dorchester County on 12 April 1816: *of a chestnut colour...born free and is the daughter of Anna Jackson* [Certificates of Freedom for Negroes 1806-64, 34].

Cecil County
1. Peter Jackson, born about 1759, enlisted in the 5th Maryland Regiment on 2 April 1782: *residence: Cecil County, age 23, 5'6" height, complexion: black.* He was due $59 pay by the end of the year [NARA, M246, roll 34, frames 400, 433 of 587].

Delaware
1. Henry Jackson, born say 1669, was called "Harry a Maletto," the servant of William Sterling, in March 1689/90 when Francis Betteley deposed to the Northampton County, Virginia court that he had been harrowing wheat in company with Harry when Harry told him where Mr. John Baron stored cloth and other goods (which Betteley later stole). Harry was called Henry Jackson, "maletto servant to William Sterling," on 29 September 1690 when he sued for his freedom. The case was resolved by the parties agreeing that Henry would serve one year and then be discharged from service with reasonable clothing. On 28 May 1697 he, called "the maletto," was presented for driving a cart on Sunday. He was discharged from the presentment on payment of the court fees [Wills, Orders, 1689-98, 46, 62, 64-5; 1698-1710, 427, 451]. He had a child by Ann Shepherd, a "Christian white woman" who was presented by the Accomack County court for having an illegitimate child. When required to identify the father of her child on 6 June 1721, she told the Accomack County court that it was "Indian Edmund," but on 6 July 1721 she admitted that it was Henry Jackson, "a Mullatto." The court ordered that she be sold for five years [Orders 1719-24, 33]. Henry and Ann may have been the parents of
2   i.   John, born say 1720.

2. John Jackson, born say 1720, may have been the John Jaxon who was taxable in Bogerternorton Hundred of Somerset County in the household adjoining Edward **Harman** in 1739 [List of Tithables, 1739]. He had a child by Jane **Harman** in Somerset County before 18 November 1740 when she confessed that he was the father [Judicial Record 1740-2, 59-60, 310]. He was a "mulatto" who baptized his son William on 15 June 1746 at St. George's Protestant Episcopal Church, Indian River Hundred, Sussex County [Wright, *Vital Records of Kent and Sussex Counties*, 91]. His children were
3   i.   William, born say 1740.
    ii. Patience, born 25 November 1748 at St. George's Protestant Episcopal Church, Indian River [Wright, *Vital Records of Kent and Sussex Counties*,

94]. She married Job **Friend** ("Melattoes") on 8 June 1772 in Sussex County [Records of the United Presbyterian Churches of Lewes, Indian River and Cool Spring, Delaware 1756-1855, 284].

iii.   ?James, called a "Poore Muloto & Several in his family" when he was a delinquent taxable in Indian River in 1789, head of a Sussex County household of 4 "other free" in 1810 [DE:455] and 3 "free colored" in Indian River Hundred in 1820 [DE:208].

iv.   ?Stephen, servant of John **Regua/ Ridgeway** in March 1754 when the Sussex County court ordered him to serve additional time to make up for thirty day's lost service worth 52 shillings [Delaware Archives RG 4815.017, 1753-1760, frame 93]. He was taxable in Indian River from 1773 to 1784, head of a Sussex County household of 5 "other free" in 1810 [DE:320] and 5 "free colored" in Dagsboro Hundred, Sussex County in 1820 [DE:388].

4   v.   ?Annanias, born say 1760.

3.   William Jackson, born say 1746, son of John Jackson, was baptized on 15 June 1746 at St. George's Protestant Episcopal Church, Indian River. He, a "mulattoe," and his wife Nelly registered the 19 October 1768 birth of their daughter, Lydia, at St. George's Protestant Episcopal Church, Indian River [Wright, *Vital Records of Kent and Sussex Counties*, 91, 98]. He was taxable in Indian River Hundred, Sussex County, in 1773 and 1774, head of a Sussex County household of 4 "other free" in 1810 [DE:458] and 4 "free colored" in Nanticoke Hundred in 1820 [DE:232]. Their children were

i.   Lydia, born 19 October 1768, baptized 20 August 1769.

ii.   ?Agnes, born say 1770, married Edward **Hermon (Harmon)** on 27 November 1788 in Sussex County.

iii.   ?Israel, married Polly **Handsor**, "free Mulattoes," on 18 April 1802 in Sussex County [Records of the United Presbyterian Churches of Lewes, Indian River and Cool Spring, Delaware 1756-1855, 302, 318].

4.   Annanias Jackson, born say 1760, and his wife Hester registered the 10 March 1785 birth of their daughter Hester at St. George's Protestant Episcopal Church, Indian River [Wright, *Vital Records of Kent and Sussex Counties*, 106]. He was head of an Indian River, Sussex County household of 8 "other free" in 1810 [DE:455] and 5 "free colored" in 1820 [DE:208]. They were the parents of

i.   Hester, born 10 March 1785, married Eli **Hitchins** on 9 September 1802 in Sussex County.

ii.   ?Katherine, married Thomas **Hanzor** on 4 February 1808 in Sussex County [Records of the United Presbyterian Churches of Lewes, Indian River and Cool Spring, Delaware 1756-1855, 318, 320].

JACOBS FAMILY

The Jacobs family of Delaware and Maryland probably descended from the Virginia branch of the family [*Free African Americans of North Carolina... by this author]..

1.   Abel[1] Jacobs, born say 1745, a "mulatto," was living in Indian River, Sussex County, when he and his wife, Sarah, registered the 10 July 1769 birth of their son Abraham at St. George's Protestant Episcopal Church, Indian River [Wright, *Vital Records of Kent and Sussex Counties*, 98]. Abel was taxable in Indian River and Angola Hundred, Sussex County, from 1770 to 1777 [DSA, RG 2535, roll 1]. His children were

i.   Abraham, born 10 July 1769, baptized 20 August 1769, head of an Indian River, Sussex County household of 5 "other free" in 1800 [DE:437].

ii.   Sarah, married Adonijah **Harmon**, "free Mulattoes," on 19 January 1795 in Sussex County.

iii.   ?Abel[2], married Nancy **Morris**, "free Mulattoes," on 18 April 1802 in

Sussex County [Records of the United Presbyterian Churches of Lewes, Indian River and Cool Spring, Delaware 1756-1855, 310, 318].

Members of the Jacobs family in Maryland and Pennsylvania were
2 i. Patty, born say 1760.
   ii. Andrew, head of a Northampton County, Pennsylvania household of 2 "other free" in 1790.

2. Patty Jacobs, born say 1760, was head of a Baltimore Town household of 6 "other free" in 1790. She may have been the mother of
   i. Phoebe, born say 1780, "free Mulatto" mother of Ann Jacobs, a five-month-old "Mulatto" baptized 19 February 1799 at St. Peter's Church, Baltimore [Piet, *Catholic Church Records in Baltimore*, 63].
   ii. Samuel, head of a Baltimore City household of 5 "other free" in the 7th Ward in 1810 [MD:84].
   iii. Nace, head of an Anne Arundel County household of 4 "other free" in 1810 [MD:70].
   iv. R., head of a Baltimore household of 3 "other free" in 1810 in the Eastern Precincts [MD:517].

JEFFERY FAMILY

1. Richard Jefferys, born say 1745, a "free Negroe formerly servant to John Willson of Kent County in Maryland," was free on 9 February 1767 when he purchased land from William **Trusty** alias William **Gibbs.** The land consisted of 12-1/2 acres in Queen Anne's County which was whatever rights William had to *Killmanning's Plains* after he had sold his 12-1/2 acres left to him by the will of John Gibbs. He mortgaged 73 acres called *Killmaners Plains* to Eleazar Massey on 13 July 1774 [Land Records RT H:56]. He was apparently the father of
   i. Jacob, a "Man of Colour" who sold 7 acres called *Killmanins Plains* in Queen Anne's County for $45 to William **Cork** and Joseph **Oliver,** "people of Colour," on 15 September 1810. They sold the same land back to him for $50 on 25 May 1811, and he sold 23 acres called *Killmanins Plains* adjoining his land for $94 on 27 May 1811 [Land Records STW-9:369; JB-1:29-31].
   ii. ?Rachel, head of a Queen Anne's County household of 3 "other free" in 1800 [MD:351].
   iii. ?George, taxable "free Negro" in Murderkill Hundred, Kent County, Delaware from 1781 to 1784 [frames 510, 550, 575, 633].
   iv. ?Simon Jeffers, "Negro" head of a Kent County, Maryland household of 6 "other free" in 1790 and 8 in 1800 [MD:162].
   v. ?James, head of a Kent County, Maryland household of 5 "other free" in 1800 [MD:162].
   vi. ?Betty, head of a New Castle County household of 2 "other free" in 1810 [DE:223].
   vii. ?Levi Jeffers, head of a Sussex County household of 5 "other free" in 1810 [DE:377].
   viii. ?Levi Jeffers, head of a Sussex County household of 7 "other free" in 1810 [DE:390].

JERVIS FAMILY

1. Margrett Jervice, born say 1697, was living in Manokin Hundred of Somerset County on 2 June 1714 when she confessed in court that Captain Arnold Elzey's "Negroe servant" was the father of her "Mallato" child. The court sold her for seven years and her child Money for thirty-one years to Mr. Worthington for 3,000 pounds of tobacco. Casah "Negroe man servant" of Major Arnold Elzey confessed that he was the father and received 30 lashes. She was the spinster servant of Mrs.

Alice Worthington of Stepney Parish on 4 June 1717 when she confessed that she had an illegitimate child by "Buboe Negroe." The court ordered her sold for seven years, sold her child to her mistress until the age of thirty-one for 500 pounds of tobacco, and ordered that Buboe receive 30 lashes. The court sold Margaret to Merrick Ellis, Gentleman, for 1,000 pounds of tobacco on 18 August 1724 [Judicial Record 1713-5, 70-1; 1715-7, 211, 235, 239-40; 1723-5, 217]. She was the ancestor of

   i.   Money, born about March 1714, apparently identical to "Mollatto" Moll Jervice whose six-month-old son Sam was sold by the Somerset County court to Alice Ellis for 31 years in August 1733 for 500 pounds of tobacco. She was called Mary Jarvice, "a free molatto woman," in August 1742 when the Somerset County court sold her son Bobo Jarvis (born 2 February 1739/40), "begott by a negro," to William Stoughton, Gent., for thirty-one years [Judicial Record 1733-5, 56; 1740-2, 316b, 317].

   ii.   ?Ann Jervis, born say 1716, a spinster living in Stepney Parish on 15 June 1736 when she confessed to the Somerset County court that she had a child by a "negroe." The court sold her for seven years and her unnamed son until the age of thirty-one to Alice Ellis [Judicial Record 1735-8, 198].

   iii.   Bobo, born in February 1739/40, sold to William Stoughton, Gent., in Somerset County in August 1742 [Judicial Records, 1740-2, 317].

JOHNSON FAMILY

The Johnson family originated in Northampton County, Virginia, before 1650. Members of the family were in Somerset County by 1665, in Delaware by 1677, and in North Carolina by 1720. Included below are the members of the family who moved to Maryland and Delaware during the colonial period.

1.   Anthony[1] Johnson "Negro," born say 1600, was in Virginia by about 1622 according to his and his wife Mary's petition to the Northampton County court on 28 February 1652/3:

> *...they have been Inhabitants in Virginia above thirty years, consideration being taken of their hard labor...and ye great losses they have sustained (by an unfortunate fire)...ordered that from the day of the date hearof...the sd Mary Johnson & two daughters of Anthony Johnson Negro be disengaged and freed from payment of Taxes* [ODW 1651-54, fol.161].

He appeared in the county records on 12 October 1647 when he purchased a cow from Edward Douglas, on 10 January 1647/8 when he purchased a calf from James Berry, and 24 December 1648 when he purchased a cow from John Winbery by deeds proved in Northampton County on 22 February 1652/3 [ODW 1651-4, 123]. He patented 250 acres in Northampton County at great Naswattock Creek for the transportation of five persons, including his son Richard Johnson, on 24 July 1651 [Patents 1643-51, 326]. On 4 August 1658 he purchased 6 cattle and a patent for land of unstated acreage or location from his son John by deed witnessed by George and Francis Parker, and on 21 December 1658 he and his son John sold 2 heifers to John Williams [ODW 1654-55, fol.35; DW 1657-61, 9, 17]. He purchased a colt from Francis **Payne** on 31 January 1659/60 [ODW 1651-54, 123; DW 1657-61, 38].

His "Negro servant" John Casor attempted to gain his freedom by claiming he had been imported as an indentured servant. In 1653 Casor appealed to Captain Samuel Goldsmith who tried to intervene on his behalf, but Johnson insisted that

hee had ye Negro for his life [ODW 1651-54, 226].

Johnson's wife and children tried to persuade him to release Casor, and his neighbor, Robert Parker, apparently allowed Casor to stay on his property. However, Johnson bought suit in Northampton County court against Parker in 1654 for detaining his "Negro servant, John Casor," and the court upheld Johnson's right to hold Casor as a slave [Orders 1655-58, 10]. On 23 November 1654 Anthony recorded a discharge to "John Caser Negro" from all service [DW 1654-5, fol. 35], but it appears that he continued to hold Casor as his servant.

In 1665 Anthony and his wife Mary, his son John and his wife Susanna, and John Casor moved to Somerset County with Randall Revell and Ann Toft who claimed them and many whites as head rights for 2,350 acres of land [Patents 8:495-6]. On 17 April 1665 Anthony and his wife Mary gave 50 acres of their land to their son Richard and assigned their right to the remaining 200 acres by deed recorded in Accomack County on 17 April 1665. They also recorded the transportation of their livestock: 14 head of cattle, a mare, and 18 sheep [Accomack DW 1664-71, fol.10; p.12-fol.12]. On 10 September 1666 he leased 300 acres in Somerset County on the south side of Wicomico Creek in Wicomico Hundred called *Tonies Vinyard* for 200 years [Land Records O-1:32-33].

His widow called herself "Mary Johnson...Negro (the relict of Anthony Johnson...Negro deceased)" on 3 September 1672 in a Somerset County deed by which she gave cattle to her three grandchildren: Anthony, Richard, and Francis, and gave her son John power of attorney over her property and authority to sue for some debts in Virginia. "John Cazara Negro" was a witness (signing) to the 3 September 1672 deed of gift to her grandchildren [Somerset County Judicial Record 1671-75, 159-62]. She renegotiated Anthony's lease in Somerset County for 99 years with the provision that her sons John and Richard would assume the lease after her death [Land Records O-2:20-21]. "John Cazara Negro servant" recorded his livestock brand in court with her consent on 3 September 1672, and she recorded her mark a few weeks later on 26 September 1672 [*Archives of Maryland* 54:760-1]. She was called "Mary Johnson of Wiccocomoco...widow" in July 1676 when she purchased a mare and assigned it to her slave John Corsala [Judicial Records 1675-7, 95]. She was called executor of Anthony Johnson deceased on 17 January 1690 when Edward Revell acted as her attorney in a suit she brought in Accomack County court [WDO 1678-82, 154]. She was living in Sussex County in March 1693/4 when Mary Okey appeared in court to support her complaint that her son John was not maintaining her as he had promised [Court Records 1680-99, 646, 655]. The children of Anthony and Mary Johnson were

2   i.   John[1], say 1631.

3   ii. Richard[1], born about 1632.

      iii. a daughter, excused from paying tax by the February 1652 Northampton County court, perhaps the Joan[1] Johnson who in 1657 received 100 acres in Northampton County from "Deabendanba, Kinge of nusangs," being land next to her brother, John [Whitelaw, *Virginia's Eastern Shore*, 671].

      iv. a daughter, excused from paying tax by the Northampton County court in February 1752.

2.   John[1] Johnson, born say 1631, received a grant for 550 acres in Northampton County on 10 May 1652 at great Naswattock Creek, bounded on the south by the main creek adjoining the land of his father for the importation of eleven persons including Mary Johnson [Patents 3:101]. A white resident of the county, also named John Johnson (Sr.), tried to take possession of the land, but John was awarded the land by the Northampton County court on 28 August 1653 [DW 1657-66, 57-58, 103; DW 1651-54, fol.200]. In November 1654 he and Mary **Gersheene**, an African American servant of his father, were punished for fornication. On 4 August 1658 he sold 6 cattle and a patent for land of unstated acreage or location to his father Anthony, and he and his father sold 2 heifers to John Williams on 21 December 1658. In 1662 he was head of a household of 2

tithables in Northampton County, called John Johnson Negro [ODW 1654-55, fol.35; Orders 1657-64, 9, 17, 103]. On 27 December 1664, in preparation for leaving for Somerset County with his father, he sold his land to George Parker, noting in the deed that he had made a gift of part of the land to Guslin Venitson earlier that year on 1 June 1664. However, he and his wife Susan did not assign the property to Parker until 18 July and 12 August 1670 by deed recorded in Accomack County on 17 July 1672 [Accomack County OW&c 1671-3, 122]. On 17 January 1664/5 his wife Susannah petitioned the Northampton County court to release him from jail where he was held for begetting a child by Hannah Leach who was probably white [Orders 1664-74, fol.92].

He was called "John Johnson Negro" on 11 March 1667/8 when he and two white men, Alexander King and John Richards, were charged in Somerset County court with stealing corn from an Indian named Katackcuweiticks. They confessed their guilt and were ordered to deliver two barrels of corn to the King of the Manoakin at Manoakin Town. John was sued by Randall Revell in Somerset County court for a minor debt on 13 January 1674/5 and appeared as a witness in a court case against Revell. The justices were at first doubtful about admitting the testimony of an African American against a white person. However, his testimony was allowed after he assured the court that he was a Christian and "did rightly understand the taking of an oath." He gave his age as thirty-seven in his deposition in 1670. He testified again in 1676 and was witness to several deeds. Edward Surman appointed him as guardian ("assistant") to his children by his will which was proved in Somerset County court on 10 January 1676/7 [*Archives of Maryland*, 54:675, 707, 712; Judicial Records 1670-1, 10, 15, 6, 205; 1671-5, 41, 260, 267-8, 429, 457-8; 1675-7, 47, 78]. He moved to Sussex County where he received a patent for 400 acres on Rehoboth Bay in September 1677. He purchased 200 acres in Sussex County and sold this land by deed which he acknowledged in court in April 1683. In August 1683 he was accused of murdering his wife Susan. The court took depositions from John Okey and Jeffry Summerford, and released him because they saw "no sign of murder." He appeared in Sussex County court as a witness on seven occasions between March 1680/81 and February 1688. He sued John Okey for debt in May 1685, and he was a defendant on 16 occasions, mainly for debts. The court postponed action on one of these cases because he was in Virginia between December 1684 and May 1685. He was identified as a "Negro" on only three of these occasions, one a case in which he had the estate of Nathaniel Bradford in his custody. In August 1704 he was called "John Johnson, Free Nigroe, Aged Eighty Years and Poor and Past his Labour" when the Sussex County court agreed to maintain him for his lifetime on public funds. He was apparently still living in November 1707 when Walter Groombridge had a suit against him for a debt of £3 [Horle, *Records of the Sussex County Court*, 103, 110, 144, 166, 190, 193, 204, 214, 216, 229, 235, 251, 253, 299, 315, 342, 356, 365, 384, 447, 462, 516, 540, 635, 797, 857, 919, 1201, 1314]. John[1]'s children were

4   i.   John[2], born perhaps 1650.

       ii.   Anthony[2], born perhaps 1655, devised a cow and a calf by the will of his grandmother, Mary Johnson. He was a sued in Sussex County court on 7 May 1706 and was a witness in a Sussex County case in November 1709 [Horle, *Records of the Sussex County Court*, 1227, 1291].

      iii.   ?Joan[2], "Negro," married John Puckham, a baptized Monie tribesman, on 25 February 1682/3 in Somerset County [Register of Liber IKL, Somerset Courthouse by Torrence, *Old Somerset*, 143]. See the **Puckham** history.

      iv.   an unnamed son, born say 1667. William Futcher claimed in February 1689 Sussex County court that Johnson's son had been bound to serve him for nine years. The suit was canceled because of Futcher's death [Court Records 1680-99, 294, 322, 342]. Perhaps this was William Johnson "Molater" who bound himself to serve Ralph Doe, carpenter, of Somerset County for four years on 2 June 1700 in order to pay his debts. On 31

March 1702 the Somerset County court ruled the indenture was insufficient and set William at liberty [Judicial Record 1701-2, 105-6].

v. ?Comfort, born say 1680, "free Nigrene," presented by the Sussex County court for having a bastard child in 1699. James Walker of Rehoboth Bay agreed to pay her fine and give her a three year old heifer in exchange for her serving him an additional thirteen months, and she bound her two year old son to him until the age of twenty-one [Court Records 1680-99, 768, 774, 775]. In February 1706 she confessed to having a bastard child by Justice William Bagwell's servant, Patrick Delany, and in May 1706 she admitted to having a child by Rice Morgan [Horle, *Records of the Sussex County Court*, 1218, 1219, 1276, 1281].[16]

3. Richard[1] Johnson, born about 1632, was one of the five persons his father claimed as head rights in 1651. On 8 February 1653 Governor Richard Bennett instructed Nathaniel Littleton to deliver a black cow to him. On 28 September 1652 he claimed two headrights, and on 21 November 1654 he received a patent for 100 acres in Northampton County adjoining his father and his brother John [ODW 1651-54, fol.103, p.133; Patents 1652-55, 296]. On 19 January 1663/4 he brought suit in Accomack County court against Richard Buckland [DW 1663-66, 54]. He remained in Accomack County on 50 acres left to him by his father when his father took the rest of the family to Maryland [Accomack DW 1664-71, p.12-fol.12]. He purchased 590 acres near Matomkin from Christopher Tompson in December 1675 and conveyed half this land to his son Francis in 1678 [WD 1676-90, 14; *Virginia's Eastern Shore*, 1088]. He was taxable in Accomack County on 2 tithes from 1676 to 1681 (called Richard Johnson, Sen.). He died before 19 March 1689 when his wife Susan Johnson, called a widow, was sued by Hendrick Johnson for some cooper's work he had performed for her after her husband's death [WDO 1678-82, 55, 155, 268, 322]. She came into court to give an account of the estate of William Silverthorne which included several yards of linen lent to "Richard Johnson Negro Since deceased" [W&c 1682-97, 142, 155, 157]. She may have been white since their son Richard was called a "Mulatto." Their children were

i. Francis, born say 1655, received a calf by his grandmother's 3 September 1672 Somerset County deed of gift. He apprenticed himself to George Phebus in Somerset County for three years to be a cooper in November 1673 [Judicial Record 1671-75, 161-2, 336-7]. He moved to Sussex County with his uncle John[1] Johnson by 8 September 1685 when he was summoned as a witness in a court case between William Futcher and John Crew [Court Records 1680-99, 99]. He sued Henry Stretcher in Sussex County court in November 1686, and he was called "Francis Johnson, the Negro" in June 1687 when the court ordered William Orion to pay him 20 shillings for taking up his runaway servant, John Martin.[17] He testified in court for Henry Stretcher in October 1687. He was in Accomack County about February 1689 (called "Francis Johnson Mollatto" and "Brother" of Richard Johnson) when he agreed to complete a fence which Richard contracted to build for Colonel John West. In 1689 he sold the land in Accomack County which his father had conveyed to him in 1678 in order to pay a debt of 6,000 pounds of tobacco [WD 1676-90, 507a, 508; W&c 1682-97, 155a, 156, 187-187a]. He was living on land adjoining William Futcher in Rehoboth Bay, Sussex County, in December 1690 and testified in Sussex County in March 1693 in a case between John Barker and

---

[16]Patrick Delaney's age was adjudged at thirteen years by the Accomack County court on 7 February 1700 [Orders 1697-1703, 84].

[17]Francis Johnson was identified by race in only one of the seven times he was named in Sussex County [Horle, *Records of the Sussex County Court*, 356, 425, 468, 481, 720, 757, 863].

Aminadab **Handsor** [Horle, *Records of the Sussex County Court*, 757; Court Records 1680-99, 600]. He was called a "Mollatto" on 30 March 1699 when he purchased 300 acres called *Rotten* on the north side of Indian River in Sussex County [DB A-1:83, 226]. On 4 November 1707 Hill Drummond brought suit against him in Accomack County court for uttering scandalous words [Orders 1703-9, 103-103a]. On 8 April 1713 he paid Comfort **Driggers**'s fine of 500 pounds of tobacco for the illegitimate child she had in Accomack County earlier that year. Perhaps Elizabeth Johnson, who gave evidence against Comfort, was a relation of his [Orders 1710-4, 56a, 58]. He was security in Accomack County court for Edward Winslow and his wife Anne who failed to appear to answer Thomas Dashiell and Ephraim Heather of Somerset County [Orders 1714-7, 19].[18] He may have been the Fran. Johnson who William **Driggus** appointed as one of the executors of his 7 June 1720 Somerset County will [WB 17:285].

ii.   Richard[2], born say 1660, received a calf by his grandmother's 3 September 1672 Somerset County deed of gift [Judicial Record 1671-75, 161-162]. He and his wife Anne Johnson were servants of John Cole of Accomack County in 1680. She was required to serve her former master, William Whittington, an additional four years for having two illegitimate children while in his service [Northampton Orders 1678-83, 34; Accomack WDO 1678-82, 288-9]. On 3 September 1679 he was called Richard Johnson, Jr., when John Cole and his wife sued him in Accomack County court for kicking Mrs. Cole. On 5 August 1681 he deposed that about Christmas of 1680 he was the servant of John Cole of Matomkin [WDO 1678-82, 108, 288]. On 3 April 1688 Adam Michael sued him for 5,000 pounds of tobacco as a penalty for his nonperformance of a bond, and on 20 December 1688 Colonel John West sued him for failure to build a fence consisting of 400 wood panels for his cornfield (called "Richard Johnson Mollatto"). Richard completed only 40 or 50 of the panels before turning the work over to "his Brother Francis Johnson" in exchange for a gun and several other items. On 16 June 1689 Captain William Custis won a suit against him for about £1. Maximillian Gore acted as his security. He was a tithable head of an Accomack County household in 1692. Esther Pharis identified him as the father of her illegitimate child who was born on 4 June 1695 [W&c 1682-97, 129a, 132a, 150a, 155a, 156, 160, 258a; Orders 1690-9, 153, 173]. He was called "Richard Johnson, Mollattoe" in September 1699 when the Sussex County court presented him for stealing a mare belonging to William Faucett of Somerset County. He was excused after explaining that he had already returned the mare, "taking of the Mare threw mistake, being so like his mare" [Court Records 1680-99, 780]. On 8 October 1707 he was called Richard Johnson "Mulatta" in Accomack County court when Hill Drummond brought a suit against him for debt [Orders 1703-9, 103-103a]. He may have been the Richard Johnson of Carteret County, North Carolina, who purchased 130 acres on Core Sound on the east side of North River from George Cogdell and sold this land on 2 October 1724 to (his nephew?) Jacob Johnson and (his niece's husband?) Theophilus Norwood. The deed was proved by John Simpson and Enoch Ward, who also proved the will of (his brother?) William Johnson [DB C:113-4].

4.   John[2] Johnson, born perhaps 1650, was named as John Sr.'s son in 1670 when they recorded their livestock brand in Somerset County [*Archives of Maryland* 54:757]. On 29 August 1677 he purchased a 44 acre lot on the east side of the

---

[18]Edward Winslow provided security for William **Driggers** in Somerset County court when he was convicted of having an illegitimate child by Mary Winslow [Judicial Records 1707-11, 95-6].

Chesapeake Bay and south side of the Wicomico River called *Angola*. This land probably adjoined *Tonys Vineyard* where his grandmother was then living [Maryland Provincial Patents, Liber 20:224-5; Davidson, *Free Blacks*, 29]. The land was escheated in 1706 with the notation, "no heirs as I understand" [Maryland Provincial Rent Roll, Vol. no. 1, 34]. He was in Sussex County in December 1680 when he was fined for singing "a scurlous disgracfull song" about Samuel Gray and his wife and would have been whipped if William Futcher had not posted security for him. He married Elizabeth Lowe (an English woman) in Sussex County on 13 March 1680/1 [Court Records 1680-99, 2, 23]. She was probably the Elizabeth Johnson who was twenty years old on 14 August 1683 when she appeared as a witness in court. He apparently left the county sometime before February 1683/4 when he was accused of killing a sow belonging to Andrew Depree and taking the meat to John Okey's house [Horle, *Records of the Sussex County Court*, 228, 260]. On 5 March 1699/1700 the Kent County, Delaware court referred to him and his wife as "John Johnson a free Negroe, and Elizabeth his wife (an English woman)" when they were accused of running away and leaving their seven-year-old daughter Susannah in the custody of Thomas Nicholls. The court bound her to Nicholls until the age of eighteen [Court Records 1699-1703, 14]. He may have been identical to John Johnson "Negro" who was sued in Cecil County court on 14 June 1710 for failure to pay his taxes in 1707, 1708 (on two tithes), and 1709. He was called a "Negro" when he was sued for debt by Paul Phillips and when he sued Anne Millener in the same court. On 31 September 1704 he bound his daughter Sarah Johnson, who was about seven or eight years old, to Paul Phillips until the age of twenty-one. Phillips had assigned the indenture to Thomas Wouleston by 9 June 1713 when the court ordered her to serve the remainder of her time to him according to her indenture [Judgment Records 1708-16, 70, 71, 85, 88-9, 202]. John was the father of

    i.   ?John[3], born say 1682, a "Malattoe" servant boy ordered by the Sussex County court in September 1698 to serve his master, Justice John Hill, another seven months for running away for a month [Court Records 1680-99, 744].

    ii. Susannah, born about 1693.

   iii. Sarah, born about 1696-1697, seven or eight years old on 31 September 1704 when she was bound as an apprentice by her father to Paul Phillips. She was probably the Sarah Johnson "Malatto" who was the servant of Nathaniel Horsey in Annamessex Hundred, Somerset County, when she admitted that she had an illegitimate child by "Ned Negroe" belonging to her master [Judicial Record 1713-15, 176, 219; 1715-17, 43].

Their descendants in Maryland and Delaware were most likely:

    i.   William, a "Molatto," died before 25 July 1778 when John Rowland was granted administration on his Sussex County estate. His inventory amounted to £122 and included a parcel of books and carpenter's tools. His widow received £16 as her third and £38 was distributed to the unnamed heirs [RG 4545, roll 132, frames 244-6].

    ii. Thomas, born say 1750, a "Melato," owed 5 shillings to the Worcester County estate of Mr. Alexander Buncle on 3 February 1761 [Prerogative Inventories 72:137-42].

   iii. Sabra, born say 1750, a "free Mallatto" admitted to the Worcester County court in June 1769 that she had an illegitimate child by Ned **Dutton** in November 1768. She paid her fine and James Riggan of Pocomoke Hundred paid her court costs [Court Proceedings 1769-79, 40].

   iv. Milby, convicted by the February 1754 Sussex County court of assaulting John **Regua/ Ridgeway** [DSA, RG 4815.017, 1753-1760, frames 49, 66, 86], taxable in Little Creek Hundred, Sussex County, from 1773 to 1777, head of a Little Creek Hundred, Sussex County household of 6 "other free" in 1800 [DE:488]. He died about 1805 when Mary Johnson was granted administration on his estate [RG 4545, roll 131, frame 290].

    v. John[5], a taxable "Molattoe" in Baltimore Hundred, Sussex County in 1777.

    vi. William, head of a Worcester County household of 7 "other free" in 1790.

    vii. George, head of a Worcester County household of 6 "other free" in 1800 [MD:798].

    viii. Levi, head of a Somerset County household of 5 "other free" in 1800 [MD:491].

    ix. Rachel, born before 1776, head of a Worcester County household of 4 "free colored" in 1830.

Other Johnson families:

1.   Margery Johnson, born say 1698, the servant of Clement Sale, confessed to the Talbot County court in November 1717 that she had a child by Phoenix, a "Negro planter" of St. Peter's Parish [Judgment Record 1717-9, 6-7]. She may have been the ancestor of

    i. Frederick, head of a Talbot County household of 5 "other free" and 2 slaves in 1800 [MD:517].

    ii. John, head of a Kent County household of 5 "other free" in 1800 [MD:162].

    iii. Robert, head of a Kent County household of 5 "other free" in 1800 [MD:162].

    iv. Suky, head of a Dorchester County household of 5 "other free" in 1800 [MD:674].

1.   Abigail Johnson, born say 1740, was the servant of Andrew Francis Chaney of Somerset Parish, Somerset County, on 16 March 1761 when she confessed that she had a child by Hector, a "Negro" slave of Thomas Williams. The court ordered her sold for seven years and ordered her son David sold for thirty-one years [Judicial Records 1760-3, 130b-131]. She was the mother of

    i. David, born about January 1762, head of a Lewis and Rehoboth, Sussex County household of 7 "free colored" in 1820 [DE:302].

Another member of a Johnson family was

    i. Abraham, a "Malatto man" listed in the inventory of the Dorchester County estate of Govert Loockerman on 18 August 1728 with one year left to serve [Prerogative Court Inventories 1728-9, 13:184].

Another Johnson family:

1.   William Johnson, born say 1705, a "free negro," petitioned the Prince George's County court on 27 June 1732 that he came into Maryland as a free man with Captain William Spaven who sold him as a slave to Colonel Joseph Belt. Captain Spaven testified that he met up with William Johnson in London, that Johnson stated that he was in great necessity, asked what voyage he was bound out on, and agreed to go with him to Maryland. When they arrived in Maryland, Spaven sold Johnson to Colonel Belt for his lifetime. The court ruled that Johnson serve five years from the time of his arrival in 1729 [Court Record 1730-2, 541]. He may have been the ancestor of some of the members of the Johnson family who were free on the Western Shore:

    i. Polly, head of a Baltimore Town household of 3 "other free" in 1790 and 5 "other free" in 1800 [MD:246].

    ii. Michael, head of a Washington County household of 7 "other free" in 1800 [MD:644].

    iii. Rachel, head of a Montgomery County household of 5 "other free" in 1800 [MD:236].

    iv. Nicholas, head of a Baltimore City household of 6 "other free" in 1800 [MD:246].

    v. Susanna, head of a Baltimore City household of 3 "other free" in 1800 [MD:246].

vi. James, head of a Baltimore City household of 3 "other free" in 1800 [MD:246].

JOLLEY FAMILY

Members of the Jolley family were
i. James, head of a Baltimore City household of 9 "other free" in 1800 [MD:248].
ii. Thomas, born about 1766, registered in Dorchester County on 15 August 1806: *blackish colour...raised by General Henry Hooper and manumitted by Elisha Cornish on 15 August 1806, aged about 40 years* [Certificates of Freedom, 1806-64].
iii. John, head of a Dorchester County household of 6 "other free" in 1800 [MD:666].
iv. Henry, head of a Dorchester County household of 2 "other free" in 1800 [MD:666].
v. Will, head of a Dorchester County household of 3 "other free" and 9 slaves in 1800 [MD:700].
vi. Harry, head of a Dorchester County household of 2 "other free" in 1800 [MD:691].
vii. Peter, "Negro" head of a Caroline County household of 10 "other free" in 1810 [MD:158].

JONES FAMILY

Anne Arundel County
1. Mary Jones, born say 1683, the servant of Jonas Twogood, was convicted by the Anne Arundel County court in March 1702/3 of having an illegitimate "Malatto" child. She may have been the ancestor of
i. John[1], born about 1718, a thirty-five year old "mulatto" whose escape from the Anne Arundel County jail was reported in the 15 February 1753 edition of the *Maryland Gazette* [Green, *The Maryland Gazette, 1727-1761*, 115]. He and two white men, Stockett Williams and John Ijams, were charged with stealing goods from a warehouse in Anne Arundel County. Williams and Ijams were pardoned in exchange for their testimony against another white man named Jeremiah Williams. Stockett Williams testified that John Jones lived for a time in Prince George's County and had a brother-in-law named John Lee [*Archives of Maryland* 28:564-8].
ii. Elizabeth, born say 1725, presented by the Anne Arundel County court in August 1746 for not listing herself as a tithable [Judgment Record 1746-8, 214].
iii. Agnes, "Negro" head of an Anne Arundel County household of 5 "other free" in 1790.
iv. John[2], head of an Anne Arundel County household of 10 "other free" in 1800 [MD:97].
v. George, head of an Anne Arundel County household of 1 "other free" in 1790.

Baltimore County
1. Mary Jones, born say 1714, was the mother of an illegitimate "Mulatto" child who was bound to Thomas Hughes by the Baltimore County court in August 1724 [Liber IS#TW#3, 26, 201]. She was the mother of
i. Mary, a "Molatto" girl valued at £18 in the 20 November 1739 Anne Arundel County inventory of Thomas Hughes [Prerogative Court Inventories 1739-41, 24:288-90].

1. Winifred Jones, born say 1707, a servant of Thomas Sheredine, confessed to the

Baltimore County court in June 1728 that she had a "Mullatto" child, and the court sold her for seven additonal years to her master for 2,000 pounds of tobacco and sold her child, "age one year the 28 December next," for thirty-one years. She was also convicted of bastardy in August 1725 and November 1733. Her son James, born in 1733, was bound to her master [Liber IS#TW#3, 313; Liber HWS#6, 16]. She was the mother of

    i.   Nan, born about 1725, a "Molatto" with 3-1/2 years to serve when she was listed in the inventory of the Baltimore County estate of Major Thomas Sheredine [Prerogative Inventories 50:174].

    ii. Sampson, born about 1730, a "Molatto" with 8 years to serve when he was listed in the inventory of the Baltimore County estate of Major Thomas Sheredine [Prerogative Inventories 48:174].

    iii. Joan, born about 1732, a "Molatto" with 10 years to serve when he was listed in the inventory of the Baltimore County estate of Major Thomas Sheredine [Prerogative Inventories 48:174].

    iv. James, born about 1734, a "Molatto" with 13 years to serve when he was listed in the inventory of the Baltimore County estate of Major Thomas Sheredine [Prerogative Inventories 48:174].

    v. Jonas, born about 1738, a "Molatto" with 16 years to serve when he was listed in the inventory of the Baltimore County estate of Major Thomas Sheredine [Prerogative Inventories 48:174].

    vi. ?Honse, head of a Baltimore County household of 3 "other free" in 1810 [MD:567].

Prince George's County

1.   Hannah Jones, born say 1740, confessed to the Prince George's County court in June 1761 that she had a "Mulatto" child. The court ordered her sold for seven years and bound her two-year-old daughter Amey to her master, Thomas Beall, Sr. [Court Record 1761-3, 47]. She was the mother of

    i.   Amey, born about June 1759.

Other members of the Jones family on the Western Shore were

    i.   Cassy, head of a Frederick County household of 4 "other free" in 1800 [MD:853], the mother of Daniel Jones who registered in Frederick County on 18 September 1820: *a black man, aged about forty three years...son of a certain Cassey Jones a free woman of Colour...as appears from the affidavit of Ignatius Jones* [Certificates of Freedom 1808-42, 113].

    ii. Michael, head of a Montgomery County household of 4 "other free" in 1790.

    iii. Lewis, head of a Frederick County household of 5 "other free" in 1800 [MD:983].

    iv. Porsey(?), head of a Frederick County household of 2 "other free" in 1800 [MD:853].

Talbot County

1.   Sarah Jones, born say 1707, was living in St. Peter's Parish in November 1727 when she confessed to the Talbot County court that she had a child by a "Negroe." The court sold her and her eight-week-old child to Thomas Wiles [Judgment Record 1727-8, 352]. She may have been the ancestor of

    i.   David, head of a Queen Anne's County household of 1 "other free" in 1790.

    ii. Aimy, head of a Talbot County household of 3 "other free" in 1800 [MD:508].

Other members of the Jones family on the Eastern Shore were

    i.   Peter, a "Negro" baptized on 10 May 1768 by Father Joseph Mosley of St. Joseph's Mission. John Tucker, "Negro," and Esther, "Negro," were the godparents [Wright, *Vital Records of the Jesuit Missions,* 4]. Peter was head of a Kent County household of 6 "other free" in 1800 [MD:162].

ii. John, "Negro" head of a Kent County household of 1 "other free" in 1790.

iii. William, a "Mulatto," admitted to the Kent County court in November 1774 that he had an illegitimate child by Rachel Clark. They were fined 30 shillings [Criminal Dockets 1774-6, dockets 63, 64].

KELLY FAMILY

1. Mary Kelly, born say 1700, servant of Moses Maccubbins, confessed to the Anne Arundel County court in June 1719 that she had a "Mallato" child by her master's "Negroe Harry." In August 1721 she confessed to having another child by Harry. She was ordered to serve seven years for each offense. Her children were bound to her master until the age of thirty-one [Judgment Record 1717-9, 380; 1720-1, 411]. Perhaps one of them was the "Mollatto Girle" (not identified as free) who was listed in the inventory of the Anne Arundel County estate of Moses Maccubbin, Gentleman, on 14 November 1733 [Prerogative Inventories & Accounts 1735-6, 78]. Mary may have been the ancestor of

    i. Catherine, head of a Baltimore City household of 2 "other free" in the First Ward in 1810 [MD:289].

COURSEY/KERSEY FAMILY

1. Mary Kersey, born say 1720, the servant of Nicholas Glen, was fined by the Talbot County court in August 1742 for having an illegitimate child. She was called "Mary Kersey Mulatto" in Glen's account that he recorded in court in November 1744 in a case he brought against her for running away for eighty days and bearing two children in his house. In June 1745 she received corporal punishment for having another illegitimate child [Judgment Record 1742-3, 289-90, 301; 1744-5, 109; 1745-6, 134]. She was the mother of

    i. Nero, born in February 1741/2.

    ii. ?James[1] Arse, head of a Talbot County household of 13 "other free" in 1790.

    iii. Jane, born about March 1745, three months old when she was bound to Nicholas Glen/ Glynn until the age of eighteen.

Other members of the Coursey/ Kersey family were

    i. George Kersey, head of a Talbot County household of 3 "other free" and a slave in 1790, perhaps identical to George Course who was head of a Frederick County household of 4 "other free" in 1800 [MD:937].

    ii. John, a "negro" taxable who was living at Jasper Petticoat's in Upper Newfoundland and Seneca Hundred, Montgomery County, in 1783 [MSA S1161-8-5, p.25].

    iii. Ralph Corse, head of a Murderkill Hundred, Kent County, Delaware household of 6 "other free" in 1800 [DE:114] and 4 in 1810 [DE:56].

    iv. William Coursey, born before 1776, head of a Broadkill Hundred, Sussex County household of 9 "free colored" in 1820 [DE:314].

    v. John Coursey, born before 1776, head of a Lewis and Rehoboth Hundred, Sussex County household of 8 "free colored" in 1820 [DE:306].

    vi. Elizabeth Hearse, born about 1767, registered in Dorchester County on 17 September 1810: *of a blackish colour...born free, raised in Talbot County, aged about 43 years* [Certificates of Freedom for Negroes 1806-64, 14].

    vii. Caesar Corse, "Negro" head of a Kent County household of 8 "other free" in 1790.

    viii. William Coursey, head of a West Sassafras, Cecil County household of 1 "other free" in 1790.

    ix. Edmund, head of a Baltimore City household of 6 "other free" in 1800 [MD:169].

    x. James[2], born about 1792, registered in Dorchester County on 4 May 1815:

yellow complexion...born free, raised in Dorchester County, aged about
23 years [Certificates of Freedom for Negroes 1806-64, 25].

KING FAMILY

1. Mary King, born say 1722, was presented by the Prince George's County court on
   22 March 1742/3 for having an illegitimate child on information of the constable
   for King George Hundred. She was not found by the sheriff, so the case was
   struck off the docket on 27 November 1744. She may have been the mother of
   Margaret King, a four-month-old child who the Prince George's County court sold
   to William Cheshire on 23 November 1742 until the age of thirty-one. (She was
   called Mary King in the court record and Margaret King in the index) [Court
   Record 1742-3, 215, 340, 612]. She was the mother of
   i.   Margaret, born about July 1742.
   ii. ?Solomon, head of a Talbot County household of 4 "other free" in 1790.
   iii. J., head of a Frederick County household of 6 "other free" in 1810
        [MD:579].

Mary may also have been the ancestor of members of the King family who were
counted in the 1810 census for nearby Prince William County, Virginia:
   i. Samuel, head of a Prince William County household of 5 "other free" and
       4 slaves in 1810 [VA:513].
   ii. Sarah, head of a Prince William County household of 4 "other free" in
       1810 [VA:518].

KNIGHT FAMILY

1. Elizabeth Knight, born say 1692, the servant of Robert Eagle, confessed to the
   Anne Arundel County court on 11 March 1711/2 that she had a child by "Negroe
   Rich belonging to Col. Charles Greenberry." The court bound the child, born 6
   February 1711/2, to her master until the age of thirty-one and ordered that she
   serve seven years for the offense [Judgment Record 1708-12, 404, 412]. She may
   have been the ancestor of
   i. William, head of a Kent County household of 4 "other free" in 1790.

1. Moses Knight, born about 1755, was head of a Frederick County household of 5
   "other free" in 1800 (Moses Night) [MD:788] and 10 in 1810 (M. Knight)
   [MD:635]. He was about 76 years old on 26 March 1831 when he appeared in
   Davis County, Indiana court and petitioned (signing) for a pension for his services
   in the Revolution. He stated that he enlisted in 1779 in South Carolina in the
   regiment commanded by Colonel Jack McIntosh. He had not applied earlier
   because he had been living in Maryland where he had owned 146 acres in 1818.
   He had a wife named Maryann (age 54), son Abraham (17), son Isaac (10),
   daughter Analisa (8-9), and grandson Elijah (9-10). He appeared in court again on
   13 May 1833 and added that he was sometimes called Moses Sharper and Moses
   McIntosh because he was raised by Colonel Alexander McIntosh. His widow
   Mariam H. Knight applied for a widow's pension in Knox County, Indiana, on 4
   December 1850 and stated that they were married about 1795 in Pleasant Valley,
   Washington County, Maryland, and her husband died on 2 April 1848 [NARA,
   W.10182, M804, http://fold3.com/image/24655780]. He and his wife Marian were
   the parents of
   i. Katy, born about 1799, registered in Frederick County on 13 August 1821:
       aged about twenty two or three years...a Dark Mulatto...Daughter of
       Moses and Mariah, free persons.
   ii. Susan, born about April 1801, registered on 14 January 1822: *aged twenty*
       years in April last...yellowish Complexion...Daughter of Moses Knight
       and Marian his wife, free persons.

iii. Israel, born about 1803, registered on 14 January 1822: *aged nineteen years in March last...Black, a flat nose...Son of Moses Knight and Marian his wife, free persons.*
iv. Rachel, born about 1805, registered on 14 January 1822: *aged Sixteen years April last...yellowish Complexion...Daughter of Moses ~~Knight~~ and Marian his wife* [Certificates of Freedom 1806-27, 123, 124].

LACOUNT/ LECOMPTE FAMILY

Members of the Lecompte family in Maryland and Delaware were
1   i. Thomas^1 Lacount, born say 1740.
       ii. William^1 Lecompte, born say 1742, a "Black Man," head of a Transquakin Hundred, Dorchester County household of 3 "Blacks" in 1776 [Carothers, *1776 Census of Maryland*, 51].

1.   Thomas^1 Lacount, born say 1740, was taxable in Little Creek Hundred, Kent County, Delaware, from 1765 to 1770, in Duck Creek Hundred from 1773 to 1776, in Little Creek from 1781 to 1787, in Duck Creek in 1788, and in 1789 his name was crossed off the Little Creek Hundred list and he was listed as a delinquent [RG 3535, Kent County Levy List, 1743-67, frames 508, 520, 553, 566; 1768-84, frames 10, 26, 66, 180, 220, 258, 270, 503, 542, 570, 583, 620; 1785-97, frame 24, 49, 72, 74, 103, 128, 174]. He died before 12 January 1796 when Hester Lacount, the widow of Thomas Lacount, Senr, declined the administration and his son William Lacount was granted administration on his Duck Creek Hundred estate with Patrick Conner as security. The inventory was valued at £39 [RG 3545, roll 132, frames 311-317]. He was the father of
       i. William^2, a "Negro" taxable in Duck Creek Hundred on a horse and 5 hogs in 1797 [RG 3535, Kent County Levy List, 1785-97, frame 490, 575; 1797-8, 358, 406].
       ii. ?John, born say 1765, taxable in Little Creek Hundred from 1786 to 1789, a "Negro" taxable in Duck Creek Hundred in 1797 and 1798 [RG 3535, Kent County Levy List, 1785-97, frame 49, 72, 74, 106, 197, 575; 1797-8, frame 358, 406].
       iii. ?Thomas^2, born say 1770, a "Negro" taxable in Duck Creek Hundred in 1797 and 1798 [RG 3535, Kent County Levy List, 1785-97, frame 490, 575; 1797-8, 358, 406], married to Letitia **Durham** on 30 June 1794 when he received her portion of the distribution of the Little Creek Hundred estate of her father John **Durham** [RG 3545, roll 68, frames 612-23], perhaps the Thomas Lecompte who was head of a Dorchester County household of 6 "other free" in 1800 [MD:724].
       iv. ?Elizabeth, head of a Duck Creek Hundred, Kent County, Delaware household of 3 "other free" in 1800 [DE:8], perhaps the mother of Joseph Lacount, born about 1780 in Delaware, a "Mulatto" head of a Spruce Ward, Philadelphia household with wife Mary in 1850 [family no. 201].
       v. ?James, a "Negro" taxable in Little Creek Hundred in 1798 [RG 3535, Kent County Levy List, 1797-8, frame 333].

LAMB FAMILY

Members of the Lamb family in Maryland were
       i. Cato, "Negro" head of a Kent County household of 7 "other free" in 1790 and 4 in 1800 [MD:163].
       ii. Nathaniel, head of a Kent County household of 7 "other free" in 1800 [MD:151].
       iii. Jeremiah, head of a Kent County household of 6 "other free" in 1800 [MD:163].
       iv. Nathaniel^2, head of a Kent County household of 5 "other free" in 1800 [MD:150].

    v.   Charles, head of a Kent County household of 5 "other free" in 1800 [MD:163].

    vi. Michael, head of a Kent County household of 3 "other free" in 1800 [MD:163].

LANTOR/ LANTERN FAMILY

1.   Thomas[1] Lantor and his wife Isabella registered the birth and baptism of their children in Christ Church Parish, Middlesex County, Virginia [NSCDA, *Parish Register of Christ Church*, 52, 60, 64, 67, 72]. Their children were

        i.   John, born 30 July, baptized 1 October 1698.

2   ii.   Peter[1], born 25 January 1699/1700.

        iii. Mary, born 9 September 1700, baptized 22 May 1709.

        iv. Margaret, baptized 21 November 1702.

3   v.   Thomas[2], baptized 5 November 1704.

2.   Peter[1] Lantor, born say 1706, and (his son?) Reubin Lantor, "Mulattos of St. Thomas's Parish...Planters," were charged in Orange County, Virginia court on 11 October 1755 with assaulting and beating John Lynch who they mistook for a runaway servant. On 24 November 1757 he and Sarah Bourn were indicted by the grand jury for fornication on the information of Andrew Bourn and Andrew Mannen. This indictment was titled "Peter Lantor and his wife" when it was dismissed on 23 June 1758 [Orders 1754-63, 178-9, 357, 368, 388, 392, 411, 443]. On 24 November 1768 the grand jury presented Peter for concealing his tithable-wife Sarah Lantor but excused him the following day [Orders 1763-9, 366, 535, 538]. On 10 March 1767 he sued John Hansford for 984 pounds of tobacco. The judgment records for the case included an untitled paper that may have been written by the lawyer for the case and read, "Underwood liberty to prove acc[t] by oath," apparently referring to the case in which Christopher **Underwood**, "a malatto," petitioned the justices for assistance in proving his case against a white man named John Branham [Judgments, September 1762-July 1763, LVA microfilm reel 121, Court Papers, May 1763, approximately frame 108]. On 2 October 1769 John Booth was charged with feloniously shooting and killing Peter. The court ordered Booth sent to the General Court for trial. (Booth was a co-defendant with Peter in a suit for debt on 24 August 1764) [Orders 1769-77, 35, 90; 1763-9, 190]. Sarah received £4 annually for five years by the 21 June 1771 Orange County will of Caleb Sesson, proved 22 August 1771 [WB 2:436-7]. Her plantation was located near a new road which was ordered to be opened on 23 June 1774 from Chestnut Mountain over the Mountain Run [Orders 1769-77, 319, 340]. Peter may have been the father of

        i.   Reuben, born say 1734, charged in Orange County court along with (his father?) Peter Lantor, "Mulattos of St. Thomas's Parish...Planters," on 11 October 1755 for assaulting and beating John Lynch who they mistook for a runaway servant [Orders 1754-63, 178-9, 331, 355, 379, 413]. On 22 June 1758 the Orange County court ordered that Thomas **Baulkham**, a "Mulattoe," be paid as a witness in William Minor's suit against him [Orders 1754-63, 404].

        ii.   Mordecai, sued William Talliaferro in Orange County court in June 1764 for £16 for building a shed, the floor for the barn and sawing 586 feet of plank [Judgments, May-August 1764, June Court Papers, LVA microfilm reel 124].

3.   Thomas[2] Lantor, baptized 5 November 1704 in Christ Church Parish, was paid 30 pounds of tobacco in King George County, Virginia, on 8 December 1722 for helping to guard a prisoner in the county jail. He was involved in several minor suits in King George County between 2 February 1722/3 and 6 March 1724/5 [Orders 1721-3, 74, 101; 1723-5, 166, 186, 208, 220, 236]. And he was involved in a number of lawsuits, mostly for debt, in Caroline County court as plaintiff and

defendant between 11 May 1732 and 13 June 1746 [Orders 1732-40, 9, 11, 62, 63, 83, 91, 125, 129, 137, 149, 165, 166, 384; 1740-6, 139, 464, 561, 590]. He was the father of Elizabeth Saunders's "mulatto" child born before 12 September 1735 when Elizabeth identified him as the father in Caroline County court. The court ordered Elizabeth to serve her master Samuel Coleman additional time and ordered the child bound to Coleman [Orders 1732-40, 307, 378, 481, 491, 503, 520]. On 10 February 1745/6 he produced a certificate in court for taking up two white servants belonging to John Glanton of Caroline County. That same day he was ordered to be placed in the stocks for half an hour, no explanation being given for the punishment [Orders 1740-6, 563, 565]. He was apparently identical to "y^r Brother Tom" who William Talliaferro listed in his account of transactions with Peter Lanter in 1752. Taliaferro paid Peter and Tom's levies in 1754 [Judgments, May-August 1764, Court Papers, May 1764]. He may have been the father of

4 i. Elizabeth, born say 1730.
   ii. Thomas^2, born say 1740, married to Mary Walker on 28 August 1783 by Rev. Aaron Bledsoe in Orange County [Ministers' Returns, 13].

4. Elizabeth Lantern, born say 1730, testified in Kent County, Delaware, on 22 November 1769 that (her son?) Peter Lantorn, who was assessed as a tithable the previous year, was born on 8 April 1750 and therefore should not have been tithable [Kent County Levy Assessments, 1768-84, Reel no.3, frame 38]. She married Robert **Game** before September 1782 when Robert named her (called Elizabeth Lanthorn) and her daughters Mary and Sarah in his Murderkill Hundred, Kent County will [WB L-1, fol. 267-8]. She was the mother of

   i. Peter^2, born 8 April 1750, father of an illegitimate child by Keziah **Dean** in Little Creek Hundred, Kent County, about December 1773 [DSA, RG 3505, MS case files, May 1774 Indictments; RG 3805.003, 1735-1779, frame 580]. He was tithable in Little Creek Hundred in 1772 and 1773, in Dover Hundred in 1778, in Little Creek in 1779 and 1780, and a delinquent Duck Creek Hundred taxable in 1781 and 1782 (called Peter Lantern/ Lanthron). In May 1785 he and Francis Day, laborers, were charged with stealing 200 pounds of flour from John Pernell and 400 pounds of bacon from Joseph Harper in Murderkill Hundred on 4 April 1785 [DSA, RG 3805, MS May 1785 Indictments]. He was head of a Murderkill Hundred household of 3 "other free" in 1800 (called Peter Lanteron) [DE:126].
5 ii. ?Joseph^1 Lantern, born say 1756.
   iii. Mary.
   iv. Sarah.

5. Joseph^1 Lantern, born say 1756, was tithable in Dover Hundred, Kent County, from 1776 to 1785. He married Elizabeth **Harmon**, widow and administrator of Daniel **Harmon**'s 10 May 1774 Kent County estate [de Valinger, *Kent County, Delaware Probate Records*, 289]. On 9 August 1786 Elizabeth was the administratrix of Daniel **Harmon**, deceased, when they were called Joseph and Elizabeth Lanthorn and summoned to answer the complaint of John **Harmon** [Brewer, *Kent County Guardian Accounts, 1744-1855, Edmonson to Hopkins*, 141]. Joseph purchased 6 acres in Halifax County, North Carolina, for £44 on 23 December 1789. On 30 October 1795 he, Moses Matthews, and John **Kelly** purchased 100 acres, tools, furniture, cattle, and hogs from John **Harmon**, and he purchased 100 acres near the road from Halifax Town to Enfield old courthouse from John **Harmon** on 3 December 1795 [DB 17:231, 920; 18:130]. Joseph was head of a Halifax County household of 7 "other free" and 7 slaves in 1800 [NC:324]. (His widow?) Charity Lantern was head of a Halifax County household of 4 "other free" in 1810 [NC:34]. He may have been the father of

   i. Joseph^2, Jr., born about 1772, head of a Halifax County household of 3 "other free" in 1800 [NC:324] and a 78-year-old "Mulatto" born in Delaware, counted in District 1 of the 1850 Montgomery County,

Alabama census with (wife?) Nancy Lanton who was born in South
Carolina and with real estate valued at $1,000.

ii. James, born say 1780, head of a Halifax County household of 2 "other
free" in 1810 [NC:33] and 7 "free colored" in 1820 [NC:155].

LAWDER FAMILY

1. Isabella Lawder, born say 1705, was the servant of John Cleaver on 18 August
1724 when George Copper paid the Kent County court 2,200 pounds of tobacco
for eight years of her service, seven years for having an illegitimate "Molatto"
child and one year for court fees. She had a child by a white man before 16 June
1730 when the court ordered that she receive twenty one lashes [Criminal
Proceedings 1724-8, 15, 127]. She may have been the ancestor of
   i. Thomas, head of Montgomery County household 3 "other free" in 1790.
   ii. James, born about 1774, head of a St. Mary's County household of 7
   "other free" in 1800 [MD:419], registered in St. Mary's County on 2
   August 1814: *aged forty years or thereabouts...complexion bright yellow -
   hair short...born free* [Certificates of Freedom 1806-64, 28]. He may have
   been married to Nancy Lawder, the mother of Elizabeth **Lewis** who
   registered in St. Mary's County on 28 July 1823: *Daughter of a free yellow
   woman by the name of Nancy Lawder, aged about twenty eight
   years...bright complexion...born free* [Certificates of Freedom 1806-64,
   62].

LAWRENCE FAMILY

1. John Lawrence, born about 1762, was head of a St. Mary's County household of
7 "other free" in 1800 [MD:422]. He registered in St. Mary's County on 7 March
1815: *aged fifty three or thereabouts...complexion yellow, hair curley...raised in
Saint Mary's County & was born free* [Certificates of Freedom 1806-64, 30]. He
was probably the husband of Ann **Mason** Lawrence, born about 1777, who
registered in St. Mary's County on 29 April 1822: *daughter of Milly Mason, about
45 years of age...light complexion* [Certificates of Freedom 1806-64, 59]. John
and Ann were probably the parents of
   i. Kitty **Brian**, born about 1797, registered in St. Mary's County on 29 April
   1822: *daughter of Ann Lawrence, about 25 years of age...very light
   complexion...born free* [Certificates of Freedom 1806-64, 59].
   ii. Cornelius, born about 1797, registered in St. Mary's County on 28
   November 1816: *aged nineteen years...light complexion...born free*
   [Certificates of Freedom 1806-64, 37] and registered in Essex County,
   Virginia, on 21 June 1824: *born free by certificate of St. Mary's County,
   Maryland, 27 years of age* [Register of Free Negroes 1810-43, p.46, no.
   115].
   iii. Henry, born about 1800, registered in St. Mary's County on 11 March
   1822: *son of Naney Lawrence...about twenty two years of age, bright
   complexion...born free* [Certificates of Freedom 1806-64, 59].

Other members of the Lawrence family were
   i. Charles, born in June 1704, a "Mulatto" servant of Windsor Kenner who
   sued his master in Northumberland County, Virginia court for his freedom
   on 18 July 1733. The court ruled that he was twenty-nine years old and
   would not be thirty-one until June 1735 [Orders, 1729-37, 102, 150].
   ii. Spencer, born 2 April 1711, a "Mullatto" servant of Richard Kenner who
   sued his master in Northumberland County for his freedom on 14 January
   1739/40. After considering the deposition of Mrs. Elizabeth Footman of
   Westmoreland County, the court ruled that he would not be thirty-one
   until 2 April 1742 [Orders 1737-43, 119, 127, 130].
   iii. William, head of Westmoreland County, Virginia household of 2 "other

free" in 1810.
    iv. Jane, head of Westmoreland County, Virginia household of 2 "other free" in 1810.

LEATHERBY FAMILY

1.   Ann Leatherby, born say 1758, was indicted by the Kent County, Maryland court for "Mul° Bast^y" in March and August 1776 [Criminal Dockets, appearances no.35, 31]. She may have been the mother of
    i. Peter Leatherberry, head of an Accomack County household of 3 "other free" in 1810 [VA:37], taxable with his wife Doll in a list of "free Negroes" 1813 [PPTL 1783, frame 833].

LEE FAMILY

Anne Arundel County:
1.   Margaret Lee, born say 1675, a servant of Lyle Welch, confessed to the Anne Arundel County court on 12 March 1705/6 that she had a "Mullattoe male child of her body by a Negro slave" [Judgment Record 1705-6, 172-3]. She may have been the ancestor of
    i. John, born say 1720, brother-in-law of John **Jones** of Anne Arundel County [*Archives of Maryland* 28:564-8].
    ii. William, head of an Anne Arundel County household of 9 "other free" in 1810 [MD:55].
    iii. Sarah, head of an Annapolis household of 5 "other free" in 1810 [MD:111].
    iv. Philip, head of a Baltimore City household of 6 "other free" in 1810 [MD:308].
    v. Jacob, head of a Baltimore City household of 4 "other free" in 1810 [MD:115].
    vi. Peter, head of a Baltimore City household of 3 "other free" and 2 slaves in 1810 [MD:67].

Prince George's County
1.   Eleanor Lee, born say 1697, was the mother of Daniel, a "Mallato" boy who was sold by the Prince George's County court to John Wright on 25 June 1717 for 400 pounds of tobacco [Court Record 1715-20, 241]. She was the ancestor of
    i. Daniel, born about January 1717, a "Mullatto boy" listed in the Prince George's County estate of John Wright, valued at £18 on 15 December 1729 and a "Mulatto" carpenter valued at £40, listed with 5-1/2 years to serve in the Prince George's County estate of Ann Wright on 21 June 1742 [Prerogative Court Inventories 1729-30, 15:397; 1742-3, 27:20].
2   ii. ?Lucy, born say 1755.

2.   Lucy Lee, born say 1755, was head of a Montgomery County household of 9 "other free" in 1790 and 4 in 1810 [MD:920]. She may have been the mother of
    i. John, head of a Montgomery County household of 6 "other free" in 1810 [MD:919].
    ii. James, born about 1790, registered in Frederick County on 14 March 1815: *a Mulatto Man, light complexion, six feet one and a half inches high...about Twenty five years of age is free born of a white woman as appears by the affidavit of William Lewis* [Certificates of Freedom 1806-27, 49], perhaps identical to J. Lee, head of a Frederick County household of 2 "other free" in 1810 [MD:596].

Dorchester County
1.   Money Lee, born say 1725, a "Spinster white woman," confessed in Dorchester County court in November 1754 that she had a "Mulatto" child by a "Negroe" on

10 December 1753 [Judgment Record 1754-5, 125-6]. She was probably the ancestor of

2   i. Rachel, born say 10 December 1753.
3   ii. David, born say 1770.
     iii. Sarah, born say 1773, head of a Dorchester County household of 3 "other free" in 1800 [MD:656], mother of Rachel **Denwood** who registered in Dorchester County on 3 August 1815: *of a light chesnut colour...born free and is the daughter of Sarah Lee who was convicted for having a child by a slave, aged about 23 years.*
     iv. Henry, head of a Dorchester County household of 5 "other free" in 1800 [MD:695].
     v. Draper, head of a Dorchester County household of 3 "other free" in 1800 [MD:655].
     vi. Robert, "Negro" head of a Worcester County household of 5 "other free" in 1800 [MD:727].

2.   Rachel Lee, born say 10 December 1753, was convicted of having a child by a slave in Dorchester County. She was the mother of
     i. Leah **Baltimore**, born say 1776, mother of Mahala **Baltimore** who registered in Dorchester County on 18 June 1815: *of a light chesnut colour...daughter of Leah Baltimore who was the daughter of Rachel Lee who was convicted and sold for having a child by a slave, aged about 19 years* [Certificates of Freedom for Negroes 1806-64, 26, 27].
     ii. Levin **Johnson**, born about 1780, registered in Dorchester County on 13 September 1815: *of a yellowish colour...born free and is the son of Rachel Lee who was convicted and sold for having a illegitimate child, aged about 35 years* [Certificates of Freedom for Negroes 1806-64, 29].

3.   David Lee, born say 1770, was head of a Dorchester County household of 6 "other free" in 1800 [MD:715]. He was the father of
     i. Nancy **Bishop** Lee, born about 1799, registered in Dorchester County on 7 December 1827: *of a light chesnut colour, was born free and raised in Dorchester County and is the daughter of Nancy Lee who was manumitted by David Lee, aged about 18 years, granted on information of David Lee* [Certificates of Freedom for Negroes 1806-64, 57].
     ii. Major, born about 1802, registered in Dorchester County on 21 April 1828: *light chesnut colour...born free, and is the son of David Lee aged about 26 years* [Certificates of Freedom for Negroes 1806-64, 58].
     iii. Pleasant **Cornish**, born about 1804, registered in Dorchester County on 18 May 1824: *of a chesnut colour...daughter of David Lee a freeman, aged about 20 years* [Certificates of Freedom for Negroes 1806-64, 50].
     iv. Abraham, born about 1804, registered in Dorchester County on 21 April 1828: *dark chesnut colour...born free and is the son of David Lee, aged about 24 years* [Certificates of Freedom for Negroes 1806-64, 58].

LENKINS FAMILY

Members of the Lenkins family of Maryland were
     i. Henley, "Mulatto" head of a Charles County household of 7 "other free" in 1790 and 5 "other free" in 1810 [MD:348].
     ii. Sarah, born say 1750, charged Leonard **Swann** in Charles County court in March 1769 with begetting her illegitimate child [Court Records 1767-70, 405A]. She was head of a Charles County household of 7 "other free" in 1800 [MD:506].
     iii. Townly, "Mulatto" head of a Charles County household of 6 "other free" in 1790.
     iv. Eleanor, "Mulatto" head of a Charles County household of 3 "other free" and 2 slaves in 1790.

v. Peter, head of a Charles County household of 5 "other free" in 1800 [MD:532] and 5 "other free," a white woman over 45 years old, and 2 slaves in 1810 [MD:325] and 10 "free colored" in 1830.

LETT FAMILY

1. Mary Lett, born say 1700, was said to be living at George Rogers's on 6 August 1728 when she was presented by the Baltimore County court for having a base born child. However, no evidence appeared against her when the case came to trial in November 1728, so she was released when Richard Gist agreed to provide security for her payment of the court fees. On 2 March 1730/1 the court bound her "Mollatto" children Sarah and Zachariah Lett to William Rogers until the age of thirty-one [HWS#6 (Court Proceedings, 1728-30), 22, 74; HWS#7 (1730-1732), 97].[19] She was apparently married to Robert **Bannaker** by 20 May 1731 (her second marriage?) when she petitioned the Maryland Provincial Court by her lawyer William Cumming:

    Mary Beneca of Baltemore County. That your Petitioner was born of a White Woman, a Servant of John Newman of the County af[t] whom your Petitioner Did Serve until she attained to the Age of thirty-one Years at which time your Petitioner was adjudged to be free by the Justices of Baltemore County af[t]. That During your Petitioners Servitude had severall Children born of her Body That your Petitioner was adjudged by the Justices of Baltemore County af[t] to pay unto the said John Newman the Sum of Seven thousand Pounds of Tobacco for maintaining & bringing up the said Children during your Petitioners said Servitude & for the payment of the said Seven thousand Pounds of Tobacco that your Petitioner before the Justices of the said court at March Court 1727 did Bind three of her Children to wit Sarah Lett, Zachariah Lett & Deborah Lett to Serve a Certain W[m] Rogers of s[d] County who undertook the Payment of the same Tobacco until they should Come to Age. That lately the said Rogers applyed to the Justices of the County af[t] & obtained the following Order to be made: March Court 1730. Upon the Motion of William Rogers to the Court & upon due Deliberation by the said Court had do adjudge Sarah Lett, Zachariah Lett and Deborah Lett the Children of Mary Lett to serve the said Rogers till Each of them attain to the Age of thirty One Years as by an attested Copy annext appears. Your Petitioner likewise Shews that the af[t] Sarah Lett one of the said Children hath now attained to above the age of Sixteen Years...And that the said Sarah by Law is entitled to her freedom. Your Petitioner therefore most humbly beseeches Y[r] Honours to Order Citation to issue against the said W[m] Rogers to answer the Premises And...adjudge Your Petitioners Children to be free when they Attain to the age of Sixteen & twenty one Years [Provincial Court Judgments, Liber R.B. no.1, fols. 425-426, MSA].[20]

    The court ordered Rogers to appear at the next session, but there is no further record of the case. She was apparently successful since her son Zachariah was married less than ten years later. Mary was the mother of

    i.   Sarah, born before about 1715, perhaps identical to Savory Lett who married Simon **Thompson** ("negroes") on 10 November 1734 at St. Paul's Parish, Baltimore [Reamy, *Records of St. Paul's Parish*, I:31]..

2   ii. Zachariah[1], born say 1720.

    iii. Deborah.

---

[19]Mary may have had white relatives in Baltimore County. Jane Lett was indicted by the court in March 1717/8 for having a bastard child and named the father James Ketcham who was a white man [Court Proceedings 1715-18, 237-8].

[20]William Cumming was also Robert Pearle's lawyer in his suit in Provincial Court.

2.   Zachariah[1] Lett, born say 1720, was married to Margaret by 1 January 1743/4 when their daughter Luzana was born. He purchased 50 acres in Baltimore County called *Noon's Chance* from William Rogers for £24 on 20 October 1759 and sold this land for £90 on 12 October 1771 [Land Records B#H (1759-61), fol. 6; AL#D (1771-2), fol. 34]. He and Margaret were the parents of.

    i.   Luzana, born 27 April 1741,

    ii.   Vashti, born 1 January 1743/4, d/o Zachariah and Margaret Lett.

    iii.   Daniel, born 29 October 1745, s/o Zachariah and Margret Lett [Reamy, *Records of St. Paul's Parish*, I:31]. He took the oath of an insolvent debtor in Frederick County and assigned all his belongings to James Stewart on 20 March 1788 [Land Records WR 8:55]. He was a "free black" taxable in Shenandoah County, Virginia, from 1807 to 1818 [PPTL, 1800-18, 366, 485, 651, 829] and head of a Shenandoah County household of 6 "other free" in 1810.

Other members of the Lett family were

    i.   Elijah, head of a Frederick County household of 6 "other free" in 1790.

    ii.   Aquilla, head of a Frederick County household of 5 "other free" in 1790.

    iii.   Rosalin, head of a Frederick County household of 5 "other free" in 1790 and 3 in Washington County in 1800 [MD:638].

    iv.   Charles, head of a Jefferson County, Virginia household of 11 "other free" in 1810 [VA:78].

    v.   Zachariah[2], taxable in Shenandoah County, Virginia, from 1801 to 1813: called a "free black" starting in 1810 when he was taxable on 2 tihes and 2 horses [PPTL, 1800-18, 54, 408, 538].

    vi.   Delilah, born about 1771, registered in Frederick County on 13 September 1826: *about fifty five years of age...a bright Mulatto Woman...free Born as appears by the affidavit of Nicholas Willson* [Certificates of Freedom 1808-42, 187].

    vii.   Benjamin, born about 1792, married Mary **Calliman**, 5 January 1809 Frederick County, Virginia bond.

LEWIS FAMILY

1.   Margaret Lewis, born say 1712, the servant of Thomas Stocketts, had a "mulatto" daughter named Ann Lewis who was born in All Hollows Parish, Anne Arundel County, on 28 November 1733 [Wright, *Anne Arundel County Church Records*, 47]. In August 1737 she confessed to the Anne Arundel County court that she had another mixed-race child. She was the servant of Thomas Hands in August 1741 when she was convicted of having a third mixed-race child named Sarah [Judgment Record 1736-8, 250; 1740-3, 252]. Margaret was the mother of

    i.   Ann, born 28 November 1733.

    ii.   a child, born about 1737.

    iii.   Sarah, born about 1741.

Other members of a Lewis family were

    i.   John, born say 1698, a "Negroe" released from prison in Prince George's County on 23 August 1720 when the court determined that he was a free man [Court Record 1715-20, 1034].

    ii.   Samuel[1], head of a Frederick County household of 5 "other free" in 1800 [MD:969] and 5 in 1810 (S. Lewes) [MD:529].

    iii.   Samuel[2], head of an Anne Arundel County household of 9 "other free" in 1810 [MD:69].

    iv.   Hannah, a "m0ulatto" who had an unsuccessful suit against Nathaniel Martin in Baltimore County court in 1772, probably the mother of two-year-old "mulatto" James Lewis who was bound out by the court that year to Stephen Fell [Court Proceedings 1772, 26, 37].

    v.   Abraham, head of a Baltimore County household of 7 "other free" in 1810

[MD:494].
vi. D., head of a Frederick County household of 4 "other free" in 1810 [MD:530].
vii. C., head of a Frederick County household of 3 "other free" in 1810 [MD:554].
viii. R., head of a Baltimore City household of 3 "other free" in 1810 [MD:518].
ix. John, head of a Baltimore City household of 2 "other free" in 1810 [MD:173].

LILES/LYLES FAMILY

1. Elizabeth Liles, born say 1698, came to Maryland from Virginia when she was sixteen years old and had a child by Thomas More in Prince George's County for which she was punished by the court. She was in Baltimore County in June 1728 when she petitioned the court that she was living in the household of Hugh Redgley when and his slave Jack were married by Reverend Jacob Henderson. Redgley mortgaged Jack, Jack was transferred to Hyde Hopton, and she went with Jack to Mr. Hopton's. Jack died and Hopton was then keeping her chikren as slaves. On 6 August 1728 the oourt ordered Hopton to deliver her children to her. Ninian Marriartee agreed to pay her court costs [Court Proceedings, 1728-30, Liber HWS#6: 29-30]. She may have been the ancestor of
   i. James, a "M°ᵗᵗ" taxable in Powhatan County, Virginia, in1799 [PPTL, 1782-1817, frame 186].

Endnote:
1. See Arlene Polk's history of this family on http://freeafricanamericans.com/lyles.htm

LITTLEJOHNS FAMILY

1. Jane Little Johns, born say 1725, was the servant of Joshua Hopkins of St. Peter's Parish in March 1747/8 when the Talbot County court convicted her of having a "Mullatto" child by a "Negro." The court sold her fifteen-month-old daughter Mary to Edward Barwick until the age of thirty-one. She was the servant of Jonathan Shannahan in June 1754 when she admitted in Talbot County court that she had a "Mulatto" child by a "Negroe." The court ordered that she serve her master another twelve months for the trouble of his house and then be sold for seven years [Criminal Record 1747-51, n.p.; 1751-5, n.p.]. She was the mother of
2   i. Mary, born about December 1746.

2. Mary Littlejohn, born about December 1746, confessed in Talbot County court on 10 May 1768 that she had a child by a "Negro" slave. The court sold her for seven years to William Rigon for 4 shillings and sold her "Mulatto" child Francis to Rigon for 3 shillings [Criminal Record 1767-74, n.p.]. She was the mother of
   i. Francis, born about 1768.

LOCKERMAN FAMILY

Members of the Lockerman family were
   i. John, born say 1760, was a "N." head of a St. Jones Hundred, Kent County, Delaware household of 7 "other free" in 1800 [DE:47]. He was married to Angelica by 3 December 1810 when Esther **Sisco** left her and Susan **Durham**, widow of William **Hanser**, 4-1/4 acres and her personal estate by her Kent County will [WB P-1:69]. She may have married, second, a member of the **Hanser** family since she was listed as Angelica **Hanzer** in the 1850 census for Dover Hundred: a 76-year-old "Mulatto" living with 54-year-old "Mulatto" Ann **Cambridge** [DE:348].
   ii. Simon, head of a Kent County, Delaware household of 10 "other free" in

1810 [DE:25].

   iii. David, "F.N." head of a Kent County, Delaware household of 4 "other free" in 1810 [DE:56].

   iv. Jacob, "F.N." head of a Kent County household of 3 "other free" in 1810 [DE:50].

   v. Sidney, born about 1777, obtained a certificate of freedom in Talbot County on 7 October 1813: *a bright Mullatto Woman was born free, and raised in the County afsd. about 36 years of age, 5 feet 4 1/2 inches high* [Certificates of Freedom 1807-15, 90]. She was head of a Wilmington Borough, New Castle County household of 2 "free colored" in 1820 [DE:191].

   vi. ?Adam Lookman, head of a Worcester County household of 5 "other free" in 1800 [MD:820].

   vii. ?James Lockman, F.N. head of a Kent County, Delaware household of 3 "other free" in 1810 [DE:65].

LONGO FAMILY

1.   Anthony Longo, born say 1625, was called Tony Longo "a negro" on 1 February 1647 when the Northampton County, Virginia court ordered him to pay his debt of 384 pounds of tobacco to Francis White. He was taxable on 1 tithe in Northampton County in 1660 [Orders 1657-64, 102]. He was called "Tony Longo Negro" in Northampton County on 28 March 1655 when he was granted a certificate for 250 acres due by (head) rights [DW 1655-68, pt. 1, 11]. Edmund Morgan in *American Slavery - American Freedom* quoted a confrontation that Anthony had with a Northampton County court official as evidence that racism had not yet taken hold on the Eastern Shore in the seventeenth century and how quickly Africans assumed typical English disdain for authority:

   Anthony Longo: What shall I go to Mr. Walkers for: go about your business you idle rascal: I told him I had a warrant for him: shitt of your warrant have I nothing to do but go to Mr. Walker, go about your business you idle rascal as did likewise his wife, with such noise that I could hardly hear my own words, when I had done reading the warrant: stroke at me, and gave me some blows [DW&c 1654-5, 60a].

He was apparently the father of

2   i. James[1], born say 1652.

2.   James[1] Longo, born say 1652, was a tithable head of household in Accomack County from 1676 to 1692 [Orders 1676-78, 32, 58, 1678-82, 17, 101; W&c 1682-97, 192, 228a, 258a]. On 17 May 1681 he purchased 200 acres which had formerly belonged to Colonel Southy Littleton in Accomack County from John Washborn [W&D 1676-90: 261]. He was a delinquent Accomack County militiaman in January 1685. On 20 September 1687 he and Jane Fitzgerald posted bond for Dorothy Bestick, servant of George Nicholas Hack of Pungoteague, who was presented by the court for having an illegitimate child by "George Francis Negro Slave to ye sd Geo Nich Hack." In 1687 Dorothy bound her daughter Sarah to him until the age of eighteen years [W&c 1682-97, 57, 119a, 142a].[21] On 20 September 1687 James was fined 100 pounds of tobacco for assaulting Richard Shulster. Shulster testified that when he passed by James Longo's house on horseback,

---

[21]On 19 February 1690 Dorothy Bestick was presented for having another illegitimate child [W&c 1682-97, 175a, 181a, 187]. Perhaps her descendants were the two John **Bosticks** who were heads of "other free" Kent County, Delaware households in 1810 [DE:185, 188].

James...leaped over his fence furiously...laye hold of ye Deponts. horses bridle...calling the deponent Rogue, Rascall, and severall other scurrilous words over and over againe threatning to beate him and asked me why I did not come to pay him a dayes work...layd his hands on my shoulder in a violent manner...caused great paine.

The next day he brought suit in court against Shulster. He was sued by William Twyford on 20 November 1689 for failing to perform carpentry work which he had contracted for, and on 16 June 1691 the Accomack County court presented him for working on Christmas [W&c 1682-97, 119, 170a; Orders 1690-9, 32]. He was called James Longo "the Molatta" on 21 February 1694 when he was presented by the grand jury for turning a road which passed through his land [Orders 1690-7, 32, 123a, 124a]. On 2 April 1706 he petitioned the Accomack County court to permit him to turn this road. The court gave him permission to do so as long as the new road was as near to or nearer to Pungoteague and was well maintained. The court was not satisfied with the new road, and on 9 October 1707 the justices ordered him to reopen the original road. On 5 May 1708 he posted bond for the illegitimate child he had by Isabel Hutton (a white woman) who was presented by the court on 3 June 1707 for having a "Mulatto Bastard Child." On 5 May 1708 she testified in Accomack County court that James Longo "negro or mullatto" was the father of the child she was pregnant with, and on 5 August the same year she was called "Isabel Hutton who lives at James Longoes" when she was convicted of "having a Bastard Child by a Mulatto." The same court ordered that he be arrested for acting in a contemptuous manner when an officer of the court attempted to serve him with a warrant [Orders 1703-9, 68, 74, 98, 101a, 114, 114a, 122, 125]. He made a 13 August 1729 Accomack will, proved 1 September 1730, by which he left 70 acres of his land to his son James, 70 acres to his daughter Mary **Huten**, and 70 acres to his daughter Elizabeth, and the remainder of his estate to his wife Isabel. His wife and daughters were executrices of the will [Wills 1729-37, pt.1, 101]. His children were

    i. James[2], taxable head of a Mattapony Hundred, Somerset County household in 1727, and head of a household in Wicomico Hundred from 1731 to 1740: taxable on Nathaniel **Morris** from 1737 to 1740 [List of Tithables]. He was called James Longer, carpenter, on 5 June 1733 when he purchased 100 acres called *Pole Hamilton* on the southeast side of the southeast arm of the Rockawakin River in Worcester County for £15 [Land Records:AZ:108]. He was a carpenter living in Somerset County on 14 February 1734/5 when he sold 70 acres in Accomack County on the south side of Revel's Branch for £12 [DW 1729-37, fol. 209]. On 17 June 1735 the Somerset County court bound out Nathaniel **Morris**, orphan son of George **Morris**, to him to make linen and woolen wheels and chairs and to read and write. James was called a wheelwright in November 1737 when he sued blacksmith John Farlo for £7. On 20 March 1738/9 the court allowed him 90 pounds of tobacco for three days testimony in the case of His Lordship against Isaac Saddler, a white man, and granted him a license to keep an ordinary. In March 1740/1 Thomas and William Selby were indicted by the Somerset County court for stealing seven turkeys from him [Judicial Record 1735-7, 14; 1737-8, 152; 1738-40, 75, 110; 1740-2, 92, 96].

    ii. Elizabeth, living in Somerset County on 1 June 1736 when she sold the 70 acres in Accomack County which she received by her father's will for £9 [DW 1729-37, 235] and living in Stepney Parish in March 1737/8 when she confessed to the Somerset County court that she had a child by Richard Jones. James Longo was her security [Judicial Record 1737-8, 208].

    iii. Mary **Hutton**, born about 1708, probably the ancestor of John **Hutton**, head of a Washington, D.C. household of 1 "other free" in 1800 and Sarah **Hutton**, head of a Kent County, Delaware household of 2 "other free" in

1810 [DE:198].

Their Longo descendant was
i. Daniel, "Mulatto" taxable in Little Creek Hundred, Kent County, Delaware, in 1797 and 1798 [Assessments, frames 7, 483].

Other members of a Longo family were
i. John Lango, a "negro" boy with 17 years to serve when he was listed in the 15 September 1674 inventory of the Anne Arundel County estate of Thomas Meeres [Prerogative Court (Inventories and Accounts), 1:67-70].
ii. Ann, born say 1683, a "Mallatta Woman" living at William Smith's who was presented by the Prince George's County court on 28 March 1703/4 for having an illegitimate child. She was called "Ann Congo," servant of William Smith, on 22 August 1704 when he paid her fine [Court Record 1699-1705, 289a, 309a].

McDANIEL/ McDONALD FAMILY

1. Johanna McDaniel/ McDonald, born say 1720, confessed in Dorchester County court in November 1745 that she had an illegitimate "Mollatta" child by a "Negroe" on 10 May 1745. Her unnamed son was bound as an apprentice to Joseph Sherwood until the age of thirty-one [Judgment Record 1744-5, 474]. On 25 March 1751 she was the spinster servant of Henry Fidderman of Queen Anne's County when she confessed to having a child by a "Negroe." The court sold her son Daniel to Thomas Dockey for 16 shillings. She was called Joanna McDonald in June 1753 when she admitted that she had another child named William by a "Negro." He was sold to John Emory for 620 pounds of tobacco. In June 1757 and November 1759 she was convicted of having other children for which she received only a fine [Criminal Record 1751-9, 13-4, n.p.]. She was the mother of
i. Daniel McDaniel, "Free Mulatto" head of a Queen Anne's County household of 2 "other free" and 4 slaves in 1790, called Daniel McDonald, when he was head of a Queen Anne's County household of 10 "other free" in 1800 [MD:355].
ii. William, born about 1753.

Another McDaniel Family:
1. Alice McDaniel, born 18 March 1705, was a twenty-one-year-old "Mallatto Born of a white Woman" who was living in Charles County on 13 August 1728 when the court ordered that she serve John Howard (the highest bidder) to the age of thirty-one. She was presented by the Charles County court for having an illegitimate child on 11 March 1728/9 on information of constable George Thomas [Court Record 1727-31, 153, 229].

MCDONALD FAMILY

1. Grace Macdonald, born say 1670, was listed in the 15 March 1713/4 Charles County inventory of Edmund Howard, Gentleman:

One Irish woman named Grace Marryed to a Negroe man	£5
1 mollatto girl	
said Man & woman &c born in Virg^a before her	
Mother's Intermarriage wth said Negroe }	£10
one D^o boy named Benj^m born since their Marriage	£6
one D^o Girl Alice also borne since Marriage	£11

[Prerogative Court Inventories and Accounts, Vol. 35A, 248-52].
Grace Macdonald was a "poor indigent Woman" who died before 14 June 1720 when the Charles County court allowed Thomas Howard 300 pounds of tobacco for taking care of her during "her long sickness" and burying her. The same court bound her thirteen-year-old "Malatto" daughter Alice to him and his wife

Elizabeth Howard [Court Record 1717-20, 335, 337; 1720-2, 38]. Grace was the mother of

  i. an unnamed "molatto girl," born say 1697 in Virginia.
 ii. Benjamin, born about 1704, a "Mollatto Boy named Benjamin 12 years old" listed in the inventory of the 9 October 1716 Charles County estate of Elizabeth Howard on 9 October 1716 [Prerogative Inventories 1716-1717, 15].
2 iii. Alice, born about 1703.

2.   Alice MacDonald, born about 1703, was a thirteen-year-old "Malatto" girl bound to Thomas and Elizabeth Howard by the Charles County court on 14 June 1720. She may have been the mother of
3   i. Joanne, born say 1733.

3.   Joanne McDonnald, born say 1733, was convicted of having a "Mulatto" child in Queen Anne's County in June 1753 [Criminal Record, n.p., cited by Hodes, *White Women, Black Men*, 220]. She was probably the mother of
   i. Daniel, head of a Queen Anne's County household of 10 "other free" in 1800 [MD:355].
  ii. Charles, head of an Octoraro, Cecil County household of 1 "other free" in 1790.

MADDEN FAMILY

1.   Margaret Madden, born say 1705, the servant of Edward Needles of St. Peter's Parish, was convicted by the Talbot County court in March 1724/5 of having an illegitimate child by a "Negroe." The following year in March 1725/6 she confessed to having another child by Sampson, the slave of Aaron Parrot. In November 1727 she confessed to having another illegitimate child by a "Negroe," and the court bound her daughter Grace to her master until the age of thirty-one. In November 1730 the court sold her to her master for twenty-eight years for four convictions and sold her son Isaac, born 29 May 1730, to her master for 4,000 pounds of tobacco. She was convicted and sold for another term of seven years in June 1733, and was called Margaret Maddin a white woman in June 1742 when the court ordered her to serve a sixth term of seven years and sold her daughter Rose until the age of thirty-one [Judgment Record 1725-6, 64-5, 480-1; 1726 (reverse), 44, 56, 62; 1727-8, 345; 1728-31, 312; 1731-3, 673; 1742, 93-4]. She was the mother of
2   i. Grace, born about 1727.
  ii. Isaac, born 29 May 1730, a "Mulatto" servant for whom Edward Needles posted £40 security in Talbot County in August 1755 for his appearance to answer charges of having a child by a white woman named Rachel Dee. Charles Manslip and Patrick McQuay were Rachel's security. Isaac and Rachel were found guilty and each paid a fine of £1.10 [Criminal Record 1751-5, n.p.; 1755-61, 12-14].
3 iii. Rachel[1], born say 1735.
  iv. Sampson, born about 1738, a fourteen-year-old "Melator" serving until the age of thirty-one when he was listed in the Talbot County estate of Edward Needles on 27 July 1752 [Prerogative Inventories 54:297-300].
4   v. Rose, born say 1742.

2.   Grace Madden, born about 1727, confessed to the Talbot County court in March 1744/5 that she had an illegitimate child for which she received ten lashes. She was called Grace Madden, Junr., in November 1747 when she was ordered to serve Edward Needles for the trouble of his house. In August 1748 the court ordered that she receive 10 lashes for fornication and bound her son John to Edward Needles until the age of twenty-one [Judgment Record 1744-5, 230-1; Criminal Record 1747-50, n.p.]. She was the "Mulatto" servant of Edward

Needles in November 1750 when the court ordered that she serve another seven years for having an illegitimate "Mulatto" child and sold her daughter Sarah to Needles until the age of thirty-one [Criminal Record 1751-5, n.p.]. In March 1752 the Talbot County court convicted her of having two illegitimate "Mullato" children by a "Negroe" slave, ordered her sold for seven years for each offense and sold her daughters Margaret and Elizabeth to Edward Needles until the age of thirty-one. In August 1753 she was convicted of the same offense, and the court sold her son Daniel to Needles until the age of thirty-one for 5 shillings. In November 1755 she had another child by a "Negro," was sold for another seven years, and the court sold her eight-month-old daughter Rachel to Elizabeth Needles for 5 shillings. And she admitted to the same offense in November 1758 and November 1761 when the court sold her daughter Jane to Edward Needles. In November 1770 the court convicted her of having a child by a free person and ordered that she pay a fine of £1.10 for having a child named Levin [Criminal Record 1747-50, n.p.; 1751-5, n.p.; 1755-61, 15-16, 255; 1761-7, 13; 1767-74, n.p.]. She was the mother of

i.   John, born about 1748.
ii. Sarah, born about 1750.
iii. Margaret, born about 1751.
iv. Elizabeth, born about 1752.
v.   Daniel, born about 1753.
vi. Rachel[2], born about March 1755, paid a 60 shilling fine to the Talbot County court in August 1777 for having an illegitimate child and refusing to identify the father. John Needles was security for her maintenance of her daughter Martha [Criminal Record 1775-7, n.p.].
vii. Jane, born about 1761.
viii. Levin, born about 1770, head of a Talbot County household of 4 "other free" and a white woman in 1800 [MD:531].

3.   Rachel[1] Madden, born say 1735, was the spinster "Mulatto" servant of Elizabeth Needles of St. Peter's Parish, Talbot County, in November 1752 when the court convicted her of having a "Mulatto" child by a "Negroe" person. The court ordered her sold for seven years after the completion of her service and sold her son Martin to her mistress for 5 shillings. In June 1755 she was convicted of the same offense, and the court sold her daughter Sarah to William Weathers until the age of thirty-one for 30 shillings. She had another daughter Ruth by a "Negroe" which she admitted to in Talbot County court in November 1756 [Criminal Record 1751-5, n.p.; 1755-61, 70-1]. She was the mother of

i.   Martin, born about September 1752, a four-year-old "Mollatto" boy listed in the Talbot County estate of Elizabeth Needles on 27 June 1756 with 27 years to serve [Prerogative Inventories 63:444], head of a Talbot County household of 1 "other free" and a slave in 1800 [MD:506].
ii. Sarah, born about January 1755, paid a 30 shilling fine to the Talbot County court in June 1780 for having an illegitimate child [Criminal Record 1777, n.p.]. She was the mother of Jeffrey Maddin who registered in Talbot County on 30 April 1807: *a Mulatto Man about 32 years of age...raised in the County...5 feet 7 Inches high & was born of a free Woman called Sarah Maddin* [Certificates of Freedom 1807-27, p.158].
iii. Ruth, born about 1756.

4.   Rose Madden, born say 1742, was a 15-year-old "Mollatto" girl listed in the inventory of the Talbot County estate of Elizabeth Needles on 27 June 1756 with 16 more years to serve [Prerogative Inventories 63:444]. She was the spinster servant of Edward Needles in March 1765 when she admitted in Talbot County court that she had a child by a "Negro." The court sold her son Dick to her master until the age of thirty-one for 7 shillings. She admitted to the same offense in August 1766. The court ordered that she be sold for seven years and sold her son

Jim to Thomas Cannon until the age of thirty-one for 12 shillings. In November 1767 she had another child by a "Negro" slave and the court sold her son Isaac for 1 shilling to John Harding until the age of thirty-one [Criminal Record 1761-7, 334-5, 468; 1767-74, n.p.]. She was the mother of

    i.   Dick, born about 1764.
   ii.   James, born about 1766.
  iii.   Isaac, born about 1767.

They were the ancestors of

    i.   Wm Tiz, born about 1740, an eight-year-old "Melator" serving until the age of twenty one when he was listed in the Talbot County estate of Edward Needles on 27 July 1752 [Prerogative Inventories 54:297-300]. Will was a twelve-year-old "Mollatto" boy bound until the age of twenty one when he was listed in the inventory of the Talbot County estate of Elizabeth Needles on 27 June 1756 [Prerogative Inventories 63:444].
   ii.   John[1], born about 1749, a four-year-old "Melator" serving until the age of twenty-one when he was listed in the inventory of the Talbot County estate of Edward Needles on 27 July 1752 [Prerogative Inventories 54:297-300]. Jack was an eight-year-old "Mollatto" bound until the age of twenty one when he was listed in the inventory of the Talbot County estate of Elizabeth Needles on 27 June 1756 [Prerogative Inventories 63:444].
  iii.   Benjamin, born about 1751, a three-year-old "Melator" serving to the age of twenty-one when he was listed in the inventory of the Talbot County estate of Edward Needles on 27 July 1752 [Prerogative Inventories 54:297-300].
  iv.   Esther, born say 1757, paid a 60 shilling fine to the Talbot County court in November 1777 for having an illegitimate child and refusing to identify the father. George Burgess was security for her maintenance of her daughter Sophia [Criminal Record 1775-7, n.p.].
   v.   Ruth, born say 1758, paid a 30 shilling fine to the Talbot County court in August 1777 for having an illegitimate child. Elizabeth Broadway was security for her maintenance of the child [Criminal Record 1775-7, n.p.].
  vi.   Rebecca Maden, born say 1767, head of a Caroline County household of 5 "other free" in 1790.
5   vii.   John[2], born say 1770.
 viii.   George, born before 1776, head of a Talbot County household of 3 "free colored" in 1830.
  ix.   William, born before 1776, head of a Talbot County household of 2 "free colored" in 1830.
   x.   Jenney, born say 1775, head of a Talbot County household of 3 "other free" in 1800 [MD:536].
  xi.   Toby, born about 1787, registered in Talbot County on 9 September 1815: *a light Black man...about 28 years of age, 5 feet 6 ½ inches high.*
  xii.   John, born about 1788, registered in Talbot County on 28 August 1811: *a black man...about twenty three years of age, five feet Seven Inches and Three quarters...rather of a bright Complexion was born free and that he was raised in the County.*
 xiii.   William[2], born about 1790, registered in Talbot County on 27 July 1813: *born free and raised in the County...about 23 years of age, five feet 4 3/4 inches high of a dark Mullatto Colour* [Certificates of Freedom 1807-15, 13, 53, 72].

5.   John[2] Madan, born say 1770, and his wife, Elizabeth, "free Mulattoes," baptized their children in St. Paul's Parish, Baltimore, on 17 September 1797. John Madden was head of a Baltimore County household of 2 "free colored" in 1830. They were the parents of

    i.   William, born 24 July 1791, baptized 17 September 1797.
   ii.   George, born 5 February 1797, baptized 17 September 1797 [Reamy,

Records of St. Paul's Parish, I:111].

MAGEE FAMILY

1. Fortune Magee, born say 1687, was a servant of Mrs. Mary Day, called "Fortune a Mallatto girl," in March 1698/9 when she was convicted by the Somerset County court of stealing goods from merchant James Maxwell. The court also charged her mistress with encouraging her to steal the goods but found Mrs. Day guilty only of concealing the goods. On 15 June 1705 the court ordered that she serve Mrs. Day until the age of thirty-one, explaining that she was the "mulatto" daughter of Maudlin Magee, a white woman living in Somerset County who was married to George Magee at the time. On 7 March 1710/11 the court presented her for having four illegitimate children: one about seven years old, one five, one three and one three months old. On 8 August 1711 she confessed that Penny, "negroe" servant to Mr. Benjamin Wailer was the father of her child. On 6 August 1712 she bound her children, Ross, Sue, and Perlina to Mrs. Day [Judicial Records 1698-1701, 129, 134, 167; 1702-5, 212, 251; 1707-11, 454; 1711-13, 40, 220]. Fortune was taxable in Baltimore Hundred, Somerset County, in 1735 [List of Tithables]. Her children were

    i.   Rose, born in March 1703, mother of Joe Magee, born 12 March 1722/3, who she bound as an apprentice to Edward Rownd in Somerset County in March 1722/3 until the age of twenty one [Judicial Records 1723-5, 3b].
    ii. Sue Magee alias **Game**, born in April 1705, a "mulatto" woman living in Stepney Parish, Somerset County, from 1741 to 1754 when her "mulatto" children, Belinder, Davey, Jenney, James, and Nelly Magee were born.
    iii. Perlina, born in April 1707, five years old "next April" in August 1712 when she was bound as an apprentice.

Their descendants in Maryland and Delaware were

    i.   Robert McGee, head of an Allegany County household of 7 "other free" in 1800 [MD:3].
    ii. Susannah Megee, head of a Sussex County household of 3 "other free" in 1800 [DE:391].
    iii. Job Mcey, head of a Sussex County household of 4 "other free" in 1810 [DE:384].
    iv. George, born before 1776, head of a Northwest Fork, Sussex County household of 3 "free colored" in 1820 [DE:242].

MAHONEY FAMILY

Patrick and Charles Mahoney won a suit for freedom against their master John Ashton in October 1797 on testimony that the family descended from a "negro" woman named Ann Joice who was carried by her owner to England and then imported to Maryland by Lord Baltimore as a slave about 1680. The parties in the case agreed that she was the mother of William Digges' Sue (a mulatto woman) and four "mulatto" men: David (a carpenter), Frank Herbert, Jack Wood, and Tom Crane.[22] Ownership of Ann Joice and her children passed to Henry Darnall of Anne Arundel County. William Digges' Sue was the mother of Warren's Poll, Hill's Nelly, and Carroll's Sue. Carroll's Sue was the mother of Nelly, who was the mother of Patrick and Charles Mahoney. The Court of Appeals reversed the ruling and found for Ashton in 1802 [Catterall, *Judicial Cases Concerning Slavery*, IV:53-5]. Nelly and Charles may have been identical to Nelly

---

[22]"Negroes" Jack Wood, Davy, and Jack Crane were sentenced to death by the Prince George's County court in July 1770 for murdering a white man named William Elson by cutting his throat with an axe. The court ordered that they have their right hands cut off, that they be hanged by the neck until they were dead, that their heads be severed into four quarters and their remains be set up in the most public place in the county [Court Record 1768-70, 25-6, 589].

Joice, head of an Anne Arundel County household of 1 "free colored" in 1830, and Charles Joice, head of an Anne Arundel County household of 9 "free colored" in 1830. (And a Moses Joice was head of a Baltimore County household of 8 "free colored" in 1830.)

Members of the Mahoney family who were free in Maryland were
1   i.   Patrick, born say 1760.
      ii.   Charles[1], born day 1768, living in Anne Arundel County on 4 May 1801 when John Ashton recorded a deed of manumission to him in Charles County [Land Records IB #6, 118]. He was head of an Anne Arundel County household of 5 "other free" in 1810 (called Charles Mahan) [MD:93]. He was the brother of Gabriel and Barney Mahoney and was living in Washington, D.C., on 16 September 1817 when he and Barney manumitted Gabriel's wife and son [Provine, *District of Columbia Free Negro Registers*, 144].
2   iii.   Gabriel[1], born say 1770.
3   iv.   Barney, born say 1771.
      v.   James, born say 1775, and his wife Teresa, "free Mulattoes," the parents of Charles Mahony, a nine-month-old child baptized on 16 November 1800 at St. Peter's Cathedral in Baltimore [Piet, *Catholic Church Records in Baltimore*, 79].
      vi.   Daniel, born about 1772, a thirty-three-year-old "yellow man" manumitted by John Ashton by deed recorded in Charles County on 13 August 1805 [Land Records IB #6, 418]. He was called Daniel Mahan in 1810, head of an Anne Arundel County household of 8 "other free" [MD:97].
      vii.   Thomas Mahan, head of an Anne Arundel County household of 7 "other free" in 1810 [MD:59].
      viii.   Robert Mahan, head of an Anne Arundel County household of 2 "other free" in 1810 [MD:74].
      ix.   John, head of an Octoraro, Cecil County household of 1 "other free" in 1790.

1.   Patrick Mahoney, born say 1760, was manumitted by John Ashton by deed recorded in Charles County on 4 May 1804 [Land Records IB #6, 117]. He was head of an Anne Arundel County household of 8 "other free" in 1810 [MD:60]. He was the father of
      i.   Gabriel[2], born about 1795, registered in Prince George's County on 5 April 1815: *a bright mulatto youth about 17 years old...was raised in the family of Benjamin Hall and afterwards sold to his father Patrick Mahony, a free man of color, who afterwards manumitted Gabriel* [Provine, *Registrations of Free Negroes*, 18].

2.   Gabriel[1] Mahoney, born say 1770, was head of a St. Mary's County household of 3 "other free" in 1810 [MD:213]. He was manumitted by Walter Leigh on 28 July 1804, and on 12 March 1810 Gabriel purchased his wife Alley and son Charles from William Zachary. He died on 26 December 1815 intestate and did not free his wife or son. His brothers Charles and Barney manumitted Alley (born about 1773) and seven-year-old son Charles on 16 September 1817 [Provine, *District of Columbia Free Negro Registers*, 144]. Gabriel and Alley were the parents of
      i.   Charles[2], born about 1810.

3.   Barney[1] Mahoney, born say 1771, his wife Linda (born about 1773), and their eight children were freed by Osborn Sprigg of Prince George's County on 15 February 1813 [Provine, *District of Columbia Free Negro Registers*, 144]. Barney and Linda were the parents of
      i.   Patsey, born about 1793.
      ii.   Ellen, born about 1797.
      iii.   Ann, born about 1801, registered in Washington on 2 August 1831: *a*

bright mulatto woman about thirty years old.
    iv. Caroline, born about 1803.
    v.   Mary, born about 1804.
    vi. Susan, born about 1807.
    vii. Daniel, born about 1809.
    viii. Barney², born about 1812.

MALAVERY FAMILY

1. Richard Malavery, born say 1695, was taxable in Manokin Hundred of Somerset County in Charles Revell's household in 1725 [List of Tithables, 1725]. He married Dinah **Mongom** (nee **Harmon**?), widow of Philip³ **Mongom**, about 1728 when she was a taxable in his Northampton County, Virginia, household. They were called Richard and Dinah Munlavery in the Northampton County list for 1731 [L.P. 1728-31]. They were probably the parents of
2   i.   Dorcas, born say 1720.
        ii. Thomas, born say 1727, taxable in the household of Isaac Baston in Manokin Hundred, Somerset County, in 1743. He was sued in Somerset County court by Smith Hersey in August 1747 for £13 which he had signed a promissory note for on 11 May 1745. Thomas claimed that he should not have had to pay the note because he had signed it under duress while in prison. The court found in his favor and ordered Hersey to pay him 1,288 pounds of tobacco for his court costs [Judicial Record 1747-9, 17].

2. Dorcas Malavery, born say 1720, was living in Coventry Parish on 20 March 1738/9 when the Somerset County court indicted her for having an illegitimate child. She confessed and named the father Jonas **Miller** who was called "Jonas Hogskin (**Hodgskin**) a "Mallatto" on 19 August 1739 when he confessed and was fined 30 shillings. She was apparently identical to the "mollatto woman Dorcas" named in the Pocomoke Hundred, Somerset County will of Robert Boyer on 27 March 1746 which was proved on 12 April 1746: *To negro man Harry, on my wife's decease, 50 acres and his freedom...To my mollatto woman Dorcas & all her children, on my wife's decease, their freedom & 4 head of good cattle* [Prerogative Court Wills 24:397]. Dorcas sued James Ottley in Somerset County court on 18 August 1747 for detaining her as a servant. She was apparently identical to Dorcas, "wife of Negro Harry," whose "Malatto" children were bound to Ottley by the same court [Judicial Record 1738-40, 74, 128, 171; 1747-49, 6, 10]. She was called Darkes Melavery when she was taxable in Pocomoke Hundred in 1749 and 1750 [List of Tithables, 1749, 1750] and called Dorcas Malavery in August 1750 when she petitioned the court that Ottley had sold one of her children to someone in Accomack County and was mistreating the other two. The case was dismissed with each party paying their own costs [Judicial Record 1749-51, 178]. The children of "Negro Harry and his wife Dorcas" were
        i.   David, born in November 1739, "Malatto son of Negro Harry and Dorcas his wife," eight years old when he was bound as an apprentice to James Ottley on 18 August 1747.
        ii. Harry, born in November 1741, six years old when he was bound to James Ottley.
        iii. Elijah, born in October 1745, two years old when he was bound to James Ottley.

MALLORY FAMILY

1. Elizabeth Murrely, born say 1682, the servant of Robert Tyler, was convicted by the Prince George's County court on 26 November 1700 of having an illegitimate "Malatta" child by a "Negro Man." The court ordered that she be sold for seven years at the expiration of her indenture. She was called "Elizabeth Mallary Servant

to Robert Tyler" on 25 November 1702 when the court ordered that she serve him 12 months for the trouble of his house in having a "Malatta" child. She was called "Elizabeth Mallary Late Servant to Mr. Robert Tyler" on 28 March 1703/4 when the court sold her for seven years to Abraham Clark who promised that "she shall not work in the Grounds" [Court Record 1699-1705, 80a, 215, 289a]. She may have been the ancestor of

   i. Aggy Mallery, head of a Richmond City, Virginia household of 3 "other free" in 1810 [VA:374].

MARSHALL FAMILY

1. William Marshall, born say 1720, a white planter, married Anne **Perle**, a "Mulatto" woman, in Prince George's County before 23 August 1743 when the court ordered that he be sold for seven years. He was ordered to be released from prison so the case could be tried at the Provincial Court [Court Record 1743-4, 17]. He may have been the ancestor of

   i. Tom, head of a New Castle County, Delaware household of 8 "other free" in 1800 [MD:269].

   ii. Clement, head of a Prince George's County household of 5 "other free" and 4 slaves in 1810 [MD:78].

   iii. William, head of a New Castle County household of 7 "other free" in 1810 [DE:301], perhaps the husband of Lucy Marshall, head of a Milford, Kent County, Delaware household of 3 "free colored" in 1820 [DE:86].

   iv. John, born say 1770, married to Susanna, "free negroes," when they registered the birth and baptism of their daughter Mary in St. Paul's Parish, Baltimore: *born 31 December 1792, baptized 3 March 1793* [Reamy, *Records of St. Paul's Parish*, I:64].

   v. Isaac, head of an Accomack County household of 9 "other free" in 1810 [VA:113].

MASON FAMILY

Members of the Mason family in Maryland were

   i. Benjamin, born say 1735, a "free Nigroe" who owed 4 shillings to the St. Mary's County estate of Richard Farris about 1760 [Prerogative Inventories 71:150-2] and was "a Mulatto fellow born at the mouth of the Patuxent" who was among three sailors who ran away from the ship *Dragon* according to an advertisement placed by their captain in the 6 August 1761 issue of the *Maryland Gazette* [Green, *The Maryland Gazette 1727-61*, 271]. He was a "blk." head of a St. Mary's County household of 4 "other free" in 1810 [MD:208].

   ii. Henny, head of a St. Mary's County household of 13 "other free" in 1790 and 15 in 1800 [MD:420].

   iii. Milly[1], born say 1755, mother of Ann **Lawrence** who registered in St. Mary's County on 29 April 1822: *daughter of Milly Mason, about 45 years of age...light complexion.*

   iv. Joseph, head of a St. Mary's County household of 6 "other free" in 1790, 5 in 1800 [MD:392] and 7 in 1810 [MD:208].

   v. Dinah, head of a Queen Anne's County household of 6 "other free" in 1790 [MD:99].

   vi. Drady, born about 1765.

   vii. Elizabeth[1], head of a St. Mary's County household of 4 "other free" in 1790.

   viii. Chester, "Negro" head of a Kent County household of 3 "other free" and a slave in 1790 [MD:82].

   ix. Henry, born about 1778, a "blk." head of a St. Mary's County household of 6 "other free" in 1810 [MD:221]. He registered in St. Mary's County on 12 November 1813: *thirty five years...complexion yellow, hair short and woolly...born free.*

- x. Milly, born about 1781, registered in St. Mary's County in August 1807: *about twenty six years of age, yellow complexion, was free born.*
- xi. John, born about 1783, registered in St. Mary's County on 23 November 1813: *aged thirty years...Complexion Copper, hair short & woolly...born free.*
- xii. Elizabeth[2], born about 1787, registered in St. Mary's County on 5 August 1807: *about twenty years of age, yellow complexion, was born free.* She was head of a St. Mary's County household of 1 "other free" in 1810 [MD:215].
- xiii. Matthew, born about 1789, registered in St. Mary's County on 12 March 1810: *aged twenty one years or thereabouts...Complexion not being black, hair short...born free.*
- xiv. Priscilla, born about 1790, registered in St. Mary's County on 21 August 1809: *aged nineteen years or thereabouts...born free.*
- xv. Rebecca, born about 1791, registered in St. Mary's County on 24 August 1809: *eighteen years...complexion yellow - hair streight...born free* [Certificates of Freedom 1806-64, 1, 2, 7, 8, 24, 59].

1. Drady Mason, born about 1765, was a "blk." head of a St. Mary's County household of 5 "other free" in 1810 [MD:222]. She registered in St. Mary's County on 2 August 1814: *aged forty nine years or thereabouts...Complexion bright yellow - hair short & Curley...born free* [Certificates of Freedom 1806-64, 28]. She was the mother of
   - i. James, born about 1789, registered in St. Mary's County on 17 August 1809: *aged 20 years or thereabouts...Complexion rather dark, hair short & nappy...son of a free born woman named Drayten Mason.*
   - ii. Perry, born about 1802, registered in St. Mary's County on 13 July 1824: *son of Drady Mason, about 22 years old, bright complexion...born free.*
   - iii. Harry[2], born about 1802, registered in St. Mary's County on 13 July 1823: *son of Drady Mason, aged 21 years...dark complexion* [Certificates of Freedom 1806-64, 7, 65, 66].

MASSEY FAMILY

Members of the Massey family in Maryland were
- i. Ame, head of a Queen Anne's County household of 2 "other free" in 1790.
- ii. Thomas, head of a Queen Anne's County household of 6 "other free" in 1800 [MD:357].
- iii. John, head of a Kent County household of 4 "other free" in 1800 [MD:151].
- iv. Abraham, head of a Kent County household of 4 "other free" in 1800 [MD:163].
- v. David, head of a Kent Count household of 2 "other free" in 1800 [MD:151].
- 1   vi. Henny, born say 1780, living in St. Mary's County on 3 November 1819 when her son Alexander registered: *son of Henny...about seventeen of a very bright complexion...born free and was borned and raised in Saint Mary's County* [Certificates of Freedom 1806-64, 53].

MATTHEWS FAMILY

Members of the Matthews family were
- i. Nicholas, head of an Anne Arundel County household of 9 "other free" in 1790.
- ii. Edward, head of a Philadelphia County, Pennsylvania household of 5 "other free" in 1790.
- 1   iii. Catherine, born about 1771.

iv. George, head of a Charles County household of 4 "other free" in 1800 [MD:561].
v. Susana, head of a Frederick County household of 3 "other free" in 1800 [MD:909].

1. Catherine Matthews, born about 1771, registered in Prince George's County on 28 July 1826: *a black woman, about 55 years old, and 5 feet 5 inches tall...born free in Prince George's County*. She was the mother of
    i. Mary **Peal**, born about 1796, registered in Prince George's County between 24 September and 15 October 1827: *a black woman, about 31 years old, and 5 feet 3-1/2 inches tall...daughter of Catherine Matthews*. Her daughter Frances **Bacon** registered the same day: *a black woman about 17 years old, 5 feet 2-1/4 inches tall...daughter of Mary Peal*.
    ii. Henny, born about 1802, registered on 28 July 1826: *a dark mulatto woman, about 24 years old, and 5 feet 1-1/2 inches tall...born free...daughter of Catherine Matthews*.
    iii. Rezin, born about 1804, registered on 29 July 1826: *a black man, about 22 years old, and 5 feet 7 inches tall...son of Catherine Matthews* [Provine, *Registrations of Free Negroes*, 58].

MAYHEW/ MAYHALL FAMILY

1. Thomas[1] Mayhew, born say 1708, may have been identical to "1 Indian Man Named Tom" who was valued at £32 and listed among the slaves of the Honorable Thomas Addison, Esquire, deceased, on 10 August 1727 when his widow Eleanor Addison brought the estate to an appraisement in Prince George's County [Prerogative Court Inventories 1727-9, 12:295-313]. Thomas India petitioned the Prince George's County court in March 1729 that he was free born, baptized in England, and imported with his mother into Maryland under indenture. However, he was detained as a slave by Madam Eleanor Addison [Court Record 1728-9, 413]. He was probably the father of
    i. Thomas[2], born say 1735.

2. Thomas[2] Mayhew, born say 1735, escaped from the Prince George's County jail according to the 29 May 1760 issue of the *Maryland Gazette*. He was described as "of a very dark Complexion, his Father being an East-India Indian...formerly lived in lower Prince George's County" [Green, *The Maryland Gazette, 1727-61*, 246]. He may have been the father of
    i. Robert Mayhall, "Mulatto" head of a Charles County household of 9 "other free" in 1790.

MEAD FAMILY

Members of the Mead family in Maryland and Pennsylvania were
1   i. Lucy, born say 1750.
    ii. Primus, born say 1760, head of a Delaware County, Pennsylvania household of 3 "other free" in 1790.

1. Lucy Mead, born say 1750, was head of a Baltimore City household of 5 "other free" in 1800 [MD:278]. She may have been the mother of
2   i. Jeffrey, born say 1773.

2. Jeffrey Mead, born say 1773, and his wife Phoebe registered the birth and baptism of their daughter Mary Anne in St. Paul's Parish, Baltimore. Their daughter was
    i. Mary Anne, born 1 April, baptized 17 April 1796 [Reamy, *Records of St. Paul's Parish*, I:96].

MILLER FAMILY

Somerset County
1. Susannah Miller, born say 1684, was presented by the Somerset County court on 13 March 1704/5 for having an illegitimate "Mallato" child, William Hickman informer [Judicial Record 1702-5, 212].

Delaware
1. Jacob Miller, born say 1705, was taxable in Little Creek Hundred, Kent County, Delaware, in 1727, taxable in Murderkill Hundred from 1735 to 1738 when he was identified as a "Negro," and taxable in Dover Hundred from 1756 to 1765. He sued Tabitha **Francisco** in Kent County in August 1731 [RG 3815.031, Common Pleas, Dockets 1722-1732, frame 509]. He was called Jacob Miller (Negro) in Kent County court when John Holliday sued him for debt in November 1737 and on 26 February 1747 when he admitted in court that he owed Robert Willcocks £27 [RG 3815.031, Common Pleas, Dockets 1733-1740, frames 347, 358; 1744-50, 388]. He may have been the ancestor of

   i.   Aaron, born say 1745, a "Negro" taxable in Murderkill Hundred, Kent County, in 1766, in Little Creek Hundred in 1772 and 1774, in Murderkill Hundred in 1778, Dover Hundred in 1779 and 1780, a "Free Negro" in Murderkill Hundred in 1782, in Little Creek Hundred in 1783, in Murderkill Hundred in 1784 and 1785, a "free Negro" taxable in Dover Hundred in 1788, 1794 and 1797 [DSA, RG 3535, 1743-67, frame 543; 1768-84, frames 129, 222, 346, 364, 429, 452, 550, 575, 598, 629; 1785-97, frames 13, 28, 111, 310, 399], head of a Kent County household of 10 "other free" in 1800 [DE:50].

   ii. Rike/ Right/ Rake, born say 1747, confessed to the Kent County court in November 1771 that he had an illegitimate female child by Elizabeth **Beckett** about July 1769, before she married Jacob **Gibbs** [DSA, RG 3805, MS, indictments]. He was taxable in Dover Hundred in 1768, called a "Free Negro" there in 1780, a Murderkill Hundred delinquent in 1780, a Dover Hundred taxable in 1780 and 1781 [DSA, RG 3535, 1768-84, frames 11, 108, 429, 432, 449, 452, 500]. He may have been identical to Drake Miller who was taxable in Dagsboro Hundred, Sussex County, in 1796, in a non-alphabetized list with Deberix and Isaac Miller in 1796 [RG 2535, 1780-96]. He was counted as white in Dagsboro Hundred in 1800 (age 26-45) and head of a Dagsboro, Sussex County household of 7 "free colored" in 1820 (over 45) [DE:374]. On 11 December 1814 Drake and his wife Polly sold 27 acres of their land in Dagsboro Hundred near Folly Road which led from Salisbury to Indian River [DB 32:98].

   iii. Debricks/ Debrix[1], born say 1750, taxable in Little Creek Hundred, Kent County, from 1777 to 1784: listed as a "Negro" starting in 1782 [RG 3535, Kent County Levy List, 1767-84, frames 310, 335, 341, 367, 369, 443, 503, 531, 542, 570, 583, 620], taxable in Little Creek Hundred, Sussex County, on 2 horses, a cow and a heifer in 1796 and head of a Sussex County household of 7 "other free" in 1810 [DE:307].

   iv. Isaac, a taxable "Negro" in Little Creek Hundred, Kent County, from 1779 to 1784, taxable on 81 acres in Little Creek Hundred, Sussex County, in 1796 [DSA, RG 2535, 1768-84, frames 367, 369, 443, 446, 503, 542, 570, 583, 620]. He was head of a Little Creek Hundred, Sussex County household of 7 "other free" in 1800 [DE:375], 4 whites (a male 26-45) and 3 "other free" in 1810 [DE:451] and 5 "free colored" in 1820 [DE:274]. He patented 81 acres in Sussex County called *Green Glade* on 14 December 1797 and sold this land for $200 on 18 September 1805 [DB AB:140].

   v.   John, a taxable "Negro" in Dover Hundred from 1770 to 1773.

   vi. Peter, a taxable "Negro" in Little Creek Hundred, Kent County, from 1777 to 1797, head of a Little Creek Neck, Kent County household of 4 "other free" in 1800 [DE:35] and 3 in Sussex County in 1810 [DE:435].

   vii. Haste, head of a Little Creek Hundred, Sussex County household of 6 "other free" in 1810 [DE:307].

  viii. Deberox[2], born 1776-1794, head of a Duck Creek Hundred, Kent County household of 7 "free colored" in 1820 [DE:49]. He left a 5 April 1841 Duck Creek Hundred will, proved 22 April 1841, which named his wife Sarah, children Josiah, Elijah, Enoch, Robert, and Rachel; and grandchildren Rachel and John **Hews**, children of his daughter Maria [WB R:197].

   ix. Charles, a taxable "Negro" in Jones Hundred, Kent County in 1780, head of a Dover Hundred household of 4 "free colored" in 1820 [DE:41].

Queen Anne's County

1.   Eliza Miller, born say 1750, pleaded guilty to "Mulatto Bastardy" in November 1770 in Queen Anne's County court. The court sold her daughter Mary for thirty-one years to M. Joshua Calk for 111 pounds of tobacco [Surles, *and they Appeared in Court, 1770-1772*, 14]. She was the mother of

    i. Mary, born say 1770.

   ii. ?John, head of a Queen Anne's County household of 9 "other free" in 1810 [MD:149].

   iii. ?Peter, head of a Queen Anne's County household of 4 "other free" in 1810 [MD:151].

MITCHELL FAMILY

1.   Anne Mitchell, born say 1705, the servant of John Edmondson of St. Peter's Parish, confessed to the Talbot County court in March 1724/5 that she had an illegitimate child by a "Negroe." In November 1725 the court sold her daughter Esther to her master until the age of thirty-one. She was convicted of having a second mixed-race child in March 1726/7. In March 1727/8 the court sold her to her master for fourteen years. In March 1730/1 she was fined 600 pounds of tobacco for having a child by Benjamin **Guy** alias **Williams**. Benjamin was ordered to serve Edmonson for one year to pay for their fines. She was fined for fornication again in March 1732/3 [Judgment Record 1723-4, 277; 1724, 38; 1725-6, 73-4; 1727-8, 23, 454; 1728-31, 349; 1731-3, 631]. She was the mother of

    i. Esther, born before 3 March 1723/4, bound to serve John Edmondson in November 1725 until the age of thirty-one. In November 1741 she was called a spinster "Mulatto" woman of St. Peter's Parish when she confessed to the Talbot County court that she had two illegitimate children and paid a 30 shillings fine for each [Judgment Record 1740-2, 318-9].

MOLUCK FAMILY

Members of the Moluck family in Dorchester County were

    i. Jimmimey Molix, a Black Man," head of a household of 5 "Negroes" in Transquakin Hundred in 1776 [Carothers, *1776 Census of Maryland*, 50].

   ii. Roger, head of a Dorchester County household of 6 "other free" in 1790.

   iii. Moses, head of a Dorchester County household of 3 "other free" and a white woman in 1790.

   iv. Isaac, purchased his wife Moriah and son Isaac from Reubin Wittgot by Dorchester County deed on 13 May 1810 for £25 and set them free [Land Records HD 17:177-9]. He was head of a Dorchester County household of 3 "free colored" in 1830.

   v. John, a "Negro" man purchased by George Ward from Levin Traverse for the purpose of manumitting him on 16 July 1792. On 29 July 1801 Peter Ferguson and John Reid sold John Molock a horse and colt, cow and calf, five sheep, eight hogs, a blacksmith bellows, anvil, vice, three pair of tongs and five hammers for £20 [Land Records HD 3:493; 26:383].

vi. Rhody, purchased her husband Isaac Molluck from John Watson by Dorchester County deed for $1 on 26 January 1814 and set him free the same day [Land Records ER-2:627-8].

vii. Polly, born about 1792, registered in Dorchester County on 22 May 1810: *a Mulatto Girl about eighteen years of age...with straight hair, was born free and raised in Dorchester County* [Certificates of Freedom for Negroes 1806-64, 12].

MONGOM/MONGON FAMILY

1. Philip[1] Mongom, born say 1625, was the slave of Captain William Hawley who claimed him as a headright in 1646 in Northampton County court [DW 1645-51, 39 by Deal, *Race and Class*, 383-93]. In 1645 he was whipped in court for entertaining and concealing Sibble Ford, a runaway English maidservant [DW 1645-51, fol.2]. He and Mingo **Mathews** were slaves hired out by Hawley to John Foster who complained that

> the Negros which hee had of Capt. William Hawley were very stubborne and would not followe his business.

In 1649 Hawley made an agreement with them that they would be free upon payment of 1700 pounds of tobacco or one white servant [DW 1654-55, fol.25, 54]. However, there is some evidence to suggest that they were freed not by this payment but by warning the local English population of an Indian plot to poison their wells in July 1650 [DW 1645-51, fol.217]. In 1651 he arranged to marry Martha Merris, an English widow, signing a deed of jointure with her to reserve her property for herself and her children [DW 1651-54, 33, fol.33]. In May 1660 he was acquitted of stealing hogs but was fined 100 pounds of tobacco for throwing some hogs ears on the table where the justices were sitting [Orders 1657-64, 68]. In 1663 he was fined for having an illegitimate child by Margery Tyer, a white woman [Orders 1657-64, fol.173, 175]. In 1666 he recorded his livestock mark in court [DW 1651-54, at end of volume, 6]. Philip was a taxable head of a Northampton County household in 1664 and was taxable with his then wife Mary (a free African American) from 1665 to 1677 [Orders 1657-64, 198; 1674-79, 190]. He and two white men, Edward Parkinson and Peter DuParks, were renting 300 acres on the bay side on Mattawaman Creek from John Savage when he made his 26 August 1678 will, and in 1680 he leased 200 acres near the Pocomoke River by the Maryland-Virginia border [Orders 1674-9, 316; 1678-83, 151; Whitelaw, *Virginia's Eastern Shore*, I:228; II:1216]. On 20 August 1678 Canutus Benne/ Bents confessed in Accomack County court to owing him 555 pounds of tobacco [Orders 1678-82, 7]. On 29 January 1684/5 he submitted to the court that he had notoriously abused and defamed his most loving friends and neighbors John Duparkes and Robert Jarvis. In November 1687 a group of his white neighbors gathered at his house with him, his wife Mary, and his son Philip, Jr. After much "drinkinge and carrousinge," his guests began beating one of the white members of the group, and Philip and his wife and son joined in the melee. The fight broke up when Philip threatened one of them with his gun. They were all fined 500 pounds of tobacco in Northampton County court [OW 1683-89, 118-9, 320-322]. He was last mentioned in the court record of 30 September 1691: "Phillip the Negro planter" [DW&c 1680-92, 306]. He was the father of

2 i. Philip[2], born say 1659.

2. Philip[2] Mongom, born say 1659, rented 200 acres in Accomack County near Guilford Creek from John Parker on 18 January 1679/80 (called Philip Mongon) [WD 1676-90, 185-6]. He and his wife Mary died before 15 June 1700 when their estate, consisting of livestock, household goods, and a sword, was sold to pay their creditors [DW&c 1692-1707, 262; OW&c 1698-1710, 44]. Their children

were
i. Philip[3], born about 1690, the twelve or thirteen year-old "Negro" son of Philip Mongom bound by the Northampton County court to his grandmother Mary Mongom until the age of twenty-one on 1 March 1702/3 [OW&c 1698-1710, 126-7]. He was granted administration on the estate of William **Harmon** on 12 January 1725/6 when William's orphans Edward and Jane **Harmon** chose him as their guardian [Orders 1722-9, 225]. He was taxable in Abraham Bowker's household in 1723, head of his own household in 1726 with Edmund and Jean **Harmon**, and taxable with his wife Dinah Mongon and (her sister?) Jane **Harmon** in 1727 [Bell, *Northampton County Tithables*, 102, 119]. He made a 5 January 1727/8 will, proved a few days later on 9 January, by which he left all his estate and a "Negro girl named Jane Harman" until she arrived at lawful age to his wife Dinah [WD 1725-33, 102, 106]. Dinah was head of a household in 1728 with Jean **Harmon**. Dinah married Richard **Malavery/Munlavery** about a year later. In one list for 1729 she was called Dinah Mongom when she and Jean **Harmon** were in Richard ___ ery's household, and in another list for 1729 she was called Dinah **Malavery** when she and Jane were tithable in Richard **Malavery**'s household. Richard and Dinah were tithables in 1731 but were not taxed again in any of the surviving lists [Bell, *Northampton County Tithables*, 169, 201, 221]. They probably moved to Somerset County, Maryland where Thomas **Malavery** was a taxable in 1743 [List of Taxable Persons].
ii. Mary, born about 1691, daughter of Philip Mongom, twelve years old on 29 December 1702 when she consented to her indenture to George Corbin in Northampton County court on 29 January 1704/5. And she consented to her indenture on 29 January 1704/5 to Thomas Roberts who obliged himself to give her a two-year-old heifer and new clothing when she came of age [OW&c 1698-1710, 122, 215]. She was tithable in Thomas Savage's household in 1724 [Bell, *Northampton County Tithables*, 66] and was presented by the grand jury of Northampton County on 11 May 1725 for having a bastard child. On 12 August 1725 the court excused Captain Thomas Savage from paying her fine because he had given due notice that she was out of the county [Orders 1722-29, 181, 189, 202, 387].
iii. Jane, born about 1693, the nine-year-old "Negro" daughter of Philip Mongom, "free Negro," deceased, bound as an apprentice to George Corbin at her own request on 29 December 1702 [OW&c 1698-1710, 122].
iv. Esther, born say 1698, chose her guardian in Northampton County court in 1714 [Orders 1711-16, 155]. She was tithable in John and Henry Smaw's households from 1724 to 1727, in the household of Jean **Left (Webb)** in 1729, and in Thomas **Drighouse**'s household in 1731. She probably married Henry **Stephens**, Thomas **Drighouse**'s neighbor, the Esther **Stephens** tithable in Henry's household from 1737 to 1744 [Bell, *Northampton County Tithables*, 72, 103, 119, 167, 226, 266].

MONK FAMILY

Members of the Monk family in Maryland were
i. Bennet, born say 1738, a "molato" boy bound to Absolom Kent until the age of twenty-one on 21 April 1745 when Kent gave Bennet to his wife by his Calvert County will, proved 27 May 1745 [Prerogative Wills 24:113].
ii. Jane, "Mulatto" head of a Charles County household of 4 "other free" in 1790.
iii. Edward, head of a Montgomery County household of 4 "other free" in 1790.
iv. William, "Negro" head of a Kent County household of 3 "other free" in

1790.

    v.   Peter, born before 1776, head of a Dorchester County household of 4 "free colored" in 1830.

   vi.   Elizabeth, born say 1785, mother of Ann Monk who registered in St. Mary's County on 6 August 1822: *daughter of Eliz. Monk...aged about 16 years, of a light complexion...born free...in Saint Mary's County* [Certificates of Freedom 1806-64, 60].

MOODY FAMILY

1.   Elizabeth Moody, born say 1755, was indicted by the Kent County, Maryland court for "Mulatto Bastardy" in March 1775, November 1775, and August 1776 [Criminal Dockets, March 1775 presentments, no. 5]. She may have been the mother of

    i.   James, head of a Kent County household of 5 "other free" in 1800 [MD:151] and 5 in 1810 [MD:904].

MOORE FAMILY

Members of the Moore family in Maryland were

    i.   Daniel, "Negro" head of a Kent County household of 5 "other free" in 1790 and 3 in 1800 [MD:151].

   ii.   Daniel, Jr., head of a Kent County household of 4 "other free" in 1800 [MD:152].

  iii.   John, head of an Octoraro, Cecil County household of 4 "other free" in 1790.

   iv.   William, head of a Baltimore City household of 9 "other free" in 1800 [MD:284].

    v.   Richard, head of a Kent County household of 6 "other free" in 1800 [MD:151].

   vi.   Hannibal, head of a Talbot County household of 5 "other free" in 1800 [MD:521].

1   vii.   Peggy, born about 1758.

2 viii.   Levi, born say 1770.

1.   Peggy Moore, born about 1758, obtained a certificate of freedom for herself and son Joseph Moore in Washington, D.C., 19 April 1808: *a colored woman named Indian Peg, who now calls herself Peggy Moore...upwards of fifty years old.* She testified that her son Joseph was born in Charles County where she lived from her childhood. Joseph was brought up by Thomas Gilpin [Provine, *District of Columbia Free Negro Registers*, 224]. Peggy was the mother of

    i.   Joseph, born in October 1779, perhaps the Joseph Moore who was being held as a slave by William Hepburn before 21 August 1786 when the Fairfax County, Virginia court ordered him discharged because he was born of free parents [Orders 1783-8, 254].

2.   Levi Moore, born say 1770, was head of a Dorchester County household of 5 "other free" in 1800 [MD:732]. He was the father of

    i.   Nancy, born about 1795, registered in Dorchester County on 13 August 1811: *of a copper colour...born free, raised in Dorchester County, Daughter of Levi Moore aged about 16 years on information of Levi Moore.*

   ii.   Matilda, born about 1799, registered in Dorchester County on 18 April 1816: *dark chesnut colour...born free...daughter of Levi Moore aged about 17 years information of Levi Moore.*

  iii.   Kitty, born about 1801, registered in Dorchester County on 18 April 1816: *dark chesnut colour...born free...daughter of Levi Moore aged about 15 years information of Levi Moore* [Certificates of Freedom for Negroes

1806-64, 17].

MORGAN FAMILY

1. Jane Morgan, born say 1750, was presented by the Queen Anne's County court for "Mulatto Bastardy" in March 1770 but struck off the docket in November 1771 [Surles, *And they Appeared at Court 1770-1772*, 9, 44]. She may have been related to
    i.   Thomas, head of a Kent County household of 5 "other free" in 1800 [MD:164].
    ii. Rose, head of a Kent County household of 5 "other free" and a slave in 1800 [MD:152].

Members of the Morgan family of St. Mary's County were
    i.   Jane, head of a household of 5 "other free" in 1790.
    ii. James, head of a household of 5 "other free" in 1790 and 5 in 1800 [MD:419].
    iii. Susanna, head of a household of 2 "other free" in 1790.
    iv. William, born about 1785, registered in St. Mary's County on 19 June 1809: *aged twenty four years or thereabouts...complexion Yellowish, hair short...raised in the County aforesaid and was born free.*
    v.   Gustavus, born about 1795, registered in St. Mary's County on 12 March 1819: *son of Eleanor Morgan, aged twenty four years...born free* [Certificates of Freedom 1806-64, 5, 45].

Other members of the family in Maryland were
    i.   Samuel, head of a Baltimore City household of 5 "other free" in 1800 [MD:310].

MORRIS FAMILY

Members of the Morris family in Maryland and Delaware may have been related to "Mallatto" William Morris who was accused in Accomack County court on 6 December 1704 of threatening someone with a gun [Orders 1703-9, 38, 42a]. Members of the Morris family in Maryland and Delaware were
1   i.   Nathaniel, born in October 1720.
2   ii. Elizabeth[1], born about 1726.
       iii. Thomas, born say 1728, a "mulato" taxable in Nanticoke Hundred of Somerset County in 1748 [List of Tithables, 1748].

1. Nathaniel[1] Morris, born in October 1720, orphan son of George Morris, was bound by the Somerset County court as an apprentice to James **Longo** to make linen and woolen wheels and chairs and to read and write on 17 June 1735 [Judicial Record 1735-7, 14]. He was taxable in the household of James **Longo** in Wicomico Hundred, Somerset County, from 1736 to 1740. He was also listed in his own household with wife Eliza in 1740 [List of Tithables]. He registered the birth of his son, Levi, in St. George's Protestant Episcopal Church, Sussex County, on 17 January 1747/8 [Wright, *Vital Records of Kent and Sussex Counties*, 93]. He may have been the Nathaniel Morres who owed the Worcester County estate of Peter **Beckett** 12 shillings on 23 January 1754 [Prerogative Inventories 60:89]. He was taxable in Broadkill Hundred, Sussex County, from 1770 to 1774. He was the father of
3   i.   Levi[1], born 17 January 1747/8.
       ii. Elizabeth[3], born say 1752, married Thomas **Clerk** (**Clark**) ("Mustees, free"), 1 July 1773 in Lewes and Coolspring Presbyterian Church [Records of the United Presbyterian Churches of Lewes, Indian River and Cool Spring, Delaware, 1756-1855, 286].

2.   Elizabeth[1] Morris, born about 1726, was a "Molatto Girle" aged twelve years old, bound until the age of twenty-one, and valued at £18 in the 25 July 1738 Talbot County estate of John Vickers [Prerogative Court Inventories 1737-9, 23:488]. She may have been the mother of

    i.   John, head of a Queen Anne's County household of 8 "other free" in 1790.

    ii.   Elizabeth[2], born say 1750, presented by the Queen Anne's County court in March 1770 for having an illegitimate child by a "negro." She was sold for seven years and her daughter Jane, born 7 January 1770, was sold for thirty-one years to William Robinson for a total of 2,600 pounds of tobacco [Surles, *And they Appeared at Court 1770-1772*, 5].

3.   Levi[1] Morris, born 17 January 1747/8, married Sarah **Hanzer** in September 1768 in Sussex County [Records of the United Presbyterian Churches of Lewes, Indian River and Cool Spring, Delaware 1756-1855, 279]. He was a delinquent taxable in Sussex County in 1767, a delinquent taxable in Lewes and Rehoboth Hundred, Sussex County, in 1787, head of an Indian River, Sussex County household of 4 "other free" in 1800 [DE:438] and 5 in 1810 [DE:456]. The Sussex County court fined him six pence for assault in February 1773 [RG 4805, General Sessions, 1767-1794, frame 132]. He may have been the father of

    i.   Nathaniel[2], born say 1775, married Alice **Handsor**, "Two free Mulatoes," on 24 December 1799 in Sussex County, and second, Sarah **Cornish**, "free Mulattoes," on 5 December 1802 [Records of the United Presbyterian Churches of Lewes, Indian River and Cool Spring, Delaware 1756-1855, 315, 318]. He was head of an Indian River, Sussex County household of 2 "other free" in 1800 [DE:438] and 8 "free colored" in 1820 [DE:220].

    ii.   Nancy, married Abel **Jacobs**, "free Mulattoes," on 18 April 1802 in Sussex County [Records of the United Presbyterian Churches of Lewes, Indian River and Cool Spring, Delaware 1756-1855, 310, 318].

    iii.   Levy[2], born 1776-1794, married ___ **Okey** in May 1805 and second, Eunice **Johnson**, "Mulattoes," on 19 December 1810 in Sussex County [Records of the United Presbyterian Churches of Lewes, Indian River and Cool Spring, Delaware 1756-1855, 322]. He was head of an Indian River, Sussex County household of 3 "other free" in 1810 [DE:416] and 5 "free colored" in 1820 [DE:208].

    iv.   Simon, head of an Indian River, Sussex County household of 3 "other free" in 1800 [DE:308].

    v.   Isaac, head of an Indian River, Sussex County household of 4 "free colored" in 1820 [DE:214].

    vi.   Minty, born before 1776, head of a Worcester County household of 9 "free colored" in 1830.

    vii.   Gabriel, born before 1776, head of a Worcester County household of 7 "free colored" in 1830.

MOLTON/MORTON FAMILY

1,   Samuel Molton, born say 1720, was a "molatto" belonging to John Welsh of Prince George's County on 24 February 1748 when Welsh directed that he be free after the death of his wife [Prerogative Court (Wills), Liber 26, folio 40]. He was apparently identical to Samuel Morton who married Molly, the sister of Benjamin **Banneker**. On 27 February 1758 Mary Welsh of Prince George's County made a deed of release to Mary **Banicker** (Samuel's mother-in-law) for a "Mealato Servant Samuell Morter" [Land Records, PP:104]. This was equivalent to a certificate of freedom for Samuel. Samuel Morton was taxable in Upper Patapsco Hundred of Baltimore County on his own tithe and Greenberry Moreton's tithe in 1773 [MSA, C428-51, 1773 Tax List] and was listed in the ledger of Ellicott & Company between September 1774 and July 1775 [Bedini, *Life of Benjamin Banneker*]. Samuel and Vachel Moton were "Negro" taxables in Elkridge

Hundred, Anne Arundel County, in 1783 [MSA S 1161-1-3, p.5]. Samuel and Molly were the parents of

    i.   Greenbury Morten, born about 1757, employed at Ellicott's Lower Mills [Bedini, *Life of Benjamin Banneker*, 62], purchased 20 acres in Baltimore County from Benjamin Banneker on 20 December 1785 [Land Records WG#Y, 653]. He registered in Baltimore County on 20 March 1807: *yellow or Brown complexion, 5 feet 8 inches high, age 50, born free in Balt^e Co^{ty}* [Certificates of Freedom, 1806-16, (not manumitted), no. 2] and was head of a Patapsco Hundred, Baltimore County household of 7 "other free" in 1810 [MD:644].

    ii. ?Deb., head of a Baltimore City household of 6 "other free" and 8 "other free" in 1810 [MD:280, 300].

    iii. Joshua, registered in Baltimore County on 23 April 1807: *Negro, yellowish colour, 5 feet 2-1/2 inches age 21, born free in Balt^e Co^{ty}* [Certificates of Freedom, 1806-16, (not manumitted), no. 3]

    iv. Charles, born about 1780, registered in Baltimore County on 8 May 1807: *Negro, yellowish complexion, 5 feet 3 inches high, age 27, born free in Balt^e Co^{ty}* [Certificates of Freedom, 1806-16, (not manumitted), no. 17].

MORTIS FAMILY

1.   Mary Mortus, born say 1702, was the servant of Thomas Wilson on 27 March 1721/2 when the Prince George's County court presented her for having an illegitimate "Malatto" child. On 26 June 1722 she confessed that her master's "negroe man" Hannibal was the father. The court sold her and her child to John Middleton and ordered that Hannibal receive fifteen lashes [Court Record 1720-2, 484, 561, 619-20]. She was probably the mother of

2   i.   Anne, about 1722.

2.   Anne Mortis, born about 1722, was the "Molatto" servant of Thomas Edelen on 22 June 1742 when she was presented by the Prince George's County court for having an illegitimate child. On 22 November 1742 she confessed to the charge, and the court ordered that she receive fifteen lashes. On 22 November 1743 the court bound her son Bob to Thomas Edelin, Jr., until the age of thirty-one. On 23 June 1747 she was called "Molatto Nan" when the court sold her for seven years to Thomas Edelin Jr. and sold her twelve month old "Mullatto" daughter Rachel to Baruch Williams until the age of thirty-one [Court Record 1742-3, 2, 240; 1743-4, 2, 147, 169, 170; 1746-7, 629]. She still had three years to serve when she was called "Mulatto Nan" in the inventory of Thomas Edelin's Prince George's County estate on 25 January 1754 [Prerogative Inventories 58:140]. She was the mother of

    i.   an unnamed "Molatto Boy" to be free at age twenty-one when he was listed in the 11 November 1754 Prince George's County estate of Mary Edelen [Prerogative Inventories 58:245].

    ii. Robert, born about 1742, a "Molatto" to be free at the age of thirty-one when he was listed in the inventory of the Prince George's County estate of Mary Edelen on 11 November 1754 [Prerogative Inventories 58:245].

    iii. Rachel, born about June 1746, a "Molatto" girl valued at £15 in the inventory of the Prince George's County estate of Baruch Williams on 8 April 1755 [Prerogative Inventories 59:345-6].

MOSELY FAMILY

Members of the Mosely family in Delaware were

1   i.   William, born say 1725.

2   ii. Ann, born say 1727.

3   iii. Absolem¹, born say 1730.

1. William Mosely, born say 1725, a "mulatto," registered the birth of his daughter, Elizabeth, on 17 January 1747/8 at St. George's Protestant Episcopal Church, Indian River Hundred, Sussex County [Wright, *Vital Records of Kent and Sussex Counties*, 93]. He was the father of

4   i.   ?John¹, born say 1746.
        ii. Elizabeth, born 17 January 1747/8.

2. Ann Mosely, born say 1727, was fined £3 by the Sussex County court in May 1744 for having an illegitimate child [RG 4815.017, General Sessions Court, 1741-53, frame 156]. She may have been the mother of

        i.   Hannah, mother of an illegitimate child in Sussex County before February 1757 for which she paid a fine in November 1757 [RG 4815.017, General Sessions Court, 1753-60, frames 320, 338, 361, 383].

3. Absolem¹ Mosely, born say 1730, was indicted by the Sussex County court in February 1749. He posted £50 bond and John Corwill was surety for another 50 pounds. The case was dismissed in August 1750 on his commitment to pay all fees [RG 4815.017, General Sessions Court, 1741-53, frames 448, 453, 470]. He purchased 104 acres called *Oliver's Folly* on the north side of Sow Bridge Branch in Sussex County from William **Winsley** for £12.10 on 4 May 1765 [DB K-10:270]. He was taxable in Slaughter Creek, Sussex County, in 1770 [RG 2535, reel 1]. He left a 25 April 1795 Sussex County will, proved 30 April 1795, by which he named his sons Purcell, Absolem, Curnell and other unnamed children [WB E:33-4]. His land was listed as half cleared and worth about 30 shillings per acre in the 1796 tax list for Cedar Creek Hundred [RG 2535, reel 2]. He was the father of

        i.   Purcell, born before 1776, head of a Sussex County household of 8 "other free" in 1810 [DE:463] and 10 "free colored" in Broadkill Hundred in 1820 [DE:334]. He was an 80-year-old "Mulatto" laborer living with John Mosely in the 1850 Dover Hundred census [DE:345].
        ii. ?Cornelius¹, married Alce **Hanzer**, "Blacks, freed" on 29 June 1779 in Sussex County [Records of the United Presbyterian Churches of Lewes, Indian River and Cool Spring, Delaware 1756-1855, 294]. He was taxable in Duck Creek Hundred, Kent County, from 1779 to 1780 [RG 3535, Kent County Levy List, 1768-84, frames 407, 429, 430, 452], a delinquent taxable in Indian River Hundred, Sussex County, in 1790 [RG 2535, roll 2] and head of a Lewes and Rehoboth Hundred, Sussex County household of 6 "other free" in 1800 [DE:414].
        iii. George, a delinquent taxable in Indian River Hundred, Sussex County, in 1790 [RG 2535, roll 2]
        iv. ?John², head of a Sussex County household of 6 "other free" in 1810 [DE:455] and 6 "free colored" in Broadkill Hundred in 1820 [DE:334].
        v.   Absolem², born about 1785, head of a Dagsboro Hundred, Sussex County household of 5 "free colored" in 1820 [DE:372], a 75-year-old "Mulatto" listed in the 1860 census for Broadkill Hundred, Sussex County.
        vi. ?Jacob, head of an Octoraro, Cecil County household of 1 "other free" in 1790.

4. John¹ Mosely, born say 1746, and his wife, Elizabeth, had their son, Billy, baptized on 9 September 1770 at St. George's Protestant Episcopal Church, Indian River Hundred, Sussex County [Wright, *Vital Records of Kent and Sussex Counties*, 100]. He purchased 50 acres in Nanticoke Hundred, Sussex County, on the southwest side of the Raccoon Swamp that empties into the Nanticoke River for £50 on 7 August 1786 [DB N-13:299]. He was taxable in Dagsboro Hundred in 1784 and in Nanticoke Hundred from 1789 to 1796 when he was listed as a "Molatto" [DSA, RG 2535, roll 2]. He was head of a Nanticoke Hundred household of 8 "other free" in 1800 [DE:342], 8 in 1810 [DE:462], and 5 "free colored" in Broadkill Hundred in 1820 [DE:330]. They were the parents of

    i.   William[2], born 1 October 17__, baptized 9 September 1770.

    ii. ?Solomon[1], taxable in Duck Creek Hundred, Kent County, Delaware, from 1768 to 1772 when he was delinquent [RG 3535, Kent County Levy List, 1768-84, frames 23, 75, 119, 148], called "Solmon Mosely the elder," a yeoman of Kent County, in November 1772 when the grand jury indicted him for stealing two bushels of wheat from Risdon Bishop of Little Creek Hundred [DSA, RG 3805, MS case files November 1772 indictments]. He was head of a Cedar Creek, Sussex County household of 9 "other free" in 1800 [DE:307].

    iii. ?Cornelius[2], born 1776-1794, head of a Murderkill Hundred, Kent County household of 4 "free colored" in 1820 [DE:6].

Other members of the family in Delaware were

    i.   Solomon[2], born before 1776, head of a Dagsboro Hundred, Sussex County household of 3 "other free" in 1800 [DE:425] and 2 "free colored" in 1820 [DE:372].

    ii. Emeline, head of a Sussex County household of 8 "other free" in 1810 [DE:445].

    iii. Benjamin, born before 1776, head of a Broadkill Hundred, Sussex County household of 3 "free colored" in 1820 [DE:334].

    iv. Hezekiah, head of a Sussex County household of 7 "other free" in 1810 [DE:410].

    v.   John[3], born 1776-1794, head of a Broadkill Hundred, Sussex County household of 5 "free colored" in 1820 [DE:334].

    vi. Isaac, head of an Appoquinimink Hundred, New Castle County household of 3 "free colored" in 1820 [DE:156].

MULLAKIN FAMILY

1.   Margery Mullakin, born say 1670, appeared in Norfolk County, Virginia court on 15 September 1689 to answer the judges' presentment that she had born a bastard child by a "Negro" during the time of her indenture [Orders 1675-86, 320]. Her descendant may have been

2   i.   Adam[1] Mullican, born say 1750.

2.   Adam[1] Mullican, born say 1750, was head of a Talbot County household of 8 "other free" in 1790. He was probably the father of

    ii. Adam[2], born about 1789, registered in Talbot County on 11 October 1813: *a black Man, about 24 years of age, 5 7-3/4 in. high...born free & raised in the County* [Certificates of Freedom 1807-28, 20].

MUNGARS FAMILY

1.   John Mungars, born say 1730, purchased 100 acres called *Hearns Quarter* in Worcester County on 4 March 1753 for £15 [Land Records C:3]. He was probably the ancestor of

    i.   Martha, head of a Worcester County household of 4 "other free" in 1800 [MD:830].

MUNT/ MUNS FAMILY

1.   Mary Munt, born say 1700, the servant of Richard Cooper, confessed to the Talbot County court in August 1719 that she had a child by her master's slave "Mallatoe Robin," and the court bound her one-month-old daughter Honner to her master. In November 1723 the court bound her daughter Matrey Munt to her master until the age of thirty-one. Mary had completed her indenture to Richard Cooper by November 1725 when the court sold her to Cooper for another fourteen years as punishment for having two illegitimate "Mullato" children [Judgment Record

1717-9, 303, 383, 386-7; 1722-3, 92; 1723-4, 142-3, 235; 1725-6, 425].[23] She left a 7 July 1758 Kent County, Delaware will, proved 14 September 1758, by which she gave her daughter Eleanor a shilling, her son Robert a bed, furniture, two mares, a colt, a horse, seven head of sheep, hogs, a cow and calf, pewter dishes and other household items; her son Robert's wife Mary Ann a calimanco gown, a black quilt, a petticoat, mantle and striped apron; her daughter Abigail all her other wearing apparel, a chest, linen wheel, looking glass and frying pan; her daughter Charity a shilling; and her granddaughter Julianna Munt a bed and wool blanket and other household items. She named her son Robert executor and named his wife Mary Ann in a codicil. Robert Munt was granted administration on the estate on 9 August 1775 [DSA, RG 3545, roll 162, frames 453-9; WB K:188-9; L:171]. Mary and Robin were the parents of

   i. Honner, born in July 1719, "spinster" of Kent County, died before 13 September 1756 when Mary Munt was granted administration on her estate [DSA, RG 3545, roll 162, frame 451; WB K:143].
   ii. Matrey, born about 1722, an illegitimate "Mallato" child sold until the age of thirty-one by the Talbot County court to Richard Cooper for 1,000 pounds of tobacco on 5 November 1723 [Judgment Record 1722-3, 142-3].
   iii. Eleanor, received a shilling by her mother's will.
   iv. Abigail, sued her brother Robert Munt, labourer, in February 1760 for detaining her property: 3 pewter plates, a pewter dish, an iron pot, a black calimanco gown, a white shalloon mantle, and a striped Holland apron but discontinued the suit before it came before the court [RG 3815.013, dockets 1760-62, frame 5].
2 v. Robert[1], say 1730.
   vi. Charity.

2. Robert[1] Munt, born say 1730, was administrator of the Kent County estate of his mother Mary Munt and was married to Mary Ann Munt when his mother made her will. He was taxable in Murderkill Hundred, Kent County, from 1759 to 1766. He was allowed £2 by the Kent County levy court on 18 November 1766 for burying a poor man named Henry Smith. He was taxable in Dover Hundred from 1770 to 1774 [Kent County Levy List 1743-67, frames 233, 276, 318, 387, 401, 417, 442, 460, 524, 529; 1768-84, frames 69, 159, 175, 216]. He died before 7 August 1775 when John Penn, Esq., was granted administration on his Kent County estate. Mary Munt was administratrix on 9 August 1775 and returned an inventory valued at £77. He owed money to William **Durham** and Cornelius **Hanser** [DSA, RG 3545, reel 162, frames 460-464]. He may have been the father of

   i. Robert[2] Muns, a "Mulatto" single man, taxable in Little Creek Hundred, Kent County, in 1798 [RG 3535, Levy List, 1797-8, frame 477], head of a Little Creek, Kent County household of 3 "other free" in 1800 [MD:31].
   ii. Nathan Mun, head of a Kent County, Maryland household of 1 "other free" in 1790.
   iii. Ann, mother of an illegitimate daughter by George **Sisco** in Duck Creek Hundred in 1782 [DSA, RG 3805.0, MS Kent County Court case papers, August 1782 Indictments].

MURRAY FAMILY

1. Margaret Murray, born say 1705, was called Margaret Murrough of Eastern Neck Hundred on 10 October 1718 when she was charged by the Kent County, Maryland court with having a "Mollatoe" child by a "Negro" man but found not guilty because there was no evidence to prosecute. She was called Margaret Murray and was the servant of Michael Miller in March 1719/20 when the court charged her

---

[23]Richard Cooper was taxable in Murderkill Hundred, Kent County, in 1746 [Levy list 1743-67, frame 58].

with the same offense but again found her not guilty [Court Proceedings 1718-20, 205, 407]. She was convicted of having a "Mollatoe" child sometime before 25 November 1725 when she completed her indenture to Michael Miller and he delivered her up to the court to be sold for seven years. The court sold her to Henry Cully for 2,500 pounds of tobacco. On 10 August 1726 she had an illegitimate child by a white man [Criminal Records 1724-8, 114, 268]. She was probably the ancestor of

    i. Penelope, born say 1725, a "spinster" who confessed to the Kent County, Maryland court on 17 November 1741 that she had an illegitimate child by a "Negro." The court ordered that she be sold for seven years and ordered her child to serve her master, Michael Miller, until the age of thirty-one. She was presented for having another illegitimate child (no race indicated) on 17 June 1746, but she was acquitted because she was then a married woman [Criminal Proceedings 1739-42, 226-7; 1742-7, 277-8, 289]. She was a "Mallatto Woman" who still had 8 years to serve when she was valued at £20 in the inventory of the Kent County estate of Mr. Michael Miller on 6 May 1747 [Prerogative Inventories & Accounts 1747-1748, 350-3].

   ii. Abigail, born say 1740, a "Mallatto Girl" who still had 24 years to serve when she was valued at £20 in the inventory of the Kent County estate of Mr. Michael Miller on 6 May 1747 [Prerogative Inventories & Accounts 1747-1748, 350-3].

  iii. Sarah, born say 1752, pled guilty in Queen Anne's County court in June 1770 that she bore a "mut." (Mulatto) child [Surles, *and they Appeared at Court, 1770-1772*, 5].

  iv. Valentine, enlisted in the Revolution for 3 years on 14 May 1778 and was discharged on 19 June 1781 [*Archives of Maryland*, 18:299, 545]. He was apparently identical to Valentine Murrin who was one of four "Black Persons being Soldiers," Thomas **Thompson**, Leonard **Turner**, Valentine Murrin, and John **Adams**, who were arrested in Orange County, North Carolina, in December 1780 for breaking into someone's house. They were forcibly rescued by their officer Major McIntosh of the Continental Army [Orange County Court Minutes 1777-82, Dec. 19 and 23, 1780].

   v. William, "Negro" head of a Kent County household of 1 "other free" in 1790 and 1 in 1800 [MD:175].

  vi. Nathan, head of a Kent County household of 6 "other free" in 1800 [MD:175].

  vii. Daniel, head of a North Susquehannah, Cecil County household of 1 "other free" in 1790.

 viii. Darkus, head of a Baltimore City household of 6 "other free" in 1800 [MD:284].

  ix. Mary, head of a Baltimore City household of 6 "other free" in 1800 [MD:284].

   x. Rachel, head of a Kent County household of 4 "other free" in 1800 [MD:163].

  xi. Samuel, head of a Montgomery County household of 4 "other free" in 1800 [MD:185].

  xii. Jude, head of a Kent County household of 2 "other free" in 1800 [MD:164].

 xiii. Nancy, head of a Talbot County household of 2 "other free" in 1800 [MD:523].

  xiv. George, a "negro" head of a Caroline County household of 4 "other free" in 1810 [MD:195].

MYERS/ MAYERS FAMILY

1.   Christian Myers, born say 1729, confessed in Prince George's County court on 23 August 1748 that she had an illegitimate "Mulatto" child. The court ordered that she serve seven years and sold her seventeen-month-old daughter Sarah to her

master John Carrick until the age of thirty-one [Court Record 1747-8, 341]. She was the mother of

    i. Sarah, born about February 1747.

2   ii. ?Molly, born say 1757.

    iii. ?Liddy, head of a Frederick County household of 3 "other free" in 1800 [MD:979].

2.   Molly Myer, born say 1757, was a "Molatto" girl valued at £15 in the inventory of the Baltimore County estate of James Dawkins on 5 April 1765 [Prerogative Inventories 86:255]. She may have been the mother of

3   i. Samuel Mayers, born say 1775.

3.   Samuel Mayers, born say 1775, and his wife Jane Mayers were the parents of Hannah Mayers, a "free Mulatto" born in June 1790 and baptized on 9 June 1794 by Rev. Mr. Oliver at St. Thomas Parish, Baltimore County [Reamy, *St. Thomas Parish Registers*, 1732-1850, 30]. Their child was

    i. Hannah, born in June 1790.

Another possible relative was

    i. Sarah Ann Myers, born about 1791, registered in Frederick County on 15 November 1819: *a bright Mulatto...about twenty eight years of age...free born woman and the daughter of Henny Taylor as appears from the affidavit of John Reign* [Certificates of Freedom 1807-28, 100].

Members of a Myers family on the Eastern Shore of Maryland were

    i. Jeremiah, "Negro" head of a Kent County household of 6 "other free" in 1790.

    ii. Rebecca Miens, head of a Talbot County household of 3 "other free" in 1800 [MD:521].

NAILOR FAMILY

1.   Elizabeth Nuller, born say 1730, a "Molo.," was paid by the Kent County, Maryland levy court in 1773 for supporting herself and her child and attending John Woodard and his wife. She was called a "Mol^a" when the court paid her to maintain herself and child for the years 1774 and 1775. She was probably the mother of

    i. Rebecca Nailer, paid by the Kent County levy court for maintaining herself and her children in 1783 [1758-1784 Levy List, 281, 292, 307, 401].

    ii. Sampson Nailer, "Negro" head of a Kent County household of 4 "other free" in 1790 [MD:80] and 5 in 1800 [MD:175].

    iii. Rachel Nailor, "Negro" head of a Kent County household of 2 "other free" in 1790 [MD:80].

    iv. Benjamin Nailer, head of a Kent County household of 7 "other free" in 1800 [MD:164].

    v. Henry, born before 1776, head of a Kent County household of 2 "free colored" in 1830.

    vi. Catherine, born before 1776, head of a Kent County household of 8 "free colored" in 1830.

NATT FAMILY

1.   Joanna Natt, born say 1737, was the white servant of John Duffey in March 1755 when she confessed to the Queen Anne's County court that she had a child by a "Negroe." The court sold her daughter Martha for 31 years to her master for 1,200 pounds of tobacco. On 25 March 1760 she confessed to the court that she had another child by a "Negro" man. The court ordered her sold for seven years after the completion of her indenture and sold her three-year-old daughter Alce to her

master until the age of thirty-one for 250 pounds of tobacco, and sold her one-year-old daughter Elizabeth for £25 [Criminal Record 1751-9, n.p.; 1759-66, 35-7]. She was the mother of
    i. Martha, born 10 May 1754.
    ii. Alce, born about 1757.
    iii. Elizabeth, born about 1759.

NELSON FAMILY

1. Mary Nelson, born say 1675, was the "malato" mother of John Nelson who was born in All Hallows Parish, Anne Arundel County, on 10 November 1695 [Wright, *Anne Arundel County Church Records*, 3]. Mary was the mother of
    i. John, born 10 November 1695.
    ii. ?Sarah, born say 1700, the servant of Henry Ridgely in March 1720/1 when she confessed to the Anne Arundel County court that she had a child by "a Negroe Man belonging to Mr. Richard Warfield." The court bound her child to her master until the age of thirty-one [Judgment Record 1720-1, 87, 355]. She was apparently the mother of "Richard Nelson (Molato)" who was listed in the inventory of the Anne Arundel County estate of Colonel Henry Ridgely on 29 June 1750 [Prerogative Inventories 1750-1751, 62-6].

They may have been the ancestors of
2   i. Ann¹, born say 1735.
    ii. Ann², "of Coller" head of a Baltimore County household of 1 "other free" and 4 slaves in 1810 [MD:710].

2. Ann¹ Nelson, born say 1735, was the servant of William Brawner of Charles County in March 1755 when she was presented for having a "Mollatto" child. She confessed to the charge, and on 10 June 1755 the court bound her five-month-old son Joseph to Timothy Carington until the age of thirty-one. On 8 November 1757 she was presented for having another mixed-race child [Court Record 1755-1756, 90, 179; 1757-8, 1]. She was the mother of
    i. Joseph, born about January 1755.
    ii. ?Hannah, a "Mulatto" head of a Charles County household of 1 "other free" in 1790.

NEWMAN FAMILY

1. Maria Newman, born say 1735, was the servant of Thomas Maccatee on 10 June 1755 when she confessed in Charles County court that she had a "Mollatto" child. The court bound her four-month-old son William to her master until the age of thirty-one [Court Record 1755-6, 127, 180]. She was the mother of
    i. William, "Mulatto" head of a Charles County household of 4 "other free" in 1790, 6 in 1800 [MD:515], and 3 in 1810 [MD:303], perhaps the William Newman who was head of a Randolph County, Virginia household of 2 "free colored" in 1830.
    ii. ?Benjamin, head of a Montgomery County household of 10 "other free" in 1790.
    iii. ?John, head of an Eastern District, Harrison County, Virginia household of 8 "free colored" in 1830.

NICHOLS FAMILY

Members of the Nichols family in Maryland were
    i. James, born say 1690, a "Mulatto" allowed 450 pounds of tobacco for his support by the Anne Arundel County court in August 1752 [Judgment Record 1751-4, 38].
1   ii. Grace¹, born say 1718.

        iii.   Menta, born about 1721, a 110-year-old from Baltimore who emigrated to Liberia aboard the schooner *Orion* in 1831 with John Nichols, a 60-year-old barber, Jane (age 45), and James Nichols (age 18) [http://fold3.com/image/46670314].

        iv.   Philip, born about 1762, a "Mulatto" man who still had nine years to serve on 30 July 1784 when Archibald Elson of Prince George's County placed an ad in the *Maryland Journal and Baltimore Advertiser* stating that Philip had run away in June that year [Windley, *Runaway Slave Advertisements*, II:314-5].

        v.   Prifry, a 96-year-old "Mulatto" counted in 1850 census for Talbot County.

1.   Grace[1] Nichols, born say 1718, confessed to the Prince George's County court on 22 August 1738 that she had an illegitimate child. The court was informed that the child was a "Mallatto" and ordered that her mistress Salome Docra bring her and the child into court for inspection and that Mary White take care of the child until the next court. On 28 November 1738 the court ruled that the child was "not a Mallatto" and paid Mary White £2.10 to teach Grace's daughter Mary Nichols to read the Bible and to give her a decent suit of clothes at the end of her indenture. On 28 November 1749 the court allowed 200 pounds of tobacco a year for Grace's support. Rachel Spriggs sued Grace on 28 August 1750 for a debt of 202 pounds of tobacco [Court Record 1738-40, 119, 192; 1748-9, 72, 133; 1749-50, 231]. She was the ancestor of

  2   i.   Mary[1], born say 1738.
  3   ii.   ?Ann, born say 1757.

2.   Mary[1] Nichols, born say 1738, was bound to Mary White by the Prince George's County court on 28 November 1738. On 22 November 1763 she confessed to the court that she had an illegitimate "Mulatto" child. The court ordered that she be sold for seven years (at the end of her service in March 1766) and bound her one-year and five-months-old son Felix to her mistress Johanna Ellson until the age of thirty-one. On 28 November the court ordered that she serve another seven-year term and bound her five-month-old "Mulatto" daughter Fido to Johanna Ellson until the age of thirty-one [Court Record 1763-4, 8, 352-3]. She was the mother of

        i.   Felix, born June 1762.
        ii.   Fido, born in June 1764.
  4   iii.   Grace[2], born say 1780.

3.   Ann Nichols, born say 1757, was head of a Prince George's County household of 5 "other free" in 1790. She appeared before the clerk of Prince George's County on 27 March 1804 and named her children: Zingr., Henry, Rachel, Mary, Ace, George, Elizabeth and Kitty Nicholls and their birth dates. She also gave the names and birth dates of three children of Mary Nicholls: Grace, Jane, and John Nicholls. And she stated that Grace Nicholls was the daughter of Mary Nicholls [Land Records JRM, no. 10, p. 273]. She recorded the certificate she received from the clerk in the Court of the District of Columbia in Alexandria on 23 July 1816 [Arlington County Register of Free Negroes, 1797-1861, no. 35, p.31]. She was the mother of

        i.   Ling, born 2 May 1775.
        ii.   Henry, born 20 August 1777.
        iii.   Rachel, born 18 February 1780.
  5   iv.   Mary[2], born 21 May 1782.
        v.   Asa, born in February 1785.
        vi.   George, born 30 March 1789.
        vii.   Elizabeth, born 14 August 1797.
        viii.   Kitty[1], born 17 September 1799.

4.   Grace[2] Nichols, born 20 August 1776, a "free woman of colour," was the mother of

        i.   John Elson, born 11 March 1802 according to the deposition of Ann

Nicholls, registered in Prince George's County on 26 July 1827: *a bright mulatto man, about 25 years old...born free in Prince George County...son of Grace Nicholls, a free woman of colour.*

ii. Kitty[2], born about 1803, registered in Prince George's County on 30 July 1827: *a copper-colored woman, about 24 years old...daughter of Grace Nicholls.*

iii. Sophia, born about 1808, registered in Prince George's County on 26 July 1827: *a copper-colored woman, about 19 years old...daughter of Grace Nicholls.*

iv. Mary[3], born about 1810, registered in Prince George's County on 26 July 1827: *a bright mulatto girl, about 17 years old...daughter of Grace Nicholls* [Provine, *Registrations of Free Negroes*, 67].

5. Mary[2] Nichols, born 21 May 1782, was the mother of John and Jane Nichols according to the testimony of Ann Nichols in Prince George's County on 27 March 1804. Mary was the mother of
    i. Jane, born 10 December 1800.
    ii. John, born 15 September 1802.

NICHOLSON FAMILY

1. Ruth Nicholson, born say 1745, was a white woman living in Queen Anne's County on 1 July 1765 when she had a "Mullatto" child by a "Negroe" man [Judgment Records 1766-7, part 1, CD image 37]. She may have been the ancestor of
    i. Samuel, head of a Chester County, Pennsylvania household of 5 "other free" in 1790.
    ii. Andrew, head of a Chester County, Pennsylvania household of 3 "other free" in 1790.
    iii. Joseph, head of a Chester County, Pennsylvania household of 2 "other free" in 1790.

NORMAN FAMILY

1. Elizabeth Norman, born say 1695, confessed in Prince George's County court on 24 March 1712/3 that she had an illegitimate child by James Carr and was ordered to serve her master Benjamin Belt a year for the trouble of his house. She was the servant of Benjamin Belt in March 1714/5 when she confessed to having another child. On 23 August 1715 the court ordered Belt to keep her and her "Mallatoe" child until the November court. The court sold her and her child to Richard Keene, the constable for Patuxent Hundred, for 3,600 pounds of tobacco later that year on 22 November. Five years later on 22 November 1720 she confessed to the court that she had an illegitimate child by a "Mullato man of William Digge's." The court sold her to her master for seven years and sold the child to William Maccoy until the age of thirty-one. On 28 August 1722 she confessed to having another "Malatto" child, and the court ordered her sold to Richard Keene for seven years and gave her child to William Harris until the age of thirty-one. She may have been the mother of two children listed in the inventory of the estate of William Harris on 1 July 1730:

1 Mollatto Girl named Beck 9 years old - £12
1 Mollatto Girl named Jane 5 years old to be free at 16 year old - £.15

[Prerogative Inventories & Accounts 1730-1732, 16-17]. In March 1749/50 the court allowed her 200 pounds of tobacco a year for her support, rejected her petition on 25 June 1751 to have a doctor, but paid Doctor Richard Smith 800 pounds of tobacco on 26 November 1751 for removing a cancerous tumor from her arm. She received 400 pounds of tobacco for her support on 23 November 1756 [Court Record 1710-5, 285, 693, 721, 790; 1715-20, 4; 1720-2, 20-1, 84, 622-3;

1748-9, 133; 1751-4, 71, 157, 355]. She may have been the mother of
2   i.   Beck, born about 1720.
3   ii. Jane¹, born say 1722.

2.   Beck (no last name), born about 1720, may have been identical to "Melattow Rebeccah" who was living at Samuel Selby's when she was presented by the Prince George's County court on 25 March 1739/40 for having an illegitimate child by information of the constable for Mount Calvert Hundred [Court Record 1738-40, 566]. And she may have been the "Mollatto Beck" whose "Molatto" daughter Jane was bound by the Prince George's County court to Joseph Bladen until the age of sixteen on 22 June 1742 [Court Record 1742-1743, 3]. On 25 November 1746 the court convicted "Mullatto Beck belonging to Samuel Selby" of "Mullatto Bastardy" and bound her six-week-old daughter Henrietta to Samuel Selby for thirty-one years [Court Record 1746-7, 200-1]. She may have been the mother of
          i.   Jane², born 1 March 1741/2, bound to Joseph Bladen, called "Mulatto Jane" and serving until the age of twenty-one when she was listed in the Prince George's County inventory of Mr. Richard Keene on 1 October 1754 [Prerogative Inventories 60:156-162].
4   ii. Henrietta, born about October 1746.

3.   Jane¹ Norman, born say 1722, was called "a Mallatto woman named Jane (no last name) Living at Mr. Richard Keen's" on 23 August 1737 when she confessed to the Prince George's County court that she had an illegitimate child by a "free Mallatto." The court ordered that she receive twenty lashes and serve her master an additional year and a half and sold her two-month-old son James to Edward Swann until the age of twenty-one. She had another child by a free person before 28 November 1738 when the court ordered that she receive fifteen lashes and serve her master twelve months for the trouble of his house, bound her male child to Keene until the age of twenty-one years, and ordered Keene to give the boy a year of schooling and a decent suit of clothes at the end of his indenture. She may have been the "Mallatto Jane" who confessed to the Prince George County court on 25 March 1739/40 that she had an illegitimate child. The court bound her two-month-old female child to Peter Albino until the age of sixteen [Court 1738-40, 569]. She was called "Jan Molato Norman" on 26 November 1745 when the court bound her son Joseph to Richard Keene until the age of twenty-one. On 28 June 1748 and 28 March 1749 she was convicted of having illegitimate children by a free person. On 27 November 1750 she was called "Mollatto Jane belonging to Richard Keene" when she confessed to having another child named Basil who was bound to Keene until the age of twenty-one [Court Record 1736-8, 497, 504; 1738-40, 176, 192, 200; 1744-6, 248, 279; 1747-8, 168; 174; 1748-9, 181; 1749-50, 244]. She was the mother of
          i.   James¹, born in June 1737.
          ii. Joseph¹, born about 26 August 1745, three months old when he was bound to Richard Keene until the age of twenty-one.
          iii. Jane³, born about 1745, a nine-year-old "Mulatto" girl bound to serve until the age of twenty-one when she was listed in the inventory of the Prince George's County estate of Richard Keene on 1 October 1754 [Prerogative Inventories 60:156-62].
          iv. Bazil¹, born in 1750, taxable in Hampshire County, Virginia, from 1796 to 1801: taxable on 3 tithes and 3 horses in 1796, 2 tithes in 1798, his own tithe in 1799 and 1800, called a "Negro" in 1801 [PPTL 1782-99, frames 426, 519, 594; 1800-14, frames 40, 59].
5   v.   ?Phebe, born say 1752.
          vi. ?Catherine, head of a Montgomery County household of 6 "other free" in 1790.

4.   Henrietta (no last name), born about October 1746, was the daughter of "Mullatto Beck" whose daughter Henrietta was bound by the Prince George's County court

to Samuel Selby until the age of thirty-one. She was apparently identical to Henrietta Norman who confessed to the Prince George's County court on 27 August 1765 that she had a "Mulatto" child. The court ordered that she be sold for seven years and bound her two-month-old child Ailce to her master William Deakins until the age of thirty-one [Record 1764-5, 195, 200]. She had two more children which she was charged with on information of William Deakins on 25 November 1766 and 28 March 1769 [Court Record 1766-1768, 15, 167; 1768-1770, 170, 174]. She was the mother of

6   i.   ?Bazil², born about 1760
7   ii. Ailce, born June 1765.
     iii. William, born about 28 January 1769, two months old on 28 March 1769 when he was bound out by the Prince George's County court until the age of twenty-one [Court Record 1768-70, 174].

5.   Phebe¹ Norman, born say 1752, was a "free negroe" living in Frederick County, Virginia, on 7 September 1784 when the court bound her children Ralph (age 6), Loise (8), James (4) and Elizabeth (2) to Gerard Briscoe [Orders 1781-4, 573]. She was the mother of

     i.   Bazil², born say 1772, "son of Phebe a free negroe," bound by the Frederick County, Virginia court to Gerard Briscoe on 7 September 1784 [Orders 1781-4, 570], probably the Bazil Norman who was taxable in Randolph County from 1814 to 1829: in a list of "Free Negroes & Mulatters over 16 years" in 1814 and 1815, a "Coul⁴" taxable in 1817 [PPTL 1787-1829, frames 444, 466, 484, 494, 505, 519, 536, 720], head of a Randolph County, Virginia household of 4 "free colored" in 1830 (born before 1776) [VA:130].
     ii. Loise, born about 1776.
     iii. Ralph, born about 1778.
     iv. James, born about 1780.
     v.   Elizabeth, born about 1782, head of a Frederick County, Virginia household of 3 "other free" in 1810 [VA:575].
     vi. ?Phebe², born 16 April 1783, a "Negro child" bound by the Frederick County, Virginia court to Robert Glass on 6 December 1791 [Orders 1791-2, 308].

6.   Bazabel² Norman, born 12 July 1760, was taxable in the same list as James Norman in a list of "free Negroes" in Frederick County, Virginia, in 1802 [PPTL 1782-1802, frame 856] and head of a Frederick County, Virginia household of 7 "other free" in 1810 [VA:569]. He gave his age as 57 "the 12ᵗʰ July last" on 14 May 1818 in Washington County, Ohio court when he made a declaration to obtain a pension, stating that he enlisted in Maryland in 1777. He gave his age as 63 on 25 July 1820 and was living in Roxbury Township, Washington County, Ohio, when he made a second declaration in court, stating that he served in the 7th Maryland Regiment and owned 100 acres of land, two old horses, and owed $125 to Joel Adams, $20 to Aquilla Norman, $6 to Charles Norman and several other debts. His only family living with him was his 63-year-old wife, a son 1 month shy of 21, and a granddaughter about 8 years old. He died on 17 July 1830, and his widow Fortune Norman applied for a widow's pension on 2 August 1837. She stated that she married her husband near the Montgomery County courthouse in September 1782, but there was no person living who could testify to their marriage but her brother James **Stephens** who testified that he saw them married by Reverend Thomas Reed in September 1782. Fortune died on 30 February 1841, and her heirs listed on 3 October 1846 were Rebecca **Grayson**, Acquilla Norman, Bazil Norman, James Norman (who had died leaving children Lucinda **Baldwin**, a widow, and Columbus Norman of Roxbury) and Joseph Norman (who died leaving children Sarah Ann, Mary Ann and Betsy Norman who were all minors). They stated that they lived in Virginia and moved to Ohio about twenty-five to thirty years previous [NARA, W.5429, M804, roll 1825]. They were the parents of

    i.   Rebecca **Grayson**.

    ii. James[2], born say 1787, taxable in the same list as Bazil Norman in a list of "free Negroes" in Frederick County, Virginia, in 1802 [PPTL 1782-1802, frame 856], head of a Hampshire County, Virginia household of 2 "other free" in 1810 [VA:770], father of Lucinda **Baldwin** and Columbus Norman. (Ned **Baldwin** was head of an Anne Arundel County household of 5 "other free" in 1810 [MD:74].)

    iii. Acquilla, a resident of Union, Washington County, Ohio, and heir of Basil and Fortune Norman on 16 January 1847 when he appointed an attorney to collect any pension due him.

    iv. Bazil[4], born about 1800, a "Mulatto" born in Virginia and counted in the 1850 census for Decatur, Washington County, Ohio, with "Mulatto" wife Sarah and a 23-year-old child born in Ohio [family no. 1].

    v.   Joseph[2], head of a Frederick County, Virginia household of 4 "free colored" in 1830, father of Sarah, Mary Ann and Betsy Norman.

7.   Ailce/ Elsey Norman, born June 1765, was the mother of Rachel **Hawkins** who registered for herself and her daughters in Washington, D.C., on 4 October 1826 [Provine, *District of Columbia Free Negro Registers*, 70]. Elsey was the mother of

    i.   Rachel, mother of Mary Ann **Hawkins** (born about 1806), Margaret (born about 1808), Martha (born about 1812), Francis (born about 1813), and William Henry (born about 1822).

Other members of the Norman family were

    i.   George, head of a Washington County household of 1 "other free" in 1790.

    ii. Betty, head of a Frederick County, Virginia household of 3 "other free" in 1810 [VA:575].

    iii. James, a "free Negro" taxable in Richmond City from 1788 to 1796 [PPTL 1787-99], father of John Norman who bound himself as an apprentice to Robert Mitchell, Esq., for 2 years in Richmond City on 20 May 1793 for £6 with the consent of his father [Hustings Court Deeds 1792-9, 69-70].

    iv. Lilly, born say 1773, a "Mulatto" living in Hamilton Parish on 22 August 1774 when the Fauquier County court ordered her bound to Judith Neale Grant [Orders 1773-80, 203].

    v.   Delpha, "Mulo." head of a King and Queen County, Virginia household of 7 "other free" in 1810 [VA:172].

    vi. Reuben, head of a Warren County, North Carolina household of 5 "other free" in 1800 [NC:822].

    vii. Samuel, head of a Warren County, North Carolina household of 2 "other free" in 1790 [NC:78].

    viii. Polly, head of a Chowan County, North Carolina household of 3 "free colored" in 1820 [NC:129].

Members of a Norman family in Delaware were

1   i.   Edward[1], born say 1720.

    ii. Bridget, one of the heirs of Aminadab and Rose **Hanser** who sold 50 acres in Little Creek Hundred, Sussex County, on 5 May 1752 [DB H-1, 329-30].

1.   Edward[1] Norman, born say 1720, a "mulatto," had his son Edwarrd baptized on 16 May 1747 at St. George's Protestant Episcopal Church, Indian River [Wright, *Vital Records of Kent and Sussex Counties*, 92]. He may have married Ann **Hanser**. He witnessed the wills of several white residents of Kent County, Delaware, between 1748 and 1765 and the will of Isabella **Hughes** in 1757 [deValinger, *Kent County, Delaware Probate Records*, 125, 136, 145, 173, 190, 215, 217]. He was taxable in Little Creek Hundred, Kent County, in 1753 and 1755. In December 1765 the Kent County court allowed Jacob Stout £1.19 for burying him [Kent County Levy List, 1743-67, frame 107, 143, 514]. His children were

    i. Edward², born say 1747.

    ii. Elizabeth, born 26 August 1748, "daughter of Edward Norman," baptized 27 September 1748 at St. George's Protestant Episcopal Church, Indian River [Wright, *Vital Records of Kent and Sussex Counties*, 94]. She married John **Hanzer** on 21 September 1768 in Sussex County [Records of the United Presbyterian Churches of Lewes, Indian River and Cool Spring, 1756-1855, 279].

NORRIS FAMILY

1.   Mary Norris, born say 1720, was living in Shrewsbury Parish on 14 November 1738 when the Kent County, Maryland court convicted her of having a "Mollatto" child by a "Negro." The court ordered her to serve her master William Woodland for seven years. She had a child by a white man in 1740 and received 20 lashes [Criminal Proceedings 1738-9, 152, 162-3, 172, 180-1]. She was apparently the ancestor of

    i. Nathaniel, born about 1736, a "Mollatto" orphan boy about nine years old and valued at £20 in the Kent County estate of William Woodland on 27 May 1745 [Prerogative Inventories & Accounts, SR 4341-2, Liber 31:312-315]. He ran away from his master John Blackstone before 22 July 1760 when Blackstone placed an ad in the 14 August 1760 issue of the *Pennsylvania Gazette*: *run away from the subscriber, living in Kent County, Maryland, near Joshua Vansant Mill, a likely Mulatto Fellow, named Nathaniel Norris, about 26 Years of Age, well set, 5 Feet 6 inches high, and is very remarkable for having thick lips. Had on when he went away, a half worn Felt Hat, light coloured Halfthick Vest, without sleeves, coarse homespun Shirt, Petticoat Trowsers, white stockings, good Shoes, with Brass Buckles, and wears his hair short, with a Linen Cap* [*Pennsylvania Gazette*, http://accessible.com].

    ii. George, a "Molatto" who was required to post security of £50 to give evidence in the case of His Lordship against "Negroe Jack" in Kent County court in June 1767 [Criminal Dockets 1766-71].

Another Norris family:

    i. Catherine, born about 1785, registered in Prince George's County court on 15 October 1815: *a mulatto woman about 30 years old...was raised in the family of Col. Patrick Sim of Prince George's County and is a free woman and was adjudged such by the Prince George's County Court at its September Term 1815 in her petition for her freedom against Sim* [Provine, *Registrations of Free Negroes*, 19].

NORWOOD FAMILY

Members of the Norwood family in Delaware were

1   i. Nathaniel¹, born about 1735.

    ii. Daniel¹, born about 1739, a 19-year-old farmer born in Angola Hundred who enlisted in the French and Indian War on 19 April 1758 and was listed in the 17 May 1758 muster of Captain McClughan's Company for the campaign in the Lower Counties [Montgomery, *Pennsylvania Archives, Fifth Series*, 142-3]. He pled guilty and was fined 5 shillings for trespass in Sussex County court in May 1758. He confessed judgment of £6.19 to Jacob Kollock, Esq., in April 1764. He was taxable in Indian River and Angola Hundred in 1773 and 1774 [DSA, RG 2535, reel 1]. The state charged him with felony in May 1786 [RG 4815.017, General Sessions Court, 1753-60, frame 423; 1761-71, frame 154; 1771-93, 385, 391, 404].

1.   Nathaniel¹ Norwood, born about 1735, was a 23-year-old planter born in Indian River Hundred who enlisted in the French and Indian War on 19 April 1758 and

was listed in the 17 May 1758 muster of Captain McClughan's Company for the campaign in the Lower Counties [Montgomery, *Pennsylvania Archives, Fifth Series*, 142-4]. He was indicted by the Sussex County court for trespass in May 1758 for which he submitted to the mercy of the court. In February 1759 he was adjudged to serve the estate of Joseph Warrington, deceased, at the rate of 30 shillings per month to pay off his debts [RG 4815.017, General Sessions Court, 1753-60, frame 423; 1761-71, frame 319]. He and his wife, Jemimy, registered the 17 June 1769 birth of their "Melatto" son, Bowen, and their son Nathan at St. George's Protestant Episcopal Church, Indian River Hundred, Sussex County [Wright, *Vital Records of Kent and Sussex Counties*, 99, 103]. Nathan was taxable in Indian River Hundred, Sussex County, from 1774 to 1784 [DSA RG 2535, reels 1&2]. Administration on his Sussex County estate was granted to (his wife) Jemima Norwood on 10 March 1786 [de Valinger, *Calendar of Sussex County Probate Records*, 173; A 91:116]. Nathaniel and Jemima were the parents of

2   i.   ?Eli[1], born say 1768.
     ii. Bowen, born 17 June 1769 (perhaps identical to Eli Norwood).
3   iii. Noble, born say 1775.
     iv. Nathan[2], born 15 February 1777, baptized 27 September 1777 [Wright, *Vital Records of Kent and Sussex Counties*, 103]. He was taxable in Indian River Hundred from 1797 to 1801 [DSA, RG 4200.027, reel 2, frames 176, 258].
     v.   ?John[1], head of a Sussex County household of 5 "other free" in 1810 [DE:354].

2.   Eli[1] Norwood, born say 1768, married Anna **Rust** on 4 December 1789 in Sussex County [Records of the United Presbyterian Churches of Lewes, Indian River and Cool Spring, Delaware 1756-1855, 304]. Anna was probably related to George **Rust**, head of a Dagsboro Hundred, Sussex County household of 3 "free colored" in 1820 [DE:388]. Eli was taxable in Indian River Hundred, Sussex County, in 1789, 1790 and 1796 [DSA RG 2535, reel 2; RG 4200.027, reel 2, frame 115], head of an Indian River Hundred, Sussex County household of 5 "other free" in 1800 (Eli Nord) [DE:437] and 5 in 1810 [DE:412]. On 13 March 1819 he and his wife Elon made a Sussex County deed for a half acre to the trustees of Harmony Meeting House: Purnall **Johnson**, Burton **Johnson**, William **Hayes**, John **Cornish** and Mitchell **Johnson** for the building of a house of worship for the use of the members of the Methodist Episcopal Church [DB 45:124]. He left a 2 January 1838 Sussex County will, proved 23 May 1838, witnessed by Whittington **Johnson**, naming his widow Elon and seven children: Eli, Stephen M., William D., Wingate P., Samuel B, Mary Jane N., and Ann **Johnson**, wife of Whittington. He was the father of

     i.   John[2], born 1 January 1794, son of Eli and Anna Norwood, baptized at St. George's Protestant Episcopal Church, Indian River [Wright, *Vital Records of Kent and Sussex Counties*, 111].
     ii.   Eli[2], married to Charity Norwood in October 1855 when they were summoned as witnesses in the case of the State against Levin **Sockum**, a "free Mulatto," for selling ammunition to Isaac **Harmon**, a "free Mulatto" [DSA, RG 3805, MS case files, October 1855 indictments].
     iii. Stephen M.
     iv.   William D.
     v.   Wingate P.
     vi.   Samuel B.
     vii. Mary Jane N.
     viii. Ann, wife of Whittington **Johnson**.

3.   Noble Norwood, born say 1775, was taxable in Indian River, Sussex County, in 1796 and 1801 [DSA, RG 4200.027, reel 2, frames 115, 258] and head of an Indian River, Sussex County household of 6 "other free" in 1800 [DE:437] and 10 in 1810 [DE:405]. Noble and Lydia Norwood were the parents of

    i. Polly, baptized 12 February 1797 at Indian River, Sussex County, "free Mulatto" daughter of Noble and Lydia Norwood.

    ii. Betsey, baptized 17 August 1799 at Indian River, Sussex County, daughter of Noble and Lydia Norwood [Records of the United Presbyterian Churches of Lewes, Indian River and Cool Spring, Delaware 1756-1855, 391, 399].

NUTT(S) FAMILY

1.   Jane Nutt, born say 1700, was living at the house of Joseph Venable in Stepney Parish, Somerset County, in June 1721 when she confessed that she had a "Mulatto" child in the month of January 1719/20. The court ordered her sold for seven years [Judicial Record 1719-22, 82, 100].

She may have been the ancestor of the members of the Nutts family in Accomack and Northampton counties:

    i. William, born say 1750, an Indian living in Accomack County on 25 October 1774 when he and Nathan Addison's slave Jacob were charged with felony [Orders 1774-7, 270, 277].

    ii. Daniel, born December 1760, a four-year-old "Mulattoe" bound to Major Joyne by the Northampton County, Virginia court on 11 September 1765 [Minutes 1765-71, 11]. He was head of an Accomack County household of 4 "other free" in 1810 [VA:45].

    iii. Edmund, born Christmas 1774, bound by the Northampton County court to Margaret Addison on 12 February 1782 [Minutes 1777-83, 336]. He was a "free Negro" taxable in Northampton County from 1798 to 1803 [PPTL, 1782-1823, frames 251, 270, 312, 353]. He married Mary **Bibbins**, 18 June 1800 Northampton County bond, Southy **Collins** security, consent of Nanny **Bibbins**. He was head of an Accomack County household of 8 "other free" in 1810 [VA:45]. He was called an Indian when his wife Mary was counted as a "free negro" in Accomack County in 1813 [PPTL 1782-1814, frame 833].

    iv. Thomas, head of an Accomack County household of 5 "other free" in 1800 [*Virginia Genealogist* 2:158].

    v. Bridget, married Toby **Stephens**, 7 September 1804 Northampton County bond, Ben Dunton security.

    vi. Sabra, married Isaac **Stephens**, 16 August 1809 Northampton County bond, Isaac Stevens, Sr., security.

    vii. Ariena, born say 1779, married Peter **Beckett**, 10 January 1800 Accomack County bond, Babel **Major**, surety. Babel **Major** was head of an Accomack County household of 6 "other free" in 1810 [VA:43]. Ariena may have been the Arena **Becket** who married Thomas **Bibbins**, 2 August 1800 Accomack County bond, Peter **Bibbins** surety.

OKEY FAMILY

The Okey family probably has some connection to John Okey and his wife Mary Vincent, early residents of Sussex County. Before marrying John Okey, Mary had a son Aminadab **Hanser** by a slave in Accomack County, Virginia [see the **Hanser** history]. It appears that there was another member of the Okey family who was named Aminadab, and he was probably mixed-race as well. However, his origin has not yet been identified. Perhaps he was another mixed-race child of Mary Okey. John Okey owned 400 acres in Sussex County called *Mollattoe Hall* in 1686 [DB A:31, 49; Horle, *Records of Sussex County*, 412-3].

1.   Aminadab Okey, born say 1680, may have been the "strang Child...which is not Certainly known Whose it is" who was living at John Okey's house in March 1682 when the Sussex County court bound him to Henry Bowman. Aminadab Okey was

sued by Aminadab **Hanser** in Sussex County court on 3 May 1704 [Horle, *Records of Sussex County*, 155, 1191]. He and Aminadab **Hanser** were apparently neighbors because on 9 April 1713 he was required to give £100 security to Aminadab **Handsor** in Sussex County court to guarantee that he would abide by the arbitrators' decision regarding the removal of a fence on their properties [DB D-4:225-6]. And Aminadab **Hanser**'s wife Rose mentioned Aminadab Okey's land adjoining hers in her 8 December 1725 deed of sale [DB F-6:220-2]. Aminadab Okey died before 1734 when the account of his estate was recorded in Sussex County court. The account totaled £44 and included £22 for the sale of land [Orphans Court 1728-44, 65]. He was most likely the ancestor of

2   i.   Robert[1], born say 1698.

3   ii.   Joseph, born say 1725.

         iii.   Thomas, born say 1726, recorded his ear mark in Sussex County court on 18 November 1747 [Q-16:301]. He submitted to the Sussex County court on the charge of assault and paid a 2 shilling fine in November 1754 [RG 4815.017, 1753-1760, frame 118]. He died before 4 February 1784 when is widow Elizabeth sold half of 106 acres in the forest of Broadkill Hundred, Sussex County, which she had purchased on 3 May 1780. She sold the remainder on 10 January 1793 [DB N-13:254, 511].

4   iv.   Jean, born say 1731.

         v.   Alexander[1], born say 1732, charged with grand larceny in Sussex County court in May 1754 [RG 4815.017, 1753-60, p.134, frame 71].

5   vi.   Saunders[2], born say 1742.

         vii.   Sinai, made to post bond in Sussex County court in November 1784 to keep the peace with William **Jackson** and Cornelius **Molsely** as her securities [RG 4805, General Sessions Court, 1767-94, frame 349].

         viii.   Robert[2], born say 1746, sued by Jesse Mackemmy in Sussex County court in May 1768 and agreed with the plaintiff in May 1769. He sued Alexander Stockley in August 1770 [RG 4815.017, General Sessions Court, 1761-71, frames 417, 435, 509, 555]. He was taxable in Lewes and Rehoboth Hundred, Sussex County, in 1774. He was called a tanner on 2 February 1789 when he and Jennett Okey, spinster, purchased as tenants-in-common 4 acres in Lewes and Rehoboth Hundred on the edge of the Rehoboth Road [DB O-14:161]. He was head of a Sussex County household of 9 "other free" in 1800 [DE:438] and 11 in 1810 [DE:462].

         ix.   Thomas[2], Jr., taxable in Lewes and Rehoboth Hundred in 1774.

5   x.   William[1], born say 1763.

         xi.   Jonathan[2], head of a Saint Jones Hundred, Kent County household of 2 "other free" in 1800 [DE:45] and 3 in Sussex County in 1810 [DE:416].

         xii.   Robert[3], head of a Little Creek Hundred, Kent County household of 3 "other free" in 1800 [DE:40] and 9 in Sussex County in 1810 [DE:468].

         xiii.   Robert[4], born 1776-1794, head of a Sussex County household of 7 "other free" in 1810 [DE:415] and 8 "free colored" in Lewes and Rehoboth Hundred in 1820 [DE:306].

         xiv.   William[2], born 1776-1794, head of a Lewes and Rehoboth Hundred, Sussex County household of 6 "free colored" in 1820 [DE:306].

         xv.   Levin, taxable in Broadkill Hundred, Sussex County, in 1784. He was indicted by the Sussex County court for petit larceny in November 1783 with Elizabeth Oaky as his security [RG 4805, General Sessions Court, 1767-94, frame 321]. He purchased 6-1/2 acres in Broadkill Hundred at the sheriff's sale for £15, made additions to the dwelling, added other buildings and improvements and sold it about two years later about 1789 for £40 [DB O-14:154, 622].

         xvi.   Betty, head of an Accomack County household of 4 "other free" and a slave in 1810 [VA:117].

2.   Robert[1] Okey, born say 1698, was living on land adjoining Samuel and Ann **Hanser** on 20 May 1733 when they sold 124 acres near Rehoboth Bay, Sussex

County. He was mentioned in the 11 June 1742 Sussex County, deed of his son Samuel who sold land which had formerly belonged to Aminadab Okey and Robert Okey [DB G-7:34-5; H-8:14]. He died before 3 September 1745 when his daughter Sabria and her husband John **Parsons** petitioned the Sussex County court to divide his land among his heirs [Orphans Court 1744-51, 17]. He was the father of

    i.   Samuel, born say 1719, called son of Robert Okey on 11 June 1742 when he sold 60 acres in Sussex County which was formerly owned by Robert and Aminadab Okey and by Aminadab **Hanzor** before them [DB H-8:14]. He was sued by William Taft in Sussex County court in November 1742, but the case was settled out of court, and he sued David McCracken in court in November 1762 but withdrew the suit before it came to trial [RG 4815.017, General Sessions Court, 1741-53, frame 45; 1761-71, 118]. He was listed in the account of the Sussex County estate of Cord Hazard, Jr., on 12 March 1750 [Orphans Court 1744-51, 80].

    ii. Richard, born say 1721, called brother of Samuel Okey in Samuel's 11 June 1742 Sussex County deed by which Samuel sold land adjoining Richard's [DB H-8:14].

    iii. Sabria, born say 1725, wife of John **Parsons**.

3.   Joseph[1] Okey, born say 1725, and Elizabeth Oakey sold 89 acres in Sussex County, part of *Ebenezer*, to John Barker for £11.10 on 8 August 1744 [DB H-8:66]. He and his wife Arcada Okey were administrators of the Worcester County estate of her father Peter **Beckett** on 23 January 1754 [Prerogative Inventories 48:98-100; 60:89; Accounts 37:65]. He sued James Pettyjohn in Sussex County court for assault in February 1759 but discontinued the suit in February 1760 [RG 4815.017, General Sessions Court, 1753-60, frames 510, 526, 585]. He purchased 212 acres in the forest of Broadkill Hundred from the sheriff on 5 August 1762 for £20 and sold this land the same day for £25 [DB I-9:390-1]. He was a "Molatto" taxable in William Burford's District, Granville County, North Carolina, in 1765. He was taxable on 2 tithes in 1769 and 1771 and was taxed on an assessment of £329 in Nap of Reeds District, Granville County, in 1780. In 1786 he was called Joseph Oakey, Sr., in Nap of Reeds District of Granville County when he was head of a household of 2 "white" men over 60 or under 21 years and 4 "white" women in the state census. He was taxable on 250 acres from 1786 to 1804 and taxable on 1 poll in 1786. He was called Joseph Oakley in 1800 when he was head of a Granville County household of 8 "other free." Perhaps his widow was Sarah Oakey who was taxable on 50 acres in Ledge of Rock District, Granville County, from 1805 to 1808 [Tax List 1803-1811, 142, 199, 212, 268]. Joseph was probably the father of

7   i.   Joseph[2], Jr., born say 1750.

    ii. Micajah, head of a household of 1 "white" male under 21 years of age and 2 "white" females in Nap of Reeds District in the state census for Granville County in 1786.

4.   Jean Okey, born say 1731, was paid in December 1770 by the Sussex County levy court for maintaining the child of Rho(?)dia **Harmon** [RG 2535, Levy Assessments, roll 1]. She was called a spinster on 2 February 1789 when she and Robert Okey purchased, as tenants-in-common, 4 acres in Lewes and Rehoboth Hundred on the edge of the Rehoboth Road [DB O-14:161]. She may have been identical to Jane and/ or Jeangull Oakey. An administration bond on Jane Oakey's estate was filed on 15 March 1793 by Robert (signing) and Jonathan Okey, and a Jeangull Oakey left a 29 September 1792 Lewes and Rehoboth will, which was proved 7 September 1793 by Jonathan Oakey and Abraham Hargis. She left all her land and household goods to her son Jonathan [RG 4545, roll 182, frames 185-189]. She was the mother of

    i.   Jonathan[1], born say 1757, perhaps the John Okey, Jr., who was taxable in Lewes and Rehoboth Hundred in 1774 [RG 2535, Levy Assessments, roll 1]. Jonathan was head of a Little Creek Hundred, Kent County household of 4 "other free" in 1800 [DE:41].

5. Saunders Okey, born say 1742, was sued for debt by Robert and Mary Jackson in Sussex County court, but the case was agreed to before coming to trial [RG 4815.017, General Sessions Court, 1761-71, frame 106]. Saunders and his wife, Mary, "melattoes," registered the 20 October 1771 birth of their daughter, Rhoda, at St. George's Protestant Episcopal Church, Indian River [Wright, *Vital Records of Kent and Sussex Counties*, 101]. He was taxable in Lewes and Rehoboth, Sussex County in 1774 and a delinquent taxable in 1787. He married, second, Johannah **Hansor**, widow of Nehemiah **Hansor**, by 12 November 1787 when they were summoned to court to give an account of Nehemiah's estate [de Valinger, *Court Records of Kent County, Delaware, 1680-1705*, 89]. He was the father of

    i.   Rhoda, born 20 October 1771.
    ii. ?Lina, married Shepherd **Harmon** on 10 October 1802 in Sussex County.
    iii. ?Nancy, married Peter **Pride** on 12 February 1803 in Sussex County [Records of the United Presbyterian Churches of Lewes, Indian River and Cool Spring, Delaware 1756-1855, 318, 319].

6. William[1] Oakey, born say 1763, and his wife Sarah registered the 5 April 1785 birth of their daughter Polley at St. George's Protestant Episcopal Church, Indian River Hundred, Sussex County [Wright, *Vital Records of Kent and Sussex Counties*, 106]. He was taxable in Indian River Hundred, Sussex County, in from 1784 to 1790. William and Sarah were the parents of

    i.   Polly, born 5 April 1785, baptized 5 October 1785.

7. Joseph[2] Okey, born say 1750, was taxable on an assessment of £1,810 in Granville County, North Carolina, in 1780. He was called Joseph Oakey, Jr. in 1790 when he was taxable in Dutch District, Granville County, and called "Joseph Oakley, Jr." in 1800 when he was head of a Granville County household of 8 "other free." He was taxable on 447 acres in Dutch District, Granville County, from 1786 to 1796 and taxable on 250 acres from 1802 to 1804. His 8 August 1804 Granville County will was proved by his wife Elizabeth in August 1805. He (signing) left 100 acres to his son Aaron, 150 acres to his son Willie and daughter Selah, and named his other children: Joseph, Susanna, Elizabeth, and Deborah [Original at N.C. Archives, CR.044.801.29]. His widow Elizabeth Okey was taxable on 250 acres in Ledge of Rock District in 1805 [Tax List 1796-1802, p.283; 1803-1811, 89, 142, 199, 212], and head of a Ledge Neck, Granville County household of 3 "free colored" women in 1820 [NC:18]. They were the parents of

    i.   Aaron.
    ii.   Selah.
    iii. William[4]/ Willie.
    iv.   Joseph[3].
    v.   Susanna.
    vi.   Elizabeth.
    vii. Deborah.

OLIVER FAMILY

Anne Arundel County

1. Ann Oliver, born say 1682, was the mother of a "mulato" son named William Oliver who was baptized in All Hollow's Parish, Anne Arundel County, on 18 October 1703 [Wright, *Anne Arundel County Church Records*, 17]. She was the mother of

    i.   William, born 18 October 1703.

They may have been the ancestors of

    i.   Robert, "free Negro" head of a Baltimore City household of 6 "other free" in 1800 [MD:320].

Kent County
1. Margaret Oliver, born say 1725, confessed in Kent County, Maryland court on 18 March 1745/6 that she had a "Mulatto" child by a "Negro" man. The court sold her for seven years and her child until the age of thirty-one. She had another child by Nicholas Fanning, a white man, about August 1748 and paid a fine of thirty shillings. John Matthews was her security [Criminal Proceedings 1742-7, 238-9; 1748-60, 21, 25, 28]. She may have been the ancestor of
    i.   Matthew, a "Mulatto" drafted from Kent County on 10 December 1781 but had not reported for service [NARA, M246, roll 34, frame 444 of 587]. He was a "Negro" head of a Kent County household of 2 "other free" in 1790.
    ii. Joseph, head of a Queen Anne's County household of 5 "other free" in 1800 [MD:363]. He and William **Cork** were called "people of Colour" when they purchased 7 acres from Jacob **Jefferys**, a "Man of Colour," in Queen Anne's County on 15 September 1810 for $45. They sold the land back to him for $50 on 25 May 1811 [Land Records STW-9:369; JB-1:29-30].
    iii. Seb, head of a Kent County household of 1 "other free" and 7 slaves in 1800 [MD:175].

ONEY FAMILY

1. Eleanor Oney, born say 1730, a "Negro," was living in Stepney Parish, Somerset County, on 18 June 1751 when she was convicted of having an illegitimate child by "Negro Quamino," the slave of Henry Lewis. Thomas Moor was her security for payment of her fine. Her "Negro" daughter Levina Oney was bound to Thomas Moor by the court until the age of sixteen. She was convicted of having another illegitimate child on or about 1 February 1762 on the evidence of Thomas Dashiell. In August 1762 she was living in Stepney Parish when the court fined her 20 shillings for an assault on Elizabeth Hull on 22 July 1762 [Judicial Records 1749-51, 293-4; 1760-3, 145d, 151, 168]. She was the mother of
    i.   Levina, born about 1750, a spinster living in Stepney Parish on 21 June 1768 when the court ordered her to pay a double fine when she refused to identify the father of her illegitimate child. Job Sirmon was her security [Judicial Records 1767-9, 149-150].
    ii. ?Patience, born say 1752, a "Negro," of her own free will bound herself as an apprentice to Robert Brown until the age of sixteen in June 1762. On 18 November 1766 the court convicted her of having a child by a "Negro" slave [Judicial Records 1760-3, 136; 1767-9, 36].
    iii. ?Perlina, born say 1762, presented by the Somerset County court on 17 March 1772 for having an illegitimate child [Judicial Records 1769-72, 279].

They were apparently the ancestors of
    i.   Daniel, head of a Northwest Fork Hundred, Sussex County household of 8 "free colored" in 1820 [DE:244].
    ii. Martin, head of a Little Creek Hundred, Sussex County household of 8 "free colored" in 1820 [DE:408].
    iii. Horatio, head of a Dagsboro Hundred, Sussex County household of 6 "free colored" in 1820 [DE:394].

OSBORNE FAMILY

1. Anne Osborne, born say 1678, the former servant of Elizabeth Smith "of ye River side," was convicted by the Charles County court on 14 June 1698 of having a "Molatto" child. She died before 10 November 1700 when Thomas Parker was paid for looking after her in her sickness and burying her [Court Record 1696-1701/2, 376; 1699/1700-1701/02, 99]. She may have been the ancestor of
    i.   Squire, head of a New Kent County, Virginia household of 4 "other free" and a slave in 1810 [VA:762].

OVERTON FAMILY

Members of the Overton family were
1   i.   Caleb, born 14 July 1750.
        ii.   John, born say 1780, husband of Sarah Ann **Davis** (born about 1782) who
              was born of free parents in St. Mary's County. She and her daughters
              Elizabeth (born August 1818) and Sarah Ann (born April 1820) obtained
              certificates of freedom in Washington, D.C., on 1 November 1827
              [Provine, *District of Columbia Free Negro Registers*, 111].

1.   Caleb¹ Overton, born 14 July 1750, was head of a Charles County household of 11
     "other free" in 1800 [MD:515]. He was the grandson of a white woman according
     to the registration of his son Caleb, Jr., in Washington, D.C., on 30 November
     1840. He married Margaret **Gates** of Charles County who was also born free.
     Margaret had a daughter named Elizabeth **Gates**, born 29 December 1782, by a
     previous marriage. Caleb obtained certificates of freedom for their children in
     Washington, D.C., in October 1814 [Provine, *District of Columbia Free Negro
     Registers*, 378-9]. Their children were
          i.   Margaret.
         ii.   Patrick.
        iii.   Richard.
         iv.   Susan.
          v.   Samuel, born say 1814.
         vi.   Mary Magdalene, born say 1816.
        vii.   Caleb², Jr., born about 1818, twenty-two years old on 30 November 1840.

OWENS FAMILY

Members of the Owens family in Maryland were
          i.   David, head of a North Susquehannah, Cecil County household of 1 "other
               free" in 1790.
         ii.   Jonas, head of a Charles Town, Cecil County household of 1 "other free"
               in 1790.
        iii.   James, born about 1786, head of an Anne Arundel County household of 2
               "other free" in 1810 [MD:93]. He registered in Anne Arundel County on
               12 June 1816: *aged about thirty years...bright complexion...free born*
               [Certificates of Freedom 1810-31, 84].
         iv.   Delila, born about 1793, registered in Anne Arundel County on 12 June
               1816: *aged about twenty three years...yellow complexion, long straight
               hair...free born* [Certificates of Freedom 1810-31, 84].

PALMER FAMILY

1.   Ann Palmer, born say 1706, was the servant of Michael Gilbert of Cople Parish,
     Westmoreland County, Virginia on 24 July 1724 when she acknowledged having
     a "Mulatto" child "begott of her body by a negro Man" [Orders 1721-31, 70a]. She
     may have been the ancestor of
          i.   John, head of a Loudoun County household of 5 "other free" in 1810
               [VA:313].
         ii.   Betty, head of a Queen Anne's County household of 2 "other free" in 1790.
        iii.   Samuel, head of a Kent County, Maryland household of 3 "other free" in
               1800 [MD:165].

Another Palmer family:
Priscilla Palmer, born say 1702, a single white woman of Christ Church Parish,
Lancaster County, Virginia, had a male child by Robert Carter's slave named "Mullatto
Billy" on 26 March 1723 [Orders 1721-9, 98-100].

PARKER FAMILY

Members of the Parker family in Anne Arundel County were
  i. Susan[1], born about 1730, 5-1/2 months to serve when she was listed in the inventory of the Anne Arundel County estate of Thomas Stockett in 1751. She was head of an Anne Arundel County household of 8 "other free" in 1800 [MD:109].
1 ii. Ann, born about 1732.

1. Ann Parker, born about 1732, "a free Mulatto," bound her "Mulatto" son Robert Parker to Thomas Stockett in Anne Arundel County court on 11 June 1751 until the age of twenty-one [Judgment Record 1751-4, 3]. She was listed in the inventory of the Anne Arundel County estate of Thomas Stockett on 10 January 1763:

Mullatto Servants Bound 31 yrs:	
Ann Parker about 22 months to serve -	*£5*
Sue Do 5-1/2 ------	*£7/10/0*
Tobit Between ten & Eleven yrs old	*£12*
Pegg between Eight & nine yrs old	*£8*
Bacon between five & six yrs old	*£8*
Isaac between three & four yrs old	*£6*
William twenty months old	*£3*
Charity about thirteen months old	*£2/10/0*

[Prerogative Inventories 82:46-7]. She was the mother of
  i. Robert, born say 1750, head of an Anne Arundel County household of 5 "other free" in 1810 [MD:92].
  ii. ?Tobit/ Toby, born about 1752, between ten and eleven years old on 10 January 1763 when he was listed in Stockett's inventory, head of an Anne Arundel County household of 1 "other free" and 2 slaves in 1800 [MD:117].
  iii. ?Peg, born about 1754, head of an Anne Arundel County household of 7 "other free" in 1800 [MD:116].
  iv. ?Bacon, born about 1757, head of a Montgomery County household of 5 "other free" in 1790 and 5 "other free" in Allegany County in 1810 [MD:7].
  v. ?Isaac, born about 1759.
  vi. ?William, born about 1761, head of a Cecil County household of 5 "other free" in 1800 [MD:224] and an Anne Arundel County household of 8 "other free" in 1810 [MD:93].
  vii. ?Charity, born about 1762, head of an Anne Arundel County household of 6 "other free" in 1810 [MD:77].
  viii. ?Priscilla, born about 1765, registered in Anne Arundel County on 7 August 1807: *aged forty two years...complexion dark...raised in Anne Arundel County* [Certificates of Freedom 1806-7, 43, 44]. She was head of an Anne Arundel County household of 3 "other free" in 1810 [MD:81].

Other members of the Parker family were
  i. Sarah[1], born about 1755, registered in Anne Arundel County on 7 August 1807: *aged fifty two years...yellowish complexion...raised in Anne Arundel County*.
  ii. Susanna[2]/ Suck, head of an Anne Arundel County household of 5 "other free" in 1800 [MD:116].
  iii. James, head of an Anne Arundel County household of 6 "other free" in 1810 [MD:75].
  iv. Andrew, head of an Anne Arundel County household of 5 "other free" in 1810 [MD:75].
  v. Jesse, head of an Anne Arundel County household of 5 "other free" in 1810 [MD:81].
  vi. Nancy, head of an Anne Arundel County household of 4 "other free" in

1810 [MD:75].

vii. Lucy, head of an Anne Arundel County household of 4 "other free" in 1810 [MD:77].

viii. Sarah[2], born about 1779, registered in Anne Arundel County on 8 April 1819: *aged about forty years...dark Complexion...free born*. She was head of an Anne Arundel County household of 4 "other free" in 1810 [MD:75].

ix. Elizabeth, born about 1782, registered in Anne Arundel County in 1807: *aged about twenty five years...yellowish complexion...raised in Anne Arundel County*.

x. William, born about 1783, registered in Anne Arundel County on 21 August 1819: *aged about thirty six years...dark Complexion...free born*.

xi. Susanna[3], born about 1784, registered in Anne Arundel County on 4 March 1819: *aged about thirty five years...brown complexion...free born*.

xii. Charity, born about 1786, registered in Anne Arundel County on 19 March 1823: *aged about thirty seven...brown Complexion...free born*.

xiii. Thomas, born about 1793, registered in Anne Arundel County on 21 August 1819: *a Mulatto man...aged about twenty six years...free born* [Certificates of Freedom 1810-31, 43, 44, 128, 129, 140, 190].

PARKINSON FAMILY

1. Moses Parkinson, born say 1750, married Sally **Cornish** ("Molattoes") on 7 January 1771 in Sussex County [Records of the United Presbyterian Churches of Lewes, Indian River and Cool Spring, 1756-1855, 282]. He was taxable in Lewes and Rehoboth Hundred in 1774 [DSA, RG 2535]. He was called "Moses Parkinson of Indian River Hundred a free Mulatto" in 1791 when the State summoned him to court for "making shooting matches and selling Liquor in smaller measure than allowed by law" [DSA, RG 4805.021, 1755-1791, MS case files]. Moses and Sally were the parents of

i. Moses **Cornish**, born 29 August 1777, "son of Moses and Sarah Parkeson," whose birth was registered at St. George Protestant Episcopal Church of Indian River Hundred [Wright, *Vital Records of Kent and Sussex Counties*, 103]. He was head of a Broadkill Hundred, Sussex County household of 10 "free colored" in 1820 [DE:326].

ii. ?Major, head of an Accomack County, Virginia household of 9 "other free" in 1810 [VA:47].

iii. ?John, married Sally **Handzor**, "Mulattoes," on 19 December 1810 in Sussex County [Records of the United Presbyterian Churches of Lewes, Indian River and Coolspring, Delaware 1756-1855, 322].

PARSONS FAMILY

1. Elizabeth Parsons, born say 1702, was called Elizabeth "Dersons" on 28 August 1722 when she confessed to the Prince George's County court that she had an illegitimate "Malatto" child. The court sold her and her child to her master John Magruder. On 24 March 1723/4 she was called "Elizabeth Parsons," the servant of John Magruder, when she was presented by the court for having an illegitimate child on information of James Magruder, the constable of Western Branch Hundred. She confessed to the offense on 25 August 1724, and the court ordered that she receive fifteen lashes. On 28 June 1726 she was called "Elizabeth Persons" when she confessed to having a "Malatto" child, and the court sold her and her child to John Magruder [Court Record 1720-2, 556, 620-1; 1723-6, 239, 338, 645-6]. She was probably the mother of

i. Page, born about 1721, a "Mollatto fellow named Page aged 29, 2 years to serve" who was listed in the inventory of the Prince George's County estate of Mr. John Magruder in October 1750 [Prerogative Inventories & Accounts 46:103-5].

Other members of a Parson family were

1   i. John, born say 1722.

      ii. Catherine, born say 1724, confessed to the Talbot County court in November 1745 that she had an illegitimate child by an Indian named William Asquash. The court ordered that she receive ten lashes [Judgment Record 1745-6, 246-7].[24]

2   iii. Thomas, born say 1726.

1. John Parsons, born say 1722, married Sabria **Okey**, daughter of Robert **Okey**, before 3 September 1745 when they petitioned the Sussex County Orphans Court to divide her father's land among his heirs [Orphans Court 1744-51, 17]. John was called a "mulatto" on 16 May 1747 when his daughter Ann was baptized on 16 May 1747 at St. George's Protestant Episcopal Church, Indian River Hundred, Sussex County [Wright, *Vital Records of Kent and Sussex Counties*, 92]. He was taxable in Lewes and Rehoboth Hundred, Sussex County, in 1774. He was the father of

      i. Ann, born 16 May 1747.

2. Thomas Parsons, born say 1726, a "mulatto," registered the 18 March 1749 birth of his son John at St. George's Protestant Episcopal Church, Indian River Hundred, Sussex County [Wright, *Vital Records of Kent and Sussex Counties*, 94]. He was the father of

      i. John², born 18 March 1749.

Their descendant in Delaware was

      i. Jacob, head of a New Castle County household of 6 "other free" in 1800 [DE:255].

PATTERSON FAMILY

1. Margery Patterson, born say 1734, was convicted in Kent County, Delaware, in April 1753 of having a female "Mulatto" child. The court ordered that she receive 39 lashes, be put in the pillory for two hours, be fined £10, and serve a total of 5 years. She was living in Duck Creek Hundred in August 1755 when she was indicted for having a child by a "Negro" [RG 3805.002, Quarter Sessions, 1734-79, frame 225 and August 1755 MS case file indictments]. She was probably the ancestor of

      i. James, "N." head of a Little Creek Hundred, Kent County household of 7 "other free" in 1800 [DE:34].

      ii. Peter, "N" head of a St. Jones Hundred, Kent County household of 3 "other free" in 1800 [DE:46].

     iii. Hannah, born 1776-1794, head of a Dover Hundred, Kent County household of 7 "free colored" in 1820 [DE:32].

PECK FAMILY

1. Ann Peck, born say 1703, confessed to the Prince George's County court on 26 March 1722/3 that she had a "Malatto" child who died before her court appearance. She named the father, "a negroe man nam'd Tom belonging to Esqr. Brooke." The court sold her to her master, Alexander Contee, for seven years. On 25 June 1723 Tom confessed to begetting the child, and the court ordered that he receive fifteen lashes. On 25 August 1724 she confessed to having another child by Tom, and the court ordered her sold for seven years and the child sold until the age of thirty-one [Court Record 1720-2, 648; 1723-6, 9, 83, 306, 339-40, 390-1, 558]. She was the

---

[24]A William Asquash was one of the Choptank Indians who sold land in Dorchester County in 1727 [Land Records 1720-32, Liber old 8, 153].

mother of

2   i.   Jane, born 15 February 1723/4.

2.   Jane Peck, born 15 February 1723/4, was called "Mulatto Jane belonging to Alexr. Contee" in Prince George's County court on 24 June 1740 when she was presented for having an illegitimate "Malatto" child. She and her daughter Sarah were sold to her master. On 27 November 1744 the court bound her son Joseph to William Beanes until the age of twenty-one years and ordered that he give the boy one year of schooling and his freedom dues at the completion of the indenture. She could not pay her fine, so she received ten lashes. The court ordered her daughter Priscilla bound to Robert and Edith Richards until the age of sixteen years and ordered that they teach her to read, spin, knit and sew. On 28 November 1749 the court bound her fifteen-month-old son John to Thomas Contee until the age of twenty-one, and on 22 March 1757 the court bound her seven-month-old son David to Thomas Contee until the age of thirty-one. On 25 November 1766 she confessed to having another illegitimate child for which the court ordered that she only pay a fine and court costs for which her son Joseph provided security [Court Record 1723-6, 340; 1738-40, 653; 1740-2, 18, 617; 1746-7, 620; 1748-9, 80, 85, 174; 1751-4, 174; 1754-8, 411; 1765-6, 27]. She was the mother of

3   i.   Sarah, born 5 February 1740.
     ii. Joseph[1], born about January 1744, bound to William Beanes on 27 November 1744. John Booker purchased Joseph from Beanes and boarded him with Robert Richards. Booker died and Beanes claimed that Joseph still belonged to him because he had had no right to sell him [Court Record 1748-9, 235-6]. He may have been identical to the Joseph Peck who head of a Baltimore County household of 7 "other free" with Thomas Peck in 1810 [MD:477].
     iii. Priscilla, born in October 1747.
     iv. John, born about August 1748, a "free negro" head of a Prince George's County household of 2 "other free" in 1800 [MD:281].
4   v.   ?David[1], born about September 1756.

3.   Sarah Peck, born 5 February 1740, was bound to Alexander Contee by the Prince George's County court on 24 June 1740. She was called "Mulatto Sarah" on 25 June 1765 when the court ordered that she be sold for seven years and sold her two year old son David to John Harrison until the age of thirty-one. She confessed to having another "Mulatto" child on 24 June 1766 and another on 22 March 1768 when the court ordered her sold for a third seven-year term and bound her seven-month-old child Beck to John Harrison until the age of thirty-one [Court Record 1764-5, 1, 115; 1766-8, 452, 576]. She was the mother of
     i.   David[2], born about June 1763, two years old on 25 June 1765 when the court sold him as an apprentice to John Harrison until the age of thirty-one [Court Record 1765-6, 115]. He was head of a Frederick County household of 6 "other free" in 1800 [MD:841]. He registered in Frederick County on 14 June 1806: *a yellow negro or Mulatto, about 5 feet 11 Inches high, stout made and of a good countenance, aged about forty three years...he was born in Prince George's County in this State, and was brought to this County in the year 1781 by a certain John Harrison, Esq., now deceased, as his servant or slave until he should arrive to the age of thirty one years* [Certificates of Freedom 1806-27, 1].
5   ii. ?Jonathan, born say 1766.
6   iii. Rebecca[1], born July 1767.

4.   David[1] Peck, born about August 1757, was seven months old on 22 March 1757 when he was bound to Thomas Contee. He was a "free negro" head of a Prince George's County household of 6 "other free" in 1800 [MD:259] and 1 "free colored" in Frederick County in 1830. He was the father of
     i.   Henny, born about 1796, registered in Prince George's County on 27 June

1815: *a dark mulatto woman, about 19 years old...daughter of David Peck Sr., a free man of color.*

ii. Polly, born about 1799, registered in Prince George's County on 27 June 1815: *a bright mulatto woman, about 16 years old...daughter of David Peck Sr., a free man of color.*

iii. David[4], registered in Prince George's County on 10 July 1830: *a free black man who was born free...on Mr. Mackall's plantation and is the son of old David Peck who I daresay you very well know as he was a tenant for Mr. Mackall for many years. He and his wife were born free* [Provine, *Registrations of Free Negroes*, 18, 156].

5. Nathaniel Peck, born say 1766, and his wife Lydia, "free negroes," registered the 1 September 1792 birth of their daughter Rebecca at St. Paul's Parish, Baltimore. He was head of a Baltimore Town household of 6 "other free" in 1790. Perhaps his widow was Mrs. Peck, head of a Baltimore City household of 6 "other free" in 1800 [MD:314]. They were the parents of

    i. Rebecca[2], born 1 September 1792, baptized 3 February 1793 [Reamy, *Records of St. Paul's Parish*, I:64].

    ii. ?Mary, head of a Baltimore City household of 5 "other free" in 1810 [MD:270].

6. Rebecca Peck, born July 1767, was bound as an apprentice to John Harrison on 22 March 1768 until the age of thirty-one by the Prince George's County court [Court Record 1766-8, 579]. She was the mother of

    i. Joseph[2], born about 1780, registered as a free Negro in Prince George's County on 11 March 1813: *a dark mulatto man, about 33 years old...raised in the town of Upper Marlboro in Prince George's County and is a free man, being a descendant of a free woman named Rebecca Peck.*

Other members of the Peck family were

    i. Thomas, head of a Baltimore City household of 5 "other free" in 1810 [MD:265].

    ii. Betty, head of a Washington County household of 3 "other free" in 1800 [MD:554].

    iii. Richard, born about 1788, registered in Frederick County on 13 January 1818: *a Yellow Negroe Man aged about Twenty six years, five feet five inches high, square made...is the son of Deborah, a free Woman of Colour and a free Born as appears by the affirmation of John Russell* [Certificates of Freedom 1806-27, 81].

Talbot County
1. Mary Peck, born about 1712, was a spinster white servant of Solomon Horney in March 1758 when she acknowledged in Talbot County court that she had a child by a "Negro." The court ordered her to serve her master another twelve months for his damages and then be sold for seven years [Criminal Record 1755-61, 161]. She was about fifty years old and still had four years to serve on 10 November 1762 when she was listed in the inventory of the Talbot County estate of Solomon Horney [Prerogative Inventories 79:453]. She was the mother of

  2   i. Frances, born say 1738.

  3   ii. Simon, born say 1750.

        iii. Patrick, born about 1757, a five-year-old "Mulatto" boy with twenty-six years to serve when he was listed in the 10 November 1762 Talbot County estate of Solomon Horney [Prerogative Inventories 79:453].

2. Frances Peck, born say 1738, won her freedom in Talbot County in 1769 by proving that her mother was a white woman. She was probably identical to Frank Peck who was head of a Talbot County household of 7 "other free" in 1790, Fanny Peck who was head of a Baltimore City household of 12 "other free" in 1800

[MD:332], and F. Peck, head of a Baltimore City household of 6 "other free" in 1810 [MD:77]. She may have been the mother of
  i.   David³, head of a Talbot County household of 1 "other free" in 1800 [MD:521].

3.   Simon Peck, born say 1750, was head of a Talbot County household of 10 "other free" in 1800 [MD:519]. He may have been the father of
  i.   Louranah, born about 1783, registered in Talbot County on 24 June 1815: *a dark mulatto Woman...about 33 yrs. of age...born free and raised in the County.*
  ii. Henry, born about 1787, registered in Talbot County on 11 September 1815: *a bright mulatto man about 28 years of age.*
  iii. Charles, born about 1790, registered in Talbot County on 23 September 1815: *a bright Mulatto man...about 25 years of age...born free & raised in the County.*
  iv. George, born about 1794, registered in Talbot County on 11 July 1815: *a Black man about five feet Seven Inches high about 21 years of age...born and raised in the County afsd. and is free born* [Certificates of Freedom 1807-15, 41, 49; 1815-28, 3].

PENNINGTON FAMILY

Members of the Pennington family were
  i.   Mahala, born say 1780, mother of Kitty **Danby** who registered in Dorchester County on 8 September 1829: *bright yellow...born free in Dorchester County and is the daughter of Mahala Pennington who was also born free about 29 years of age* [Certificates of Freedom for Negroes 1806-64, 64]. Kitty **Danby** was probably related to Mary **Dansby**, head of a Talbot County household of 6 "other free" in 1800 [MD:530] and Andrew **Danberry**, head of a Talbot County household of 6 "other free" in 1800 [MD:510].
  ii. James, head of a Talbot County household of 2 "other free" in 1790, 4 "other free" and a white woman 26-46 years old in 1800 [MD:522], 5 "other free" in New Castle County, Delaware, in 1810, and 8 "free colored" in Red Lion Hundred, New Castle County, in 1820 [DE:168].
  iii. Philip, head of a New Castle County, Delaware household of 4 "other free" in 1810 [DE:303].
  iv. Elias, a "mulatto," bound out in Cecil County on 30 July 1796 to serve until the age of 21.

PENNY FAMILY

1.   Ann¹ Penny, born say 1680, was the mother of a "Mallatto" man named Sam Penny who was about twenty-six years old on 14 March 1726/7 when the Charles County court ruled that he was born in Charles County, the son of a white woman named Ann Penny, and should have been bound until the age of thirty-one [Court Record 1725-7, 411-2]. Ann was the mother of
2   i.   Sam, born about 1701.

2.   Sam Penny, born about 1701, was living with Cleborn Lomax, Sr., on 14 June 1726 when the Charles County court ordered that he appear in court. On 14 March 1726/7 the court bound him to serve John Cox for five years [Court Record 1725-7, 236, 344, 411-2]. He may have been the father of
  i.   Ann², "Mulatto" head of a Charles County household of 1 "other free" in 1790 and 6 "free colored" in 1830.
  ii. Sarah, "Mulatto" head of a Charles County household of 1 "other free" in 1790 and 10 "other free" and 3 slaves in 1810 [MD:329], perhaps the Sarah Penny who was presented by the Charles County court in March 1774 for

having an illegitimate child [Court Record 1773-4, 77].

Another member of the family was
    i. Nancy, born about 1755, a "Mulatto" counted in the 1850 census for Charles County.

PERKINS FAMILY

1. Isaac Perkins, born say 1690, was taxable in Murderkill Hundred, Kent County, Delaware, in 1729 and 1730: responsible for the tax of Winsley **Driggers** [DSA, RG 3535, 1726-42, frames 354, 364]. He may have been related to the Perkins family of Accomack County, Virginia [*Free African Americans of North Carolina, Virginia...* by this author]. Sarah Redman sued him in Kent County for a debt of £5, and he was committed for want of bail in May 1727 [RG 3815.031, frames 147, 155]. He may have been the ancestor of
    i. Caleb[1], born say 1715, perhaps ill or unable to support himself and his family in November 1740 when the Sussex County court allowed £7 for the support of his wife and daughter. He was sued by James Fisher in Sussex County court in May 1742 [RG 4815.017, General Sessions, 1707-41, frame 638; 1741-53, frame 75].
    ii. William, born say 1728, no race indicated when he was tried for felony in Accomack County on 22 September 1746: found guilty of "taking but not breaking" (in). On 24 November 1747 he was charged with stealing 8 yards of linen, given 25 lashes, and ordered to leave the county within six days [Orders 1744-53, 221, 224, 233, 236]. He was probably the William Perkins who was indicted in Sussex County court on an unspecified charge in February 1747/8 [DSA, RG 4815.017, General Sessions Court, 1741-53, frame 330], a taxable "Molatto" in Little Creek Hundred, Sussex County, on a cow and calf and 3 shoats in 1796. He was head of a Sussex County household of 6 "other free" in 1800 [DE:343] and 6 in 1810 [DE:300]. Another William Perkins was head of a Sussex County household of 7 "other free" in 1810 [DE:363].
    iii. Luke, taxable in Mispillion Hundred, Kent County, in 1773, a delinquent taxable in 1774, taxable in Little Creek Hundred, Kent County, in 1780 in the same list as Caleb Perkins, taxable in Broadkill Hundred, Sussex County in 1790 in the same list as Caleb Perkins [DSA, RG 3535, 1768-84, frames 171, 204, 369, 419, 446, 489; RG 2535, 1780-96].
    iv. Caleb[2], taxable in Little Creek Hundred, Kent County, Delaware from 1780 to 1789 when he was a delinquent [RG 3535, Kent County Levy List, 1768-84, frames 446, 489; 1784-97, frames 49, 72, 75, 107, 136, 177], a delinquent taxable in Broadkill and Little Creek Hundred, Sussex County, in 1790 [DSA, RG 2535, 1780-96], a "Negro" taxable in Duck Creek Hundred in 1797 and 1798 [RG 3535, 1784-97, frames 498, 577; 1797-8, frame 420], and head of a Kent County household of 5 "other free" in 1800 [DE:18].
    v. James, head of a Sussex County household of 4 "other free" in 1800 [DE:101] and 8 in 1810 [DE:363].
    vi. Aaron, head of a Sussex County household of 6 "other free" in 1800 [DE:438].
    vii. Peter, head of a Sussex County household of 8 "other free" in 1810 [DE:363].
    viii. Adam, head of a Kent County, Delaware household of 3 "other free" in 1810 [DE:62].
    ix. Frank, head of a Talbot County household of 5 "other free" in 1790 and 6 "other free" and a white woman in 1800 [MD:514].
    x. Sampson, born in December 1751, Mulatto son of Esther Perkins, bound to Southy Littleton by the Accomack County court on 28 May 1755, to Thomas Webb on 25 February 1755 and to David James to be a weaver on

26 April 1757 [Orders 1753-63, 45, 81, 184]. He was a "Molatto" taxable in Pitts Creek, Worcester County, in 1783 [MdHR, MSA S1161-11-9, p.4].

PERLE/ PEARL FAMILY

1. Robert[1] Perle, born about 1686, was freed by the 14 April 1713 Prince George's County will of Richard Marsham. Marsham called him "Robert (a molatto)...age 28 years" and stipulated that he should serve until the age of thirty-five at which time Robert, his wife and child were to be free. He also stipulated that Robert should build his grandson Leonard Brooke a twenty foot dwelling house and a fifty foot tobacco house, clear of carpenter's wages. Any other children born to Robert's wife while she was a slave were to continue as slaves [Prerogative Court (Wills), Liber 13, fols. 514-20]. Robert was listed in Marsham's 15 June 1713 Prince George's County inventory:

Negroes:

one Malato Man Robin 7 years to serve, age 27	£16
one Malato boy Jemmy 17 years to serve, age 18	£20
one Malato woman nanny, 7 years to serve	£14
one Malato boy Daniel, sickly, 2 yrs old	£5

In Negroe Robins house:	
one Indiff good flock bed boulster & old blankett	0/10/0
3 worne Stript & Duffils matchcoats	0/9/6
old Iron carpenter's tooles a sett	0/10/0
one Chest	0/5/0
brown thread	0/20/0
2 Casters hatts	0/10/0
12 Ells brown Oz"	0/9/6
1 felt hat	0/2/6
1 p¹ french falls	0/3/0
1 ream writing paper, ink powd'	0/8/0
an old Syth	0/1/6
44 hogs 3 yrs old or thereabts.	26/8/0
6 a yr. old dᵒ	1/16/0
3 Shoetes	0/9/0
Hair cloth for sailes	0/14/0
and old plow	0/9/0
a Creens bagg	0/0/6
a p¹ old Scales and weights	0/2/6
plate at 5-2 per ounce, 82 ounces	21/3/8

[Prerogative Court Inventories and Accounts, Vol. 35A, 299-308].
He was called "Robert Pearl, carpenter of Prince George's County, alias Mulatto Robin," when he purchased land in Prince George County near the Patuxent River and the Beaver Dam Branch from John Cranford for £20 on 14 January 1722/3 and purchased a 100 acre part of Archer's Pasture from Jonathan Prather on 11 July 1724 [Land Records I:429-30, 443, 568]. He sued Charles Drury for assaulting him on 6 October 1727, but the court ruled unanimously on 26 March 1728 that the plaintiff was "a Malata born of a negroe slave and though manumitted by his late master's will" was not qualified to take the oath and prosecute any action at law in the court [Court Record 1728-9, 129]. He was called "Robert Perle of Prince George's County, free Mullatto," on 18 October 1727 when he petitioned the Assembly that he was rendered incapable by the justices of the county court from recovering his just debts [*Archives of Maryland* 36:20]. And in May 1729 he took his case of assault against Charles Drury to the Provincial Court which awarded him £45 sterling and his costs [Provincial Court Liber R.B., no. 1, fols. 135-7, MSA]. On 5 February 1728 Benjamin Loyd mortgaged to him and Peregrine Makanesse, blacksmith, a 52 acre part of *Taylortown* in the freshes on the west side of the Patuxent River, a 12-1/2 acre part of *Taylortown*, and two Negroes, fifteen

cattle, two horses, a mare, sixteen hogs, household goods, a dwelling house and 1,100 pounds of tobacco due Loyd from Charles Gervis for rent of land. On 23 August 1729 he mortgaged slaves Harry and Lucy to sheriff Richard Lee for 8,411 pounds of tobacco [Land Records M:460, 464]. He was called "alias Malatto Robin" when he appeared in Prince George's County court between 1728 and 1735. He sued John Bursh in March 1728, but the case was agreed between them before trial, and he was sued for 972 pounds of tobacco in June 1728. On 25 March 1729 he and Peregrine Mackanesse petitioned the Prince George's County court that they had provided £200 security for Benjamin Lloyd's administration of the estate of his father Thomas Lloyd. They testified that Lloyd had mortgaged two parcels of land, two Negroes, one white lad, fifteen head of cattle, two horses, three mares, sixteen hogs, household goods, corn and tobacco on the plantation by a deed executed and acknowledged on 5 February 1728. However, Mackanesse and Perle were unable to get Lloyd to complete the administration of the estate, and they asked that the court either appoint them administrators or release them from their bond, but the court rejected their petition. On 27 November 1733 Richard Marsham Waring had a suit against him which was agreed to before coming to trial. In November 1735 he petitioned the Prince George's County court that the main road ran through his plantation and people riding through were always leaving the gate open. The court appointed a jury to view the road and make a decision. On 22 June 1736 he and Thomas Swann provided £71 security for John Orchard's administration of Darby Rine's estate, and he purchased the thirty-one-year indenture of Mary Wedge's "Malatto" child [Court Record 1728-9, 52, 209, 220, 410; 1732-4, 323-4, 452-4, 587, 655, 672-3; 1734-5, 642; 1736-8, 51, 60-1]. On 26 November 1736 he and his wife Ann sold 44 acres of *Archer's Pasture* near Cabbin Branch to Henry Holland Hawkins, Gentleman, of Charles County for £10 and 650 pounds of tobacco [Land Records T:423]. He was the overseer of the highway in the lower part of Monocacy Hundred on 23 August 1748 when the grand jury presented him for neglecting his duty, and the court fined him 500 pounds of tobacco [Court Record 1746-8, 332; 1748-9, 45]. He and (his son) Thomas Pearl recorded their cattle marks in Frederick County court on 20 January 1748/9. By 7 October 1751 Frederick County deed he sold 124 acres of *Archer's Pasture* on the west side of the Patuxent River to the Rev. John Eversfield, rector of St. Paul's Parish in Prince George's County, for 6,000 pounds of tobacco. On 8 November 1756 he purchased 150 acres called *Flint's Grove* on the west side of Seneca Creek in the part of Frederick County which became Montgomery County in 1776 and sold this land on 2 December 176_. He left a 3 September 1765 Frederick County will, proved 4 October 1765, by which he gave slaves Peter, Rachel, Nan and Harry, a horse and furniture to his son Daniel; gave slaves Lucy, Peg, Jenney, Jo and Lids to his son James; gave slaves George, Bess, Seney, Bill and Jeney to his son Basil; named his children Thomas Pearl, Charles Pearl, Ann **Marshall** and Catherine **Dean** and gave four barrels of corn and a barrel of wheat to Elizabeth Jervis [Frederick County Land Records B:1; F:93-5; G:318; Will Records A-1:257]. Elizabeth Jervis, widow, was convicted by the Frederick County court of stealing sixty-seven pieces of silver Spanish dollars and a gold French Guinea from his estate. Thomas Pearl, James Pearl, Basil Pearl, William Graves and Mary Marshall were witnesses against her. She received thirty lashes, a half hour in the pillory and was ordered to pay 3,992 pounds of tobacco to Robert's executors James and Basil Pearl [Judgment Record 1763-6, 800, 807, 808-10, 822].[25] Robert was the father of

2   i.   Daniel[1], born about 1711.

      ii. Anne, born say 1722, a "Mulatto" woman who married a white planter named William Marshall. The Prince George's County court ordered that he be sold as a servant for seven years. On 23 August 1743 the court ordered him released from prison so the case could be tried at the

---

[25] See http://www.lindapages.com/genealogy/robertpearl-jeske.htm by Mary Clement Jeske for more on Robert Perle.

Provincial Court [Court Record 1743-4, 17].

iii. James, died before 12 May 1774 when his widow Elizabeth returned the inventory of his Frederick County estate, valued at £582 and named Basil and Thomas Pearl as his next of kin [Inventories, C-3:194].

iv. Catherine, born say 1729, living at Monocacy Hundred on 25 August 1747 when the grand jury of Prince George's County presented her for bastardy. The presentment was quashed on 24 November 1747, perhaps because she was married [Court Record 1747-8, 90, 297]. She was married to a member of the **Dean** family when her father made his will.

v. Thomas, son of Robert Pearl, recorded his cattle mark in Frederick County court on 20 January 1748/9. He confessed in Frederick County court to assault against Elizabeth Jervis in June 1763 [Judgment Record 1763-6, 28, 42].

vi. Basil[1], head of an Allegany County household of 8 "other free" in 1800 (Basil Perril, Sen[r]) [MD:1].

vii. Charles, master of John **Grimes** who was bound to him as an apprentice carpenter until the age of twenty-one by the Prince George's County court on 22 June 1762 [Court Record 1761-3, 188]. Charles was head of an Allegany County household of 5 "other free" and 5 slaves in 1800 [MD:5].

2. Daniel[1] Pearl, born about 1711, a "Mullato," married a white woman named Elizabeth Graves before November 1742 when the Prince George's County court presented her for the offense on information of Thomas Wilson and Edward Mobberly. The case was dismissed by order of the attorney general on 26 March 1744/5. Daniel was sued on 25 March 1745/6 by William Cumming for a debt of 1,600 pounds of tobacco [Court Record 1742-3, 191; 1744-6, 26, 504, 578]. He gave his age as fifty-seven and named his father Robert Pearl when he made a deposition in a Frederick County land dispute on 1 April 1768. He left a 5 September 1774 Frederick Town will, proved 15 November 1774, by which he directed that slaves Nann and Rachel be sold to pay his debts, gave a cow and calf to his son Basil, gave 5 shillings to his daughter Ann **Burgis** and divided the remainder of his estate among his children Joseph, Robert, Jeremiah and Sary Pearl who he ordered to take care of his son William Pearl; ordered his boy Kitt to be set free at age twenty-one; ordered his boy Jack who was given to him by the court to be delivered to his daughter Sary Pearl; and named his sons Joseph and brother Basil as executors [Land Record Liber L:518-20; Will Records A-1:520]. He was the father of

i. Basil[2], head of an Allegany County household of 3 "other free" in 1800 (Bazel Perril, Jun[r]) [MD:3].

ii. Joseph, sued John Johnson in Frederick County court in March 1764 for assault [Judgment Record 1763-6, 197].

iii. Robert[2].

iv. Jeremiah.

v. Sarah, posted bond of £10 to appear in Frederick County court in August 1766 to testify against Margaret and Samuel Park [Judgment Record 1763-6, 1034], perhaps identical to S. Pearl, head of a Frederick County household of 3 "other free" and 4 slaves in 1810 [MD:598].

vi. Ann **Burgis**.

vii. William.

Other Perle/ Pearl/ Perrill descendants were

i. Mary Perrill, head of an Allegany County household of 6 "other free" in 1800 [MD:7], perhaps the Mary Perl who was a 90-year-old "Mulatto" counted in the 1850 census for Frederick County in the household of Jacob Perl (age 39).

ii. Daniel[2], head of a Prince George's County household of 6 "other free" in 1810 [MD:42].

iii. P., head of a Frederick County household of 5 "other free" in 1810

[MD:598].

PHILLIPS FAMILY

1. Elizabeth Phillips, born say 1700, was the servant of Eliza Stevens of St. Peter's Parish in March 1720 when the Talbot County court ordered that she serve her mistress an additional year for stealing petticoats and a bonnet from her mistress. In March 1724/5 she confessed to the court that she had an illegitimate child by "Negroe Will, the slave of Elizabeth Phillips." The court ordered that she be sold as a servant for seven years. She confessed to having another child by William in March 1725/6. In November 1728 she admitted to having another child by a "Negroe" and the court ordered her and her child sold to William Stevens. She was the servant of William Stevens in November 1731 when she was convicted of fornication and given thirty lashes [Judgment Record 1720, 14; 1725-6, 64-5, 485-6; 1726, 89; 1728, n.p.; 1731-3, 463]. Elizabeth may have been the ancestor of

   2   i. Jane, born say 1748.
   3   ii. Richard, born say 1760.
        iii. Stephen, born before 1776, head of a household of 2 "free colored" in Election District 3 of Caroline County in 1820. In 1843 Jacob Charles (counted in the 1820-1840 census for Election District 3 of Caroline County) received Stephen's pay of $13.33 for serving in the Revolution [*Archives of Maryland Online*, 595:422].
        iv. John, "Negro" head of a Kent County household of 2 "other free" in 1790.
        v. Henry, head of a Kent County household of 5 "other free" in 1800 [MD:165] and 6 in 1810 (H. Phillips) [MD:871].
        vi. Robert, head of a Kent County household of 7 "other free" in 1810 [MD:845].

2. Jane Phillips, born say 1748, was the servant of Moses Alford in August 1767 when she was convicted by the Kent County court of having a "Molatto" child. The court sold her son Anthony Phillips until the age of thirty-one to her master for 5 shillings [Criminal Docket 1766-71, n.p.]. She was the mother of
        i. Antony, head of a Harford County household of 5 "other free" in 1810 [MD:800].

3. Richard Phillips, born say 1760, was head of a Caroline County household of 6 "other free" in 1790, 13 in 1800 [MD:471], and 8 in 1810 [MD:178]. He was probably the father of
        i. Daniel, registered in Caroline County on 31 October 1809: *yellow complexion, free born and raised in the said county* [Certificates of Freedom, 33].

Anne Arundel County
1. Mary Phillips, born say 1714, servant of William Lock, was convicted by the Anne Arundel County court in June 1734 of having an illegitimate child "begott by a Negro." The court bound her six-month-old daughter to her master until the age of thirty-one, and in March 1735/6 the executor of Lock's estate brought her into court to be sold for seven years [Judgment Record 1734-6, 4, 410]. She was listed in the inventory of the Anne Arundel County estate of William Lock, Esquire, in 1734:
Mary Phillips infirm 2 years & 4 months to serve -   £5
Molato Dick 6 years to serve -   £22
Negroes:
Sam a Molato 2 years old to be free at thirty one -   £6
[Prerogative Inventories & Accounts 1734, 191-4]. She was probably the ancestor of
        i. John, head of an Anne Arundel County household of 2 "other free" in 1790.
        ii. Betsey, born about 1770, registered in Anne Arundel County on 7 August 1807: *aged thirty seven years...complexion yellowish...raised in Anne*

Arundel County [Certificates of Freedom 1806-7, 43].
  iii. Poll, head of an Anne Arundel household of 3 "other free" in 1810 [MD:81].

PICKETT FAMILY

1. Mary Pickett, born say 1703, was the servant of Edward Offutt on 27 August 1723 when she confessed in Prince George's County court that she had a "Malatto" child. The court sold her and her child to William Offutt [Court Record 1723-6, 77, 139]. She was probably the mother of
  i. Sarah Pickart, born say 1725, mother of a "Molatto" son Stafford who was born in Overwharton Parish, Stafford County, Virginia, on 22 October 1757 [Overwharton Parish, Stafford County, Registry 1724-76, 192].
  ii. William¹, head of a Montgomery County, Pennsylvania household of 5 "other free" in 1790, perhaps the William Pickett who was head of a Philadelphia County household of 5 "other free" in 1790.

PLOWMAN FAMILY

1. Mary Plowman, born say 1685, was a "Spinster" presented by the Kent County, Delaware court in May 1704 for having a bastard child by Frank, "A Negro Slave lately belonging to Cornelia Curtis." The court ordered that she receive twenty-one lashes and that she serve her master, Daniel Rutty, additional time for paying her court fees. Frank received thirty-nine lashes, and his master, Hugh Luffe, was ordered to pay his costs. In August 1706 she came into court and bound her "Mollatoe" daughter, Rose, to Daniel Rutty and his wife Eleanor until the age of twenty-one [Court Records 1703-1717, 5b, 50b]. She was the mother of
  i. Rose, born about 1704.

PLUMMER FAMILY

The Plummer family descended from a young white woman who was convicted by the Calvert County court of having a child by a "Negro" in January 1692. In August 1693 her father, Thomas Plummer of Anne Arundel County, appealed to the Council of Maryland to reduce her fine of 6,000 pounds of tobacco [*Archives of Maryland* 8:351-2]. Her daughter was probably the ancestor of
1 i. Cupid, born say 1760.
  ii. Thomas, head of Kent County, Delaware household of 3 "other free" in 1800 [DE:16].

1. Cupid Plummer, born say 1760, was head of a Prince George's County household of 6 "other free" in 1790 and 6 in 1800 [MD:281]. His wife was identified as Milly Plummer when their children obtained certificates of freedom in Prince George's County. They were the parents of
  i. Eliza, born about 1786, registered in Prince George's County between 29 June and 28 July 1826: *a dark mulatto woman, about 40 years old...daughter of Milly Plummer.*
  ii. Becky, born about 1790, registered in Prince George's County on 1 April 1820: *Dr. William Beanes proved to the clerk's satisfaction that Becky Plummer, a black woman about 30 years old...has a dark complexion...daughter of a free man of color named Cupit Plummer and his wife Milly who is also free. Becky was born and raised in Prince George's County.*
  iii. Milly, born about 1798, registered on 10 March 1828: *about 30 years old...daughter of Milly Plummer* [Provine, *Registrations of Free Negroes*, 34, 57, 73].

POULSON FAMILY

1. Hannah Polson, born say 1725, was the servant of Edward Day on 6 November 1745 when she confessed in Baltimore County court that she had "a Negro basterd child latly born of her body." The court ordered that she serve her master an additional seven years and sold her daughter Nan to her master until the age of thirty-one [Proceedings 1743-6, 748-9]. Her descendants were
    i.   Joseph, born about 1769, a seven-year-old "Mulatto" bound to William Smith of Harford County in 1776 [*Maryland Historical Society Bulletin*, vol. 35, no.3]. He was head of an Allegany County household of 5 "other free" in 1800 [MD:15].
    ii. John, born before 1776, head of a Wilmington Borough, New Castle County household of 9 "free colored" in 1820 [DE:186].

PRATT FAMILY

1. Elizabeth Pratt, born about 1694, was an eighteen year old "mallatto Girle" who successfully petitioned the Charles County court for her freedom in August 1712. Her mother, Dido, was freed by the last will of Major Thomas Truman, and Elizabeth was then a servant of John Southern's widow [Judicial Records 1711-5, E-2:152]. She may have been the ancestor of
    i.   Daniel, head of a Mispillion Hundred, Kent County household of 4 "other free" in 1800 [DE:126], 4 in 1810 [DE:85], and 7 "free colored" in 1820 [DE:79].
    ii. Polly, born about 1770, registered in Talbot County on 19 October 1816: *a negro woman...now about 43 years of age...rather of a light Complexion...born free and raised in the County* [Certificates of Freedom 1815-28, 48].
    iii. Samuel, born before 1776, head of a Kent County, Maryland household of 6 "free colored" in 1830.

PROTEUS/ PRATTIS FAMILY

1. Sarah Protice, born say 1715, was presented by the Queen Anne's County court in March 1770 for failing to list herself as a taxable. In May 1771 the court approved her petition to be levy free for the future [Judgments 1771-80, 6]. She may have been related to Isaac **Bently** who was described as a "mulatto fellow...alias Protus" on 14 August 1760 when Richard Tilghman Earle of Queen Anne's County advertised in the *Maryland Gazette* that he had run away with an English convict servant man named Benjamin Williams [Green, *The Maryland Gazette, 1727-61*, 251]. She may have been the ancestor of

    3   i.   Rebecca Protes, born say 1735.
    3   ii. Charles[1] Pratis, born say 1750.
        iii. William Prattice, "F.N." head of a Kent County, Delaware household of 6 "other free" in 1810, listed twice [MD:33, 47], head of a Murderkill Hundred, Kent County household of 8 "free colored" in 1820 [DE:13].

2. Rebecca Proteus, born say 1735, was a spinster "Mulatto" woman living in Queen Anne's County in March 1754 when the was fined 30 shillings for having an illegitimate child named Margaret. Charles Conner was her security for her maintenance of the child [Criminal Record 1751-9, n.p.]. She was a spinster of Christ Church Parish who was convicted in Queen Anne's County court of stealing a hog worth 100 pounds of tobacco in June 1768 [Judgment Records 1766-7, part 1, CD image 100]. She was the mother of
    i.   Margaret, born 10 April 1753.

3. Charles[1] Prattis, born say 1750, was head of a Caroline County household of 6 "other free" in 1790. He may have been the father of

    i. Charles², born 1 October 1769, registered in Caroline County on 20 July 1815: *free born yellow complexion aged 46 in October next.*

    ii. Isaac, born 28 October 1792, registered in Caroline County on 14 November 1814: *negro man Isaac Prattis was free born yellow complexion raised in County of Caroline 22 years old 28 October last* [Certificates of Freedom 1807-1863, pp. 68, 72].

PRISS/ PRESS FAMILY

1. Priscilla, born say 1688, was called "Priss alias Priscilla a Malatta or Mustees bagg with a bastard Child got in Somerset County in Maryland" in Accomack County court on 7 August 1706 when Edward Bagwell, "Indian," appeared in court and agreed to have her child bound to him [Orders 1703-9, 75]. Her child was

2   i. William, born in 1706.

2. William Priss/ Press, born in 1706, was called "an Indian who was born in Accomack (County) of the body of a free Negro called Priscilla" in March 1730/1 when he was fined 1,000 pounds of tobacco for failing to list himself as a tithable in Northampton County, Virginia. Thomas Fisherman, who was also an Indian, was paid 1,000 pounds of tobacco for informing on him [Mihalyka, *Loose Papers 1628-1731*, 239]. William was apparently the ancestor of the following members of the Press family:

    i. Littleton, married Molly **Fisherman** 14 December 179_ Northampton County bond, Reubin **Reed** security.

    ii. Elsey, head of an Accomack County household of 3 "other free" in 1800 [*Virginia Genealogist* 2:160].

    iii. Tabby, married Thomas **Francis**, 26 December 1796 Northampton County bond, Edmund Press security.

    iv. Molly, married Sam **Beavans**, 19 August 1797 Northampton County bond, Abraham Lang security.

    v. Edmund, security for the 24 September 1796 Northampton County marriage of Solomon **Beavans** and Esther **Casey**.

    vi. ?John, head of a Sussex County family of 8 "other free" in 1810 [DE:375].

PRICE FAMILY

Delaware
1. Eleanor Price, born say 1685, was living in Mispillion Hundred, Kent County, Delaware, in May 1703 when she was presented by the court for "Fornication with A Negro Man named Peter Belonging to Mr. John Walker" (their master). She pleaded guilty, received twenty-one lashes and was ordered to serve her master an additional eighteen months [Court Records 1699-1703, 80b]. In May 1708 the Kent County court bound her child Jeremia to John and Daniel Walker, the sons of John Walker, until the age of twenty-one [Court Records 1703-17, 72b]. Her son was

2   i. Jeremiah¹, born 15 March 1703.

2. Jeremiah Price, born 15 March 1703, was bound to John and Daniel Walker of Kent County, Delaware, in May 1708 until the age of twenty-one [Court Records 1703-17, 72b]. He may have been the ancestor of

    i. Jacob, a "Mollater" man, taxable in the North West Fork Hundred, Sussex County, in an undated tax list, about 1780.

    ii. William, head of a Montgomery County, Pennsylvania household of 7 "other free" in 1790.

    iii. Peter, head of a Delaware County, Pennsylvania household of 5 "other free" in 1790.

    iv. Josiah, head of a Franklin County, Pennsylvania household of 2 "other free" and a white woman in 1790.

    v. Thomas, head of a Montgomery County, Pennsylvania household of 2 "other free" in 1790.

vi. Catherine, head of a Chester County, Pennsylvania household of 1 "other free" in 1790.

Maryland

1. Jane Price, born say 1727, was the indentured servant of Hugh Eccleston of Great Choptank Parish, Dorchester County, on 10 November 1745 when she confessed to having a "Molatto" child by a "Negroe" [Judgment Record 1744-5, 475]. She was a "Malatto Woman" who still had ten years to serve when she was listed in the inventory of the Dorchester County estate of Thomas Eccleston on 31 August 1747 [Prerogative Inventories & Accounts 1747-1748, 264]. She may have been the ancestor of

   i. Rachel, born say 1757, a spinster servant who had a "Mulattoe" child during her service and was sold by the Caroline County court for seven years after the completion of her service. The court also sold her son Stephen, born 22 May 1777, until the age of thirty-one for £25 [Criminal Record 1774-8, 369-70].

   ii. Isaac, head of a Caroline County household of 5 "other free" in 1790.

   iii. Jere², head of an Octoraro, Cecil County household of 1 "other free" in 1790.

PRIDE FAMILY

1. Southy Pride, born about 1738, was born in Sussex County, and was 21 years old when he enlisted in Captain John Wright's Company in the French and Indian War on 11 May 1759 [Public Archives Commission, *Delaware Archives*, 18, 25]. He married Eunice **Hermon (Harmon)**, "Melattoes," on 13 May 1772 in Sussex County [Records of the United Presbyterian Churches of Lewes, Indian River and Cool Spring, Delaware 1756-1855, 284]. He was taxable in Indian River Hundred, Sussex County in 1774 [DSA, RG2535, reel no. 1]. They may have been the parents of

   i. Thomas, head of a Broadcreek, Sussex County household of 4 "other free" in 1800 [DE:391] and 5 "free colored" in Nanticoke Hundred in 1820 [DE:314].

   ii. Peter, married Nancy **Oakey** on 12 February 1803 in Sussex County [Records of the United Presbyterian Churches of Lewes, Indian River and Cool Spring, 1756-1855, 319]. He was head of a Sussex County household of 7 "other free" in 1810 [DE:466] and 4 "free colored" in Broadkill Hundred in 1820 [DE:314].

   iii. Ben, head of Kent County, Delaware household of 2 "other free" in 1800 [DE:27].

   iv. Comfort, head of a Lewes and Rehoboth Hundred, Sussex County household of 2 "other free" in 1800 [DE:413].

   v. Edward, head of an Appoquinimink Hundred, New Castle County household of 8 "free colored" in 1820 [DE:147].

PRICHARD/ PRITCHET FAMILY

Members of the Prichard family were

   i. Obediah Pritchard, Sr., born about 1746, a 30-year-old "black" man counted in the Susquehannah Hundred, Harford County census in 1776 [Carothers, *1776 Census of Maryland*, 117].

1 ii. Ann, born say 1748.

   iii. Stephen Pritchard, born about 1761, a 15-year-old "black" man counted with Obediah in the Susquehannah Hundred, Harford County census in 1776 [Carothers, *1776 Census of Maryland*, 117].

1.   Ann Pritchard, born say 1748, was a spinster living in Queen Anne's County on 10 May 1767 when she had an illegitimate "Molatto" child by a "Negro man." The court ordered that she be sold for seven years after she completed her service to James Sudler [Judgment Records 1766-7, part 1, CD image 100]. She was probably the mother of the five-year-old "Mulatto" girl serving until the age of twenty-one who was listed in the Queen Anne's County inventory of James Sudler on 8 April 1773 [Prerogative Inventories 113:199]. She may have been the ancestor of

      i.   James, head of a Talbot County household of 3 "other free" in 1800 [MD:531].

Other members of a Prichard/ Pritchet family were

      i.   Silas Pritchett, manumitted by Solomon Barwell in Kent County, Delaware, on 20 October 1786 [DSA, RG 3555.55], head of a Kent County, Maryland household of 5 "other free" in 1800 [MD:63].

PROCTOR FAMILY

1.   Elizabeth[1] Proctor, born say 1687, was the servant of Mrs. William Boreman (Boarman), Jr., on 12 June 1705 when the grand jury of Charles County presented her for having an illegitimate "Mollatto" child. She was ordered to serve her master another two years after the expiration of her indenture and her child was bound to Boarman on 14 August that year when she appeared in court and admitted her guilt. She was presented for the same offense on 9 March 1708/9. She admitted her guilt in court on 8 June 1709, and the court ordered her to serve an additional seven years and ordered her child bound to Boarman until the age of thirty-one [Court Record 1704-10, 126, 146, 448, 469-70]. She was living on 60 acres of land in Charles County which belonged to William Boarman, Sr., when he made his 8 April 1720 will. And she was living on land adjoining William Boarman of Charles County on 26 February 1728/9 when he wrote his will [Baldwin, *Maryland Calendar of Wills*, V:10; VI:118]. Her own 3 February 1740 Charles County will was proved 15 March 1743. She left her entire estate to her son Charles Proctor [WB AC:166]. She was the mother of

2   i.   Charles[1], Sr., born say 1705.
3   ii.   a child, born before 9 March 1708/9.

2.   Charles[1] Proctor, Sr., born say 1705, received a Charles County deed of gift from his mother, Elizabeth Proctor, of four cows, a steer, two calves, a heifer, nineteen hogs, and household goods on 4 June 1727 [Land Records L-2:366]. He was a taxable in Trinity Parish Upper Hundred, Charles County, in 1758: head of a household which included (his sons?) Benjamin and Charles, Jr. He owned land in Charles County on 1 January 1762 when he leased a tract adjoining his called *Chesam* from his neighbor Barton Wathin for ten years at 1,000 pounds of tobacco per year. The lease required that he use no more than three taxables besides himself to work the land [Liber L-3, 140-1]. He was sued for debt in Charles County court by John and James Jameison in November 1771 [Court Records 1770-2, 126]. He was counted in the constable's census for Charles County in 1778 and taxable in the 3rd District of Charles County in 1783 [MSA 1161-4-10, p.10]. He may have been the father of

      i.   Benjamin, born say 1738, taxable in Charles County in 1758, sued for debt in Charles County court by Samuel Hanson in November 1767 [Court Records 1767-70, 39]. He was counted in the constable's census for Charles County in 1778 and was taxable in the 3rd District of Charles County in 1783 [MSA 1161-4-10, p.9].

      ii.   Charles[2], Jr., born say 1740, taxable in Charles County in 1758, a taxable in the 3rd District of Charles County in 1783 [MSA 1161-4-10, p.10] and a "Mulatto" head of a Charles County household of 7 "other free" in 1790. On 12 November 1760 the Charles County court presented him for begetting an illegitimate child by Jean Robinson, the servant of John Hanson, Sr. Thomas James Boarman was his security [Court Record 1760-2, 88, 90].

 iii. Leonard, born say 1742, sued in Charles County court by Samuel Hanson in November 1767 for a debt of 1,350 pounds of tobacco owed since 23 February 1765 [Court Records 1766-7, 687]. He was listed among Charles County residents who took the oath of fidelity in 1778 and was a "Mulatto" head of a Charles County household of 1 "other free" in 1790.

3. ____ Proctor, born before 9 March 1708/9, an illegitimate child born to Elizabeth Proctor in Charles County, may have been the parent of

 i. Catherine, born say 1730, presented by the Charles County court in March 1748/9 for having an illegitimate child (no race indicated). The court ordered that she receive twelve lashes and serve her master Thomas Reading an additional year and a half [Court Record 1748-50, 350-1].

4 ii. William, born say 1730.

 iii. Thomas[1], born say 1734, taxable head of a Trinity Parish Upper Hundred, Charles County household in 1758, counted in the constable's census for Charles County in 1778, and taxable in the 3rd District of Charles County in 1783 [MSA 1161-4-10, p.10]. He and Samuel **Collins** were "Mulatto" heads of a Charles County household of 12 "other free" in 1790.

4. William Proctor, born say 1730, was a taxable head of a Trinity Parish Upper Hundred, Charles County household in 1758. He was sued in Charles County court for debt by John and James Jameison in November 1771 [Court Records 1770-2, 126]. He took the oath of fidelity in Charles County in 1778. He was a "Mulatto" head of a Charles County household of 5 "other free" in 1790 and 5 "other free" and a slave in 1800 [MD:512]. He was the father of

 i. Charles[3], born say 1755, called "Charles Proctor (of William)" when he was counted in the 1778 constable's census for Charles County [Liber X-3:630-40]. He enlisted in the Revolution for 9 months on 5 July 1778 and was listed in the muster of Captain Henry Gaither's Company in August and at White Plains in September 1778 (the same company as John and Adam **Adams**, Joshua and Charles **Scott** of Charles County) and died in the service [NARA, M246, roll, frames 153, 159, 162 of 526; [*Archives of Maryland* 18:150].

Other members of the family in Maryland were

 i. Walter, enlisted in the Revolution for 9 months on 5 July 1778 and was listed in the muster of Captain Henry Gaither's Company in August and at White Plains in September 1778 and died in the service [NARA, M246, roll, frames 153, 159, 162 of 526; *Archives of Maryland* 18:150].

 ii. Basil, born say 1755, counted in the constable's census for Charles County in 1778, head of a Charles County household of 2 "other free" and a slave in 1800 [MD:511] and 2 "other free" and a slave in 1810 [MD:315].

 iii. Francis, born say 1755, counted in the constable's census for Charles County in 1778 and taxable in the 3rd District of Charles County in 1783 [MSA S1161-4-10, p.10], a Mulatto" head of a Charles County household of 1 "other free" in 1790.

5 iv. Henry, born say 1755.

6 v. Joseph, born say 1760.

7 vi. Thomas[2], born say 1762.

 vii. Eleanor, "Mulatto" head of a Charles County household of 2 "other free" in 1790 and 7 in 1800 (Eleaius Proctor) [MD:565].

8 viii. Isaac, born say 1769.

 ix. Alexander, head of a Charles County household of 6 "free colored" in 1830.

 x. Robert, head of a Charles County household of 6 "free colored" in 1830.

    xi. Cloe, "Mulatto" head of a Charles County household of 1 "other free" in 1790.

    xii. Michael, "Mulatto" head of a Charles County household of 1 "other free" in 1790.

    xiii. Elizabeth[2], "Mulatto" head of a Charles County household of 1 "other free" in 1790, married John **Butler** in St. Mary's Mattawoman Parish, Charles County, on 10 February 1793. The couple required a dispensation because they were related within the third degree of consanguinity which was equivalent to being second cousins [Colonial Dames of America, *Records of St. Mary's Parish, 1793-1861*, 161].

    xiv. Jacob, "Mulatto" head of a Charles County household of 1 "other free" in 1790 and 3 "other free" in Montgomery County in 1800 [MD:216].

    xv. Tenney, "Mulatto" head of a Charles County household of 1 "other free" in 1790.

    xvi. Susanna, "Mulatto" head of a Charles County household of 1 "other free" in 1790.

    xvii. Milley, "Mulatto" head of a Charles County household of 1 "other free" in 1790.

    xviii. Jennett, "Mulatto" head of a Charles County household of 1 "other free" in 1790.

    xix. James[1], "taxable in the 3rd District of Charles County in 1783 [MSA 1161-4-10, p.9], a Mulatto" head of a Charles County household of 1 "other free" in 1790 and 7 in 1800 [MD:517].

    xx. Ann, "free Mulatto" head of a Prince George's County household of 7 "other free" in 1800 [MD:267].

    xxi. Raph, head of a Charles County household of 2 "other free" in 1810 [MD:331].

5.   Henry Proctor, born say 1755, was counted in the constable's census for Charles County in 1778 and was a "Mulatto" head of a Charles County household of 6 "other free" in 1790 and 11 in 1810 [MD:315]. He served in the Revolutionary War and was discharged on 3 December 1781 [*Archives of Maryland* 48:10]. He and his wife Ann were the parents of

    i. Cornelius, baptized 29 March 1807 in St. Mary's Mattawoman Parish in Charles County with Elenora Proctor as the godmother.

    ii. Catherine, baptized 21 September 1817 [Colonial Dames of America, *Records of St. Mary's Parish, 1793-1861*, 16, 20].

6.   Joseph Proctor, born say 1760, was a "Mulatto" head of a Charles County household of 6 "other free" in 1790. He and his wife Elizabeth were the parents of

    i. Elizabeth, baptized 2 March 1794 in St. Mary's Mattawoman Parish, Charles County [Colonial Dames of America, *Records of St. Mary's Parish, 1793-1861*, 7].

7.   Thomas[2] Proctor, born say 1762, was a "Mulatto" head of a Charles County household of 5 "other free" in 1790 and 3 in 1800 [MD:512]. He may have been the Tom Proctor whose burial was recorded in St. Mary's Mattawoman Parish between 1816 and 1819. He and his wife Anney(?) were the parents of

    i. Cornelius, born 16 September, baptized in St. Mary's Mattawoman Parish in 1806 [Colonial Dames of America, *Records of St. Mary's Parish, 1793-1861*, 15, 23].

8.   Isaac Proctor, born say 1769, was a "Mulatto" head of a Charles County household of 1 "other free" in 1790 and 5 in 1800 [MD:512]. He married Elizabeth **Butler** in St. Mary's Mattawoman Parish on 29 September 1794. The couple required a dispensation because they were related within the second degree of consanguinity which was equivalent to being first cousins. They were the parents of

    i. Ann, born 1 March, baptized in St. Mary's Mattawoman Parish on 1 April

1795 [Colonial Dames of America, *Records of St. Mary's Parish, 1793-1861*, 9].

Talbot County and Delaware:
1. Mary Proctor, born say 1727, was a "Mulatto" spinster living in Saint Peter's Parish, Talbot County, in November 1747 when the court convicted her of having a child by a "Negro" person. The court sold her for seven years and her nine-month-old child Daniel to William Moodey for thirty-one years [Judgment Record 1747-50, n.p.]. She was the ancestor of
    i.   Daniel, born about 1747, convicted in Talbot County court in June 1767 of stealing 50 clapboards belonging to Samuel Bowman. He was ordered to receive 30 lashes, stand in the pillory and pay four times the value of the goods which amounted to 120 pounds of tobacco [Criminal Record 1767-74, n.p.]. He was head of a Talbot County household of 2 "other free" in 1790. He was the father of John Proctor who registered in Talbot County on 7 August 1809: *a Mullatto man...5 ft. 8 in. high, yellow complected...about 23 years of age. Is the identical person named in a manumission from Daniel Procter his Father to him* [Certificates of Freedom 1807-15, 76].
    ii. ?James[2], born before 1776, head of a Sussex County household of 4 "other free" in 1810 [DE:325] and 6 "free colored" in Dagsboro Hundred, Sussex County, in 1820 [DE:396]. He was called a "free Negro" in May 1793 when the Sussex County court charged him with having an illegitimate child by Nicey **Dutton** [RG 4805, General Sessions, 1767-1794, frame 521].
    iii. Renney, born 1776-94, head of Dagsboro Hundred, Sussex County household of 2 "free colored" in 1820 [DE:396].

PROUT FAMILY

Members of the Prout family of Maryland were
    i.   Ann, head of an Anne Arundel County household of 3 "other free" in 1790 and 4 in 1800 [MD:101].
    ii.   Arthur, born about 1743, registered in Anne Arundel County on 21 June 1807: *aged sixty four years...Complexion Black...raised in Anne Arundel County* [Certificates of Freedom 1806-7, 40].
    iii. Isaiah, head of an Anne Arundel County household of 9 "other free" in 1800 [MD:97].
    iv.   Jacob, head of an Anne Arundel County household of 7 "other free" in 1800 [MD:97].
    v.   Catherine, born about 1761, registered in Anne Arundel County on 15 May 1807: *free born...about the age of forty one years, her complexion is a mulatto and was raised at the head of south river in Anne Arundel County.*
    vi.   Sarah, born abut 1768, registered in Anne Arundel County on 30 June 1807: *thirty nine years of age...her complexion is yellowish...raised in Ann Arundel County* [Certificates of Freedom 1806-7, 14, 42].
    vii. James, head of an Anne Arundel County household of 3 "other free" in 1800 [MD:101].
    viii. William, head of an Anne Arundel County household of 3 "other free" in 1800 [MD:101].
    ix.   Fanny, head of a Baltimore City household of 6 "other free" in 1800 [MD:316].
    x.   Philip, head of a Baltimore City household of 4 "other free" in 1800 [MD:316].
    xi.   Cate, head of a Baltimore City household of 4 "other free" in 1800 [MD:330].
    xii. Robert, head of an Anne Arundel County household of 1 "other free" in 1800 [MD:101].

xiii.   Nancy, head of a Washington, D.C. household of 1 "other free" in 1800.
xiv.   Kitty, born about 1789, registered in Anne Arundel County on 15 June 1819: *aged about thirty years...brown Complexion...free born.*
xv.   Richard, born about 1783, a 45-year-old who emigrated to Liberia from Baltimore aboard the brig *Nautilus* in 1828 [http://fold3.com/image/46670275].
xvi.   Frederick, born about 1790, registered in Anne Arundel County on 2 September 1811: *about twenty one years of age...dark mulatto...free born.*
xvii.   Philip, born about 1793, registered in Anne Arundel County on 29 May 1816: *about twenty three years...brown complexion...free born.*
xviii. Harriet, born about 1797, registered in Anne Arundel County on 13 November 1818: *aged about twenty one years...light Complexion...free born* [Certificates of Freedom 1810-31, 14, 82, 125, 138].

PUCKHAM FAMILY

1. John[1] Puckham, born say 1660, was an Indian who married Anthony **Johnson**'s granddaughter Joan **Johnson** in Stepney Parish, Somerset County, on 25 January 1682/3:

    John Puckham an Indian baptised by John Huett minister on 25th day of January one thouseand six hundred eighty two And the said John Puckham & Jone Johnson negro were married by the said minister ye 25th February Anno Do./ Maryland.

    Clayton Torrence surmised that John may have been from the Monie Indian Town which was not far from the home of Joan **Johnson**'s likely father, John[1] **Johnson** of Wicomico Creek [Torrence, *Old Somerset*, 142-3]. And Thomas Davidson suggested that the name Puckham may have been derived from the Nanticoke Indian village of Puckamee which then existed in northern Somerset County [Davidson, *Free Blacks*, 32]. John Puckham may have been deceased on 13 June 1699 when Joan Puckham bound her sons John and Richard as apprentices in Somerset County court [Judicial Record 1698-1701, 162]. Their children were

    2   i.   ?Abraham, born say 1685.
            ii.   John[2], born 1 December 1686, bound as an apprentice by his mother on 13 June 1699.
            iii. ?Susannah, born say 1688, admitted in Somerset County court that she had an illegitimate child by John Candley in 1706 and by Anthony Smith in 1708 [Judicial Record 1705-6, 302; 1707-11, 100, 133]. She was probably identical to Sue Puccum whose illegitimate child by Thomas Britt was baptized in St. Anne's Parish, Anne Arundel County on 28 February 1719/20 [Wright, *Anne Arundel County Church Records*, 86]. He may have been identical to the Thomas Britt who was the servant of Captain Tunstall of Somerset County on 10 August 1708 when his age was adjudged at fifteen years [Judicial Record 1707-11, 133].
    3   iv.   Richard[1], born 10 March 1690.

2. Abraham Puckham, born say 1685, was taxable in the Wicomico Hundred, Somerset County household of Jacob Crouch in 1723 and 1724 [List of Taxables]. In March 1723/4 Elizabeth Crouch, administrator of Robert Crouch, sued Abraham in Somerset County court for £2.6 which he had owed since December 1718. He was taxable in the household of Giles Boushaw in Wicomico Hundred in 1725, in the Monie Hundred household of Philip Covington in 1727, and in his own household in Manokin Hundred in 1728. In November 1729 his wife Honor Norgate, the servant of Philip Covington, and he, called "husband of aforesaid Honour," sued Covington for her freedom dues. And in 1730 they were sued by Covington [Judicial Record 1729-30, 205]. Abraham was not taxable in 1731, so he and his wife may have left the county that year. In the March 1742 session of

the Dorchester County court he and his wife Margaret were accused of stealing a parcel of thread from Elizabeth Proctor, and in June 1743 he was sued by Carr, apparently in a case for debt that was agreed to by both parties before coming to trial [Judicial Records 1740-3, 237-8]. He owed the Dorchester County estate of Colonel Joseph Ennalls £9.2 on 19 March 1760 [Prerogative Inventories 76:200].

3. Richard[1] Puckham, born 10 March 1690, was bound as an apprentice to Benjamin Colman in Somerset County court on 13 June 1699 by his mother Joan Puckham [Judicial Records 1698-1701, 162]. He was taxable in the Wicomico Hundred, Somerset County household of Reverend Alexander Adams (minister of Stepney Parish) in 1723 and 1724, taxable in Wicomico in his own household from 1727 to 1734, in Manokin Hundred in 1736 and taxable in Monie Hundred in 1738 and 1739 with (his son?) John Puckham. He was head of a Manokin Hundred household with (his sons?) John, Richard, Matthew, Solomon, and David from 1744 until 1754. He probably died before 1756 when (his sons?) Saul/ Solomon and David were taxable in the Monie Hundred household of Mary Puckham. In 1759 (his children?) Priscilla, David, Matthew, and Solomon were taxables in the Manokin Hundred household of Mary Puckham. Mary may have been his widow or his daughter Mary. Richard was the father of

    i. Mary, born say 1721, daughter of Richard Puckham "of Manokin," fined by the Somerset County court in 1742 for bearing a bastard child [Judicial Record 1742-4, 160]. She was head of a household with John Puckham in Nanticoke Hundred in 1740, in Manokin Hundred in 1743, and in 1746 she was head of a Manokin Hundred household with Richard Puckham, although not taxable herself. She rented a lot and house in Somerset County from George Wilson on 5 January 1746/7 [Land Records X:225].

    ii. John[3], born say 1723, first taxable in the Monie Hundred household of (his father?) Richard in 1739, taxable in John Bell's Manokin Hundred household in 1746, taxable in his father's Manokin household in 1748 and taxable in William Polk's household in 1753.

4   iii. Richard[2], born say 1725.

    iv. Matthew, born say 1734, first taxable in Manokin Hundred in 1750, received a patent for 30 acres on the east side of Princess Anne Town in 1762, sold this land to Charles Redding on 2 April 1771 and sold 50 perches called *Chance* on the east side of the Chesapeake to Charles Redding for 5 shillings on 17 January 1764 [Liber C:199]. He was a taxable "free Negro" in Dover Hundred, Kent County, Delaware, in 1781 and 1782 and taxable with his brother Richard in Broadkill Hundred, Sussex County, in 1784 and 1790. He may have married Eleanor **Durham**, the Eleanor Puckham who witnessed the 9 April 1788 Kent County will of John **Durham** [WB M-1, fol. 171].

    v. Solomon, born about 1735, taxable in the Manokin household of (his father?) Richard Puckham in 1751. In August 1762 he was called a planter when Ephraim Wilson brought a successful suit against him for a £4 debt for a bay mare Solomon purchased from Wilson in November 1760. On 21 March 1769 William Giddes sued Solomon and (his brother?) Matthew, carpenters, in Somerset County court for a £26.15 debt, and on 19 November 1771 Wilson Heath sued them for a £4.5 debt [Judicial Records 1760-3, 166b-167; 1769-72, 11-2, 31-2, 261, 264].

    vi. David, born say 1737, first taxable in 1754, called "David Pucham, planter" on 19 March 1771 when William Pollett sued him in Somerset County court for a debt of £1.19 [Judicial Record 1769-72, 173-4].

    vii. Priscilla, born say 1743, taxable in Mary Puckham's household in 1759. On 16 June 1767 and 15 August 1769 she confessed to the Somerset County court that she had illegitimate children (by a free person) and was fined £3 by the court for each offense [Judicial Record 1766-7, 51, 145; 1769-72, 66].

4.   Richard[2] Puckham, born say 1725, was taxable in the Manokin Hundred, Somerset County household of Henry Ballard in 1743 and 1744, in John Bell's household in 1748, in his father's household in 1749 and head of his own household in 1759. In 1762 he received a patent for 192 acres in Somerset County. On 20 August 1767 he sold a mare and two cows to John Anderson to pay a debt he owed William Polk, and he sold a mare, a cow and a bull to George Miles on 8 January 1771. He and his wife Ann mortgaged 117 acres called *Labour* to William Miles on 28 February 1769, sold the land for £80 on 19 March 1772, and sold 75 acres to Levi Lankford on 21 June 1772 [Liber B:16; D:111, 265; E:33, 175]. William Giddes sued him for a debt of £4.10 on 20 June 1769 [Judicial Record 1769-72, 32, 209]. He was taxable in Broadkill Hundred, Sussex County, in 1774 and taxable with his brother Matthew in Broadkill Hundred from 1784 to 1788, crossed off the list in 1789 [RG 2535, 1780-1796]. He was renting 135 acres in Broadkill Hundred on 5 September 1787 when the sheriff sold it to pay a judgment against the estate of the owner, Nicholas Little, deceased [Mason, *Land Records of Sussex County*, 78]. Nicholas Little sued him for debt in Sussex County court in February 1790 [DSA, RG 4815.006, frame 38]. He may have been the father of

   i.   Stephen, born say 1758, enlisted in Colonel David Hall's Company in the Delaware Regiment on 3 February 1776 and was listed in the muster in the barracks at Lewes Town on 11 April 1776 [Public Archives *Commission, Delaware*, 43-5].
   ii. George, born say 1766, taxable in Little Creek Hundred, Kent County, Delaware, in 1788 and 1789, head of a Wicomico Hundred, Somerset County household of 5 "other free" in 1800 [MD:480] and 5 "free colored" in 1820 [MD:120].
   iii. Levin, born say 1768, taxable in Little Creek Hundred, Kent County, Delaware, in 1788 and 1789 and taxable in Little Creek Hundred, Sussex County, in 1790. He was head of a Somerset County household of 3 "other free" and a white woman over forty-five in 1810 [MD:257] and 4 "free colored" in 1820 [MD:120]. He was assessed on 40 acres in Wicomico and Nanticoke Hundreds, Somerset County, in 1813 and 1814 [Assessment Records 1813-16].
   iv. Ephraim, born say 1769, taxable in Little Creek Hundred, Kent County, Delaware, in 1789.
   v.   John[4], born say 1770, a delinquent taxable in Little Creek Hundred, Sussex County, in 1790, head of a Nanticoke Hundred, Somerset County household of 3 "other free" and a white woman in 1810 [MD:257]. On 9 April 1804 he purchased 32 acres in Somerset County on the west side of Dividing Creek and the main road leading to Stephen's Ferry at the head of Wicomico River near Turkey Pen Ridge and sold this land on 16 January 1808.

Other members of the family were
   i.   Iby, born say 1745-50, head of a Talbot County household of 11 "other free" in 1790 [MD:116].
   ii. Lemuel H., born after 1775, head of a Worcester County household of 3 "free colored" in 1830.

QUANDER FAMILY

1.   Henry[1] Quando, born say 1675, and Margaret Pugg, "negroes," were freed by the 13 October 1684 Charles County will of Henry Adams which was proved on 9 July 1686 [Wills, 2:101]. He petitioned the Charles County court on 11 August 1702, "being a free Negroe," asking whether his wife should have to pay taxes, and the court ruled that she was taxable [Court Record 1701-4, 80]. He rented 116 acres called *Wheeler's Folly* in Charles County from Ignatius Wheeler for 3,200 pounds of tobacco on 11 February 1695/6 and sold the rental to Edward Stevens on 1 January 1718/19 [Land Records Q-1, 83; Prince George's County Land Records

JRM, 1]. His wife was apparently Margaret Quander who complained to the Provincial Court about that Thomas Wheeler had convinced her daughters Mary and Elizabeth to bind themselves as servants for seven years as security for the appearance in Charles County court of Anne Reyny (a white woman charged with having a child by a slave) in December 1720, then transporting Reyny to Virginia and taking her daughters as his servants for the seven years. The Provincial Court referred the case back to the Charles County court which ruled in her favor on 13 March 1721/2 and ordered Wheeler to pay her 2,148 pounds of tobacco for her costs [Court Records 1717-20, 188; 1720-2, 201]. Margaret was a "free negroe woman" who petitioned the Prince George's County court on 25 June 1723 to allow her and her daughters to be levy free. Her petition was rejected, but she petitioned again on 26 November 1723 citing the law, and the court ordered that she and her three daughters be levy free in the future. Henry was called a planter on 22 June 1731 when he was sued in Prince George's County court by Richard Cross. The plaintiff failed to prosecute, so he was ordered to pay Henry his costs of 360 pounds of tobacco. On 28 August 1733 Margaret complained to the court that she was charged for tax on herself and daughters in 1732 and 1733, but the court rejected her petition. She claimed to have been upwards of seventy years old on 26 June 1739 when she successfully petitioned the court to be levy free because she was unable to labor and was dependent on her children for support [Court Record 1723-6, 83, 312; 1730-2, 142, 631; 1732-4, 66-7, 398; 1738-40, 349].[26] He died before 16 April 1743 when his Prince George's County estate was appraised by John Lawrence with Henry Adam Quando as nearest of kin [Prerogative Court (Inventories) DD-10:139-40]. Henry and Margaret were probably the ancestors of

   i.   Maria, born say 1704, confessed in Prince George's County court on 23 March 1724/5 that she had an illegitimate child. George Hardy, carpenter, undertook to pay her court fees [Court Record 1723-6, 420].

   ii. Mary, born say 1706, confessed in Prince George's County court on 22 June 1725 that she had an illegitimate child. Thomas Edelen undertook to pay her court fees and to keep the child from being a charge to the county [Court Record 1723-6, 420].

  iii. Elizabeth, illegally held as a servant in 1721.

  iv. Henry Adam, born say 1725, the servant of Joseph Green Simpson in March 1743/4 when he was charged with twenty-two days runaway time [Court Record 1743-4, 275]. He may have been identical to Adam Quander who owed £1.10.8 to the estate of Edward Neale in 1765 [Prerogative Inventories, 1765, 132].

   v. Henry², "free Negro" head of a Prince George's County household of 1 "other free" in 1800 [MD:272].

  vi. Cecilia Quander, born about 1769 in Fairfax County, Virginia, a "Mulatto" listed in the Fairfax County household of "Black" Ause(?) Quander in 1850.

  vii. Nancy, head of a Georgetown, Washington, D.C. household of 3 "other free" in 1800.

QUEEN FAMILY

The Queen family won its freedom from slavery on testimony that they descended from a native Indian of South America, and in 1810 members of the family sued for their freedom claiming descent from a white woman. Deponents testified for the trial in 1810 that they had heard talk that the ancestor of the family was Mary Queen who was brought into the country by Captain Larkin and sold for seven years [Catterall, *Judicial Cases Concerning Slavery*, IV:49-54; Circuit Court District of Columbia Minutes 1808-11, 285, 287, cited by Brown, *Free Negroes in the District of Columbia*, 69-70].

---

[26]Free Negro women and the mixed-race children of white women were taxables according to a law passed in 1725 [*Archives of Maryland* 35:427].

Members of the family in Maryland were
1   i.   Mary¹, born say 1755.
      ii.   Edward¹, sued John Ashton for his freedom in Prince George's County on 15 October 1791 and won his case in the General Court of Maryland in May 1794. In April 1796 he sued Ashton for having kept him enslaved during the period his case was being decided, but the court found in Ashton's favor. Edward, a "free negro," died 23 February 1798 and was buried 24 February 1798 at St. Peter's Church in Baltimore [Piet, *Catholic Church Records in Baltimore*, 193].
     iii.   Simon, born about 1760, registered in Prince George's County on 15 June 1810: *a black man...appears to be upwards of 50 years old. He was raised at the white marsh in Prince George's County and is free by judgment of the Prince George's County Court at its April Term 1796 on his petition against Reverend John Ashton.*
     iv.   William¹, born about 1767, head of a Prince George's County household of 4 "other free" in 1800 [MD:298]. He registered in Prince George's County on 3 September 1827: *a black man about 60(?) years old...obtained his freedom by judgment of the Prince George's County Court dated 15 April 1796 on his petition for freedom against John Ashton.*
     v.   Nicholas, born about 1775, registered in Prince George's County on 25 April 1810: *a Negro man with a dark complexion, about 35 years old...raised in Prince George's County and was adjudged free by the Prince George County Court at its April Term 1796 on his petition against Reverend John Ashton..*
     vi.   Susannah, head of a Charles County household of 5 "other free" and a slave in 1810 [MD:348].
     vii.   Fanny, born say 1780, mother of Mary Angelique Queen, a two month old "Mulatto" baptized in St. Peter's Church, Baltimore on 20 November 1800 [Piet, *Catholic Church Records in Baltimore*, 99].
     viii.   Stephen, born about 1785, registered in Prince George's County on 23 August 1819: *a black man...about 34 years old. He obtained his freedom by filing a petition in Prince George's County against John Ashton* [Provine, *Registrations of Free Negroes*, 6, 19, 29, 68].

1.   Mary¹ Queen, born say 1755, was head of an Anne Arundel County household of 10 "other free" in 1800 [MD:97] and 7 in 1810 [MD:58]. She was the mother of
     i.   ?Ann, head of an Anne Arundel County household of 4 "other free" in 1800 [MD:93].
     ii.   ?Nancy, born about 1776, head of an Anne Arundel County household of 8 "other free" in 1810 [MD:59]. She registered in Anne Arundel County on 1 November 1816: *aged about forty years, dark complexion., free born.*
2   iii.   ?Charity, born about 1777.
3   iv.   ?Eleanor, born about 1779.
     v.   Isaac, born about 1793, registered in Anne Arundel County on 18 August 1815: *a negro man...aged about twenty two years...of a dark complexion...born of Mary Queen.*
     vi.   William³, born about 1794, registered in Anne Arundel County on 18 August 1815: *negro man...aged about twenty one years...dark complexion...free born of Mary Queen* [Certificates of Freedom 1810-31, 92].

2.   Charity Queen, born about 1777, was head of an Anne Arundel County household of 3 "other free" in 1810 [MD:73]. She registered in Anne Arundel County on 8 September 1818: *aged about forty one years...dark Complexion...free born.* She was the mother of
     i.   Edward²/ Ned, born about 1794, registered in Prince George's County on 24 July 1815: *very dark complexion, is about 21 years old...son of Charity Queen who recovered her freedom in Prince George County Court April*

term 1796 from the Rev. John Ashton.

3. Eleanor Queen, born about 1779, registered in Anne Arundel County on 8 September 1818: *aged about thirty nine years...dark Complexion...free born.* She was the mother of
    i.   William[4], born about 1797, registered in Anne Arundel County on 11 March 1817: *Son of Nelly Queen, aged about twenty years...dark complexion...free born.*

Other members of the Queen family in Anne Arundel County were
    i.   Thomas[1], head of a household of 9 "other free" in 1810 [MD:60].
    ii.   Thomas[2], head of a household of 8 "other free" in 1810 [MD:71].
    iii.   Lewis, head of a household of 7 "other free" in 1810 [MD:71].
    iv.   John, head of a household of 6 "other free" in 1810 [MD:74].
    v.   Sally, head of a household of 8 "other free" in 1810 [MD:73].
    vi.   Robert, born about 1779, registered in Anne Arundel County on 30 May 1817: *aged about thirty eight years...brown complexion...free born.*
    vii.   Betty, head of a household of 5 "other free" in 1810 [MD:75].
    viii. Philis, head of a household of 4 "other free" in 1810 [MD:73].
    ix.   Winnifred, head of a household of 4 "other free" in 1810 [MD:77].
    x.   Rachel, head of a household of 4 "other free" in 1810 [MD:92].
    xi.   Protus, head of a household of 3 "other free" in 1810 [MD:75].
    xii.   Jemima, head of a household of 2 "other free" in 1810 [MD:75].
    xiii. James, born about 1791, registered in Anne Arundel County on 21 October 1815: *aged about twenty four years...brown complexion...free born.*
    xiv.   John, born about 1791, registered in Anne Arundel County on 9 February 1819: *aged about twenty eight years...black complexion was free born.*
    xv.   Paul, born about 1793, registered in Anne Arundel County on 7 April 1818: *aged about twenty five years...black complexion...free born.*
    xvi.   William[2], born about 1793, registered in Anne Arundel County on 7 August 1815: *a negro man...aged about twenty two years...light complexion...free born.*
    xvii. Dennis, born about 1794, registered in Anne Arundel County on 10 March 1818: *aged about twenty four years...dark complexion...free born.*
    xviii. David, born about 1795, registered in Anne Arundel County on 14 August 1817: *aged about twenty two years...brown complexion...free born.*
    xix.   Gabriel, born about 1796, registered in Anne Arundel County on 9 September 1815: *a negro man...dark complexion...free born.*
    xx.   John, born about 1797, registered in Anne Arundel County on 17 September 1816: *aged about nineteen years...brown complexion...free born.*
    xxi.   Mary[2], born about 1799, registered in Anne Arundel County on 1 November 1816: *aged about seventeen years...bright complexion...free born* [Certificates of Freedom 1810-31, 60, 62, 63, 89, 92, 95, 98, 103, 110, 112, 121, 127].

RANDALL FAMILY

Members of the Randall family were
    i.   David, enlisted as a substitute under the command of Captain Charles Williamson in the 2nd Maryland Regiment on 24 May 1778 and was discharged on 3 April 1779 [*Archives of Maryland*, 18:156, 327]. He was head of an Anne Arundel County household of 2 "other free" in 1790 and 1 "free colored" over the age of 55 in 1830.
    ii. Stephen Randle, head of a Baltimore City household of 6 "other free" in 1810 [MD:352].

RAY FAMILY

1. Isabella Ray, born say 1694, was the indentured servant of Benoni Thomas in July 1713 when she admitted in Charles County court that she had a "Mallato" child by a "negroe." The court ordered that she be sold for seven years and that her child be bound out until the age of thirty-one. She was the servant of Thomas Stone on 14 June 1715 when she confessed to the same offense, and on 9 June 1719 and March 1722 when she admitted in Charles County court that she had two more mixed-race children. On 10 March 1723/4 the court sold her to Stone for twenty-one years [Court Records 1711-5, 250, 255, 483, 499; 1720-2, 307; 1723-4, 217]. She was listed in the inventory of Thomas Stone, Sr.'s Charles County estate on 28 November 1728:

    One white woman named Issabella to Serve ab^t 25 yeares for Mallatto
    Bastard- £10
    One Mellatto born of a white woman named James ab^t 15 y^{rs} old- £18
    One Ditto named Bridgett ab^t 9 y^{rs} old- £15
    One Ditto named Charles ab^t 6 y^{rs} old- £10

    [Prerogative Court Inventories 1728-9, 13:314-5].
    She was probably the mother of
    i.   James, born about 1713.
    ii. Sarah, born say 1715, presented for having an illegitimate child about 1735. On 9 June 1747 Anne Fowke petitioned the Charles County court that Sarah Ray, her "Mallatto Servant," had a child about twelve years previous, and she had neglected to have her adjudged for the expenses of having the child. The court ordered that Sarah serve an additional two years [Court Record 1746-7, 84].
    iii. Bridget, born about 1719, a "Mulatto" presented by the Charles County court in March 1749 for having an illegitimate child. She was presented for the same offense in August 1743 with no race of the mother or child indicated [Court Record 1741-44, 627; 1748-50, 603].
2   iv. Charles^1, born about 1722.

2. Charles^1 Ray, born about 1722, was a "Molatto" married to Bridget Rae in November 1757 when the Charles County court granted his petition to have her declared levy free [Court Record 1756-7, 297]. They may have been the parents of
    i.   Charles^2, a "Mulatto" head of a Charles County household of 4 "other free" in 1790, 4 "other free" and a slave in 1800 [MD:531] and 12 "other free" and 2 slaves in 1810 [MD:348].
    ii. Thomas, "Mulatto" head of a Charles County household of 6 "other free" in 1790.
    iii. James, "Mulatto" head of a Charles County household of 5 "other free" in 1790 and 7 in 1800 [MD:523].
    iv. Daniel, "Mulatto" head of a Charles County household of 2 "other free" in 1790.
    v.   Sadley, head of a Petersburg household of 2 "other free" in 1810 [VA:119b].
    vi. Adam Rea, head of a Northampton County, Pennsylvania household of 8 "other free" in 1790.
    vii. Aaron, head of a Charles County household of 5 "other free" in 1810 [MD:331].
    viii. Abednego, head of a Charles County household of 5 "other free" in 1810 [MD:334].

REARDON FAMILY

1. Nelly Reardon, born about 1768, registered in Dorchester County on 24 November 1812: *a bright mulatto...born free and being the illegitimate child of Jesse Reardon who was convicted at November Term 1768 and was sold at that term to Ezekiel*

Keene until she arrived to the age of 31 years, now being 43 years [Certificates of Freedom for Negroes, 1806-64, 20].

REDDING/ REDDEN FAMILY

1. Mary Redding, born say 1728, was taxable in the Pocomoke Hundred, Somerset County household of Purcell Newbold from 1747 to 1750: called Mary Redding in 1747 and 1748, called "molatto Moll" in 1751 and in 1753 when she was in Joyce Newbold's household, listed with "molatto Patience" [List of Tithables]. On 19 March 1750 the Somerset County court presented her for having an illegitimate child in March 1749. In June 1751 she was called the "Molatto" mother of "Molatto Patience" when Patience was bound to Purnall Newbold until the age of sixteen and she was given fifteen lashes as punishment for having an illegitimate child [Judicial Record 1749-51, 292-3, 295]. She was the mother of
      i. Patience, born about March 1749.
2   ii. Nell, born say 1751.

2. Nell Redding, born say 1751, was called "Nell a free Molatto" on 15 November 1768 when she confessed to the Somerset County court that she had a child named Moses by a "Negro." The court ordered that she be sold for seven years and sold her son to her master, Purnall Nubold, until the age of thirty-one. She was called "Nell Redding, a free Melotter" on 21 August 1770 when she had another child by a "Negro" slave. The court ordered that she serve for seven years and sold her son Ibbe to her master, Samuel Wilson, until the age of thirty-one [Judicial Record 1767-69, 238; 1769-72, 152]. She was the mother of
      i. Moses Redden, born in 1768, head of a Broadcreek Hundred, Sussex County household of 6 "other free" in 1800 [DE:391], 7 in 1810 [DE:318] and 5 "free colored" in 1820 [DE:398].
     ii. Ibbe, born in 1770.
    iii. ?Spencer, born before 1776, head of a Worcester County household of 3 "free colored" in 1830.

REED FAMILY

1. Elizabeth Reed, born say 1710, was the servant of Thomas Wilkinson of Saint Paul's Parish, Queen Ann's County, on 1 November 1729 when she had a "mullatto" child named Anne by a "negro." The court sold her daughter to her master until the age of thirty-one for 500 pounds of tobacco, ordered that she be sold for seven years and ordered her to serve 30 days for running away. In June 1732 the court convicted her for another illegitimate child. She was called a "Mullatto woman convict of fornication with a Negro" when the court sold her to Wilkinson for £12.17 [Judgment Record 1730-32, 56-7, 143-4, 526]. She may have been the ancestor of
      i. Sarah, born say 1736, a spinster "Mulatto" woman who was fined 30 shillings by the Queen Anne's County court in March 1754 for having an illegitimate child on 10 April 1753. Richard Small was her security for maintaining the child. In March 1755 she was convicted of having another child on 10 May 1754 [Criminal Record 1751-9, n.p.].
     ii. Charles, head of a Dorchester County household of 3 "other free" in 1800 [MD:695].

Other members of a Reed family in Maryland were
      i. Henny, head of a St. Mary's County household of 4 "other free" in 1800 [MD:431].
     ii. Sarah, head of a St. Mary's County household of 2 "other free" in 1800 [MD:412].
    iii. Darky, head of a Baltimore City household of 8 "other free" in 1800 [MD:328].

iv. Nell, head of a Baltimore City household of 6 "other free" in 1800 [MD:346].
1   v. Sarah¹, born day 1780.
2   vi. Catherine, born say 1780.

1. Sarah¹ Reed, born say 1765, was head of a St. Mary's County household of 5 "other free" in 1790 and 3 in 1800 [MD:431]. She was the mother of
    i. Jeremiah, born about 1788, registered in St. Mary's County on 5 April 1819: *son of Sarah Reed...complexion dark - about thirty one years of age...born free.*
    ii. William, born about 1788, registered in St. Mary's County on 21 April 1820: *Son of a free black woman by the name of Sarah Reed...about thirty two years of age, and is of a dark complexion...born free* [Certificates of Freedom 1806-64, 47, 54]. He was head of a St. Mary's County household of 1 "other free" in 1810 [MD:228].

2. Catherine Reed, born say 1780, was the mother of
    i. Attaway, born about 1800, registered in St. Mary's County on 4 May 1819: *daughter of Catherine Reed...about nineteen years of age, of a light complexion...long and curly hair, was born free.*
    ii. Susanna, born about 1802, registered in St. Mary's County on 4 May 1819: *daughter of the above (Catherine Reed)...about seventeen years of age, a tolerable dark complexion...born free* [Certificates of Freedom 1806-64, 50].

RHOADS FAMILY

1. Mary Roades, born say 1675, was called a widow in June 1707 when Richard King petitioned the Anne Arundel County court to have her "Mullattoe" daughter Elizabeth Roades bound to him instead of to John Harwood to whom she was originally bound. The court refused to grant his petition unless he could better prove his case [Judgment Record 1707-8, 532]. She was the mother of
    i. Elizabeth, born say 1700.

They may have been the ancestors of
    i. Maria Road, head of a Baltimore City household of 5 "other free" in 1810 [MD:32].
    ii. Pere Rhoads, head of a Kent County household of 4 "other free" in 1810 [MD:885].
    iii. Jacob Rhoads, head of a Kent County household of 4 "other free" in 1810 [MD:885].
    iv. Samuel Rodes, head of a Prince George's County household of 6 "other free" in 1810 [MD:44].
    v. Clement Rhoads, "blk." head of a St. Mary's County household of 1 "other free" in 1810 [MD:190].
    vi. Sandy Rodes, "N." head of a Murderkill Hundred, Kent County, Delaware household of 6 "other free" in 1800 [DE:111] and 4 "free colored" in Wilmington Borough, New Castle County in 1820 [DE:195].
    vii. Thomas Roads, "N." head of a Mispillion Hundred, Kent County, Delaware household of 3 "other free" in 1800 [DE:93].
    viii. Robert Roads/ Rhoads, head of a New Castle County household of 2 "other free" in 1810 [DE:239] and 7 "free colored" in White Clay Creek, New Castle County, in 1820 [DE:107].
    ix. Joseph Roads, head of a New Castle County household of 2 "other free" in 1810 [DE:239].
    x. Caesar Rhoad, "N." head of a Sussex County household of 4 "other free" in 1810 [DE:416] and 4 "free colored" in Lewis and Rehoboth Hundred, Sussex County in 1820 [DE:306].

RICHARDS FAMILY

1. Ann Richards, born say 1727, was the servant of Peter Comerford of St. Peter's Parish in March 1747/8 when the Talbot County court convicted her of having a child by a "Negro." The court sold her son Stephen to her master until the age of thirty-one for £15 [Criminal Record 1747-50, n.p.]. She was the mother of
   i. Stephen, born about 1747.

RIDGEWAY FAMILY

1. John[1] Rigway, born say 1720, a "mulatto," had his daughters Mary and Comfort baptized on 22 May 1748 at St. George's Protestant Episcopal Church, Indian River Hundred, Sussex County [Wright, *Vital Records of Kent and Sussex Counties*, 94]. He may have been identical to John Ridgway who called himself a French Man when he recorded his ear mark in Sussex County on 5 May 1746 [DB Q-16:301]. He was called John Regua when he purchased 148 acres in Indian River Hundred on the west side of a branch of Swan Creek from Cord Hazzard for £15 on 1 May 1753 and another 147 acres adjoining this land from Hazzard for £18 on 16 August 1754 [DB H-8; I-9:28]. In February 1754 he charged Milby **Johnson** in Sussex County court with assault but discontinued the suit when **Johnson** agreed to pay court costs. In March 1754 he petitioned the court that he had lost thirty day's service worth 52 shillings from his servant Stephen **Jackson**. The court ordered **Jackson** to make up the cost in time of service. Robert Pack sued him in August 1757 and the court allowed a continuance so John could take the deposition of Thomas Baker. John sued Abraham Wiltbanck, Sr., for trespass in February 1758 and sued William Shankland and Robert Pack in November 1758, William Vaughan in August 1759. Cornelius Kollock sued him in April 1761 and the jury ruled that he pay Kollock £7 in August 1762 when the case came to trial. The court required him to post £50 for his good behavior in May 1762 and discharged him on payment of a fine in August 1762. He sued Thomas Worrington in August 1762 but discontinued the suit before it came to trial [DSA RG 4815.017, 1753-1760, frames 66, 86, 93, 370, 390, 409, 413, 489, 492, 508, 525, 544, 551, 564, 567, 584, 586, 600, 602, 629; 1761-1771, frames 23, 37, 54, 64, 76-7, 81, 87, 89, 99, 106]. He was taxable in Indian River Hundred from 1770 to 1791 [DSA, RG 2535, rolls 1 & 2]. On 20 April 1781 he charged Burton Prettyman with breaking and entering his property in Indian River Hundred and carrying away thirty fence panels containing eight logs each. He was charged with assaulting Prettyman and paid a 6 pence fine in November 1783. In November 1793 the court ordered the sheriff to secure his property which included a yoke of oxen, a steer and a cow which Joshua Ingram was detaining, and ordered the sheriff to recover a yoke of oxen, two cows, a desk, and other items from William Rigwah [RG 4815.017, 1761-1771, August Term Case Files, narrative 1-31; RG 4815.017, 1771-93, frames 284, 325; November 1793 MS case files, nos. 29 & 30]. On 11 April 1797 Zadock Barker entered a caveat against him and was given title to land they both claimed [DSA, Book of Caveats, 1796, p. 251]. He was the father of
   i. Mary, born say 1746.
   ii. Comfort, born say 1748.
2 iii. ?William[1], born say 1753.
3 iv. ?Isaac[1], born say 1763.
   v. ?Peter, head of a Sussex County household of 3 "other free" in 1810 [DE:400]. He died before 7 September 1830 when Philip Mariner was granted administration on his Sussex County estate which was valued at $60 and included a wagon and harness. (His wife?) Nancy Rigware, Jacob **Collins**, "Negro," James Rigware, George **Moseley**, and Return **Johnson** purchased items at the sale of the estate [RG 4545.009, roll 208, frames 167-174].
   vi. ?Simon, born before 1776, head of an Indian River, Sussex County household of 4 "free colored" in 1820 [DE:208]. His "free Mulattoe" son

Isaac² Ridgway was baptized on 30 July 1803 at Indian River, Sussex County [Records of the United Presbyterian Churches of Lewes, Indian River and Cool Spring, Delaware 1756-1855, 403].

2. William¹ Riguway, born say 1753, was taxable in Indian River Hundred, Sussex County, from 1774 to 1791, and a "Negro" head of a Sussex County household of 5 "other free" in 1810 [DE:407]. He and his wife, Jane, were the parents of an unnamed child, born 29 August 1784 and baptized 31 July 1785 at St. George's Protestant Episcopal Church, Indian River [Wright, *Vital Records of Kent and Sussex Counties*, 106]. Jane was probably the Jane Ridgeworth who witnessed the 26 October 1784 Sussex County will of William **Handsor**. William Rigware was indicted by the Sussex County court for forgery in November 1784 but was discharged on payment of court fees. John Rigwaw was his security [RG 4815.017, General Sessions Court, 1771-93, frame 375]. William was head of a Sussex County household of 5 "other free" in 1810 [DE:407]. He was called William Rigware, Senʳ, of Indian River Hundred when he sold (signing) by 1 February 1813 deed to Philip W. Mariner the land he had purchased from John B. Frame as well as a piece of warranted land adjoining, amounting to about 60 acres in the fork of Swan Creek [DB 31:134]. He died before 7 November 1826 when his Sussex County estate was administered [RG 4545.009, roll 208, frames 178-9]. He may have been the father of

    i. Francis(?) Rigwan, head of a Sussex County household of 3 "other free" in 1810 [DE:429].

    ii. John Rigware, head of a Sussex County household of 4 "other free" in 1810 [VA:400].

    iii. Jacob, head of a Sussex County household of 4 "other free" in 1810 [DE:454].

    iv. William², born before 1776, head of a Sussex County household of 2 "other free" in 1810 [DE:404] and 4 "free colored" in 1820 [DE:220].

    v. John², born about 1777, head of an Indian River, Sussex County household of 4 "free colored" in 1820 [DE:220], a 73-year-old "Mulatto" counted in the 1850 census for Lewes and Rehoboth Hundreds with 56-year-old Nathaniel **Clark** and (his wife?) Unicey [family no. 852].

3. Isaac¹ Riguway, born say 1763, and his wife Lydia registered the 15 July 1785 birth of their daughter Allender at St. George's Protestant Episcopal Church, Indian River [Wright, *Vital Records of Kent and Sussex Counties*, 106]. He was taxable in Indian River and Angola Hundred in 1789. Isaac and Lydia were the parents of

    i. Allender, born 15 July 1785, baptized 11 September 1785.

    ii. ?Polly Rigware, married William **Huggins** on 29 April 1809 in Sussex County [Records of the United Presbyterian Churches of Lewes, Indian River and Cool Spring, Delaware 1756-1855, 320]. William was head of a Dagsboro Hundred, Sussex County household of 3 "other free" in 1810 [DE:453] and 6 "free colored" in 1820 [DE:372].

Other members of the family were

    i. Ben Ridgeway, head of a Talbot County household of 4 "other free" in 1790 and 7 in 1800 [MD:531].

    ii. Thomas Ridgway, head of a Nansemond County, Virginia household of 7 "whites" in 1783 [VA:57] and a "Mulatto" head of household in 1784 [VA:74].

    iii. Thomas, born before 1776, head of a Talbot County household of 3 "free colored" in 1830.

RISNER FAMILY

1. George Risner, born say 1765, was head of a St. Mary's County household of 5 "other free" in 1790. He may have been the father of

i. Sarah, born about 1795, registered in St. Mary's County on 16 March 1825: *aged about thirty years, daughter of Susan Bullock...of bright complexion...born free and raised in Saint Mary's County* [Certificates of Freedom 1806-64, 68].

ROACH FAMILY

1. Rose Roach, born about February 1718, was apparently identical to "Rose Mullatto," a four-month-old child on 19 June 1718 when the Somerset County court ordered Mary Fountain to bring her to the next court. She was a "Mollatto Girl about 10 years old to serve till she is 31 years old" when she was listed in the inventory of the Somerset County estate of Mary Fountaine on 7 July 1723, so she apparently the child of a white woman [Judicial Record 1718, 112; Prerogative Inventories & Accounts 1725-1727, 150-4]. She was called a "free born Mullato woman named Rose" in August 1738 when the Somerset County court convicted her of having an illegitimate child and sold her nine-month-old son Jack to Mrs. Mary Fountain until the age of thirty-one. In March 1740/1 she was called a "Mulatto" woman who had been bound as an apprentice to Mary Fountain until the age of thirty-one and still had eight more years to serve when the Somerset County court convicted her of having a child by Tom, the slave of Nicholas Fountain. She was called "Malatto Rose" in August 1749 when the court sold her to Ezekiel Hall for seven years, to commence 20 July 1749, and sold her son George for thirty-one years [Judicial Records 1738-40, 8; 1740-2, 58-9; 1749-51, 6]. She was apparently the ancestor of

    i. Jack, born in December 1737.
    ii. Charles, head of a Worcester County household of 5 "other free" in 1790.
    iii. James, head of a Worcester County household of 4 "other free" in 1790.
    iv. Moses, head of a Talbot County household of 4 "other free" in 1790.
    v. Richard, head of a Cecil County household of 1 "other free" in 1790.
    vi. Sylvia, born before 1776, head of a Worcester County household of 3 "free colored" in 1830.
    vii. George, head of a Sussex County household of 4 "other free" in 1800 [DE:375], 11 in 1810 [DE:312], and 3 "free colored" in 1820 [DE:400].
    viii. Gillis, born 1776-1794, head of a Northwest Fork, Sussex County household of 3 "free colored" in 1820 [DE:248].
    ix. David, a "Blackman," purchased 6 acres called *Hog Quarter* in Pitts Creek Hundred for $60 on 13 May 1807. He manumitted a "negro woman named Priscilla Roach" of the age of forty-three years by Worcester County deed of 4 February 1826 [Land Records Z:53-4; AR:294-5] and was head of a Worcester County household of 4 "free colored" in 1830.

ROBERTS FAMILY

1. Alice Roberts, born say 1712, was the spinster servant of Mr. George Thorpe in March 1732 when she admitted in Queen Anne's County court that she had a child by a "Negroe" and bore a "mullatto" child. The court ordered that she be sold for seven years and sold her daughter Jane, born in November 1731, to George Thorpe for 700 pounds of tobacco. She was indicted for the same offense in the same court, but the attorney general decided not to prosecute [Judgment Record 1732-5, 14-16]. They may have been the ancestors of

    i. William, born say 1734, charged in Talbot County court in March 1759 by Francis Duling (the tax collector) for failing to pay tax on his wife Rachel, but the court's attorney decided not to prosecute the case [Criminal Record 1755-61, 228-9].
    ii. Tom, head of a Talbot County household of 9 "other free" in 1800 [MD:534], perhaps identical to Tom Roberts who was counted as head of a Talbot County household of 7 "other free" in 1800 [MD:532].
    iii. Adam, head of a Talbot County household of 7 "other free" in 1800

300   *Roberts Family*

[MD:522].
iv. Moses, a free African American who was indicted by the Dorchester County court in 1797 for marrying a white woman named Mary Webb. The justices agreed with Moses's contention that "there have been Marriages in the said County similar to his own, and that no prosecutions have taken place in consequence thereof" [Governor and Council, Pardon Papers, 1782-1830, MdHR, 7:66, 1797, cited by Daniels & Kennedy, *Over the Threshold*, 259-60].
v. Leven, head of a Talbot County household of 8 "free colored"in1830.
vi. Samuel, head of a Talbot County household of 6 "free colored" in 1830.

Somerset County
1. Mary Roberts, born say 1705, was the servant of John Ricketts of All Hollows Parish on 18 June 1723 when the Somerset County court convicted her of having a child by her master's "Negro man Simon." She was called a mollatto" on 17 March 1723/4 when the court ordered that she receive ten lashes for having an illegitimate child on 1 September 1723 [Judicial Record 1723-5, 48, 145]. She was probably the ancestor of
i. Esther, head of a Worcester County household of 5 "other free" in 1810 [MD:657].
ii. Robert, head of a Worcester County household of 3 "other free" in 1810 [MD:657], perhaps the husband of Leah Roberts, daughter of Samuel **Collick** and his wife Esther. Leah Roberts was one of their children who sold a tract called *Red Oak Ridge* and an adjoining 8-1/2 acres called *Equantico Savannah* in Worcester County on 16 October 1801 [Land Records, U:405].
iii. Sarah, head of a Worcester County household of 3 "other free" in 1810 [MD:657].

ROBINSON FAMILY

1. Isabella Robertson, born say 1727, was the servant of Elizabeth Bradford of Christ Church Parish in August 1747 when she confessed to the Queen Anne's County court that she had a child by a "Negro" and bore a "Mulatto" child on 10 July 1746. The court sold her for seven years to William Hopper for 750 pounds of tobacco on 22 September 1748 when her previous indenture was completed. In November 1750 she was called "Isabella Robinson spinster servant to William Hopper" when she confessed in court that she had a "Mulatto" child by a "Negroe." The court sold her daughter Henrietta to Hopper for 2 shillings, and in June 1752 the court bound her "Molatta" daughter Sarah Robinson to William Scott until the age of twenty-one, noting that Isabella had died during her delivery [Judgment Record 1747-8, 4, 197, 238; 1750, 115-6; 1751-2, 240]. She was the mother of
i. Henrietta, born in November 1750.
ii. Sarah, born 18 February 1752.

They may have been the ancestors of
i. Thomas, a "Molatto" taxable on 100 acres in Acquango Hundred, Worcester County, in 1783 [MSA 1161-11-5, p.8], head of an Indian River Hundred, Sussex County household of 3 "other free" in 1800 [DE:438], 7 in 1810 [DE:453] and 6 "free colored" in 1820 [DE:206].
ii. Rhoda, head of a Sussex County household of 4 "other free" in 1810 [DE:390].
iii. Moses, head of a Sussex County household of 7 "other free" in 1810 [DE:467].
iv. Jacob, head of a Sussex County household of 5 "other free" in 1810 [DE:445] and 4 "free colored" in Indian River Hundred, Sussex County, in 1820 [DE:212].

Members of the Robinson family in Dorchester County were

    i. David Robertson, born say 1760, a "yellow/ freckled" soldier born in Dorset (Dorchester) County who enlisted in the Revolution in Northampton County, Virginia, and lived in Middlesex County [Register & description of Noncommissioned officers & Privates, LVA accession no. 24296 by http://revwarapps.org/b69.pdf (p.54)].

2   ii. Levi, born say 1768.

    iii. Isaac, head of a Baltimore City household of 6 "other free" in 1800 [MD:338].

    iv. Anthony Robertson, born before 1776, head of a Dorchester County household of 7 "free colored" in 1830.

    v. Enoc, head of a Dorchester County household of 6 "other free" in 1800 [MD:690].

    vi. Margaret, born say 1775, died before 18 July 1818 when her son Robinson **Hill** registered in Dorchester County: *of a bright yellow complection, born free and raised in Dorchester County and is the son of Margaret Robinson, now deceased, about 22 years old* [Certificates of Freedom for Negroes 1806-64, 38].

2. Levi Robinson, born say 1768, was head of a Dorchester County household of 8 "other free" in 1800 [MD:689]. He and his wife Nelly were the parents of

    i. Richard, born about 1794, registered in Dorchester County on 10 January 1815: *of a chestnut colour, was born free, the son of Nelly who was the wife of Levi Robinson who formerly belonged to Henry Hooper...aged about 21 years.*

    ii. Levin, born about 1800, registered in Dorchester County in 1822: *of a dark chestnut colour...born free and is the son of Nelly Robinson the wife of Levi, aged about 22 years* [Certificates of Freedom for Negroes 1806-64, 20, 47].

ROGERS FAMILY

1. Grace Rogers, born say 1710, was the mother of a "Mulatto" child named Ishmael who was being cared for by Jacob Bull in Baltimore County in August 1728 [Liber HWS#6, 30]. She was the ancestor of

    i. Ishmael, born before August 1728.

    ii. ?James, head of a Queen Anne's County household of 5 "other free" in 1790.

    iii. ?Samuel, head of a Queen Anne's County household of 1 "other free" in 1790.

    iv. ?William, head of a St. Mary's County household of 6 "other free" in 1800 [MD:412].

    v. ?Edward, head of a Baltimore City household of 4 "other free" in 1800 [MD:352].

    vi. ?Sucky, head of a Talbot County household of 1 "other free" in 1800 [MD:531].

ROLLINS FAMILY

1. Elizabeth Floid, alias Rollins, born say 1738, a servant of John Brown, confessed in Prince George's County court on 22 November 1757 that she had a "Mulatto" child. The court ordered her sold for seven years and bound her seven-month-old daughter Jane to her master until the age of thirty-one [Court Record 1754-8, 540]. She was the mother of

    i. Jane, born April 1757.

    ii. ?Benjamin, head of an Essex County, Virginia household of 7 "other free" in 1810 [VA:198].

    iii. ?Charlotte, head of a Petersburg household of 3 "other free" in 1810

[VA:334b].

ROSS FAMILY

1. Margaret Ross, born say 1736, the servant of Ann Lewis, was presented by the Anne Arundel County court in August 1756 for having a "Molatto Bastard" [Judgment Record 1754-6, 705, 706, 714]. She was the mother of
    i. Patience, born say 1756, bound by the Anne Arundel County court to Ann Lewis until the age of twenty-one.

They may have been the ancestors of
    i. Robert, "Negro" head of a Harford County household of 7 "other free" in 1790.
    ii. Joseph, head of a Washington County household of 7 "other free" in 1800 [MD:654].
    iii. Tamer, head of a Baltimore City household of 6 "other free" in 1800 [MD:352].
2   iv. Hammond, born say 1770.
    v. James, head of a Frederick County household of 2 "other free" in 1800 [MD:853].
    vi. Henry, head of a Queen Anne's County household of 5 "other free" and a slave in 1810 [MD:152].
    vii. John, "Negro" head of a Caroline County household of 5 "other free" in 1810 [MD:158].
    viii. Charles, head of an Anne Arundel County household of 3 "other free" in 1810 [MD:97].
    ix. Sarah, head of an Annapolis household of 4 "other free" in 1810 [MD:117].

2. Hammond Ross, born say 1770, was married to Mary, "free Mulattoes," when the birth and baptism of their daughter Mary was recorded in St. Paul's Parish, Baltimore. Ham was head of a Baltimore City household of 4 "other free" in 1800 [MD:328]. Hammond and Mary were the parents of
    i. Mary, born 6 October, baptized 29 December 1793 [Reamy, *Records of St. Paul's Parish*, I:74].

ROUNDS FAMILY

1. Benjamin Rounds, born say 1750, was free according to the certificates of freedom granted to his grandchildren, Matilda and Mary Ann Rounds, in Washington, D.C., on 16 October 1835. He was the father of
    i. ?Treasy, born about 1768, registered in Washington, D.C., on 25 January 1813: *a mulatto woman about forty-five years old...born free and raised in St. Mary's County.* Her daughters Betsy and Mary **Swann** registered on 11 June 1821.
    ii. ?Nancy, born about 1769, about forty-four years old on 28 January 1813 when she registered in Washington, D.C.: *Nancy Scott alias Nancy Rounds, a mulatto woman...raised in St. Mary's County.*
    iii. ?Off, born about 1772, registered on 25 January 1813: *a mulatto man aged about forty-one, was born free and raised in St. Mary's County.* He served *for a considerable time as an apprentice to Michael Cusick.* He was probably identical to Theophilus Rounds, husband of Milly **Turner**, whose stepson Lewis **Turner** registered in Washington, D.C., on 19 July 1830. Richard Briscoe, a justice of the peace, testified that Lewis's parents moved from Maryland to Washington about 1800.
2   iv. Hezekiah, born about 1774.
    v. ?Stephen Round, head of a Worcester County household of 3 "other free" in 1800 [MD:784].

2. Hezekiah Rounds, born about 1774, was about thirty-nine years old on 28 January 1813 when he registered in Washington, D.C.: *a Mulatto man...born free and raised in St. Mary's County*. He served as an apprentice "for a long time" with Michael Cusick of St. Mary's County. He was married to Kitty Rounds on 4 September 1821 when their children obtained certificates of freedom. Kitty was the daughter of a white woman named Nancy Collier [Provine, *District of Columbia Free Negro Registers*, 7, 8, 68, 280-1, 181]. Hezekiah and Kitty were the parents of

    i. Eliza, born about 1798, twenty-three years old when she registered in Washington, D.C., on 4 September 1821.
    ii. Leathy, born about 1802, about nineteen years old when she registered on 1 September 1821.
    iii. Hudson, born about 1803, eighteen years old when he registered on 4 September 1821.
    iv. Sarah, born about 1805, about sixteen years old when she registered on 5 June 1821.
    v. Matilda, born about 1811, about ten years old when she registered on 4 September 1821.
    vi. Alfred, born about 1813, about eight years old when he registered on 4 September 1821.
    vii. Kitty, born about 1814, about seven years old when she registered on 4 September 1821.
    viii. Mary Ann, born about 1816, about five years old when she registered on 4 September 1821.

RUSSELL FAMILY

1. James[1] Russell, born about 1690, a "Mallatto belonging to Mr. Notley Rozier," petitioned the Charles County court for his freedom on 13 March 1721 that he was the son of a white woman and had reached the age of thirty-one. He was married to a woman named Mary on 27 Augusgt 1728 when John Pritchett complained to the Prince George's County court that he had a "Malatto wench" who had been bound to his predecessor and wife until the age of thirty-one, that she married James Russell five years previous, that they had three children which gave him much trouble in maintaining, besides the loss of her labor while she was pregnant, and that James was using his house when he was out of work. James complained that his own former master Notley Rozier and Pritchett had both consented to the marriage and that he had paid Pritchett 3,000 pounds of tobacco for the children's support. The Prince George's County court called him a "Malatto Man" on 26 August 1729 when it ordered that he take his three children who were with John Pritchett into his own care [Court Record 1723-6, 148-9; 1728-9, 9, 129; 1729-30, 136]. He may have been the ancestor of

    i. Richard, head of a Baltimore City household of 10 "other free" in 1800 [MD:328] and 11 in 1810 [MD:194].
    ii. _____, born say 1750, an unnamed "mulatto" freeman who married Mary, the daughter of Mary Spanow (a white woman of Montgomery County) and a "Negro" man. Their daughter Rachel was a widow in Bladensburg, Maryland, on 28 February 1822 when her daughter Elizabeth **Thomas** registered as a free Negro in Washington, D.C. [Provine, *District of Columbia Free Negro Registers*, 18].
    iii. Jane, born say 1750, called a "yellow woman now deceased" by Richard Ponsonby on 21 September 1802 when he made an affidavit in Bladensburg and recorded it with the Prince George's County court that she was free born, had lived with his family many years previous and that her twenty-three-year-old son William was born while she was in his service [Land Records JRM #11, 166].
    iv. James[2], head of a Baltimore City household of 2 "other free" in 1810 [MD:323].

> v.   Sarah, head of a Washington County household of 1 "other free" in 1810 [MD:534].

RUSTIN FAMILY

1.   Margaret Ruston, born say 1670, the servant of Colonel Edward Pye, admitted to the Charles County court on 12 January 1691/2 that she had an illegitimate child. The court ordered that she receive twelve lashes. A year later on 1 January 1692/3 Pye brought her into court to have her adjudged for the damages he sustained by her giving birth to a child during her indenture, and the court noted that her child was a "Molattoe and ye father of ye s^d Child a Negroe slave belonging to ye s$^{d.}$ Edwd. Pye." She may have been the first white woman in the county to give birth to a mixed-race child under the law of 1692 because the justices were undecided about how to rule on the matter and referred it to the next court so that "ye old Lawes Concerning Negroes & Slaves may be Enquired into" [Court and Land Record 1690-2, 334; 1692(3)-4, 9]. She was probably the mother of "Two Malatta boyes not slaves" who were valued at £8 each in the 10 June 1697 inventory of the Charles County estate of Col. Edward Pye [Prerogative Court (inventories and Accounts) 15:481-2]. And she was probably the mother of

2   i.   Thomas^1, born about 1691.

2.   Thomas^1 Rustin, born about 1691, was living in Charles County on 12 June 1750 when the court ordered that his wife Lucy should be levy free due to an infirmity. On 10 August 1756 the court ordered his goods attached to pay his debt of 1,003 pounds of tobacco to William Gammell. On 12 June 1759 the court ordered that he be levy free for the future. He may have had children by a slave. A slave named Thomas Rustin was called "Thomas Rustain, Junior" and "Molatto Thomas Rustain" in Charles County court in November 1756 [Court Record 1748-50, 724; 1756-7, 2, 3, 117-8, 144, 201; 1759-60, 177]. Perhaps he was the father of

> i.   Robert, born say 1720, the slave of William Neale on 13 November 1750 when he, Ned Boy (also a slave of William Neale), and "Negroe James" (the slave of Ledstone Smallwood) were presented by the Charles County court for stealing goods from the storehouse of Hugh Mitchell [Court Record 1750, 140].
>
> ii.   Thomas^2, born say 1725, the slave of William Neale on 8 June 1756 when the Charles County court convicted him of stealing a hat which belonged to Thomas McPherson and ordered that he receive thirty-nine lashes and be put in the pillory for one hour. On 10 August 1756 he was called "Thomas Rustain Junior (Slave to William Neale)" when the Charles County court presented him for stealing a saddle which belonged to James Carroll. He was called "Molatto Thomas Rustain" in November 1756 when he was acquitted of the charge. On 8 November 1757 the Charles County court presented him for striking Richard King. On 9 November 1758 the court presented his master, William Neale, for allowing him to keep a horse or horses as his own property [Court Record 1756-7, 2, 3, 117-8, 201; 1757-8, 1, 566].
>
> iii.   George, born say 1728, the slave of William Neale on 9 November 1758 when his master was presented by the Charles County court for allowing him to keep a horse or horses as his own property [Court Record 1757-8, 566].

Other members of the Rustin family were living in adjoining Prince George's County about the same time.

1.   Abigail **Tent**, born say 1670, claimed to be about sixty-seven years old on 28 August 1733 when the Prince George's County court granted her petition that she be supported on public funds. The county continued to provide 600 to 750 pounds of tobacco for her support between 22 November 1748 and 27 November 1753 due

to her old age and blindness. Her daughter, Elizabeth Rustin, testified in Prince George's County court on 24 August 1736 that her mother was a "Molatto born of a white woman" and her father a white man. Abigail was probably related to John Tent who paid Elizabeth Rustin's fine in Prince George's County court on 23 August 1715 [Court Record 1710-5, 766, 790; 1732-4, 405-6; 1736-8, 155-6; 1748-9, 3; 1751-4, 316, 503]. She was the mother of

2   i.   Elizabeth Riston, born say 1692.

2.   Elizabeth Riston, born say 1692, confessed in Prince George's County court on 23 August 1715 that she had an illegitimate child but refused to identify the father. John Tent paid her fine. She confessed to having another illegitimate child on 27 March 1721/2, and the court ordered that she receive nineteen lashes. She petitioned the Prince George's County court on 28 August 1733 saying that she was that year counted as a taxable and conceived that she should not have been because her mother was a "Molatto born of a white woman" and her father a white man, but her petition was rejected. She petitioned the court again on 24 August 1736 that she was the daughter of a white man who had a child by Abigail **Tent**, a "free Molatto" woman and the court granted her petition. Samuel Magruder, Sr., sued her in Prince George's County court on 27 March 1738/9, but the matter was agreed before it came to trial [Court Record 1732-4, 405-6; Court Record 1720-2, 488-9; 1736-8, 155-6; 1738-40, 320]. She was the mother of

     i.   Ann, born say 1715, petitioned the Prince George's County court together with her sister Alice on 24 August 1736 saying that they were the children of Elizabeth Riston by a white man and asked that the constable where they lived be ordered to remove them from the list of taxables. The court granted their request [Court Record 1736-8, 151]. She was probably the Ann Rustin who pled not guilty to the charge of fornication with Thomas **Baulkham**, a "Mulattoe," in Orange County, Virginia, on 23 November 1758. The case was dismissed on 23 August 1759, probably because they were married [Orders 1754-63, 479, 491].

    ii.   Alice, born say 1718.

They were probably the ancestors of

     i.   James, a "Mulatto" head of a Charles County household of 3 "other free" in 1790.

    ii.   John, "free negro" head of a Prince George's County household of 7 "other free" in 1800 [MD:298].

   iii.   Charlotte, the ancestor of William Rushten who registered in Prince George's County on 13 September 1822: *a bright mulatto man, about 24 years old...is free, being the descendant of Charlotte Rushten, a free woman of color* [Provine, *Registrations of Free Negroes*, 43].

SALMONS/ SAMMONS FAMILY

1.   Jane Salman/ Salmond, born say 1683, was the indentured servant of Francis Makemie on 3 December 1701 when she was presented by the Accomack County court for having an illegitimate "Mullatto" child. On 2 March 1702/3 she testified that "Peter Negro belonging to the sd Makemie" was the father of her child. She was convicted again of "haveing a basterd Child borne of her body begat by a Negro" on 4 October 1704, 5 June 1706, and on 4 May 1707. The court ordered that she be sold to pay her fine [Orders 1697-1703, 122a, 126a, 140a; 1703-9, 35a, 66, 72, 107a, 114]. She was probably the ancestor of

2   i.   Joseph[1], born say 1747.

3   ii.   Benjamin[1], born say 1748.

4   iii.   Solomon, born say 1750.

2.   Joseph[1] Salmons/ Sammons, born say 1747, was taxable in Indian River, Sussex County, in 1770, 1774, and 1777. He and his wife Ann registered the 14 December

1772 birth of their daughter Nela at St. George's Protestant Episcopal Church, Indian River [Wright, *Vital Records of Kent and Sussex Counties*, 101]. He was a "Melatto" taxable in Broadkill Hundred in 1788. In 1789 he was listed as an Indian River delinquent taxpayer with the notation that he had paid in Broadkill Hundred and he was also listed as a "Melatto" in the list for Broadkill in 1789 (called Joseph Salmon). In 1800 he was called Joseph Sammons, head of a Delaware household of 7 "other free" [DE:328]. He was the father of

 i. Nela, born 14 December 1772, baptized 13 June 1773.

3. Benjamin[1] Salmons/Sammons, say 1748, was taxable in Indian River Hundred, Sussex County, in 1770, in Little Creek in 1777, in Nanticoke Hundred in 1787 and 1789 (with Benjamin Sammons, Jr.), and a delinquent taxpayer in Little Creek Hundred in 1790. In 1796 he was taxable on 50 acres in Little Creek. He was head of a Sussex County household of 4 "other free" in 1800 [DE:343] and 11 in 1810 [DE:363]. He may have been the Benjamin Salmons who died before 31 March 1812 when (his widow?) Pruda Salmons was granted administration on his Sussex County estate which was valued at $182. After payment of debts, she and his thirteen children divided the balance of $76.42 [DSA, RG 4545.009, reel 217, frames 154-160]. He may have been the father of

 i. Benjamin[2], born 1776-1794, head of an Indian River Hundred, Sussex County household of 6 "free colored" in 1820 [DE:220].

4. Solomon Sammons, born say 1750, was taxable on the southside of Broadkill Hundred, Sussex County, in 1770 and a "Molat" taxable on 50 acres in Little Creek Hundred in 1796. He received a certificate for 4 acres in Sussex County in 1795 [DB 20:11]. He was head of a Sussex County household of 5 "other free" in 1800 [DE:343]. He may have been the Solomon Sammons who married Jinny Veezy on 19 January 1784 at Lewes and Coolspring Presbyterian Church [Wright, *Vital Records of Kent and Sussex Counties*, 131]. He may have been the father of

 i. William[2], head of a Sussex County household of 4 "other free" in 1810 [DE:368].

Other members of the Salmons/ Sammons family in Delaware were:

 i. Isaac[1] Sammons, born say 1760, taxable in Indian River in 1789, head of a Broadkill Hundred, Sussex County household of 4 "other free" in 1800 [DE:328] and 8 in 1810 [DE:374].

 ii. Isaac[2], Jr., born say 1769, taxable in Indian River Hundred in 1789, head of a Sussex County household of 8 "other free" in 1810 [DE:375].

 iii. Eli, born say 1770, taxable in Broadkill Hundred in 1790 and a "Mul." taxable in Broadkill in 1791, head of a New Castle County household of 12 "other free" in 1800, called "Elihu Sammons & C. N. (Negro)" [DE:154].

 iv. William[1], head of a Sussex County household of 10 "other free" in 1810 [DE:375]

 v. John, head of a Dagsboro Hundred, Sussex County household of 7 "other free" in 1800 [DE:424] and 6 "free colored" in 1820 [DE:380].

 vi. Nathan, head of a Mispillion Hundred, Kent County household of 5 "other free" in 1800 [DE:106] and 8 "free colored" in Murderkill Hundred, Kent County, in 1820 [DE:7].

 vii. James[1], born before 1776, head of a Dagsboro Hundred, Sussex County household of 7 "free colored" in 1820 [DE:372].

 viii. Moses, head of an Indian River Hundred, Sussex County household of 3 "other free" in 1800 [DE:437].

 ix. Cyrus, head of a Sussex County household of 8 "other free" in 1810 [DE:467].

 x. Benjamin[3], born 1776-1794, head of an Indian River Hundred, Sussex County household of 6 "free colored" in 1820 [DE:212].

 xi. Zachariah, born 1776-1794, head of Nanticoke Hundred, Sussex County household of 3 "free colored" in 1820 [DE:230].

- xii. James[2], born 1776-1794, head of an Indian River Hundred, Sussex County household of 4 "free colored" in 1820 [DE:208].
- xiii. Henry[1], born before 1776, head of a Dover Hundred household of 5 "free colored" in 1820 [DE:32].
- xiv. Henry[2], born 1776-1794, head of a Mispillion Hundred, Kent County household of 4 "free colored" in 1820 [DE:71].

Members of the family in Maryland were
- i. Thomas, head of a Frederick County household of 5 "other free" and a white woman in 1800 [MD:828], perhaps the father of Joseph[2] Salmon who registered in Frederick County on 7 September 1821: *a yellow Man, aged about Twenty nine years, five feet six Inches high, a Mulatto...free Born as appears by the affidavit of George Littlejohn* [Certificates of Freedom 1806-27, 121].
- ii. Sampson, head of a Baltimore City household of 6 "other free" in 1800 [MD:348].

SAMPSON FAMILY

Members of the Sampson family of the Eastern Shore of Maryland were probably the mixed-race children of a white servant woman of Thomas Martin of Talbot County. The 27 September 1734 inventory of his estate listed the following Sampson family members [Prerogative Court Inventories 1734-6, 19:156-9]:
- i. Elizabeth, born about 1707, a "Molattoe" having 4 more years to serve in 1734.
- ii. Mag, born about 1715, a "Molatto" having 11 or 12 more years to serve in 1734.
- iii. William, born about 1716, a "Molattoe" having about 13 years to serve in 1734, perhaps the William Sampson who was a "Negro" head of a Kent County household of 2 "other free" and a slave in 1790.
- iv. Sisly, born about 1721, a "Molattoe" having about 17 or 18 years to serve in 1734.
- v. Priscilla, born about 1724, a "Molatto" having about 21 or 22 years to serve in 1734.

The inventory of the Calvert County estate of Henry Broome listed 1 "Molatta Boy named James Sampson" (not identified as free) on 16 December 1736, and the inventory of the Calvert County estate of John Broome listed "Mulatto Jam[s] Simpson 2-1/2 y[rs] to serve" [Prerogative Court Inventories and Accounts, 1736-7, 147-9; 1749, 335-7].

Other members of the Sampson family were
- i. Mary, a "Negro" head of a Kent County household of 3 "other free" in 1790 and 4 in Baltimore City in 1800 [MD:358].
- ii. Sarah, a "Mulatto woman" manumitted by John Cadwalader by deed of manumission in Kent County on 20 October 1783 [Chattel Records Liber DD, no.3, 138] and a "Negro" head of a Kent County household of 3 "other free" in 1790.
- iii. James, a "Negro man" set free by John Cadwalader by deed of manumission in Kent County on 20 October 1783 [Chattel Records Liber DD, no.3, 137].
- iv. Jacob, head of a Dorchester County household of 7 "other free" and a slave in 1800 [MD:670].

SAUNDERS FAMILY

1. Rebecca Saunders, born say 1680, was the servant of Adam Johnson when she was presented by the grand jury of Kent County, Delaware, for "lyeing Commonly with the said Johnsons Nigroe man As man and Wife," living secretly in caves from

May 1700 to November 1705 and pilfering hogs, cattle, corn and other goods. She was given 31 lashes and made to stand in the pillory for an hour [Court Records 1703-17, 32a]. Members of the Saunders family on the Eastern Shore of Maryland and in Delaware were

i. Ann, head of a Kent County, Maryland household of 5 "other free" in 1800 [MD:154].

ii. Richard, head of a Kent County, Maryland household of 4 "other free" in 1800 [MD:166].

iii. William, head of a Kent County household of 3 "other free" and 2 slaves in 1800 [MD:166], perhaps the Bill Sanders who was head of a New Castle County household of 5 "other free" in 1810 [DE:250] and 2 "free colored" in Pencader Hundred, New Castle County, in 1820 [DE:100].

iv. Daniel[1], head of a Kent County, Delaware household of 10 "other free" in 1800 [DE:19] and 2 "free colored" in 1820 [DE:45].

v. Daniel[2], head of a Kent County, Delaware household of 6 "other free" in 1800 [DE:23].

vi. John[2], born say 1751, a delinquent "Negro" taxable in Dover Hundred from 1771 to 1772, taxable in Lewes and Rehoboth Hundred, Sussex County, in 1774, a "Mulattoe" taxable in Dover Hundred in 1797 and 1798, head of a Little Creek Hundred, Kent County household of 8 "free colored" in 1820 [DE:24].

vii. Isaac, head of a New Castle County household of 4 "other free" in 1810 [DE:283].

viii. Caesar, "free Negro" head of a Kent County, Delaware household of 3 "other free" in 1810 [DE:186] and 3 "free colored" in 1820 [DE:140].

ix. Asa, born before 1776, head of a Little Creek Hundred, Kent County, Delaware household of 3 "free colored" in 1820 [DE:27].

x. Perry, born before 1776, head of a Pencader Hundred, New Castle County household of 6 "free colored" in 1820 [DE:24].

Another Saunders family:
1. Elizabeth Saunders, born say 1716, appeared before the Caroline County, Virginia court on 12 September 1735 and identified Thomas **Lantor** as the father of her illegitimate child. The court ordered the child bound to Samuel Coleman and on 8 October 1736 ordered her to serve her master Samuel Coleman additional time for having an illegitimate "mulatto" child [Orders 1732-40, 307, 378]. She may have been the ancestor of

i. Elizabeth **Lantorn**, testified in Kent County, Delaware, on 22 November 1769 that (her son?) Peter Lantorn, who was assessed as a tithable the previous year, was born on 8 April 1750 and therefore should not have been tithable [Kent County Levy Assessments, 1768-84, Reel no.3, frame 38]. She married Robert **Game** before September 1782 when Robert named her (called Elizabeth Lanthorn) and her daughters Mary and Sarah in his Murderkill Hundred, Kent County, Delaware will [WB L-1, fol. 267-8].

ii. John[1], born about 1734, a 23 year old "Mulatto" who ran away from William Pickett of Prince William County, Virginia, on 27 March 1757 according to the 2 September 1757 issue of the *Virginia Gazette* [Hunter edition, p.3, col.2], perhaps the John Sanders who was head of a Somerset County household of 5 "other free" in 1800 [MD:466].

iii. Rebecca, married Charles **Game**, 15 September 1812 Worcester County bond.

SAVOY FAMILY

1. Mingo Savoy, born say 1680, was a planter living in Anne Arundel County in August 1705 when John Edwards and the court sued him for 2,000 pounds of tobacco for trading with a slave named Mingo belonging to Edwards. He was found not guilty. He appeared in court in November 1709 in accordance with his

bond of £10, but no one appeared to prosecute him. In June 1717 he petitioned the court that he had inadvertently bound his grandchildren to John Durden and that they were being misused by Samuel Burgess who had become their master. The court bound his "Negroe" grandchildren to Burgess, the boy until twenty-one and the girl until sixteen. In June 1719 he was among twenty residents of the county who were ordered to work on the road for South River Hundred. In June 1723 he bound his daughter Judy to Humphrey Godman for six years, ending 1 November 1729 [Judgment Record 1705-6, 80; 1708-12, 8; 1717-9, 13-14, 553; 1722-3, 22-3]. He paid 4 shillings to the Anne Arundel County estate of Thomas Simpson before 5 August 1710 [Prerogative Court Inventories and Accounts, Vol. 32A, 342]. He was probably the ancestor of the members of the Savoy family who won their freedom after bringing suit in the General Court of Maryland [Catterall, *Judicial Cases Concerning Slavery*, IV:54]. He was the father of

2   i.   ?Arthur, born say 1712.
3   ii.   Judith, born 1 November 1713.
     iii. ?Sarah, married William **Barton** on 25 October 1731 in All Hallow's Parish, Anne Arundel County [Wright, *Anne Arundel County Church Records*, 45].

2.   Arthur Savoy, born say 1712, was a defendant in Anne Arundel County court in August 1735 when he was required to post bond of £10 for his appearance in court and for his good behavior towards John Mariarte. He was discharged when on one appeared against him. He was called a "labourer" in August 1737 when he was acquitted by the Anne Arundel County court of stealing a cow which belonged to Ann Jones. In August 1741 he was convicted of stealing a mare from Robert Killeson on testimony of Anthony **Hill** and Peter **Impey**. He was given 35 lashes and ordered to pay fourfold the value of the mare. In March 1741/2 he was ordered to serve John Watkins, administrator of John Mariartee, for two years for a debt of 1,643 pounds of tobacco. Watkins was ordered to deliver him up to the court at the end of his servitude to serve the county for criminal fees. In June 1744 Matthew Elliott undertook to pay 714 pounds of tobacco which he owed the county. In August 1746 he was presented by the court for failure to list his wife as a taxable [Judgment Record 1734-6, 283a, 304, 374; 1736-8, 249; 1740-3, 237, 248, 251, 401; 1743-4, 472; 1746-8, 214, 285]. He was living in Prince George's County on 23 November 1756 when he was presented by the court for not listing his wife and daughter as taxables by information of William Bright, constable for Mattapony Hundred. He submitted to the court and was discharged after paying court fees. He and his wife Jane, by their attorney, Attorney General Henry Darnell, sued Bright for assault. The court found in favor of Bright for the assault on Jane but against Bright for the assault on Arthur [Court Record 1754-8, 350, 372-4, 456]. He was among seventy-eight persons imprisoned for debt who were released by an act of the Assembly on 19 December 1769 after surrendering up all their real property [*Archives of Maryland* 62:169]. Arthur and Jane may have been the ancestors of

     i.   Archibald, born say 1755, "Mulatto" head of a Charles County household of 9 "other free" in 1790.
    ii.   Philip, born about 1758, a "Man of Colour" about 60 years old when he appeared in Anne Arundel County on 2 April 1818 and stated that he enlisted in Annapolis in the 1st Maryland Regiment in 1778 and served his time. He had a wife and ten children who were all slaves [NARA, S.35057, M804, roll 2125, frame 302; M246, roll 34, frame 177 of 526].
   iii. William[1], born say 1762, "Mulatto" head of a Charles County household of 5 "other free" in 1790 and 8 in 1800 [MD:568].
   iv. Jane, born about 1765, registered in Anne Arundel County on 28 April 1807: *about the age of forty two years...Complexion a bright Mulatto was born free...born & bred in the City of Annapolis* [Certificates of Freedom 1806-7, 11].
    v. Francis, born say 1768, "Mulatto" head of a Charles County household of 1 "other free" in 1790 and a "free Negro" head of a Prince George's County

household of 6 "other free" in 1800 [MD:262]. He married Mary **Curtis** on 16 February 1795 in St. Mary's Mattawoman Parish, Charles County [Colonial Dames of America, *Records of St. Mary's Parish, 1793-1861*, 162].

    vi.   Martha, born say 1769, "Mulatto" head of a Charles County household of 2 "other free" in 1790.

4   vii. Thomas, born say 1775.

5   viii. Milly, born say 1778.

3.   Judith Savoy, probably born 1 November 1713, was bound as an apprentice by her father Mingo Savoy to Humphrey Godman in Anne Arundel County until 1 November 1729. She was a "free Negro" who petitioned the Anne Arundel County court in November 1740 that Walter Phelps was holding her as a servant for debts he had paid for her over the previous eight or nine years. They included her fine for having an illegitimate child. She was presented for bastardy again in June 1743 [Judgment Record 1740-3, 90, 131, 224; 1743-4, 7]. She was probably the mother of

    i.   Sarah, a "free Negro" bound to Walter Phelps in November 1741 until the age of twenty-one with the consent of her unnamed mother [Judgment Record 1740-3, 319].

4.   Thomas[1] Savoy, born say 1775, was a "free Negro" head of a Prince George's County household of 3 "other free" in 1800 [MD:259]. He may have been the husband of Katherine Savoy and father of

    i.   Harry, born about 1798, registered in Prince George's County on 10 July 1828: *a bright mulatto man, about 30 years old, and 5 feet 10-1/2 inches tall...son of Negro Kitty, a free woman of color.*

    ii. William[3], born about 1801, registered in Prince George's County on 26 August 1826: *a bright mulatto man, about 25 years old, and 5 feet 10-3/4 inches tall...born free in Prince George's County, being the son of Katherine Savoy, a free woman of color* [Provine, *Registrations of Free Negroes*, 59, 74].

5.   Milly Savoy, born say 1778, obtained a certificate of freedom in the District of Columbia on 14 August 1823, for herself and sons Elijah and Horatio on testimony of James Barron. He swore that he had known her for about forty years and that she was born on his grandfather's plantation in Charles County. She was freeborn because her grandmother was a white woman [Provine, *District of Columbia Free Negro Registers*, 25]. She may have been identical to Milly Savoy whose son Thomas registered in Prince George's County on 19 September 1827. She was the mother of

    i.   Elijah, born about 1802.

    ii. Horatio, born about 1805.

    iii. Thomas[2], born about 1806, registered in Prince George's County on 19 September 1827: *a black man, about 21 years old, and 5 feet 9 inches tall...born free in Prince George's County...son of Milly Savoy, a free woman of color* [Provine, *Registrations of Free Negroes*, 69-70].

Other members of the family in Maryland were

    i.   Thacy, born about 1750, a 100-year-old "Mulatto" woman counted in the 1850 Charles County census.

    ii. Peter, born say 1770, head of a Frederick County household of 8 "other free" in 1800 [MD:971].

    iii. Samuel, head of a Frederick County household of 3 "other free" in 1800 [MD:983].

6   iv. William[2], born say 1780.

    v. Juliet, born about 1785, registered in Anne Arundel County on 20 April 1807: *about the age of twenty two years...Complexion brown, was born free. her mother and grand mother being free.*

vi. Mary, born about 1787, registered in Anne Arundel County on 15 June 1807: *aged twenty years...complexion black...raised in Anne Arundel County* [Certificates of Freedom 1806-7, 10, 38]. She may have been the Mary Savoy who was married to John Allerson's slave named Francis when their son, John Savoy, born 17 March, was baptized in St. Mary's Parish, Charles County, on 26 April 1807 [Colonial Dames of America, *Records of St. Mary's Parish, 1793-1861*, 16].

vii. Richard Savoy **Garrett**, born about 1792, registered in Anne Arundel County on 25 January 1819: *aged about twenty seven years...brown complexion...free born*. He was probably related to Peggy **Garrett** who registered in Anne Arundel County on 6 February 1819: *aged about nineteen years...brown Complexion...free born* [Certificates of Freedom 1810-31, 126, 127].

6. William[1] Savoy, born say 1780, and his wife Hannah, "free blacks," registered the birth and baptism of their daughter Harriet in St. Paul's Parish, Baltimore. Their daughter was

i. Harriet, born August 1803, baptized 4 January 1804 [Reamy, *Records of St. Paul's Parish*, II:26].

SCARLET FAMILY

1. Susannah Scarlett, born say 1734, was the servant of Robert Dade in November 1753 when she confessed to the Charles County court that she had an illegitimate "Molatto" child. The court ordered her sold for seven years, ordered her to serve her master another year for the trouble of his house, and sold her son Lawrence Scarlett for thirty-one years to her master for £3.4 [Court Records 1753-4, 221]. She was called a white woman servant named Susan with two years to serve when she was listed in the inventory of the Charles County estate of Captain Robert Dade on 27 July 1756 [Prerogative Inventories 62:27-8]. She was the servant of Dade's widow Eliza Dade on 9 March 1757 when she was presented by the court for having another "Molatto" child. She confessed to the charge and was ordered to serve seven years and another year for the trouble of the house. In November 1758 she was indicted for having "Mulatto" twins [Court Record 1755-6, 382; 1756-7, 205; 1757-8, 566]. She was the mother of

i. Sarah, born about 1750, a six-year-old "Mulatto" girl to serve until the age of thirty-one when she was listed in the inventory of the Charles County estate of Robert Dade in 1756.

ii. Lawrence, born about 1753, a three-year-old "Mulatto" boy to serve until the age of thirty-one when he was listed in the Charles County estate of Robert Dade in 1756.

iii. a child, born about 1757.

iv. twins, born about 1758.

SCOTT FAMILY

1. Anne Scott, born say 1695, was the servant of Philemon Hemsley on 10 November 1713 when she was presented by the Charles County court for having a "Mallato" child by information of John Sanders [Court Record 1711-5, 318]. She was probably the mother of

2 i. Mary, born say 1713.

2. Mary Scott alias Flemer, born say 1713, a "Mallatto Girl" born of a white woman, was living in Charles County on 13 August 1728 when the court ordered that she serve John Bruce ("with whom she had been brought up from a child") until the age of thirty-one. She was listed in the inventory of the Charles County estate of Mr. John Bruce on 8 April 1737: "Mallato Mary £18, Mallato Judith £30, Negro

Luke £25, Mary Scott for 12 years £18" [Prerogative Inventories & Accounts 1736-1737, 280]. She was called "Scotty a Mullatto Woman of Mrs. Sarah Bruce" on 8 November 1737 when the Charles County court presented her for having an illegitimate "Malatto" child by information of George Hatton and called Mary Scott on 13 June 1738 when she was convicted of having a male "Mullatto" child by information of George Hatton [Court Record 1727-31, 153; 1734-9, 382, 459, 494]. She may have been the ancestor of

    i.   Joshua, enlisted in Captain Henry Gaither's Company of the 1st Maryland Regiment on 27 May 1778, was sick in camp at White Plains on 2 September 1778, in Fish Kill Hospital later that month, present in March 1780 [NARA, M246, Roll 33, frames 162, 168 of 526]. He was a "Mulatto" head of a Charles County household of 3 "other free" in 1790 and 2 in 1800 [MD:513].

    ii. Crecy, "Mulatto" head of a Charles County household of 1 "other free" in 1790.

   iii. Charles, enlisted in Captain Henry Gaither's Company of the 1st Maryland Regiment on 28 May 1778, was sick in camp at White Plains on 2 September 1778, in Fish Kill Hospital later that month, present in March 1780 [NARA, M246, Roll 33, frames 162, 168 of 526]. He was head of a Frederick County household of 11 "other free" in 1800 [MD:798].

   iv. Ann, head of a Frederick County household of 2 "other free" in 1800 [MD:849].

    v. Robert, head of a Frederick County household of 4 "other free" in 1800 [MD:843].

1.   Judith Scott, born say 1717, was a "Mullatto" woman living in Queen Anne's County in June 1737 when she was convicted by the court of having an illegitimate child. She was called a spinster of Saint Paul's Parish in November 1739 when she had another child [Judgment Record 1735-7, 308; 1740, 18]. She may have been the ancestor of the following members of the family in Maryland:

    i.   Timothy, head of a Kent County household of 5 "other free" in 1790 and 3 "other free" and 3 slaves in 1800 [MD:176].

    ii. John, "Negro" head of a Kent County household of 5 "other free" in 1790 and 7 in 1810 [MD:912].

   iii. Hannah, head of a Talbot County household of 1 "other free" in 1800 [MD:522].

   iv. Thomas, head of a Kent County household of 2 "other free" in 1800 [MD:166].

    v. Richard, head of a Kent County household of 5 "other free" in 1800 [MD:176] and 3 in 1810 [MD:911].

   vi. Abraham, head of a Kent County household of 4 "other free" in 1810 [MD:859].

SHAVER FAMILY

1.   Tabitha Shaver(s), born say 1732, ran away from her master Jedidiah Ewell in Accomack County for 6 days in July 1750 [Orders 1744-53, 426]. She was the indentured servant of William Pullitt in June 1757 when she admitted in Somerset County court that she had an illegitimate child by a "Negro." The court ordered that she serve an additional seven years and bound her daughter Rachel until the age of thirty-one [Judicial Records 1757-60, 40b]. She was the mother of

    i.   Rachel, born about 1757.

They may have been the ancestors of

    i.   Samuel, born before 1776, head of a Mispillion Hundred, Kent County, Delaware household of 4 "other free" in 1800 [DE:83] and 6 "free colored" in 1820 [DE:71].

SHAW FAMILY

1. Mary Shaw, born say 1690, a "Free Negro," was indicted by the Baltimore County court on 6 March 1710/1 for having an illegitimate child [Proceedings 1708-10, Liber IS#A, 205, 214]. She was apparently the mother of

    2   i.   Catherine[1], born say 1710.
         ii. Hannah, born say 1720, indicted for bastardy in Baltimore County court in June 1739 and November 1741. In March 1741/2 she was the servant of William Grafton when she confessed to having a child by a slave. Her one-year-old child was sold to Grafton until the age of thirty-one. She was indicted again in March 1746/7 [Liber HWS#6, 401; TB#TR, 152, 333; TB#TR#1, 378, cited by Barnes, *Baltimore County Families, 1659-1759*, 573-4].
         iii. ?Mamouth, born say 1731, bound by his mother Mary Shaw to William and Elizabeth Wright in Baltimore County on 20 November 1736 for sixteen years [Land Record HWS#IA, fol. 50].

2. Catherine[1] Shaw, born say 1710, had an illegitimate child before August 1728 when John Moorcock paid her court costs in Baltimore County court. On 5 November 1728 Loyd Harris paid her fine of 30 shillings. She was indicted for the same offense in August 1733 and March 1736/7. On 7 March 1736/7 the court sold her for seven years and her son that she had by a slave for thirty-one years to Richard Gist for £37. In November 1738 the court She was the servant of William Grafton of Baltimore County in March 1737/8 sold her daughter Sarah for thirty-one years and ordered her to serve another seven years, noting that she was then the servant of William Grafton since Gist had assigned his rights to her and her child to Grafton. Her daughter Ruth was bound by the court to Grafton in March 1744/5. On 6 August 1745 she confessed in court that she had a "Negro Basterd lately borne of her body." The court ordered her to serve Grafton an additional seven years and sold her daughter Temperance to her master until the age of thirty-one. She had another child by a slave before June 1750 when she was sold for another seven-year term [Liber HWS#6, 22, 74; Liber HWS#9, 69; Liber HWS#IA, 35, 173, 321; Liber TB&TR#1, 220; Liber TR#5, 10; Proceedings 1743-6, 473, 645]. She was the mother of
    i.   ?Susannah, born 28 February 1724/5, a "Molatto" child bound to Thomas Biddison by the Baltimore County court in August 1729 "until the age perscribed for Molattos Servitude." She was indicted for bastardy in November 1745 and November 1746 [Liber HWS#6, 274; TB&TR#1, 220; Proceedings 1745-6, 734].
    ii. Sarah, born about September 1738, six weeks old when she was bound for thirty-one years to William Grafton.
    iii. Ruth[1], born before March 1744/5.
    iv. Temperance, born about 1745.

Other members of the Shaw family were
    i.   Allender, head of a Middlesex Hundred, Baltimore County household of 2 Free Negroes age 16 and upwards and 4 females 16 and upwards [Carothers, *1776 Census of Maryland*, 163].
    ii. Cate[2], born about 1752, head of a Baltimore City household of 10 "other free" in 1800 [MD:336]. She registered in Baltimore County on 9 November 1809: *yellowish complexion, 5 feet 4-1/2 inches high, age 50, born free in Harford Co[ty]* [Certificates of Freedom, 1806-16, (not manumitted), no. 45].
    iii. Ruth[2], born about 1771, registered in Baltimore County on 12 November 1810: *Mulatto, yellow complexion, 5 feet 4-1/4 inches high, age 39, born free in Balt[o] Co[ty]* [Certificates of Freedom, 1806-16, (not manumitted), no. 67].
    iv. Joshua, head of a Baltimore City household of 9 "other free" in 1800

[MD:360].
v. Eleanor, born say 1771, married Moses **Stevenson** on 21 April 1789 in St. Paul's Parish, Baltimore [Reamy, *Records of St. Paul's Parish*, I:52].
vi. Rachel, born about 1783, registered in Baltimore County on 1 May 1807: *Dark complexion, 5 feet 1-1/4 inches high, age 24, born free in Balt° Co°* [Certificates of Freedom, 1806-16, (not manumitted), no. 8].

SHELDON FAMILY

1. Elizabeth Sheldon, born say 1724, had an illegitimate daughter named Rachel by "Negro Phill" in Kent County, Delaware, before May 1743 when the court ordered that she receive twenty-nine lashes [DSA, RG 3805.002, 1734-1779, frames 81, 84]. They may have been the ancestors of
    i. Richard, head of a Dauphin County, Pennsylvania household of 1 "other free" in 1790.

SHEPHERD FAMILY

1. Mary Shepherd, born say 1705, was the servant of William Powell on 22 March 1725 when she was presented by the Prince George's County court for having a "malatto" child [Court Record 1723-6, 557]. She may have been the ancestor of
    i. Margaret, "Negro" head of a Kent County, Maryland household of 3 "other free" and 4 slaves in 1790.
    ii. York, "Negro" head of a Kent County, Maryland household of 2 "other free" and a slave in 1790 and 3 "other free" and a slave in 1810 [MD:833, 912].
    iii. Benjamin, a "mulatto" taxable in Upper Langford Bay, Kent County, Maryland, in 1783 [MSA 1161-7-2, p.11], head of a Kent County household of 8 "other free" in 1800 [MD:177] and 11 in 1810 [MD:842].
    iv. John, a "mulatto" taxable in Upper Langford Bay, Kent County, Maryland, in 1783 [MSA 1161-7-2, p.11], head of a Kent County household of 6 "other free" in 1810 [MD:844].
    v. Margaret, born about 1767, registered in Anne Arundel County on 9 June 1807: *freeborn about forty years of age, her complexion is black...raised at the fork of Patuxent* [Certificates of Freedom 1806-7, 87].
    vi. Samuel, born say 1770, married Sarah **Orrick**, "free blacks," on 28 April 1792 in St. Paul's Parish, Baltimore [Reamy, *Records of St. Paul's Parish*, I:65].
    vii. James, born before 1776, head of a Kent County household of 6 "other free" in 1810 [MD:849] and 4 "free colored in Northwest Fork, Sussex County, in 1820 [DE:262].
    viii. Sarah, born 1776-1794, head of a Murderkill Hundred, Kent County household of 4 "free colored" in 1820 [DE:6].
    ix. Joseph, "negro" head of a Caroline County household of 22 "other free" in 1810 [MD:187].
    x. Polly, head of a Baltimore City household of 4 "other free" in 1810 [MD:169].
    xi. Emery, head of a Baltimore City household of 2 "other free" in 1810 [MD:169].

SHORTER FAMILY

1. Elizabeth[1] Shorter, born say 1662, was the servant of William Roswell of St. Mary's County in 1681 when she was married to Little Robin, a "negro man," by a priest named Nicholas Geulick. Roswell gave the couple to Anthony Neale of Charles County, and at Neale's request, Rev. Geulick made an affidavit on 15 June 1702 that he had performed the marriage. On the same date Roswell's wife, Emma Roswell, deposed the same facts about the marriage and added that Elizabeth and

Robin had three "mulatto" children: Mary, Jane, and Martha. Both affidavits were recorded in the registry of King and Queen Parish, St. Mary's County. Elizabeth was the mother of

2   i.   Mary, born say 1683.
        ii. Jane[1], born say 1685, transferred to Roswell Neale in 1723 by the St. Mary's County will of his father Anthony Neale.
3   iii. Martha, born say 1687.

2.   Mary Shorter, born say 1683, was the daughter of Elizabeth Shorter according to Emma Roswell's testimony on 15 June 1702 which was offered into evidence in a suit brought before the General Court of Maryland by Basil Shorter in October 1794 and another Shorter descendant in the Court of Appeals in 1808. According to testimony at the case held in 1808, Martha Shorter was devised in 1723 to Edward Neale by the will of his father Anthony Neale. Mary may have been identical to the "Malatta woman called Mary" who was valued at £28 in the inventory of the Charles County estate of Anthony Neale in 1724 [Prerogative Inventories & Accounts 1723-1724, 327-8]. She was called a "molatto" in June 1747 when she sued Edward Neale in Charles County court with Edmund Machatee, James Gates and Thomas Douglass as her witnesses [Court Record 1746-7, 78]. According to Basil Shorter's October 1794 suit for freedom in St. Mary's County, Mary was the mother of

4   i.   Linda, born say 1710.

3.   Martha/ Pat Shorter, born say 1687, was given to Raphael Neale by the St. Mary's County will of his father Anthony Neale in 1723. Raphael Neale gave Martha to John Lancaster after he married Neale's daughter Elizabeth according to testimony of Mary Lancaster on 24 August 1803. The petitioner in the 1808 Appeals case testified that Martha was the mother of Betty, who was the mother of Sarah, who was the mother of Betty, who was the mother of the petitioner. Martha was the mother of

5   i.   Elizabeth[2]/ Betty, born say 1710.

4.   Linda Shorter, born say 1710, was the mother of Basil Shorter who sued for his freedom in St. Mary's County in 1794. She was the mother of
        i.   Basil, sued for his freedom in St. Mary's County in 1794.
6   ii. ?Rachel, born say 1745.

5.   Elizabeth[2]/ Betty Shorter, born say 1710, was the mother of
7   i.   Sarah, born say 1735.

6.   Rachel Shorter, born say 1745, was head of a Washington, D.C., household of 5 "other free" in 1800. She obtained a certificate of freedom in Washington County on 7 October 1807 and registered it in the Court of the District of Columbia in Alexandria on 30 May 1815: *I do certify that to the best of my recollection Rachael Shorter and her children Matilda, Anna, Belinda, Catherine, John and Barrett obtained their freedom sometime in May 1795. M. H. Rozer* [Arlington County Register of Free Negroes, 1797-1861, no. 29, p.27]. She was the mother of
        i.   Matilda.
        ii. Anna.
      iii. Belinda.
      iv. Catherine, born say 1770, registered in Washington, D.C., on 28 March 1806. Robert Brent certified that she and her children Oswald, Henry, Peter, Thomas, Grace and Betsy were freed by Notley Young by the judgment of the General Court of Maryland [Provine, *District of Columbia Free Negro Registers*, 169].
       v.   John.
      vi. Barrett.

7.   Sarah Shorter, born say 1735, was the daughter of Betty Shorter. John Lancaster gave her to Henry Digges of Charles County who married Lancaster's daughter Henrietta. Digges sold Sarah's daughter Betty to Boswell, the defendant in the Court of Appeals case in 1808 [*Cases in the General Court and Court of Appeals of Maryland*, 238-40; *Cases in the Court of Appeals of Maryland*, 359-62]. Sarah was the mother of

     i.   Elizabeth³/ Betty, born say 1760.

They were the ancestors of

     i.   Edward, born about 1752, registered in Anne Arundel County on 15 May 1807: *of the age of fifty two years, his Complexion black, was born and bred in Charles County and now resides in the City of Annapolis* [Certificates of Freedom 1806-7, 19].

     ii.   Jane², born say 1760, obtained her freedom from the Mathews family. She was the mother of Monica Shorter and grandmother of Theresa Shorter who married Joseph **Colson** on 4 November 1819 and registered as a free Negro in Washington, D.C., on 28 June 1821 [Provine, *District of Columbia Free Negro Registers*, 4].

     iii.   Clement, born say 1765, registered his granddaughter Mary Ann Shorter in Washington, D.C., on 9 June 1825. He was called a "free black man," husband of Phillis Shorter, "a free mulatto woman." They were the parents of Letitia Shorter **Dorsey**, mother of Mary Ann Shorter. Mary Ann was born about 1808 [Provine, *District of Columbia Free Negro Registers*, 39]. Members of the **Dorsey** family were heads of "other free" households in 1810 in Annapolis (Nicholas and Samuel **Dorsey** [MD:116]) and Baltimore (Bill, John and Isaac **Dorsey** [MD:421, 517, 641]).

     iv.   Ignatius, born about 1767, registered in Frederick County on 21 April 1807: *at a Court in Frederick Town the sixteenth day of November 1795, Ignatius Shorter was set free and discharged from the servitude of a certain William Emmit his then master. Said Ignatius Shorter (is) five feet four and a half Inches high, about forty years of age, middling black* [Certificates of Freedom 1806-27, 4]. He was head of a Frederick County household of 4 "other free" in 1800 [MD:889].

     v.   Elizabeth⁴/ Betty, head of a Frederick County household of 5 "other free" in 1800 [MD:901].

     vi.   Nelly, born about 1772, registered in Frederick County on 13 August 1810: *about Thirty eight years of age, a dark Mullatto, about Five feet six and three quarter inches high, slender made...by the Judgment of the said Court August Term Eighteen hundred and Ten was adjudged free* [Certificates of Freedom 1806-27, 21].

     vii.   Charity, head of a Charles County household of 3 "other free" in 1800.

     viii.   Thomas, "free negro" head of a Prince George's County household of 2 "other free" in 1800 [MD:301] and 7 in 1810 [MD:71].

     ix.   Henry, "blk." head of a St. Mary's County household of 2 "other free" in 1810 [MD:174].

     x.   Henny, born about 1790, "blk." head of a St. Mary's County household of 5 "other free" in 1810 [MD:191], registered in St. Mary's County on 12 August 1812: *aged twenty two years...complexion not very black - hair long & woolly...born free being the daughter of Lucy Shorter who obtained her freedom in the late General Court of Maryland from Henry Neal* [Certificates of Freedom 1806-64, 19].

     xi.   Joe, born about 1791, registered in Frederick County on 22 October 1818: *a dark Mulatto, about five feet Six and a half Inches high, twenty seven years of age...has always since his arrival ta the age of twenty one years passed as a free man...as appears from the affidavit of Col. John Huston* [Certificates of Freedom 1806-27, 86].

SIMITER FAMILY

1.   Catherine Scimter, born say 1688, was a "free woman" and wife of "Negroe John," slave of Colonel Ernault Hawkins, on 23 November 1731 when she confessed in Queen Anne's County court that she had received stolen goods from two servants of Mr. Walter Carmichel & Company. She was ordered to pay 2,000 pounds of tobacco for each of the two offenses. Otho Coursey, John Holden, Richard Holden and Joseph Elliott gave bond on 24 March 1732 to appear in court to testify against Catherine Cymeter, Jonathan Cymeter, and Solomon Cymeter. The sheriff won a judgment against her for his part of the 2,000 pounds of tobacco in November 1733, and he recorded a list of her property which included a small horse, old mare, two 3-year old horses, eight sows, two old feather beds, an old prayer book, an old gun, two feather beds and other household items. The court rejected her petition to be maintained by the county in June 1739 but called her a poor old woman when it allowed Peter Marnie Columbell 1,000 pounds of tobacco to maintain her in March 1747 until November that year. The court also allowed for her maintenance in 1747 and 1748 [Judgment Record 1730-32, 329-30; 1732-5, 2, 40, 93-4, 364, 423-5; 1735-9, 488; 1746-7, 144; 1747-8, 39, 238]. She owed the Queen Anne's County estate of Solomon Clayton (who died in 1739) a debt of 4 shillings [Prerogative Inventories Liber 98:18-22]. Her husband was apparently John Symeter who was about 72 years old when he was listed as a slave in the inventory of the Queen Anne's County estate of Mr. Edward Neal on 8 February 1761 [Prerogative Inventories 81:260-1]. They were apparently the parents of

2   i.   Jonathan Simeter, born say 1708.
    ii. Solomon[1], born say 1710, gave bond on 25 March 1732 to appear in Queen Anne's County court. He was called Solomon Simiter, Labourer of St. Paul's Parish, in June 1732 when the court found him not guilty of spoiling twenty wooden logs set aside by Otho Coursey, Gentleman, for building a house and when Matthew Dockery won a suit against him for 4,000 pounds of tobacco [Judgment Record 1732-5, 2, 3, 413, 436].

2.   Jonathan Simeter, born say 1708, gave bond on 25 March 1732 to appear in Queen Anne's County court [Judgment Record 1732-5, 2]. He owed the Queen Anne's County estate of Solomon Clayton (who died in 1739) a debt of £1 [Prerogative Inventories Liber 98:18-22]. In 1741 the constable for Worrell Hundred testified that he failed to list a member of his household (his wife?) Mary Cymiter, a taxable person of the age of sixteen and upwards, but the court found him not guilty. He died before March 1747 when his sons Solomon and William Simmiter were bound by the court to David Register until the age of twenty-one. Perhaps his wife or daughter was the Mary Scymiter to whom Joseph Dockery owed £3.13 in August 1767 [Judgment Record, 1741-2, 184, 267; 1746-7, 146; 1767, 68-9]. He was the father of

3   i.   ?Elizabeth, born say 1731.
    ii. Solomon[2], born 2 February 1738, eight years old when he was bound out to be a blacksmith in 1747. His master David Register was indicted for abusing him and William Simmater but not further charged in November 1749 [Judgment Record 1749, 266].
    iii. William, born 12 May 1743, four years old when he was bound to David Register to be a blacksmith in March 1747.
    iv. Mary, born about 1746, "poor orphan...Daughter of Jonathan Simmater" maintained by the county in 1748, bound to John Clemmonds until the age of sixteen in March 1749 [Judgments 1747-8, 238; 1749, 20].

3.   Elizabeth Simiter, born say 1731, had an illegitimate child before March 1752 when John Nabb was her security in Queen Anne's County court that her daughter Susanna would not become a charge to the county and before November 1754 when he was security for her illegitimate daughter Frances. She was called a

"Mulatto" woman in court when she had an illegitimate child before 26 August 1760 by an unknown person. The court ordered that she receive fifteen lashes. She had another child before August 1762 when Joseph Nabb was her security that her daughter Sarah would not become a charge to the county [Criminal Record 1751-9, n.p.; 1759-66, 50, 149]. She was the mother of

    i.   Susanna, born about 1751.
    ii. Frances, born about 1754.
    iii. Sarah, born about 1762.

They were probably the ancestors of

    i.   John, presented by the Kent County, Maryland court in November 1775 for not giving in his tax [Criminal Dockets 1774-6, no.37]. He was head of a Kent County household of 6 "other free" in 1800 [MD:154].
    ii. Hannah Simmeter, "F.N." head of a Queen Anne's County household of 6 "other free" in 1790.
    iii. Darkey Simmeter, "F.M." head of a Queen Anne's County household of 3 "other free" in 1790.
    iv. Hager Simiter, head of a Baltimore City household of 2 "other free" in 1810 [MD:196].
    v. Doney Simiter, head of a Baltimore City household of 1 "other free" in 1810 [MD:192].

SISCO
(see the Francisco family)

SKINNER FAMILY

1.   Mary Skinner, born say 1740, deserted her white husband and went to live with a slave who was the father of her child according to a notice placed by her husband in the 12 October 1769 issue of the *Maryland Gazette* [p.2, col. 3; http://msa.maryland.gov/megafile/msa/speccol/sc4800/sc4872/001281/html/m1 281-0892.html, p. 164]. She was probably the mother of

    i.   Salada, head of a Dorchester County household of 8 "other free" in 1800 [MD:691].
2   ii. Harry, born say 1770.

2.   Harry Skinner, born say 1770, was head of a Talbot County household of 6 "other free" in 1800 [MD:521]. He may have been the father of

    i.   Thomas, born about 1791, registered in Talbot County on 21 October 1815: *a mulatto man...about 24 years of age, 5 feet 9 Inches...born free & raised in the County.*
    ii. Henry, born about 1796, registered in Talbot County on 15 June 1816: *born free and raised in the County...about 20 years of age, 5 feet 6 Inches high of a light Complexion* [Certificates of Freedom 1815-28, 7, 33].

SMITH FAMILY

1.   Ann Smith, born say 1740, was the servant of John Fendall, Esq., on 12 February 1759 when the Charles County court presented her for having an illegitimate "Melato" child [Court Record 1759-60, 175]. She may have been the mother of

    i.   Eleanor, "Mulatto" head of a Charles County household of 4 "other free" in 1790.

1.   Hannah Smith, born about 1736, was a 40-year-old head of a Prince George's County household of 8 "free blacks" in 1776:

    i.   a female, born about 1754.
    ii. a female, born about 1763.

    iii. a male, born about 1764.
    iv. a male, born about 1767.
    v. a female, born about 1767.
    vi. a female, born about 1769.
    vii. a female born about 1775 [Carothers, *1776 Census of Maryland*, 137].

1.   Mary Smith, born say 1747, was the spinster servant of Robert Goldsborough of Talbot County in August 1761 when the court sold her daughter Sarah to her master for 33 shillings and ordered her sold for seven years after the completion of her service for having a child by a "Negro." The court sold her for seven years to Adam Gray in November 1766 for 2,350 pounds of tobacco for having an illegitimate child by a "Negro." She was the servant of Jonathan Nichols in March 1767 when she was convicted of the same offense [Criminal Record 1761-7, 493, 505, 536]. She may have been identical to Poll Smith who was head of a Talbot County household of 1 "other free" and 4 slaves in 1790. She was the mother of

    i. Sarah, born about 1761.
    ii. ?Moses, head of a Talbot County household of 7 "other free" in 1790 and 10 in 1800 [MD:518].
    iii. ?Lucy, head of a Talbot County household of 5 "other free" in 1790.
    iv. ?Ben, head of a Talbot County household of 6 "other free" in 1800 [MD:532].

Other Smith families were
    i. Anthony, a "Mullatto" runaway taken up in Accomack County, Virginia, who confessed that he was the servant of Joseph Vansweringham of St. Mary's County [Orders 1719-24, 6].
    ii. James, taxable on "Mulatto" Mary Smith in Pocomoke Hundred of Somerset County from 1756 to 1759 [List of Tithables, 1757], perhaps related to Linah Smith, head of a Worcester County household of 6 "other free" in 1810 [MD:657].

Delaware
1.   John Smith, born say 1730, was called Smith John Lower(?), a "Molatto," when David Ford gave security to the Kent County Levy court to keep him from being a charge to the county [RG 3220, MS Levy Proceedings, p.1]. He was a "Negro" taxable in Little Creek Hundred from 1766 to 1774, taxable in Duck Creek Hundred in 1775 and 1779 [RG 3535, Kent County Levy List, 1743-67, frames 521, 566; 1768-84, frames 11, 27, 104, 259, 273, 337, 371]. He may have been the father of

    i. Isaac, a "Negro" taxable in Little Creek Hundred in 1769 [RG 3535, Kent County Levy List, 1768-84, frame 66], perhaps one of the Isaac Smiths who were heads of Sussex County households of 8 "other free" and 7 "other free" in 1810 [DE:360, 373].
    ii. William, a "Negro" taxable in Duck Creek Hundred in 1775 and 1778 [RG 3535, Kent County Levy List, 1768-84, frame 259, 273, 337].

SMITHER/ SMOTHERS FAMILY

1.   Sarah Smither, born say 1702, was a "free Mullatto Woman" who had a child called "Mullatto Nanny" by a white man. In August 1743 Nanny brought a successful suit against Mrs. Holland, widow of Col. William Holland, in Anne Arundel County court for her freedom [Judgment Record 1743-4, 170]. She was the mother of
    i. Nanny, born say 1722, granted her freedom in August 1743.

They may have been the ancestors of
    i. Thomas Smothers, head of a Frederick County household of 8 "other free"

in 1800 [MD:959] and 6 in 1810 [MD:557].

 ii. Elisha Smothers, head of an Anne Arundel County household of 6 "other free" in 1810 [MD:83].

 iii. Diana Smother, head of a Baltimore City household of 1 "other free" in 1810 [MD:169].

SNOW FAMILY

1. Rebecca Snow, born say 1750, admitted to the Kent County, Maryland court in March 1770 that she had a "Molato" child, and the court sold her son Felix to Samuel Hodges for 5,000 pounds of tobacco [Criminal Dockets 1766-71, November 1769, no. 4; appearance March 1770, no. 17]. She was the mother of

 i. Felix, born about 1769.

 ii. ?Ben, head of a Kent County household of 5 "other free" in 1810 [MD:841].

 iii. ?John, born before 1776, head of a Little Creek Hundred, Kent County, Delaware household of 7 "free colored" in 1820 [DE:26].

SOCKUM FAMILY

1. John Scokem, born say 1736, was taxable in Nanticoke Hundred, Somerset County, with (his wife?) Rachel Scokem in 1757 [List of Taxables]. She was probably the widow Sockem who was taxable in Dagsboro Hundred of Sussex County, from 1784 to 1788, listed near James Sockem [DSA, RG 2535, Levy List 1780-96]. They were probably the parents of

 i. James Sockum, taxable in Dagsboro Hundred of Sussex County in 1777 and from 1784 to 1796 [DSA, RG 2535, Levy List 1767-80; 1780-96], a "Negro" head of a Dagsboro Hundred, Sussex County household of 4 "other free" in 1800 [DE:425], 8 in 1810 [DE:308] and 5 "free colored" in 1820 [DE:372]. He lived on land adjoining Levin **Thompson** in 1810, and his suit Sockum vs. Thompson was listed in the account of Levin's estate [DSA, RG 4545.009, roll 240, frame 280].

 ii. Isaac, taxable in Dagsboro Hundred in 1777 [RG 2535].

 iii. Lowder Sockum, taxable in Dagsboro Hundred in 1795 [RG 4200.027, Levy Court, Roll 2, frame 70], and 1796, living on the land of Robert Hopkins on 27 August 1807 when Hopkins made his Sussex County will [WB F-6:303].

 iv. Stephen, "free Negro" taxable in Murderkill Hundred, Kent County, Delaware, in 1789, "runaway" in 1790 [DSA, RG 3535, Levy List 1785-1797, frames 150, 173].

SONGO FAMILY

1. Joan Songo, born say 1655, was named in the 25 November 1682 Talbot County will of Timothy Goodridge, proved 27 May 1685, which she witnessed (signing). Goodridge left all hs estate to his well beloved friend Phebe Loftis, directed that four "Molattoe" children were to serve Phebe until the age of thirty-one, and the child that Joan Songoe was then pregnant with, as well any other children Joan might have, were to also serve until the age of thirty-one [Wills Liber EM#1:60]. Joan was apparently the mother of

 i. Kendall, born about April 1673, a "Mall'" servant woman having fifteen months to serve when she was listed in the inventory of the Talbot County estate of Mrs. Phebe Bowdle on 14 January 1702/3 [Prerogative Inventories and Accounts 1:618-9].[27]

---

[27]Phebe Loftis later married Thomas Bowdle [Prerogative Testamentary Proceedings, I3:120].

    ii. Sarah, born about 1676, a "Mall"' servant having three years to serve when she was listed in the inventory of the Talbot County estate of Mrs. Phebe Bowdle on 14 January 1702/3.

    iii. Grace, born about 1678, a "Mall"' servant having five years and six weeks to serve when she was listed in the inventory of the Talbot County estate of Mrs. Phebe Bowdle on 14 January 1702/3 [Prerogative Inventories and Accounts 1:618-9].

    iv. William^1, died before 5 June 1722 when Sarah and Solomon Songo signed the Talbot County inventory of his estate which consisted of a cow and calf, 581 pounds of tobacco, 5 bushels of corn and 2 shoats [Prerogative Inventories 7:244].

2   v. William^2, born say 1730.

2. William^2 Songo, born say 1730, was taxable in Duck Creek Hundred, Kent County, Delaware, in 1757, 1758 and 1766, in Little Creek Hundred from 1770 to 1771, in Duck Creek Hundred in 1772, Dover Hundred in 1773 and 1774, and in Murderkill Hundred from 1778 to 1780 [RG 3535, Kent County Levy List, 1743-67, frames 199, 212, 228, 518; 1768-84, frames 66, 104, 120, 183, 216, 347, 376, 425, 430, 461]. He was paid £8.6 by the estate of John **Durham** of Little Creek Hundred before 26 February 1789 [RG 3545, roll 68, frame 615]. He may have been the father of

    i. Ann, born say 1748, living in Little Creek Hundred, Kent County, Delaware, when the August 1768 session of the court indicted her and Isaac **Durham** for having an illegitimate female child [DSA, RG 3805, case papers, August 1768 indictments].

    ii. James, born about 1757, in the muster roll of Captain McLane's Delaware Company for March to June 1779 [*Delaware Archives, Military* I:539]. He enlisted again on 25 December 1781 and was sized in a Delaware muster roll on 28 January 1782; *age 25 years, 5'7", born in Delaware, a resident of Kent County, black hair, yellow complexion*. He was listed as a deserter who was taken up and deserted again on 28 July 1782 [NARA, M246, roll 30, frames 347 & 405 of 532]. He was advertised as a deserter in an ad placed in the *Pennsylvania Journal* and the *Weekly Advertiser* on 14 September 1782: *James Songo, a mulatto, born in Kent County, Delaware State, 25 years of age, 5 feet six inches high, has lost some of his toes* [Boyle, Joseph L, *He Loves a good deal of rum...Military Desertions during the American Revolution, 1775-1783*, Vol. 2, June 1777-1783, 249, 298-9]. He was head of a Worcester County household of 2 "other free" in 1800 [MD:786].

3   iii. Daniel, born say 1765.

3. Daniel Songo, born say 1765, was taxable in Little Creek Hundred from 1788 to 1789, in the list of "Mulatto's & Negro's" in 1797 and 1798 [RG 3535, Kent County Levy List, 1784-97, frames 75, 107, 138, 75, 473]. He was paid £8 by the estate of John **Durham** of Little Creek Hundred before 26 February 1789 [RG 3545, roll 68, frame 615]. He was not taxed in Little Creek Hundred in 1800 because he was "sickly" [RG 3535, Kent County Levy List, 1798-1800, frame 414]. He was head of a Little Creek Hundred household of 8 "other free" in 1800 [DE:33] and 2 "free colored" (a man and woman born before 1776) in 1820 [DE:25]. He was bondsman for the Delaware marriage of Asa **Street** and Rebecca **Durham** on 23 January 1811 [Marriage Records 18:292]. He may have been the father of

    i. Isaiah, born 1776-1794, head of a Little Creek Hundred, Kent County household of 7 "free colored" in 1820 [DE:29].

SOUTHWOOD FAMILY

1.   Sarah Southwood, born say 1749, was the servant of Benjamin Richardson in August 1768 when she admitted in Queen Anne's County that she had a "Mulatto" child about November 1766 [Judgment Records 1766-7, part 1, CD image 102]. She may have been the mother of
     i.   Mary, head of a Baltimore City household of 3 "other free" in 1810 [MD:165].

SPARKSMAN FAMILY

1.   Elizabeth Sparkman, born say 1692, was the servant of Nathaniel Roach of Coventry Parish at Annamessex on 8 March 1711/2 when she confessed to the Somerset County court that she had a child by Indian Robin. The court ordered that she receive 20 lashes, serve her master another two years for the trouble of his house and the court fees and bound her son George to her master. She was the servant of Alexander Hall of Annamessex on 22 May 1718 when she pled guilty to having another illegitimate child [Judicial Record 1711-13, 133-4; 1718, 91]. She was the mother of

2   i.   George[1], born 6 August 1711.

2.   George[1] Sparkman, born 6 August 1711, and Jonas **Hodgskin** paid a fine of 6 pence for assaulting Henry Reynolds in Somerset Parish in 1735 [Judicial Record 1711-13, 133-4; 1735-7, 98]. He was taxable in Henry Scolfield's Pocomoke Hundred, Somerset County household in 1739 and 1740 [List of Tithables]. He was probably the father of

3   i.   Stephen, born say 1737.

3.   Stephen Sparksman, born say 1737, was taxable in the Somerset County household of Thomas White in 1753 [List of Tithables] and was taxable in Little Creek Hundred, Kent County, Delaware, from 1765 to 1797 when he was a "Mulattoe struck off" the list (probably due to old age). He was called a cordwainer in May 1772 when the Kent County grand jury found in his favor when he was accused of stealing eight bushels of corn from William Corse the previous month on 8 April [DSA, RG 3805, MS case files, May 1772 indictments]. He was head of a Little Creek Hundred, Kent County household of 5 "other free" in 1800 [DE:32]. Perhaps he was the father of
     i.   Caleb, a delinquent taxable in Duck Creek Hundred, Kent County, in 1781.
     ii. George[2], born before 1776, head of a Worcester County household of 7 "free colored" in 1830.

Another member of the Sparksman family was
     i.   Leah, born say 1778, a "free Mulatto" who married William Wilson, a slave, on 24 March 1799 in St. Paul's Parish, Baltimore, Maryland [Reamy, *Records of St. Paul's Parish*, I:126].

SPEARMAN FAMILY

1.   Mary Spearman, born say 1710, confessed to the March 1730/1 Kent County, Maryland court that she had an illegitimate child by a "Negro." The court ordered that she be sold for seven years. She was the servant of Richard Davis in March 1733/4 when she was convicted of stealing goods which belonged to Mrs. Margaret Shippey [Criminal Proceedings 1728-34, 160, 185, 489]. She was the ancestor of
     i.   Peter, head of a Kent County household of 5 "other free" in 1800 [MD:154].
     ii. Philip, head of a Kent County household of 5 "other free" in 1800 [MD:154].

SPENCER FAMILY

1. Sarah Spencer, born say 1752, confessed to the Kent County court in March 1762 that she had a "molatto" child. The court sold her and her child Jere to Kinvin Wroth [Criminal Record 1761-72, 24]. She was the mother of

    i. Jere, born about 1762.

    ii. ?Samuel, head of a Baltimore City household of 8 "other free" in 1810 [MD:186].

    iii. ?James, head of a Montgomery County household of 7 "other free" in 1810 [MD:966].

    iv. ?Pambla, head of a Queen Anne's County household of 3 "other free" in 1810 [MD:148].

    v. ?Isaac, head of a Kent County household of 2 "other free" in 1810 [MD:908].

STANLEY FAMILY

1. Mary Stanley, born say 1708, a "Spinster" of Great Choptank Parish, Dorchester County, confessed on 12 November 1728 that she had a "Molatto" child by a "Negro." The court ordered her sold as a servant for seven years after the completion of her indenture [Judgments 1728-9, 84]. She was probably the ancestor of

2   i. Jane, born about 1748.

3   ii. James[1], born say 1760.

    iii. George, born say 1761, head of a Dorchester County household of 1 "other free" in 1790. On 25 February 1792 he manumitted three slaves he purchased from Daniel Parker: Rachel to be free immediately, Leah Standly to be free at sixteen and Jonathan Standly to be free at twenty-one [Land Records HD 6:428]. Perhaps he was deceased in 1800 when Rachel Standley was head of a Dorchester County household of 6 "other free" [MD:686].

4   iv. Salad, born say 1762.

    v. Sophia, born say 1763, purchased a forty-year-old "Negro" man named Jerry then in her possession by Dorchester County deed from Elizabeth Ennalls for £50 on 27 May 1799 and set him free [Land Records HD-15:18, 23].

    vi. Ezekiel[1], head of a Dorchester County household of 4 "other free" in 1790 and 8 in 1800 [MD:726].

    vii. Ezekiel[2], head of a Dorchester County household of 5 "other free" in 1800 [MD:736]. He mortgaged 30 head of sheep, 4 cows, 5 heifers, 3 mares, a horse, 3 colts and 15 hogs for $300 on 15 August 1814 [Land Records ER-3:123].

    viii. Robert[2], head of a Dorchester County household of 3 "other free" and a slave in 1800 [MD:725] and 8 "free colored" in 1830. On 13 March 1798 he manumitted his wife Easter and her daughter Easter whom he had purchased from Daniel Parker [Land Records HD-12:607].

    ix. Ailse, head of a Dorchester County household of 2 "other free" in 1790.

    x. Elizabeth, head of a Bohemia, Cecil County household of 1 "other free" in 1790.

5   xi. John, born about 1771.

    xii. Draper, born about 1774, registered in Dorchester County on 17 September 1807: *of a Chesnut Colour...born free...aged about 33 years.*

    xiii. Joseph, manumitted his "negro woman" Alce **Pendergrass** by Dorchester County deed on 17 October 1805. He purchased 12 acres in Dorchester County called *Turkey Swamp* from Joseph Ennalls on 3 February 1808 [Land Records HD-23:112; 24:577].

xiv. Betty, born say 1780, mother of Harriet **Hopkins** who registered in Dorchester County on 24 August 1836: *of a chesnut colour...born free...daughter of Betsey Stanley who was also born free, aged about 36 years.*

xv. Levin, born about 1782, registered in Dorchester County on 15 June 1807: *copper colour...born free...aged about 25 years* [Certificates of Freedom for Negroes 1806-64, 4, 5, 106].

xvi. William, a "free Mulatto," bound himself to serve David Harvey of Dorchester County for three years on 1 August 1802 [Land Records HD-20:92].

2. Jane Stanley, born about 1748, was a "Molatta" woman with ten years to serve on 5 January 1769 when she was listed in the inventory of the Dorchester County estate of James Hodson with a five-year-old "Molatta" boy bound until the age of thirty-one [Prerogative Inventories, 98:311-4]. She may have been the mother of

6   i. Robert[1], born say 1764.

ii. Sall, a "Mulatto" girl valued at £20 in the 3 September 1772 Dorchester County estate of William Langrell [Prerogative Inventories 105:410-11].

3. James[1] Stanley, born say 1760, was head of a Dorchester County household of 6 "other free" in 1790, 7 in 1800 [MD:686], and 7 in 1810 (called James, Sr.) [MD:402]. He and his wife Rachel were the parents of

i. Esther, born about 1800, registered in Dorchester County on 26 July 1830: *Dark complected...raised in Dorchester County and is the Daughter of Rachel and James Stanley, about 30 years of age* [Certificates of Freedom for Negroes 1806-64, 67].

4. Salady Stanley, born about 1756, was probably identical to the "Negro Boy named Salad" who still had seven years to serve when he was listed in the 7 June 1770 Dorchester County estate of Edward Smith [Prerogative Inventories 105:144]. He was head of a Dorchester County household of 1 "Free Negro or Mulatto" over 16 and 5 slaves in 1790 [MD:439] and 5 "other free" in 1800 [MD:657]. He was a "coloured man" who enlisted in the 4th Maryland Regiment on 4 September 1781 and was discharged at Fredericktown at the end of the war. He appeared in Dorchester County court on 4 April 1821 to apply for a pension, stating that he was about 67, had served for 3 years and had 9 people in his family including his wife Sally (aged 30), son Charles (aged 12), son Garretson (aged 10), daughter Sally (aged 9), Mary (aged 7), Priscilla (aged 6), son Jim (aged 5) and son Joe (aged 3). He died on 31 November 1831. Charles **Cornish** testified on 15 August 1853 that Saladda was in the Revolution, that his wife died on 15 August 1853, and that he assisted in her burial. Garrison Stanley, "free negro," was granted administration on the estate of Sarah Stanley, "free Negress," on 12 August 1857. He filed for the widow's pension of Sarah and included a statement from Matthew **Dixon**, an "old Negro man" aged one hundred and three, that her maiden name was **Blake** and that they were married by an Episcopalian minister in Cambridge on 25 December 1792 [NARA, R10057, M804, roll 2269]. Salady and Sarah's children were

i. Charles, born about 1809.

ii. Garretson/ Garrison, born about 1811.

iii. Sally, born about 1812.

iv. Mary, born about 1814.

v. Priscilla, born about 1815

vi. James[2], born about 1816.

vii. Joe, born about 1818.

5. John Stanley, born about 1771, registered in Dorchester County on 21 August 1810: *of a yellowish colour...born free, raised in Dorchester County, aged about 39 years* [Certificates of Freedom for Negroes 1806-64, 14]. He was head of a

Dorchester County household of 3 "free colored" in 1830. He and his wife Sally were the parents of

    i. John, born about 1811, registered in Dorchester County on 15 May 1832: *of a chesnut colour...free born and is the son of John and Sally Stanley who were also free born, aged about 21 years* [Certificates of Freedom for Negroes 1806-64, 83]. He was probably the John Stanley whose request for free papers so that he could trade in Baltimore was recorded in Dorchester County court on 4 May 1832 [Court Papers 1743-1846, MSA C695-1].

6. Robert[1] Stanley, born say 1764, was a "Mulatto" boy valued at £20 in the Dorchester County inventory of William Langrell on 3 September 1772 [Prerogative Inventories 109:410-11]. He was head of a Dorchester County household of 3 "other free" in 1790 and 9 "other free" and a slave in 1800 [MD:736]. He purchased and manumitted "negro woman" Dianna from Hannah Hodson for £50 by Dorchester County deed on 29 December 1798 and purchased "negro woman" Rhoda and her children Hannah and Ben from William Whittington for £18 on 4 January 1799. He may have been deceased on 22 June 1805 when (his wife?) Dinah Stanley purchased a "Negro girl Nancy Standley" by Dorchester County deed from Hannah Robertson and manumitted nineteen-year-old Nancy Stanly on 29 November 1810 [Land Records HD 14:385-9; 21-723; 23:48; ER 3:606]. He may have been the father of

    i. Nancy, born about 1792, registered in Dorchester County on 22 December 1815: *of a chesnut colour...raised by Robert Stanley and manumitted by Dinah Stanley on the 19 December 1816, aged about 24 years* [Certificates of Freedom for Negroes 1806-64, 30].

STEPHENS FAMILY

Members of the Stephens family in Maryland were

    i. James, born say 1760, testified for the pension application of his sister Fortune **Norman** on 2 August 1837 that he saw her marry Bazil **Norman** near Montgomery County courthouse in September 1782 [NARA, M804, W5429, http://fold3.com].

    ii. Fortune, born say 1762, married Bazil **Norman** in Montgomery County in September 1782.

    iii. Isaac, born about 1765, a "free Colored Man" aged between 70 and 80 years on 18 August 1840 when he testified in Anne Arundel County court on behalf of Mary Butler's Revolutionary War application that she was the widow of Nace **Butler** [NARA, R1549, M804, roll 438].

    iv. Betty, head of an Annapolis household of 5 "other free" in 1810 [MD:113].

STEVENSON FAMILY

1. Moses[1] Stevenson, born say 1745, a "Malotto Man," and his wife Eleanor registered the birth of their children in St. Paul's Parish, Baltimore County [Reamy, *Records of St. Paul's Parish*, I:53, 56]. They were the parents of

    i. Eleanor, born 12 February 1766.

    ii. Moses[2], born 17 August 1767, married Eleanor **Shaw** on 21 April 1789 in St. Paul's Parish [Reamy, *Records of St. Paul's Parish*, I:52]. He was head of a Baltimore Town household of 3 "other free" in 1790 [MD:19]. He registered in Baltimore County on 13 March 1813: *Mulatto descendant of a White Female Woman, yellow colour, 5 feet 8-1/2 inches, age 46, born free in Balt° Co^y* [Certificates of Freedom, 1806-16, (not manumitted), nos. 36, 94].

    iii. Meshack, born 28 June 1768, married Esther **Jones**, "free negroes or mulattoes," on 21 April 1794 in St. Paul's Parish [Reamy, *Records of St.*

Paul's Parish, I:78]. He was head of an Anne Arundel County household of 8 "other free" in 1810 [MD:63]. He registered in Baltimore County on 13 March 1813: *Mulatto, yellow colour, 6 feet, age 44, born free in Balt° Co°* [Certificates of Freedom, 1806-16, (not manumitted), no. 95].

iv. John, born 28 January 1770, head of a Baltimore County household of 10 "other free" in 1800.

v. William, born 31 July 1771.

vi. Samuel[1], born 5 April 1776, married Elizabeth **Feathers** in St. Paul's Parish on 5 July 1795. They were the "free Mulato" parents of Rachel, born 27 May 1798 and baptized 13 February 1799 [Reamy, *Records of St. Paul's Parish*, I:52, 89, 125]. He was head of a Baltimore City household of 6 "other free" in 1810 [MD:378].

vii. Shadrack, born 18 February 1781 [Reamy, *Records of St. Paul's Parish*, I:53], registered in Baltimore on 21 November 1839: *personally appeared Mrs. Ellen Webb who made oath that Shadrick Stevenson, aged 56 years, light complexion, hair very thin on top of head, was born free in Maryland and raised in Baltimore* [Negroes Manumitted & Born Free, 1829-1840, MdHR microfilm CR 12,262-2].

viii. Jacob, born 1 March 1783.

ix. Jesse, born 1 March 1785.

x. Charlotte, born 28 January 1789.

xi. Kesiah, born 17 August 1790.

Other members of the family were

i. Nace, head of a Baltimore City household of 7 "other free" in 1810 [MD:391].

ii. Joshua, head of an Eastern Precinct, Baltimore City household of 6 "other free" in 1810 [MD:503].

iii. Samuel[2], head of an Eastern Precinct, Baltimore City household of 4 "other free" in 1810 [MD:523].

STEWART FAMILY

Queen Anne's County
1. Jane Steward, born say 1690, was convicted of having a "Malatto" child during her term of service to Major William Turlo. She had completed her service to Turlo on 26 November 1712 when he brought her into Queen Anne's County court, and the court bound her to John King for seven years to commence on 24 October 1712. King agreed to set her free one year early and to pay her freedom dues at the end of her service [Judgment Record 1709-16, 200]. She may have been the ancestor of

i. Charles, had of a Queen Anne's County household of 2 "other free" in 1790.

ii. John, head of a Kent County household of 7 "other free" in 1800 [MD:154].

Baltimore County
1. Elizabeth Stewart, born say 1696, was a runaway servant whose "Mulatto" child Elizabeth was bound until the age of thirty-one to John and Ann Norris by the Baltimore County court in November 1716 [Liber IS#IA, 61, cited by Barnes, *Baltimore County Families*, 1659-1759, 610]. She may have been the ancestor of

i. Ark, head of a Baltimore City household of 8 "other free" in 1800 [MD:350].

ii. Samuel, head of a Baltimore City household of 6 "other free" in 1800 [MD:376].

iii. John, head of a Baltimore City household of 5 "other free" in 1800 [MD:348].

STREET FAMILY

1. David Street, born about 1736, was a 23-year-old, born in Sussex County, who was listed in the 11 May 1759 muster of Captain John Wright's Company in the French and Indian War, in the same list with Samuel and Thomas **Hanzer** of Sussex County and Andrew McGill, an Indian born in Maryland [Montgomery, *Pennsylvania Archives, Fifth Series*, 278-9]. He and his wife Mary had a daughter Hannah who was born in 1770 and baptized in St. George's Episcopal Church in Indian River Hundred in 1785 (called David Strite) [Wright, *Vital Records of Kent and Sussex Counties*, 106]. He purchased land in Indian River Hundred, Sussex County, from Smith Frame on 15 February 1777 and sold it on 21 April 1783 [DB N-13:2]. He was taxable on the north side of Broadkill Hundred in 1770, in Indian River Hundred in 1784, and a delinquent taxable there in 1787 [DSA, RG 2535, roll 1 & 2]. He was head of an Indian River, Sussex County household of 3 "other free" in 1810 [DE:454]. He died before 11 March 1816 when administration on his Sussex County estate was granted to Jeremiah Street. His inventory totaled $130 [DSA, RG 4545, frames 758-767]. He may have been the father of
    2   i.   Jeremiah, born say 1763.
           ii.   Hannah, born 15 August 1770, baptized 31 July 1785 in St. George's Episcopal Church [Wright, *Vital Records of Kent and Sussex Counties*, 106].

2. Jeremiah Street, born say 1760, was taxable in Indian River Hundred, Sussex County, in 1784 and 1789 [DSA, RG 2535], head of an Indian River, Sussex County household of 8 "other free" in 1800 [DE:438], 8 in 1810 [DE:454] and 4 "free colored" in 1820 [DE:208]. He was administrator of the Sussex County estate of David Street. In his account of the estate he listed a debt David owed him for eight months work his son Haslet had done for David as well as feeding his cattle and providing corn and firewood for him [DSA, RG 4545, frames 758-9]. He or perhaps a son by the same name and Betty **Clark** (Colour'd) married in Sussex County on 19 December 1816 [Records of the United Presbyterian Churches of Lewes, Indian River and Cool Spring, Delaware 1756-1855, 327]. He was a 97-year-old "Mulatto" counted in the Indian River Hundred census for 1850 with (his son?) Wingate Street [family no. 24]. He was the father of
           i.   Hazlet, head of an Indian River, Sussex County household of 5 "free colored" in 1820 [DE:206]. He and Jenny **Harmon** (Colour'd) married in Sussex County on 23 December 1812 [Records of the United Presbyterian Churches of Lewes, Indian River and Cool Spring, Delaware 1756-1855, 323]. He was called a "Negro" when administration on his Sussex County estate was granted to Jacob **Tingle** "Negro" in December 1833 [DSA, RG 4545, frames 786-789].
           ii.   ?Priscilla, born about 1780, a 70-year-old "Mulatto" woman counted in the 1850 census for Indian River Hundred, Sussex County, with Major and Letty **Drigas** [family no. 106].
           iii. ?Wingate, born about 1782, head of an Indian River, Sussex County household of 2 "other free" in 1810 [DE:454]. He was married to Mary **Thompson** on 16 February 1816 when they received a legacy of $34.58 from her father's estate. On 29 March 1817 they sold for $170 their rights to Tresham's Mill which Mary received by the will of her father Levin **Thompson**, a "Blackman" [DB 33:299; DSA, RG 4545.009, roll 240, frames 264-78]. Wingate was head of an Indian River household of 4 "free colored" in 1820 [DE:206], and a 68-year-old "Mulatto" farmer with $500 real estate counted in Indian River Hundred with (wife?) Nancy in 1850 [family no. 24].
           iv.   ?Asa, married Rebecca **Durham**, 23 January 1811 bond, Asa Street (signing) and Daniel **Songo** bondsmen [DSA, Marriage Records 18:292].

STRICKLAND FAMILY

1. Margaret Strickland, born say 1702, was the mother of a "Mallatto" daughter who was sold by the Charles County court to Rando. Morris until the age of thirty-one [Court Record 1723-4, 4]. She may have been the ancestor of

    i.   David, "f. Negro" head of a Fairfax County, Virginia household of 1 "other free" and 1 slave in 1810 [VA:301].

SUITOR FAMILY

1. Grace Suitor, born say 1730, a spinster "Mullatto," had an illegitimate "Molatta" child by a "Negroe." The Queen Anne's County court sold her to John Falkner for 1,587 pounds of tobacco in June 1751 [Judgment Record 1750-1, 269; Criminal Record 1751-9, 26-8]. She was the mother of

    i.   Edward, born 1 January 1749/50, "Malatto" son of Grace Suitor sold by the Queen Anne's County court to Mr. John Downes, Ju', for 1,225 pounds of tobacco in June 1751.
    ii. ?Guy, "Negro" head of a Harford County household of 10 "other free" in 1810 [MD:817].

SUMMERS FAMILY

1. Sarah Summers, born say 1742, was the servant of Edward Kelly in November 1760 when the Kent County, Maryland court presented her for having a "Molatto Bastard" child. She confessed to the charge in March 1771 and was ordered to serve seven years as punishment [Criminal Record 1761-72, 2]. She was apparently the ancestor of

    i.   Jesse, head of a Kent County, Maryland household of 1 "other free" in 1800 [MD:177].
    ii. James, a "N." head of a Mispillion Hundred, Kent County, Delaware household of 6 "other free" in 1800 [DE:101], 7 in 1810 [MD:37] and 5 "free colored" in Murderkill Hundred in 1820 [DE:3], probably the father of Thomas Summers, head of a Murderkill Hundred household of 6 "free colored" in 1820 [DE:3].

SWAN FAMILY

1. Sarah Swann, born say 1688, was a "Mollatto Hired woman" servant of Col. Hoskins on 9 September 1707 when the Charles County court presented her for having an illegitimate child by a "Negroe." She admitted her guilt to the same offense on 8 June 1714, and the court ordered that she serve her master an additional four years. On 10 June 1718 the court presented her for having another illegitimate child, and on 12 August 1718 the court sentenced her to 12 lashes "so that ye blood appear" because she had no one to pay her fine. Jacob Miller, innholder, was security for the payment of her court fees. On 11 November 1718 the court rejected the petition of William Hoskins that his "mollatto" servant Sarah Swann had born a child in his house for which he had received no reparation [Court Record 1704-10, 373; 1711-5, 402; 1717-20, 104, 142]. She was the ancestor of

    i.   Mary, Jr., "Mulatto" head of a Charles County household of 11 "other free" in 1790 and a 9 in 1800 [MD:497].
    ii.   Leonard, father of an illegitimate child by Sarah **Lenkins** in Charles County before March 1769 [Court Records 1767-70, 405A].
    iii. Elizabeth, "Mulatto" head of a Charles County household of 5 "other free" in 1790.
    iv.   Elizabeth, Jr., "Mulatto" head of a Charles County household of 1 "other free" in 1790.

v. Jennett, "Mulatto" head of a Charles County household of 4 "other free" in 1790.
vi. William, "Mulatto" head of a Charles County household of 3 "other free" in 1790.
vii. Linder, "Mulatto" head of a Charles County household of 1 "other free" in 1790.
viii. Charity, "Mulatto" head of a Charles County household of 1 "other free" in 1790.
ix. Richard, a "molatto" taxable in the 2nd District of Charles County in 1783 [MSA 1161-4-8, p.7] and head of a Charles County household of 5 "other free" in 1800 [MD:524].
x. Ann, "free Mulatto" head of a Prince George's County household of 4 "other free" in 1800 [MD:266].
xi. Polly, head of a Charles County household of 3 "other free" in 1800 [MD:563].

TAYLOR FAMILY

1. Elizabeth Taylor, born say 1690, confessed in Prince George's County court on 27 August 1711 that she had an illegitimate child by Mr. Thomas Wainwright's "Negro George." In November that year the court bound her five-month-old "Mallatto" daughter Sarah to James Gibbs until the age of thirty-one. On 22 June 1714 and 6 March 1716/7 she confessed to having "Mallotto" children, and the court sold her and her children to William Marshall, she for a total of fourteen years and her children until the age of thirty-one [Court Record 1710-5, 80, 126, 611; 1715-20, 181, 185]. She was the ancestor of
   i. Sarah, born about June 1711.
   ii. ?William[1], a "Mulatto" head of a Charles County household of 5 "other free" in 1790, perhaps identical to William Taylor who was head of a Queen Anne's County household of 2 "other free" and 3 slaves in 1800 [MD:381]. He was described as "yellow (Mulatto) complexioned, aged 29, 5'7-3/4" high, born in Maryland, from Montgomery County, enlisted April 2, 1782," when he was listed in the Revolutionary War Maryland roll [NARA, M246, roll 34, frame 436 of 586].
   iii. ?John, head of a Kent County household of 2 "other free" in 1800 [MD:167].
   iv. Henny, born say 1770, mother of Sarah Ann **Myers** who registered in Frederick County on 15 November 1819: *a bright Mulatto...about twenty eight years of age...free born woman and the daughter of Henny Taylor as appears from the affidavit of John Reign* [Certificates of Freedom 1807-28, 100].

THOMAS FAMILY

Charles County:
1. Elizabeth Thomas was a free white woman who had a child by an African American in Maryland [Catterall, *Judicial Cases Concerning American Slavery and the Negro*, IV:52]. She was the ancestor of
2 i. Mary, born about 1772.
3 ii. Terry, born say 1775.
   iii. ?Henry[1], head of a Charles County household of 1 "other free" and 2 slaves in 1800 [MD:511].
   iv. ?Eleanor, head of a Charles County household of 2 "other free" in 1800 [MD:564].

2. Mary Thomas, born about 1772, won a judgment against her master Thomas

Lancaster in the General Court of the Western Shore in October Term 1795. She recorded a copy of the judgment in Charles County court on 9 September 1805: *about twenty-three years old, 5 feet four inches...a tolerable bright mulatto*. She also recorded the birth dates of her children [Land Records IR#6, 452-3]. Her children were

 i. Letty, born 10 August 1788.
 ii. Robert, born 4 October 1791.
 iii. John, born 14 July 1793.
 iv. Richard, born 18 September 1795.
 v. Elizabeth, born 6 February 1797.
 vi. Baptist, born 26 May 1799.
 vii. Sarah, born 7 March 1801.
 viii. Edward, born 24 June 1804.

3. Terry Thomas, born say 1775, may have been the sister of Mary Thomas since Mary made a deposition in Charles County on 30 August 1805 in which she recorded the birth dates of Terry's children [Land Records IR#6, 452-3]. Terry was the mother of

 i. William, born 30 December 1793.
 ii. Henry^2, born 14 February 1796.

Prince George's County:
1. Katherine Thomas, born say 1728, the servant of Philip Mason, confessed in Prince George's County court in August 1747 that she had a "Mulatto" child. The court sold her for seven years and sold her son Jesse to her master until the age of thirty-one [Court Record 1746-7, 606; 1747-8, 91-2]. She was the mother of

 i. Jesse, born 3 February 1746/7.

Baltimore:
1. George Thomas, born say 1750, was head of a Baltimore City household of 9 "other free" in 1800 [MD:370]. He may have been the father of

 i. Abby, married John **Smith**, "free Mulattoes," on 25 May 1799 in St. Paul's Parish, Baltimore [Reamy, *Records of St. Paul's Parish*, I:115].

Members of the Thomas family on the Western Shore were

 i. Rachel, "Negro" head of a Kent County household of 5 "other free" in 1790.
 ii. Surey, head of a Cecil County household of 5 "other free" in 1790.
 iii. Grace, "Negro" head of a Kent County household of 3 "other free" in 1790.

THOMPSON FAMILY

Members of the Thompson family in Maryland were
1 i. Thomas^1, born say 1710.
 ii. Simon, born say 1713, married Savory **Lett**, "negroes," on 10 November 1734 at St. Paul's Parish, Baltimore County [Reamy, *Records of St. Paul's Parish*, I:31].
 iii. Catherine, born say 1734, a "Melater" presented by the grand jury of Prince George's County on 26 March 1754 for having an illegitimate child by information of Benjamin Duvall, the constable of Western Branch Hundred [Court Record 1751-4, 540]. She may have been identical to Catherine Thomson who was head of a Baltimore County household of 5 "other free" in 1810 [MD:489].
 iv. Jacob, born about June 1756, a "Mullatto" living with Peter Becraft on 13 March 1764 when the Frederick County court bound him to Becraft as an apprentice until the age of twenty-one. Becraft was ordered to give him one

year of schooling and provide him with a suit of clothes worth £5 at the end of his apprenticeship [Court Minutes 1763-8, June 1763, March 1764 (n.p.)].

    v. Samuel², head of a Frederick County household of 1 "other free" in 1800 [MD:955 & MD:961].

    vi. Charles, head of a Jefferson County, Virginia household of 11 "other free" in 1810 [VA:78].

    vii. Joseph, head of a St. Mary's County household of 5 "other free" in 1800 [MD:419].

    viii. John, head of a St. Mary's County household of 5 "other free" in 1800 [MD:410].

    ix. Pheaton, head of a Baltimore City household of 7 "other free" in 1800 [MD:368].

    x. Benjamin, head of a Baltimore City household of 4 "other free" in 1800.

1. Thomas¹ Thompson, born say 1710, was a "Mullatto" who was acquitted by the Charles County court on 10 August 1736 of stealing goods worth £5 from Mary Ancrum. Timothy Carrington and James Glascock were his securities. Samuel Hanson sued him and Benjamin **Day** in Charles County court for a debt of 4,020 pounds of tobacco on 13 November 1770. He was called "Thomas Thompson Mulatto" when William Cunningham & Company sued him for a debt of £12 in November 1773. He sued James **Gates** on 8 August 1774 in a case that was agreed to before coming to trial [Court Record 1734-9, 228-9; 1770-2, 216; 1772-3, 174, 577; 1773-4, 60, 519, 695]. He may have been identical to Thomas Thompson, a "Mul.," who took the oath of fidelity in Charles County in 1778 [Liber X-3:641-51] and was head of a Charles County household of 1 "other free" in 1790. He was the father of

    i. ?Henry, "Mulatto" head of a Charles County household of 6 "other free" in 1790, 10 in 1800 [MD:525] and 15 in 1810 [MD:333].

    ii. Mary, called "daughter of Thomas Thompson" on 12 November 1771 when she was presented by the Charles County court for having an illegitimate child [Court Record 1770-2, 169, 492; 1772-3, 174]. She was a "Mulatto" head of a Charles County household of 4 "other free" in 1790.

    iii. ?Thomas², one of one of four "Black Persons being Soldiers," Thomas Thompson, Leonard **Turner**, Valentine **Murrin**, and John **Adams**, who were arrested in Orange County, North Carolina, in December 1780 for breaking into someone's house. They were forcibly rescued by their officer Major McIntosh of the Continental Army [Orange County Court Minutes 1777-82, Dec. 19 and 23, 1780].

    iv. ?Jane, confessed to the Charles County court on 8 August 1774 that she had an illegitimate child. Thomas Thompson "Mulatto Planter" was her security [Court Record 1773-4, 389].

    v. ?William, "Mulatto" head of a Charles County household of 1 "other free" in 1790.

    vi. ?Alexander, "Mulatto" head of a Charles County household of 1 "other free" in 1790.

    vii. ?Joseph, "Mulatto" head of a Charles County household of 1 "other free" in 1790.

    viii. ?Ann, "Mulatto" head of a Charles County household of 1 "other free" in 1790.

Members of the Thompson family on the Eastern Shore of Maryland and in Delaware were

    i. John, born about 1724, a "molatto man" with 15 years to serve when he was listed in the inventory of the Queen Anne's County estate of William Phillips on 7 August 1740 [Prerogative Inventories 25:166-8].

1   ii. Levin, born say 1750.

    iii.   Charles, head of a Kent County household of 6 "other free" in 1800 [MD:155].

    iv.   Rachel, born say 1770, mother of Jane Thompson who registered in Dorchester County on 31 May 1815: *aged about 24 years...born free and raised in Dorchester County, Daughter of Rachel Thompson a free woman* [Certificates of Freedom for Negroes 1806-64, 26].

1.   Levin Thompson, born say 1750, may have been identical to Levin **Game** (originally from Somerset County) who was taxable in Little Creek Hundred, Sussex County, in 1777 and from 1788 to 1791 and Levin **McGee/ Magee** who enlisted in the 1st Company of the 2nd Battalion of Colonel Williams's Delaware Regiment and was listed in the muster for July and August 1780, transferred in September, delivered a coat at Lewis Town in March 1780, delivered clothing in Dover on 13 June 1780 [NARA, M246, reel 29, frames 312, 393, 402, 495]. Levin Thompson was offered as a witness in a suit between two white men (Collins vs. Hall) in Sussex County. When the case was heard by the Delaware Supreme Court in November 1793, he was called "Levin Thompson negro...a freeman." His mother and grandmother had been free and had lived in and come from Maryland [Catterall, *Judicial Cases* IV: 217]. As Levin Thompson he was taxable in Little Creek Hundred, Sussex County, on 100 acres in 1796, 40 of them cultivated, with a house and kitchen, a yoke of oxen, and four horses [DSA, RG 2535, roll 2]. He was called a "Free negro" when he patented another 35 acres in Little Creek Hundred on the south side of Broad Creek about a half mile from Houston's Mill for $17.57 [DB T-19: 509]. He had acquired 428 acres in Little Creek Hundred which included a sawmill and gristmill and 135 acres in Dagsboro Hundred by 1816. The mill was called Tresham's Mill but had once belonged to John Houston according to the 2 July 1808 deed by which he bought two parcels for $35, one called *Providence*. He was head of a Little Creek Hundred household of 5 "other free" in 1800 [DE:375] and in 1810 was listed as heads of two households: one with 18 "other free" producing 200 yards of linen and 60 yards of woolen cloth per year [DE:308] and another with 13 "other free" [DE:313]. In the 1808 deeds he was called a "Black man" and "free blackman." The deeds included:
-   1/8th part of *Tresham's Saw Mill* in Little Creek Hundred with 1/4th part of the pond belonging to it on 3 November 1808 for $162.50.
-   1/8th part of *Tresham's Mill* on 4 September 1809 for $130.
-   128-1/2 acres called *Wood's Grove* for $300 on 4 October 1809.
-   12 acres and improvements on Broad Creek formerly belonging to James Tresham for $25 on 6 November 1809.
-   42-1/2 acres in Broad Creek Hundred on 14 June 1811.
-   1/4th part of Tresham's saw and grist mill with its pond for $250 on 2 March 1814.
-   the remainder of the grist mill and pond on 30 July 1814 for $155.

[DB R-17:269; Z-24:273; AB-25:103; AD27:318; 28:251, 425; AH-31:210, 366; AK-33:54, 180, 216; Williams, *Slavery & Freedom in Delaware*, 204].[28] He called himself a "Blackman" in his 11 October 1806 will and added two codicils as he acquired more land, the last one on 7 October 1810, proved by Betsey Thompson on 16 February 1816. He left his land on the road from Laurel to Tresham's Mill to his wife Leah during her lifetime and widowhood and then to his son Isaac. He left his daughter Betsy 2 acres, left son Clemmon the place where James **Sockam** formerly lived with 5 acres and a house for his daughter Lovey and divided his carriage between his daughters Mary and Nancy. He gave a bull yearling to Nathan **Harmon**'s son Zadock. In a codicil he divided land in "Sockum" between his daughters Lovey and Betsey, but if they died the land was to go to Zadock

---

[28]Belinder **Magee** alias **Game** appears to have been identical to Belinder **Houston** who was head of a household of 4 "other free," perhaps taking the name of her master John Houston of Worcester County.

Harmon. He left $40 to his son James and left his daughter Mary 8 acres of "Chauncy" where Eady Short(?) **Street** (?) was then living. He named his children Littleton and Betsy executors, but Littleton refused. And he asked that his part of the mills be rented out to pay his debts. The estate paid Wingate **Street** and his wife Mary a legacy of $34.58, Littleton Thompson $12.21, Zadock **Harmon** $10, Leah Thompson $59.70, Clement Thompson $74.66, Lovey Thompson $19.58, Nancy Thompson $31.58, Betsey Thompson $68.50 and Peter Robinson, Esquire, $91.39 for judgment costs in the suit of **Sockum** vs. Thompson [DSA, Probate Files, RG 4545.009, roll 240, frames 264-280; WB 7:75-7]. Leah, born before 1776, was head of a Little Creek Hundred household of 2 "free colored" in 1820 [DE:410]. Levin was the father of

    i.   Isaac, born before 1776, head of a Lewis and Rehoboth household of 4 "free colored" in 1820 [DE:310].

    ii.   Betsy, married to a member of the **Green** family on 2 March 1814 when she paid Menean Bull $117.50 which completed the payment of $150 for his part of *Tresham's Mills* [DB 33:54].

   iii. Lovey.

2   iv.   Littleton, born say 1785.

    v.   Nancy.

    vi.   Mary, wife of Wingate **Street**. They sold their rights to Tresham's Mills on 29 March for $170 [DB 33:299].

   vii. Clement, born before 1795, head of a Little Creek Hundred household of 4 "free colored" in 1820 [DE:410]. He and his wife Milly sold their rights to Tresham's Mills on 20 January 1817 for $250, and on 26 September 1817 sold two tracts in Dagsboro Hundred: one of 44 acres for $66 and one of 89 acres adjoining James **Sockam** for $170 [DB 33:126, 208].

  viii. James.

2.   Littleton Thompson, born say 1785, was head of a Little Creek Hundred, Sussex County household of 3 "other free" in 1810 [DE:307] and 8 "free colored" in 1820 [DE:400]. He sold his rights to Tresham's Mills for $120 on 13 August 1817 [DB 33:182]. He made a 17 March 1823 Sussex County will, proved 29 March 1823, by which he left his plantation to his wife Levina during her widowhood and then to William Wesley Tomson (no relationship stated) as well as a heifer from a cow formerly belonging to Sarah **Harmon**. If William Wesley died without heirs, the land was to go to Jeremiah **Streat** (?), son of Seeny **Harmon**. He left a bed, furniture and a loom to his daughter Eliza Cooper Tomson and divided the remainder of his property between Sarah **Harmon** and Eliza Tomson. The estate included a book due from Jonathan **Harmon** and William **Harmon**. Levina died before 2 August 1825 when William Woolen was granted administration on her estate with Elijah **Harmon** and Zadock **Harmon** providing security. The estate paid $4.86 to Isaac Copes, assignee of Wingate **Street**, and $6.96 to Leah Thompson [Probate Files, RG 4545.009, roll 240, frames 291-301, 283-5]. He was the father of

    i.   ?William Wesley.

    ii.   Eliza.

Cecil County

1.   Margaret Thompson, born say 1708, was living in Cecil County on 10 November 1730 when the court convicted her of having "Mullatto" children by a "Negro" man [Criminal Record 1730-2, 254]. She may have been the father of

    i.   Samuel[1], head of a Charles Town, Cecil County household of 1 "other free" in 1790.

TILLS FAMILY

1. Elizabeth Tills, born say 1704, confessed in Prince George's County court on 27 August 1723 that she had a "Malatto" child by a "negroe man named Peter" who was a slave of her master, Jonathan Covell. On 26 November 1723 Peter confessed to the offense, and the court ordered that he receive twenty-five lashes [Court Record 1723-6, 141]. She was probably the ancestor of
   i. Samuel, "negro" head of a Prince George's County household in 1776, taxable on 1 "female black" [Carothers, *1776 Census of Maryland*, 129].

TIPPETT FAMILY

1. Martha Tippett, born say 1713, confessed to the Kent County, Maryland court in June 1733 that she had a "Mollatto" child by a "Negro." The court ordered that she be sold for seven years [Criminal Records 1728-34, 348, 379]. She may have been the ancestor of
   i. Isaac Tibbets, head of a Talbot County household of 5 "other free" in 1800 [MD:547].
   ii. Shadrack Tippett, "blk." head of a St. Mary's County household of 1 "other free" in 1810 [MD:229].
   iii. Lias Triplett, head of a Loudoun County, Virginia household of 4 "other free" in 1810 [VA:265].

TONEY FAMILY

1. James Tony, born say 1698, was a "mulatto man Servant" of Thomas Jefferson (grandfather of the president). In February 1719/20 he confessed to the Henrico County, Virginia court that he was absent from his master's service for eighteen days without permission [Minutes 1719-24, 7]. He may have been related to the Toney family of Maryland:
   i. Anthony[1], "Negro" head of a Kent County, Maryland household of 3 "other free" and a white woman in 1790, and 3 "other free" and a slave in 1800 [MD:177].
   ii. John[3], head of a Kent County household of 6 "other free" in 1800 [MD:167].
   iii. William[2], head of a Kent County household of 5 "other free" in 1800 [MD:167].
   iv. Abram, head of a Talbot County household of 1 "other free" and a white woman in 1800 [MD:517].

TOOGOOD FAMILY

1. Mary Toogood, born say 1715, was taxable in Baltimore County in William Dullam's household in the Lower Hundred on the north side of Gunpowder River in 1737 [Wright, *Inhabitants of Baltimore County*, 16]. In October 1782 Mary's descendant, Eleanor Toogood, won her freedom from Doctor Upton Scott in Anne Arundel County by proving that she was the granddaughter of a white woman, Mary Fisher, who was married to a slave in Saint Mary's County and had a daughter named Ann **Fisher**. Mary Toogood's descendants were
   i. E. (Eleanor?), head of a Frederick County household of 5 "other free" in 1810 [MD:466].
   ii. Betty, born say 1765, head of a Duck Creek, Kent County, Delaware household of 4 "other free" in 1800 [DE:9].
   iii. Nicholas, head of an Anne Arundel County household of 4 "other free" in 1800 [MD:101] and 3 in 1810 [MD:59]. (And there were two other Nicholas Toogoods who were heads of Anne Arundel County households of 3 "other free" in 1810 [MD:60, 79]). He may have been the husband of Eleanor Toogood, born say 1750, daughter of Ann **Fisher** of Anne Arundel County.

           Eleanor won a suit for freedom from Doctor Upton Scott in October 1782 by reason of her descent from a free white woman [*Cases in the General Court and Court of Appeals of Maryland*, 26-31].

    iv. Jacob Twogood, head of a Frederick County household of 2 "other free" in 1800 [MD:989] and 4 in Anne Arundel County in 1810 [MD:76].

    v. Robert, born about 1780, registered in Frederick County on 31 July 1810: *Robert Toogood or Robert Patterson about thirty years of age, a dark mullatto, about five feet ten inches high, stout made...free born...has been an apprentice to Mr. John Ross Key of the said county to learn the blacksmith trade* [Certificates of Freedom 1808-42, 20, 21].

    vi. Mrs., head of a Baltimore City household of 7 "other free" in 1810 [MD:368].

    vii. Joshua, head of an Anne Arundel County household of 6 "other free" in 1810 [MD:58].

    viii. Benjamin, head of an Anne Arundel County household of 2 "other free" in 1810 [MD:79].

TROUT FAMILY

1.   Sarah Trout, born say 1760, was head of an Anne Arundel County household of 5 "other free" in 1790. She may have been the mother of

    i. Dicey, born in May 1789, a twelve year old "Mulatto" bound to William Mills by the Buncombe County, North Carolina court in October 1801.

    ii. Andrew, born about 1790, an eleven-year-old "Mulatto" bound to William Mills by the Buncombe County, North Carolina court in October 1801 [Minutes 1798-1812, 103].

TRUSTY FAMILY

Members of the Trusty family, perhaps children of Wealthy **Gibbs** or (her daughter?) Rachel **Gibbs**, were

1   i. William, born say 1745.

2   ii. Stephen, born 28 March 1755.

    iii. Rebecca, head of a taxable household in the Upper District of Queen Anne's County in 1783 [Assessment of 1783, MSA S1437, p.9], head of a Queen Anne's County household of 6 "other free" in 1790.

    iv. Joseph, owed £6 to the Kent County estate of William Comegys on 13 June 1764 [Prerogative Inventories 84:11]. He was head of a Kent County, Maryland household of 6 "other free" in 1800 [MD:155], and a New Castle County household of 4 "other free" in 1810 [DE:223].

    v. Michael, a "free negro" taxable in the 3rd District of Kent County, Maryland, in 1783 [Assessment of 1783, MSA S1437, p. 6], head of a Kent County household of 4 "other free" in 1800 [MD:155] and 8 in 1810 [MD:858].

    vi. John, head of a Kent County, Maryland household of 2 "other free" in 1800 [MD:155] and 8 in New Castle County in 1810 [DE:299].

1.   William Trusty, born say 1745, called himself William **Gibbs**, "one of the Free Negroes and Heirs or Legatees of John Gibbs," when he sold 12-1/2 acres called *Killmannings Plains* by Forge Road in Queen Anne's County to William Clark on 18 June 1768 [Land Records RT-H:266]. On 9 February 1767 he called himself "William Trusty, otherwise called William Gibbs of Kent County in Delaware" when he sold to Richard **Jeffereys**, "free Negroe formerly servant to John Willson of Kent County in Maryland," for £10 whatever remaining interest he had in 12-1/2 acres called *Kilmannin's Plain* on the Chester River sold by him to William Clark [Land Records RT-H:56-7]. He was a "N." taxable in Little Creek Hundred, Kent County, Delaware, in 1789 [DSA RG 3535, Tax Assessments 1727-1850, frame

138], a "Negro" head of a Kent County, Maryland household of 4 "other free" in 1790 and head of a Duck Creek Hundred, Kent County household of 4 "other free" in 1800 [DE:4]. He may have been the father of

    i. Abraham, a "free Negro" taxable in Dover Hundred of Kent County, Delaware, in 1785 and 1786 [RG 3535, Assessment List 1727-1850, frames 10, 46].

    ii. Richard[1], born before 1776, a "free Negro" taxable in Dover Hundred of Kent County, Delaware, in 1788 [Assessment List 1727-1850, frame 108], head of a St. Jones Hundred, Kent County household of 3 "other free" in 1800 [DE:44] and 2 "free colored" in Duck Creek Hundred, Kent County, Delaware, in 1820 [DE:38].

    iii. Mary, "N." head of a Duck Creek, Kent County household of 1 "other free" in 1800 [DE:8].

    iv. Jacob, head of a Duck Creek Hundred, Kent County, Delaware household of 13 "free colored" in 1820 [DE:52].

2.   Stephen Trusty, born free 28 March 1755, was head of a Caroline County household of 3 "other free" in 1790. He purchased 80-1/2 acres called *Sansborough* in Caroline County from Colonel William Whitely for £300 on 18 October 1799. He was called a miller in the 20 March 1801 Caroline County deed by which he mortgaged (signing) this land to Whitely for £363. He sold this land to George Turner on 31 July 1804 for £565 [Land Records G:322; I:40-1]. He was head of a Kent County, Maryland household of 8 "other free" in 1810 [MD:858] and 5 "free colored" in Dover Hundred, Kent County, Delaware, in 1820 [DE:41]. He registered in Caroline County on 27 July 1818: *molatto man Stephen Trusty senior free born 63 years of age the twenty eighth day of March last molatto complexion...resided about twenty eight years in Caroline County* [Certificates of Freedom 1807-1827, p. 113]. He may have been the ancestor of

    i. Priscilla, born 19 January 1798, registered in Caroline County on 19 October 1816: *molatto woman...free born light complexion raised in Caroline County.*

    ii. Jonathan, born 13 October 1800, registered in Caroline County on 27 July 1818: *free born molatto lad 18 years of age...born and raised in Caroline bright molatto complexion.*

    iii. Henry, born 27 August 1801, registered in Caroline County on 27 July 1818: *free born.*

    iv. Sarah, born 22 December 1803, registered in Caroline County on 27 July 1818: *born free...molatto girl.*

    v. Alice, born 2 April 1806, registered in Caroline County on 27 July 1818: *molatto complextion* [Certificates of Freedom 1807-1827, p. 115].

    vi. Stephen, born 4 July 1807, registered in Caroline County on 27 July 1818: *molatto complextion born in Caroline County.*

    vii. William, born 25 September 1810, registered in Caroline County on 27 July 1818: *free born molatto boy.*

    viii. DeWitt Clinton, born 15 December 1812, registered in Caroline County on 27 July 1818: *molatto boy.*

    ix. Joseph, born 25 March 1815, registered in Caroline County on 27 July 1818: *free born...molatto complexion* [Certificates of Freedom 1807-1827, pp. 113-118].

TUNKS FAMILY

1.   Elizabeth Tunks, born say 1740, was a spinster servant of Hugh Rice of Talbot County in November 1759 when the court ordered her to serve her master seven years after the completion of her indenture for having a "Molattoe" child by a "Negro." The court sold her son John to her master until the age of thirty-one for 13 shillings. In June 1761 she admitted in court that she had another child by a

"Negro." The court sold her daughter Anne to her master until the age of thirty-one for 10 shillings and sold her for seven years to Hugh Rice for £12. She had a child by a free person for which the court fined her 30 shillings in March 1764, and in November 1766 she admitted in court that she had another illegitimate "Mulato" child named William Tunks who the court sold to Hugh Rice until the age of thirty-one [Criminal Record 1755-61, 284-5, 463-4, 517; 1761-7, 254, 505]. She was the mother of

    i. John, born about 1759, head of an Anne Arundel County household of 12 "free colored" in 1830.
    ii. Anne, born about 1761.
    iii. William, born about 1766, registered in Talbot County on 2 October 1810: *a Mulatto Man...about forty four years of age, five feet seven inches high...son of Eliz* Tunks, a white woman...sold by the court to Hugh Rice to serve until the age of thirty one years, when he became free* [Certificates of Freedom 1807-27, p.119].

TURNER FAMILY

1. Mary Turner, born say 1695, was the servant of Robert Hopkins in November 1716 when she confessed in Talbot County court that she had two children by a "Negro slave named Jo." The court bound her two "Malattoe" girls to William Clayland until the age of thirty-one. Mary and Joe received thirty-one lashes for each offense. Mary was the servant of Eliza Hopkins in November 1718 when she confessed to having another child by Joseph [Judgment Record 1714-7, 147, 153-4; 1717-9, 192, 226]. They were the parents of

    i. Mary, born 7 September 1715.
    ii. an unnamed daughter, born about September 1716.

They may have been the ancestors of

    i. Margarete, "Negro" head of a Kent County household of 4 "other free" in 1790.
    ii. Jesse, head of a Back Creek, Cecil County household of 1 "other free" in 1790.
    iii. Andrew, head of North Millford, Cecil County household of 1 "other free" in 1790.
    iv. William, born about 1793, registered in Talbot County on 18 July 1810: *five feet four inches and three Quarters of an inch high...about 17 years of age, was raised in the County afsd, is the son of Ann Turner, a Woman born free* [Certificates of Freedom 1807-15, 118].

Another Turner family:
1. Mary Turner, born say 1710, deposed in Prince George's County court on 28 November 1728 that she had a child by Peter Smith, a "Negro man belonging to William Pile." The court ordered that he receive 25 lashes "well laid on so that the blood appear." The court sold her daughter Jane to James Weems to serve him until the age of thirty-one [Court Records 1726-7, 625; 1728-9, 344-5]. She was the mother of

    i. Jane, born 15 August 1728, bound to James Weems.
    ii. ?Benjamin, born about 1729, a free Negro counted in the 1776 census for Prince George's County with (wife?) Patience (age 32) a child age 8 and two slaves [Brumbaugh, *Maryland Records*, I:42].

They may have been the ancestors of

    i. Leonard, born say 1760, one of four "Black Persons being Soldiers," Thomas **Thompson**, Leonard Turner, Valentine **Murrin**, and John **Adams**, who were arrested in Orange County, North Carolina, in December 1780 for breaking into someone's house. They were forcibly rescued by their officer

Major McIntosh of the Continental Army [Orange County Court Minutes 1777-82, Dec. 19 and 23, 1780]. Leonard was head of an Anne Arundel County household of 10 "other free" in 1810 [MD:84].

2   ii.   Eleanor, born say 1765.

2.   Eleanor Turner, born say 1765, was head of an Anne Arundel County household of 7 "other free" in 1800 [MD:106]. She may have been the mother of
   i.   James, born about 1790, registered in Anne Arundel County on 1 August 1812: *aged about twenty two years...light complexion...free born.*
   ii. James, born about 1792, registered in Anne Arundel County on 22 May 1818: *about twenty six years old...brown complexion...free born.*
   iii. Alley, born about 1792, registered in Anne Arundel County on 27 October 1818: *aged about twenty six years...yellowish Complexion...free born.*
   iv. James, born about 1796, registered in Anne Arundel County on 22 May 1818: *a Mulatto man...aged about twenty two years...yellow complexion...free born* [Certificates of Freedom 1810-31, 24, 115, 116, 124].

UPTON FAMILY

1.   Mary Upton, born say 1740, was presented by the Charles County court on 13 November 1759 for bearing a "Molatto" child by information of constable Notley Dutton [Court Record 1759-60, 358]. She was probably the mother of
   i.   William, "Mulatto" head of a Charles County household of 3 "other free" in 1790.

VALENTINE FAMILY

1.   Caesar Valentine, born say 1730, was taxable in Little Creek Hundred, Kent County, Delaware, from 1763 to 1766 and in 1771: a "N." (Negro) taxable in 1770, a Dover Hundred delinquent in 1792 [Kent County Assessments, RG 3535, 1743-67, frames 377, 383, 398, 437, 509, 521, 535, 553, 566; 1768-1784, frames 10, 27, 66, 104; 1785-97, 237]. He petitioned the Kent County court on 12 May 1772 to release his son Elijah Valentine from his apprentice indenture made to John Ham, yeoman, of Little Creek Hundred until the age of twenty-one on 6 February 1771. By the terms of the indenture, it could be cancelled by Caesar and his wife within fifteen months if they reimbursed Ham for the clothes he had provided Elijah up until that time [DSA, RG 3505, MS court papers, May 1772 Petition to release from indenture]. He was the father of
   i.   Elijah, born say 1755, taxable in Little Creek Hundred from 1780 to 1785 [RG 3535, Kent County Levy List, 1768-84, frames 443, 503, 542, 571, 583, 608, 620; 1785-97, frames 9, 24].
   ii. ?Abraham, taxable in Little Creek Hundred from 1786 to 1790 [RG 3535, Kent County Levy List, 1784-97, frames 49, 72, 138, 176], perhaps the A. Valentine who was head of a Kent County, Delaware household in 1810 [DE:161]. His wife may have been Jance Valentine, head of a Little Creek, Sussex County household of 2 "free colored" in 1820 [DE:214].

1.   Thomas Valentine, born say 1753, was probably identical to slave: "Valentine aged 16 years/ free born" who was valued at £12 in the 1 March 1769 St. Mary's County estate of Francis Thompson [Prerogative Inventories, 101:322]. He was head of a St. Mary's County household of 4 "other free" and a white woman in 1790. He may have been the Thomas Valentine, "mulatto," who broke jail in St. Mary's County and was thought to be in Alexandria according to the 4 August 1785 issue of the *Virginia Journal and Alexandria Advertiser* [Headley, *18th Century Virginia Newspapers*, 347].

VERDIN/ VIRDEN FAMILY

1. Anthony Verdin, born say 1770, was head of a Murderkill Hundred, Kent County, Delaware household of 6 "other free" in 1800 [DE:118]. He may have been the father of
    i. Nancy, married Silas **Lewis**, "Mulatoes," on 21 December 1800 in Sussex County [Records of the United Presbyterian Churches of Lewes, Indian River and Cool Spring, Delaware 1756-1855, 316].
    ii. James, head of an Indian River, Sussex County household of 7 "free colored" in 1820 [DE:208].

WALKER FAMILY

1. Mary Walker, born say 1683, was the servant of Samuel Hopkins in Somerset County on 11 June 1701 when she confessed to having a "Mulatto" child by a slave named Lawrence. The court ordered that Lawrence receive fifteen lashes, and on 10 August 1703 the court sold her to Samuel Hopkins, Jr., for seven years for 3,000 pounds of tobacco [Judicial Record 1698-1701, 508; 1702-5, 53]. She may have been the ancestor of
    i. Daniel, "Free Mulatto" head of a Queen Anne's County household of 3 "other free" in 1790 and 3 in 1800 [MD:385].

WALLACE FAMILY

Members of the Wallace family of Maryland and Delaware were
    i. Richard, head of a Talbot County household of 4 "other free" and a slave in 1790 and 3 "other free" in Mispillion Hundred, Kent County, Delaware, in 1800 [DE:103].
    ii. Prince, head of a Kent County, Maryland household of 6 "other free" and a slave in 1800 [MD:168].
    iii. Roger, head of a Murderkill Hundred, Delaware household of 5 "other free" in 1800 [DE:121].
    iv. Isaac, head of a Murderkill Hundred, Kent County, Delaware household of 5 "other free" in 1800 [DE:129] and 5 in 1810 [DE:50].
    v. Briscoe, head of a Kent County, Maryland household of 4 "other free" in 1800 [MD:156].
    vi. Rachel, born about 1785, registered in Anne Arundel County on 12 April 1813: *dark complexion, about twenty eight years of age...free born* [Certificates of Freedom 1810-31, 33].
    vii. Robert, born about 1790, registered in Somerset County on 21 June 1825: *born free in Somerset County...black Complexion...thirty five years of age* [Certificates of Freedom 1821-32, 50].

WANSLEY FAMILY

1. Sherry Wansey, born say 1635, and Freegift Wansey were "negroes" freed by the 22 June 1764 Kent County, Delaware will of Joseph Jones who also gave them 200 acres of land and named Sherry as his executor before leaving for England [WB A-1:1]. Sherrey registered in Dorchester County on 10 December 1681 [de Valinger, *Kent County General Court Records 1680-1725*, 73]. Sheery was a "poor decriped free Negro" who the Talbot County court allowed 500 pounds of tobacco for maintenance in June 1715 [Judgment Records 1714-17, 227]. They were apparently the ancestors of
2   i. Charles, born say 1745.
    ii. Peter, born say 1750, taxable in Little Creek Hundred, Kent County, Delaware, in 1767, 1771 and 1773 [Kent County Levy List, 1743-67, frame 552; 1768-84, frames 104, 129, 185] and head of a Kent County household

of 6 "other free" in 1810 [DE:43]. He was called a "Negro yeoman" when he was charged with assaulting Henry Cowgel in Little Creek Hundred on 6 August 1782 [DSA, RG 3805, MS August 1782 Indictments].

2.   Charles Wansey, born say 1745, was living in Kent County, Delaware, on 20 March 1790 when Bancroft Woodcock advertised a reward in the *Delaware Gazette* for the return of Charles's "mulatto" son Elijah Wansey who was apprenticed to Woodcock [Wright, *Delaware Newspaper Abstracts*, 12]. He was the father of
    i.   Elijah, born say 1770.
    ii.   ?Isaac Wamsley, a "free Negro" taxable in Little Creek Hundred, Kent County, Delaware, in 1787 [Levy List 1785-97, frame 73].

WARD FAMILY

1.   Anne Ward, born say 1710, was the servant of Joseph Young on 17 March 1729/30 when she admitted in Kent County, Maryland court that she had a "Mullatto" child by a "Negroe." The court ordered that she be sold for seven years and sold her child to Joseph Young until the age of thirty-one [Criminal Proceedings 1728-34, 107]. She was probably the ancestor of
    i.   Honorio, convicted of adultery with a "Mulatto" person by the Talbot County court in March 1744/5. Anthony Guy, planter, was security for payment of her fine of £3 [Judgment Record 1744-5, 231].
    ii.   Mole, a "Negro" head of a Kent County household of 3 "other free" in 1790.
    iii.   Peggy, head of a Baltimore City household of 9 "other free" in 1800 [MD:391].
    iv.   Sarah, head of an Anne Arundel County household of 3 "other free" in 1800 [MD:113].
    v.   Nancy, head of an Anne Arundel County household of 2 "other free" in 1800 [MD:116].
    vi.   Ann, head of an Anne Arundel County household of 2 "other free" in 1800 [MD:116].

WATERS FAMILY

Members of the Waters family were
1   i.   George[1], born say 1750.
2   ii.   Nace, born say 1760.
    iii.   York, a "negroe" in the 2[d] Regiment who was allowed to receive sufficient cloth for a pair of breeches on 10 February 1780 [*Archives of Maryland*, 43:82].
    iv.   Ephraim, head of an Anne Arundel County household of 4 "other free" in 1800 [MD:93].
3   v.   William, born say 1765.

1.   George[1] Waters, born say 1750, was head of a Talbot County household of 11 "other free" in 1800 [MD:510-1/2]. He may have been the father of
    i.   Rachel, born about 1792, registered in Talbot County on 8 May 1816: *a Black woman...about 24 years of age, 4 feet 11 Inches high* [Certificates of Freedom 1815-28, 30].

2.   Nace Waters, born say 1760, was head of a Baltimore City, Maryland household of 10 "other free" in 1800 [MD:387]. He may have been the parent of
    i.   Charlotte, born about 1784, a 15 or 16 year old "free mulatto" who was baptized at St. Paul's Parish, Baltimore on 30 December 1790 [Reamy, *Records of St. Paul's Parish,* vol. I, 135].

3.   William Waters, born say 1765, was head of a Kent County, Delaware household

of 7 "other free" in 1800 [DE:64]. (His widow?) Elizabeth Waters was head of a Little Creek Hundred, Kent County household of 4 "free colored" in 1820 [DE:22]. Their children were most likely

    i. George², born 1776-1794, head of a Dover Hundred, Kent County household of 11 "free colored" in 1820 [DE:22].

    ii. Samuel, born 1776-1794, head of a Little Creek Hundred, Kent County household of 4 "free colored" in 1820 [DE:20].

WATSON FAMILY

1. Elizabeth Watson, born say 1716, confessed to the Anne Arundel County court in March 1735/6 that she had an illegitimate child which the court adjudged to be "begot by some Negro." The court bound her five-week-old daughter Sabrina to Richard Watts until the age of thirty-one [Judgment Record 1734-6, 451]. They may have been the ancestors of

    i. Thomas, head of a Philadelphia County, Pennsylvania household of 2 "other free" in 1790.

    ii. Mary, head of a North Millford, Cecil County household of 1 "other free" in 1790.

    iii. C., head of a Frederick County household of 6 "other free" in 1810 [MD:615].

WEBBER FAMILY

1. Sarah Webber, born say 1750, pled guilty to "Mulatto Bastardy" in Queen Anne's County court in November 1771. Her daughter Ann was sold until the age of thirty-one to Philemon Phillips for 108 pounds of tobacco. The court sold Sarah for seven years to Philemon Phillips for 1,000 pounds of tobacco on 26 August 1774. She was probably the mother of James Webber who the court paid Philemon Phillips to maintain in November 1779 [Surles, *And they Appeared at Court 1770-1772*, 93; *1774-1777*, 27, *1779-1787*, 33]. She was the mother of

    i. Ann, born 22 November 1771.

    ii. ?Primus, "F.N." head of a Kent County, Delaware household of 6 "other free" in 1810 [DE:45].

    iii. ?Amos, born before 1776, "N." head of a Duck Creek Hundred, Kent County, Delaware household of 2 "free colored" in 1820 [DE:52].

WEBSTER FAMILY

Members of the Webster family were

    i. Thomas, born say 1745, presented by the Charles County court in August 1772 for failing to list as a tithable his wife who was a slave hired to him. He was fined 500 pounds of tobacco for the offense in November 1772 [Court Records 1772-3, 2, 171]. He was a "Mulatto" head of a Charles County household of 3 "other free" in 1790.

    ii. Daniel, born about 1752, head of a Prince William County, Virginia household of 6 "other free" in 1810 [VA:501], a 60-year-old "free Negro" living in Prince William County in 1812 when he petitioned the legislature to allow him to free his wife and children who were his slaves [Petitions, Prince William County, 1812, cited by Russell, *The Free Negro in Virginia*, 92]. He and his wife Lucy were residing at Accoquan Mills in Prince William County on 28 September 1821 when their son William **Armstead** Webster registered in the Court of the District of Columbia in Alexandria: *free born, twenty-three years of age, a bright mulatto* [Arlington County Register of Free Negroes, 1797-1861, no. 89, p.65].

    iii. John, head of a Talbot County household of 8 "other free" in 1800 [MD:549].

iv.   Joseph, head of a Baltimore City household of 6 "other free" in 1800 [MD:391].

WEDGE FAMILY

1.   Mary Wedge, born say 1709, a white servant woman of St. Barnard's Parish, Patuxent Hundred, Prince George's County, was presented by the court in March 1727 for having a "Mulatto" child. In June 1727 she admitted that the father of her child was Robert Tyler's slave named Daniel. The court bound her daughter Violetta to her master Thomas Harwood until the age of thirty-one. She had at least four more children who were sold until the age of thirty-one: William, born 8 February 1732/3, sold to Dr. Thomas Boswell; Ned, born about 1734; a child who died before June 1735 when the case came to trial; a child born in 1736 and sold to Robert **Perle**; a girl, born 9 June 1737, sold to Henry Boteler; and Samuel, born 31 October 1738, sold to her master Thomas Harwood [Court Records 1726-7, 230, 358-9; 1732-4, 164, 297-8; 1734-5, 108, 351, 410; 1736-8, 15, 46, 60-1, 504; 1738-40, 192]. She was the mother of

      i.   Violetta, born before March 1727.

2   ii.   ?Eleanor, born say 1729.

      iii.   William, born 8 February 1732/3, head of a Montgomery County, Pennsylvania household of 4 "other free" in 1790.

      iv.   Ned, born about 1734.

      v.   a child, born in 1736 who was sold to Robert **Perle**.

      vi.   a girl, born 9 June 1737.

3   vii.   Samuel, born 31 October 1738.

2.   Eleanor Wedge, born say 1729, a "free woman of colour" of Prince George's County, was the mother of

      i.   Elijah, born about 1748, registered in Prince George's County on 30 November 1822: *a colored man, about 74 years old...dark complexion...raised in the neighborhood of Dr. Thomas Marshall...son of Eleanor Wedge, a free woman of colour* [Provine, *Registrations of Free Negroes*, 44].

      ii.   ?George, "free Negro" head of a Prince George's County household of 11 "other free" in 1800 [MD:278] and 14 in 1810 [MD:24].

      iii.   ?James, head of a Charles County household of 8 "free colored" in 1830.

3.   Samuel Wedge, born 31 October 1738, was bound to Thomas Harwood until the age of thirty-one. He and his wife Jean petitioned the Frederick County court on 15 November 1763 to have one of their children bound to Battis Trout. The same court ordered that Anthony Wedge, a three year old "Molatto Child," be bound as an apprentice to Battis Trout at the request of his unnamed father [Judgment Record 1763-6, 126, 143; Court Minutes 1763-8, November 1763, n.p.]. He enlisted in the 3^{d} Maryland Regiment on 1 January 1782 and was due £45 pay on 16 November 1783 [NARA, M246, Roll 34, frames 403, 511 of 587]. He was the father of

      i.   Anthony, born 20 September 1760, bound as an apprentice to Battis Trout until the age of twenty-one.

WELSH FAMILY

1.   Mary^{2} Welch, born say 1710, was the servant of Thomas Harwood on 13 November 1728 when she admitted to the Prince George's County court that she had a "Malatto" child. The court bound her for an additional seven years and bound her two-month-old son Henry to her master until the age of thirty-one [Court Records 1728-9, 346-7]. She was the mother of

2   i.   Henry^{1}, born 28 September 1728.

      ii.   ?Sarah, a "Mulatta girl" listed in the 3 February 1748/9 inventory of the

King George County, Virginia estate of Thomas Bartlett [Inventories, 1745-1765, 36].

2. Henry[1] Welch, born 28 September 1728, son of Mary Welch, may have been the ancestor of

   i.   Henry[2], born about 1762, enlisted in the Revolution from Culpeper County for 18 months on 19 March 1781 and was sized about a month later: *age 19, 5'3-3/4" high, yellow complexion, born in King George County* [The Chesterfield Supplement or Size Roll of Troops at Chesterfield Court House, LVA accession no. 23816, by http://revwarapps.org/b81.pdf (p.35)].

Other members of a Welch family in Maryland and Virginia were

   i.   Thomas, head of a Kent County, Maryland household of 5 "other free" in 1800 [MD:168].
   ii. James, head of a Charles Town, Cecil County household of 1 "other free" in 1790.
   iii. Rebecca, head of a Loudoun County, Virginia household of 3 "other free" in 1810 [VA:291].
   iv. Clary, head of a Stafford County, Virginia household of 2 "other free" in 1810.

WHITTAM FAMILY

1. Rebecca Whitham, born say 1715, was the spinster servant of Timothy Lane of St. Paul's Parish in June 1734 when she admitted to the Queen Anne's County court that she had an illegitimate child and received fifteen lashes. In November 1735 she admitted to the court that she had a "Mullatto" child by a "Negroe," and the court sold Rebecca and her daughter Elizabeth to Walter Lane for £19 [Judgments 1732-5, 274-5; 1735-9, 322]. She was the mother of

   i.   Elizabeth, born about 1735.
2 ii. ?Sall, born say 1738.

2. Sall Whittam, born say 1738, was the free "Mullato" servant of Vincent Price on 25 November 1760 when she confessed to the Queen Anne's County court that she had a child by a "Negroe" man. The court sold her son Peter to her master for 500 pounds of tobacco and ordered her sold for seven years after the completion of her service [Criminal Record 1759-66, 60]. She was the mother of

   i.   Peter, born in 1760.

WILKINS FAMILY

1. Susanna Wilkins, born say 1683, was the servant of Richard Marsham on 10 December 1703 when she was presented by the Prince George's County court for having an illegitimate child, "the begetter thereof supposed to be an Ethiopian Dye or Couler." She confessed to having an illegitimate child but identified a white man named Henry Crumpton as the father. On 28 March 1705 the court agreed with Crumpton that both he and the mother had fair complexions and the child was a "Perfect Malatta." However, there was still some doubt, so the court ruled that her master should keep her and the child for twelve months and then deliver both up to court for further judgment [Court Record 1699-1705, 338, 358]. She may have been the ancestor of

   i.   Chester, head of a Kent County household of 7 "other free" in 1800 [MD:179].
   ii. Catherine, head of a Kent County household of 4 "other free" in 1800 [MD:178].

WILKINSON FAMILY

1. Margaret Wilkinson, born say 1712, the servant of John Howard, was the mother of a "Molatto" girl, born 4 October 1731, who was bound by the Anne Arundel County court to her master in June 1735 until the age of thirty-one. She confessed her guilt, but the court delayed their ruling because they were undecided as to whether the child was "begot by an Indian or Negro." On 9 August 1748 the court bound her daughter Moll to Ruth Todd until the age of thirty-one, the child "being adjudged by the Court to be a Mulatto begot by a Negro man" [Judgment Record 1734-6, 238, 241; 1748-51, 74]. Margaret was probably the ancestor of
    i.   Jacob, head of a Baltimore Town household of 3 "other free" in 1790.
    ii. John, head of a Baltimore City household of 8 "other free" in 1800 [MD:387] and 3 in 1810 [MD:379].
    iii. Samuel, head of a Baltimore City household of 4 "other free" in 1810 [MD:10].
    iv. Robert, head of a Baltimore City household of 4 "other free" in 1810 [MD:216].
    v.   Mrs., head of a Baltimore City household of 1 "other free" in 1810 [MD:158].

Eastern Shore of Maryland
1. Mary Wilkinson, born say 1724, was the servant of John Carroll on 1 March 1745 when she confessed in Kent County court that she had a "Mulatto" child by a "Negro." The court ordered her sold for seven years after the completion of her indenture and bound her child to her master until the age of thirty-one [Criminal Records 1742-7, 376]. She may have been the ancestor of
    i.   Jacob, head of a Baltimore Town household of 3 "other free" in 1790, perhaps the husband of "Mrs. Wilkinson" who was head of a Baltimore City household of 1 "other free" in 1810 [MD:216].
    ii. John, head of a Baltimore City household of 8 "other free" in 1800 [MD:387] and 3 in 1810 [MD:379].
    iii. Robert, head of a Baltimore City household of 4 "other free" in 1810 [MD:216].
    iv. Samuel, head of a Baltimore City household of 4 "other free" in 1810 [MD:10].

WILLIAMS FAMILY

Anne Arundel County
1. Guy Williams, born say 1678, a "Negroe planter," was sued in Anne Arundel County court on 11 March 1711/2 by Michael Moore for a debt of 2,000 pounds of tobacco which he had promised to pay in October 1710 [Judgment Record 1708-12, 433-4]. He was probably the father of
    i.   Mark, born say 1698, identified as the father of an illegitimate "Mollatto" child by Sarah Empy (**Impey**) in Anne Arundel County court in June 1717 [Judgment Record 1717-19, 10-11].
    ii. Sarah[1], born say 1712, married Anthony **Hill** on 18 December 1732 in All Hollow's Parish, Anne Arundel County [Wright, *Anne Arundel County Church Records*, 46].
    iii. Catherine, mother of Moses Williams, born 31 October 1740, and John Williams ("mulato"), born 25 January 1742, whose births were registered in All Hallow's Parish [Wright, *Anne Arundel County Church Records*, 51]. John may have been identical to John Williams, "Mulatto" head of a Charles County household of 1 "other free" in 1790.
    iv. Elizabeth, born say 1724, called "Eliza, Anthony Hill's Daughter in Law" in August 1741 when she was charged with bastardy by the Anne Arundel County court. However, the charges against her were dismissed because she

was a "free Negro woman." On 11 June 1745 she was called Elizabeth Williams when she was presented by the court for assaulting Elizabeth Jacobs. Anthony **Hill** was security for her appearance in court. She was found guilty in August 1745 and fined 20 shillings [Judgment 1740-3, 248-9; 1744-5, 322].

   v. Sarah[2], born say 1725, mother of Anna Williams, a "malatto" who was born in St. Margaret's, Westminster Parish, Anne Arundel County, on 13 June 1746 [Wright, *Anne Arundel County Church Records*, 121]. She was the servant of Joseph Crouch in August 1746 when she confessed to the Anne Arundel County court that she had an illegitimate child which the court adjudged to be a "Molatto." She was ordered to serve seven years, and her daughter Ann was bound to her master until the age of thirty-one. Crouch purchased her seven-year term for £4.5 in March 1748/9. She had another child named Sarah who was bound to Crouch in August 1750 until the age of sixteen [Judgment Record 1746-8, 216; 1748-51, 197, 629].

Another Williams family in Anne Arundel County:

1. Sarah Williams, born say 1725, was the servant of Joseph Brewer in August 1746 when she confessed to the Anne Arundel County court that she had a "Molatto" child. The court bound her five-month-old daughter Ruth to her master until the age of thirty-one. She was ordered to serve for seven years and indicted for perjury for charging a white man named Charles Hanshaw with being the father [Judgment Record 1746-8, 214]. She was the ancestor of

      i. Ruth, born about March 1746.
2   ii. ?Henry[1], born say 1760.
     iii. ?Sidney[1], head of a Baltimore Town household of 5 "other free" in 1790.

2. Henry[1] Williams, born say 1760, was a "man of color" from Anne Arundel County who enlisted in the Revolution in Annapolis about 1777 and died in Baltimore on 5 January 1850. His widow Esther applied for bounty land for his services in March 1855 and was about 90 years old on 20 June 1857 when she made a declaration in Baltimore City court. She stated that her husband served in the war and also drove wagons. Her maiden name was **Giles** and she was married to Henry on 14 August 1785 by a Methodist minister named Reverend Charles Dorsey three miles from a place called Poplar Spring in Anne Arundel County. Her application included a record of the birth of their children who were all deceased by 20 June 1857 [NARA, M804, roll 2588, W3638, Bounty land warrant 6767F-160-55]. Their children (and grandchildren?) were

      i. Hannah, born 22 October 1790.
     ii. Harry[2], born 6 August 1811.
    iii. Sary, born 31 July 1812.
    iv. John, born 11 October 1814.
     v. Warner, born 21 November 1816.
    vi. Cidney[2], born 24 October 1818.
   vii. Joshua, born 16 December 1820.
  viii. Emily, born 23 November 1822.
    ix. Perry, born 5 December 1824.
     x. Hanson, born 25 November 1827.
    xi. Basil, born 20 February 1831.

Prince George's County

1. Richard Williams, born about 1713, was freed by order of the Prince George's County court on 28 August 1744 on the petition of Elizabeth Palmer against his master Philip Mason. Elizabeth testified that he was a "Molatto" bound to Rebecca Hunter until the age of thirty-one-years and that his time was then expired [Court Record 1743-4, 515]. He may have been the ancestor of

      i. Abraham, "free negro" head of a Prince George's County household of 6 "other free" in 1800 [MD:262] and 6 in 1810 [MD:262].

ii. Robert, head of a Frederick County household of 3 "other free" in 1800 [MD:853] and 5 in Anne Arundel County in 1810 [MD:56].

iii. Liddy, born about 1794, registered in Frederick County on 6 May 1814: *a mulatto woman...20 years old* [Certificates of Freedom 1808-42, 44].

Kent County
1. Robert Williams, born say 1699, was held as a slave by John Rogers before 16 June 1730 when he sued for his freedom in Kent County court. Robert won his case as well as his costs for the appeal to the Provincial Court in May 1731 [Provincial Court Judgments, Liber R.B. no.1, fols. 462-4, MSA]. He may have been the father of

i. Thomas, a "Mulatto" who owed 240 pounds of tobacco to the estate of William Rasin of Kent County on 24 February 1764 [Prerogative Inventories 83:1-7]. He was head of a Kent County household of 2 "other free" in 1790 and 3 in 1800 [MD:168].

ii. Chester, "Negro" head of a Kent County household of 2 "other free" in 1790.

iii. William, head of a Kent County household of 8 "other free" in 1800 [MD:156].

iv. Duke, head of a Kent County household of 7 "other free" in 1810 [MD:852].

Talbot County
1. Elizabeth Williams, born say 1711, the servant of Risdon Bozeman of St. Michael's Parish, confessed to the Talbot County court in August 1731 that she had a child by a "Negroe." The court bound her son to her master until the age of thirty-one [Judgment Record 1731-3, 446]. She may have been the ancestor of

i. Richard, born say 1731, a "Mulatto" labourer fined 30 shillings by the Talbot County court in March 1757 for having an illegitimate child by Ruth **Dyas**, a free "Mulatto" [Criminal Record 1755-61, 93].

2   ii. Ann, born say 1732.

iii. Levin, head of a Talbot County household of 5 "other free" in 1800 [MD:528].

2. Ann[1] Williams, born say 1732, was a spinster living in Talbot County in November 1752 when she admitted to the court that she had a "Mullato" child by a "Negro." The court sold her for seven years to Josiah Coleman, innholder, for 2,300 pounds of tobacco [Criminal Record 1751-5, n.p.]. She may have been the mother of

i. Ann[2], born say 1752, admitted in Queen Anne's County court in March 1773 that she had a child by a "Negroe" slave [Judgments 1771-80, digital images 102-3].

Members of a Williams family in Worcester County and adjoining Accomack County, Virginia, were

i. Daniel, head of a Worcester County household of 5 "other free" in 1790, and a "Negro" head of 10 in 1800 [MD:791]. He was 78 years old on 4 May 1835 when he appeared in Philadelphia County court to make a declaration to obtain a pension for his service in the Revolution. He stated that he was born in Accomack County where he enlisted. He served for 5 years and was in charge of a wagon and two horses. He returned to Accomack County after the war, then removed to Maryland where he resided for 13 years, and moved to Philadelphia where he resided for 27 years. John **Blake**, a 76-year-old "Coloured man," testified on 1 April 1835 that he was born in Accomack County and knew Daniel Williams, a "Coloured man," since childhood and that Daniel was freeborn and spent 4 to 5 years in the service. He met up with Daniel again when he came to Philadelphia about thirteen years previous. John's wife Hester testified that she knew Daniel from her earliest recollection near Horntown in Accomack County (which is near the

Worcester County line) [NARA, M804, reel 2586, R11,569].

ii. Abraham, "Negro" head of a Worcester County household of 10 "other free" in 1800 [MD:730].

iii. Levin, head of a Worcester County household of 5 "other free" in 1800 [MD:832].

WILLIS FAMILY

1. Ann Willis, born say 1690, was the mother of a "Mallato...a small Child" who was brought before the Charles County court on 10 November 1710 by Kenett Mackenzey who stated that Ann had left the child at his home. The court bound the child to him [Court Records 1711-5, 321]. Ann may have been the ancestor of

   i. Henry, head of a Queen Anne's County household of 5 "other free" in 1800 [MD:387].

WILSON FAMILY

1. Sophia Wilson alias Jane Smith, born say 1735, was the mother of two "Mulatto" children, Elizabeth and Aquilla, who were sold to William Rogers by the Baltimore County court in March 1754 [Liber BB#A, 15, 20, 26]. Rogers gave his right to the three unnamed Mulatto children of Sophia Wilson to his daughter Sarah by his 5 June 1761 Baltimore County will [Wills 1721-63, 319]. Sophia was the mother of

   i. Elizabeth, born say 1751.

   ii. Aquilla, born say 1753.

   iii. an unnamed child, born say 1755, sold to William Rogers before 1761.

They may have been the ancestors of members of the Wilson family in Baltimore County:

   i. Abraham, head of a household of 8 "other free" in 1810 [MD:461].

   ii. Rachel, head of a household of 8 "other free" in 1810 [MD:479].

   iii. Elen, head of a household of 3 "other free" in 1810 [MD:697].

Eastern Shore
1. Samuel Wilson, born say 1715, petitioned the Queen Anne's County court in November 1744 to be excused from paying taxes on his "free Molatto" wife [Judgment Record 1744-6, 73]. He was probably the ancestor of

   i. William, perhaps the William Wilson who owed 4 shillings to the Queen Anne's County estate of Joseph Evens on 9 July 1751 [Prerogative Inventories 48:414-8], head of a Queen Anne's County household of 10 "other free" in 1790 and 11 in 1800 [MD:385].

   ii. Solomon, "F.M." head of a Queen Anne's County household of 9 "other free" in 1790 and 11 in 1800 [MD:385]. He was married to Rachel, the daughter of Sherry **Grinnage**, on 1 November 1790 when Sherry gave Rachel £5 by his Caroline County will [WB JR B:168-170]. He mortgaged a mare, milk cow, two yearlings, a sow, 1,500 pounds of tobacco and household furniture for a debt of 2,900 pounds of tobacco he owed James Stenson of Queen Anne's County on 9 February 1788. He was called a "free negro" when he purchased 50 acres in Queen Anne's County called *Mount Hope* and *Rollings Chance* for £50 from George Elliott on 14 May 1802. He purchased 15 acres from Nathan Davis for $210 on 17 March 1810 and 3 acres called *Scotland* for £140 from Davis on 22 December 1810. He and William **Chester** purchased two cows and a heifer from Rebecca Matthews for $20 by Queen Anne's County bill of sale on 23 August 1810 [Land Records STW-6:151; STW-9:325, 423-4; STW-10:19, 528-9; CD-2, 431-2]. William **Chester** was head of a Talbot County household of 4 "other free" in 1790, 7 in Queen Anne's County in 1800 [MD:329] and 3 in 1810 [MD:147].

iii. Robert, called a "mol°" in 1782 when he and (his wife? Mary Wilson, a "mul°", were charged with assault and battery in Queen Anne's County [Surles, *and they Appeared at Court*, 1779, 1782, 1785, 1786, 1787, 40]. He was a "F.M." head of a Queen Anne's County household of 8 "other free" in 1790 and 6 in Baltimore City in 1800 [MD:388]. He was called a "free Mulatto" when he purchased 3 mares, 3 cows, 2 heifers, 22 hogs, a horse cart, a plow, 3 axes, 3 horses, 2 bedsteads, 2 flag-bottomed chairs, 3 iron pots, a pewter plate and dishes, 8 bushels of wheat and 40 barrels of corn in Queen Anne's County for £42 on 22 October 1792 [Land Records STW-2:285-6].

iv. David, born about 1756, "a man of Colour" who was about 64 years old when he appeared in Washington County court on 1 August 1820 to apply for a pension for his service in the Revolution. He enlisted in June 1778 under Captain Josiah Johnson in the 5th Maryland Regiment in the 1st Brigade under General Smallwood, served until the end of the war and was discharged in Annapolis. He had a wife aged 48 and a small boy. Captain Phil Reed testified that he grew up in the same neighborhood with David in Kent County, Maryland, and that David enlisted and served in the war [NARA, S.35119, M804, reel 2605].

v. John, born about 1760, enlisted in the Revolution in Delaware and was sized on 25 June 1782: *age 22, 5'5" high, a weaver, born in Maryland, residence: Sussex County, hair black, complexion yellow, enlisted as a substitute for James Messix.* He deserted the following month [NARA, M246, roll 30, frames 347, 406].

vi. Thomas[1], a "black" head of an Upper Hundred, Queen Anne's County household of 7 Blacks in 1776 [Carothers, *1776 Census of Maryland*, 148], "F.M." head of a Queen Anne's County household of 3 "other free" in 1790 and 8 in 1800 [MD:383].

vii. Thomas[2], head of a Queen Anne's County household of 4 "other free" in 1800 [MD:383].

viii. James, a "black" head of a household in Queen Anne's County in 1776: 1 male over 21, 2 females under 12, 1 female over 21 [Carothers, *1776 Census of Maryland*, 149], head of a Queen Anne's County household of 9 "other free" in 1790 and 12 in 1800 [MD:383].

ix. ____, "free mulatto" head of a Mill Hundred, Talbot County household of 1 "Black" person in 1776 [Carothers, *1776 Census of Maryland*, 156].

x. Samuel, "F.M." head of a Queen Anne's County household of 1 "other free" and 3 slaves in 1790 and 3 "other free" in Kent County in 1800 [MD:684]. He purchased a "negro woman" called Winny Wilson, a "negro girl" called Eliza Wilson, and a "negro boy" named Samuel Y. Wilson from Samuel Y. Keene in Queen Anne's County on 10 August 1807. On 15 April 1811 Sarah Keene certified that Samuel Y. Keene had stipulated in his will that a Mulatto woman named Winny and her four children were to be manumitted if a free man of Color Samuel Wilson who was husband to Winny should pay $400, and she stated in her deed of release that the money had been paid [Land Records STW-10:9; STW-9:506].

xi. Richard, a "black" head of an Upper Hundred, Queen Anne's County household of 7 Blacks in 1776 [Carothers, *1776 Census of Maryland*, 148], head of a Queen Anne's County household of 4 "other free" in 1790.

xii. Thomas, son of Sherry **Grinnage**'s deceased daughter Ann Willson, received £5 by Sherry's 1 November 1790 Caroline County will [WB JR B:168-170].

xiii. Henry, purchased his 28-year-old wife Teney Wilson and son Joshua by Queen Anne's County deed on 6 February 1799 and sold a mare for $50 on 16 May 1811 [Land Records STW-4:566; STW-9:538].

xiv. Sherry **Wansey** Wilson, nephew of Sherry **Grinnage**, received a "negro boy Dick" by **Grinnage**'s 1 November 1790 Caroline County will [WB JR

B:168-70]. He sold a mare, colt, old walnut desk, and a horse cart in Queen Anne's County for $50 on 7 November 1825 [Land Records TM-3:548].

WINGATE FAMILY

1.   Alley Wingate, born say 1742, was presented by the Somerset County court for having a "black Bastard Child" in January 1763. She confessed to the fact, named William Hast an Indian as the father, and paid a fine of 30 Shillings [Judicial Records 1760-3, 249b-250]. She may have been the mother of
   i.   Foss, born before 1776, head of a Dagsboro Hundred, Sussex County household of 4 "free colored" in 1820 [DE:370].

WINSLOW FAMILY

1.   Mary Winslow, born say 1688, had a child by Daniel **Francisco** about 1708 when William **Driggers** carried her out of Somerset County to avoid prosecution. She returned to the county and was charged with bastardy in court on 9 June 1708 [Somerset County Judicial Record 1707-11, 74, 94, 96; 1713-15, 26]. She was probably the mother of
   i.   William Winsly, born about 1715, a "Molatto" boy aged fourteen years old in September 1729 when he was bound by the Sussex County Orphans court to serve William Sill and his wife Mary until the age of twenty one [RG 4840, 1728-1743, docket #1]. He purchased 354 acres in Cedar Creek Hundred, Sussex County, at the head of Prime Hook Neck on 4 May 1748 and sold 100 acres of this land to Absolom **Mosely** on 4 May 1765, 100 acres to John Lofland, Sr., on 15 September 1772, and the remainder on 24 February 1776 to John Lofland, Jr., to be held by Winlsy and his wife Tabitha during their natural lives with the exception of 1/4 acre for a graveyard [DB K-10:270; L-11:304; M-12:79].

WISE FAMILY

1.   Mary Wise, born say 1714, was the servant of Robert Wells on 21 August 1732 when she appeared in Prince George's County court and admitted that she had given birth to an illegitimate "Malatto" child. The court bound her nine-week-old child Becky to serve for thirty-one years and sold her and the child to her master for 1,500 pounds of tobacco [Court Records 1732-4, 14]. She was the mother of
   i.   Becky, born in June 1732.

They may have been the ancestors of
   i.   Agnes, head of an Accomack County, Virginia household of 4 "other free" and 2 slaves in 1800 and 11 "other free" in 1810 [VA:35].
   ii. Thomas, head of an Elizabeth City County, Virginia household of 5 "other free" and a slave in 1810 [VA:185].
   iii. Peter, head of a Norfolk County household of 6 "other free" in 1810 [VA:839], perhaps the Peter Wise, born before 1776, who was head of a Dagsboro Hundred, Sussex County household of 4 "free colored" in 1820 [DE:380].

WISEMAN FAMILY

Members of the Wiseman family were
   i.   James, "Mulatto" head of a Charles County household of 1 "other free" in 1790 and 2 "other free" and 3 slaves in 1810 [MD:325].
   ii. Zachariah, "Mulatto" head of a Charles County household of 1 "other free" in 1790.
   iii. John, head of a Charles County household of 5 "other free" in 1800

[MD:562] and 9 in 1810 [MD:319].

iv.   William, head of a Charles County household of 4 "other free," a white woman 26-45 years old, and two slaves in 1810 [MD:321].

v.   Robert, head of a Charles County household of 1 "other free," a white woman 26-45 years old, and 2 slaves in 1810 [MD:343].

vi.   Thomas, married to Sarah in 1819 when their daughter Mary Ann, born 27 August 1819, was baptized in St. Mary's Mattawoman Parish, Charles County, with Elizabeth **Butler** as the godmother.

vii.   Smith, married to Anne on 23 April 1826 when their daughter Catherine Anne was baptized in St. Mary's Mattawoman Parish with Elizabeth **Proctor** as the sponsor [Colonial Dames of America, *Records of St. Mary's Parish, 1793-1861*, 26, 122].

WOOD FAMILY

Members of the Wood family on the Western Shore of Maryland were

i.   Mary, a "Negro" indented servant of Jesse Ford of St. Mary's County who was valued at £10 in the inventory of his estate taken on 5 January 1768 [Prerogative Inventories 98:119].

i.   Joseph, a "Negro" indented servant of Jesse Ford of St. Mary's County who was valued at £10 in the inventory of his estate taken on 5 January 1768 [Prerogative Inventories 98:119].

ii.   Jack, still had seven years to serve on 27 March 1764 when he was listed in the St. Mary's County inventory of the estate of Mr. James Mills [Prerogative Inventories, 87: 30-1].

iii.   Charles, head of a St. Mary's County household of 7 "other free" in 1790.

iv.   Jane, "Mulatto" head of a Charles County household of 5 "other free" in 1790.

v.   Henrietta, head of a St. Mary's County household of 2 "other free" in 1790.

vi.   John **Curtis** Wood, born about 1780, registered in St. Mary's County on 12 March 1810: *aged thirty years or thereabouts...complexion Dark, hair Short...born free.*

vii.   Henry, born about 1787, registered in St. Mary's County on 28 March 1809: *aged 22 years or thereabouts...Complexion Yellowish, hair is short & woolly...born free* [Certificates of Freedom 1806-64, 4, 8].

1.   Margaret Wood, born say 1718, a spinster living in Saint Paul's Parish, confessed to the Kent County, Maryland court on 14 November 1738 that she had a "Mollatto" by a "Negro" [Criminal Proceedings 1738-9, 36, 81-2, 110-1]. She may have been the ancestor of

i.   James, head of a Sussex County household of 7 "other free" in 1810 [DE:332].

ii.   George, born before 1776, head of a Kent County, Delaware household of 6 "other free" in 1810 [DE:74] and 2 "free colored" in Mispillion Hundred in 1820 [DE:76].

WOODLAND FAMILY

Members of the Woodland family were

1
i.   Luke, born say 1740.

ii.   Sarah[1], head of a St. Mary's County household of 10 "other free" in 1800 [MD:427], perhaps the Sally Woodland who was committed to the jail of Fairfax County, Virginia, on 17 June 1801 on suspicion of being a runaway. She was released after the court was satisfied she was a free woman [Fairfax County Orders 1800-1801, 180-1].

iii.   Abraham, head of a Kent County household of 8 "other free" in 1800 [MD:156].

   iv. Thomas, head of a Kent County household of 5 "other free" in 1800 [MD:156].
   v. Margarette, head of a Kent County household of 4 "other free" in 1800 [MD:156].
   vi. Thomas, born about 1775, registered in St. Mary's County on 26 July 1816: *aged thirty nine years...complexion bright yellow - hair long & woolly...raised in Saint Mary's County, born free* [Certificates of Freedom 1806-64, 27].
   vii. Cato, head of a Kent County household of 2 "other free" in 1800 [MD:156].
   viii. Rose, head of a Kent County household of 2 "other free" in 1800 [MD:156].
   ix. Jacob, head of a Queen Anne's County household of 1 "other free" and 5 slaves in 1800 [MD:385].
   x. Mary, born about 1787, registered in St. Mary's County on 24 August 1809: *aged twenty two years...complexion bright...born free* [Certificates of Freedom 1806-64, 7].
   xi. Charles, born about 1789, registered in St. Mary's County on 30 May 1809: *aged twenty years or thereabouts...Complexion rather dark...born free* [Certificates of Freedom 1806-64, 5, 7].

1.   Luke Woodland, born say 1740, was head of a St. Mary's County household of 7 "other free" in 1790 and 2 in 1800 [MD:407]. He may have been the father of
2   i. Sarah², born say 1770.
     ii. Thomas, born about 1775, registered in St. Mary's County on 26 July 1816: *aged thirty nine years...complexion bright yellow - hair long & woolly...raised in Saint Mary's County, born free.*
3   iii. Jane¹, born say 1776.

2.   Sarah² Woodland, born say 1770, was head of a St. Mary's County household of 8 "other free" in 1800 [MD:412]. She was the mother of
     i. Harry, born about 1795, registered in St. Mary's County on 12 September 1829: *aged about 34 years...dark complexion son of Sarah Woodland* [Certificates of Freedom 1806-64, 27, 81].

3.   Jane¹ Woodland, born say 1776, was head of a St. Mary's County household of 4 "other free" in 1800 [MD:406]. She was the mother of
     i. Celia, born about 1795, registered in St. Mary's County on 12 August 1829: *daughter of Jenney Woodland, aged about 34 years...dark complexion...long woolly hair.*
     ii. Verlinda, born about 1800, registered in St. Mary's County on 1 September 1824: *aged twenty four years...light complexion, long hair...born free, being the daughter of Jane Woodland.*
     iii. Ellen **Wilson**, born about 1804, registered in Prince George's County on 2 November 1827: *a bright mulatto woman, about 23 years old...born free in Saint Mary's County...daughter of Jane Woodland.*
     iv. Jane², born about 1805, registered in St. Mary's County on 12 November 1822: *Daughter of Jinny Woodland...about 17 years of age and is of a bright complexion...free born* [Certificates of Freedom 1806-64, 60, 67, 72, 81]. She was twenty-two when she registered on 22 October 1827 in Washington, D.C. [Provine, *District of Columbia Free Negro Registers*, 87].

Perhaps one of their descendants was
     i. John Woodlin, born 1776-1794, head of a Little Creek Hundred, Sussex County household of 5 "other free" in 1810 [DE:311] and 9 "free colored" in 1820 [DE:410].

WOODWARD FAMILY

1. Thomas Woodward, born say 1730, was presented by the Prince George's County court on 24 August 1756 for failing to list his "Molatto" wife as a taxable in Prince Frederick Hundred [Court Record 1754-8, 307]. He was probably the father of
    i.   Bazel Woodard, head of an Anne Arundel County household of 5 "other free" in 1790.
    ii. Ann, born say 1755, the servant of Archibald Allen in November 1777 when she confessed to the Montgomery County court that she had an illegitimate child by a "Negro." The court ordered that she be sold for seven years and that her child be sold until the age of thirty-one [Court Proceedings 1777-81, 33-4].
    iii. ?Neptune Woodyard, "F.N." head of a Back River, Baltimore Town household of 3 "other free" in 1790.

WRIGHT FAMILY

Anne Arundel County
1. Sarah Wright, born say 1724, was charged with "Molatto Bastardy" in Anne Arundel County court on 9 August 1748 but acquitted when it was shown that she was a married woman [Judgment Record 1748-51, 81].

Somerset County
1. Comfort Wright, born say 1720, was a "molatto" taxable in James Baker's household in Pocomoke Hundred, Somerset County, in 1739 [List of Tithables]. She may have been the mother of
2   i.   Early, born say 1740.

2. Early Wright, born say 1740, was a "Molatto" woman living in Stepney Parish in August 1760 when she confessed to the Somerset County court that she had a child by "Negro Edmond." She paid her fine of 30 shillings. She was a spinster living in Coventry Parish on 16 June 1767 when she confessed to the court that she had a child by Stephen **Dutton** [Judicial Record 1760-3, 42; 1766-7, 152]. She was probably the mother of
2   i.   Stephen, born say 1760.

2. Stephen Wright, born say 1760, was taxable on 150 acres, called *Friends Folly* in Rewastico, Somerset County, in 1783 [MSA S1161-9-10, p.60] and head of a Somerset County household of 7 "other free" in 1800 [MD:459]. He may have been the father of
    i.   Nicholas, born say 1778, married Mary Wright, "free Mulattoes," on 21 November 1799 in Sussex County [Records of the United Presbyterian Churches of Lewes, Indian River and Cool Spring, Delaware 1756-1855, 314]. He was head of a Dagsboro Hundred, Sussex County household of 3 "other free" in 1800 [DE:425] and 6 in 1810 [DE:437].
    ii. Daniel, head of a Sussex County household of 3 "other free" in 1810 [DE:353].
    iii. Sarah, head of a Sussex County household of 4 "other free" in 1810 [DE:363].

Other members of the Wright family in Little Creek Hundred, Kent County, Delaware were
    i.   George, head of a household of 6 "other free" in 1800 [DE:12].
    ii. Ham, head of a household of 4 "other free" in 1800 [DE:40].
    iii. Philip, head of a household of 5 "other free" in 1800 [DE:40].

YOUNG FAMILY

Members of the Young family were
   i.   Grace, "Negro" head of a Kent County household of 5 "other free" and a slave in 1790.
   ii. Stephen, head of a Talbot County household of 5 "other free" in 1800 [MD:522].
   iii. Frank, head of a Talbot County household of 2 "other free" and a slave in 1790.
   iv. Jacob, head of a Frederick County household of 1 "other free" in 1800 [MD:861].
   v.   Polly, born about 1784, registered in Dorchester County on 25 November 1829: *of a chesnut colour...born free, raised in Dorchester County and is the Daughter of Alex Fitzgerald who was also born free, aged about 46 years* [Certificates of Freedom for Negroes 1806-64, 65].

YOUNGER FAMILY

1.   Edward[1] Younger, born about 1763, registered in Prince George's County on 8 September 1809: *about 45 years old...dark complexion...free by virtue of a deed of manumission from Overton Carr of Prince George's County* [Provine, *Registrations of Free Negroes*, 5]. He was head of a Frederick County household of 5 "other free" in 1800 [MD:843]. He was married to Polly on 3 April 1812 when his son Edward registered in Frederick County. Perhaps she was identical to Polly **Bentley** by whom he had a child named William **Bentley**. His children were
   i.   Edward[2], born about 1790, registered in Frederick County on 3 April 1812: *a Dark Mulatto, about twenty two years of age...issue of Edward Younger and Polly his Wife, free negroes, and that this same Mulatto Edward was born free as appears by the Affidavit of Mary Wandle.*
   ii. ?William **Bentley**, born about 1792, registered in Frederick County on 22 April 1811: *Son of Edward Younger and Polly Bentley free negroes residing in Frederick Town...aged about nineteen years...of middling dark complexion...as appears by the affidavit of Abraham Levy who obtained a judgment for his freedom from a certain P.H.N.B. Tot Bostrop in Frederick County Court at Novr. Term in the year 1796.*

Other members of the Younger family were
   i.   Edward[3], born about 1796, registered in Frederick County on 3 April 1812: *a dark Mulatto Boy aged about Sixteen years...was free born as appears by the affidavit of Mary Wandle.*
   ii. Philip, born about 1799, registered in Frederick County on 8 March 1815: *a dark mulatto boy, aged about sixteen years and seven month sold...is free born as appears by an affidavit of Mary Wandle* [Certificates of Freedom 1806-27, 28, 36, 48, 71].

DELAWARE

<u>Manuscript and Microfilmed Manuscript Documents</u>
Kent County General Court Records, Court Dockets 1680-February 1725, microfilm RG3800, reel 1, Hall of Records, Dover, Delaware.
Sussex County Court Records 1680-1699, microfilm RG4800, reel 2.
Delaware Archives, Sussex County Assessments, Levy Lists 1770-1796, microfilm RG2535.
Delaware Archives, Kent County Assessments, Levy Lists 1727-1850, microfilm RG3535.
Delaware Archives, Kent County Wills, A-1 through R-1, microfilm.
Delaware Archives, Sussex County Deeds, A-1 through L-11, microfilm.
Delaware Census Records, 1800 Census: microfilm M32-4; 1810 Census: M252-4; 1820 Census: M33-5.
Delaware Archives, Kent County Wills, Will Books
Sussex County Orphans Court 1728-1793, State Archives Hall of Records, Dover Delaware microfilm
Kent and Sussex County wills and deeds, microfilms at the Historical Society of Pennsylvania.

Delaware Church Records:
Records of the United Presbyterian Churches of Lewes, Indian River and Cool Spring, Delaware 1756-1855. Micro-reproduction of original records at the Genealogical Society of Pennsylvania..

<u>Printed Sources</u>
Corle, Craig W. 1991. *Records of the Courts of Sussex County, Delaware, 1677-1710.* 2 volumes. University of Pennsylvania Press.
Mason, Elaine Hastings & F. Edward Wright. *Land Records of Sussex County, Delaware,1782-89, Deed Book N, No. 13.*
de Valinger, Leon, Jr. 1944. *Calendar of Kent County, Delaware Probate Records 1680-1800.* Dover.
de Valinger, Leon, Jr. 1964. *Calendar of Sussex County, Delaware Probate Records 1680-1800.* Dover.
Wright, F. Edward. 1986. *Vital Records of Kent and Sussex Counties, Delaware, 1686-1800.* Silver Spring, Md.
Wright, F. Edward. 1984. *Delaware Newspaper Abstracts, 1786-1795.* Silver Spring, Maryland.

MARYLAND

Manuscript and Microfilmed Manuscript Documents
Census Records, 1800 Census: microfilm M32-9, 10, 11, 12. 1810 Census: M252-13, 14, 15.
Marayland deeds, all counties:
http://mdlandrec.net/main/dsp_viewer.cfm?cid=WO&view=bookview&imtyp=current&di=y&srt yp=l&status=a
<u>Prerogative Court, Inventories & Accounts, 1686-1717</u>
MSA SM 13, Rolls 65 to 72
Prerogative Court (Inventories), 1718-1777, MSA CDs
Prerogative Court (Wills), 1635-1777, http://familysearch.org
Provincial Court Judgments, 1679-1778, http://familysearch.org

<u>Anne Arundel County</u>
Court Minutes 1725-1775, MSA 11,668-1
Convict Record: 1771-1775, CR 40,516-1
Certificates of Freedom:
1806-1807, Liber A1, CR 47,242-1
1807-1811, Liber B 2, CR 79,177-2
1810-1831, CR 47,242-2

<u>Baltimore County</u>
HWS#6 and #7, MSA
Court Proceedings:
1743-1746, CR 40,707
Convict Record:
1770-1783, Liber AL, CR 40,516-2
Chattel Records:
1750-1757, Liber TR no.E, MSA R 115-3
1763-1773, Liber B, no. G, MSA R 118-2
Certificates of Freedom:
1806-1816, CR 12,262-1
1832-1841, CR 12,262-2

1830-1832, CR 12,262-3

Caroline County
Certificates of Freedom 1806-27, 1827-1851, Liber IR A, CR 47,245-2, 3.

Cecil County
Judgment Record:
1695-1702, 1708-1716, Liber E, MSA CR 6397-3a.
1769, reverse of Land Records Liber BY 4, MSA WK 948-1b, 1c.

Charles County
Court Records:
1685-1686, Liber M 1, MSA CR 35,692-1
1686-1688, Liber N 1, MSA CR 35,692-2
1687-1688, Liber O 1, MSA CR 35,692-3
1688-1690, Liber P 1, pp. 1-203, MSA CR 35,692-4
1690-1693, Liber R 1, MSA CR 35,693-1
1693-1694, Liber S 1, MSA CR 35,693-2
1696-1698, Liber V 1, MSA CR 35,698-1
1699-1700, Liber X 1, MSA CR 35,698-2
1700-1702, Liber Y 1, MSA CR 35,698-3
1702-1704, Liber A 2, MSA CR 34,653
1704-1710, Liber B 2, MSA CR 34,654-1
1710-1711, Liber D 2, MSA CR 35,693-3
1711-1715, Liber E 2, MSA CR 34,654-2
1717-1720, Liber I 2, MSA CR 34,655-2
1720-1722, Liber K 2, MSA CR 34,655-3
1722-1725, Liber N 2, pp. 1-396, MSA CR 34,655-4
1722-1725, Liber N 2, pp. 397-476, MSA CR 34,656-1
1725-1727, Liber P 2, MSA CR 34,657-1
1727-1731, Liber Q 2, MSA CR 34,657-2
1731-1734, Liber R 2, pp. 1-300, MSA CR 34,657-3
1731-1734, Liber R 2, pp. 301-538, MSA CR 34,658-1
1735-1739, Liber T 2, MSA CR 34,658-2
1741-1744, MSA CR 34,658-3
1744-1746, Liber Y 2, MSA CR 34,659-2
1747-1748, Liber Vol. 41, MSA CR 34,660-1
1749-1750, Liber Vol. 42, MSA CR 34,660-2
1750, Liber Vol. 44, MSA CR 34,660-3
1752-1753, Liber B 3, MSA CR 34,661-1
1753-1754, Liber D 3, MSA CR 34,661-2
1755, Liber C 3, pp. 1-278, MSA CR 34,671-4
1755, Liber C 3, pp. 278-318, MSA (CR 34,672-1
1755-1756, Liber E 3, (CR 34,661-3)
1755-1756, Liber E 3, pp. 401-502, MSA (CR 34,662)
1756-1757, Liber F 3, MSA CR 34,662-2
1757-1758, Liber H 3, MSA CR 34,662-3
1758-1760, Liber I 3, MSA CR 34,663-1
1760-1762, Liber K 3, MSA CR 34,663-2
1762-1764, Liber M 3, pp. 1-332, CR 34,664
1762-1764, Liber M 3, pp. 333-372, CR 34,665-1
1764-1766, Liber N 3, pp. 1-536, (CR 34,665-2
1764-1766, Liber N 3, pp. 535-823, MSA CR 34,666-1
1766-1767, Liber P 3, MSA CR 34,666-2
1767-1770, Liber Q 3, pp. 1-470, MSA CR 34,666-3
1767-1770, Liber Q 3, pp. 471-607, MSA CR 34,667-1
1770-1772, Liber T 3, MSA CR 34,667-2
1772-1773, Liber U 3, MSA CR 34,668-1
1773-1774, Liber W 3, MSA CR 34,669-2
1774-1778, Liber X 3, CR 50,840
1778-1780, Liber Y 3, MSA CR 50,841
Certificates of Freedom 1826-1860, CR 47,246-2, CM 972-1
Oaths of Fidelity, 1776, Liber X, No.3, MSA CR 50,840, CM 1236-1

Dorchester County
Judgment Record:
1690-1692, Liber Old 4-1/2, MSA CR 49,048-4, CM 438-1.
1728-1729, MSA CR 49,050-3, CM 438-2.
1742-1743, Liber Old 11, reverse, MSA CR 49,052-1, CM 438-3.

1742-1743, Liber Old 12, reverse, MSA CR 49,053, CM 438-4.
1742-1743, Liber Old 13, pp. 483-529, MSA CR 49,052-2, CM 438-5.
1744-1745, Liber Old 13, pp. 1-479, MSA CR 49,052-2, CM 438-6.

Certificates of Freedom: 1806-1851, MSA CR 34,728-1, CM 1283-1.

Frederick County
Judgment Record:
1748-1750, Liber A, MSA CR 11,668-3, CM 482-1.
1763-1766, Liber M, MSA CR 11,669-1, CM 482-2.
Court Minutes:
1750-1757, MSA CR 12,257-1, CM 497-1.
1756/11, MSA CR 12,257-2, CM 497-2;
1758-1762, MSA CR 12,257-3, CM 497-3.
1763-1768, MSA CR 11,669-2, CM 497-4.

Certificates of Freedom: 1806-1827, MSA CR 47,246-3, CM 1198-1.

Kent County
Court Proceedings:
1676-98 (CR 80,150); 1700-1 (CR 80,151); 1701-5 (CR 80,152); 1707-1709; 1714-1715 vol. JS W
(CR 6398)
1716-1717, Liber JS X, (CR 6398); 1718-20 (CR 80,153);
1722-3 (CR 80,154); 1731-3 (CR 80,155); 1733-4 (CR 80,156); 1759-1761, Liber DD 1,
MSA (CR 50,847), Minutes 1774-88 (CR 50,842)

Criminal Court:
1724-1728, Liber JS AD, MSA CR 42,838-1, CM 649-1.
1728-1734, Liber JS WK, MSA CR 42,838-2, CM 649-2.
1738-1739, Liber JS 22, MSA CR 42,838-3, CM 649-3.
1739-1742, Liber JS 23, MSA CR 42,839-1, CM 649-4.
1742-1747, Liber JS 24, MSA CR 42,839-2, CM 649-5.
1748-1760, MSA CR 42,839-3, CM 649-6.
1761-1772, Liber DD 1, MSA CR 42,840-1, CM 649-7.

Levy Court 1758-1784 (Levy List) MSA CR 50,569, CM 857.

Chattel Records:
1750-1764, Liber A, MSA CR 50,240, CM 1256-1.
1764-1775, Liber DD, No.1, MSA CR 50,241, CM 1256-2.
1775-1785, Liber DD, No.3, MSA CR 50,242, CM 1256-3.

Montgomery County
Court Proceedings:
1777-1781, MSA CR 12,253

Prince George's County
Microfilmed Court Records:
1726-34, MSA CR 34,712;1742-3, Liber AA, MdHR 5761
1696-1699, MSA CR 49,514-1
1699-1705, Liber B, MSA CR 34,707-1
1705-1708, MSA CR 49,514-2
1708-1710, Liber D, MSA CR 49,515-1
1710-1715, Liber G, pp. 1-450, MSA CR 34,707-2
1710-1715, Liber G, pp. 435-836, MSA CR 34,708-1
1715-1720, Liber H, MSA CR 34,708-2
1720-1722, Liber K, MSA CR 34,709-1
1723-1726, Liber L, MSA CR 34,709-2
1726-1727, Liber N, MSA CR 34,710-1
1728-1729, Liber O, MSA CR 34,710-2
1729-1730, Liber P, MSA CR 34,711-1
1730-1732, Liber R, MSA CR 34,711-2
1732-1734, Liber S, MSA CR 34,712-1
1734-1735, Liber V, MSA CR 34,712-2
1736-1738, Liber W, MSA CR 34,713-1
1738-1740, Liber Y, MSA CR 34,713-2
1740-1742, Liber Z, MSA CR 34,714-1
1742-1743, Liber AA, MSA CR 34,714-2
1743-1744, Liber CC, MSA CR 34,715-1

1744-1746, Liber DD, MSA CR 34,715-2
1746-1747, Liber FF, MSA CR 34,716-1
1747-1748, Liber GG, MSA CR 34,716-2
1748, Liber HH, MSA CR 34,717-1
1748-1749, Liber KK, MSA CR 34,717-2
1749-1750, Liber LL, MSA CR 34,718-1
1751-1754, Liber MM, MSA CR 34,718-2
1754-1758, Liber OO, MSA CR 34,719-1
1761-1763, Liber SS, MSA CR 34,719-2
1763-1764, Liber VV, MSA CR 34,720-1
1765-1766, Liber WW, MSA CR 34,720-2
1766-1768, Liber 28, MSA CR 34,721-1
1768-1770, Liber AA 1, pp. 1-659, MSA CR 34,721-2
1768-1770, Liber AA, No.1, pp. 658-701, MSA CR 34,722-1
1770-1771, Liber BB, No. 1, MSA CR 34,722-2
1771-1773, Liber CC, No.1, MSA CR 34,722-3
1773-1774, Liber DD No.1, MSA CR 34,723-1
1774-1775, Liber DD No.2, MSA CR 34,723-2
1775-1777, Liber EE, No.1, MSA CR 34,724-1
1777-1782, Liber EE, No.2, MSA CR 34,724-2

Queen Anne's County
Judgement Records 1709-1716, MSA CR 6397

Saint Mary's County
Certificates of Freedom: 1806-1851, MSA CR 47,251-1

Somerset County
Judicial Records:
1689-1690, MSA CR 45,672
1690-1691, Liber AW, MSA CR 45,671-2
1691-1692, MSA CR 45,673
1692-1693, MSA CR 45,674
1693-1694, MSA CR 45,675
1695-1696, MSA CR 45,676
1696-1698, MSA CR 45,677
1698-1701, MSA CR 45,678
1701/08-1702/09, MSA CR 50,304
1702-1705, Liber GI, pp. 1-299, MSA CR 34,365
1705-1707, Liber AB, MSA CR 34,366
1707-1711, MSA CR 6396-1
1711-1713, MSA CR 6396-2
1713-1715, 1722, Liber AC, pp. 1-264, MSA CR 6396-3
1715-1717, pp. 1-254, MSA CR 6396-4
1715-1717, pp. 251-487, MSA CR 6397
1718, Liber EF, pp. 1-7, 12-195, MSA CR 34,368
1719/03-1719/08, MSA CR 50,305
1719-1722, Liber IK, MSA CR 49,017
1722, Liber AC, pp. 416-430, MSA CR 6396-3
1722, Liber GH, MSA CR 34,369
1723/03-1725/03, MSA CR 50,279
1725/03-1727/06, MSA CR 50,280
1727/06-1730/06, MSA CR 50,281
1730/08-1733/06, MSA CR 50,282
1733/06-1735/03, MSA CR 50,283
1735/03-1737/03, MSA CR 50,284
1737/03-1738/06, MSA CR 50,285
1738/08-1740/08, MSA CR 50,286
1740/08-1742/08, MSA CR 50,287
1742/08-1744/11, MSA CR 50,288
1745/03-1746/08, pp. 1a-193a, MSA CR 50,289-1
1746/08-1747/06, pp. 193b-306a, MSA CR 50,289-2
1747/08-1749/08, MSA CR 50,290
1749/08-1751/06, MSA CR 50,291
1751/06-1752/11, MSA CR 50,292
1752/11-1754/08, MSA CR 50,293
1754/11-1757/03, MSA CR 50,294
1757/03-1760/03, MSA CR 50,295
1760/03-1763/06, MSA CR 50,296

1763/06-1765/08, MSA CR 50,297
1765/08-1766/08, MSA CR 50,298
1766/08-1767/08, MSA CR 50,299
1767/08-1769/03, MSA CR 50,300
1769/03-1772/03, MSA CR 50,301
1772/03-1774/03, MSA CR 50,302
1774/03-1775/03, MSA CR 50,303
1775-1784, MSA M 1301

County Tax Lists 1723-57, MdHR 20,397; MSA CR 51,864-1 to CR 51,864-31
Certificates of Freedom, 1821-1851, MSA CR 47,251

Talbot County
Judgment Records:
1686-1689, Liber NN No.6, MSA CR 78,566
1692, Liber NN 6, MSA CR 78,566
1692-1698, Liber LL7, MSA CR 78,567
1696-1698, Liber AB, no. 8, part 2, MdHR 9596-2.
1699, Liber MW 1, MSA CR 78,568
1705-1706, Liber RF 10, MSA CR 78,571
1706-1708, Liber RF 11, MSA CR 78,572
1714-1717, Liber FT 1, MSA CR 6399-2
1717-1748, C1875-22 to C1875-46
Chattel Records 1689-1692, Liber NN, No.6, CR 78,566

Certificates of Freedom: 1807-1815, MSA CR 47,252-1
1815-1828, pp. 1-183, MSA CR 47,252-2

Worcester County
Court Proceedings: 1769, MSA CR 46,934-3
1778-1779, Liber K, pp. 1-120, MSA CR 37,386-1
Land Records: 1794-1796, Liber Q, MSA CR 77,908-2
1796-1797, Liber R, MSA CR 77,909-1
1797-1798, Liber S, MSA CR 77,909-2

Internet Sources
Maryland State Archives Web Site, Assesment of 1783, MS1161:
http://mdarchives.state.md.us/msa/stagser/s1400/s1437/html/ssi1437e.html
http://familysearch.org

Printed Sources
Barnes, Robert W. 1989. Baltimore Families, 1659-1759. Genealogical Publishing. Baltimore, Maryland.
Brackett, J.R. 1889. *The Negro in Maryland*. Johns Hopkins University, Baltimore.
Brown, William Hand, ed., et.al., 68 vols. 1883-. Archives of Maryland. Baltimore.
Bureau of the Census. 1965 [1908]. *Heads of Families at the First Census of the United States Taken in the Year 1790: Maryland*. Baltimore.
Carothers, Bettie Stirling. 1970. *1776 Census of Maryland*. Lutherville, Maryland.
Daniels, Christine and Michael V. Kennedy, ed. 1999. *Over the Threshold: Intimate Violence in Early America*. Routledge.
Davidson, Thomas E. 1991. *Free Blacks on the lower Eastern Shore of Maryland: the colonial period - 1662 to 1775*. Maryland Historical Trust. Crownsville, Maryland.
Green, Karen Mauer. 1990. *The Maryland Gazette 1727-1761*. Frontier Press. Galveston, Texas.
Hodes, Martha. 1997. *White Women, Black Men, Illicit Sex in the Nineteenth-Century South*. Yale University Press.
Humphreys, David, *An Historical Account of the Incorporated Society for the Propagation of the Gospel in the Foreign Parts...to the Year 1728*. London. 1730
Porter, Frank W., *Quest for Identity: The Formation of the Nanticoke Indian Community at Indian River Inlet, Sussex County, Delaware*. University of Maryland Doctoral Dissertation. 1978.
Provine, Dorothy S. 1990. *Registrations of Free Negroes 1806-1863, Prince George's County, Maryland*. Washington D.C.
Reamy, William and Martha. 1988. *Records of St. Paul's Parish, Baltimore, Maryland*, Volume I. Family Line Publications. Westminster, Maryland.
Scott, Kenneth & Janet R. Clarke. 1977. *Abstracts of the Pennsylvania Gazette 1748-55*. Genealogical Publishing. Maryland.
Weslager, C. A., *Delaware's Forgotten Folk: The Story of the Moors & Nanticokes*. University of Pennsylvania Press. 1943.
Williams, William H., *Slavery & Freedom in Delaware 1639-1865*. SR Books. 1996.

Windley, Lathan A. 1983. *Runaway Slave Advertisements: A documentary History from the 1730s to 1790. Volume 2.* Greenwood Press. Westport Connecticut.
Wright, F. Edward. 1993. *Inhabitants of Baltimore County, 1692-1763*. Baltimore.
Wright, F. Edward. *Maryland Eastern Shore Vital Records,* 1684-1725 (Book 1), 1726-1750 (Book 2), 1751-1775 (Book 3), 1776-1800 (Book 4). Silver Spring, Md.
Wright, J. M. 1921. *The Free Negro in Maryland, 1634-1860.* Columbia University, New York.